AF378931

Overcoming the Oppressors

Overcoming the Oppressors

White and Black in Southern Africa

ROBERT I. ROTBERG

OXFORD
UNIVERSITY PRESS

Oxford University Press is a department of the University of Oxford. It furthers
the University's objective of excellence in research, scholarship, and education
by publishing worldwide. Oxford is a registered trade mark of Oxford University
Press in the UK and certain other countries.

Published in the United States of America by Oxford University Press
198 Madison Avenue, New York, NY 10016, United States of America.

© Oxford University Press 2023

Library of Congress Cataloging-in-Publication Data
Names: Rotberg, Robert I., author.
Title: Overcoming the oppressors : white and black in Southern Africa / Robert I. Rotberg.
Description: New York : Oxford University Press, [2023] |
Includes bibliographical references and index.
Identifiers: LCCN 2022040706 (print) | LCCN 2022040707 (ebook) |
ISBN 9780197674208 (hardback) | ISBN 9780197674222 (epub)
Subjects: LCSH: Africa, Southern—History. | Decolonization—Africa, Southern. |
Africa, Southern—Politics and government. | Apartheid—Africa, Southern.
Classification: LCC DT1099 .R683 2023 (print) | LCC DT1099 (ebook) |
DDC 320.968—dc23/eng/20221013
LC record available at https://lccn.loc.gov/2022040706
LC ebook record available at https://lccn.loc.gov/2022040707

DOI: 10.1093/oso/9780197674208.001.0001

1 3 5 7 9 8 6 4 2

Printed by Integrated Books International, United States of America

for
JOANNA
in memory

Contents

Illustrations

Figures

By Joanna G. Cloutier

Maps

By Dylan A. Gattey

Preface

The countries of sub-Saharan Africa have ruled their postcolonial selves for many decades. The Sudan shed the constraints of an Anglo-Egyptian condominium to become an independent nation in 1956. A year later, President Kwame Nkrumah turned the Gold Coast into Ghana, energizing and emboldening many of the aroused populations of Africa's remaining British, French, Belgian, Portuguese, and Spanish colonial possessions and trust territories to agitate for their own liberation.

In southern and eastern Africa, where entrenched white settler elites joined standard-issue British colonial administrators in governing disparate territories, the process of decolonization took much longer than in West Africa. As the Algerian war against France raged along the Mediterranean shores, so Africans from central Kenya in the 1950s attacked settlers and British installations. Farther south, after indigenous civil protests failed to halt the imposition of a white-dominated Federation of Rhodesia and Nyasaland, Africans turned violent and, under determined new leadership legitimized by months in prison, in 1964 transformed Northern Rhodesia into Zambia and Nyasaland into Malawi. Peacefully, Bechuanaland emerged as Botswana in 1966, just as Tanganyika had amicably gained its independence in 1961 (eventually as Tanzania in 1964). Both places had relatively few white residents. Nor were white numbers an impediment to nationhood when the Crown Colony of Basutoland became Lesotho in 1966 and monarchical Swaziland (now Eswatini) followed suit in 1968.

Those contested and little-contested exits from British colonial oversight left the much more heavily populated white redoubts at the end of the continent under the tight-fisted control of minorities. After an increasingly bitter civil war, white settlers were next eased out of power in Zimbabwe by African antagonism and British diplomacy in 1980. Namibia, which South Africa had incorporated into its own territorial domain in defiance of United Nations' rulings, was the locus of another struggle until the demise of the Soviet Union and skilled American diplomatic intervention caused South Africa to give way to a United Nations electoral exercise and, in 1990, to convey Namibia to independence. (The Lusophone territories of Angola and Mozambique were fought over by colonial rulers and liberation movements until the Portuguese dictatorship was overthrown from within in 1974, leading to the emergence of both new African nations in 1975. Thereafter, both countries harbored anti–South African and anti-Rhodesian guerrilla bases, assisting cross-border operations for freedom in neighboring Zimbabwe and Namibia, and also against distant South Africa.)

Whites in South Africa were much more numerous than they were in Kenya, the Rhodesias, or Namibia. They had governed themselves and their majority African, Coloured, and Asian subject peoples for eighty years before African internal unrest and external attacks, combined with outside financial pressure, finally forced white hegemonists to release famed political prisoners from prison and negotiate a peaceful transfer of power.

The Long Walk to Freedom

This book is about southern Africa's long walk to freedom, about the overturning of colonial rule in the northern territories and the dissolution of backs-to-the-wall white settler suzerainty first in what became Zimbabwe and then in South Africa. Chapters on the individual countries detail the stages along their sometimes complicated and tortuous struggle to attain the political New Zion. We learn how and why the Federation of Rhodesia and Nyasaland failed, how and why apartheid eventually collapsed, and exactly how the various components of this heavily white-conquered and later white-oppressed domain transitioned via diverse fits and starts into today's assemblage of proud, politically charged, and still mostly fragmented nation-states.

But what did the new republics make of their hard-won freedoms? That is the subject of more than half of this book. Having liberated themselves successfully, several soon dismantled democratic safeguards, established effective single-party states, closed their economies, deprived citizens of human rights and civil liberties, and exchanged economic progress for varieties of central planning experiments and stunted forms of protected economic endeavors. Only Botswana, of the new entities, embraced full democracy and good governance. The others, even South Africa, at first tightly regimented their economies and attempted severely to limit the degrees of economic freedom and social progress that citizens could enjoy.

Largely because of its emphasis on delivering high-quality and abundant quantities of positive governance, a result of remarkable political leadership, Botswana prospered steadily from independence until today; it became the most successful (across several dimensions) of all mainland African countries and a tribute to the remarkable political culture that its first president introduced, nurtured, and elaborated.

Botswana achieved its spiritual and material advance in part because achieving good governance meant putting the public interest of citizens before a leader's ethnic or family interests, and well ahead of personal preferences and concerns.

The second half of this book examines the many ways in which leadership else-where in southern Africa was often deficient, self-serving, and neglectful of the needs of large groups and numbers of citizens. It shows how almost everywhere except Botswana, presidents followed presidents who solemnly promised to up-lift their nations and their constituents, and fell far short of their own declared aspirations.

In every section of southern Africa except Botswana, ruling political elites be-came greedy. They indulged in manifold varieties of corruption: procurement over-invoicing with kickbacks, large-scale bribe taking in exchange for conces-sionary opportunities for plunder, play for pay, pay for jobs, the wholesale theft of payrolls, enrolling ghost employees, the appropriation of public resources for private enrichment, straightforward embezzlement, and even the purchase of privately consumed goods with state funds. In fact, as this book shows, corrupt actions and behavior strew boulders across the highways of progress, preventing many of the new countries (even South Africa) from delivering essential political goods like schooling and electric power to their loyal, underprivileged, and end-lessly enduring constituents.

The New Rulers

Chapters in this book hence examine what the new rulers of southern Africa did with their hard-won patrimony. The chapters reveal how in some cases out-going oppressors were succeeded by new manifestations of oppression. In 2022, the presidents of South Africa, Malawi, and Zambia were each attempting to scrub their countries of the blemishes left by previous presidential regimes and excesses. The new leadership in several other countries was busy undoing—or at least attempting to undo—the errors of their predecessors.

Fortunately, southern Africa is on the mend. This book is thus about how the southern African nations of today are attempting to recover from earlier vicissitudes and egregiously self-indulgent forms of leadership. New leaders are overcoming latter-day oppressors. Even Botswana contends with new kinds of internal struggles, just as South Africa's key areas of consternation are both within the ruling political party and between the African National Congress and its rivals.

The book's concluding chapter weaves these separate but interlocked na-tional stories into an analysis of the contribution of good leadership to southern Africa's growth, to sub-Saharan Africa maturity more generally, and to improved conditions and the alleviation of poverty in most countries. Indeed, every chapter describes how responsible or self-absorbed leadership influenced the ways in which each state dealt with its post-colonial challenges and opportunities, and how well. The conclusion assesses the extent to which the peoples of southern Africa have been served well by their leaders and what may now be done to strengthen the leadership factor in this and future decades. The conclusion discusses the impact of the coronavirus pandemic on southern Africa, and what it has meant and will mean. That last chapter also sets out the litany of challenges ahead—vexing ones that each nation will need to confront if southern Africa is to take its rightful place as a beacon of prosperity and good governance within Africa and the world.

This book is an analytical narrative throughout. It is prescriptive. It is informed by my own personal observation of, engagement with, and contemporary commentary on much that transpired in southern Africa from 1959 to 2022. I was close to the action on many telling occasions, and carefully followed the political, economic, and social developments that affected the peoples of southern Africa as they liberated and commenced to rule themselves. Hence this book is in significant parts about peoples whom I know and respect and leaders with whom I have interacted over considerable time. It reflects, too, my abiding interest in securing uplifting outcomes for the disparate peoples of southern Africa—peoples who have too often been neglected by ambitious political elites. There is much to be done, and too little time to accomplish all that now remains on southern Africa's ambitious agenda of modernization.

R. I. R.
June 17, 2022

1

"Partnership" and Multiracialism in the New Africa

Sub-Saharan Africa in the late 1950s and early 1960s was thoroughly contested, exciting, vibrant, and—for an embryonic researcher eager for knowledge and intellectual as well as political adventure—ripe for social scientific exploration. The sub-continent was in ferment; colonial rule was obviously threatened, but not necessarily in full flight. Nationalism was the cry of the day, thanks to successful devolutions of power in the Sudan and Ghana, in Guinea, and shortly in the remainder of francophone West and Central Africa and the ex-Belgian Congo. The Mau Mau rebellion in Kenya was in retreat, too, but colonial rulers were uniformly anxious to avoid similar kinds of militant protests elsewhere in their far-flung imperial domains.

The old order was giving way, and the young researcher out from Oxford arrived fortuitously amid the tumult with a natural affinity for the underdog—for those teachers, clerics, and shopkeepers who were challenging the established order and seeking a new dawn and the gaining of full democracy for themselves and their long subservient and (in many cases) oppressed brethren. Nowhere in this era was the need for new dispensations and (radically) novel solutions more necessary and more adversarial in 1959 and 1960 than in southern Africa. The juggernaut of white-devised and white-enforced brutal segregation (apartheid) anchored the end of the continent.

Wrapped to some degree around South Africa's northernmost province were the African protectorates of Swaziland (Eswatini) and Bechuanaland (Botswana), and white-run Southern Rhodesia (Zimbabwe). The last (locally governed) country was in turn linked officially to its northern and African neighbors, Northern Rhodesia (Zambia) and Nyasaland (Malawi), African British protectorates with copper mines, tea plantations, and white settlers and white mine-workers of some duration. The last three unlikely bedfellows had been yoked together by Britain in 1953 as the Federation of Rhodesia and Nyasaland over the vehement protests of Africans of all classes and backgrounds in the northern protectorates and in Southern Rhodesia, and to the great applause of conniving, greedy, white planters and industrialists in the colony.

This was the bitterly contested setting for my introduction to Africa and its political conflicts. Despite African concern and opposition, much of the British

Overcoming the Oppressors. Robert I. Rotberg, Oxford University Press. © Oxford University Press 2023.
DOI: 10.1093/oso/9780197674208.003.0001

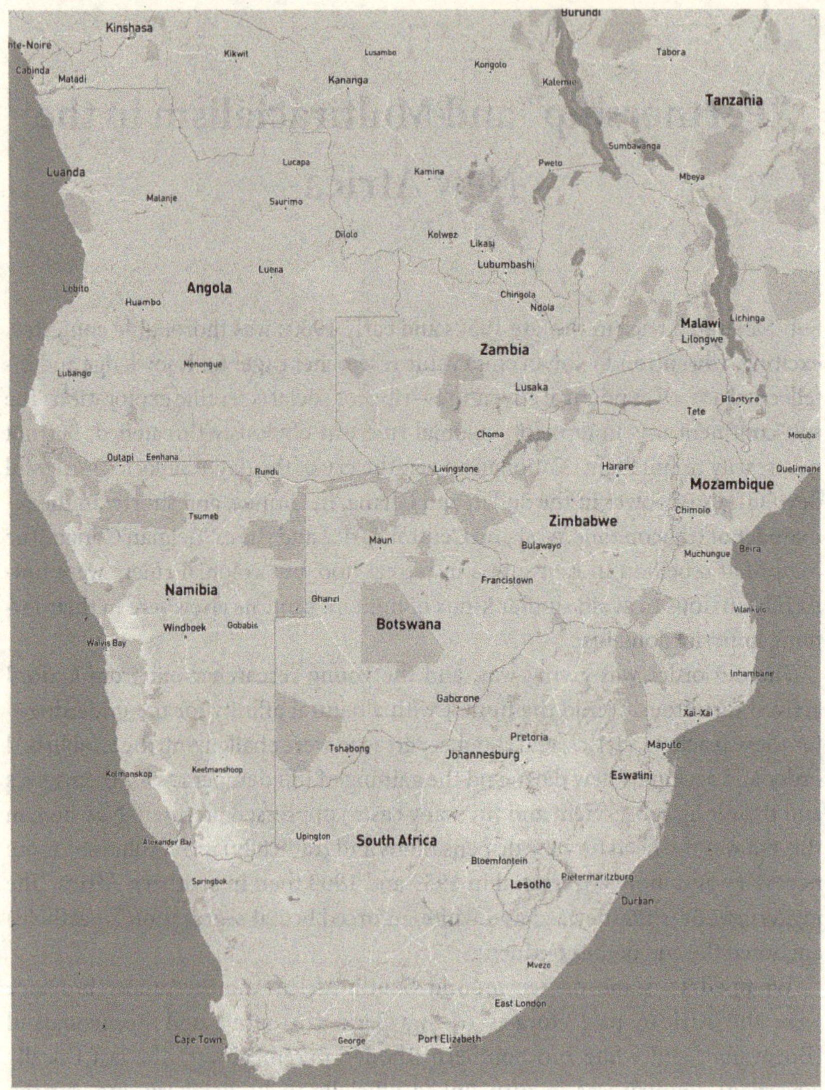

Map 1.1. Southern Africa

political establishment, even a smattering in the academy, and some well-intentioned Americans, viewed the Federation as a bold experiment in multi-racial partnership, linking white and black harmoniously in a manner capable in theory of halting the spread of odious apartheid northward into white-run Southern Rhodesia while simultaneously avoiding the dangers of "premature" African rule and mayhem of the Mau Mau variety in the protectorates. The knowledgeable and liberal Britons who had helped to engineer the Federation, push it through Parliament after bargaining with the whites of the Rhodesias, and deftly snub South Africa by snatching Bechuanaland and Swaziland (and Basutoland) from the clutches of apartheid, congratulated themselves on a clever maneuver that would help to give much of southern Africa an opportunity to modernize and develop without inter-communal strife. The plan was to let white rule by entrenched settlers and mine-workers gradually "uplift" the larger mass of less well-educated Africans. Northern Rhodesia's copper riches would support the new edifice, support the otherwise impecunious Africans of the protectorates (and of Rhodesia), and subsidize the weak economy of Southern Rhodesia while Southern Rhodesia in turn supplied (white) managerial talent to the entire Federal enterprise.[1]

The partners would evolve. At first the junior partners would remain junior, but gradually they would help to oversee their own destiny politically as they gained in economic parity. In this manner, reckoned Whitehall and the Southern Rhodesian and Northern Rhodesian (white) political establishments, the settlers would remain content and profit, and Africans would—over decades—share the benefits that were bound to accrue to such a Machiavellian arrangement. And African nationalism—African representative home rule—would be sidestepped for a long time, possibly forever.

Even from my limited prior knowledge before landing in the heart of the Federation in very early 1959, I knew that such a runaround was unlikely to provide anything of value to the African populations of the three Federal component territories (more than 2.5 million Africans in each territory, with only 223,000 whites in Southern Rhodesia, 76,000 in Northern Rhodesia, and 9,000 in Nyasaland). I understood, too, that Africans in all three components had voiced overwhelming opposition to the Federation, and that there were some prominent local liberal whites declaiming that the Federation was less a sensible experiment than a thoroughgoing sellout to settler interests. But I could not have known (nor could others) as I walked off a lumbering propeller aircraft after an eighteen-hour journey to Harare from London, exactly how the Federal question was going to be resolved and how I was going to participate as a researcher in its dissolution and the political convolutions that ensued.

As a young doctoral student in a distant and unfamiliar land, I could not have been more energized, more open-eyed, more concerned to learn everything there was to learn about British Central Africa, and to write about its new and upcoming insurgents both as a budding scholar and as a sometime stringing journalist for the *New York Times*. (I had been employed by the *New York Times* in New York before going up to Oxford. From Oxford I contributed articles to the newspaper via its London bureau. In Africa I was the proud possessor of a

Times telex account, so could file stories occasionally from Zambia and beyond. The *Times* then had no correspondent in Africa.) The moment was very ripe for inquiry, learning, and engagement.

Along the Cairo Road

Based for that first year in Africa at Zambia's premier, still colonially run, research institute at the edge of what was still a sleepy national capital of 82,000, I quickly set about gleaning everything I could about the kidney-shaped future nation, then of 3 million, now 18 million, people. There were three urgent tasks: (1) to try to explore the entire country (11 percent larger than Texas and roughly equivalent to the size of France, Spain, and the Low Countries) during my allotted year away from Oxford so that I could begin to appreciate how its different peoples and regions interacted with each other, and formed the whole; (2) to investigate throughout the Protectorate how colonial rule and accompanying Christian missions (Zambia then had a remarkable number of distinct churches and sects operating mission establishments across the length and breadth of the country) influenced indigenous Zambians for good and ill; and (3) to grasp the political differences that (how much I hardly imagined at the beginning) were about to rend the country's colonial legacy and create a virile indigenous drive to independence.

Lusaka, the capital of the Protectorate only since 1935, was originally merely a station on the sole rail line, half way between Victoria Falls and the old capital of Livingstone and Ndola and Kitwe, the chief mining towns of the Copperbelt. Zambia then was one of the three largest copper producers in the world. Copper ore provided 97 percent of the nation's and about 75 percent of the Federation's export earnings. The rail line carried copper ore south from the Copperbelt through Botswana and South Africa to freight terminals in Port Elizabeth (now the Nelson Mandela Bay Metropolitan Municipality) on the Indian Ocean, and thence to the United Kingdom, the United States, Japan, and other overseas consumers and fabricators.

Alongside the rail line that drove straight through Lusaka's commercial center, with its many small white- and Indian-owned shops, its larger depots for maize, and scattered office buildings, was the Cairo Road, the city's sole paved artery. Named that way to acknowledge Cecil Rhodes' dream of a British transportation route from Cape to Cairo, the tarmacked road carried automobiles and trucks beyond Lusaka in northern and southern directions. But to go east, past my institute and the country's best high school, and onward to distant Malawi, vehicles traversed gravel. And to the west, toward the far-distant Kafue and Zambezi Rivers, and the semiautonomous state of Barotseland, the tracks were largely composed of scraped and packed earth, muddy and dangerous during the yearly rains.

Eventually, I managed to visit every corner of Zambia, even evangelical mission stations near the headwaters of the Zambezi River adjacent to Angola and extremely isolated Roman Catholic outposts located near the same mighty river—but separated by 684 miles—nestled near Mozambique. I went back and forth on the Great East and Great North Roads, went west carrying big drums with the fuel required to attain remote Mongu and Sesheke en route to the border with Angola, traveled far off the usual beaten paths to see the second longest uninterrupted waterfall in Africa—a narrow plunge of 772 feet called Kalambo Falls, near Lake Tanganyika, and made several journeys into the Gwembe Valley alongside the lower Zambezi River to observe how callously Federal and colonial officials were ousting 30,000 Tonga villagers to make room for the lake (280 km long) that would form behind the mighty Kariba Dam, completed on my watch in 1959. On the Copperbelt I went underground, to the deepest point in the Mufulira mine, to try to understand how ore was dynamited and collected, and to observe the obscenely difficult conditions under which African miners labored.

There was much to see and peoples of seventy different linguistic groups and four dominant ones to meet and to understand and appreciate. There were chiefs and missionaries to interview; district commissioners and their assistants to accompany on their journeys in order to learn how the colonial system ran itself and governed its protected charges; local students and others to travel with and learn from, especially when they were within their home provinces; and villagers who took us in, miles from the line of rail.[2]

Quickly, too, I realized that Africans were mobilizing against Federal rule, and against colonial oversight, much more forcefully and determinedly than had been reported to me in Britain and the United States. Zambians (and Malawians) were agitating with a new fervor for freedom. The African townships around Lusaka and elsewhere in Zambia were embracing nationalism and independence in new ways. The colonial and Federal authorities were becoming increasingly nervous. More than once I was summoned to the office of the colonial secretary for native affairs in Northern Rhodesia (the third official after the governor) and instructed to pay strict attention to my doctoral research on missions only and to cease involving myself (even as an observer) in politics. Essentially, I was told forcefully to stop meddling.

But even by the time (Sir) Glyn Jones (later governor of Malawi and member of the Pearce Commission in Zimbabwe, and someone I subsequently came to know well) tried to warn me away from studying political evolution, hardly anyone aware of the depths of African discontent could avoid being captured by the promise of gifted new leadership and the prospect of transformational change.

Within days of my January arrival in Lusaka, it was clear to me and to others that Africans were challenging authority and demanding rights in ways that were new, provocative, and inspirational. No longer could Britain's Colonial Office remain complacent.

The governor of the nascent Zambia, together with his colonial civil servants and a cadre of mostly Oxbridge trained district commissioners and their mostly white and some black assistants, provided the core of "native" administration. This was a tidy and largely inefficient but somehow effective way of governing colonial territories. The district commissioners, each responsible for a rural collection of chiefdoms and villages, collected taxes, arbitrated disputes, prosecuted and tried local offenders, and projected a kind of British imperial "rightness" over the indigenous terrain. This method and its rationale was reasonably well accepted in rural Zambia especially since, to some degree, the district commissioners ruled together with indigenous chiefs, many of whom prospered alongside the foreign administration.

But the urban areas, growing in size and importance, were less content with an absence of real political participation under foreign governance. Urban residents throughout the colonies were better educated, more aware, and with broader horizons than their rural counterparts. They appreciated the fact that Ghana and the Sudan had already achieved independence. They resonated with the grievances of Kenya and had many of their own. Some well-traveled Zambians had been to India or knew details of Mohandas K. Gandhi's successful struggle against British domination in India (and what he had failed to accomplish earlier in South Africa).

The missionaries in Zambia had also instructed well. The more liberal denominations, such as the United Free Church of Scotland, the British Wesleyan Methodists, and the Church of England, had been teaching their communicants to value individual freedom and initiative, to deprecate any limitations on human freedom, and to value the humane teachings of the Gospel. Those messages penetrated deeply into the Zambian consciousness. Many Africans schooled and catechized by liberal missionaries naturally came to want the same rights as whites and believed that they deserved them, especially in their own country.

White Zambians helped to rule the territory through an elected national assembly called the Legislative Council (Legco). By 1959, after decades of devolution, it had a strong say in making laws and running the territory. The governor still had the final word, but he and the other "officials" largely tried to avoid conflict with Legco and its white leaders. There had long been an appointed white assemblyperson who nominally represented "native interests," and four Africans had recently been elected to Legco. In addition, the Federation's own parliament included two Africans from each of its constituent parts.

At the same time, Zambia's colonial rulers relied for the articulation of indigenous views as much on the African Representative Council as on subordinate councils established in each of the Protectorate's provinces. These were lively, often vigorously argumentative, talking shops. The administration largely viewed them as expressive outlets, not as core components of the territory's governing apparatus. The fact that nearly all of these councils had strongly opposed the creation of the Federation in 1953 had not deterred the Colonial Office from foisting the Federal scheme on Africans in the northern lands. The fact that the indigenous leaders of these councils, and that leaders of the emerging African elites in both territories, had separately and together pleaded with the Colonial Office not to yoke their futures to that of Southern Rhodesia had made no difference. Africans, on these grounds alone, felt ignored and abused.

The Federal Experiment

What was wrong with the Federal experiment? By 1959, it was clear to African opinion in the northern lands, and also in Zimbabwe, that multiracial partnership was a sham, as indigenous spokesmen had long suspected. Africans would, it was envisaged by Federal Prime Minister Sir Godfrey Huggins (later Lord Malvern) and (Sir) Roy Welensky, his successor, in some far-off day play a probably minor part in ruling the Federation and its three components. But for the present and the near future, at least, whites would control the Federal policy levers in their own interest. Africans would not be segregated particularly (although that was still the case in Southern Rhodesia), but their educational and social perquisites would remain inferior to whites. And the existing color bar would remain social policy everywhere; Africans were forced in the Rhodesias to purchase meat from hatches at the back of butcheries, to stand in separate queues at airports, to use different entrances to hospitals and administrative offices, and so on. Budgetary expenditures obviously favored whites despite the fact that the Federal population of 7.2 million was 97 percent African.

Welensky, a bluff, burley, locomotive driver who had earlier been a white political leader in Northern Rhodesia, had openly declared that "partnership" could never mean "equality": whites would always remain "the senior partner."[3] Huggins, rarely wavering, even laid out his conception in public in 1951 for all to hear: his callous metaphor was a partnership that consisted of a rider and his horse. He went on to say, "[w]e do not pretend there is any equality of partnership at the present time, but the Native has joined the firm and has his foot on the lower rungs of the ladder; he will have to learn the wisdom of trying to help himself."[4] Huggins, a longtime leader of whites in Southern Rhodesia, also affirmed that "Africans are all liars, until they are very much advanced."[5] As Cyril Dunn, a perspicacious British journalist, later reported after interviewing Africans in the northern territories, "The most suitable definition of 'partnership' was: '[a] political system existing in a multiracial society where the blacks are kept permanently subservient to the whites and are persuaded that this is not the case.' "[6] Kenneth Kaunda's own contemporaneous comment on Huggins, Welensky, and the paradigm of partnership was, "Lord Malvern [Huggins] . . . has . . . never hidden his crude scorn for African opinion. . . . It is to these prophets of apartheid posing, circumspectly, as believers in partnership that the British Government sold us when they imposed the Federation . . . in 1953."[7]

There was nothing obviously redeeming about the Federal experiment from the African point of view. Admittedly, creating the Federation had blocked any extension of extreme racial politics northward from South Africa, but that had never been much of a reality or a threat, and, although Afrikaners were numerous proportionally in Southern Rhodesia, it had been a "British" self-governing colony since 1923. Admittedly, too, the creation of the Federation probably helped to attract foreign investment; the three sections of the Federation were stronger economically together. Impoverished Nyasaland (Malawi) certainly benefited from Zambian copper revenues being expended on roads and airfields and other facilities within its territory.

Southern Rhodesia gained the most from the experiment, however, as Huggins knew that it would. With northern copper royalties finding their way into the Federal exchequer, and with the Federation being administered from Salisbury (Harare) in what became Zimbabwe, it is no wonder that Zambian Africans, especially, felt misused and cheated. The expression *bamba zonke* ("grab the lot" or "skim the cream") was widely used in the north as an epithet for Salisbury's growth on the back of Zambian sweat equity.

Consistently strong prices for copper helped to build the imposing Kariba Dam athwart the Zambezi River and to supply relatively inexpensive power to both Rhodesias and to the mines. Salisbury came to resemble the sky-scrapered cities of western America. New immigrants, white miners, white (and Asian) shopkeepers, and bankers all grew impressively wealthy. Locomotive drivers like Welensky prospered. Similarly African living standards probably rose, albeit more slowly and more hesitantly than original promises of what the Federal scheme would deliver. Under Federation, Africans saw little improvement in their generally miserable lot, especially when compared to recent white immigrants.

Before going north to Zambia for the first time, I listened carefully to Julian Greenfield, successively Federal minister of education, minister of law, and minister of home affairs, and a long-established white political figure in Southern Rhodesia, when he explained in idealistic terms how the Federal scheme was going to benefit blacks as well as whites. By managing the kind of proficient operation that Africans could hardly hope to emulate, he said, the Federation was boosting incomes overall, and some (he said "most") of those rewards were trickling down to the mass of Africans. But he could not cite more than a mere handful of Africans who were rising in the Federal civil service (there were nine in 1959), or who were beginning to lead corporate endeavors. (As Jaspar Savanhu, the most highly placed of those nine Africans in the Federal governing apparatus said when he resigned in disgust in 1962: "I have finally reached the decision that your government . . . has failed or has no intention of fully implementing the policy of partnership. . . . As matters stand today I feel that my presence among an all-white Civil Service is only tolerated and I feel lonely, a piece of window dressing. . . .")[8] Greenfield, however, naturally insisted that Africans were well off and that the Federation was an opportunity for whites to create a future British dominion, on the New Zealand and Australian models, with Africans as (subordinate) citizens. Even someone like Greenfield, the careful and well-modulated antithesis of a rabble-rouser, was content to live out a major exercise in hypocrisy. The Federation was a con job.

Socially, lip service was paid in the territories and in the United Kingdom to pretense that the Federation was genuinely multiracial and that Africans were going to be treated well. But everyone closely involved, not only aggrieved African elites, understood that it was a charade. By 1959, a broad-based response by all strata of educated and working-class Africans in both Northern Rhodesia and Nyasaland appreciated with alacrity that the whites were conspiring to place Africans firmly under white rule, whatever Britain preferred to the contrary, and calling the result a federation. Even as early as 1948, the Northern Rhodesian African Congress opposed what was happening: "[S]ome people may think that the African does not see clearly the meaning of Federation. We see its meaning and it means to enslave the African." Moreover, "The secret of Federation is to subordinate African interests. . . ." Indeed, the Congress continued, "Partnership . . . is a ladder for Europeans . . . to climb on us." Dr. Hastings Kamuzu Banda, an American-trained physician practicing in London and later president of Malawi, in 1949 wrote in horror together with Harry Nkumbula, a Zambian student at the London School of Economics, that protected Africans had no wish to exchange their status as wards of the British government for that of "slaves" of the settlers. Moreover, Banda predicted that whites would be "advanced in all spheres to the detriment of Africans." The British policy of abolishing discrimination was "doomed."[9]

Educated, middle-class and working-class African Northern Rhodesians were adamantly opposed. "The word [partnership] itself has a good sound," reported Mufana Lipalile to the Northern Rhodesia Western Provincial Council (one of the Protectorate's regional indigenous talking shops), but when there are two oxen, "one black and one white," the white one can say, "I must go ahead and you must come behind me all the time." "Partnership," said Donald R. Siwale in Northern Rhodesia, "is only used on lips and papers and not in practice." (Siwale, a former Church of Scotland mission teacher and government civil servant, also looked forward to the day when Africans would rule Northern Rhodesia, as they already did in Ghana).[10]

The Northern Rhodesian African Representative Council petitioned the Secretary of State for the Colonies: "While appreciating the principle of partnership," its submission read, "it should be clearly understood that the Africans' home is in Africa, whereas the Europeans can have access to other parts of the British Commonwealth. If opportunities for advancement of our race are denied in Africa, where else . . . shall we be found?"[11]

In Nyasaland, where James Frederick Sangala had become president of the nationally representative Nyasa African Congress, forty delegates from its fifteen branches confirmed their opposition to the federal scheme and promised that "Nyasas have and will still protest at all costs."[12] In Zambia, the Mporokoso Native Welfare Association voted against federation. So did the Luwingu and Mwenzo welfare associations, the Northern Rhodesian Northern and Western Provincial Councils, and a number of other official and unofficial forums of African opinion.[13] (The provincial councils were government-initiated but African-controlled voices in their local areas, as were the various district welfare associations that existed in both protectorates.) Later in 1951, a special meeting of African delegates from a number of local organizations repudiated "partnership" in any form, any guise. "Officials [must be] getting tired of their responsibilities" to think of leaving, they said. Africans were being pawned by His Majesty's Government. Just afterward, a regular session of the African Representative Council refused even to help Governor Sir Gilbert Rennie to define "partnership."[14]

In 1951, Dauti Yamba and Pascale Sokota, teachers and subsequent politicians, with the knowledge of Northern Rhodesia's African National Congress, tested partnership by demanding parity of positions with white "unofficials" on the Executive Council of the Northern Rhodesian Legislative Council, to which august body they had both just been appointed. They were rebuffed. Banda later exclaimed that "partnership" could not be brought to Central Africa by force. "We, the Africans of Nyasaland and Northern Rhodesia, are people."[15] Africans could hardly believe, even as late as 1951, just how cavalierly Whitehall was prepared to strip their rights way and assign their fate to their present and future oppressors.

Even chiefs, such as Bemba senior chief Mwamba and Malawi chiefs Mwase of the Cewa and Philip Gomani of the Ncheu Ngoni opposed partnership and federation. Most members of the Barotseland paramount chief's council voted against federation.[16] "Every African in Northern Rhodesia does not want to be federated with Southern Rhodesia," wrote Paul Sikazwe. He explained the sense of his associates graphically: "If a man is given food and he vomits it, can he again eat what he had already vomited? . . . Most of us know that our friends in Southern Rhodesia are slaves."[17]

In Northern Rhodesia, the Chinsali African Welfare Association, led at the time by Kenneth Kaunda, Simon Kapwepwe, and Rueben Kamanga, teachers and all later leaders of the new Zambia, rejected federation outright.[18]

The Man with the Monocle

It was on one of my several tours of Zambia's Northern Province—a heartland of dissent and agitation—that I arrived at Shiwa Ngandu ("the lake of the royal crocodiles")—near Chinsali, to meet, interview, and learn from the accumulated wisdom of Lt. Col. Sir Stewart Gore-Browne, J.P. He had at one time been the leader of the Northern Rhodesian "unofficials"—the white settlers—giving way to Welensky, the rough-hewn former prizefighter. Gore-Browne had subsequently become the representative in Legco for African interests. He was antagonistic to the Federal scheme, very supportive of African nationalist grievances, in favor of giving more political participatory rights to Africans, friendly with Kaunda and Kapwepwe (their homes and mission station were near Shiwa Ngandu), and passionate regarding the components of an honest partnership between white and black.

Yet, Gore-Browne also was a monocle-wearing patrician of mature years who was more settler than most settlers. After having first arrived at Shiwa Ngandu (originally Lake Young) in 1914, he decided that he would make a permanent home there after returning from shelling Germans on the French front in World War I. He established a plantation where he grew limes for the French perfume market. Lime oil could travel more easily and inexpensively (per value) than some other crops. Shiwa Ngandu was several days' journey from the line of rail, and lime oil had a chance—slim though it was—of helping to defray the costs of establishing a Tuscan-type manor house with a view of the lake, keeping a medley of servants, eventually supporting a family (and many retainers), and enabling Sir Stewart (as he was to become) to travel back and forth to Lusaka and onward to London.[19]

Gore-Browne always excelled as an effortless host. As early as 1925, entertaining Sir Herbert and Lady Stanley, the new governor of Northern Rhodesia and his wife, Gore-Browne reported to Dame Ethel Locke-King in London that the evening had been a wild success: "White soup with new asparagus was followed with fresh lake fish fried, wild duck, and cheese straws, all washed down [513 miles from Lusaka] with champagne." Stanley said that it was the best food he had had anywhere, telling Gore-Browne, "Give me some more of that wild duck, and then shut me in my sty."[20]

When Nadine Gordimer, the celebrated South African novelist and future Nobel laureate, visited the estate forty years later, Gore-Browne's warmth and keen appreciation of "proper" hospitality was still strong. "Sir Stewart," she wrote, "is a handsome Englishman of eighty-three, remarkable not in the conventional sense of the grand old man representing the good or bad old past, but in the flexibility of mind that enables him to span . . . the recorded history of the country he lives in. . . . We dined on jugged wart-hog."[21] Guests were treated royally at Shiwa Ngandu, even neophyte researchers like myself who may have been surprised that a man with such a formidable bearing could be so respected by African politicians and subsistence farmers despite his old world, albeit avuncular, manner.

Some of the early settler politicians had been rabidly antagonistic to Africans and African advancement. Leopold Moore, a cranky Livingstone pharmacist, and Welensky were in that mold. White self-interest consisted of having a ready supply of inexpensive labor and of not spending much time, money, or effort providing schooling opportunities or medical care to the laborers, to a vast array of little-educated rural Africans, or even to those who worked in the cities and towns located along the rail line in white-farmed, maize-growing districts or on the Copperbelt.

In any event, settler whites had their voices heard in Legco throughout the 1920s and 1930s, but it was not until the 1940s, and the fallout from World War II, that unofficials were allowed to outnumber officials in Legco and to have what amounted to a shadow form of responsible government.

Gore-Browne had been a steady member of Legco from 1935. By the time that I was fortunate enough to enjoy his hospitality at Shiwa Ngandu, I had become fully aware that African nationalists, and especially Kaunda and Kapwepwe, were very fortunate that such a well-respected, internationally known political voice harmonized with their own. Gore-Browne well knew the white Rhodesians and their penchant for manipulating Whitehall to gain ascendancy over blacks while covering up their hypocritical motives about the true nature of multiracial "partnership." What they had long wanted, as Gore-Browne foresaw and articulated, was to create white rule in perpetuity. Sharing and uplifting was never the true goal.

Gore-Browne had evolved as a political statesman since 1935. He had helped to settle railway and copper-mining strikes, had served on two decisive land tenure and land allocation commissions, had promoted free compulsory universal education for Africans, had demanded that Africans receive passports, had served as commissar of thousands of Polish evacuees interned in Northern Rhodesia during World War II, and had become a confidant of successive British governors. He helped to create state secondary schools for Africans and sought to send Zambians overseas to universities. He also demanded political representation for Africans and, during World War II, persuaded the Colonial Office to establish first provincial councils and then the African Representative Council as a way of giving Africans "voice." He appreciated and welcomed the likelihood that the majority should some day govern itself.

Gore-Browne shocked some of his white unofficial colleagues in Legco as early as 1943 by decrying the "unnatural" color bar: "I do feel that so long as there is an artificial restriction . . . on the black man rising as far as he is able . . . we are asking for trouble and heading for ultimate disaster." He continued: "I regard the white man's interest and the black man's as irrevocably interlocked." He urged whites to make Africans their (real) partners and to recognize their "common humanity."[22] A few years later he recommended giving "qualified" Africans the vote in elections to the Legislative Council: "I cannot do anything so repugnant to my sense of justice as to deny a man who is adequately qualified the right to vote, merely on account of the colour of his skin."[23] In 1947, he even persuaded officialdom to refer to their ultimate constituents as "Africans," not "natives." That was a revolutionary act for the time, but not for someone fluent in CiBemba and comfortable living mostly on his own in the heart of Bemba country as both a lord of the manor and a colleague of increasingly militant nationalists.

Throughout the later 1940s, when whites like Huggins and Welensky were agitating locally and in Whitehall for some form of amalgamation between the three English-speaking Central African territories, Gore-Browne was warning against tying Zambians and Malawians to Rhodesians. He was hardly fooled by the "multiracial partnership" concept that was being hawked locally and in London by such well-meaning paternalists as the founders of the Capricorn Africa Society. At a major conference with white representatives from all three territories and officials from the Colonial and Commonwealth Offices, Gore-Browne said that he would never "be a party to putting our Africans in any way under Southern Rhodesian Government."[24] Gore-Browne also discerned ahead of most others that the Federal idea had aroused a new political consciousness among Africans.

Although he failed almost singlehandedly among whites to prevent the Federation from coming into existence in 1953, he observed its operations carefully. By 1956, along with politicized Africans in all three territories, he concluded that partnership "was humbug." Discrimination and near-segregation were just as strong as before. "Federation . . . has not only done nothing towards bettering race relations, but has even made things worse by failing to do anything constructive and by seeming to be satisfied with platitudes about a vague partnership. . . ." He urged whites to stop penalizing Africans for having "the black face which the Lord provided him at birth."[25]

By the time of my first visit to his estate, Gore-Browne was publicly aligned with the Zambia Congress, a most unusual action for white person of such standing in Africa. That is why I felt privileged to be in his company and share his expansive and well-considered views. He, almost alone of whites in Zambia, was favorable to universal suffrage for Africans, approved the busting up of the Federation, and argued for the transition to some form of African home rule.

Gore-Browne had obviously been on a remarkable political journey by the time that I arrived on his doorstep at Shiwa Ngandu. Later, before his death in 1967 at eighty-four, and Zambia's first state funeral, I was to visit Shiwa Ngandu many times, often with my wife, to be entrusted by Sir Stewart with boxes and boxes of his personal papers, and (much later) to write his biography—*Black Heart: Gore-Browne and the Politics of Multiracial Zambia* (1977).

A New Political Ferment

Plunged headlong into the debates over Federation and freedom in early 1959, I rapidly appreciated that the wheels of African nationalism were rolling relentlessly, and at a newly accelerated pace. I had landed in Zambia just in time to hear heated exchanges between advocates and opponents of the Federation and to sense that the Federal experiment, having failed in the eyes of the bulk of its citizens, would have to fight interminably to prevent its unraveling.

Malawi's Kamuzu Banda led the charge: "To hell with Federation," he shouted, and promised to die for the nationalist cause. "Whatever the consequences," Kaunda exclaimed in Lusaka, "we are prepared to pay the price of freedom in this country." Both Kaunda and Banda vilified settler oppression. Muna Sipalo, a vibrant follower of Kaunda, demanded self-government "now," and promised to create "nonsense [if] we must create nonsense." Africans threw stones at motorists in Blantyre and Zomba (Malawi). Masauko Chipembere said that "we (the Congress party and its adherents) were red hot."[26] The Malawians (where I was soon to visit) were consciously trying to test the resolve of the colonial authorities.

Zambians, too, in those first few weeks of 1959, were voicing themselves more militantly but, aside from a few cases of arson that might have had political origins, Northern Rhodesia was comparatively quiet. Nkumbula had not uttered the kinds of challenges that Banda and Chipembere were articulating, but there was discontent everywhere within the Federation, and an ominous foreboding that I quickly sensed.

The nationalist standard-bearer in Northern Rhodesia had long been the Northern Rhodesian African National Congress (ANC). It had fought the Federal concept from its inception in the late 1940s and early 1950s. Nkumbula, its combative leader since 1951 (whom I interviewed both in Lusaka and in his Ila village near Namwala on the Kafue Flats), was a doughty opponent of the Federation and an assertive, even flamboyant, advocate of African independence. As one of the Protectorate's better formally educated citizens, he had been schooled at Makerere University College in Uganda before continuing for a few years at the London School of Economics.

By the month of my arrival in Zambia, however, Nkumbula's political standing had been compromised by his willingness to call off not one but two boycotts of Asian- and white-owned shops that still discriminated against African customers. He had opposed a mineworkers' strike and had been persuaded by white liberal politicians to moderate his advocacy of indigenous home rule. None of his nuanced tactics pleased younger, many CiBemba-speaking, militants. Nkumbula seemed to be selling out. And he tried to rule the ANC in a high-handed, authoritarian, manner.

Nkumbula's arrogance and attitudes did not please his deputy, the young Kenneth David Kaunda, or his treasurer, Kaunda's close friend Simon Mansa Kapwepwe. They and many others in the Congress believed that Nkumbula was not forceful enough in representing them—that he was too receptive to Colonial Office and white settler blandishments. Nkumbula drank heavily, too, and sometimes he was impaired. There were suggestions as well that he had mishandled Congress finances, to his personal advantage. He was inefficient, famously forgetful, and seriously undisciplined.[27] But the major issue may well have been that Nkumbula was from the Southern Province, the home of the Tonga and the Ila, and that the rising cadre of new militants were mainly from the Bemba heartland in the north, from CiBemba-speaking communities on the Copperbelt, or from Zambia's CiNyanja-speaking Eastern Province. The Bemba are Zambia's largest ethnic group; the Tonga, and especially the Ila, are much less numerous.

At a lonely United Free Church of Scotland (Presbyterian) mission in the remote far north of Bemba-speaking Zambia, a black cleric from neighboring Malawi had long preached an advanced form of the Gospel together with the Highland Scottish missionaries who were his nominal superiors. The cleric was David Kaunda, from northern Nyasaland (Malawi), where the United Free Church of Scotland had established pioneering settlements along the shores of Lake Malawi as early as 1894. The Reverend Kaunda's son, Kenneth David, grew up near Chinsali (and Shiwa Ngandu) on the Lubwa mission station in Zambia, was schooled there and in Lusaka through the equivalent of the U.S. tenth grade, and, with Kapwepwe, a fellow student in the Lubwa school, and a number of other like-minded young mission-trained proto-democrats, established the Zambia African National Congress (ZANC) in late 1958. To differentiate themselves and their new organization from Nkumbula and the older Congress, the ZANC said that it stood for an end to all discrimination, demanded universal suffrage and African home rule, and favored secession from the Federation. The ZANC claimed 900 members when it applied for official registration on December 1, 1958.[28]

There were personality as well as character and linguistic differences. Kaunda had already done a study tour of Britain and India and had returned to Zambia as a determined champion of rapid political change. He was also persuaded of the virtues of non-violence. Instinctively a "humanist," as he later declared himself, Kaunda was a less fiery speaker than Nkumbula. He reasoned more than he exhorted. Kapwepwe, on the other hand, was a powerful spokesman for change, employing African and CiBemba aphorisms with skill and panache. Kaunda and his followers sought "natural justice," and immediate improvements in African political and social rights.

It was because Kaunda and the ZANC had emerged strongly on the local Zambian political scene a few weeks before my arrival in Lusaka that I soon located Kaunda in his home in Chilenje, a crowded African township within greater Lusaka. I went to Hut 280 (now a historic designation) at the beginning of February 1959 and listened carefully to Kaunda's well-thought-out plan to bring about new political dispensations in his native land. Wearing a starched white shirt and his characteristic Ghanaian kente-cloth wraparound, and with his hair brushed straight up, Kaunda patiently explained to this relatively jejune interrogator that he had the winds of change at his back—that Zambians under his kindly but tough-minded leadership could achieve in their nation what

Figure 1.1. Kenneth Kaunda

Ghanaians had achieved in theirs. (Nigeria was soon to follow Ghana, as were many francophone polities.)

The gist of our conversation was encapsulated in an article of mine that ran in the February 24, 1959, edition of the *New York Times*. As a result, Kaunda became more widely known as a man in the Gandhian mode who was trying to lead a successful, if determinedly peaceful, revolution in the heart of Africa. The article was appropriately subtitled "New Movement in Northern Rhodesia Plans Campaign of Civil Disobedience." Kaunda told me that first his party would "withdraw our labor from . . . employers." I asked him if passive resistance would succeed. His response was "a shrug and a smile." Then he said: "But the weapons of violence are in the hands of the imperialists; we will not use them."[29]

That long interview began a cherished acquaintance that endured for sixty years despite disagreements over strategy and tactics. We flew together to Tanzania one day when Kaunda dryly noted that one of the propeller engines had caught fire, met on innumerable occasions in Zambia's State House during his twenty-seven-year presidency, and visited on the banks of the Luangwa River when he was finally ousted from power. We shared meals in Cambridge, Massachusetts, especially after his visit to Saddam Hussein's Iraq to observe a mock election. A remarkable humanist and honest politician, he nevertheless made major mistakes—as future chapters discuss.

As I described Kaunda to readers in 1959, and again in a series of articles in 1962, Kaunda was a self-described moderate. Never a drinker, never a smoker, and man who in so many ways behaved as the antithesis of the stereotyped African male, and especially African male politicians, he was an unshakable Gandhian by belief and persuasion. "When Kaunda speaks, his eyes flash but his voice is mild." He had a "ready, warm smile for his friends and supporters, but charity for those who oppose him." Even when talking about his arch-rival Welensky, all he said, mildly, was "misguided, unfair, dishonest." On the move to battle internationally for Zambia in London, Accra, or Dar es Salaam, he often wore a frayed trench coat and carried a book by someone of Gandhian teaching, plus—too frequently—a collection of old newspapers, to be perused in time.[30]

What was apparent to me, and to *New York Times* readers, was that Kaunda was a new kind of African nationalist leader. Deeply religious without being pious, liberal theologically beyond nearly all of his peers, gentle of speech, an environmentalist before that was a category, and a vegetarian amid an overwhelming assembly of carnivores, Kaunda was unique, and uniquely qualified to lead Zambia to independence from British rule outside the Federation.

Kaunda had a following among the handful of college graduates and the many high school graduates of his country. But he was also trusted by conservative chiefs and admired for his political positions and his humane character by African mine-workers on the Copperbelt, many of whom were CiBemba speaking, as well as by indigenous urban dwellers of all backgrounds. They wanted change and felt that Kaunda, Kapwepwe, Reuben Kamanga, Sikota Wina, and many others of different ethnic groups could express their increasing dismay at colonial and Federal oversight, and lead the nation to independence.

The growing power of the ZANC and some disturbances on the Copperbelt, together with widespread agitation and scattered violence, soon aroused the Federal authorities and their colonial counterparts. Within weeks of my *New York Times* article, the Federal and territorial authorities declared an "emergency," rounded up the African nationalist leaders in both protectorates and in the colony, and bundled them off to prisons in Zimbabwe or to a series of rural rustication holding camps in distant parts of Zambia.

Federal troops arrived in Nyasaland on February 20 and proceeded to quell the disturbances that were roiling the Protectorate. Six days later, the Prime Minister of Southern Rhodesia banned the local African National Congress and incarcerated around 500 of its members. The Nyasa Congress was banned on March 3, and Banda and 200 others arrested. Before dawn on March 12, the governor of Northern Rhodesia closed down the ZANC and arrested Kaunda and forty-five other committed leaders. Northern Rhodesia's governor, (Sir) Arthur Benson called gentle Kaunda the "head of Murder Incorporated."[31]

Banda and many of his closest adherents were imprisoned in Gwelo (now Gweru) prison and in Bulawayo's Khami prison in Zimbabwe. Kaunda was first rusticated in the remote Kabompo district of northwestern Zambia and then abruptly hauled off to prison in Lusaka and Harare.[32] Other Zambians, like Wina and Kapwepwe, were sent to remote districts where they were presumed to know no one and to be unable to converse in a local language that was not their own.

The governor's actions and words and the decisive moves of the Federal authorities seemed an overreaction. Most of us who were close to the new nationalist movements thought so, as did the overseas press. After all, Kaunda was a pacifist, and the Zimbabweans had not hitherto been particularly militant. An official inquiry "failed to produce a single instance of violence" attributable to the new Zambian party.[33] Banda's rhetoric was heated, and so was Chipembere's, but it was verbal. However, what we did not know, until one of the participants later told me at length, was that informers had infiltrated a clandestine meeting of activists from all three territories.

Seventeen miles from Fort Jameson (Chipata) in late February 1959, Kaunda, Muna Sipalo, Sikota Wina, Dunduzu Chisiza, and George Nyandoro met and agreed to what they called the Farmhouse Declaration. Banda and Joshua Nkomo of the Southern Rhodesian Congress were supposed to arrive for the tripartite discussions, but instead sent substitutes (Chisiza and Nyandoro). The cabal convened over one long evening and well into the next dawn. Those plotting together "felt that instead of taking national action country by country, we must strike on the same day in order to divide the Federal forces so they couldn't quell anything." "But we knew that we were going to be arrested."

The Farmhouse Declaration "was the call to a general revolt simultaneously throughout . . . the Federation. It was a general call towards guerilla warfare which should be organized from the rural areas because the security forces were not sufficiently strong there. . . ." This was a "desperate" move. "We wanted just to draw attention of the world to the fact that there [was] a lot of injustice going on here."[34] The plotters expected, apparently, that their efforts "would . . . draw attention to their movements and their struggle." After all, only the Nyasa Congress was capable at that point of mobilizing throughout its home territory. The other two movements were still consolidating themselves and gaining legitimacy within their respective territories.

By the time that I managed to make my way to Malawi during the emergency, and also to Zimbabwe, the African politicians whom I would have interviewed were packed off to their respective detention centers. But there were white and Asian nationalist sympathizers whom I interviewed in Malawi, and even some comparatively responsive security officials. My visits to Blantyre and Zomba were less engaging than they were to become, as subsequent chapters indicate.

Zimbabwe was politically quiet, too. By the time of my return there during the emergency I could connect only with enterprising independent black newspaper editors such as Nathan Shamuyarira, later President Robert Mugabe's chief sugarcoating publicist and sometime cabinet minister. In later years he and I were to agree to disagree about Zimbabwean corruption and dictatorship, but in 1959 and for a few years thereafter he was a deeply connected colleague in touch with liberal white and African elements within Southern Rhodesia.

Harare was also the home of academic colleagues, many of whom were instrumental in fighting against the color bar, especially by desegregating swimming pools as well as ending blatant racial discrimination in shops and on the street. Of importance, too, throughout Harare and the entire Federation, were the efforts of Clyde Sanger and the staff of the *Central African Examiner*, a liberal newsweekly. Sanger ran the only uncompromised journalistic enterprise throughout the entire Federation, although Richard Hall eventually managed to open an independent weekly (and later a daily) in Lusaka after battling to keep Ndola's *Northern News* from being taken over by owners hostile to African nationalism.[35] The Blantyre, Bulawayo, Lusaka, and Salisbury (Harare) daily newspapers all sang government praises.

I wrote for the *Examiner*, but not always on political matters. Sometimes I wrote about the threat of locusts or about water shortages, and also managed to review a wealth of relevant books.

During the emergency, life went on pretty much as before across the Federation, except that much of the newly prominent African political leadership was sidelined for at least the balance of the year. Very few high-level members of the congresses were left outside. The Federal authorities presumably thought that they could buy time to dampen political movement followership, and at least to deprive the new indigenous politicians of opportunities to spread their message and organize. White farmers and businessmen breathed relief, especially in Malawi, where there were rumors that the local Congress had planned to poison whites and massacre them as they slept.

There were fewer marches, fewer flights of rhetoric, less attention to opposition to the Federation. But since almost every place else in Africa was breaking its colonial bonds, especially in francophone West and Central Africa and the Trust Territory of Tanganyika (Tanzania), it was clear to at least some local and many metropolitan observers that not even the local emergency could deflect the drive to overturn Federal rule. As Kaunda wrote, "They have banned the great name of Zambia but the greater name of *freedom now* is spiritual. It is beyond their reach and so they cannot ban it . . . we are just beginning."[36] Additionally, those confined to remote districts were able to spread the nationalist word to areas that hitherto had been little politicized. Likewise, the prisoners in Gweru and Khami became much more consolidated and determined than before.

During the year, as I drove the roads of the country to visit mission stations and tour districts on foot with colonial officials, it became more and more evident that Africans were not to be deterred from the quest for independence. How that would ensue was at first not clear. Locally, Kaunda and his colleagues had impressed and electrified the nation. They had masses of followers, especially as Nkumbula's Congress lost favor.

As I toured the vast country, I visited many of the detained United National Independence Party (UNIP) leaders. At Luwingu, in the Bemba-speaking heartland, I found Wina, a Lozi-speaker, stuck in a relatively primitive holding area at the end of a long road from the district headquarters. We reviewed the philosophical undermining of African nationalism and examined its underpinnings in the local context. He assured me that the emergency marked the beginning of a nationalist triumph, not its end. Wina had been a journalist and a publicist, so he was able to articulate the demands of the people and of his putative political party with ease and persuasion. It was the first of many discussions over sixty years, sometimes amid his political or personal crises. Wina was a cabinet minister many times over in Zambia, and deputy speaker of its parliament. His brother Arthur, trained in economics at the University of California at Los Angeles, became the country's first minister of finance and another friend and maker of modern Zambia.

Detention and incarceration in both Zambia and Malawi solidified both respective new nationalist movements. The prisoners learned whom they could and could not trust. They gained a sense of mutual solidarity that later proved supportive and essential. The Nyasas in both the Gweru and Khami prisons prepared themselves, whenever they were to be released, intellectually for a continuation and escalation of the struggle. Some of the more dangerous Malawian "threats to peace and good order" schooled their less well-educated brethren in politics, in English, and in history. Five of the Malawians in Khami Prison possessed university degrees. They passed what they knew to their less formally advanced fellow Congress prisoners. Many of the members of Banda's first postindependence cabinet were in Khami, together with a future university chancellor.

Establishing UNIP

Outside, during the emergency in both protectorates, nationalist activity slowly resumed despite the absence of the detained leaders. Much of this post-emergency political maneuvering had to be discreet, but I was aware that the locking up of leaders only temporarily halted the spread of dissidence. In Zambia a few new, small political parties tried to substitute temporarily for the ZANC. In the old ANC, Titus Mukopo, Nkumbula's chief deputy, tried to stage a coup and oust his increasingly erratic boss. Failing there, he and several other defectors consolidated two other political groupings to form UNIP, pledging to keep the presidency of UNIP open for Kaunda.

In Malawi, young Aleke K. Banda (no relation to Kamuzu Banda, and of a different ethnic background) was released early in July from prison in Zimbabwe, returned to his ancestral home in Malawi (which he had never even visited), and created with Orton Chirwa, freed from prison in September, and several others the new Malawi Congress Party (MCP) to replace the Nyasa Congress. The presidency of the MCP was reserved for Dr. Banda, who monitored—even guided—events from his prison cell in Zimbabwe.

Kaunda was not released from detention until early 1960, by which time I was returning to Oxford. Kamuzu Banda remained incarcerated until April 1960. But each returned home to surf the swelling waves of nationalist fervor. They had both become authentic liberators. It was only a matter of time before they could present credible demands to the colonial authorities. Kaunda campaigned afresh for self-government with a dearly earned legitimacy as a prison graduate. "One man, one vote" became the war cry in both future countries. I joined UNIP before leaving the Zambia that was soon to be, and a part of Africa to which I was to return many times before the achievement of independence. My professional and literary life became thoroughly engaged henceforth in the Africa that was emerging. Their peoples were my adopted compatriots.

Kaunda, Kapwepwe, the Winas, Mark Chona, Lishomwa Lishomwa, Simon Katilungu, the unrelated Bandas, Chipembere, Dunduzu Chisiza, and Gore-Browne were among the more remarkable Zambians and Malawians that I came to know well while immersing myself in Africa, in rapidly evolving Zambia and Malawi, and in research on missions, political change, and colonial devolution. As future chapters show, I also came to be heavily engaged in political affairs in Zimbabwe, Namibia, Botswana, South Africa, Lesotho, Kenya, Uganda, and Tanzania. The battles against continued colonial rule, against apartheid and South African white repression, engaged me mightily as a scholar, as a teacher, as a wannabe opinion shaper and writer of press articles, as a critic of authoritarian and corrupt rule, and as a friend of Africa and Africans.

The Road South

Conscious that my first year in Africa would be finite, I tried to cover as much Zambian territory as possible and to visit neighboring lands as well. Within Zambia, those valuable and informative adventures included gliding down the upper Zambezi River in a royal barge during the annual Lozi *kwamboka* festival, helping a young assistant district commissioner construct a camp for future tourists along the upper reaches of the Luangwa River, driving very slowly in the dark down an earth path east of the same river toward Fort Jameson (now Chipata) amid roaming herds of elephants, going on *ulendo* with district commissioners as they made their periodic rounds of villages and districts, and visiting closely related colorfully garbed and brightly beaded Lunda chiefs who lived on both sides of, and were officially separated by, the Congo/Zambia border.

South of Zambia, I often drove the 300 miles to Harare—still the political hub of the Federation and the locus of its own developing indigenous political ferment—and to Bulawayo, the country's second city. From Ft. Victoria (now Masvingo), I paid the first of a number of visits to Great Zimbabwe, the sometime center of a major southern African indigenous trading state. There was much to see all over Southern Rhodesia, from Inyanga in the northeast to the Matopos mountains in the southwest. Over succeeding years I was to come to know the interstices of Zimbabwe almost as well as the ins and outs of Zambia and Malawi.

I visited Lesotho, too, especially the areas around Maseru and Quthing. Prince Constantine, whom I had known at Oxford, was to return home in 1961 as King Moshoeshoe II. He advised me whom to see, especially the nationalist firebrands Ntsu Mokhehle and Godfrey Kolisang, both pan-Africanists and graduates of Fort Hare University College. Mokhehle, with clear ideas about how to drive the Basutoland Protectorate to independence, and how to keep that independence free of South African control, was then the leader of the Basutoland Congress

Party and a fierce proponent of rapid political change. I spent many hours with him and Kolisang, his key political associate. Long after those first and subsequent visits to Lesotho, once when King Moshoeshoe II entertained me in his palace, Mokhehle and his party were outmaneuvered by South African–backed conservative forces as the Protectorate gained freedom but continued its role as a labor reservoir for surrounding South Africa.[37]

In my little vehicle I drove the strip roads of Southern Rhodesia to the bustling port of Lourenço Marques (Maputo) in then Portuguese-ruled Mozambique. But the most memorable journey down these same strip roads and then over the border into apartheid-dominated South Africa took place toward the very end of 1959. After an almost 1,000-mile journey from still sleepy Lusaka, across the Zambezi and Limpopo Rivers, and then through the vastness of the northern Transvaal (now Limpopo and Guateng provinces), I finally crested a hill and—in the far distance—saw the bright beams of city lights that were entirely novel (to me) in Africa. Ahead was Johannesburg and troubled ancillary cities such as Soweto. I knew how apartheid rules would constrain my behavior and my interactions with ordinary citizens of all complexions.

In order to find out more and to interview experts, I flew from Johannesburg to Cape Town in order to visit learned authorities in the University of Cape Town—many of whose writings I had already consumed. There, and in Johannesburg, I also became acquainted with opponents of apartheid who were to become life-long friends. But this early visit to South Africa was just an opening glimpse of what was later to become a major part of my professional life and interest. (See chapters 6 and 7.)

The Road North

All too soon it was time to leave the Africa that had so much become my joy and my passion and depart for dissertation writing in Oxford. Dar es Salaam, then the capital of the Trust Territory of Tanganyika (Tanzania), was the first stop. Julius Nyerere, soon to become chief minister and then president of the republic, spoke mightily under the whirling fans of the old New Africa hotel of his vision for the country that he would soon run. He anticipated a more gradual progression to independence than in fact occurred. At the beginning of 1960, he envisaged and seemed content with a stately progression toward the promised land. His socialist views were less pronounced than they became, and the idea of incorporating Zanzibar into the nation was still embryonic.

I interviewed both Bomani brothers, Paul and Mark, and spent many hours with Oscar Kambona, later minister of home affairs, and a person of sensible and progressive ideas with whom I liaised each time that I returned to Dar es Salaam in future years. Paul Bomani became a minister and then a very successful businessman. Mark Bomani became attorney general.[38]

The short hop over the Indian Ocean to Zanzibar led to interviews with Sheikh Ali Muhsin, a moderate leader of a political faction of the Arab minority on the main island, and Abdulrahman Mohamed Babu, a Marxist-inclined strategist who was to become the architect of the Protectorate of Zanzibar and Pemba's first independence of 1963. I learned a little of the complicated Arab/African competition for primacy in the islands, less than I should have about the needs of the African majority on the islands, and not enough about the distinct cleavages within in the Afro-Shirazi Party—the primary vehicle for African political representation. I became imperfectly acquainted with the clove-growing dependency that was to be convulsed in 1964 by an African-led military coup that surprised nearly everyone on the island, its former British masters, and occasional visitors like myself.[39]

From Zanzibar I flew to Nairobi to link up again with Tom Mboya, whom I had hosted at Oxford, and to visit Karen Blixen's famed Ngong Hills, where giraffe at that time still roamed numerous and free. Mboya was the enfant terrible of nascent Kenyan politics. A bright, very articulate, and abundantly self-confident round-faced young Luo from the shores of Lake Victoria, he was the leading indigenous advocate of Jomo Kenyatta's release from detention, and of "one man, one vote" for all Kenyan Africans. My wife and I were later to join Mboya and Kenyatta on the occasion of the latter's first public speech to the Kenyan nation in 1961.

A two-engined DC-3 transported me on the next stage of my journey north. Although I later learned that the DC-3's range was only about 900 miles, we flew at least the official 897 miles to Hargeisa, the capital of British Somaliland (now Somaliland, an unrecognized but successfully self-ruled territory). The capital consisted of many camels and a few streets of sand. It was, nonetheless, a vibrant trading crossroads between the Aden Colony, and overpowering Ethiopia. By the time of my early 1960 arrival, Somaliland had agreed to join together with the Italian-administered Trust Territory of Somalia whenever it managed to gain the independence that had been promised. This urge to link up with very different clans to create a modern state was understandable but, to my untutored mind, dangerously premature.

However the politics of union were to be realized, discussion of such weighty matters were immediately superseded when I was greeted at the flimsy Hargeisa airport building by the colonial secretary (the number two official to the governor) of the British administration: "Dinner jacket?" he asked. It was a Saturday night but, no, I had not come in full regalia. The local administrators dressed up on Saturday nights, it seemed, and I was soon consuming camel kebabs on a paper plate and listening to canned classical favorites coming from a wind-up portable Victrola in some kind of administrative clubhouse. It was my introduction to a part of Africa that was enormously different from the one from which I had just come. Later, I was to see a great deal of the rest of Somalia before everything fell apart; Hargeisa in its unformed, still British, dispensation provided important insights into the diverse other Africas that I was to come to know. Certainly then, and before, I was conscious that there could never be one Africa. There were disparate cultures, disparate peoples, disparate colonial and non-colonial experiences, varied needs, and a plenitude of possible responses, not all of which were to make easy sense.

That was certainly the case when I went on to Addis Ababa, where the fabled monarchy was still all-powerful, Amharic-speakers dominated, and the Coptic Orthodox Church was largely unchallenged by the empire's internal Muslim plurality. I did not shake Emperor Haile Selassie's hand until 1973, months before the coup that ousted him, but in 1960 I spent many hours with his chief advisor, an American lawyer, and came quickly to appreciate the canny ways in which Haile Selassie continued to lord it over his uncommonly complicated and dangerously fragile kingdom.[40]

Fortunately, too, my timing was propitious. I was in Addis Ababa during Timkat, the celebrations in the Orthodox calendar of Epiphany. Row after row of brilliantly garbed priests, many carrying arks of the covenant, passed along the hilly roads of the Ethiopian capital. On and on they came, each priest more colorful than the next. The power of the church was expressed in that festival decades before I was able to spend time inside the rock churches of Lalibela and amid the stelae of Axum in Tigray.

Oxford beckoned with its dreaming spires, but Africa remained in all of its glory until the first of my many return visits, in 1961. By then, the drive for independence had developed an unstoppable momentum.

Consummating Zambian Nationhood

By incarcerating Kaunda and the other leaders of UNIP, Governor Sir Arthur Benson and the Northern Rhodesian authorities had blessed him and his cohorts with legitimacy, and positioned Nkumbula and members of what was left of the ANC as overly moderate "sellouts." Support of the masses of future Zambians thus shifted to UNIP. Kaunda clearly commanded the allegiance of the politically minded intelligentsia of the Protectorate, and gained the backing of influential patrons like President Kwame Nkrumah of Ghana and anticolonial assemblies in the United Kingdom.

From early 1960, when I was writing my dissertation in Oxford, Kaunda and his colleagues repeatedly denounced the Federation, thundered the slogan of nationalism—"one man, one vote"—and tirelessly campaigned up and down the country, gathering UNIP members as they convened boisterously in urban and rural settings. Kaunda and Kapwepwe, particularly, feared what settlers could still do to derail their indigenous drive toward independence. Any delay in gaining self-government could, they worried, give Welensky and white voters an opportunity to deter the consummation of Zambia's drive to freedom. Whether promoted or not by Kaunda, who publicly preached non-violence, the later months of 1960 witnessed attacks by Africans on public property; schools and hospitals were set alight. There were frequent clashes with the police.

The die was largely cast before the year ended when a hastily convened British commission chaired by Lord Monckton took evidence throughout the Rhodesias and Nyasaland and recommended a rapid transition to majority rule in both Northern Rhodesia and Nyasaland, and the consequent breaking up of the Federation. The commission went to Shiwa Ngandu explicitly to take evidence from Gore-Browne and from his staff. Despite vivid signs strung there by UNIP declaring, "Settlers are Bloodsuckers," Gore-Browne said that he favored home rule by Africans. "My own clear convictions," he told Monckton and the commissioners and wrote afterward, "are that African opposition to Federation is now so strong that it would be disastrous to force it on them any longer." He further said that the franchise should be liberalized "to give Africans a *genuine* share in the government of the country . . . immediately."[1] Gore-Browne, further, strongly backed Kaunda as the country's future leader, and was not shy about making that case locally and overseas. My droll friend Richard Hall, stalwart

Overcoming the Oppressors. Robert I. Rotberg, Oxford University Press. © Oxford University Press 2023.
DOI: 10.1093/oso/9780197674208.003.0002

Map 2.1. Zambia and Malawi

editor of the newly established, progressive *African Mail*, urged Gore-Browne to get back into politics, full time, despite his advanced age.[2]

In Malawi, meanwhile (as we shall see in a subsequent chapter), the British government had begun to concede the kinds of reforms that Kamuzu Banda, Aleke Banda, Orton Chirwa, and the Malawi Congress Party were demanding. An election was scheduled for 1961 that was intended to give Kamuzu Banda a commanding position in the territory. The Zambians, led by Kaunda, requested parity, even though the Colonial Office still thought that it might somehow cleverly be able to keep the Rhodesias together while letting Nyasaland (with its comparatively small handful of white settlers) separate. Kaunda sought a constitutional advance encompassing the shift to "responsible" government that the British government had now promised to Malawi. As Kaunda wrote reasonably to me, "We have been having an awfully busy time trying to influence those in authority to make decisions about our future that were acceptable to the majority of our inhabitants—as you can well imagine this has not been an easy job at all." He went on hopefully to suggest that the "end was not very much in view," but what little progress was being made, he believed, was a "by-product of our pressure," and the "economic chaos" that could follow.[3]

British colonial secretary Iain Macleod initially gave way to Kaunda. Then, after Welensky, Greenfield, and others persuaded him that Northern Rhodesia's move in parallel with Malawi would undermine prospects for a "sensible" political outcome for Southern Rhodesia, Macleod backed down, altering crucial provisions in the proposed constitution for Northern Rhodesia that had been expected to provide UNIP with substantial seats in a revamped territorial Legislative Council. Whoever controlled Northern Rhodesia controlled Central Africa. Once it seceded along with Nyasaland, the white redoubt of Southern Rhodesia would be cut adrift, and white rule there would be compromised as well.

After interminable talks in London and Lusaka, and much blustering by Welensky (he threatened to cut Zambia off from Kariba power and to strike the copper mines), Macleod proposed in early 1961 to hold an election that would tilt in favor of majority rule but give the balance of power between Welensky and Kaunda's followers to a new Liberal Party recently established by Sir John Moffat (grandson of the famous missionary). The new party was genuinely multiracial in design, but with limited black and white following. Moreover, Moffat in his own aloof way was just as much a paternalist as Welensky, the sometime trade unionist and locomotive driver.[4] Gore-Browne refused to join the Liberals, preferring to cast his lot with UNIP.

Kaunda was obviously pleased, and wrote from New York, where he was testifying before the UN's Commission on Decolonization, "My policy must prove correct, i.e., that it pays to be non-violent in these matters. The way independence came to the Congo [in 1960] and the way its affairs have been conducted do sandwich me. . . ." If talks with Britain break down, he continued, "God help us—I don't know what might follow."[5]

They did break down. Macleod gave way to Welensky in order to help ensure a peaceful and positive result when whites went to the polls in Southern Rhodesia in July 1961 to approve a constitution that would give Africans led by Joshua Nkomo fifteen seats in a sixty-five-seat local parliament. That was useful for Southern Rhodesia (see chapter 9), but a perceived double-cross in Zambia. Macleod now favored an election in Zambia based on a very complicated formula that devalued African votes and gave whites a virtual veto in many constituencies.

By the time of a short visit to Lusaka by me in mid-1961, the territory was on fire. For three months, Africans blocked roads, destroyed bridges, stoned cars, burned down schools and dispensaries, and demonstrated their displeasure violently—but mostly across the northern half of Zambia. Gore-Browne put a loaded revolver beside his bed, just in case.[6]

Macleod promised yet a further rethinking of the Northern Rhodesian situation if Kaunda could control violence, which Kaunda could and did. In late 1961, by which time I was teaching my first classes at Harvard University, Reginald Maudling replaced Macleod as colonial secretary and visited Lusaka to come to his own conclusions after hearing from Kaunda, Gore-Browne, Moffat, Welensky, and many others. His carefully crafted ultimate compromise was issued in early 1962. Importantly, the percentage of racial cross-voting required for winning election in the decisive "multiracial" seats (as a third were so designated) was lowered to give UNIP a better chance of winning a clear majority. The new Northern Rhodesian elections were scheduled for late 1962. Although a far less clear-cut arrangement than that prepared for Malawi, the road to independence was now open and the end of the Federation near.

Shortly thereafter, Kaunda (in a purple toga) and Gore-Browne (with his distinctive monocle) were testifying together before the UN Special Committee on Decolonization in New York. Together they addressed a rapturous meeting at the African-American Institute in New York, and then both came to Cambridge, Massachusetts, Kaunda to address my welcoming students and many others, and Gore-Browne to spend Easter weekend with me and my wife.

Then living in a cramped garret, we put Gore-Browne, in his stiff tweeds, patrician bearing, and all, up in one of Harvard's undergraduate living houses. He became a short-term visiting fellow. There he was feted and dined well, surrounded by curious young Harvard males.

But there was an unanticipated problem with these comfortable arrangements: My wife and I discovered belatedly that Gore-Browne had some unavoidable eating discomforts. En route to New York and Boston, he had stayed, as was his custom, at the Army-Navy Club in London. Steeping in its deep luxurious baths that he had known for sixty years or so, his false teeth slipped down the wide tub wastes. So Gore-Browne struggled to eat with difficulty the potato chips on which undergraduates dined, and much else. Joanna, my dear wife, therefore prepared dinner for our honored guest and proceeded to make *paschka*, a Russian Easter exotic soft dessert (molded in a flower pot) that was just right for Gore-Browne's sore gums, and much enjoyed.

He and I were together again in mid-1962 in Lusaka and Shiwa Ngandu, when my wife and I were in Lusaka, engaged in further research, and in Malawi, before traveling north by car to Tanzania and Uganda. But although I was destined unfortunately to miss the vicissitudes of final campaigning in Zambia, I was party to UNIP and Liberal Party calculations of advantage and disadvantage before the actual vote itself. In Lusaka, we stayed for weeks at my old research institute—long enough to introduce Joanna to the culinary delights of roasted termites (caught next to our bungalow) and to several six-foot-long steel-gray black mambas slithering overhead in the canopy.

An Enormously Contorted Multiracial Election

A British political apparatus caught between militant African nationalism and the defensive thrashing of white engine drivers, farmers, and townsmen imagined that its civil servants and colonial masters could devise an excessively ingenious, liberal mechanism to entrench plural multiracialism in the future Zambia much more completely and decisively than the creators of the Federation had done. The forty-five parliamentary seats to be contested electorally were divided into fifteen upper-roll (white) seats, which Welensky's United Federal Party was sure to win, and fifteen common-roll (black) seats, of which UNIP would likely win the majority, but would lose a few to Nkumbula's ANC. Then there were fifteen more seats on the so-called national roll: Those were deciding positions because each was a double constituency, designed for a black and a white pair running together. But succeeding in the contest for these national roll seats could only be accomplished if African candidates gained 10 percent of the white votes cast in each constituency and white candidates also gained 10 percent of the votes cast by persons of the other color. The Britons who devised this scheme foresaw the new Liberal Party of multiracialists taking these decisive seats, holding the balance of power as well-intended moderates friendly to Africans and therefore ushering in an era of "good feeling." But that was a wild-eyed dream of constitutional architects little acquainted with hard-edged retail politics among worried white miners and rail workers.

In the ensuing October 1962 election, black and white voters were asked to choose, but not along normal party or color lines. Furthermore, UNIP could form a new government only if it could attract sufficient white voters. Welensky's United Federal Party could keep control only if it could win national constituencies or persuade another party to join it. Victorious national-roll candidates would absolutely need to appeal in their statements and policies across the color line.

Kaunda accepted this Hobson's choice. Ever the optimist, he persuaded himself that whites would be reasonable and realistic. He was comfortable campaigning to bring white and black back together in true partnership. A majority of the Protectorate's 72,000 white voters would need to cast ballots for UNIP, and blacks would need to vote for UNIP-aligned whites across multi-member constituencies. Gore-Browne, for example, stood for UNIP in a double-member constituency that encompassed territory from the Copperbelt to Tanzania. Andrew Sardanis, a Cypriot businessman close to Kaunda, stood in another expanded constituency stretching westward from the Copperbelt to the border with Angola.

Kaunda, insouciant, may have been almost the only Zambian to accept the golden web of last-hope multiracialism that British colonial officials had spun. Kapwepwe and Sikota Wina thought that the entire exercise was a futile waste of time. But Kaunda loyally and energetically attempted to bring whites and blacks together and to make the difficult constitutional arrangements work. Well before the election itself, I was with him when he drove himself to exhaustion; on the hustings every day, he gave speeches to mixed and unmixed audiences, exhorted his UNIP followers to work harder, tried to fend off the UFP's dirty campaigning, prepared press releases, enlightened visiting journalists, and spent almost every late evening closeted with Kapwepwe, the Winas, Mainza Chona, and others to plan strategic moves. As Sardanis recalled, "KK was indefatigable. . . . His energy had no limits."[7] He went on television and radio and attempted to assuage white fears. A strictly abstemious person, he went to cocktail parties so that he could woo whites and demonstrate his reasonableness. By my own calculation, he covered at least 25,000 miles in a largely fruitless exercise to counter Welensky's poisonous attacks.

Most of the voters of the territory, however, had little patience for an electoral exercise that was meant to slow, rather than to accelerate, progress toward majority rule. October's balloting was profoundly inconclusive. Africans voted massively for UNIP, whites for the Federal Party. Of the 106,000 ballots cast, UNIP won 64,000 and 80 percent of the African total. Nkumbula's ANC won 17,000 votes. Of the nearly 29,000 whites, 21,500 backed the UFP, 4,500 UNIP, 1,500 the Liberals, 1,000 the ANC. But the popular vote mattered little: Thirteen of the fifteen national seats had returned no one; they were declared "vacant" since no candidate secured sufficient crossover votes. Nevertheless, Welensky's party had won one more seat than UNIP and could, theoretically, have claimed the right to direct the next Northern Rhodesian government.

Instead, the British government decided that because so many of the balance-of-power seats had returned no one, it would stage a series of by-elections in December for those decisive constituencies. Yet, the runoff contests in December were frustrated as well by the unwillingness of the electorate to cast ballots for erstwhile opponents of a different color. Gore-Browne, for example, received 93 percent of black votes and only 1 percent of potential white votes in October and 94 percent of black votes and almost 3 percent of white votes in December. Sardanis did a little better, but his vote totals were equally lopsided. Nationalists would not vote for unfriendly white candidates; white settlers and their ilk could not bring themselves to choose UNIP-inclined candidates.

Northern Rhodesia nonetheless needed a new government. UNIP feared that Nkumbula would throw his seven seats in with those sixteen won by John Roberts, Welensky's Northern Rhodesian surrogate, and his UFP, and thus thwart incipient black-led responsible government.[8] (Kamuzu Banda had been running Malawi's "responsible" government for a year.) UNIP held only fifteen seats, the remainder being still "vacant." Fortunately, Nkumbula came to his anti-Federal, indigenous nationalist senses and was finally persuaded in very late 1962 to share power and share responsible government authority and cabinet seats with Kaunda, who became minister of local government but was also acknowledged as the incipient country's chief political leader.[9]

A momentous political shift had occurred under the guise of a failed multiracial balloting exercise. Africans had outmaneuvered white settlers, almost without the help of British machinations, and the obvious next step after running the new (temporary) government of the Protectorate was to agree on a proper transition to majority rule. Already, Britain had transferred power to Julius Nyerere and the Tanganyika African National Union (TANU) in an independent Tanganyika, and to Apolo Milton Obote and the Uganda's People's Congress in that country. Jomo Kenyatta's Kenya, was next in line, for 1963. Britain had also agreed to let Malawi secede from the Federation. Kaunda wanted as much, and again demanded parity with Banda's Malawi in gaining full independence.

It took a little bluster and guerrilla theater, and some well-timed walkouts during meetings between Kaunda, Nkumbula, and the new Secretary of State for the Colonies, but by April 1963, Kaunda and Nkumbula knew that Northern Rhodesia could make its way to nationhood in 1964, after yet another election. This one would be run on standard first-past-the-post lines for sixty-five parliamentary places, with ten additional ones reserved for whites for four years. Equally, the Federation experiment would be wound up by the end of 1963. Power was to be transferred effectively and finally to the majority in both northern territories, with Southern Rhodesian Africans (as we shall see in chapter 9) left to pursue their own lonely and much more contorted nationalistic endeavor.

The Northern Rhodesian parliamentary elections of early 1964 gave UNIP fifty-five seats and the ANC ten, eight in the south. Roberts' party won the ten reserved seats. Kaunda quickly became prime minister en route to an independence day set for October 1964, when he would become the embryonic nation's first president. In choosing his first cabinet, he accomplished what he was to continue to accomplish for the next twenty-seven years—to balance the competing regional interests within his party, to shuffle ministerial portfolios so that competence and sectional favoritism were equally regarded, and to keep those who might have been envious of his own preeminence off-balance and appeased. "One nation, one Zambia," was his professed mantra.

Not all of Kaunda's key followers were university graduates. Nor was the Zambia that was soon-to-be well stocked with trained personnel for the subministerial positions in the new government. By some estimates, Zambia had no more than one hundred university graduates available for governmental service; only a small handful of trained indigenous lawyers, doctors, engineers, surveyors, chartered accountants, and so on, existed. There may have been as few as 1,000 Zambians who had completed high school. Who was to staff the ministries, the civil service, the embassies overseas, and help to run even the mines as their managements were gradually (over years) Africanized?

After October, the Northern Rhodesia Protectorate would become Zambia, a name derived from Zambezia and suggested by Kapwepwe and Arthur Wina.

Influenced by Nkrumah's replacement of the colonial Gold Coast appellation with Ghana, the name of a historic empire in roughly the same part of West Africa. Kaunda (and UNIP) obviously needed a new national name unaffiliated with a capitalistic British imperialist like Cecil John Rhodes. But unlike the hoary Zimbabwean empire, the territory that was to become Zambia had no traditional kingdoms other than Barotseland, the Lozi domain in the far west. And (aside from the Winas and a few others) there was no affinity among Bemba, Nyanja, Tonga, or anyone else, with Barotseland. Anyway, the Litunga, or ruler of the Lozi, had opposed UNIP and had favored continued white rule. The Bemba had a paramount chief, and the Lunda of the far northwest had many chiefs, but "Zambia" proved a happily made-up name with no dissenters.

I was teaching, and could not observe (as I had done first-hand in Malawi) the British flag fluttering down in October 1964 and the new Zambian standard being raised. But I had been in Lusaka and elsewhere in Zambia during the middle of the year, had talked at length to the new prime minister and both Winas about their heady prospects, and had long conversations with (Sir) Richard Luyt, the chief secretary and the person self-charged with moving Zambia as expeditiously as possible out of white hands and into black control. He was an advocate in Whitehall for Kaunda, and a judicious behind-the-scenes opponent of Welensky and the whites in Southern Rhodesia. Sir Richard became a close acquaintance, and we saw much of each other in Zambia and later in South Africa, when he became vice chancellor of the University of Cape Town.

The big question after 1964 was whether Kaunda, a gentle vegetarian and soft-spoken disciple of Gandhi, could successfully guide his more pugnacious followers, and especially his fellow (and finally victorious) nationalist politicians, into a New Jerusalem that kept the copper engine of prosperity roaring, held a plural society of ethnically dissimilar groups together, and demonstrated conclusively to its retreating colonial overlords and skeptical Federal adherents that Africans could indeed run their own show well, fairly, and without discrimination. There was much to do, little time, and abundant competing priorities.

Aggregating Power, Commanding the Heights

Establishing a new country, especially in southern Africa after ten years of Federal domination, was less straightforward than we might imagine. Kaunda naturally appointed a mixture of recent university graduates and struggle captains to help him to govern the new Zambia, but they all lacked experience. Their predecessors were largely uninterested, and in some cases were uninvited, to introduce their Zambian successors to governmental machinery. As an inevitable result, the new cabinet members and the upper ranks of officialdom entered office largely unacquainted with their portfolios and responsibilities. Moreover, everyone inducted into government scrambled to acquire "appropriate" perquisites. There were new houses to be found, automobiles and fancy furniture to be procured, subordinate staff to be hired, and altered pecking orders to be established. Many white civil servants and many from the merchandizing community fled en masse. Some incoming cabinet members and deputies were able, others floundered. Two of the initial set of ministers accepted bribes, and were sacked. Only the mines kept operating normally and profitably—thanks to the acceleration of a futile war in distant Vietnam. Throughout, even on the Copperbelt, the new nation contemplated novel names, novel postures, novel expectations, and novel social and operating assumptions. The goal, pursued haphazardly and opportunistically by a cadre of Kaunda's governing associates, was to establish an "effective" Africanized apparatus of oversight and implementation as rapidly and as fully as possible. However, as Sardanis, a new appointee himself, later wrote: "It all looked like a muddle...."[10]

Muddle was understandable and excusable, as I experienced whenever I paid a yearly visit to Lusaka and Kaunda in State House to learn how the nascent government was maturing. Like so many inside and outside government who wished Zambia well, and had faith in Kaunda's exceptional leadership promise and the capabilities of the university graduates on his team, I presumed that Zambia could escape the greediness and curtailing of civil liberties that had begun to distinguish the ruling regimes of youthful Ghana, Guinea, and the Congo / Zaire.

Kaunda was a leader of whom much was expected despite his own lack of formal higher educational attainment. He seemed an estimable guide of a people liberated from oppression. He possessed, as far as I and other close participants could see, a sensible vision for the new nation, a deft administrative hand, a sense of moral self-mastery (and Adam Smith's "perfect prudence"), and an integrity that was absent in many of his peers.[11] Other recent "liberators" of Africa were clearly more self-important, more impressed with their own rightness for the role of national leadership (such as Nkrumah, Félix Houphouet-Boigny, Jomo Kenyatta, Kamuzu Banda, and Sékou Touré). Zambia's road ahead appeared comparatively smooth despite the comparative abruptness of the transition of power, despite relentless settler and Rhodesian antagonism, and despite the strident approaches of some of Kaunda's more assertive Zambian colleagues.

On the Front Line

We did not reckon, however, that white Rhodesians would declare independence unilaterally from Britain in late 1965 and that Zambia would be enmeshed for the next fifteen years in a global sanctions endeavor meant to bring Rhodesia (as it came to call itself) to heel. Zambia became a "Front Line State," one of five nations hosting supposedly secret training camps of African insurgents against Rhodesia, and also against apartheid South Africa. (I was to spend time in Lusaka over the years with leaders of the Zimbabwean, Namibian, and South African guerrilla contingents.)

The Rhodesian breakaway, and responsive sanctions, strained landlocked Zambia logistically. Its supplies traditionally came from Rhodesia and South Africa and its vital copper exports hitherto had traveled by rail through Rhodesia, Botswana, and South Africa. Its liquid fuels came from Rhodesia. Instead of being able quietly to develop in its own way, the infant Zambia now had to behave militantly against its neighbor while simultaneously looking out cagily for the economic and political self-interests of its own citizens and industries.

Zambia rationed petrol, expensively airlifted fuel to Ndola, and then began a massive exercise to import petrol in forty-five-gallon galvanized drums and other essential goods along the graveled, oft-treacherous Great North Road from the line of rail all the way (1,200 miles) to Tanzania's main (but clogged) port of Dar es Salaam. (I drove up and down that atrocious road—the "Hell Run"—to visit Shiwa Ngandu and various research sites in the Northern Province, but always amid great clouds of hazardous dust from speeding fuel trucks. In the rainy season slippery mud replaced the clouds of dust.) Eventually—but it took several years and immense expense—450 state-owned trucks plied up and down the Hell Run artery, keeping Zambia supplied and exports of copper flowing until a pipeline and a railway could be constructed.

For a new nation to be on the front line against remaining white, entrenched interests (and Rhodesia's unilateral declaration of independence naturally led to a guerrilla war against the white regime partially pursued from bases in Zambia) and to be forced to reinvent itself logistically (because of sanctions imposed by Britain, the United States, and the UN on Rhodesia) was harmful.[12] But the unexpected Rhodesian consternation in 1965 was matched, eventually, by unanticipated ideological adventures that began in Tanzania.

Zambia is a tragic example of how ill-considered decisions led to the immiseration of the state and widespread poverty. Three years after independence, particularly, Kaunda and UNIP made a series of unforced errors that started the process of unraveling the nation's democratic underpinnings. Following a rather trivial but racially charged incident involving a Lusaka white butcher's misconstrued gift of a turkey to the national vice president's wife (she claimed that he had sent her a spoiled bird), UNIP Youth Brigade members a few days later rioted and destroyed the butchery. The leader of the brigade said that his followers would not allow "a white chap" to treat us "like in the colonial days." Kaunda rightly condemned the rioters for taking the law into "their own hands."[13] The judge trying the case later sentenced the Brigade leader to twelve months in jail. But

Kaunda, pressed by local UNIP bigwigs, pardoned the chief culprit, the master-mind of the riot, and consequently and lastingly undermined the sanctity of the rule of law in Zambia. Expatriate judges were condemned as insensitive to local cultural matters and, as a result, the Zambian judiciary almost never again func-tioned independently. It became a creature of the executive and the ruling party.

Kaunda, moreover, refused to rein in the Youth Brigade when it attacked the local Lusaka *Times of Zambia* and its crusading white editor, my old liberal friend Richard Hall. His newspaper had supported judicial independence and had crit-icized the Youth Brigade for foolish vigilantism. Kaunda failed to act, too, when the Brigade attacked the hapless butcher's white lawyer and caused him and the butcher to flee to Rhodesia.

Juridical niceties and freedom of expression were no longer regarded as obstacles to the wishes of the state and its major political party. That was the clear message of these series of leadership errors of omission and commission; they forced Kaunda's hand, moreover, and produced multiple consequences that were poorly appreciated and too little understood at the time.

I shopped at the same butchery and was living in Zambia when the case of the supposedly unwholesome fowl occurred. I wrote it up for the *New York Times* and later for the *Central African Examiner* and *Africa Report*. My wife and I and our then two very young daughters (one learning to crawl up and down steep stairs and her elder sister mischievously using a garden hose to spray her sister and herself) were then living for much of the year (I was on sabbatical) in Lusaka's first racially mixed experimental enclave close to the city's municipal hospital. We had black and white neighbors, each in almost identical comfort-able but small brick houses recently erected by a well-meaning philanthropist who sought to integrate a populace that was still largely segregated by income and color. There was a BBC correspondent in one house, an American researcher and family in another, a leading woman UNIP figure and future minister in a third, and the celebrated South African exiled jazz pianist Todd Matshikiza and Esme, his wife, in a fourth (there were others, too). With Matshikiza, the com-poser of the South African musical *King Kong* and the author of *Chocolates for My Wife*, and their son John (later a London stage star), we spent many convivial hours long before Todd's sudden and unexpected death.

Behind our modest mansion in this sometime wasteland between an African township, a thriving Anglican mission, and the city's main hospital was a path used every hour by Africans heading to the hospital. We were therefore the ob-ject of frequent attention and notice, especially when I—a youngish white man—carried or played with my daughters. But it was when I put Nicola, not quite two, into a child carrier, put her on my back, and started walking that heads swiv-eled and Africans pointed, commented, and guffawed. What was a *mzungu*—a presumed white bwana—doing women's work? Men in Africa never carried their children, and certainly never carried them on their backs in the manner of women wrapping their cloaks around themselves, with babies and small children snugly inside and on the back.

Joanna was in Zambia to research her Tufts University thesis, "Aggression and Affection in a Multiracial Schooling Setting." Having begun to learn CiBemba, I was involved in my usual way in politics and political development. But I was also attempting to write a history of the Bisa people, who spoke a language similar to CiBemba and who lived in the Northern and Luapula Provinces, especially in and around Lake Bangweulu (where David Livingstone died). I traveled frequently up and down the Great North Road to the Bisa, and also to visit Gore-Browne, whose lengthy diaries I was reading into a tape recorder in the months before he died. I was also frequently with my UNIP friends (I was still a member) and with congenial backers of Kaunda like Hall, Trevor and Carol Coombe (of the University of Zambia), and Denis and Oenone Acheson (he managing one of the copper behemoths and she producing great art).

The new University of Zambia was a beehive of activity, too, under its energetic Canadian vice chancellor and with an assembly of committed neo-Marxist and non-Marxist pioneering lecturers from Europe and Africa. It was a time—despite the incident of the unwholesome fowl and its unfortunate aftermath—when everyone concerned could still remain optimistic that Zambia would succeed in building a nation much more effectively and painlessly than other young African polities—despite the Rhodesian war, despite potential fuel shortages, and despite what by late 1967 seemed to be serious fissures within UNIP. After all, the Vietnam War called for copper, and the Zambian mines were still producing well.

The Kaunda doctrine and his "Little Red Book" of approved ideas dates from the same year. In April, humanism became official as the national creed. He served notice by his Doctrine of Humanism that he intended to banish all tribal or personal power blocs within UNIP and the nation. Articulating ideas that he had long cherished and publicized, but never before set out in an official document, he enunciated a full social, economic, and political program to which he as the "father of the nation" expected all of his followers (by which he meant all Zambians) to adhere. Echoing Nyerere's Arusha Declaration of Socialism and Self-Reliance (*ujamaa*, or brotherhood) of earlier in the year, and especially drawing on the Arusha Declaration's formulations of proper economic development, Kaunda called for a return to the imagined "classless" society of pre-colonial Zambia.[14] Wealth would have to be redistributed to make that return possible. Man, the Doctrine of Humanism declared, was designated as the proper focus of society and of the energies and policies of UNIP. "African society has always been man-centred . . . all human activity centres around MAN."[15] For Kaunda, humanism and this man-centeredness transcended both capitalism and communism, yet incorporated the best features of each ideological tendency. In accord with the new doctrine, economic development should be pursued only to the extent that it benefited individuals. A governmental Ministry of Guidance was established to advance these new doctrines and the overall cause of humanism.

Zambia's humanism differed from Tanzanian socialism, and Soviet communism, by condoning private property and, most of all, by seeking to avoid rather than to provoke and glorify class conflict. For Kaunda (most Zambians were indifferent, and party members also) a man-centered society valued human relations over material possessions. Pre-colonial village life was imagined as a communal man-centered paradise motivated by a sense of ethical universalism that would stimulate a new moral national culture.

These sentiments were romantic and, for Kaunda, uplifting. But Zambia already had a striving proto-middle class, a working group of acquisitive miners, and the makings of a striving culture that could never embrace agrarian socialism or revert to a pre-modern approach to everyday life. Moreover, by 1973, Zambia was more urbanized than the typical new African nation. Kaunda (and Nyerere) were shutting barn doors long after the horses of everyday avariciousness, and competition, had left the African barn.

As a near contemporary critique concluded, "The ability of Humanism to provide an ideological basis for action and a cohesive and coherent direction for development was, however, inhibited by its own weaknesses. The first was its ambiguity. . . . Moreover the prescriptions for development were based on a utopian notion of Zambian traditional society that . . . scarcely applied in the countryside, let alone to the realities of urban life."[16] Humanism further failed to address problems of factionalism and patronage, the mainstays of Zambian and many other political cultures.

Tellingly for policy purposes, the stated enemies of humanism accordingly were apathy, deviance from the party line, ill discipline, and selfishness. Tribalism, provincialism, racialism, and bureaucracy were also anathema. "All these evils are dangers not only within the Party but perhaps even more so in Government." At a UNIP annual congress later in 1967, Kaunda told the delegates that they should all be working hard to establish a "man-centered society." "It is most important to state," he informed party members, "that the most important single unit in our democracy is man himself, and let me emphasize that this man is not defined according to his color, tribe, religion, creed, or political leanings." Man was the "beginning and end of everything on earth."[17] ("Man" presumably included women, but such inclusion was never addressed.)

Such lofty sentiments were brushed aside at the party convention and within UNIP indefinitely. The delegates were determined to vote along ethnic lines for positions within the party and the government. Persons of Bemba background gained more and more control of UNIP, to the president's chagrin. Even Kapwepwe annoyed his old schoolmate, Kaunda, by using Bemba voting power to gain the vice presidency of the party (and, automatically, the national vice presidency after the upcoming 1968 elections) and to oust the stalwart on whom Kaunda had come to rely. Kapwepwe also rallied Bemba forces to oust many non-Bemba from the party central committee and from important positions within UNIP. Even Arthur Wina, the minister of finance, was pushed out because of his Lozi ethnicity (and the fact, probably, that he evidently was more knowledgeable and sophisticated than other local university graduates).

Humanism and Spoils

Humanism sounded positive in general, and was welcomed by donors, but party operatives were more interested in the direct spoils that came with positions in government and the ruling party. The result—despite humanism—was to give UNIP a more sectionalized and grasping character than Kaunda wanted. The balancing at which he was so effective was now more difficult. Personally, he always rose above ethnic particularities because even though he grew up in the Bemba heartland, his intonation and his accent were those inherited from his parents, northern Malawians. So he was seen to be beyond tribalism, and that enabled him to lead a party that—like so many in Africa—was roiled bitterly and ethnically (belying the UNIP "one nation, one Zambia" slogan). Kaunda, in disgust, told party members the next year that he was "not prepared to preside over a federation of tribes."[18] From the national perspective, Kaunda was indispensable, but sections of the ruling party wanted more control and easier access to the perquisites of power.

Conceivably in order to improve his indispensable status within UNIP, and to some limited extent to appease the Kapwepwe faction, in early 1968 Kaunda fatefully decided to confiscate 51 percent of nearly all business operations within the country. He did so because other African leaders had demanded similar control of economic activity within their own nations, because Nyerere's Arusha Declaration had started a similar process in Tanzania, and because—sensibly—he wanted to give opportunities to Africans and to replace the whites and Asians who had previously discriminated against Africans and commanded too many of the remaining local economic levers. "From the standpoint of developing an African capitalist class, eliminating the Asian middleman made sense" politically, if no sense economically.[19] Zambia hence proceeded to purchase 51 percent of small, medium, and large enterprises (including the twenty-five most important foreign-owned concerns) and put Zambians in charge. That was the point of the reforms that emerged from the Mulungushi Conference in 1967, but turning commercial establishments into parts of the bureaucracy (through the ministry of trade and industry) and using them as patronage sumps, was bound to frighten away foreign investors and make owners of property insecure. Capital flight could follow.

In 1969, a similar process was pursued concerning the copper mines—providers of 95 percent of export earnings and 56 percent of government revenues. After tense negotiations, the Anglo-American Corporation of South Africa (with massive holdings in that country as well) and Roan Selection Trust of the United States, the two mine owners, reluctantly agreed to Zambia's evaluation of what the mines were worth, to a new tax methodology in lieu of well-established but anachronistic royalty payment arrangements, and to management and oversight by the government.[20] Africanization would obviously be accelerated, as would increases in the bargaining power of the African Mine Worker's Union and an end to many of the privileges of white unionized miners. Through this extension of the 51 percent rule, Kaunda's actions were helping to minimize the national appeal of Kapwepwe and others who criticized his leadership. In 1970, Zambia's banks also received the 51 percent treatment. The varieties of corporate endeavor were henceforth organized as Indeco (industry), Mindeco (mines), and Findeco (banks), huge parastatal ministries with innumerable government-managed (formerly private) corporations within them.

These several socialistic arrangements were tidy, ideologically secure, and probably consonant with what Kaunda and a few close associates genuinely believed were advantageous for Zambia and its people's prosperity and the national spirit. They were transformative acts. Kaunda, unwittingly and unthinkingly, as I came to believe at the time, assumed that these initiatives sensibly redirected capital away from foreigners and exploiters. Whether or not these state-owned operations made good economic policy for the infant Zambia and for the welfare of its citizens in the short and medium runs, however, they were to prove disastrous in the long run. Zambians would have lived better and enjoyed better state services, as well as higher incomes, if Kaunda's Zambia had followed the more modest and purposeful Botswanan rather than the Tanzanian (and Ghanaian) models.

Kaunda and I often talked about his indispensability and his growing desire to turn the nation more and more fully into a humanistic socialist showcase. We discussed philosophy more than we discussed opportunity costs, human consequences, and margins of error. But those considerations were very real, and, unlike Nyerere, Kaunda was not a deep reader or a fully aware thinker. Nor was he numerate. Too often he was expedient, but with an ability to draw upon Gandhian principles to make the results appear spiritually desirable, and therefore uplifting.

Only Kaunda in those early days could have commanded the loyalties of Zambians and successfully have led them into battle against the arrayed forces of white Rhodesia and South Africa (both of whom periodically raided insurgent establishments in Zambia). Only Kaunda could have gained the full support of Tanzania for Zambia's commercial lifeline. And only Kaunda could have persuaded donors and some students of African development that the Mulungushi reforms and humanism were worthwhile. Indeed, there were skeptics even within Zambia that Kaunda never won over. His "improvements," turmoil from sanctions, and Bemba greediness led in 1968 to a loss of parliamentary seats in Barotseland to a newly created Lozi political party. This rejection of UNIP proved a wake-up call for Kaunda that led, in a few years, to a major political shakeup—and to even more difficulties.

In the immediate term, however, the electoral losses forced Kaunda to reassert some measure of control over the fractious party. In 1969, he dismissed the central committee and appointed an eleven-person interim executive committee of the party loyal to him and to humanism. Four were from the Bemba heartland, one was a Lozi. He renamed Barotseland as the new Western Province, and removed many of the sometime kingdom's privileges.

His break with Kapwepwe became more and more serious, too, especially when Kapwepwe left UNIP and created the United Progressive Party (UPP), a largely Bemba grouping, in 1971. Kaunda soon had them all arrested, with the stage set for an even more fateful rearrangement of the Zambian political and constitutional landscape. To make the arrests Kaunda used the very colonial-era laws that Governor Benson had earlier and fatefully employed to arrest him and the others involved in "Murder Incorporated."

Kaunda's general decency and caution did not prevent mistakes. Privately to me, after creating them and realizing their flaws, he rationalized. He admitted that some had been hasty, like an episode of misguided racialism in 1969 that caused the departure of the country's new white, Irish, chief justice, a UNIP supporter who was targeted in a misguided way by subordinates of the president. Nor did his good intentions prevent economic mismanagement and an acceptance (for party ends) of ministerial incompetence.

Streamlining Political Participation

The defining judgmental errors occurred in 1972, however, when Kaunda decided fully to nationalize the mines (along with minor zinc and coal operations) and also to ban competing political parties (on the Tanzanian model).

With regard to creating a single-party political system, and confining representation of the people to that entity, UNIP could justifiably claim that the party harbored within itself various competitive factions and that the public interest would be well safeguarded by single-party members representing the varied citizen initiatives. Instead, this Nyerere-similar rationalization allowed a powerful oligarchy within UNIP to make decisions about national priorities without consulting constituents or taking contrary opinions into account. (What Kaunda did not explain publicly was that Kapwepwe's smaller UPP was gaining strength, and was perceived as a threat to UNIP). In this manner, Zambia joined the many authoritarian governments within sub-Saharan Africa that effectively ignored the needs and preferences of their citizens and existed mostly to convey power, prestige, and riches to its ruling elite—an echo of Fanon's provocative warnings amid the Algerian war for independence: "The single party is the modern form of the dictatorship of the bourgeoisie, unmasked, unpainted, unscrupulous, and cynical."[21]

Nyerere, with whom I had conversed in 1960 and with whose ministers (Oscar Kambona, particularly) I had kept in contact ever since, decided in 1965 not only to help Kaunda relieve Zambia's logistical nightmare by establishing a mutual transport consortium and planning a pipeline and a railway connecting the two countries, but also to stifle his country's reasonably well-functioning democratic system. Nyerere abolished Tanzania's political pluralism in favor of an all-knowing, all-controlling, single-party state, and that abrogation of democratic participation had fateful reverberating consequences for Zambia.

Nyerere rationalized his derogation of standard multi-party parliamentary democracy. Africans, Nyerere decided (with a glance at the Soviet Union, China, and parts of West Africa)—had in pre-colonial times achieved consensus without the strife and the "harmful" competition that was fundamental to Western-style electoral politics. So Nyerere effectively neutered political participation for all of his countrymen, except in theory within the all-powerful ruling political party—Chama Cha Mapinduzi, the party of the revolution (formerly TANU).

In terms of policy and social welfare, as the (elected) party leader, Nyerere would decide and a subservient parliament would ratify. This was authoritarianism at its fullest, but cloaked beneath a paternalistic notion of development that took choice and voice away from citizens and gave it to and kept it within the party, but really gave it to Nyerere (and his successors) alone.[22]

Like Kaunda, Nyerere was personally likable, modest, gentle, and effective at persuading donors and many of his own people that such autocratic doses of state-centered cod liver oil were good for economic progress in low-income states and essential for nation-building in Africa. Nyerere gulled even skeptical American and British researchers with this self-serving pablum. But not me. (Many years later, he and I spent a delightful evening in Arusha reminiscing, with Nyerere confessing his many overconfident "foolish" errors of all-knowing dominance.)

This single-party subterfuge was also adopted by Kenya and by a number of other African countries, by default: Malawi, Somalia, Zaire/Congo, the Central African Republic, and Idi Amin's Uganda. Zambia might have retained its British-delivered standard issue constitution (as independent-minded Botswana did) and stayed true to its parliamentary beginnings (with Nkumbula's ANC as the main opposition). But Nyerere was Kaunda's mentor. They were close personally, largely because neither enjoyed playing "the big African man." Neither was a bully, as so many of their contemporaries as rulers were. And so Kaunda, well before he fully considered the disadvantages of banning political choice, followed Nyerere down this common Cold War corridor of single-party authoritarianism. Years later, Kaunda assured me that creating a single party state was definitely "not a mistake." It "stopped internal conflicts within UNIP."[23]

Never an ideologue in the manner of Kwame Nkrumah or Robert Mugabe, and less insistent on establishing a cult of personality than Banda, Kenyatta, and Mozambique's Samora Machel (despite the Little Red Book), Kaunda nevertheless stifled his incipient democracy well before its people learned how to participate transparently and vigorously. Decisions were taken after 1965 by Kaunda alone or by Kaunda and the party grandees that would eventually be seen as both premature and misguided.[24]

Killing the Copper Calf

After the Mulungushi reforms and the relentless 51 percent takeover of much of the faltering Zambian economy, it was probably inevitable (although unexpected) that Zambia would try to bring the main engine of its prosperity fully under state control. Botswana tried a different strategy with its diamonds, but Kaunda apparently believed that a total transfer of the mines and mine wealth to the nation (and the loss of expatriate management and expertise) would improve its and his political fortunes. Kaunda committed "many blunders for political reasons," but reneging on the earlier arrangements with the mining companies was hardly to serve Zambia well. Moreover, imprudently and prematurely redeeming at a premium the bonds that Zambia had used to repay the mining companies produced shady profits for persons who had recently purchased those bonds on the open market and cost the Zambian exchequer dearly. Highly placed Zambians—but not Kaunda—may well have benefited.[25]

The nationalization of the Anglo-American Corporation and the Roan Selection Trust (which had become American Metal Climax) mining properties on the Copperbelt claimed existing profits and royalties for the state, and also provided abundant patronage opportunities for well-placed cabinet ministers. In 1972, Zambia was producing about 500,000 metric tons of copper a year, an amount it never again exported until the twenty-first century. Its GDP per capita in 1995 dollars was $624, just before nationalization occurred. In 1999, again in 1995 dollars, Zambia's per capita GDP was $369. Full nationalization was, as so many of us tried to tell Zambians before and after the deed were done, the wrong move at the wrong time for the wrong reasons. But some of my university colleagues thought it a smart maneuver—until it wasn't.

The takeover of the copper industry culminated a socialist process of turning virtually all Zambian private enterprise into sections of a state-owned conglomerate, with disastrous results for African standards of living and social services. Kaunda doubtless had the idealistic motives that at length he described to me. But other bright-eyed politicians saw the attractions of patronage and accepted quiet payoffs. The inexperienced, the partially trained, and the incompetent gained plum positions in the newly acquired industries and companies. Some of the incoming managers were better at plundering than at administering. Wage bills rose. Nationalized companies developed cash flow problems that often caused—as Zambia became relatively less affluent—financial chaos. Moreover, with the winding down of the Vietnam War, copper became less valuable. Its price per pound almost halved between 1972 and 1978. And then there were the oil price shocks that rocked the world and made petroleum imports and everything else much more expensive for countries like Zambia.[26]

Not understanding the full economic consequences, but in a forlorn attempt to mitigate urban unrest in and around Lusaka and other Zambian cities, the government subsidized urban consumers and miners by keeping maize meal and cooking oil prices artificially low through price controls and, simultaneously, paying farmers unrealistically depressed prices for their produce.[27] That made farming unprofitable and drove families from the rural areas into the already congested cities. More than 50 percent of Zambia soon became urbanized, with new pressures on services in cities where water supplies and electric power were already limited. These were self-defeating policies, but Kaunda and his UNIP advisors would not listen to those who tried to explain how public ownership of the main means of production and cosseting urban voters were driving the nation to economic ruin amid continuing troubles in Rhodesia and the steadily falling price of Zambia's only significant source of foreign exchange. Kaunda, despite my gentle efforts now and then to offer a new perspective, never appreciated the extent to which his policies of personal and state control were at the root of virtually all of the country's difficulties, and that they constituted a permanent, not a temporary, dilemma.

By 1978, Zambia was broke. It cost more to mine copper than the ore fetched on world markets. And Zambia had to keep producing, no matter what, because the nation had few other sources of ready earnings. Indeed, the nation had hardly any reserves of foreign exchange, payments for imports were a full year in arrears (and the gap was to grow), and the country had a debt to overseas lenders that approximated more than 100 percent of annual export earnings. Firms could hardly import machinery to upgrade the mines or industries. Nor could merchants import consumer goods since the state, which licensed all imports, had no cash. Even the Chinese construction of the Tazara railway from Kabwe to Dar es Salaam was going to be of little help. By this time the state had killed agriculture by making fertilizer expensive, credit scarce, and state market prices for maize and peanuts laughable. The International Monetary Fund (IMF) proposed drastic reforms, not once but on several occasions. But Kaunda could never bring himself to accept those tightening up initiatives. He (and UNIP) preferred to continue to muddle, and to hope vainly for increased global demand and better prices for copper.

The president of Zambia was wedded to his 1972 prescriptions, and to the humanistic socialism that was embodied in his, and UNIP's, design for national economic activity. State control of most of the country's industry, and a notorious lack of efficiency within state-run enterprises, inflated the cost of most goods and was responsible for periodic scarcities and the kinds of consumer dissatisfaction that could lead to rioting. When Rhodesian aircraft bombed Zimbabwe African National Union and Zimbabwe African Peoples Union training camps within Zambia, killing hundreds, regular Zambians saw how powerless the nation had become and understood again how costly it was to keep to the prevailing anti-Rhodesian sanctions regime. (See also chapter 9.) Shortages of tea, coffee, salt, flour, and other basic consumer goods resulted from adherence to the sanctions effort and the plunge in copper export earnings. Not for the first time, Zambians wondered whether the high cost of principles and humanism were worth it.

Hosting Guerrillas

Tanzania and Zambia, and Angola and Mozambique after 1975, all hosted anti-Rhodesian and anti–South African guerrilla encampments. Dar es Salaam and Lusaka, the southern bush in Tanzania and the lands near the Zambezi River, and later the Tete corridor and coastal cities in Mozambique, plus sections of Angola close to Namibia, housed the South African ANC, the South-West African People's Organization (SWAPO), the Zimbabwe African National Union (ZANU), and the Zimbabwe African People's Union (ZAPU) soldiers in training and their political commissars Thabo Mbeki, Herbert Chitepo, George Silundika, James Chikerema, George Nyandoro, and Eddison Zvobgo—several of whom I saw now and again, or sometimes often. Joshua Nkomo was often in Lusaka and Dar es Salaam as well. The fact that these militant exiles made their presence known to the local populations may indeed have irked residents, especially in Zambia, but neither UNIP nor Kaunda ever retreated from their unexpected role in the vanguard of the front line.

Indeed, Kaunda played a robust role throughout the 1970s both in supporting the several guerrilla detachments that used Zambia as a forward operating base, in attempting to mediate between contending ZANU and ZAPU factions (Kaunda always was pro-Nkomo, Nyerere less so), and in promoting a range of negotiating initiatives to end Rhodesian unilateral independence and bring a sustainable peace to the region. Kaunda arranged fruitless meetings with Prime Ministers Ian Smith of breakaway Rhodesia and Prime Minister B. Johannes Vorster of South Africa. He stimulated and modulated British and American peace making in the region. He arrested suspects after Herbert Chitepo's murder and ignored Nkomo's receipt of heavy arms from the Soviet Union while bemoaning Cuban activity in the region and urging U.S. Secretary of State Henry Kissinger and his successors to keep the Cubans and the Soviets who had battled with the MPLA (Movimento Popular de Libertação de Angola) in Angola out of the remainder of southern Africa. Later, after failed British attempts to square the Rhodesian circle with an African-led, but non-guerilla, series of power shifts, the successes of the *chimurenga* insurgency and deft British intervention boosted by Kaunda finally resulted in Zimbabwe's independence, a result for which Kaunda could claim abundant credit.

But as actively as Kaunda and Mark Chona, his chief emissary, tried throughout the 1970s to transfer power from whites to blacks in Rhodesia, and thus to reopen Zambia's logistical routes from the south, Kaunda still had to deal daily with economic and political crises at home. Indeed, much of what Kaunda and his colleagues were trying to do regionally had to be kept separate from more insular local politics. And a good deal of what they were attempting in the regional realm was clandestine, or at least known primarily in guerrilla and international circles. (A fuller story, and much of the backstory of the drive to Zimbabwe's freedom, is presented at length in chapter 9.)

Kissinger's Red Neck

It was during this active period of supporting guerrilla movements, attempting diplomatically to reduce white rule in Rhodesia and to deal domestically with lowered copper prices and increasing consumer agitation, that President Ford invited Kaunda and a massive entourage to Washington for a state dinner and visit. The date chosen happened to be the 200th anniversary of the battle of Lexington, the spark that ignited the American Revolution. During the morning, President Ford visited Lexington, shook hands with my fittingly Revolutionary-costumed fourth-grade daughter Nicola, and then (by dint of our fast flying and rapidly changing into proper evening dress) greeted my wife and me in a White House receiving line that night.

President Ford was very pleased to welcome "President Kovanda," such a good friend of the United States, to America. Or was it "President Kayunder?" Or maybe "President Kavunda?" President Ford could never quite get the name right. Nor did he seem to know where Zambia was. Fortunately, my wife and I had old Zambian official friends at our tables. And I was positioned in such a way behind Secretary of State Kissinger's table that I could see his neck visibly redden in annoyance when President Ford couldn't get the name of his guest right and failed to say anything remotely sensible about Zambia's relations with the United States (Zambia then supplied 15 percent of all copper imports into the United States).

But Kissinger's neck reddened even more when, in some strange breach of protocol after dinner had been served, Kaunda brought out his guitar and he and the Zambians moved into an adjoining room and started singing Zambian national political party and freedom songs. The American ambassador to Lusaka even joined in, which made Kissinger even angrier at the impropriety of it all. US-Zambian relations suffered until President Carter replaced President Ford.

A Deepening Morass

Despite this diversion in Washington, and while Kaunda was busily trying to end white rule in Rhodesia, Zambia was becoming more and more ungovern-able. Students at the university marched on State House to protest the mire into which the nation had floundered. Rural dwellers downed tools and headed for the crowded cities on the line of rail. When the election of 1978 occurred at the end of that year, there was no way of voting against Kaunda since there was no other candidate. But voters could simply refuse to turn up at the polls and deny Kaunda the 50 percent turnout that a successful election required. But even that option was deprived of many; the party and police apparatuses forced people to go to the election stations and cast ballots. In a single-party state, voters also had no choice about their legislators, even though in some constituencies UNIP had held primary elections prior to the main vote. Yet, UNIP had denied the victors in a number of those primary elections certification as candidates. The party executives and Kaunda were all-powerful.[28] Parliamentary representation, as it was developing in Zambia (to my dismay), was an irrelevant oxymoron.

Kaunda had already declared UNIP to be the supreme and sole custodian of the people's interests. The preferences of the dominant party took precedence over regular political institutions like parliament or the courts. Socialism, or what passed for socialism in much of Africa, prevailed. Indeed, humanism began to be superseded by "pure" socialism as an ideology. But that was a cover for naked state (really party) control of most aspects of Zambian life. Blaming capitalism for distorting the incentives of everyday affairs, Kaunda banned real estate agents and property sales; nationalized all cinemas (because of perceived moral depravity), tourist resorts, fishing operations, and crocodile farms; and extended the party's authority over the national newspapers, television, and radio so that they would thereafter reflect the thinking and dictates of the party. Sovietism-lite was running amok in Zambia even though most of the people of the nation shrugged in dismay and disbelief.

Even the arrival of Zimbabwe's independence (see chapter 9) in 1980 failed to alleviate Zambia's parlous economic and fiscal plights. Although shorter routes to the sea were thereafter available, world copper returns were still far below the Zambian producer price. Cobalt, Zambia's only other significant export, provided little help with the country's urgent cash flow needs. By 1982, Zambia was one of the five most heavily indebted nations in the world. Payments to overseas creditors were often twenty-five months in arrears. Cash and barter had replaced full faith and credit in most international transactions.

Activity in Zambia was grinding to a halt since most domestic sources of manufacturing and employment depended on unaffordable, scarce, imported raw materials and machinery. The local kwacha currency was depreciating rapidly, too. Zambia imported 50 percent of its food, so cash shortages led to scarcities of staples. Fertilizer came largely from outside, too, so farmers grew less maize than before. And there were few seeds, so farmers could not plant. Supermarket shelves were bare of consumer goods. Textbooks became unavailable. Even the university library could buy no books. The ministry of health could not ensure steady supplies of basic vaccines, a soft drinks monopoly manufacturer could produce nothing without caps for its bottles, and local flour mills made flour from local crops, but had no sacks. Overall, most of the industries created in the first decades of independence to give Zambia self-sufficiency—the tire makers and the auto assemblers—could do nothing without imported parts and raw materials.

In the colonial period, Zambia was largely fully supplied with maize, meat, and milk from local sources. But with rising African incomes, neglect of the indigenous farming community, and hostility toward the handful of still-productive, white-run maize, tobacco, and beef producers, Zambian consumers found it more and more difficult in the 1970s and into the 1980s to find what they needed on local market shelves. Zambia, like so many other African nations of the era, had made the mistake of appeasing urban voters through subsidies and failing to ensure adequate economic returns for its rural providers. Every subsidy drained productive capital and lowered the returns to farmers, who eventually gave up.

Since the government had gained control of virtually all aspects of economic existence, permits were required for everything that moved. Obtaining permission to import items to fill the bare shelves, for example, depended on bureaucratic decisions; there was now ample room for personal enrichment by the permitting authorities. Persistent foreign exchange shortages led to a thriving black market and profitable arbitraging by those within the party who enjoyed favorable access to dollars or pounds. "The temptation for officials to embezzle, steal, and be bribed is common," I wrote at the time.[29] The minister of power, transport, and communications was charged with taking large sums from a disaster relief fund. Others were using contract negotiations to construct an unneeded (and never completed) steel mill to enrich themselves. Perhaps $100 million was wasted.

There were many in high places, but not Kaunda, who were fleecing the nation for private gain. It was for that reason that Kaunda borrowed a methodology from Hong Kong and created an Anti-Corruption Commission (ACC) that attempted until 1991 to keep swindling to containable levels. The Hong Kong Independent Commission Against Corruption, established in 1974 with the ambitious goal of eradicating rampant corruption in the British city-colony and with educating citizens, officials, and businessmen to shun corrupt dealings, had succeeded brilliantly by 1984 in curbing the wild excesses of corruption that had been the Hong Kong norm. Kaunda asked a British police superintendent who had been in charge of the local Police Mobile Unit (a SWAT team) and had helped to guard the president in State House, to visit Hong Kong and come back with a plan. Paul Russell did so, and then proceeded to "expose as much corruption as possible." In the Hong Kong manner, he also "began seriously to get people . . . educated and better informed on corruption." Citizens began to report likely instances of the malady. The ACC, Russell later said, "was seen as a place where if you made a report someone would help. . . ."[30] The ACC came to be trusted. Unlike later presidents in Zambia and Malawi for whom Russell became the leader of anti-corruption efforts, Kaunda interfered little in the investigation and prosecution of corrupt persons within UNIP and the parastatal corporations.

Russell and his team examined Mindeco, the steel scheme, the state-owned supermarket chain's general manager, the head of the National Insurance Company, the shady activities of a governor of the Bank of Zambia, the private actions of the chief immigration officer, the appointed UNIP governor of the Lusaka Urban District, and many illicit smugglers of ivory and emeralds, and supervised antipoaching patrols. The Commission prosecuted a minister of mines in the Supreme Court, accusing him of corruptly soliciting an expensive Mercedes Benz sedan from a German company seeking mining concessions. A managing director of the state-run Zambia Airways was sacked after Russell stormed into its London headquarters on Kaunda's orders and, flourishing a large pair of scissors, cut up the Zambian-issued official credit cards of the director and his employees.

Several cabinet ministers were removed from their positions after Russell and his team had done due diligence and presented Kaunda with evidence of wrongdoing. On one occasion, with Kaunda's blessing, Russell arranged a road block to ensnare a cabinet minister who mistakenly thought that he was politically immune. Another was removed from office for behaving arrogantly and crossing Russell.

Between 1984 and 1990, the Zambian ACC pursued 1,011 cases, prosecuted 480 of the 1,011, and obtained 128 convictions and 47 acquittals. Some of cases were not prosecuted because doing so "was against the public interest." That meant that Kaunda or the attorney general decided to spare the culprit to prevent a schism within UNIP. But, for the most part, the Zambian ACC was freer of political interference than most of the commissions in Africa, and in Zambia subsequently. Nevertheless, even Russell was prevented from going after some of the most egregious, large-scale cases of possible corruption.

The doings of the mighty, shady Lonrho Corporation (originally the London and Rhodesian Gold Mining Corporation), which was unusually close to Kaunda and curried economic favor from the president, were off-limits. It is evident that Roland "Tiny" Rowland, Lonrho's domineering chief executive, had special access to the Zambian State House, and that he gained commercial benefits from that privileged access. But exactly how Rowland obtained such advantages, and what he did in terms of sharing the wealth are not known. *The Economist* said that "in furtherance of business he dispensed generous bribes to leaders of newly independent black countries." British Prime Minister Edward Heath called him "the unacceptable face of capitalism." But Nelson Mandela and Kaunda praised his assistance to their countries and what he did to advance the economies of South Africa and Zambia.[31]

Hubris and State Decay

After a long period of economic weakness exacerbated by its own poorly conceived decision-making, Zambia was palpably unable to satisfy the aspirations of its urban and increasingly middle-class population. The impact of the world recession, and a bout of drought, compounded these miseries. Unemployment was growing, housing for migrants to the cities was short, water and sanitary sewerage equipment were scarce, and the parastatals simply could not satisfy consumers. The morass into which the new nation had fallen may have been clear to critics, but obvious remedies—a return to the market economy (the IMF answer), selling off the parastatals and halting a challenging attempt to manage all aspects of economic productivity, and accepting renewed participatory democracy—were politically impossible both for Kaunda and for UNIP, or so the grandees of the nation thought. The ascendancy of the single party had empowered a proliferation of "incompetent self-seekers and time servers who formed an iron curtain between Kaunda and reality. . . ."[32]

Kapwepwe had died in 1980, but Kaunda somehow still felt that he needed to be more left-leaning than anyone else to maintain his hold on the party. Or maybe (I couldn't really tell despite prolonged conversations) he believed that his standing among other African heads of state depended on a more and more strenuous expression of anti-capitalistic rhetoric.

Kaunda, after all, was head of the Front Line States during this period. That meant that he attempted to become a peacemaker across the color line. He had met with a sour president of South Africa athwart the Victoria Falls. He conversed with Ian Smith and Abel Muzorewa of Rhodesia to see if he could broker an end to the civil war that inflamed Zambia's neighbor. These were politically dangerous (and ultimately inconsequential) exercises, so Kaunda needed domestic cover.[33]

Then the rains failed in southern Africa for three years running, piling climatic disaster atop man-made economic weaknesses. Even the farmers themselves were short of staple foods. Famine manifested itself as shortages of cash with which to purchase foodstuffs as well as the absence of local crops for sale.

By the end of the 1980s, Zambia was in permanent economic crisis, with rampant inflation. Because of natural and human-imposed calamities, and because authoritarianism had for so long deprived citizens of voice and of a sense of "belonging" to the nation, Kaunda and UNIP were both losing legitimacy. I was in and out of Zambia throughout the 1980s, and could sense Zambian socialism's lack of appeal, especially to young Zambians. Jobs were scarce. There was no safety net for the poor. The university was in shambles, my old family living quarters were decayed, and Lusaka—although five or ten times larger than the sleepy city that I had first known—was shabby and its inhabitants (as far as I could gather) depressed. The great dreams of Mulungushi were deferred, if not derided.

The authorities had to contend with periodic rioters demanding political change, and access to food. France in the late eighteenth century had come to Zambia. There was a rising clamor for multiparty instead of single-party rule. African trade unionists on the Copperbelt demanded democracy. So did Western-educated Zambians (the rising middle class) and students at the main and other universities. Donors echoed these sentiments, so pressure for a new political dawn grew exponentially.

An attempted coup led by a junior army officer in 1989, followed by extensive protests in the cities and large-scale protests in Lusaka, brought Kaunda sharply to his senses. In 1990 he promised to introduce a new constitution and democracy, permit other political parties, reform the economy, and begin to privatize state-owned enterprises. But it was far too late. A real dictator or an African military potentate might have tried to hang on. But Kaunda, deep down, harbored sincere obligations to the people of Zambia.

The end of the Kaunda regime came in 1991. I flew with him to the presidential retreat along the South Luangwa River in eastern Zambia to await the electoral results and to review the missteps that may have marred his twenty-seven year presidency and tainted his legacy. He was expecting victory, based on all that he had done for the Zambian people. I could hardly begin to explain why his people might now differ. He had brought the nation to independence, broken the Federation, fostered schooling, promoted an emerging middle class, placed Zambians in control of industries and virtually all sectors of political and social life, and contributed to the rapid modernization of the nation despite harassment from the south and logistical nightmares. He had supplied a heady vision and mobilized his followers behind ambitious national goals.

But participatory democracy had been forced into government-controlled channels. Representation meant nothing. Kaunda's security forces had imprisoned dissidents. Much of the press was government owned, and a propaganda mouthpiece. Corruption was not unknown (although less venal than it later became). Whatever Kaunda decreed as positive for the collective national welfare had not always pleased citizens. As we sat talking in the presidential lodge on the Luangwa River, Kaunda could not begin to believe that many of his initiatives had backfired—that there had been a better way to govern and policy directions that might have brought higher returns to his people. Kaunda cared deeply, but had been expedient instead of intellectually rigorous.

The voting returns, when they reached us, showed that UNIP had lost badly to the new Movement for Multiparty Democracy, led by Frederick Chiluba, a promising trade unionist of evangelical leanings. Kaunda became one of the very few African autocrats to retire peacefully from office. (Later he was persecuted.) Chiluba at first seemed to favor the kinds of reforms that Zambians wanted. But his reign soon proved anything but promising, as the next chapter discusses.

3

King Cobra and Other Menaces

Zambia Banishes Autocracy

We welcomed the demise of single-party rule in Zambia after twenty-seven volatile years. We, in this usage, encompasses the broad mass of Zambian citizens, most of the region's important churches and NGOs, foreign embassies, corporate executives, farmers of all backgrounds and colors, some (but not all) of the neighboring state governments, most of the local and foreign media representatives, the heads of a range of international organizations, and all friends of the nation. It was long past time for a return to democracy. That is what citizens wanted and voted for (see chapter 2) and what outgoing longtime president Kenneth Kaunda accepted as his unfortunate just deserts. Despite my close acquaintance with Kaunda, I could not have been more pleased as well with the popularly expressed judgments (and donor pushing) that had brought about the final ending of a troubled reign.

Voters decisively chose a leader and a party that campaigned on a platform that combined modernizing promises together with earnest anticorruption declarations. In Zambia, incoming President Frederick Chiluba and his Movement for Multiparty Democracy (MMD) put themselves forward as a new broom capable of cleaning out the UNIP stables and reviving revenues from copper, still Zambia's only significant source of foreign exchange earnings and urban employment.

The Man of Seventy-Two Shoes

Although many of my longtime UNIP friends had been ousted from power, others had switched sides and remained in parliament, or in business. Chiluba drew several prominent defectors from UNIP into his crusading new administration. At least it was intended, and sold to the Zambian electorate, as a developmentally innovative advance after the long years of quasi-socialist decay under Kaunda. What transpired instead, alas, was an era of renewed muddle and purposeful malfeasance, accompanied by a steady determination to steal as

Overcoming the Oppressors. Robert I. Rotberg, Oxford University Press. © Oxford University Press 2023.
DOI: 10.1093/oso/9780197674208.003.0003

much as possible from a state already weakened and impoverished by a want of integrity.[1]

Chiluba and the MMD had gained voting strength by promoting an end to Afro- socialism, humanism, and nationalization. They declared themselves in support of real democracy and free enterprise, argued for smaller and less-expensive public services, and proclaimed themselves against corruption. One clear objective was re-privatizing the copper mines—Zambia's most essential economic engine. Another was to sell off the non-mineral enterprises that dominated and strangled the nation's economy: the agricultural marketing boards, the state-controlled business entities, the national airline, and more.

These were all worthy goals. But redirecting the Zambian economy so that it would no longer be dominated by the state, and no longer be run by, and to suit, patronage appointees beholden to their backers in UNIP rather than to shareholders, soon gave way to a rash of politically sanctioned looting adventures that dwarfed anything that Zambia had ever previously experienced. Chiluba was no more interested in the welfare of his citizens, it soon transpired, than were Idi Amin in Uganda or Mobutu Sese Seko in Zaire/Congo. Chiluba was acquisitive, as well as being uncommonly paranoid, and, according to a well-connected local businessman who interacted with him on a number of formative occasions, Chiluba was an implausible leader stretched far beyond his intrinsic capabilities: "The vanity displayed by his [natty] attire seemed to underline his empty head; his inability to think and put what he heard to logical test and make a judgement." Moreover, the businessman epitomized Chiluba's political compatriots in the MMD prophetically, as "crooks and drug dealers . . . whose aim was to get into government in order to have a free hand to pursue their nefarious activities."[2] The key technocrats, many holdovers from the Kaunda era, were much more professional and public spirited.

The empty head sat atop a diminutive body. But for all of his five-foot height (Kaunda, usually well tempered in his remarks, dismissed Chiluba as a "four-foot dwarf"), Chiluba had vaulted to the presidency at the head of an MMD that he had helped to create on account of his evident charisma and his reputation as a provocative and captivating speaker. Born to CiBemba-speaking parents in Kitwe, on the Copperbelt, and schooled (only) as far as Form II (grade 10) in Kawambwa in the CiBemba-speaking Luapula Province, Chiluba had gained business experience as a bus driver and an accounts clerk on the Copperbelt. There he rose to prominence as a Pentecostalist preacher, becoming a city councilor in Ndola, and—in time—the head of the Zambia Congress of Trade Unions, all well before Kaunda finally ended single-party rule under pressure from donors and his own followers.

Chiluba and his political movement's victory in the 1991 election proved too conclusive (75 percent of the vote for the MMD, only 25 percent for UNIP) for the incoming president's own good. Inexperienced at even the national level and totally unacquainted with the world outside, Chiluba misread his mandate and the meaning of his polling success.[3] Nevertheless, it buoyed him into believing that he was more a gift from the Almighty than a mere new broom: among his first initiatives was a declaration announcing that Zambia was a "Christian nation," as if fiat could alter the way Zambians regarded themselves or were regarded by others.

All of his regime's main accomplishments, such as they were, were in the economic sphere, with some others social, and a few political. No longer did the state try to control every aspect of commercial and corporate life. The new administration preached openness and sought to adhere to the structural adjustment strictures of the International Monetary Fund (IMF). That meant that the state could no longer borrow recklessly and hope for international bailouts. Advised by a macroeconomic expert team sent out from the Harvard Institute for International Development and funded by European donors, Chiluba's government abolished exchange controls; this relaxing of what had hitherto been a tightly regimented fiscal regime encouraged new individual entrepreneurial awakenings and Zambian-organized innovative enterprises. State-owned operations on the road to privatization attracted new competitors—all to the benefit of consumers. New firms entered the transport sector, for example, adding to the country's road chaos but lowering consumer costs in that area.

Harvard's advisors also persuaded Zambia's finance ministry to introduce many reforms, including the introduction of a value-added tax mechanism on consumer and other goods and enhancements to the important ways in which the mines remitted considerable sums to the government. The finance ministry overhauled how income taxes were levied and collected—a first for southern Africa—established a state revenue authority, and, together with the economists from Harvard, helped the Zambian Reserve Bank to straighten out its books and its accounting system. Harvard's advice helped to reduce Zambia's hyperinflationary tendency and supported Zambian officials in their debt relief negotiations with the IMF. All of these efforts were intended to smooth the path toward privatizing the key engines of Zambia's post-Kaundan economy.

Even so, overall, Chiluba's eight years in office hardly produced positive returns for individuals or the nation. Formal employment levels fell from 563,000 in 1990 to 513,000 in 2001 even as Zambia's population increased. Zambia's GDP per capita also slid backward, from the equivalent of $419 in 1990 to $350 in 2001. Lower copper prices and years of severe drought played a role in these falling returns, but so did reduced outputs, attributable to the running down of the mines under Kaunda, and to the failure of the new government to privatize with deliberate speed, evenhandedly. Farmers lost access to guaranteed crop prices thanks to the premature liquidation of a major national marketing board. Additionally, Chiluba's treasury allowed average base interest rates for commercial lending and the like to rise from a punitive 61 percent in early 1993 to a destructive 262 percent later in the same year, with not quite so high rates of inflation persisting for several more years.[4] All Zambians were quickly worse off than even during the most desperate Kaunda years.

Chiluba and company only began unbundling the various copper mine properties after he had been reelected as president in 1996 (UNIP had foolishly refused to contest parliamentary seats in the same election) and the pressure to do so from donors and the international finance community had become difficult to resist. Until then, Chiluba and his ministers treated the mines as assets to be plundered. So they were reluctant to let go—despite campaign promises in 1991 and the expectations then and later of the international lending agencies that the point of a post-Kaundan transformation was the return of the mines to free enterprise.

The Zambian Privatisation Agency eventually sold 150 state-controlled entities that comprised 280 types of commerce. Just as in contemporaneous Russia, hotels, dairies, tire firms, pharmaceutical companies, banks, insurance providers, and textile operations were all auctioned off, frequently to well-connected MMD politicians, cabinet ministers, and other grandees with inside access. Many of these privatizations were manipulated, with favored purchasers learning from cronies how to bid successfully. A cobalt mining and production concession was won by an Israeli company, with most of the proceeds going to MMD insiders, not to the agency or the state. One smallish copper mine fell into the hands of a Canadian company, again with much of the cash outlay detouring into political pockets. An Indian firm with little experience gained the Luanshya mine, possibly after giving shares to Chiluba. (Investigators later discovered that Chiluba had purchased property in five overseas jurisdictions, and kept bank accounts in the British Virgin Islands.) Chiluba may also have profited personally from the sale of an emerald mine. Moreover, according to one contemporary investigative report, most of the mining properties that Kaunda had (mistakenly) nationalized in 1972 were sold off at the end of the twentieth century for pittances redeemed to the national treasury, plus extensive kickbacks to MMD politicians.[5] Some of the more productive mines were acquired by Glencore, an avaricious Swiss firm. The Anglo-American Corporation of South Africa, the original owner of the better-worked mines on the Copperbelt, obtained many of them back by 2000, again for very little, plus a host of concessions relating to taxes, power supplies, the provision of housing and other amenities for workers, and more. Needless to say, it was many years before Zambia resumed its traditional world role as a major exporter of copper ore.

Bullying Losers

Chiluba's much-touted Christian nation, and its presumed Christian leader, demonstrated no greater humility or statesmanlike behavior in the social sphere than he and it did economically. Becoming president by promising a return to democracy, Chiluba immediately, on day one, proceeded peremptorily to frog-march out of their offices—without any semblance of due process—holdover African mining company executives and their assistants, in a sheer show of force. Other UNIP officials in state-owned corporations were also purged, as were slogans popularized by UNIP to unify the nation, and almost anything even remotely connected to the persons and regime that had previously ruled the country. Moreover, Chiluba deprived Kaunda arbitrarily of his pension and the post-presidency house to which he was entitled. Further, Chiluba claimed erroneously that his stately and saintly predecessor had stolen books from State House, and sent police to search through the former president's possessions.[6]

With regard to his predecessor, Chiluba soon discarded whatever democratic instincts that he may have exhibited as an up-and-coming opposition politician and trade unionist. Viewing Kaunda as a continuing threat to his own prominence—despite Kaunda's advanced age, gentlemanly behavior, and overwhelming defeat at the polls—Chiluba attempted in 1992 to declare Kaunda a non-citizen and deport him to Malawi. Subsequently, he persuaded parliament to amend the constitution to prevent anyone born of non-Zambian parents from becoming president. Kaunda, born at the Lubwa mission near Chinsali, obviously was a Zambian, albeit of Malawian extraction and Malawian parents. Eventually, Zambia's constitutional court invalidated Chiluba's machinations, confirming Kaunda's right to Zambian nationality in 2000.[7] (By then I had interviewed Kaunda over two days and at length in his rented quarters regarding the good and bad decisions of his own long presidency, about the serious errors that he and others had committed, and about the scourge of HIV/AIDS that had taken one of his sons. We refrained from discussing Chiluba and how Kaunda had been mistreated by Chiluba, but we did discuss a "cardinal error"—Kaunda's decision to merge UNIP and the state, and to appoint rather than elect district governors. He and I talked a second time by telephone, and then several more times during his lengthy sojourn at Boston University in 2002–2003.)[8]

Chiluba pounced on anyone and anything in Zambia that displeased him or threatened his hold on power. In 1993, he declared a state of emergency and arrested twenty-six UNIP leaders, charging them with preparing a coup with the preposterously alleged assistance of Iran and Iraq! Several were soon released, but others were tortured severely after being deemed "treasonous."[9] Once the Supreme Court declared the emergency and the detentions illegal, Chiluba started rounding on his own MMD ministers. (Arthur Wina, my old colleague and minister of education under Chiluba, soon had enough and denounced Chiluba's corruption and inefficiencies.) Levy Mwanawasa, a lawyer and Chiluba's first vice president, also retired early, having soured on his president's integrity. (Mwanawasa claimed, too, that he had been the target of an assassination attempt.) Several who criticized Chiluba indeed lost their lives in suspicious vehicular accidents. So did a lawyer investigating fraud and a recent finance minister. Kaunda and Roger Chongwe, Chiluba's own minister of justice, were attacked at a rally in 1997. Shots were fired at Kaunda's vehicle; observers thought that the incident constituted an assassination attempt on Kaunda. A little later, on Christmas morning of the same year, Chiluba ordered Zambian police to arrest Kaunda and haul him off to a maximum-security prison for supposedly fomenting a coup; six months later, but only after an intervention by South African President Nelson Mandela, Chiluba did release Kaunda. (Others linked to the alleged coup were tortured brutally.) But a year later, Major Wezi Kaunda, the former president's third son, was pulled from his automobile and fatally shot in what appeared to be a political murder.[10] There were more outrages: Princess Nakatindi Wina, a prominent member of the MMD from Barotseland, a cabinet minister, and the wife of my friend and politician Sikota Wina, fell afoul of Chiluba for more obscure reasons and was imprisoned and tortured, suffering a miscarriage. "Chiluba was very serious about revenge."[11]

A correspondent covering Kaunda's trial portrayed the two adversaries well: "The two could hardly be more different. Mr. Kaunda is tall and solid, wears Nehru suits and affects a large white handkerchief into which he alternately storms and weeps; as a liberation leader he combed his hair [straight up], but now, at 73, he has a gray beard and lives on raw vegetables. . . . Chiluba, 54, is tiny and efficient, a fundamentalist Christian who wears natty suits and does without a scurrying entourage. In his rapid-delivery speeches, he quickly lapses into tart scorn, doing imitations while telling folksy stories deriding . . . Kaunda, African and Western leaders and other critics. . . . He's driven by a fear of appearing weak. . . ."[12]

In addition to torture and killings, revenge and psychological quirkiness meant the taking of political prisoners, curbing free speech, and seeking to shut down *The Post*, an independent newspaper in Lusaka that had been a voice of protest against Kaunda's government, as well as skeptical first and then openly critical of its successor. *The Post* harried Chiluba editorially, and reported on a number of the initiatives and botched endeavors of his government. It also tried to hold him and his associates to their campaign promises. But, most galling of all, *The Post*'s widely read columnist had strong opinions about Chiluba, calling him "a vain, cross-dressing, high-heel wearing, adulterous, dwarf thief."[13]

The columnist referred in part to Chiluba's several tumultuous divorces; his decided preference for English-tailored suits (he owned several hundred bespoke versions); Swiss-crafted shoes—including the green, crocodile leather model, with two-inch heels, that he was wearing when I first met him; and dozens of fancy ties. Clearly, dressing up elevated Chiluba in his own mind. He had expensive tastes that were only whetted by gaining the Zambian presidency. Indeed, when running for that same office in 2010, Michael Sata made sure that audiences knew that he was not another Chiluba—by then reviled: "We are not going to steal money, we are not going to plunder, we are not going to buy suits, we are not going to buy shoes. We are not going to give girls houses.…"[14]

I caught up with Chiluba in mid-1997, shortly after *The Post* had been harried and the president and the police had moved strongly to stifle opposition. Despite his diminutive stature, Chiluba was attempting to run a heavily autocratic enterprise based more on plunder than on estimable governance. Indeed, Zambia's developmental accomplishments were steadily receding; poverty numbers were rising, along with widespread crime. The reform platforms on which he had been elected in 1991 and 1996 had largely been replaced by a series of questionable half-hearted endeavors, including personally lucrative deregulation exercises.

He and I met in State House, where I had so often talked with Kaunda. But Chiluba led me not to a drawing room or the dining room where Kaunda frequently received me but to a very tiny, tucked-away hideout off the library where Chiluba preferred to preside. In an expensive suit and tie, he sat behind a very imposing desk, heatedly denying that he had imprisoned politicians, editors, and other regime opponents, or that he had sought to close *The Post*. I found the interview and experience surreal. Chiluba by the time of our talk was clearly less in touch with reality than many other heads of state. And why he insisted on spinning untrue tales and attempting to persuade me of their veracity when the global press was filled with exact tales of his excesses, I could not fathom. My direct questions about press freedom, human rights violations, and the possible flaws of his economic program were all answered—but with falsehoods that spoke more to his growing paranoia than to his capacity to continue to rule a once-prosperous and promising nation.[15]

Chiluba was immensely temperamental, as I discerned, and neither reflective nor possessing of anything that might conceivably be termed "a vision" for Zambia. He obviously saw his leadership of the nation as a chance to grow tall in esteem, become a man of the world, and travel widely. At the time of the interview, however, he had not sponsored the assassination of Kaunda's son or messed a second time with the father; otherwise I would have tried to engage Chiluba on those questions as well as less inflammatory ones. I found it easy to conclude, exiting State House, that the land of my old research frontier and second home had truly fallen on very hard times. How someone like Chiluba vaulted to the apex of the political tree was unfathomable. But, at the time, I hardly knew how much Chiluba had already stolen from the state and its people, and how much more mendaciously he was soon to grasp.

Thefts of Millions

The extent of Chiluba's thievery only revealed itself during the presidency of his successor. But the head of his own Anti-Corruption Commission, a holdover from the Kaunda era, had quickly realized that Chiluba's avariciousness was extreme. Despite the new president's evangelical history and pretensions, it became evident as early as 1992 that Chiluba believed that his own fortunate turn had come, that it was now his moment in life and politics to gain riches and have a "free-for-all."[16]

Chiluba looted state resources systematically. A particularly brazen method involved dipping into a secret Zambian bank account held in London for state security purposes by the state-owned Zambian National Commercial Bank. Ostensibly controlled by the director general of the Zambian Security Intelligence Services, the secret account usually was employed to obtain defense equipment, spy materials, and the like. A woman in the Zambian ministry of finance was the only person authorized to make transfers to the intelligence services via the London account. However, she could be bribed to do as she were told, and to keep quiet. So could the director general of the intelligence services be relied upon to stay silent. Accordingly, the person with the metaphorical keys shifted moneys into the London account; Chiluba used those funds to satisfy his acquisition of flashy suits, crocodile shoes, and other clothing—literally hundreds and hundreds of items—in Britain and Switzerland. He paid more than $1 million to a Swiss boutique. He also purchased imposing properties in Belgium (costing about $4 million) and South Africa. He made arrangements to profit from trafficking in (nonexistent) arms meant to be transferred by a Bulgarian dealer to the Zambian army. Chiluba was further implicated in the "disappearance" of sixty-seven fully loaded fuel trucks destined for Lusaka from Dar es Salaam. Innumerable other schemes to profit from the presidential incumbency were eventually revealed when Chiluba was tried in Britain and later in Zambia. Curiously, Zambia's auditor general knew about many of the peculations in real time but feared challenging Chiluba.[17]

In order to protect himself, Chiluba sacked the top police, special branch, and military chiefs whom he inherited from Kaunda. He marginalized the Zambian ACC that Kaunda had created and was relieved when Paul Russell, its no-nonsense head, left Zambia for a similar position in Malawi. As a result of the purposeful undermining of Zambia's instruments against corruption, scams proliferated. Drug trafficking became even more pervasive than during the last years of Kaunda's government and animal poaching depredations became much more frequent than before. The Species Protection Department within the ACC tried to continue to operate effectively until it realized that Chiluba was implicated in "some highly dubious dealings."[18]

Immediately on becoming president, Chiluba found various ways to obstruct Russell and the work of the ACC. Cases of the kind that had previously moved smoothly from investigation to prosecution were now increasingly hindered by counter-orders from State House. As Chiluba effectively neutered the Commission, so graft and fraud in their many guises flourished in Zambia as never before. By some estimates, the number of corrupt incidents rose by 40 percent from 1991 to 1996, and exponentially thereafter. From 1997 to 2001, of about 4,800 suspected breaches of the law, the ACC could only investigate 1,500. Convictions accordingly fell over that period to a low of ninety-one.[19]

One infamous example of presidential interference with the operations of ACC concerned the minister of local government. Investigators from the ACC, following up on a tip, decided at length that the minister was definitely "on the take." Russell presented a detailed indictment to the director of public prosecutions; after a long wait, Russell learned that—"on presidential orders"— no prosecution would ensue, quashing the ACC's investigations. Michael Sata, later president, was the minister of local government at the time, and someone deservedly critical of Chiluba's peculations—but well after the fact.[20]

President Levy Mwanawasa established a commission to ferret out all of his predecessor's misdeeds, but the real disclosure of much of Chiluba's corrupt acts came in a London court, in an action brought by Zambia's attorney general when Chiluba had settled in Britain to enjoy the illicit winnings of his big presidential extravaganza. There the ex-president was convicted in 2007 in a civil suit of converting the equivalent of $58 million worth of kwacha to his own purposes for the purchase, inter alia, of 349 monogrammed shirts, 206 monogrammed jackets and suits, 72 pairs of handmade shoes (also monogrammed), and innumerable other items of attire. The judgment in the High Court ordered Chiluba to repay $58 million to Zambia, together with sizable reimbursements from a host of other culprits.[21] However, none of this money was ever recovered, largely because the Zambian attorney general had neglected to discover and sequester Chiluba's assets beforehand. (In a separate criminal action, Chiluba's third wife was subsequently jailed in Zambia for more than three years for purchasing three houses on the Copperbelt with government funds and taking $300,000 worth of goods from State House.)[22]

Unfortunately for justice, a magistrate in Lusaka decided in separate proceedings in 2009 that the criminal case against the ex-president had not been proven, Chiluba claiming that the moneys that he had misappropriated were— somehow—political donations. Two Zambian business associates facing similar charges were sent to prison for three years each, however. A Zambian scholar termed the acquittal a major complication in the battle against corruption: "Most people will think he . . . was just forgiven. . . . and . . . no one will take the fight seriously."[23] The little man whom I privately thought an implausible buffoon and whom a knowledgeable observer called endlessly manipulative, had punched far above his height.[24]

To compound the confusion for Zambians and Africans more generally, political impunity appeared to be the ultimate victor. When Chiluba collapsed and died two years later in 2011, President Rupiah Banda gave him a state funeral, so honorably concluding one of the more blatant and egregiously corrupt performances by an African head of state.

Third-Term-itis and Succession

Well before the extent of Chiluba's abuse of public office for private gain had been exposed, he claimed indispensability and decided to flout the Zambian constitution's prohibition against more than two consecutive presidential terms. Like so many other African heads of state then and more recently, he reckoned that Zambia could hardly do without his assertive leadership. The constitution needed to be amended to suit his ambitions. This scheme might even have succeeded, on the back of a presidentially ordered flamboyant giveaway of municipality-owned houses to their tenants, were it not for the implacable opposition of church groups, NGOs, and the national law association. An uproar ensued, and Chiluba was startled enough by popular antagonism to his maneuver that he unexpectedly backed down (as Bakili Muluzi had been forced to do in neighboring Malawi).[25] Only Robert Mugabe in Zimbabwe consistently and Sam Nujoma in Namibia, once, evaded such constitutional safeguards in their own southern African principalities.

Without Chiluba as its presidential candidate in 2001, the ruling MMD had no one to put forward. This result compelled Chiluba, who planned to remain as party chairman and give orders to an elected substitute for himself, to search everywhere for a plausible presidential heir. Instead of Sata, who expected to be selected, he chose Mwanawasa, a decidedly non-charismatic lawyer from Ndola who had served as vice president ten years before and was hardly gifted as a speaker. Moreover, short-tempered, Mwanawasa possessed few political instincts. All he could claim was support from Chiluba, still a crowd favorite, and backing by the formidable MMD political machine.

Mwanawasa eked out a narrow plurality of the vote—29 percent for him and 27 percent for his closest competitor (of eleven running). Two of my longtime gifted acquaintances—Gwen Konie, a former neighbor in Lusaka, and Inonge

Mbikusita-Lewanika—both sadly polled less than 1 percent.[26] Local and external electoral monitors declared the poll rigged and flawed in several additional ways. But Mwanawasa took office regardless as the nation's third head of state and proceeded to bumble his way through a series of presidential misadventures. In the economic sphere, his administration neglected the needs of farmers (a common Zambian government failing); drove the kwacha to surprisingly high levels, thus damaging the competitiveness of agricultural exports, especially flowers, cotton, and tobacco; borrowed heavily, hence increasing Zambia's debt-servicing obligations in an unsustainable manner; and saw inflation again rise to high levels. Later, Mwanawasa sold off key copper-mining properties for far less than they were worth, perhaps gaining personal benefits from the Indian buyers.

But the most notable feature of Mwanawasa's reign was his turning on Chiluba and orchestrating with glee the investigation and pursuit of his predecessor for rampant corruption. There was much to uncover, of course, and Mwanawasa's government had the resources to follow the elaborate trail of graft and fraud that had permeated Chiluba's eight years in office. It initiated the civil case in London that led to a conclusive judgment against Chiluba, but it neither had the resources or the know-how to obtain the redress ordered by the court. Nor could Mwanawasa ultimately pursue Chiluba to the kinds of punitive conclusion that the third president obviously sought. Mwanawasa won the 2006 presidential election with great ease, winning 43 percent of the vote, and appointed Rupiah Banda vice president. (Michael Sata's Patriotic Front came second, with 29 percent of the vote, and Hakainde Hichilema's United Democratic Alliance came third with 25 percent. Two other parties also contested the poll.)[27] Two years later, at an African Union conclave in Egypt, Mwanawasa, massively overweight and with a history of minor strokes, suffered a severe stroke and died a few months later, having failed to crush Chiluba and having done too little to set Zambia on a clear path to social or economic success—even with high prices for copper and the beginnings of heavy Chinese involvement in its affairs.

Banda, a former UNIP stalwart from the Eastern Province and a politician of many decades (I knew him from his early career days), did not automatically replace Mwanawasa. According to the Zambian constitution, he had to contest a new election, eventually barely beating out Sata, who had also served the Kaunda and Chiluba administrations and ran on an anti-Chinese platform, by 41 percent to 39 percent of the vote. Hichilema, again contesting from his secure southern Zambian base, won 20 percent of the ballots cast.[28]

Banda was more like Kaunda than Chiluba and Mwanawasa in his gentle personification of leadership. Uncomfortable before crowds, and more self-effacing than most of his peers in Zambia or other African countries, he nevertheless ran Zambia well, without too much controversy and with comparatively little large-scale corruption. Fortunate that his period in office coincided with an era of good rains and of high world copper prices despite a global financial meltdown and a slow recovery, Banda could claim the best returns for decades for Zambia's farmers, corporation plantations and smallholders alike, as well as revenues from copper exports that were adequate, if less than they might have been because of the mistaken sale of key properties.

Thanks in part to the timely distribution of seeds and fertilizer to rural areas, and better pricing policies than before, maize, wheat, cotton, Virginia tobacco, peanuts, sunflower seeds, rice, sorghum, and soy all doubled or trebled their past output levels. This bonanza for the farmers, the majority of whom were peasant rather than industrial agriculturalists, also benefited from the steady way in which the Banda government operated, with few sudden policy shifts.

In the industrial arena, also, more new jobs appeared than ever before, formal employment levels rising by 23 percent, per capita annual average GDPs increasing from $1,200 in 2008 to $1,672 in 2011.[29] In these years Zambia was growing at about 8 percent a year. All of these positive outcomes showed how sensible, steady, and not necessarily populist policies could engender solid returns for the mass of the inhabitants of middle-income sub-Saharan African countries.

King Cobra Cuffs China

As positive as these results were, Sata, backed by urban CiBemba-speaking workers on the Copperbelt and rural CiBemba speakers in the Northern and Luapula Provinces, overwhelmed Banda, a CiNyanja speaker (with a smaller ethnic constituency) at the next Zambian election in 2011. Sata had been mayor of Lusaka in Kaunda's day, then a minister for ten years under Chiluba. Passed over to succeed Chiluba, he formed the Patriotic Front party. Bull-chested and always forceful, Sata was far more colorful than Banda. He promised a rash of new jobs. Furthermore, he campaigned against both Banda and Chinese influence in Zambia, calling the Chinese "infesters," not investors. By 2010, Chinese firms had acquired Zambian coal mines and sections of the copper fabrication infrastructure. They had developed a reputation for extreme social distancing, for refusals to integrate themselves into Zambian society, and for running enterprises in Zambia without much consideration for the welfare or the views of their local employees. Moreover, Banda was regarded as the Chinese-backed candidate, campaigning with Chinese cash, and of failing to prosecute two Chinese managers charged with attempted murder for shooting protesting Zambian coal miners in the Southern Province during a labor dispute. Sata, known as King Cobra because of his venomous tongue, played on this resentment, calling Chinese in Zambia bloodsuckers and more. When voters went to the polls, Sata swept 42 percent of the total, Banda only received 35 percent, and Hichilema won 18 percent.[30]

I had heard a version of this commonly employed political attack on China when I invited Sata to speak at Harvard University in 2010 before a large, mostly student, audience. He explained how Chinese managers demonstrated contempt for African miners and other kinds of workers, and how they nearly completely kept to themselves. "We want the Chinese to leave . . . ," he said. They paid "slave wages," he continued, flouted safety and environmental standards, corrupted African leaders, and were generally hostile to their African employees. "Western capitalism had a human face," but the Chinese were "only out to exploit us."[31] In contrast, he praised Taiwan and implied that it was its own independent country.

There was much truth in what Sata was alleging in public at Harvard and on the political campaign trail at home. Indeed, my own research had discovered that Chinese employers in Africa sadly believed that their own national personnel were more obedient, more efficient, more reliable, and more trustworthy than Africans. As alien managers, they were aware that African employees would report them when they tried to cut corners or behaved in an unconscionable manner. Outrages on the Zambian mines hence showed the extent to which Chinese owners and managers ignored safety regulations, reduced wages, and pushed their local workers hard—all in attempts to fulfill or over-fulfill quotas for mining output or construction timeliness. Zambian miners preferred to seek comparable work at Swiss-, Canadian-, South African-, or Indian-managed copper mines that were reputedly safer and their employees better paid; Human Rights Watch rated the Chinese operations subpar, as it did on the copper mines in nearby Katanga, Congo. Chinese operations in both locations, ironically, were distinctly unfriendly to the local unions and to unionization.[32]

Chinese managers in Africa kept their social distance from Africans, another source of resentment. Most Chinese middle managers and other employees refrained from mingling with their local workers, reserving social outreach for official engagements with politicians and high-level bureaucrats. This practice did not endear the Chinese in Africa to their local counterparts. Furthermore, the communities that Chinese firms created in Africa to support their imported enterprises were socially thin, and isolated. Even, or especially, members of the imported laboring force were discouraged from associating after work with Africans. Sometimes the Chinese living quarters were even ringed with barbed wire and other barriers to discourage fraternization in Lusaka and on the Copperbelt.[33]

Despite his anti-Chinese vituperations, King Cobra turned out to be a chameleon. As soon as Sata, seventy-four, emerged victorious in the election, he tried to reassure China of his positive intentions: "Foreign investment is important to Zambia and we will continue to work with foreign investors who are welcome in the country . . . but they need to adhere to the labor laws."[34] Shortly thereafter he dispatched ex-president Kaunda to Beijing to add further reassurances. In Lusaka, he began to praise China and how its efforts and friendship contributed to Zambian development.

In many other policy areas, Sata was more assertive than measured, declaring radical governing shifts without much prior consideration, and without listening very much to the advice of his ministers or officials. He decentralized the rural administration of his unitary state, creating many patronage openings without having the funds to make appointments and establishing new districts and an additional province—all at untold expense and for purposes that were barely articulated. Inconsistent and impulsive, he proved capricious in hiring and firing ministers and associates of all kinds. Whereas Banda was steady and almost too calm, Sata hopped around from subject to subject, frequently blindsiding his ministers and perplexing officials.

When I next encountered him in 2012, it was in State House, but not in the closet of a room where I talked with Chiluba. I was directed to a stately boardroom, with the president sitting behind a vast credenza of a desk, distant from me. He was very agitated, and I learned shortly afterward that he had just exchanged rather heated (on his side) and perfunctory (on the other side) words with former U.S. President George W. Bush. Apparently, President Bush expected a sensible conversation about American interests in Zambia (he was in the country accompanying former First Lady Laura Bush's visits to several cervical cancer clinics that she was funding generously). Instead, Sata ranted at Bush about United States' colonialism and its supposed poor performance in Africa. That breached protocol and ended the Bush visit in a hurry.

I unknowingly followed Sata's foolish reversion to his King Cobra persona; I tried to discuss China's role in Zambia and how the West could help Zambia achieve its development goals. But it was a waste of time. Sata was distracted by his wayward encounter with President Bush (whom I shortly thereafter met at a lavish July 4 reception at the U.S. embassy—and heard the story of Sata's blunders from the ambassador) and was full of platitudes about the accomplishments of his administration. Candid discussion was out of the question, even after our lengthy shared time at Harvard. (Fortunately, that evening in Lusaka I caught up at some length at a dinner organized by the U.S. ambassador with a number of very old and lasting friends who had all played significant roles in Zambia's modern political and economic growth: Sikota Wina, former cabinet minister and deputy speaker of the parliament; Mark Chona and Lishomwa Lishomwa, both out of politics and successful in business; the outgoing chief justice, busy writing the country's new constitution; and several other younger opinion makers. The discussion was much livelier, more informative about Zambia, and more pointed than my talk with Sata.)

About a week later, I happened to be at Livingstone airport (after revisiting Victoria Falls) and ready to fly back to Lusaka, when I saw Sata arrive in a major motorcade in another part of the airport. We spoke again, surprisingly warmly, mostly about how to develop the nation's touristic potential.

Sata's presidency compromised the nation's future, somewhat echoing Chiluba's time in office, but with the spread of sleaze kept to more modest levels. Sata berated, hired, and fired cabinet ministers and important parastatal heads frequently and without giving them time to learn about their ministerial responsibilities. Revamping the provinces and districts also churned press coverage for the sake of gaining attention more than it enhanced developmental prospects. But Sata also constructed 1,000 miles or more of badly needed roads with Chinese help and by giving contracts to concerns from China; he attempted to upgrade Zambia's fraying electric power infrastructure, build new health clinics, and construct housing for government employees. He raised the minimum wage and civil service salaries. In the process, Zambia again borrowed heavily, raising debt to GDP ratios to precarious levels (still an acute problem as I write), and perversely kept interest rates high while reimposing foreign exchange controls, a clanging echo from the past. But, thanks to copper price booms and Chinese investments, plus moneys from Eurobond borrowings, Zambia continued to grow economically during Sata's time as a result of copper revenues and new debt. The reckoning came later.

Sata's most invidious influence on Zambian political maturity resulted from his contempt for the rule of law and his unwillingness to complete an oft-promised revision of the country's 1996 constitution. Becoming increasingly intolerant of dissent and vocal opposition, Sata and his close associates, including Edgar Lungu, successively minister of home affairs, minister of defense, and minister of justice, deposed judges, interfered in court cases and judgments affecting cronies and financiers of the president, and deported longtime residents who found themselves involved in commercial or religious disputes with supporters of Sata.

The president tried with some success to overturn the election of opposition parliamentarians. He resuscitated the use of the Public Order Act to chill freedom of assembly and freedom of speech. Especially in Barotseland, where a high-level separatist movement was underway that threatened Zambia's integrity, Sata instructed the police to use all manner of force, including abducting secessionist advocates, prolonged interrogations, and torture. These and other harsh measures, including sudden house invasions ostensibly to search for banned narcotics, were employed by the Zambian Drug Enforcement Commission to harass businessmen, journalists, and others who dared campaign against Sata or his supporters.

His administration compelled NGOs to list themselves and their backers with the Ministry of Home Affairs, Russian style, and decreed the registration of all mobile SIM cards, as in Zimbabwe, the better to eavesdrop on citizens and potential dissenters. Chinese experts installed a special mechanism to monitor all internet traffic within Zambia. Elias Chipemo, an articulate would-be politician and the leader of a small political party, declared these surveillance efforts part of a "growing erosion of all the gains of democracy Zambians fought so hard to reintroduce when they successfully brought down the one party state." Chipemo flatly said that Zambia was becoming a "police state."[35] Archbishops and bishops of the Catholic Church in Zambia also expressed their alarm at these abuses by the Sata-dominated nation.

Many of these issues continued to fester, making Zambians uneasy and irritated, well into 2014. Economically, too, the country was by then underperforming its promise. Weak copper production was one depressive agent; another was the failure of large-scale farmers to contribute as much as previously to national incomes. A third constraint proved to be the enduring issue of corruption. Zambians, especially urbanites, were confronted with bureaucratic and police-perpetrated instances of extortion. Grand corruption existed, too, especially as tenderpreneurship grew and South African and other externally based would-be concessionaires looked to Zambia's growing consumer class for lucrative custom. Likewise, mineral-drilling prospects in (mostly) western Zambia attracted the kinds of investors who could be relied upon to pay for influence. None of this activity was new, but it was corrosive, and it reached high up into the ruling Patriotic Front party.

Transparency International's Corruption Perceptions Index ranked Zambia 85th least corrupt of 180 countries in 2014, after El Salvador, Morocco, and Bosnia, and before the Philippines, Thailand, and Peru, with a raw score of 38 of 100—100 being perfectly noncorrupt. In 2005, Zambia had tied with Zimbabwe for 107th place (out of 159) with a score of 26. In 2000, when the CPI rated only 90 jurisdictions, Zambia scored 34 and was 57th least corrupt on the index after Argentina and before Latvia and Mexico. From the Chiluba through the Sata administrations, and despite CPI's scoring methodology having changed, Zambia was perceived as a steadily corrupt place, particularly when it was ranked as low as Zimbabwe (under Mugabe). Sata's reign produced some improved results, but not very robustly.[36] And worse was to come. (In 2020, Zambia fell to 117th place on the CPI, together with Sierra Leone, Egypt, Ukraine, and Nepal, with a raw score of 33.)[37]

Zambia was of concern on many fronts—social, political, and economic—and being closely watched by international lending agencies, donors, and China—a major investor and lender—when Sata died in a London hospital after suffering a massive heart attack (having endured a smaller one in 2008 and becoming seriously ill early in 2014). Guy Scott, his white Zambian-born vice president, became a caretaker president prior to an election to fill out Sata's term. (Scott and

I had known each other over many years; I had visited him just before seeing Sata in 2012.)

Reverting to Autocracy

As Sata was dying, Lungu, a second-generation political operative who had been too young (born in 1956) to be politically active during the Kaunda and Chiluba regimes, eased himself toward power by winning battles within the Patriotic Front (PF) against Scott (who was ineligible to become president because of his non-Zambian parentage) and Wynter Kabimba, Sata's favorite and the secretary of the PF. Lungu, an ethnic Nsenga, grew up on the Copperbelt speaking CiBemba and drawing support from Bemba workers despite his Eastern Province family affiliation. Lungu studied law at the University of Zambia and joined a firm in Lusaka, practicing (with two years out for military service) until 2010, when the Law Association of Zambia suspended his license because of "professional misconduct." He had stolen K27,000 ($800) belonging to a client (represented by Lungu) who had successfully sued Zambia's largest cement company.[38]

By the time of his suspension, Lungu had joined the PF, being elected to parliament in 2011 from a Lusaka constituency on Sata's ticket. Sata quickly made him a junior minister in the office of Vice President Scott. Either because of his talents or his sharp elbows, Lungu swiftly gained prominence within the party, first as minister of home affairs in 2012, minister of defense in 2013, and minister of justice in 2014, while Sata was fading. Significantly, Lungu gained control of the PF's committee on discipline and became its secretary general in mid-2014 after helping to oust Kabimba, his best-placed rival, from that central post—achievements that Sata may or may not have approved, but was by then too ill to prevent. When Sata was hospitalized in London, he left Lungu in charge of presidential affairs, Lungu becoming the titular ruler of the country in place of Scott or others.

In order to become president fully, Lungu had to win a 2015 election for a twenty-month stint to fill out Sata's term and then to compete in 2016 for a full five-year incumbency. In both contests the surprisingly youthful looking sixty-year-old barely defeated Hichilema, first by 48 percent to 47 percent of the vote, the second time by 50.3 percent to 47.6 percent, in both cases with several other candidates gaining tiny percentages of support.[39]

Hichilema, a businessman who profited from Zambia's privatization of its parastatal corporations, was regarded as comparatively untainted by corrupt dealings. Six years younger than Lungu, he established the United Party for National Development in 2006, and sought the presidency ever after. From the Monze district in the Southern Province and ethnically Tonga, the fourth largest of Zambia's seventy or so language groups, Hichilema studied economics at the University of Zambia and gained an MBA degree at the University of Birmingham, thereafter becoming the head of two accountancy firms in Lusaka.

In each case, after narrowly losing the presidential poll, Hichilema cried foul. He claimed that the PF had rigged each election, stuffing ballot boxes and rearranging final counts. But whether or not Hichilema had been defeated fairly, Lungu looked for any excuse to curtail his persistent opponent's criticisms.

In 2017, their motorcades clashed. That is, Lungu asserted that Hichilema's vehicles had refused to give way to him, presumably a traffic offense that could have been prosecuted. Instead, Lungu sent the police to raid Hichilema's residence at night, tear-gassing his frightened wife and children and carting the defeated candidate off to Zambia's maximum-security prison, where he was tortured and held in solitary confinement for eight days without food or water. Lungu also declared a state of emergency. His prosecutors charged Hichilema with treason.

The three largest church bodies in Zambia condemned the assault on Hichilema, terming it the actions of a dictator. So did nearly every embassy, on behalf of their governments (but not President Jacob Zuma's South Africa), and human rights groups around the globe. Julius Malema, the flamboyant leader of one of South Africa's opposition parties, the Economic Freedom Front, called Lungu a coward and said that locking up his main adversary was reminiscent of actions taken under apartheid. The prison authorities, on Lungu's orders, barred former president Kaunda; Mmusi Maimame, then leader of South Africa's main opposition party, the Democratic Alliance; and Hichilema's wife from visiting the prisoner. Eventually, former Nigerian president Olusegun Obasanjo and Baroness Patricia Scotland, secretary general of the Commonwealth of Nations, were allowed to see Hichilema in prison and to plead for his release. Never prosecuted, he emerged from detention after four months, pledging to continue his political campaigns against Lungu and the PF.

The attack on Hichilema confirmed Lungu's authoritarian impulses. In 2016, he tried to shut *The Post* by alleging financial irregularities, forcing the newspaper to publish away from its premises and in a clandestine manner for several weeks. In 2020, he shut it down completely and closed PrimeTV, a leading local outlet, permanently. In 2019, the police abruptly arrested Chishimba Kambwili, formerly Lungu's minister of information, a contender in the next presidential election, and leader of the National Democratic Congress, a minor political party, for allegedly defaming the president by alluding to him (but not by name) as a dog. Two days earlier, the registrar of societies had revoked his party's official registration. Another former cabinet minister, Henry Kalaba, minister of foreign affairs, left the PF in 2018, claiming that Lungu permitted "swelling" corruption within Zambia. In 2020, Pastor Nevers Mumba, head of the MMD (Mwanawasa's party) was detained in the Congo on Lungu's orders for attempting to solicit political campaign funds there. In the same year, the police harassed Hichilema once again, summoning him for questioning about the purchase of property in the Eastern Province in 2004. Also in 2020, a well-known local rapper who composed songs referring to Lungu's crushing of civic freedoms was once more arrested.

In the same year Lungu replaced a governor of the central bank who had refused to let Lungu's administration print money. Local headlines throughout these years asserted that Lungu was learning dangerous lessons from the adjoining governments of Zimbabwean presidents Robert Mugabe and Emmerson Mnangagwa. Wherever he acquired his venom, Lungu certainly emerged in 2016, after winning the presidency a second time, as a pretentious despot. (I was in Zambia in 2015, but never saw him then or later. Nor did I meet with Inonge Wina, Lungu's well-placed and highly regarded vice president and the widow of Arthur Wina.)

Many of these hostile acts demonstrated Lungu's intolerance of competition and impulses of disobedience. But they were motivated largely by his determination to keep power and contest a third election in 2021, when he would be violating the Zambian constitution and succumbing to the debilitating African leadership disease of third-term-itis.[40] He managed, however, to persuade Zambia's constitutional court (previously packed with loyalists) to opine that serving twenty months during his first, abbreviated, presidency did not constitute a real or full term. Indeed, the campaign to be reelected president began almost as soon as he won his second presidency in 2016 and continued with his persecution of rivals like Hichilema and anyone else whose aspirations dared to pop above the political parapet.

In order to assist, Mugabe-like, in furthering his election prospects, in 2020 Lungu cleverly canceled the existing voters' roll and replaced it with a new one. Mugabe had performed the same maneuver in 2013. (See chapter 9.) Zambians had a month at the end of the year to sign their names onto the roll. Opposition strongholds had unequal opportunities to do so—naturally. A University of Zambia authority commented that "Lungu hopes to disenfranchise as many opposition supporters as possible."[41]

In 2020, amid the coronavirus, Zambia's economy teetered on the brink of ruin. The price of copper (Zambia was still 70 percent reliant on copper export earnings) fell by 16 percent due to diminished demand because of Covid-19, with royalties due to Zambia falling as well from the previous year, a slide that had begun in 2013. (Copper prices rallied substantially in 2021.) Yet, tumbling over themselves to accumulate rents and cover debts, Lungu and his associates drove taxes on the copper companies to levels among the highest in the world. In 2019, the government tried to take back one of its more profitable mine properties from an Indian company. Glencore said it would stop mining at Mopani. As a result of such endeavors and the higher taxes, production of copper slumped to 700,000 metric tons in 2020, lower than 750,000 metric tons in 2019 and far below the 858,000 metric tons of 2018.[42]

Despite all of this cautionary financial news, in late 2020, to bolster his election chances, Lungu promulgated an expansive budget that included the equivalent of $275 million (up 300 percent from the previous year's budget) to provide farmers (and voters), who comprised half of the country's population, with inputs such as the fertilizer and seeds that are typically in Africa supplied by the state through marketing boards or other bureaucratic mechanisms.

Falling Prey to China

Consumed by power, Lungu also drove Zambia deeply into debt. Like Sata before him, Lungu's government splurged on excessively expensive roads (including a freeway that did not quite make it to Lusaka), with many new arteries costing twice the African average per mile; Lungu's government built dams, stadiums, and other infrastructural improvements. It also raised civil service pay several times. As a result, the total of Zambian borrowings in foreign currencies and pledged to foreigners tripled between 2014 and 2018 relative to GDP. Its debt had grown by 1,000 percent since 2011, to $12 billion.[43] Of that amount, nearly a third was owed to China, a quarter to holders of largely agricultural financing Eurobonds from the Sata era and after, and only a fifth—but a worrying fifth because it had to be remitted sooner—to foreign commercial banks.[44] In 2020, the amounts needing to be repaid equaled more than 8 percent of Zambia's annual GDP, a dangerous total.

Critics aver that not only did debt service charges comprise more than a third of Zambia's budgetary allocations, starving social services and neglected school-building and teacher-training needs, but the accompanying financial mismanagement across a host of ministries, including the treasury, was "calamitous." The IMF refused in 2020 to help Zambia refinance its Eurobond loans because of an overwhelming lack of "transparency."[45]

Widespread corruption, probably even exceeding the good old Chiluba excesses in size, and certainly more skillfully masked, hardly helped. The manner in which the public exchequer and the long-suffering citizens of Zambia had been fleeced certainly contributed to Zambia's financial woes. Another, possibly unrelated, discovery showed that multinational mining companies and other investors in Zambia may have (legally but damagingly to Zambia) for several years remitted profits overseas, removing those large amounts from the Zambian economy.[46]

Another economic and fiscal blow came from corrupt proceedings. A critical account from 2018 placed Zambian grand corruption near the head of its sub-Saharan African class. It declared that the real reason why Zambia had run up debts equal to 59 percent of GDP from 2005 to 2018 was not because of the fall in the price of copper, but because the nation-state was "run by an inept and venal elite who used easy credit to line their own pockets. Much of the money Zambia borrowed was squandered or stolen. Bigwigs skimmed from worthy-sounding contracts. When the country brought bright new fire engines their price somehow ballooned by 70 percent, to more than $1 million each. Its new roads mysteriously cost twice as much per kilometer as its neighbours'. Its airport terminal was designed to accommodate an improbable ten-fold jump in traffic. A slide into authoritarianism made corruption harder to check."[47]

A Central Asian mining concern that had purchased the Chambishi copper smelter to process ores from Katanga bribed political leaders, including three presidents, lavishly.[48] Furthermore, the trusted Financial Intelligence Centre of South Africa reported that Zambian shady transactions and illicit money-laundering totals had risen from $382 million in 2017 to $520 million in 2018.[49] A parliamentarian who had left the PF called "the levels of looting and gross mismanagement of state resources . . . disheartening and unprecedented and threaten[ing to] national security and unity."[50]

By the end of 2020, Zambia blamed the coronavirus and copper problems for its severe money problems. But corruption and wild spending by Lungu and his ministers played a larger, possibly more conclusive, role. The nation could not pay its bondholders, either. So it became the first African nation to default on its external euro borrowings. Bondholders turned down a six-month extension request for the first of notes that had come due for $43 million. Two more notes subsequently fell into default, with debts to China and international lending institutions also at risk.[51]

Voters Opt for Democracy

Lungu had attempted to inveigle parliament to give him unusual powers to rule by decree and to extend the term of the presidency to seven years. He wanted a "constitutional dictatorship" of unprecedented reach.[52] To the surprise of many observers, however, in late 2020 legislators turned down this attempt to subvert the national constitution. Without such enhanced powers, in August 2021 Lungu once again attempted to beguile Zambian voters when they went to the polls. But this time the Lungu regime's intimidation of the electorate and its attempt to prevent campaigning by Hichilema and his followers failed. Zambian civil society—especially the churches and the lawyers—closely observed the balloting and ran a parallel count, thus making any rigging of the results difficult. Hichilema, a more pronounced democrat than Lungu, won overwhelmingly, by 2.8 million to 1.8 million votes. This was an especially encouraging and unexpected result given Lungu's anxious determination to continue his autocratic rule.

Voters were tired of being poor and being victimized by a crudely corrupt administration. Consumed by power, Lungu had driven Zambia deeply into debt. Zambia's public debt as a share of GDP had doubled from 66 percent to 113 percent, the value of the local kwacha currency having fallen precipitously; food prices had soared and copper production slumped. Zambia's debts in foreign currencies and pledged to foreigners tripled between 2014 and 2018 relative to GDP.

Under Lungu, too, with copper revenues falling and corruption rising, Zambians had suffered from high food prices and shortages of staples together with stagflation—a combination that ensured unprecedented levels of fiscal distress. Hichilema's sixth successive electoral campaign hence rode to victory on the back of the country's prevailing sense of economic discontent and anger at Lungu's tightfisted policies, including his curtailing of free speech and assembly. The nonprofit Freedom House had rated Zambia under Lungu in 2021 as only "partly free," with a low score of 52 out of 100.

Hichilema's victory also showed that African voters were finally able to eschew ethnic preferences. In few other countries has a minority candidate triumphed over a representative of a majority constituency, with policy and character trumping identity. Although Lungu is ethnically an easterner, his party is strongly linked to the northern Bemba, Zambia's largest ethnic group. Since independence in 1964, speakers of CiBemba and their eastern allies have mostly dominated political life in Zambia. Presidents Kaunda, Chiluba, and Sata all spoke CiBemba, as did President Mwanawasa, a Lenje from the Copperbelt, and Lungu (who matured on the mostly CiBemba-speaking Copperbelt). Hichilema, now sixty, a British-educated CiTonga-speaking businessman, broke the political hold on the nation of CiBemba speakers.[53]

Whether the new president and his administration could quickly improve Zambia's economic prospects was the big imponderable as Hichilema took office. He said that he could. He promised to root out corruption—a major and difficult task for any incoming African president. After winning, he said that his government would have "zero tolerance" for corruption. He revealed that his administration had inherited an "empty" treasury and had discovered "a lot of people who are not working, but are on the payroll" of the government. "Horrifying" amounts of money had been stolen, he revealed. "People are still trying to make last-minute movements of funds . . . which are not theirs."[54]

If Hichilema is as good as his word—"We are not masters of the people, we are their servants" –and if he manages well to revive honest dealings and shows that his professed reform agenda is real, then Zambia's relatively well-educated and resilient people will doubtless respond with alacrity. But as this writing the debt overhang is real and so is massive unemployment.[55]

Zambia required a bailout from the IMF due to the default in 2020 and the country's critical shortage of foreign exchange reserves. In 2022, the country's new administration finalized an arrangement backed by the IMF to restructure approximately $17 billion worth of debt. The IMF lent Zambia $1.4 billion so that it could service Lusaka's many creditors, each of which would have to cancel substantial sums of money owed. Zambia was indebted to China for about 40 percent of the total owed externally.

The IMF also insisted on curtailing the subsidies that buoyed up urban life in Zambia while increasing the national deficit. The IMF wanted its $1.4 billion worth of assistance to "re-establish fiscal sustainability" and to reorient public resources "away from inefficient public investment" toward increased investment in health, education, and social benefits.[56] Hichilema's administration's task will be to use this boost in funding progressively, and for the benefit of all Zambians. Hichilema's self-proclaimed "new dawn" government has trumpeted its openness and transparency, its determination to root out corruption, and its restoration of the media and speech freedoms that Lungu's administration had curtailed. Democracy, Hichilema said, was in Zambia to stay. "The government has set in motion measures that build a diverse and inclusive government but uphold human rights and promote the rule of law." The "new dawn" also encompasses giving more power to rural authorities than ever before, doing everything possible to "put the country on a sound [economic] footing" and creating jobs "in the countryside."[57] That was Hichilema's message.

Nevertheless, as Zambia in 2022 endured renewed coronavirus anxieties, there was no guarantee—only lofty promises—that Hichilema's incumbency would transform and uplift his citizens. His electoral victory was a harbinger of Zambia's and Africa's growing political maturity. So was his appearance at President Biden's Democracy Summit in December 2021 an affirmation of an evident probity and an espousal of anticorrupt values, but in 2022 Zambia still had rocky economic roads to traverse as a deep debtor, and a legacy of decades of mismanagement and poor governance to overcome. Whether Hichilema will deliver the positive results that his people and critics expect will surely depend on his leadership and political capabilities, but also on an ability to vaccinate the mass of Zambians and the absence of unanticipated climatic or other natural calamities. In mid-2022, the pandemic had given Zambia more than 322,000 coronavirus cases, but barely four thousand deaths, a possibly vastly understated total.[58]

A Zambia whose fortunes have slid precipitously downward since President Kaunda's day may, under Hichilema, finally grasp a golden opportunity to recover, and to benefit all Zambians.

4

The Hijacking of Malawi

Banda's Uptight Despotism

"I will denounce you in public, when I get around to it." That was the message contained in a letter that came to me in late 1965 from President Hastings Kamuzu Banda, Malawi's liberating leader and all-powerful head of state. Indeed, months later, Banda ranted and raved at a public meeting in Zomba, Malawi's colonial capital, about a Harvard academic who had dared to challenge his omnipotence. He spared no niceties of language in excoriating me and my (allegedly malign) contribution to the Malawian freedom struggle. His house organ, the *Malawi News*, carried a full report.

Banda's unexpected vitriolic exercises were triggered by the publication of my *The Rise of Nationalism in Central Africa: The Making of Malawi and Zambia, 1873–1964*, which the Harvard University Press issued in mid-1965. The bulk of the book was non-controversial as far as Banda was concerned. He featured favorably in the sections of the book that detailed the final battles against the Federation, and Banda's uncompromising on-the-ground leadership of the Malawian freedom struggle from 1958 to independence in 1964. (See chapter 1.) Banda had no complaints about the contents of the book (I had sent him a copy before its publication), but he was livid about a short postscript added after the book was in proof. That postscript discussed a post-independence political rebellion by the members of Banda's initial cabinet who had quickly become disenchanted with his narcissistic character and overweening leadership tendencies.

Led by Henry Masauko Chipembere and Dunduza Chisiza, a month after independence most of the ministers of his cabinet rose up against Banda's incipient authoritarianism. The postscript was fully objective, took no sides, cast no blame, and simply set out the reasons why most of Banda's successful fellow nationalists had resigned from their new ministerial portfolios and fled the country. But the mere mention of the cabinet "rebellion" was sufficient to enrage Banda. It also marked the first stage of dictatorship. He had become an uncompromising autocrat, dismissing the democratic preferences of the younger Malawians who had engineered his own rise to power, nullifying my positive words about him in the bulk of the book, and making mockery of everything that he had earlier confided to me and promised to his younger colleagues.

Overcoming the Oppressors. Robert I. Rotberg, Oxford University Press. © Oxford University Press 2023.
DOI: 10.1093/oso/9780197674208.003.0004

Figure 4.1. Kamuzu Banda

Denouncing me and castigating the postscript was unanticipated both because of its neutral language and because Banda had previously been so cordial and welcoming. He had visited me in Cambridge, Massachusetts. I had accompanied his victorious electoral campaign in 1961 (discussed below) and had held lengthy discussions with him then and in 1962 and 1963. Moreover, I had attended Malawi's independence celebrations in 1964 at his invitation, as his guest, and at the new state's expense. Little did I know then, or suspect, how thoroughly Banda was to hijack his nation's freedom struggle.

Establishing Malawi and Boosting Banda

James Frederick Sangala, a bookkeeper, clerk, and court interpreter, motivated the creation of the Nyasaland African Congress during World War II. A Blantyre Native Association already existed, but Sangala saw the need for a national body to represent and articulate the political aspirations of Africans, to seek redress for their grievances, and to act collectively against colonial rulers. Sangala wanted "all Africans and leaders of this country to give their support . . . so that our race should have a place among the civilized."[1]

The Congress was formally established in Blantyre in early 1944. Its several dozen creators asked the colonial government for improved educational opportunities, modern housing, the right to form trade unions, and the return of the lands that had been taken from Africans and given to white settlers but never developed. They sought direct representation of Africans by Africans on the Protectorate's Legislative Council. And they rejected any form of amalgamation with the Rhodesias.[2]

These events were welcomed from afar, and supported financially, by a Malawian living in the north of England with whom Sangala and his Congress cohorts had had no previous contact. This was Banda, an assistant medical officer at a hospital in North Shields, near Newcastle upon Tyne. He had fled Kasungu, in Malawi's central province, during World War I, settling first at a mine in Southern Rhodesia and then in South Africa. Young Banda, probably born about 1898, labored first as an oiler underground, then as a pumper of water at a colliery near Dundee, KwaZulu-Natal, and later as an interpreter on the Witwatersrand Deep (gold) Mine near Boksburg in what is now Gauteng province. There he became a member of the African Methodist Episcopal Church, an American missionary establishment. That church sponsored Banda's subsequent visit to the United States in 1935 to enroll first in the high school section of the Wilberforce Institute (now Central State University in Wilberforce, Ohio) and then as a premed student at the Universities of Indiana and Chicago. He became a physician at Meharry Medical College in Nashville, Tennessee, obtaining high marks. After graduating, he obtained a further degree at the Edinburgh Royal College Medical School, and learned about tropical diseases at the University of Liverpool.[3]

All the while, Banda tried to keep abreast of political developments in his native Nyasaland, in many cases through his contacts with missionaries of the Church of Scotland. When he heard about the establishment of the Nyasaland African Congress, he began giving unsolicited advice to Sangala and others from afar, and contributing small but useful sums of money toward the costs of the Congress. He urged the Congress to centralize its operations, and not to rely on branches with divergent views and methods of operation. He offered to pay the salary of a full-time organizer, a proposal that was rejected. At home in Britain, Banda pressed the Fabian Bureau to join him in lobbying members of the House of Commons to improve conditions in Nyasaland. In 1948, he and a delegation from the Congress led by Charles Matinga and A. J. Mponda tried to persuade the colonial authorities in London to upgrade educational facilities in Nyasaland, but to no avail.[4]

From the late 1940s, as discussed in chapter 1, Banda was active from Brondesbury Park, London, where he had opened a private medical practice, vehemently opposing the federating of Nyasaland to the Rhodesias. Federation was the "thin edge of the wedge of amalgamation . . . coated with the sugar of federation to make it easier for the Africans and the Imperial government to swallow."[5] In 1953, just before the Federation was imposed on antagonistic Africans, Banda accused the British government of handing Africans over to whites in a "cold, calculated, callous and cynical betrayal of a trusting, loyal people."[6] When neither his heated words, nor the opposition of Northern Rhodesian spokespersons and enlightened Britons, halted the Federal juggernaut, Banda quit Britain in disgust, decamping to the Gold Coast (soon to become Ghana).

At home, chiefs and many congress-persons urged their followers to disregard agricultural and other colonial regulations, some choosing prison over obedience. There were riots and road-blocking incidents, particularly in the white-run tea plantation district of Cholo (Tyolo). Further disturbances and attacks on plantations occurred in the Chiradzulu and Chikwawa districts. Police were stoned. In the Mlanje and Port Herald districts, Africans refused to pay their yearly taxes. In Domasi, police fired on protesters. Fearful, the leaders of the Nyasa Congress tried to distance themselves from the agitators. They warned their followers against provoking the government.

The Nyasa Congress gained more backbone when younger, educated, members returned from universities abroad. Chipembere, the chubby, open-faced, articulate son of a revered Anglican cleric on distant Likoma Island, came home from Fort Hare University College in South Africa. Murray William Kanyama Chiume, slight and querulous, returned from Makerere College in Uganda and high school teaching in Dodoma, Tanganyika. Styling themselves "Young Turks," Chipembere and Chiume pressed the colonial government to declare Nyasaland an African state and to let it secede from the Federation.

In 1956, thanks to a revised constitution, Chipembere and Chiume were both elected to the Protectorate's Legislative Council, along with three other Congress members. Chiume and Chipembere peppered the government benches in the Council with barbed questions concerning wages, housing, the non-alienation of trust land belonging in theory to Africans, and expanding compulsory education.[7] Both demanded the end of racial discrimination and the use of the offensive word "native." Intemperate sometimes, Chipembere called white settlers "bloodsuckers." Both youthful leaders were still engaged in this kind of verbal jousting when I arrived on the Central African scene in 1959.

By then, too, bewhiskered, sharp-eyed Dunduzu Chisiza had been deported to Nyasaland from Southern Rhodesia by Prime Minister Garfield Todd because of Chisiza's militancy as a key member of the protean Southern Rhodesian African National Congress. (See chapter 9.) Chisiza had abundant organizing experience, which he was to put to good use in what became Malawi. He was a theoretician, too, with knowledge of the Indian independence struggle, and an owlish demeanor that I was to come to know well. He had also become a Baha'i believer.

A few months before my arrival in the region, Chipembere had finally persuaded Banda to return home to lead the Nyasa national movement against the

Federation. This was a fateful move, and in more ways than Chipembere, Chiume, and others could have then appreciated. "Human nature is such," Chipembere had written, "that it needs a kind of hero to be hero-worshipped if a political struggle is to succeed."[8] He, Chiume, and Chisiza, the other plausible leaders of a future Malawi, were too young and too immature—or so Chipembere believed. Orton Chirwa, an older, cautious, lawyer, was politically too inexperienced and a little too moderate for Chipembere's tastes. So Banda was chosen to be the father figure of the nationalist insurrection that Chipembere had spearheaded and now expected to manage.

By 1957, Chipembere had become confident that he could motivate and mobilize Malawians to mount a massive campaign of civil disobedience. But the movement lacked a supreme leader like Nkrumah or Kenyatta around whom all manner of Malawians could rally. Chisiza was too new in Malawi and Chiume was too arrogant. Chipembere knew that he himself was sufficiently respected and could play a leading role. He was popular, and well regarded by strong-minded youth members of the Congress. But he himself, Chipembere fatefully believed, was not right for the task. He lacked confidence in his ability as a twenty-seven-year-old to lead. He did not think that he spoke well enough extemporaneously. A mere stripling in his own eyes, Chipembere believed that for the Malawian freedom struggle to succeed in toppling the Federation, it needed a head more gray than black to guide the cause and to drive it toward independence.

"I felt that I needed ten years or more of experience in leadership," he wrote, "before I could shoulder such responsibilities . . . I . . . would make a mess of things. . . ."[9]

With such modest words and thoughts, Chipembere sealed his own fate and placed the political future of what was to become Malawi in Banda's hands. Without Banda, however, Malawi might have emerged as a progressive nation instead of the impoverished authoritarian mistake that it became under Banda.

Chipembere's choice of Banda made good, strategic sense if experience, reputation, and maturity were the main criteria. But Chipembere chose to overlook Banda's autocratic streak, revealed to Chipembere after visits to Banda in Ghana and Britain and in correspondence between the younger and the older nationalist. Chipembere thought that he could groom Banda appropriately for his new political position despite Banda's inability to speak a local language. Chipembere assumed that he could build excitement among the Malawian masses for Banda, provide adulation and applause for someone who appreciated and needed flattery, and continue himself to steer the ship of nationalism to a friendly harbor.

Chipembere and Chiume were so focused in the late 1950s on seceding from the Federation that they tolerated some of Banda's heavy-handed idiosyncrasies. Chipembere concentrated on ends, not means, and believed that the Nyasa Congress had the colonial and Federal forces on the run. By then (1958) Banda was settling into his presidency of the Congress; he persuaded delegates to its annual conference to give him total control of appointments to the party's central committee. Already, Banda was overhauling procedures and according himself unchecked power.

None of these maneuverings overly concerned Chipembere and Chiume at the time. They were more and more intent on forcing he government's hand. Chipembere had been jailed earlier for sedition. They both anticipated martyrdom; the mayhem that they purposely unleashed in late 1958 and early 1959 was designed to provoke the authorities, and it did. There were numerous militant incidents in October and November 1958.[10] Police opened fire on demonstrators at Fort Hill, in the far north, in February 1959. There were similar confrontations in Mzuzu, Mzimba, Ekwendeni, Loudon, and Fort Manning, and even in Blantyre and Zomba (the seat of colonial authority). Federal troops swooped into the Protectorate by air in late February 1959, and its British governor banned the Nyasa Congress and arrested 350 so-called troublemakers on March 3 ("Operation Sunrise").

The Malawians detained by the Federal forces in Gweru and Khami (Bulawayo) prisons in Zimbabwe could transition rapidly to being legitimate liberation heroes. In detention, too, the leaders of the Congress came to accept Banda's name for the country that they would build: Malawi, from the name of the Maravi peoples who lived around the great Rift Valley lake that parallels and gives meaning to much of the nation.[11]

The Coming of the Malawi Congress

By the time that Secretary of State for the Colonies Iain Macleod released Banda from prison in mid-1960, a new Malawi Congress Party (MCP) was up and running, legitimacy was clearly slipping away from the Federation and the colonial authorities, and (unlike the situation in Northern Rhodesia) Whitehall had little appetite to continue denying Malawians their freedom. Orton Chirwa and Aleke K. Banda—"a young man of twenty with a flair for organization"—had a well-running political machine to transfer to Kamuzu Banda.[12] Homburg on his head and lion-hair fly-whisk in hand, the latter was more than ready to claim the rewards of independence together with the prize of untrammeled party chieftainship. He called himself *Ngwazi* (or conqueror), a CiCewa sobriquet chosen to echo Nkrumah's *Osagyefo*, or "redeemer" in Fante.

The MCP had 15,000 members by the end of 1960, thanks to Aleke Banda's aggressive, widely circulated weekly outlet, the *Malawi News*.[13] MCP members were confident and well motivated now that a positive end was in sight. By mid-1961, the MCP claimed 1 million members.

Secretary of State for the Colonies Macleod realized the game was up in Malawi, at least, when he ordered Kamuzu Banda's release from Gweru prison. Macleod appreciated that Banda's leadership would prove essential during the forthcoming period; shifts of predominant power in East Africa and southern Africa had become inevitable. He immediately invited Banda to confer in London. But Banda refused to compromise or temporize. The happy result for Banda and Malawi was a new constitution, an election for Legislative Council seats in 1961, and—presuming the MCP won handily—an expectation that Kamuzu Banda would head the territory's pre-independence government. The elder Banda had usurped Chipembere and had begun to covet a paramount chieftainship over Malawians.

The *Ngwazi* was able to behave in 1960 and 1961 without many checks to his authority because Aleke Banda was very young and had no entrenched position, Orton Chirwa and Kanyama Chiume were willing to work under Kamuzu Banda, and those stalwarts (Chipembere, for one) who might have moderated Banda's overweening pretensions were still incarcerated.

Chipembere and both Dunduzu Chisiza and his elder brother Yatuta Chisiza, a former Tanganyikan policeman, were "uneasy" in their prison cells that Kamuzu Banda was acting as if the MCP were an agency of his personal authority. Autocratic rule was antithetical to local African traditional or political rule.[14] In early 1961, too, Chipembere (after a few months out of detention) was further prosecuted (possibly with Kamuzu Banda's connivance and with the assent of Sir Glyn Jones, the Protectorate's governor) for sedition and inciting violence, and sentenced to what amounted to two more years in jail. Chipembere, despite his protestations to the contrary, was a fiery speaker in CiNyanja or CiCewa, and Banda may have felt his own control of the freedom campaign threatened by Chipembere's unquestioned crowd appeal.

It was at this heady moment, with Banda poised to lead Malawi into a decisive election, with victory and freedom soon to follow, that he and Aleke Banda, who had become his aide-de-camp, visited London (to a mixed reception) and New York (where they were received with admiration and uncritical praise). Then I persuaded the Bandas to come to Cambridge, Massachusetts, to talk about decolonization and Malawi with my students and to meet prominent local persons interested in Africa.

I was then driving a Volkswagen Beetle. When my wife and I arrived to transport the Bandas to a special dinner that I had arranged with suitable dignitaries, I naturally waved the future president into the front passenger seat. But no, he would only sit in the cramped back, as befitted a big-man politician, homburg on his head. Aleke took the front seat and we went off to what turned out to be a socially disruptive dinner hosted by a distinguished judge and his wife, and including the president of a great university, his wife, and younger faculty and wives. All went reasonably well until the hostess unwittingly repeatedly referred to her guest as the prime minister of Tanganyika. "Nyasaland," he would mutter. She would then ask brightly about conditions in "Tanganyika," and he would mutter back "Nyasaland." Meanwhile the judge and the president, old friends, chatted across the table about local political issues, ignoring their foreign guests. Then we adjourned to the next room for coffee. But Banda had had enough. Very politely he asked me to take him back to the Harvard student house where I had arranged quarters for the two Bandas. So, to the shock of the hosts (who were unaware of hurt feelings) we took our leave, driving the Bandas across campus to Harvard's Winthrop House. Then my wife and I sat in the car and wondered: Should we go back? If we did, should we say anything about Kamuzu Banda's bruised ego or should we just let lèse-majesté go unremarked? After much debate, my wife and I decided to return (it was still very early) and enjoy the conversation. The hostess never realized how she had offended the famously thin-skinned American-trained physician who was now in charge of a new country soon to be called Malawi.

(Subsequently, I arranged a full undergraduate scholarship at Harvard for Aleke Banda, who had served time in prison rather than university. But Kamuzu Banda would not let his chief aide leave his side, so Aleke Banda, then twenty-four, lost an opportunity that might have given him a very different life trajectory. Young Banda and I remained in close contact, however, even after my public disagreements with Kamuzu Banda. Until Aleke Banda's untimely death in 2010, we were in frequent friendly contact, especially during his own times of obloquy and danger, and we worked closely together from his time as finance minister in the 1990s.)

I could not see Chipembere when my wife and I spent many weeks in Malawi to observe the 1961 elections, but we sent messages into Zomba Prison while traversing much of the southern part of the country with Kamuzu Banda, Aleke Banda, and Dunduzu Chisiza. I spent fewer hours with Chiume and Chirwa, but the campaign of 1961 was a whirlwind of political hustling, so we were constantly in motion from our base in Limbe.[15]

Kamuzu Banda canvassed all sections of his lengthy country before the 1961 vote, condemning "the stupid so-called Federation," leading songfests, and calling upon Africans to vote en bloc for MCP candidates. The Chisiza brothers, in charge of MCP fundraising, sold badges bearing the beaming face of Banda.

My wife and I watched the final poll numbers arrive: 98 percent of eligible voters participated. The MCP won all twenty of the lower-roll (African) seats and two of the eight available upper-roll (white) seats. The governor soon granted five, later seven, of the ten available seats on the Protectorate's executive council to the MCP.

From the beginning of 1962, Kamuzu Banda, nominally only Minister of Lands, Natural Resources, and Local Government, was effectively Nyasaland's first and final prime minister. Although Governor Jones still formally held the reins of government, Banda decided policy, approved legislation, and ordered his subordinate ministers around. (He was to be styled Chief Minister in the following year, after another London conference that promised secession from the Federation.) With surprising alacrity, he and they expanded secondary educational opportunities, revamped the Native Courts, improved the conditions of agricultural labor, reformed produce-marketing arrangements, and replaced chiefs with elected district councils. With the help of experts from across the world, Dunduzu Chisiza prepared an ambitious five-year economic resurgence plan.

The Power of One

Tragedy struck Malawi, however, in September 1962. One dark winter night racing home from a meeting in Blantyre, Chisiza slammed his car into the abutments of a high-level concrete bridge. Malawi lost one of its most principled and most able politicians. I attended the funeral along with devastated mourners from throughout Malawi. (My wife and I were then living in the country, both of us doing research in the Malawi Archives at the foot of Zomba Mountain, lunching on tasty Indian food from stall sellers near the Archives, and playing tennis at the Zomba Club before retreating up a single-lane road to our mosquito-infested house on the edge of the mountain.)[16]

Despite the great loss of Chisiza's ideas and problem-solving ability, all should have been proceeding well in a state poised to achieve independence two years later.[17] Chipembere was finally released from prison in 1963. But the state that Chipembere, Chiume, the Chisizas, and others had worked so hard and long to perfect had a basic central design flaw. Kamuzu Banda had for some time been making every decision affecting state and party. In early 1963, before Chipembere's release, Banda demanded and was given "absolute discretion" over the affairs of the party and its members. He had declared the party "supreme," as Julius Nyerere in Tanzania was soon to do and Kenneth Kaunda was to do a decade hence in Zambia.

Whatever dissension existed in the MCP was not loudly voiced in the preparations for the new red, green, and black Malawian flag to be raised aloft above Zomba's stadium shortly after midnight on July 6, 1964. It was bitterly cold, especially for those of us in dinner jackets (tuxedos) appropriate for the occasion. Fortunately, the person sitting next to me in a reserved seat was the

Irish envoy. He pulled a silver flask out of an inner pocket of his dinner jacket and offered me a quick nip of whiskey as we cheered Prince Philip, the Duke of Edinburgh, lowering the Union Jack for the last time on Malawian soil and relinquishing the ceremonial diadem of imperial might to Kamuzu Banda and his team.

A day or two later, in the warming winter sun, the troubles of independence began. The younger men and women who occupied positions of responsibility as cabinet ministers, junior ministers, and parliamentary secretaries in the new Malawi government resented being treated by President Banda as schoolchildren. In public, he invariably referred to them as "my boys." They preferred to begin to exercise the power that went with their portfolios, but Banda was a consummate micromanager, and kept tight-fisted control. "I say a thing and when I say a thing nobody must say anything else and my ministers must do nothing before I approve of it. . . ."[18] As Chisiza had written before his death, "When too much trust is reposed in a leader . . . the thing goes to his head and makes him believe he is infallible."[19]

Ministers almost to a person differed with Banda over key international policy issues, especially those related to recognizing China or Taiwan. They objected to his dealing diplomatically with East Germany, trading with South Africa and Southern Rhodesia, and his unwillingness to give aid and comfort to Zimbabwe's two guerrilla movements.[20] Banda insisted, against the preferred will of his ministers, to open relations with Portuguese-controlled Mozambique, where another anti-colonial struggle was underway. Finally, Banda refused to let Malawi join the "nonaligned" states such as Zambia and Tanzania in their opposition to white dominance in Southern Rhodesia and South Africa. His ministers believed that Banda was turning Malawi into a "Quisling" state by consorting with colonial and apartheid regimes and opposing pan-Africanism. (See chapter 5.)

Within weeks after independence, Kamuzu Banda made several speeches critical of the Organization of African Unity (OAU). After delivering one such attack in Cairo, he returned home to Malawi to belabor various ministers, including Chipembere, on the tarmac at Blantyre airport. He told the crowd of well-wishers that criticism of him and his foreign policies was equivalent to treason, and that opponents "should be watched."[21]

As president, Banda refused to Africanize the civil service, preferring to retain holdover white principals. He refused to integrate the new nation's schools. He balked at increasing the salaries of black employees. Banda, probably sixty-eight years old at the time, was old-fashioned, conservative in dress and manner, supremely narcissistic, arbitrary, bossy, and politically insecure. "Whenever you criticized him, he flared up so violently that you had to consider your own position. . . . You didn't want to risk a split at this stage [because] anyone who tried to pick a quarrel with Dr. Banda . . . would be hated by the people."[22]

By the time that a scrum of his ministers decided in August 1964 that they had had enough, Banda had accumulated unassailable power personally. He controlled the party and the press, and commanded official vigilante enforcers known as the Young Pioneers. Holdover whites were still in charge of the army and the police, and were loyal to Banda. Nevertheless, at first Banda agreed to moderate his authoritarianism. But, a month later, he turned against the democrats, and sacked Chiume, Chirwa, Yatuta Chisiza, Augustine Bwanausi, Willie Chokani, and Rose Chibambo—the most widely respected members of the party, the cabinet, and the new nation. (They all soon fled Malawi, and my friend David Rubadiri left his position as Malawi's first ambassador to the United Nations. He had been a school headmaster and later wrote esteemed novels and poetry, taught at Uganda's Makerere University College, the University of Nairobi, and the University of Botswana, and, after Banda's removal, again became Malawi's ambassador to the United Nations and vice-chancellor of the University of Malawi.) Colin Cameron, a key white supporter, had already resigned his cabinet position to protest Banda's arbitrary decision to reintroduce preventive detention. Chipembere, who had been overseas at a conference in Canada, returned home that same night, and received a note from Banda asking for support.

For Chipembere, the choices were stark. He could attempt to reform Banda, in many ways the Frankenstein monster that he had created, or he could join his colleagues in a bitter and lopsided battle for the soul of the new Malawi. He doubtless understood that Banda would not fight fair, but he greatly underestimated with what underhanded and undemocratic means Banda would battle a popular figure such as Chipembere. Arriving at parliament the morning after his return, Chipembere assured the crowd of anti-Banda supporters surrounding parliament that he would resign: "It gives me a really heavy heart that Malawi, which people were regarding as a paragon of political organisation and discipline and understanding, has now broken down. . . . Wherever Welensky is today, he must be rejoicing." He continued, "Rightly or wrongly, I regard myself as a man of some principles, a man of some honesty, a man of some courage, a man with some respect . . . I wouldn't dare for a moment retreat from my principles [now that] Malawi [has] broken down."[23]

The above paragraphs capture the gist of what I wrote more chastely and with a little less detail in the five-page book postscript that described the events of August and September 1964. Not only was Kamuzu Banda determined to denounce me for writing the postscript, he also banned the book in Malawi, and for the remainder of his reign (through 1993) prevented me from visiting Malawi for research or any other purpose. Several American ambassadors to Malawi saw this ban as unnecessarily restrictive, and tried to use their good offices to change Banda's mind, especially after twenty years or so. Instead, I had to keep abreast of political change in Malawi by other means, especially by keeping in close contact with Aleke Banda.

Chipembere was also exiled. But first he went forlornly to war. After resigning his ministerial portfolio and giving his "heavy heart" speech in parliament, he went home to the Mangochi district east of Lake Malawi. There he gained a following of supporters, was "restricted" by Banda to that area (meaning that he was not allowed to travel) and began life on the run. With 200 armed followers, he attacked the Mangochi district headquarters in February 1965, and attempted to carry the flag of rebellion all the way to Zomba. But he and his legionnaires were stopped by white-officered troops at the Liwonde ferry crossing of the Shire River. Even so, the rebellion led by Chipembere continued for a few more months, but Malawi's army easily outgunned and outmanned Chipembere's followers. Banda's Young Pioneers turned nasty, too, unleashing a reign of terror in the districts loyal to Chipembere.[24]

This was the beginning of long years of repression in Malawi (see "The Dark Decades" below), the hunting down and killing of several of Chipembere's compatriots, the killing of Yatuta Chisiza after another under-resourced attempt to invade Malawi from Tanzania (in 1967), and the assassination of dissidents within the MCP like Secretary-General Albert Muwalo (in 1977). Even Aleke Banda eventually fell out with Kamuzu Banda and was confined to his ancestral home of Nkhata Bay (near Livingstonia) for twelve forlorn years.

Chipembere knew the worst excesses of the Banda regime only from a distance. He was eased out of the country in April 1965 with Banda's knowledge and through the good offices of Governor Jones and American embassy personnel. Andrew Ross, a Scottish missionary who had been chaplain to Chipembere and others confined during colonial rule's final days to prison in Malawi, was the go-between. He arranged a rendezvous north of Lake Chirwa, from which point a darkened Land Rover took Chipembere to Zomba's grass airport. A small U.S. aircraft flew him to Dar es Salaam.[25] Chipembere's family escaped up the lakeshore from Likoma Island and joined him in the Oyster Bay suburb of Dar es Salaam, where I caught up with them some months later.

Chipembere taught at Kivukoni College in Dar es Salaam from 1966 to 1969, after gaining a master's degree from the University of California at Los Angeles (UCLA). He returned to Los Angeles after Kivukoni to work on a doctoral degree in history and to obtain treatment for diabetes. From 1970, he was also assistant professor of history at UCLA. At the same time, he began working on his autobiography; I found funding to bring Chipembere to Harvard and MIT (where I taught from 1968), and to spend parts of several summers with me and my family in New Hampshire. Among the mountains and lakes of that state, he took lengthy walks down dusty, unpaved roads, returning to his quarters in our rustic house laboriously to write a few pages in longhand on yellow lined paper, and then to muse some more, and write again. He devoted himself to this alien craft just as he did to preparing lectures for his UCLA undergraduates.

Chipembere died in 1975 in Los Angeles, from complications connected to diabetes. He had not quite finished the autobiography. Nor had he and I finished interpreting some of what he had managed to write. Nevertheless, thanks to Ericka Albaugh's assiduous transcription of his handwriting, the autobiography came to fruition and was published and launched successfully in Malawi in 2002 before a large crowd at State House in Lilongwe. President Bakili Muluzi presented *Hero of the Nation* to the country for which Chipembere had fought so fiercely. It was a fitting, but much too belated, tribute to Banda's nemesis and to one of the true originators of modern Malawi. In my introduction, I called the autobiography an "intensely personal, ever honest" account of "a vigorous life of leadership in politics, of an enduring struggle, and of personal integrity under trial." Malawi, I continued, could claim few "greater, more genuine, and more committed heroes."[26]

The Dark Decades

Kamuzu Banda was neither Africa's only homegrown oppressor in the decades after Malawi's independence nor its most compulsive violator of the human rights of his own citizens. But he was the only despot who preached Victorian morals, dressed soberly and formally in black three-piece English wool suits, and wore a trademark gray homburg hat. He had been trained professionally and at length in the United States and the United Kingdom. He spoke no African language, had only vague memories of the village life he had forsaken at an early age, and had little appreciation of the African livelihoods and cultures over which he ruled. Despite his oft-articulated scruples and heavy-handed imposition of an alien moral code on Malawi, he consorted openly with a younger woman who was not his wife, and welcomed aid from and diplomatic relations with all of those pariah places—South Africa, Portugal, Rhodesia—shunned by fellow African presidents. Banda was an anomaly, a polished megalomaniac despite his Western background and sophisticated veneer.

Banda, as those of us who wished Malawi well were soon to learn, believed more in oppression than in uplift. Immediately after independence and the ensuing cabinet crisis, plus Chipembere's rebellion, he swiftly pulled the curtain down on democracy. He tolerated no independent thinking or ideas, demanded obeisance from his ministers, parliamentarians, and civil servants, and paid little attention to the economic and social betterment of his citizenry. As a potent symbol, his motorcades were among the longest and the most antagonistic of any other African heads of state; anyone whose vehicle still dared to linger near the motorcades was arrested and often beaten. Those who lined the roads to watch had to bow their heads. Banda fancied himself some kind of monarch.

In 1965, he told the party faithful that "a Government chosen by the people themselves—whether it is a dictatorship or not, as long as it is the people who choose the dictator, it is not a dictatorship. That's all. That is what democracy is." As long as a state was not a police state, it was a democracy.[27]

Subsequently, the MCP gave Banda the power to make and revoke all public service appointments, appoint the chief justice, make or terminate other judicial appointments, and command the armed forces. He could acquire emergency powers to enable him to rule by proclamation. "I do not want all the powers of the Czar of Russia, Peter the Great, or Ivan the Terrible," he said. "No, I do not want those powers. No, no. I just want enough powers to guide this country in the right way and in the right direction."[28] In fact, Banda was hell-bent on governing Malawi on his own, with as little interference as possible from the electorate, from his politically neutered new cabinet ministers, from his subservient officials, or from major foreign ambassadors. He declared himself President-for-Life in 1970. Despite his own words, he thought of himself as a czar, ruling over serfs.

Banda believed in himself. He required every business building to have his official picture hanging on the wall; no poster, clock, or picture could be higher than his portrait. Before any film played in a city cinema, a video of Banda waving to the people was shown while the national anthem played. When Banda visited a city, he demanded that a contingent of women greet him at its airport or landing strip and perform an African dance. A special wrap-around cloth, bearing the president's picture, was the required attire for these performances. Houses of worship needed government approval to operate, and the Jehovah's Witnesses and similar evangelical bodies were banned entirely.

Banda was fanatical about codes of dress, appearances, and anything avant-garde. He banned women from wearing trousers, appearing in see-through clothing or miniskirts, showing cleavage, or appearing "immodest." Skirts and dresses had to cover the knees to conform to Government regulations. Banda explained that such restrictions were designed to instill respect and dignity for women, not to oppress them. He also prohibited kissing in public.

Men had to wear trousers, never shorts (in Africa!!). Men's hair had to be no longer than collar length, and foreign visitors at the international airport were given mandatory haircuts, if necessary. Any man who ventured into public with long hair could also be seized by police and subjected to an involuntary trim. These rules were even imposed on U.S. Peace Corps teachers and health workers, who found them absurd and burdensome. Banda demanded that that the Peace Corps teach English grammar very strictly, without affectations or conversational simplifications.[29] (At Harvard, I trained the second Peace Corps contingent to go to Malawi.) "Hippies" were denied entry to Malawi at all border crossings and airports.

Censorship was a Malawian specialty. Communist literature, erotic magazines, and Lonely Planet's *Africa on a Shoestring* guides were all banned. Offensive pages in *Time* or *Newsweek* were snipped out before distribution. Books for sale throughout the nation were carefully screened for objectionable content. Bizarrely, many books discussing Malawi's history before Banda's arrival were burned. He was inexplicably hard on books and literature about the Tumbuka, a northern Malawi people. He also banned the speaking and writing of that language. (The Chisizas were Tumbukas.)

The Malawi Censorship Board reviewed all movies, barring anything that showed nudity, kissing, or scenes that were "socially or politically unacceptable." Even personal videotapes had to be submitted to and screened by the Censorship Board. Once edited, a film was given a sticker stating that it was now suitable and sent back to the owner.[30]

Mass media in those days consisted of a single radio station, a single daily newspaper, and a single weekly newspaper—all tightly controlled outlets for governmental propaganda. Banda refused to permit television.

Enforcement of many of these diktats was left to the Tontons Macoutes of Malawi—the Young Pioneer vigilante paramilitary organization that Banda created in 1964. In the manner of so many anti-democratic African (and other) rulers, Banda smartly employed that enthusiastic Praetorian guard of enforcers to harass and terrorize his citizens and to protect his presidency from potential opposition. They operated as his bodyguards, as shock troops who demanded MCP cards from civilians and churchgoers; they bullied, imprisoned, and killed Jehovah's Witnesses; they hunted down Chipembere's supporters; and they enjoyed arbitrary actions against otherwise innocent passersby or long-haired youths.

MCP cards, signifying membership in the country's political party, had to be carried at all times and presented by adults for random police and Young Pioneer inspection. The cards were sold, often forcefully, even to young children and to persons like the Witnesses who saw the party cards as professing fealty to an earthly domain. At least 40,000 Jehovah Witnesses were brutalized by the Young Pioneers because they refused to carry cards. Thousands languished in prison for years. Many others were tortured and killed.[31]

Banda was an Elder of the Church of Scotland, and—theoretically—a God-fearing Presbyterian. His Malawian critics, especially those close to the two Scottish-derived Protestant denominations that had played such a formative role in Malawi's colonial history, were bitterly critical of their failures to oppose Banda's despotism: "During more than thirty years of [Banda's] atrocious reign of terror, never once did the Scottish-orientated Church in Malawi raise a voice of protest."[32]

Although the 1963 Nyasaland Constitution, which Banda backed, included a long chapter on the "Protection of the Fundamental Rights and Freedoms of the Individual," those provisions were downplayed in the post-independence 1964 constitution and utterly removed in the 1966 constitution of the nascent Republic of Malawi. Doing so made it easier over the next quarter century for President Banda's national police force to imprison thousands for peacefully exercising their basic human rights of expression, assembly, and religion.[33]

Banda authorized his security forces—the police, the army, and the Pioneers—to act against opponents, even those (like many of his former cabinet ministers) who had fled to neighboring countries. The excesses were many, including clandestine abductions and assassinations—precursors of Rwandan President Paul Kagame's murderous pursuit of his opponents.[34]

Orton Chirwa, a distinguished lawyer and one of the founders of the MCP, was kidnapped in Zambia and trundled with his wife back to Malawi to face a trumped-up trial for treason in 1981. Sentenced to life in prison, he died there in 1992.

In 1983, three cabinet ministers—Dick Matenje, Twaibu Sangala, and Aaron Gadamna—and Member of Parliament David Chiwanga—died in what was labeled officially as a "traffic accident."

Banda had invited an "internal debate on pending multiparty democracy" in Malawi. During a cabinet meeting, the three ministers had voiced support for the multiparty idea, effectively challenging Banda's claim to his life presidency. Angered, Banda promptly "dissolved cabinet" and announced that parliament would meet immediately. At the end of that sitting of parliament, everyone in the chamber was effectively stripped of his/her political status. The three men were then rounded up at the Zomba parliament buildings for questioning. Chiwanga happened on them being tortured in a back room and had to be silenced, too. The four were bundled into Matenje's Peugeot 604 and driven to Thambani in the Mwanza district, west of Blantyre, where the car accident was staged: sources reported that their car had "overturned" while the men had been attempting to escape into neighboring Mozambique.[35] Later, it was discovered that they had been cruelly killed by having tent pins hammered into their heads. Banda ordered a secret burial under cover of darkness and mandated that the caskets not be opened for a last viewing.

Amnesty International reported on numerous occasions during Banda's reign that opponents had been tortured after mass arrests. Amnesty charged him with 6,000 murders.[36]

For these crimes, especially for murdering Matenje and the other three in 1983, Banda and his relative and close aide, former Minister of Finance John

Tembo, were tried in 1995 (after Banda's ouster) in Malawi's High Court. A special Commission of Inquiry had investigated the alleged murders and issued what amounted to an indictment in January of the same year. A jury acquitted Banda, Tembo, and others for want of evidence and the Malawi Supreme Court of Appeal confirmed the acquittal in 1997.[37]

Banda's foreign policy ideas were antithetical to the Young Turks, to neighboring state presidents, to the OAU, and to progressives everywhere. Nevertheless, Banda saw merit in cavorting with his counterparts in South Africa, welcoming Prime Minister B. Johannes Vorster to Lilongwe in 1970 and paying his own official visit to Pretoria and Johannesburg in 1971. Banda further banned liberation movements from his soil. He was equally friendly, even cozy, with Ian Smith's breakaway Rhodesian regime, and with the Portuguese colonial overlords in neighboring Mozambique.

Following independence in Malawi, Banda strengthened his relationship with the Portuguese colonial government by appointing an honorary consul in Maputo, Mozambique, in 1964. He also worked actively against Frelimo, the Liberation Front of Mozambique. Despite the OAU's designation of Malawi as a Front Line State, Banda refused to help Frelimo battle Portuguese-controlled Mozambique. He even directed Malawi's army and the Young Pioneers to assist the Portuguese in their (losing) battles against the forces of Frelimo. After independence in 1975 in Mozambique, Banda and his security forces continued to oppose Frelimo, bolstering the rearguard efforts of the Mozambique National Resistance Movement (Renamo), a Mozambican counter-Frelimo military front sponsored by South Africa and Rhodesia. Malawi even channeled South African aid to Renamo.[38]

The End of Despotism

With the collapse of Soviet communism, Britain, the United States, and other donors embraced the idea of multiparty democracy in Africa. This external pressure on countries such as Malawi and Zambia coincided with a welling-up of popular sentiment in those countries and elsewhere in Africa partial to democrats over autocrats. Malawi and Zambia alike were caught up in the third wave of democratic transition that spread across the continent following such critical markers as the end of apartheid after Nelson Mandela's release from prison and the independence of Namibia in 1990. (See chapter 10.) Banda and the MCP's total control of political participation and economic development in Malawi had come to a new reckoning.

Western political leaders no longer had as much use as before for developing-world anti-communist dictatorships, all of which came under mounting pressure to democratize. As a condition of further aid, European and American donors told Banda that he had to implement reforms aimed at making his government transparent and accountable to the people and the international community. The British government stopped financial support. In early 1992, the Roman Catholic bishops in Malawi issued a Lenten pastoral letter that criticized Banda and his government. Students of the University of Malawi and the Malawi Polytechnic joined protests and demonstrations to support the bishops, forcing authorities to shut both campuses. A month later, a leading trade union leader echoed the bishops and demanded a referendum on Malawi's future—on whether to move from single-party to multiparty rule. He was arrested, but his courageous advocacy, the raised voices of the Catholic and Presbyterian hierarchies, and the urgings of the international donor community finally, in late 1992, persuaded Banda to accede to the clamor for a public vote on his total control of Malawi.[39] Banda was then about ninety-four years old and was to die in 1997, aged ninety-nine.

In mid-1993, to Banda's shock and genuine surprise, the citizens of Malawi voted 64 percent in favor of scrapping Banda's one-party dictatorial regime.[40] The die was cast. Uncharacteristically, but perhaps as a consequence of his age, Banda also agreed to give up his presidency for life and most of his autocratic powers. The Malawi army disarmed the Young Pioneers and disabled its spying and informer networks. Overall, the shift back to the democratic structures that Chipembere, Chiume, and both Chisizas had preferred was peaceful, but those men were no longer available to welcome Malawi's second political dawn.

Banda tried to claim that his long reign had been positive for Malawi, and that his heavy-handed leadership had protected Malawi from the evils of modernity that were engulfing its neighbors, from internal strife and external war, and from want. But, in addition to being terrorized by the Young Pioneers and poorly cared for in terms of educational opportunity and medical care, Malawians at the end of twenty-seven years of Bandadom were (despite his fervid boasts to the contrary) hungry, and as poor as they had been in 1964. The record of his long years in office is lamentable.

During the 1970s, Malawi achieved modest successes as a developing nation. Yet it remained astonishingly deprived with a per capita income through the 1980s and into the 1990s of under $200 a year. At the end of the Banda era in 1993, the country's 10 million people were the eighth poorest in the world. Only 500,000 of its people were in wage employment, a full 100,000 working for the state. Inflation was running at 40 percent per year, its kwacha currency had greatly depreciated, and critical imports such as fuel, wheat flour, and hospital sutures were correspondingly scarce. Just as Presidents Idi Amin in Uganda and Julius Nyerere in Tanzania had been suspicious and ignorant of the useful role of (largely) Asian petty traders and their commercial networks across the rural areas of both vast countries, Banda had also displaced Asian merchants in Malawi. Thus, the country lost its accustomed informal economic backbone; no longer were these small-scale merchandisers able to import, export, supply credit, and act significantly as Malawian up-country entrepreneurs of first resort.

For foreign exchange and staple foodstuffs, Malawians were heavily dependent on the export of flue-cured tobacco (for sale mostly to China) and on maize. Both crops are rain fed, and Malawi through the Banda years and beyond suffered from frequent droughts, periodic seasons of food insecurity, and occasional starvation. Little had been done to extend irrigation beyond a few white-owned tea plantations (tea was a long-standing cash crop, entirely in non-indigenous ownership, but a minor contributor to GDP); to improve conditions for the growing of maize, the national staple; to sponsor tourism; or to elevate the overall difficult economic horizons of nearly all Malawians. Scandalously, too, Banda's dictatorship had forbidden peasants to grow profitable cash crops like groundnuts (peanuts) and had restricted the cultivation for home use of cassava (manioc), a basic food subsistence staple.

Meanwhile, the dictator had constructed a large and sprawling personal industrial and agricultural empire, skimming outside donor developmental assistance and appropriating profitable internal opportunities for himself. He personally controlled and profited from the monopolistic endeavors of the Press Corporation, a conglomerate with holdings in all aspects of Malawian commerce throughout the nation. (He was its sole shareholder, "on behalf of the people of the nation.") Banda hindered the growth of competing indigenous firms, and used commercial and agricultural regulations to advantage his own holdings.

Critics speak of Banda's harmful strangulation of the Malawian economy over three decades. There was never any official reckoning, however, of how much Banda had taken for himself and his close associates, and how much had been stashed overseas. He ran a corrupt government, but how much he profited and what he did with his winnings has never been investigated in Malawi. On the other hand, Malawians were spared petty corruption of the kind that bedeviled neighboring countries. After all, Banda—not subordinates—was there to collect for himself as many of the riches of the country as possible.

The major internal symbols of Banda's self-aggrandizement were his thirteen opulent state residences or palaces, each erected and maintained at national expense. He rarely visited any of them and stayed only for few nights at the largest and most outrageous of all. This last grandiosity, sitting in the center of 1,500 green acres, was constructed just outside Lilongwe, the capital city for much of the Banda years. Three hundred gardeners and 500 house servants maintained the grounds and the Persian-style residence. It took a full twenty years to build, contained 150 rooms, and cost $120 million (1994 values). The non-residential side of this palace contained phalanx after phalanx of expensively appointed offices, waiting annexes, boardrooms, and smaller meeting salons. In its residential side, there were bedrooms for Banda and his consort, plus entertainment rooms, kitchens, and so on, each suite furnished differently. The main bathrooms had gold-handled taps. But the pride of this edifice was a massive, three-story, spiral staircase that connected the palace's two halves, and was endlessly reworked and rebuilt.

Who knows what this monument to megalomania was intended by Banda to signify and what its utilitarian purpose might have been. After I toured this Roman emperor's folly of a building, inside and out, following Banda's removal in 1994, its banquet hall for a few years served as the meeting place of Malawi's new parliament. Later, President Bingu wa Mutharika decided to move in and make the palace his glorified abode, forcing parliamentarians to scramble until China came to their rescue. (See chapter 5.)

In the educational realm, Banda claimed expertise and a compassion for the needs of his people. Yet, for all of the regime's attention to tertiary and secondary education, it neglected primary schooling. Banda restricted access to primary schools by charging high fees, and refused to expand instructional opportunities in the rural areas. He was especially reluctant to increase schooling choices for girls.

At the secondary schooling level, Banda created his only lasting achievement, an elite institution called Kamuzu Academy, styled after a British public school. He staffed it with white foreigners and ordered a severely classical curriculum based on his faulty imagination of what elite nineteenth-century British public schoolboys learned.

As self-appointed chancellor of the University of Malawi, he decreed what could be taught and who could teach there. His prejudices were Edwardian if not Victorian. Overall, he retarded the development of education throughout the country, especially at the university level. Furthermore, his informers and the Young Pioneers identified students opposed to Banda's regime, and silenced them.

In the medical field, despite his American and British training and his own professional life as a physician, Banda refused to expand clinics and hospitals, and starved those budgetary areas of needed capital. In 1994, only 122 physicians served all of Malawi, giving the country one of the lowest medical personnel ratios per capita in the world. By the time that Banda left office, HIV/AIDS was rampant, infant mortality and maternal mortality rates were among the highest in the world, and family planning was virtually non-existent.

Banda did almost nothing to modernize his country. Indeed, when I led a team of Harvard economists to Malawi in 1994, it was hard to escape the conclusion that Banda really had had little use for his "backward" countrymen. He was a despot who disdained and feared his own people.

The final pages of the Banda political era turned when Malawians went to the polls in 1994 to vote for a new parliament and a new head of state. Several parties, including the MCP, contested the 1994 national elections. Bakili Muluzi, a southern Malawian and a trucking entrepreneur who had once served in Banda's cabinet, led the United Democratic Front to a triumphant victory (47 percent) over Banda and the MCP (33 percent). Among Muluzi's winning team was Aleke Banda, who became minister of finance, and Justin Malawezi, who became vice president. They had both been prominent officials during the long reign of Kamuzu Banda, but at various times had been imprisoned, cashiered, or otherwise pushed aside. (Malawezi had been an all-American soccer star at Columbia University in 1967 and, in time, a language trainer for Harvard's Peace Corps Training Program for Malawi in the summer of 1965. We always kept in touch thereafter—well into the twenty-first century. In Banda's government he had served as permanent secretary in several ministries, ending up as the president's last secretary and as secretary to the cabinet.)

Malawi now had an opportunity to grow economically and socially, and its people to enjoy new freedoms of religion, speech, and press, not to mention the end of onerous dress and other social controls. Malawians had finally thrown off the Banda yoke, openly could criticize their rulers, could clamor for help with agricultural uplift, and could hold their heads high in the African Union and other international meetings. With Kamuzu Banda's removal, Malawi was reborn.

5
Promises, Promises

Modern Malawi Seeks Prosperity and Plenty through Pot

With Banda deposed and his Malawi Congress Party (MCP) the decided loser in the 1994 parliamentary elections, the nation that the outgoing president had organized as if it were a private (rotten) pocket borough prepared itself for substantial regeneration. Still a desperately poor elongated sliver of a country, Malawi required a big boost of creative thinking to pull the nation smartly out of the economic cocoon into which it had been enveloped by long years of purposeful neglect.

This was to be the anointed task of several successive governments, the first led by President Bakili Muluzi after his United Democratic Front (UDF) attained solid backing from the voters (47 percent to 33 percent for Banda, with a third party gaining 18 percent).[1]

The victorious party included a number of persons who had broken with Banda or had otherwise left the MCP at various times before the decisive referendum in 1993. Muluzi, a gregarious, prosperous, Muslim trucking entrepreneur and would-be sugar and rice monopolist from southern Malawi, had been minister of education and minister of transport under Banda, as well as secretary general of the MCP, leaving that party only in 1983. Incoming Vice President Justin Malawezi had been in charge of Banda's own office and the cabinet before 1990. Aleke K. Banda had been President Banda's faithful chief aide-de-camp from 1961 (see chapter 4) until 1981, when the elder Banda came to suspect (erroneously) that the younger Banda (they were not even distantly related) was plotting to succeed him. Banda rusticated Aleke Banda, putting him under house arrest for twelve years in a remote northern location. He became Muluzi's first minister of finance after the 1994 election. Innumerable other prominent members of the UDF assumed ministerial positions after having defected from the MCP or after having returned from enforced exile in neighboring countries.

Muluzi immediately released political prisoners, relaxed Kamuzu Banda's draconian dress and decorum codes, and restored essential freedoms of speech, press, assembly, and religion—those actions and innumerable other initiatives signifying that a new dawn (*kwacha*) had indeed arrived. But the neophyte Malawi government also had to contend with a plethora of social and economic needs that Banda and his close associates had refused to ameliorate, or had left

Overcoming the Oppressors. Robert I. Rotberg, Oxford University Press. © Oxford University Press 2023.
DOI: 10.1093/oso/9780197674208.003.0005

unaddressed. This callous preference for backwardness—for letting Malawians miss out on the kinds of educational, public health, and living standard advances that had been enjoyed by newly emancipated Africans elsewhere on the continent—had typified nearly all aspects of civic and rural affairs during the life presidency of Banda. Muluzi and his ministers thus had much to do, an agenda of change and modernization that was only compounded by the three-year drought that beset the country as the UDF took office.

Malawi, landlocked, 520 miles long, and a little larger than Virginia in total area, had nearly 11 million inhabitants in 1994 and was multiplying its population at a startling 3.2 percent a year. Its annual average GDP per capita was $121, compared to Zambia's $412, and its life expectancy was forty-six years, two years more than that for Zambia. Tobacco comprised nearly $200 million worth of exports, tea $30 million, cane sugar $18 million, and coffee $15 million. It imported $50 million worth of petroleum products, $38 million of maize, and much smaller values of electrical machinery, automobiles, etc. All exports and imports traveled tortuous miles by road or rail from distant coastal ports, or expensively by air. At one point amid this era, Malawi's freight and transport insurance rates were among the very highest in the world.

An agricultural subsistence economy, with household survival dependent on growing of, or access to, maize and lesser amounts of manioc (cassava), most Malawians relied for their livelihoods and the avoidance of famine on ample and timely rains as well as on governmentally supplied seeds and fertilizer. Irrigation was very limited, confined mostly to white-owned sugar, tea, and coffee estates in the country's south. Industrious though Malawians doubtless were (many had long worked in distant South Africa), the country counted hardly any factories or mines, and no globally focused service or manufacturing enterprises.

In the short run from 1994, the continued dependence on the increasingly despised crop of tobacco remained Malawi's last best hope of accumulating foreign exchange earnings and thus accruing the cash (together with puny local tax and import fees) with which to afford increasing services for its citizens. Malawi was well placed geographically and climatically for little else. But fewer and fewer people outside of China and Indonesia would continue to smoke, and the market for flue-cured tobacco (Malawi's specialty) would shrink faster than that for the Virginia tobacco of Zimbabwe and parts of the United States. Unfortunately, Malawi in 1994 could not just fall back on industry—although stitching garments might have proven competitive—on selling other crops, or on services—even imaginative ones like call centers—despite the reputation of its better-educated citizens as well-articulated communicators in English. It was going to be difficult to expand the export of its famed tea and coffee, and local sugar and cotton could not compete well on the world market. Furthermore, the country at that point had no known caches of exploitable minerals. Tourism later provided a minor source of foreign exchange earnings, but the potential of this sector had never been nurtured by Banda's regime.

Scottish Presbyterian missionaries, English Anglicans, and Roman Catholic White Fathers had long educated Malawians, and found them eager to learn. But Banda had achieved little for most of his countrymen in this area. Nor, despite his medical background, had he done much to improve the country's clinical facilities or public health accomplishments.

The economically and socially destructive policies of Banda's dictatorship (see chapter 4) had compounded many of those deficits. Farmers had long been prevented from growing profitable cash crops, and paltry state-controlled purchasing programs for such products of the soil as peanuts, legumes, other vegetables, and fruit, made sowing staples unattractive.

The Muluzi government further inherited a currency, the kwacha, that was rapidly depreciating. In U.S. dollars, it lost half of its value between mid-1994 and early 1995. That made critical imports such as motor fuel, wheat flour, immunizations, and medicines prohibitively costly. Inflation during the Muluzi government's first year ran at about 40 percent annually.

Set against these formidable problems, and the country's recent history of regimentation and repression, was the undoubted talent in Muluzi's new government. Its cabinet ministers, junior ministers like Catherine, Masauko Chipembere's widow, a gifted Reserve Bank governor like Matthews Chikaonda (who had an American doctorate and had taught economics in Canada), and a cadre of trained civil servants held a well-nuanced understanding of how poor economies might develop themselves in the age of globalization: by opening up their markets and by liberalizing economically, with some speed. Muluzi's government was slow to do the last, being reluctant despite a galaxy of outside advice to become thoroughly open. To do so, the new administrators knew, would limit state control and, especially, minimize handsome benefits potentially accruing to key figures in and near the government. Malawi much too reluctantly listened to the donors (and outside advisors) and only hesitantly began privatizing formerly state-owned enterprises.

Muluzi's administration accepted that educating young women was essential, both for family planning and economic growth needs. Malawi's population was doubling every twenty years; many women wanted to reduce the number of live births per mother down from 6.7 to a figure closer to the 2.1 replacement rate, but Banda had forbidden family planning. The Muluzi government's sensible answer was quickly to abolish fees for primary school and to urge families to send their girls to be instructed (an advance that Banda had always opposed).[2] But removing obstacles to learning, training more teachers, and constructing new schools could not speedily enough overcome the skills' shortages that the Muluzi regime inherited from the lost years of Banda. Moreover, doing so at a time when the system had too few teachers, too few suitable premises, and almost no textbooks, compounded the immense problem of doubling school enrollments overnight.

Every kind of professional was in short supply, acutely so in the medical arena: in 1994, only 122 licensed physicians served 11 million Malawians (or one physician for every 82,000 persons), one of the lowest physician per capita ratios in the world. In that arena, as in so many others, Malawi lacked human resource capacity and required foreign assistance. During Banda's time, and later, about 50 percent of each annual budget came from donors. Moreover, in 1995, "Domestic revenues amounted to 16 percent of GDP. Government revenues amounted to just $19 per capita—for funding all manner of political goods, i.e. $19 per head paid for schools, health centers, courts, roads, and public administration."[3]

With such a shortage of physicians it was hardly unexpected that Malawi, by 1994, should—along with the rest of southern Africa—have begun to endure one of the globe's highest HIV-positive prevalence rates. Infant mortality (106 per 1,000 live births in 1998) and maternal mortality numbers (752 deaths per 100,000 live births) were also unusually high, even for Africa.[4]

Muluzi and his ministers inherited a formidable array of problems, a backlog of political and other voices waiting to be heard, an impulse toward gaining economic reward that was ready to be unleashed, and a long unmet demand for modernization on the part of its constituents. Fortunately, foreign donors wanted to help, and the new government exuded energy, optimism, and inventiveness.

Multipartyism flourished, as well, along with democracy. The UDF won the second post-Banda election in 1999 with 52 percent of the vote to 45 percent for the MCP, led by Gwanda Chakuamba, and with less than 1 percent going to future president Bingu wa Mutharika. The MCP remained largely a Central Province party, with strong support from the CiCewa-speakers whom Banda had favored and cultivated. The UDF was popular in the Southern Province and, after having merged with the Alliance for Democracy in 1997, also in the Northern Province. The government kept control of radio and television throughout, but allowed the press, with a proliferation of newspapers, to run free. It also respected the desire of judges to regain the independence that they had lost during the Banda years. Imperative for Malawi and the victorious UDF was rapid economic development and capacity building. Banda had left Malawi underdeveloped and impoverished. With his removal, the time had come to propel Malawi forward.

Harvard to the Rescue

Naturally, I was pleased to be back in Malawi and to be in a position to offer assistance to the new government, especially to Aleke Banda's influential ministries of finance and economic planning and development. He explicitly asked for the kinds of advice that the experienced personnel of the Harvard Institute of International Development (HIID) were able and willing to provide. They had worked extensively in Pakistan, Indonesia, South Korea, Malaysia, Kenya, Nigeria, Zambia, and other developing countries and had long helped finance and planning ministries and central banks to organize themselves and to benefit from a keen awareness of global fiscal and investment realities.

After a reconnaissance on my first trip back to the country in 1993 and another in 1994, and following extensive consultations with HIID in Cambridge, Massachusetts, we agreed quickly to produce an official report recommending a comprehensive strategy that the Malawian government could pursue in order to raise the economic trajectory of the country and to improve the standards of living of its inhabitants as rapidly as possible. We soon assembled a relatively large team to produce a systematic examination of Malawi's prospects and challenges.

In order to satisfy President Muluzi and Aleke Banda's desire to begin the next calendar year with an action plan raising incomes and meeting the pent-up demands of their constituents, my colleagues and I assessed Malawi's needs and wrote "Trickle-Up Growth: A Development Strategy for Poverty Reduction in Malawi" before the very end of 1994. When I presented our comprehensive findings to Muluzi and his assembled cabinet ministers, and answered their many searching questions, it was clear that HIID and Malawi were to partner effectively to uplift the country economically and, we earnestly hoped, socially. We and I intended that our efforts could make a difference in elevating household incomes, ameliorating agricultural practices, spreading literacy, bettering public health outcomes, and much more.[5]

"With 60 percent of the [nation's] population below the poverty line," we proclaimed, "economic growth [could] only be achieved and sustained if growth emanate[d] from the poor, that is, if the majority of the poor increase their own productivity and income." Only if the poor "participate in a growing economy" could Malawi reduce poverty. Moreover, sustained growth and substantial poverty reduction were dependent upon growth in the traditional sector of the overall economy. "Modern sector growth" would not necessarily do enough to transfer wealth to the poor (and reduce inequality).

"Trickle-Up" hence proposed to improve the productivity of agricultural smallholders and rural workers through research and investment in maize and tobacco growing, the two crops together accounting for about 25 percent of Malawi's annual GDP. Moreover, maize was the basic caloric source for nearly all Malawians and tobacco earned 75 percent of the nation's foreign exchange receipts.

If we could assist Malawi in strengthening the production of both crops we could raise incomes of smallholders and farm laborers directly, and also—indirectly—the incomes of other rural workers who supplied goods and services to farmers. "No other approach to development," the report asserted in bold type, and no other investments in Malawi, "can come close to raising incomes for so many people. . . ."[6]

Our report further advocated protecting the country's natural resource base and thus soil fertility, curtailing overfishing, arresting the clear-cutting of woodlands, and improving the quality of the nation's precious and easily wasted water supplies.

We made it absolutely clear that uplifting the productivity of smallholders depended in large part on better public health and family-planning outcomes, and on educating girls (as well as boys). Doing so would require major governmental investments.

Diversification of the country's economic base made obvious good sense. Growing horticultural and legume crops would help. So would very small-scale irrigation schemes (to counter shortages of rain), the promotion of tourism, and initiating labor-intensive manufacturing—activities in which the private sector should, we said, be encouraged to invest.

"Government's only tasks," we declared rather sententiously, were "to deregulate markets," welcome foreign and domestic investors, "promote competition while reducing economic concentration, invest in the country's [very weak] transportation and communications infrastructure, and, otherwise, stay out of the way." We advocated reducing budgetary deficits, avoiding inflation, and stabilizing Malawi's new kwacha against foreign currencies. "In order to break the vicious circle of inflation and currency depreciation," we said, budget deficits had to be eliminated and a new cash budget introduced. That meant, we knew, drastic reductions in expenditure combined with major revenue increases.[7]

In sixty-four closely set pages, the report detailed what the Government of Malawi should do to enhance food security and agricultural productivity, to stabilize its macroeconomy and the national treasury, to exercise prudent fiscal management, to school its young people, to slow population growth, and to provide better health services.

We offered seventy-eight specific recommendations, ranging from aggressively expanding a new crop-buying program to reduce marketing monopolies, imposing new policies on the proper use of fertilizers, eliminating the quotas that the Banda administration had invoked on the growth of particular commodities, urging new lending to farmers from government-affiliated parastatal enterprises, enabling the formation of fishery associations, streamlining tariffs to reduce import controls, raising interest rates to reduce inflation, and boosting civil service salaries.[8]

We recommended that Malawi focus on trickle-up growth practices, on lifting the incomes of tobacco and maize smallholders, and on letting multiplier effects flow from those initiatives across the populous and needy rural areas. We further urged the new government to let entrepreneurs, local and foreign, make most agricultural and industrial investments—not to rely exclusively as heretofore on governmental initiatives. We wanted to wean Malawi abruptly away from state-supplied and state-dominated entities. The proper role of government, we said, was to reduce the size of the civil service in order to shrink budget deficits and to help stabilize the difficult fiscal situation that Muluzi and his team had inherited from Banda.

Growth with equity was one of our motifs. We further indicated how best to reduce poverty and make the massive educational improvements that were—everyone agreed—necessary. With what we had proposed, reasonable falls of rain at the right times, project assistance from the US Agency for International Development (USAID) and other donors, responsible "liberal democratic" governance, and a new national political will, Malawi would grow robustly and well. But it would "have to do it itself." Then the country's renaissance could surely become "a model for the new Africa."[9]

Two follow-up analyses by HIID authorities emphasized that reducing poverty depended on increasing the demand for unskilled labor in Malawi. In contrast to a heavily interventionist top-down initiative that sections of the Malawian government were advancing in opposition to the "Trickle-Up" plan, ours was bottom-up and growth making. "Direct interventions by government . . . may harm the poor [and] can . . . invite corruption," one analyst wrote. Another emphasized that the only way to reduce poverty was through "accelerated economic growth . . . involving . . . smallholder farmers." The author urged the government to cease protecting Malawian commercial firms and to force them to compete "in a wider market." Doing so meant keeping the kwacha exchange rate competitive.[10] These approaches, and many other helpful ideas offered by HIID, were welcomed by President Muluzi, Aleke Banda, and the entire Malawi cabinet, but careful implementation, in practice, was rarely a priority.

Nonetheless, with funding from USAID, HIID placed superbly qualified advisors in three ministries. They worked mightily to assist Aleke Banda and Malawezi, his successor when Banda became minister of agriculture in 1997, to strengthen accountability and transparency, to modernize operational processes within the finance ministry, to try to coordinate bureaucratic responses across ministries and the central bank, and, in 1998, to overcome a debilitating exchange-rate crisis involving a rapidly sinking Malawian kwacha, steep inflation rises, and a significant decline in real wages.

Achieving these objectives proved a struggle because not all relevant Malawians accepted policy advice that impinged upon their own self-interests. And Muluzi embraced the reforms advocated by foreign advisors only verbally, rarely in practice. In the agricultural domain, however, where food insecurity was often dire and robust maize harvests separated political, social, and economic success from abject failure, the notion that Malawi should routinely subsidize smallholder maize production gained credibility. For example, at a time of acute maize scarcity in 1998, HIID's advisor recommended routinely distributing hybrid seed and fertilizer packs to Malawi's farmers. In time, giving rather than selling bundles of seed and fertilizer to dependent smallholders proved a catalytic idea. "Nothing help[ed] . . . [more to] quell inflation and dispel the current state of . . . insecurity." A "Best Bet" starter pack containing a few kilos of seed and fertilizer enabled smallholders, many tilling a hectare or less, to farm with reduced risk.[11] It also could show smallholders the advantages of using modern seeds and ample fertilizer. Moreover, if the "Best Bet" scheme worked, farmers would clamor in future for high-quality seeds and a rich market would be established. (Organic practices were never considered at this early stage.)

These were among the ongoing and ultimately successful reforms initiated by our persons on the ground. (I was "backstopping," i.e., supporting our persons in the field. Later, after writing a new proposal, I did the same with and for our Harvard mission to Mozambique.)

As gifted and wise as were the economists that Harvard recruited to assist Malawi, they were in Malawi to advise, to explain why particular policy innovations would perform better than alternative options, to help the government to develop tools for economic management, and to indicate how citizens would benefit more by following one practice instead of another. Ministers and their officials listened to the advisors, but did not always take heed. Often, political demands trumped technical cautions to the contrary. Or personal proclivities and the influence of other stakeholders led ministers to ignore the well-intended advocacy of the technocrats, both the foreign advisors and their Malawian counterparts.

Most of all, the advisors rarely appreciated fully, and anyway could not on their own have barred, the kinds of nefarious deal makings that occurred outside of the bureaucratic compounds. Corruption distorted governmental priorities, as it always does, and seriously undermined the developmental reform efforts to which the Muluzi government had ostensibly committed itself to its constituents, to Harvard's team, to USAID, and to me.

Temptations Too Many, Results Too Few

Muluzi's ten years in office were characterized by endemic corruption, with the president and many of his cabinet ministers using their offices as springboards to great wealth. Muluzi's family controlled 60 percent of all national sugar sales and ran most of the nation's buses. Others had their own scams. In one case the minister of education took kickbacks from a British printer in connection with the supply of school exercise books worth more than $2 million. (The exercise books arrived months late, well after schools had opened.) Another cabinet minister paid a motor vehicle firm large sums for repairs to government vehicles that were never completed, or perhaps to vehicles that were never even conveyed to the shop. The National Audit Office in 2003 discovered thousands of improper government accounts invented to hide peculation. A major corruption scandal cost three cabinet ministers their positions; Muluzi was also compromised. As a Malawian proverb intoned: "Raise a python and he will swallow you."[12]

There was the lurid exceptional case of Precious Kalonga Stambuli, Muluzi's sometime economic advisor and, previously, permanent secretary of the ministry of economic planning and development (where he hindered the work of the HIID advisory team). Allegedly, he stole K354,000 ($24,000) from the president's International Appeal Fund for Clean Water in 1997. But an arrest on this charge followed his decision to leave government service and criticize Muluzi's failure seriously to address Malawi's critical economic problems.[13] In 2003, after Stambuli had returned from exile to official favor as the head of a bank owned by Muluzi, someone strangled him in his bed, allegedly on Muluzi's orders, which Muluzi denied.

That should have been the end of at least one supposed case of corruption in Malawi. But, many years later, notes that Stambuli had made before he died surfaced in the Malawian opposition press. They claimed, at length, that Muluzi had always been a thief, citing chapter and verse beginning with the taking of petty amounts of money over long periods well before he became an important person in Kamuzu Banda's MCP. His fingers kept going into various tills, according to the notes, pocketing moneys from the sale of MCP cards, and even stealing cured tobacco from farms. Finally, in 1982, Banda's intelligence officers caught him taking motor vehicles belonging to Banda and the party. At about the same time, Muluzi illicitly, it was claimed, gave himself permits to buy, sell, and transport sugar; he charged Asian traders inordinate sums under the table to move "his" sugar and thus to fleece Malawian consumers.[14]

After he became president in 1994, Muluzi supposedly continued to pilfer. He took $2 million intended to build army barracks. In that same year, Muluzi dispatched Stambuli to Britain to pick up an envelope filled with cash from a company involved in a major scam in Malawi, and to Mauritius on a similar errand. In 1995, substantial moneys from multiple citizen deposits in the Malawi Postal Savings Bank found their way to Muluzi, draining scores of individual accounts.[15] None of these accusations was ever tried in court. Nor was Stambuli's murderer ever found and put on trial.

Petty corruption flourished as well. Given a particularly "inefficient and ineffective public service delivery [system] and rigidity in the bureaucracy, [a] ... lack of automation in most government departments in Malawi, and the fact that almost every transaction ha[d] to be supported by official stamps, signatures and copious documentation, busy clients were ready to bribe officials to obtain faster action. Moreover, public officials were known to develop 'rules and norms different from those that were expected by the public'" and intentionally to slow down the process so as to encourage speed payments. "This," wrote a Malawian expert, had "given rise to opportunities for public officials to apply rules and regulations selectively and discriminatorily, thus perpetuating corruption."[16]

Muluzi and I talked often in the 1990s. He was always genial, welcoming, and deceptively open to hearing about the diverse impediments to rapid economic development that I brought to his attention. On several occasions, I felt bold enough to ask him when he was going publicly to speak out against "creeping corruption." With a big smile, he always assured me that he well recognized the problem and promised "next week" to give that speech and also to ferret out those in his administration who were feeding at the public trough. But he never did, and it was only later that I understood how thoroughly enmeshed in capturing and looting the state were he and his close associates. (We had further discussions about the problems of rural food scarcity, and the struggle against Malawian corruption, in 2002, when Muluzi, at a lavish event in State House, reverently launched the posthumous autobiography of Masauko Chipembere that I had prepared for publication. The political elite turned out to remember the man who first decried Kamuzu Banda's authoritarianism instincts, rebelled, and lived his few remaining years in exile.[17] Chipembere would have railed against state laxity, and Muluzi, had he survived.)

But, perhaps as a diversionary tactic, in 1995 Muluzi did follow Kaunda in Zambia and countries such as Kenya, Tanzania, Mauritius, and Botswana in establishing an Anti-Corruption Bureau (ACB) on the Hong Kong model. Two years later, he asked Paul Russell, by then discouraged by President Chiluba's evisceration of the comparable commission in Zambia, to be the chief advisor to Malawi's own anti-corruption entity. (See chapter 3.) The ACB (drawing on Zambian legislation) focused, as did other anti-corruption endeavors in sub-Saharan Africa, on bribery, fraud, misappropriation of funds, and the abuse of authority and public office.[18] But its jurisdiction never extended, as had Hong Kong's entity, to the private sector. Nonetheless, the ACB, especially in its later years, was mandated to prevent corruption and to educate against it in the manner of Hong Kong's commission, but with distinctively fewer resources.

Under Muluzi (even with Russell's intervention), the ACB was severely hampered in its activities: it could initiate no prosecutions without permission from the Director of Public Prosecutions (DPP), a Muluzi crony. Despite the ACB's investigation of a number of serious cases, no prosecutions of cabinet ministers were approved by the DPP during Muluzi's entire reign. The ACB developed incriminating dossiers about the questionable actions of an attorney general and a minister of local government. But the DPP would not take those cases and others to court. Even so, the ACB tried to do what it could to uncover and develop prosecutable cases.

The ACB revealed a number of brazen fraudulent schemes. In early 1998, to discuss but one example from the Bureau's early years, a complaint arrived alleging that the general manager of the state Petroleum Control Commission (PCC) had purchased an expensive motor car worth more than K1 million ($67,000), far in excess of his stated income. The general manager and the minister of energy and mining, it became apparent, had corruptly awarded a contract to supply imported petrol at inflated prices to the PCC. The contractor was a Tanzanian who had been barred from operating in Malawi, but apparently knew how to pay well. As per the new regulations, all of Malawi's petrol had to be trucked in, overland, from Tanzania to the contractor's depot and allocated to local filling stations by the state-owned body. As a result of such an inflated contract, local prices to consumers rose appreciably.

The fuel supplier had meanwhile opened bank accounts for the general manager and the minister in Guernsey and elsewhere in Europe. More than $1.7 million was paid to the general manager, who was prosecuted by the ACB in 2001. The minister, a close associate of Muluzi, was implicated but never prosecuted.[19]

In another common case, the minister of finance in 1999 prevailed upon his staff and the chair of an official tender evaluation body to throw its support illegally to an untried new firm and away from the incumbent Swiss holder of a contract to inspect imports to Malawi. The ACB declared in 2000 that the minister of finance had "acted in a manner conducive or connected to corrupt practices" and that his principal official had done the same. "The tender process . . . was tainted with bad practice and strong suspicion of corruption." The ACB recommended that the false award be rescinded and that the president of Malawi be asked to take "appropriate action" against the minister and his key official. But nothing was ever done, and the minister of finance (Cassim Chilumpha) later became vice president during President Bingu wa Mutharika's reign and minister of energy under President Joyce Banda.[20]

There were many procedural ways in which the actions and successes of Africa's anti-corruption commissions were compromised and well-meaning enforcement endeavors frustrated. Malawi's ACB during the Muluzi era, and under President Bingu wa Mutharika after 2004, failed to indict more than a handful of miscreants despite the rampant purchasing of politicians and other instances of suspected corruption. The ACB was allowed to open cases only after the registering of a complaint. In 2002, it was dealing with about 1,700 complaints but had only investigated and concluded 118 cases. In 2009, Malawi's ACB received more than 500 complaints, investigated about 100, and recommended for prosecution about 20.[21] It was during this period that Global Integrity, an American-based

NGO, investigated Malawi and accused the ACB of not targeting "the big fish." It also indicated that nearly all investigations were stalled because key personnel were regularly absent.

Hunger and Graft

Peculation, graft, and all kinds of financial sleight of hand cost lives in Malawi, as well as in neighboring Zambia and Zimbabwe. Across those three countries the rains had failed in 2001, leading to a poor maize yield, followed by weak rains in the 2001–2002 planting season and another insubstantial harvest. "Hunger is again stalking southern Africa," I wrote "In the markets of [Zomba, a] . . . former capital town, in the nearby markets of Blantyre, Malawi's largest commercial center, and throughout the length of this already impoverished country, there is no maize (corn), the staple food. Cassava (manioc), a substitute stomach filler, is also hard to find. So are yams. Moreover, no one seems to be doing anything to avert the coming starvation. Official denials of the seriousness of the situation are standard."

"On the rainy slopes of towering Mount Zomba," my commentary continued, "I purchased small white potatoes and could have bought dead and live animals that were dangled from outstretched arms, a scattering of vegetables, and a variety of herbs and charms. But nothing was on sale to fill the belly in the local African manner."[22]

Neighboring Zambia was also bereft of maize and cassava. So was Zimbabwe, traditionally a much wealthier land that usually exported maize to its neighbors. In Zimbabwe, too, cooking oil and sugar (both of which Zimbabwe usually provided in abundance) were hard to find. Bread had been unavailable for months. In these three countries, as many as 30 million people were at risk of going hungry throughout 2002, and millions of children were certain to become even more malnourished than they already were.

Malawi, the poorest of the three, suffered the most. In the midst of this developing national food crisis, Malawi relied on its previously created National Food Reserve Agency and a Strategic Grain Reserve (SGR), the latter managed by officials of the state's Agricultural Development and Marketing Corporation (ADMARC), which stored maize purchased for and donated into the SGR. But it soon transpired that the Strategic Grain Reserve was empty when Malawi needed it most. About 160,000 metric tons of maize had been sold as early as August 2000, when food shortages were becoming evident and 3 million Malawians required food assistance; 60,000 metric tons were even exported to Kenya.

Without authority, ADMARC had sold most of its accumulated supplies of maize, instead of holding them in reserve, thus harming the public; when great shortages of maize in 2001 occasioned hunger and hundreds of deaths throughout the nation, ADMARC and others had to purchase new supplies of maize from South Africa. The government consequently lost many millions of kwacha as a result of these maladroit maneuvers while a slew of well-connected traders and politicians, previously given preferential access to stored supplies of the staple grain, profited considerably by selling inexpensive pre-crisis maize expensively to the public once shortages became apparent. One of those scam buyers of SGR maize was Joyce Banda, later the nation's president; she sold 841 tons of SGR maize, to great personal gain. (Banda, an ADMARC board member, was subsequently also accused of benefiting from a contract awarded to her by ADMARC to construct a transit depot.)

Nationwide, the swindle was enormous. The ACB discovered that maize husbanded to alleviate famine had in fact been sold illegally to favored clients; the manager of the marketing board and presumed prime culprit had apparently used his $15 million profits to purchase a five-star hotel (and much else), but he (Friday Jumbe), arrested in 2004 at Blantyre's Chileka airport, promised to reimburse the state, and later became minister of finance.[23]

Major crises of governance in Malawi accompanied these swindles and the onset of hunger. Judges were impeached, a tough and honest finance minister sacked, university students shot, and democracy made more precarious by the inept and self-serving policies of the Muluzi government. (Stambuli was also strangled at about the same time.) In a country where donors provided as much as 15 percent of the annual GDP, Denmark withdrew its mission in disgust, Britain withheld balance-of-payments support, and the United States reduced its overall funding.

Going for the Third Term

Amid these crises of legitimacy, the encroaching famine, and Malawi's inability to cope, in 2002, Muluzi decided that Malawi could not possibly do without him as its leader. The constitution that he and his followers had adopted in 1994 specifically prohibited a third consecutive presidential term. Nevertheless, like so many "indispensable" and ambitious African political figures before and since, Muluzi (succumbing like others to the virulent disease of third-term-itis) thought that he could persuade parliament to amend the constitution accordingly, and the courts to ratify.

Muluzi's campaign for a constitution-breaking third presidential term included operation "Moving with a Bag of Money"—the bribing of forty opposition members of parliament. But most other legislators and judges were unwillingly to be bought. When demonstrators against prolonging Muluzi's time in office took to the streets en masse, Muluzi backed down and constitutionalism prevailed. That was when he also cast about, like Chiluba in Zambia, for a potentially compliant replacement, and chose as a successor Bingu wa Mutharika, Muluzi's largely unheralded minister of economic planning and development.

During the ten-year Muluzi administration, clientelism had prevailed. The bureaucracy was characterized by "patronage through appointment, offers of lucrative contracts, and enticement of party loyalists and opposition MPs with cash."[24]

At the end of the Muluzi presidential era, Transparency International reviewed Malawi's anti-corruption efforts: It declared that the ACB was "ineffective in both prevention and prosecution of corruption in the country." It also commented that there was no strong political will to fight corruption. The country's political leadership merely wanted to "save face."[25] Public opinion polls revealed that 65 percent of Malawians believed that politicians and officials were not to be trusted. They were uniformly corrupt.[26] The Corruption Perceptions Index in 2003 gave Malawi only 28 points out of 100, ranking it 83rd out of 133 countries, below Romania and just ahead of India.[27]

The Mutharika Maneuvers

When Bingu wa Mutharika, another southern Malawian and originally named Brightson Webster Ryson Thom, became president of Malawi in 2004, he had served as a cabinet minister, as governor of the nation's reserve bank, as a loans officer at the World Bank, and as a director of the Economic Commission for Africa, as well as head of the Common Market for Eastern and Southern Africa—an aspirational structure (from which body he had been sacked for "abuse of office"). He claimed a PhD in development economics that, in fact, had been purchased from an unaccredited for-profit online diploma mill—Pacific Western University—in Encino, California. He would not have been elected without Muluzi's strong support and the backing of Muluzi's UDF party. (Muluzi later apologized to Malawians for "imposing" Mutharika on them.)[28]

During his swearing-in ceremony as president, Mutharika declared that under his administration there would be "zero tolerance of corruption." He promised "swift investigation, prosecution, and punishment" of all public officials who stole and abused their positions.[29] But that was just fancy talk.

Even so, during his first presidential term, Mutharika married sensible agricultural pricing policies and the effective distribution of "Best Bet" seeds and fertilizer with the arrival of bountiful rains. His constituents prospered, and fewer Malawians than usual went hungry. Because Mutharika and Foreign Minister Joyce Banda jettisoned diplomatic relations with Taiwan and embraced ties to mainland China, Malawi gained new budgetary support and Chinese developmental attention, some of which contributed to farming prosperity. China constructed or refurbished important roads, such as the critical artery along Lake Malawi from Salima to Liwonde and Machinga; built and gave to parliament a brand-new legislative chamber in Lilongwe, and erected an ostentatious hotel nearby. Trade with China also rose appreciably as Beijing started purchasing more Malawian tobacco than ever before. All of these initiatives greatly increased the country's annual per capita GDP outcomes from about $289 in 2005 to $438 in 2009.[30] Malawians appreciated the prosperity of the first Mutharika era.

They also welcomed his attacks on his predecessor. Mutharika broke with Muluzi shortly after being inaugurated and spent the next several years pursuing wrongdoers from his predecessor's period in office. His new Democratic People's Party (DPP) claimed in early 2004 to be investigating the finances of ten former senior ministers; a new era in anti-corruption pursuit seemed about to begin. The ACB was involved, working closely with a responsive public prosecutor and following up on the many reports of official malfeasance that it had received (a total of more than 3,000 from 1997 to 2006).[31] The prosecutor, the ACB, and the attorney general together paraded suspects before the media, but the few cases that eventually made it into court were badly prepared and many acquittals followed. Local observers believed that the 2004–2006 anti-corruption blitz was essentially an exercise in political persecution, but it impressed citizens. Mutharika was never secure in office; but becoming plausibly active on the anti-corruption front thrilled the donors on whom Malawi had long been dependent for project and budgetary support.

The ACB and public prosecutor could claim success when they jailed a mayor of the nation's largest city, and a political ally of Muluzi, for two years for stealing from his administration's road maintenance fund. (Muluzi remained chair of the UDF after he unwillingly left the presidency in 2004.) Two members of Mutharika's own cabinet were accused of illicitly retaining funds for canceled overseas journeys but were excused when they promised to reimburse the nation.

The ACB further tried to investigate Muluzi's shady involvement with a business park that had been constructed on prime land in Blantyre and then leased to the government. Subsequently, the ACB learned that more than $7 million had been paid into various accounts controlled by Muluzi from sources in Libya, Morocco, Rwanda, and Taiwan. The ACB believed that it had discovered major diversions of foreign assistance moneys into Muluzi's pocket. Libyan-supplied tractors were but one item. Muluzi claimed that he was simply receiving funds for the UDF.

Nevertheless, when the ACB tried to arrest Muluzi in 2006, Mutharika suspended the director of the ACB, completely vitiating its independence. The prosecutor, presumably on orders, dropped all forty-two counts of theft and abuse of office against the former president. Mutharika needed the support in parliament, where he lacked a majority, especially of UDF politicians still close to or controlled by Muluzi. Mutharika may also have wondered if prosecuting Muluzi provided a proper precedent. He, too, would eventually become an ex-president.

Two years later, the government accused Muluzi of plotting to overthrow Mutharika, arresting him at the country's main international airport. Twelve months afterward, the state alleged that Muluzi had earlier purloined $12 million of foreign assistance moneys from Taiwan, Morocco, and Libya meant for poverty alleviation. Muluzi by then openly opposed Bingu wa Mutharika and threatened to run against him for the presidency in 2009. (Muluzi's embezzlement trial proceeded in fits and starts in 2009, 2011, 2016, and 2019. It was still in process in 2022.)

Contemporaneously, Mutharika reckoned that it was his moment to benefit from the proverbial fatted calf. He evicted members of parliament from their opulent Banda-built chamber in Lilongwe so that he could leave his official presidential palace in Blantyre and move into the 300-room folly that Kamuzu Banda had erected just before he was forced to abandon the life presidency.[32] Mutharika ordered a new official automobile—a Mercedes Maybach limousine costing more than $400,000, paying for it from funds in an official Emergency Drought Recovery Programme account financed by donors. He purchased a $13.6 million jet aircraft for presidential use. But, much more by way of venal scale presidential peculation was occurring during this period, cleverly concealed.

Mutharika, advised by his brother Peter, was systematically misappropriating or stealing large amounts from the national treasury and depositing it in banks in Southeast Asia for his and his brother's own personal use, and with which to contest future elections. The total amount discovered in 2015 by a German-sponsored audit conducted by a major global accounting firm was about $47 million. Peter, on behalf of his brother, apparently made frequent visits to Singapore and Malaysia to deposit substantial dollars in their names.[33]

Peter Mutharika, tall and calculating, with hooded eyes, taught law in Africa and then for many years in the United States. He held an American green card, although Malawians suspected that he had become an American citizen, and returned to Malawi only to help his brother and to join the profiteering pursuits that Muluzi and Bingu Matharika had so successfully inaugurated. Peter and I talked ("as fellow academic Americans") several times in and near Malawi's parliament in early 2012 after he had become an MP and the new head of his brother's DPP. It was clear to me then that he was prepared to be ruthless politically, in pursuit of personal and family ambitions. He also thought that his American experience gave him more wisdom and a fuller perspective than other Malawians.

After Bingu wa Mutharika was re-elected president overwhelmingly in 2009 (66 percent over John Tembo of the MCP's 30 percent), and Peter Mutharika had left his professorship of international and comparative law at Washington University after thirty-seven years, their governance methods altered profoundly. Together they began to rule Malawi more and more autocratically. Criticism annoyed the president. So the brothers sought to censor the press, overpower the judiciary, and intimidate members of parliament who belonged to their own DPP as well as its MCP and UDF rivals. They attempted to "impose draconian clamp downs on freedom of expression and freedom of the press." And Bingu wa Mutharika, seventy-seven, started quarreling over policy and precedence with the several international lending institutions and foreign aid organizations on which poor Malawians still depended. The British High Commissioner, subsequently expelled, averred that Bingu wa Mutharika was "evermore autocratic and intolerant of criticism."[34]

His harsh initiatives, the president's volatile and "erratic" behavior, and what civil society called an "arrogant and out of touch" regime that was doing little to alleviate economic distress and systematically mismanaging finances, led to a burst of citizen action in Malawi's major population centers, even in Mzuzu in the far north. "Sleepy Malawi grew angry." The president responded petulantly and threateningly. He ordered his soldiers "to shoot to kill." "Even if you hide in holes, I'll smoke you out," the untethered would-be despot declared. In the country's first significant repression of civilians since the days of Kamuzu Banda's presidency, protesters were killed and many arrested. A local human rights leader was attacked inside a church compound, with the police behaving like "animals."[35]

The Bingu wa Mutharika presidency rapidly lost legitimacy. Malawians turned against him, not knowing the turmoil that would soon ensue. When Bingu Mutharika suddenly died in April 2012, after a massive heart attack, Peter Mutharika wanted to succeed him. So Peter engineered the spiriting of the decomposing corpse, inadequately disguised as someone needing medical attention, out of Malawi by air ambulance to South Africa. Peter Mutharika and eleven senior politicians close to Bingu Mutharika thought that by resorting to such a bizarre and easily unmasked cover-up that they could prevent Vice President Joyce Banda from becoming president. (A year later, a Malawian investigative commission concluded flatly that Peter Mutharika had been the plot's "mastermind.") If they could but keep the news and timing of Bingu Mutharika's death quiet for a few days, the elder brother could somehow gain time and support to subvert the authorized pattern of succession—or so they schemed.

The Mutharikas and Joyce Banda had fallen out in 2011, when she opposed their plan to turn Peter into Bingu's successor (at the next regular election). President Mutharika responded by tossing her out of the ruling DPP (she formed her own new political party) and attempted to cancel the vice presidential position to which she had been elected on his own winning ticket. He derided her as a "mere market woman," and his wife piled on by calling her someone who merely sold fritters (*mandasi*) and was therefore unfit to succeed to the presidency. (Banda, a prosperous entrepreneur owning many businesses, retorted that she was proud to stand with the *mandasi* sellers.) A cat-fight continued in that unseemly manner.

After his brother's sudden fatal heart attack, Peter Mutharika and other DPP leaders, according to the special commission, "approached the army, police and the attorney general's office over the next 24 hours to try to find a way to stop Banda, but all three institutions insisted that the Constitution was clear that the vice-president should succeed Mutharika."[36] Malawi's vaunted constitutionalism prevailed, as it often did. But, in addition, Peter Mutharika had won few friends in Malawi; he was regarded in many quarters as a bully and an opportunist.

When the air ambulance arrived from South Africa, its medical team refused to carry a dead body back to South Africa. But, by then, Malawian state media had announced that Bingu wa Mutharika was ill and being flown to Johannesburg for treatment. South African intelligence, about the same time, caught wind of the scheme and asked its Malawian counterparts exactly what kind of maladroit maneuver was underway.

In the early hours of the next day, Bingu wa Mutharika's body arrived at a South African air force base near Pretoria, thanks to assistance from the South African foreign ministry. Quickly, at the South African military hospital in Pretoria, the corpse was indeed pronounced dead. But at a meeting the same morning in Lilongwe, the Malawian cabinet, minus Joyce Banda, decided to seek a court writ to stop Banda's accession and succession, and to appoint an acting president (presumably the surviving Mutharika). But by the evening of that second contorted day, South Africa said that they were ready to announce the former president's demise. That meant that Peter Mutharika and his fellow plotters had to accept defeat, and to declare the dead president truly dead and the very alive vice president his proper heir. So ended law professor Peter Mutharika's attempt to subvert Malawi's constitution and abridge the rule of law. It was not to be his last such travesty.

By the time that South Africa forced Peter Mutharika's hand, Banda had secured the backing of Malawi's army chief, who sent troops to protect her. Muluzi, an enemy of the Mutharikas, also declared that constitutional processes must be followed. Banda had served in Muluzi's second cabinet as well as Bingu wa Mutharika's first one. Thwarting Peter Mutharika's ambitions and his scheme (which might well have succeeded in other African countries), Joyce Banda promptly became Africa's second female head of state, after Ellen Johnson Sirleaf of Liberia.

A Woman President

Banda's two-year presidency (fulfilling the remainder of Bingu wa Mutharika's term) was notable for her successful attempt to repair relations with donors, with most of whom Bingu wa Mutharika had battled until they withdrew and ceased extending support. Breaking with the African Union, she boasted that she would arrest President Omar al-Bashir of the Sudan, an indicted war criminal, if he dared to enter Malawi. Taking advice from the IMF, Banda also sharply devalued the kwacha, leading to escalating bouts of inflation without otherwise stabilizing Malawi financially.

She sold the presidential jet that Bingu wa Mutharika had purchased wantonly in 2011, promising to devote the proceeds of the sale to poverty reduction. She also cut her own official salary back by 30 percent to a paltry (for Africa) $42,000 a year, saying that "we have a nation to build."

Banda sacked a national police chief who was widely feared and disliked, and who had enforced many of Mutharika's authoritarian acts. Likewise, she fired the head of the national broadcasting service for having facilitated her predecessor's propaganda and pledged to honor all media freedoms. Transparency, she said, was to be cherished. (She also discharged the minister of information, a woman, because the latter had earlier termed Banda "unqualified.")

"In these and so many other ways," I wrote enthusiastically, "Banda is obviously cut from a very different cloth than her presidential predecessors." I instanced the plethora of fraud that had punctuated both the Muluzi and Mutharika interludes and implied that Joyce Banda's promise to "put the people of Malawi's needs foremost," and not to be yet "another male petty despot," were very positive omens.

"President Banda says that she intends to uplift Malawi in sustainable ways," I continued, "to minimize the corruption which has long sapped the national vitality, to diversify the economy, to build roads, and to demonstrate that a woman can lead Malawi with integrity and dignity toward prosperity for all." If only she can, I concluded my overly optimistic panegyric, "she will have demonstrated that male leadership is overrated in Africa, and that the era of women leading benighted countries forward has at last arrived."[37]

Unfortunately, however, her days in office were remarkable less for the real policy accomplishments that she had promised than for an explosion of corruption that reflected badly on her leadership even if little of the abundant proceeds reached her directly and even if promiscuous filching from the national treasury had begun under her predecessors. According to auditors, large-scale corruption and money laundering had consumed Malawi's bureaucracy and cabinet ministers. The scandal, called "Cashgate," was exposed in 2014 but had been festering for several years. Twenty-five cabinet ministers lost their positions for joining in fraudulent over-invoicing schemes and the falsification of payrolls worth at least $54 million. (Two years before, I dined unwittingly with one of the culprits, a former journalist and protégée of Aleke Banda who had become finance minister. Over dinner he articulated politically correct bromides about the evils of thieving from the state and the people.)

The looting of the national treasury reached "a fever pitch" in 2013, reported the auditors, when a third of the total amount was pilfered, much of it on a single day. The managers of eight local commercial banks and senior officials in the office of the accountant-general were in league with the rogue politicians, and profited from rubber-stamping suspicious payment vouchers. The nation's budget director was killed during these investigations, presumably to keep him from exposing the scheme.[38]

Given the massive corruption that punctuated the Mutharika and Joyce Banda eras, whatever the ACB had been doing or not doing, the "biggest fishes" had been acting with impunity. "Ordinary Malawians," explained one commentator, "look at abuse of state resources by those in power as acceptable." Anyway, he continued, "people join politics in Malawi mainly to make money."[39] Hindered by Muluzi and Bingu wa Mutharika and at least the first public prosecutor, the understaffed, underfinanced, and largely powerless Malawian ACB had hardly been able to contain corruption, much less curtail its sustainable growth throughout the first twenty years of its existence. (Russell had departed in 2005.)

Return of the American

Given the startling nature of the auditor's report and the difficulties of governing what had become a severely fractured country in the wake of the DPP's failed coup, it is no wonder that Joyce Banda lost to the remaining Mutharika brother in the election of 2014. In a balloting that was hardly well run, and may have been rigged, Mutharika won 36 percent of the vote, the Rev. Lazarus Chakwera of the MCP (having replaced Tembo as its leading candidate) 27 percent, and Banda only 20 percent.[40] Banda soon fled to the United States, fearing political persecution and potential prosecution sponsored by her erstwhile successor.

After Peter Mutharika, seventy-four, became president in 2014, he installed a new director of the ACB and urged him to engage in an all-out attack on Malawian corruption. As he told the Council on Foreign Relations in New York, "we can get rid of [corruption] . . . we are fighting corruption, no question about it. But you know, there will always be corruption, I suppose, in every society, in the sense that there will be some people who are always going to—you know, to have shortcuts to get riches. But I think there are serious penalties if you are caught, and I assure you that, and they know that I will not abide—that my government will not abide corruption."[41] The second President Mutharika spoke as vigorously and assuredly as had his predecessors about how corruption would be curtailed. But there was never any evidence that his regime was moving any more energetically against corrupt politicians and other public servants than had its predecessors.

Peter Mutharika's period as president was marked from the start by food shortages (the rains had failed and maize crops had withered), foreign exchange deficiencies that led to severe power cuts, and renewed leanings toward autocracy. He tried to dial back media autonomy and to prevent judges from deciding cases against the government. Again, these authoritarian displays and prevailing unsatisfactory economic and social results led thousands to demonstrate in 2018 against the paltry economic growth achievements of this Mutharika presidency. But crowds of dissidents also protested new corruption scandals, later including allegations that Mutharika himself had received a $200,000 kickback from a local businessman who had "won" a multi-million-dollar contract to provide food rations to the police.

These troubling occurrences and disquiet in large parts of Malawi influenced the national mood when Mutharika and Chakwera once more in 2019 contested Malawi's presidency. Chakwera, sixty-five at the time, came from the Central Province, where his father was a farmer and a preacher. He graduated from the University of Malawi during the Kamuzu Banda era, and then obtained three theological degrees, the first two from South African universities and the third a doctorate in ministry from an evangelical Christian university in Illinois. Afterward, he taught at Kenya's Pan-Africa Theological Seminary and India's new All Nations Theological Seminary in West Bengal. Subsequently, he became general superintendent of the Assemblies of God church in Malawi, a self-governing affiliate of a worldwide Pentecostal movement that began in and is headquartered in the United States. Prime Minister Abiy Ahmed of Ethiopia and former Prime Minister Scott Morrison of Australia are both Pentecostal disciples; Pentecostalism is a rapidly growing Christian creed in Nigeria and South Africa.

Chakwera says that he left the church for politics in 2013, succeeding Tembo as head of Kamuzu Banda's old MCP, when "one day, God spoke to my heart, and God was not saying I'm pulling you out of ministry—God was saying I'm extending your ministry."[42]

The conduct of the 2019 election battle between Mutharika and Chakwera, two candidates strikingly separated by age, region, religiosity, apparent probity, and temperament more than by policy preferences, was more blatantly disturbed than the contest in 2014, and probably more than any other in the history of Malawi. In two southern districts officials allegedly switched vote counts to favor Mutharika. An election monitor in one of those polling areas was caught tampering with the forms on which results were listed. Thugs employed by the DPP threatened opposition voters in the Central Province and throughout the tea-growing areas of the Southern Province. These were tactics familiar to poll watchers in Zimbabwe, Kenya, and elsewhere. But in Malawi, and perhaps for the first time anywhere in Africa, Mutharika's supporters used plain correction fluid or whiteout to cover over and replace tally sheet results that listed Chakwera's large vote totals. Despite credible reports of such fraud, the Malawi Election Commission certified Mutharika's victory, saying that he had won almost 159,000 more votes than Chakwera, and 800,000 more than the United Transformation Movement's Saulos Chilima, who had previously been Mutharika's vice president.

Peter Mutharika began his second presidential term in 2019 but served only until early 2020, when Malawi's Constitutional Court demonstrated its surprising independence by nullifying the 2019 result and ordering a rerun of the contest. In Africa only Kenya, in 2007, had ever experienced a similar judicial overturning of an election result, in that case after weeks of heavy violence. In Malawi, the court acknowledged in a judgment that took seven hours to read that the contest had been marred by blatant improprieties, including numerous instances of vote totals altered by whiteout. "The integrity of the result was severely compromised," opined the five judges.[43] The polling exercise had been farcical in its malevolence and incompetence.

When the election was held chastely a second time, in the late southern autumn of 2020, Chakwera easily triumphed. The final, fully accepted, totals were Chakwera, 59 percent of the votes; Mutharika, 40 percent.[44] The new government subsequently froze Mutharika's bank accounts and opened a corruption investigation. For the remaining Mutharika brother, the game was up. (In 2021, Bingu wa Mutharika's valet, later Peter Mutharika's chief "bodyguard," was investigated for massive fraud, holding personal assets amounting to at least $2.2 million, and the murder of an anticorruption official.)[45]

The Pentecostal Pledge

Chakwera promised to transform Malawi. In a forthright inaugural address, he told Malawi's people: "It is no secret that we have had one administration after another shifting its post to the next election, promising prosperity, but delivering poverty; promising nationalism, but delivering division; promising political tolerance, but delivering human rights abuses; promising good governance, but delivering corruption; promising institutional autonomy, but delivering state capture." The nation had been left in "ruins," so Chakwera pledged to get rid of the rubble of corruption and to replace lazy officials with energetic, conscientious ones. Government, he said, is service.[46]

According to the Corruption Perceptions Index for 2020, reflecting the Mutharika years, Malawi had sunk to 129th place (of 180), with a low raw score of 31.[47] Thus, over the course of the present and future Chakwera presidencies the effective combat of all manner of graft should be reflected in such future benchmark ratings—if any leader can overcome the structural lag of corrupt practices in a polity as deprived as Malawi.

One of Chakwera's first actions, amid the coronavirus pandemic, was to impose mask-wearing, physical distancing, and many other sensible restrictions on his country's 19 million citizens. He took responsibility for curtailing the disease much more seriously than did his predecessor and most of his peers across Africa. At the end of the first month of 2022, Malawi listed 85,000 confirmed cases and only 2,550 deaths, so luck, the country's very youthful population, and Chakwera's sensible measures may have helped to slow the spread of the pandemic in that one country.[48] But the Omicron variant was only then beginning to attack southern Africa, spreading probably from South Africa, and almost all African reported numbers were, anyway, likely undercounts because of prevailing statistical weaknesses.

Chakwera made a series of appealing statements about the restoration of democratic practices in a nation that had suffered bouts of authoritarianism and corruption since the ouster of dictator Kamuzu Banda in 1994. He promised to declare his personal assets annually—a first for Malawi and most African nations—and to establish a truly independent anti-corruption bureau to investigate those—such as Mutharika—who stole from the public. Calling for enhanced scrutiny of the executive by parliament, and enhanced accountability all around, he even said he would introduce legislation to reduce the powers of the presidency.

He railed against tribal nepotism but packed his first cabinet largely with CiCewa-speaking representatives from the Central Province, several of whom were husbands and wives. Because of this last, heavily criticized, action, Malawians in 2022 still were not sure whether Chakwera was a serious improvement over the mendacity of their previous leaders, or someone conceivably with a refreshing belief in public service.

In attempting to expand Malawi's economic growth potential, Chakwera planned to exploit mineral deposits in his nation's northern reaches. Chakwera became anxious to take advantage of the artisanal gold mining that exists outside official purview. Chakwera's administration also impressed outsiders by its broadmindedness in exploring a range of other promising commercial possibilities to enhance the nation's traditional and paltry foreign exchange-earning capabilities.

At the end of his first one hundred days in office, Chakwera gave himself a reasonably positive rating, excusing the relatively slow pace of reform. Progress would take time. "The focus of my administration for the first 100 days has been to turn Malawi around," Chakwera said. "For, our nation has long been a flooding ship sailing in hostile waters and heading in the wrong direction. As any good sailor will tell you, stopping a flooding ship from sinking and turning around in such hostile conditions of the pandemic, are not small feats."[49]

Malawi nevertheless continued to struggle with the economic downturn that accompanied Covid-19 throughout the world, and in Africa. Chakwera's administration still needed to ensure adequate seeds and fertilizers for farmers at the beginning of the 2022–2023 planting season, to pray for good rains for 2022, and to encourage donors to restore their funding of Malawi's budget and key projects. Because the economy grew less than 1 percent in 2020, thanks to collateral damage from the global pandemic, Chakwera's government proposed a range of innovative new ways to gain much-needed foreign exchange.

In 2021, the most innovative of these initiatives was a determination to cultivate and export large quantities of marijuana, joining South Africa, Zimbabwe, Lesotho, Nigeria, Morocco, Ghana, Eswatini, and Zambia in a rush to profit from pot. Malawi's parliament voted to legalize cannabis farming and the government created a Cannabis Regulatory Authority. By the end of 2021 it had issued more than seventy licenses to cooperatives and newly established commercial enterprises. How profitable their total production will be, and how much employment pot growing will bring, was to be determined in 2022 and beyond. But the hope was that as export revenues from tobacco growing continued to recede—in 2020 tobacco exports fell by 31 percent, leading to a 26 percent fall in earnings from the crop—marijuana profits would gradually take tobacco's place as a critical contributor to foreign exchange returns.[50]

Neither in his inaugural address nor in his one hundred days report did Chakwera reflect on what should be the consuming issue of his and future administrations. A desperately poor country where the annual average GDP per capita is still no more than $500, Malawi is doubling its population every twenty or thirty years. the UN Population Division forecasts that the country, about 20 million in 2021, will host nearly 50 million people in 2050 and approximately 70 million in 2100.

Where will and how will that vast human surge live? How will they feed themselves, especially given climatic shifts that are making rainfalls much more unpredictable and droughts more frequent and destructive? These new millions will mostly be young; the median age in 2021 was only seventeen, and the bulk of the people for many decades will be of working age, or younger. But formal jobs are scarce and farming, Malawi's main labor occupation, has never absorbed swelling numbers of workers and seems unlikely to do so in this or later decades. The bromides of "Trickle-Up" remain relevant. Tobacco exports are unlikely to increase and diversification, promised by both Mutharikas and Joyce Banda, has yet to occur despite talk of encouraging the production of cannabis, macadamia nuts, and peanuts. It is also not certain that donors will continue collectively to invest $1 billion a year in Malawi—as much as its own annual collection of tax revenue. And Chakwera and parliament in 2020 did raise Malawi's monthly minimum wage by 43 percent, to K50,000 ($65).[51]

Fertility and poverty go hand in hand. Globally, Malawian women deliver the globe's eighth highest number of babies per mother. Sending girls to school, and keeping them there through at least the secondary level, is known dramatically to reduce fertility rates and increase incomes. But to take such a leap forward, Malawi will need to do what Muluzi tried to accomplish in 1994—to encourage school attendance by girls, to upgrade teaching and teachers, and to improve such necessities as the availability of potable water—so permitting girls to spend fewer of their days fetching water from distant wells or standpipes. It is not clear in 2022 that Chakwera or his advisors are ready to tackle such immense and enduring problems.

Nor do they, in common with most governments in Africa, fully appreciate how their cities will become metropoles and their villages and towns mushroom in size despite an absence of adequate housing, supplies of potable water and electricity, and waterborne sanitation. Lilongwe and Blantyre are not going to compete in size and squalor with Kinshasa and Lagos but, in a relative sense, they will be equally hard to manage. Possibly Chakwera's team will address these and other problems of today's Africa in a timely and prudent fashion. If not, sustainable trickle-up growth—as we advocated in 1994—will remain as distant as ever.

In one respect, however, Chakwera's administration acted decisively in 2021 against the kinds of corrupt peculation that had long plagued Malawi. The Covid-19 pandemic had brought temptation. Indeed, 6.2 billion kwacha ($7.95 million) had been allocated for the country's coronavirus response program. But, months later, none of those funds could be found. Minister of Labor Ken Kandodo had taken foreign trips with some of the money and thirteen other national and district council employees, including an immigration official and someone working directly for the president, were arrested. President Chakwera sacked Kandodo and said that there were no "sacred cows." "If the finger of evidence point to you . . . you are going to prison."[52]

A little later two key officials from the second Mutharika administration were arrested for falsifying data delivered to the IMF. The former governor of the Malawi Reserve Bank and the former finance minister had allegedly lied to the IMF about the extent to which Malawi was meeting its loan conditions. A former minister of local government was also arrested for fraud in a similar crackdown.[53] Additionally, a businessman who had attempted to bribe judges to rule in favor of President Peter Mutharika in 2019 was jailed for nine years.[54] Impunity for corruption, common in the pre-Chakwera era, seemed at the end of 2021 to be receding in Malawi.

The Chakwera administration even cracked down on the hitherto largely immune perpetrators of wildlife poaching. Malawi, described by conservationists as "one of the biggest wildlife trafficking hubs in southern Africa," had rewritten its formerly weak laws and started prosecuting the heads of poaching syndicates, whoever they might be.[55] Prosperous entrepreneurs who had often bribed investigators and prosecutors to continue their profitable trade found themselves arrested and sentenced to prison for illegally taking wild game. A Chinese citizen, for example, was jailed for fourteen years in late 2021 for possessing rhino horn, ivory, live pangolins, and illicit arms, and for money laundering; allegedly, he was a kingpin in Malawian and East African animal-smuggling networks. His wife and son-in-law had previously been caught smuggling ivory. A Malawian associate who spoke fluent Mandarin was also imprisoned for his part in the running of the vast Chinese poaching and smuggling network that had ensnared Zambian, Tanzanian, and Mozambican gunmen and endangered mammals in its malevolent maw.

Even so, it was not yet evident in 2022 that Chakwera could manage these and innumerable other critical problems energetically and wisely. Church groups and civil society representatives urged him to be more decisive in combating corruption. They claimed that too many of his existing cabinet ministers were still sticking their fingers into public pockets. In a bold move toward the end of the first month of 2022, Chakwera consequently sacked his entire cabinet. But then he reappointed twelve of the thirty-three old ministers and added only two new individuals.[56]

In mid-2022, it was still an open question whether Chakwera could reform and uplift the conduct of politics in Malawi, and improve life-chances for its citizens. Would he rise to the many challenges and become the political leader for whom Malawians have long waited, and have suffered for in the meanwhile? Other African presidents have entered office with equally positive messages and perhaps even the intention of being effective and accountable heads of state. If Chakwera can turn his grand promises into reality, Malawi will be the better for them, and Africa can claim a victory for representative democracy and the delivery of good governance. Muluzi and the Mutharikas were largely self-interested. Chakwera may in fact care for and promote the interests of the public even though local critics say, "Malawians are now tired with the way the president is handling affairs. . . . They are no longer interested in his speeches. They are now looking for action."[57]

6

Mandela's Triumph

The Liberating of South Africa

"Who let you in?" Piet Koornhof, South Africa's beady-eyed Minister of Cooperation and Development, asked in horror when he saw me walking into South Africa's Parliament building with Helen Suzman, MP, in 1978. Earlier that year the police had intercepted letters from me to my wife and from Suzman to Winston Churchill Jr.; as a result, my pronounced anti-apartheid sentiments had been disseminated widely across South Africa's lively daily press, and been commented upon in editorials. South Africa's official response to the disclosures had been lampooned in several stellar newspaper cartoons. Koornhof and his fellow Afrikaner legislators were aware that, a few years before, their much feared, bluff, compatriot Cornelius (Connie) Mulder, Minister of Interior, had pronounced me a "prohibited immigrant."

Suzman was the leading opposition politician—a sharp-tongued stalwart of the Progressive Party, and then the Progressive Federal Party, and for thirteen earlier years a staunch antagonist of apartheid in Parliament as the sole representative of the liberal opposition. I often stayed with her and her husband, a leading medical diagnostician, when I was in South Africa, so it was perfectly reasonable that we should lunch together in the parliamentary dining room in Cape Town. It was also very reasonable that Koornhof (and Minister of Justice Kobie Coetsee, whom we would also encounter) would wonder how I managed to arrive not only in South Africa, but in their very parliamentary midst.

After all, I was a known writer of critical commentary about the cruelties and injustices of apartheid. I was friendly with many key members of Suzman's political party, had demonstrated since 1972 a decided aversion to the policies propounded by the ruling National Party, and—in the intercepted letter— had discussed viewing a banned documentary movie (*the Search for Sandra Laing*—1977) about the devastating and dehumanizing consequences of South Africa's legalized color bar. From several earlier conversations with me, too, both Koornhof and Coetsee (relatively enlightened apartheid ministers) knew not only how opposed I was to what they were doing to fulfill and further the nation's odious apartheid endeavor, but also how misguided and hypocritical I thought that they and their enabling operations were.

Overcoming the Oppressors. Robert I. Rotberg, Oxford University Press. © Oxford University Press 2023.
DOI: 10.1093/oso/9780197674208.003.0006

Map 6.1. South Africa and Botswana

A Structure of Fear and Domination

By 1978, South Africa had established an elaborate system of dehumanization, invidious classification, and petty and grand regulation that was intended to sanctify and sustain white rule over Africans, Coloureds, and Asians—in perpetuity. The nation was ghettoized both in and around cities, and through imposed rural labor reservoirs called Bantustans (homelands). Mingling, copulation, marriage, and anything else of importance across the color (called racial) line was illegal and punished decisively in order to maintain the myth of white superiority, and in order (like the caste system in India) to buttress white (or Brahmin) power.

Draconian legislation (unlike many totalitarian societies, South Africa had enacted perniciously well-crafted laws to support its arbitrary abrogation of human rights) and the tough enforcement of those rules by the police, the military, and the rest of the state security apparatus, pressed firmly on the necks of the underclasses in the country. By 1978, 4.3 million whites ruled over 15 million

Figure 6.1. Helen Suzman

Zulu, Xhosa, Pedi, Sotho, et al., 2.5 million Coloureds, and 786,000 Asians. Of the African majority, a sizable number were better educated than many whites, with decisively middle-class ideas and aspirations.[1] But, instead of accommodation and tolerance, the nation was ruled capriciously by terror and fear.

I had visited in 1959, but had purposely stayed away ever since because of the Sharpeville Massacre, the hounding of the African National Congress (ANC) and Nelson Mandela, the deadly Rivonia trial, and Mandela's incarceration on Robben Island (from 1962).

In 1972, I had decided to go back, and to see for myself how terrible things were. After all, my teaching included sections on South Africa. It was time I took the measure of apartheid directly.

By 1972, South Africa had been thoroughly transformed from a segregated state where most Africans were third-class citizens but where an educated African elite could follow professional pursuits and, especially in urban townships, participate in social and economic activities and celebrate their own cultural norms, into a regimented and bitterly demarcated society consumed by color and color differences. No longer could Africans mix legally with whites or persons of other classifications. No longer could they walk city streets without identification and the hated "pass." No longer could they complain or protest at the actions of officialdom without being labeled a communist and a treasonous enemy of the white-run state. Africans had lost the fundamental human rights that they once possessed, and so also had all residents of South Africa been deprived of the essential freedoms of speech, press, religion, and assembly.

The electoral triumph of the Afrikaner-dominated National Party in 1948 had proved revolutionary. Not only had hard-line Afrikaners, including many who had been interned in World War II for their pro-Nazi sympathies, successfully appealed to fears of black advancement (in West Africa, the Gold Coast was becoming Ghana) and competition, but they had campaigned to rewrite laws in order to guarantee permanent white dominance. Their parliamentary majorities allowed them systematically to undermine representative democracy and to set about altering the social, economic, and—particularly—the political structure of what since 1910 had been a respected (if color-conscious and segregated) British-oriented dominion and an ally of Britain in both World Wars I and II.[2]

The racist Afrikaners who controlled the National Party lacked the inherited shared values of the still segregationist-inclined Cape Dutch politicians who had led South Africa from 1910. Indeed, South Africa's new governing class viewed its victory as an ethnic one, with Afrikaners having finally ousted the hated British and reversed the adverse military result of the Anglo-Boer war of 1899–1902.[3] If they lost power again, these new rulers feared, the humiliations of the past would be revisited. From their optic, the introduction of apartheid after 1948 was fully justified: it was a question of survival as a people and a culture, and the fittest would survive. Or, to put the issue in the words of Afrikanerdom's greatest historian, ". . . apartheid [was] chiefly a means to maintain white power, wealth, and privileges."[4]

The Afrikaners entrenched themselves in power—they thought for all time—by using methods common on the African and Asian continents. They employed legal and extralegal means to hinder the voices of opposition groups inside and outside Parliament, to eliminate dissent, to equate dissent with communism and treason, and to emphasize conformity. They emasculated much of the independence of the judiciary, despite its proud Roman-Dutch legacy, and especially curtailed the courts' ability to question Parliament's supremacy. They rewrote constitutional provisions that had guaranteed the franchise for mixed-race voters, rescinded habeas corpus and restricted writs of mandamus, barred all manner of transracial intercourse (and marriage), and introduced a Population Registration Act to assign all persons to racial categories. The Group Areas Act segregated Coloureds and Asians as well as Africans commercially and residentially. The Prevention of Illegal Squatting Act allowed the government to remove

Africans from public and private land and to send those removed to resettlement camps. The Native Laws Amendment Act of 1952 eliminated homeownership and other long-held rights of Africans resident in cities and urban townships, and restricted rights of residence to defined exceptional categories.

The so-called Pass Act of 1952 required all "natives" to carry "reference" books listing everything about them. By this act, the ruling National Party sought tightly to control the movement of Africans in and out of urban areas and to stem the growth of the black population in the cities (now theoretically but impossibly reserved solely for whites). Soon, millions of Africans were carrying reference books and hundreds of thousands were being arrested for not carrying them— for "pass" and influx control offenses. In Johannesburg alone in the 1970s, 151 Africans were arrested each day for violating provisions of the Pass Act.[5]

To infuriate Africans even more, and to shift Africans farther away from white residential areas, the Native Resettlement Act of 1953 moved Africans in Johannesburg to Soweto, a new satellite city twelve miles away. In 1956 and 1957, Sophiatown, a storied black freehold area next to Johannesburg, was rezoned for whites, with Africans and Coloureds being ousted forcibly.[6] In Cape Town, the Group Areas Act enabled the government to remove mixed-race families from District Six, within the city; many had lived there for generations. In another ten or so cities and numerous towns, the same procedure eliminated Africans, Coloureds, and Asians from commercial and residential competition with whites. At least 500,000 had been relocated by the time of my return to South Africa in 1972.

Compelled to carry a pass, made subject to influx control, and being "endorsed out" or compelled to leave urban areas, were all crushing blows. No African could remain in an urban area for more than seventy-two hours unless he/she had resided there since birth, worked continuously for a single employer for ten years, and so on. But since gainful employment of almost any kind was scarce in the rural areas (and in the homelands), thousands of Africans naturally sought to evade police dragnets and entered urban areas without reference books or passes. If caught, they were summarily tried and "endorsed out"—sent to their real or their imagined homes in some distant Bantustan even though large numbers had always lived in and around the major cities.

A directive from the secretary for Bantu administration and development was illustrative: "The Bantu in the European areas who are normally regarded as non-productive and as such have to be resettled in the homelands are . . . the aged, unfit, widows, women with dependent children; Bantu on European farms who become superfluous as a result of age; professional Bantu [who are not] essential for the European labour market. . . ."[7]

Everywhere in South Africa in 1972 there were signs saying "For Europeans Only" or "Not for Non-Whites." Even if legally married (before 1953), couples of differing colors could not (legally) cohabit or "mix." These strictures obviously affected whites, blacks, Coloureds, and Indians, but what about Chinese and Japanese who lived in the country? A young Afrikaans-speaking woman was forced to realize, I wrote in the press, "that she could not continue to love her Japanese karate teacher openly" although Japanese citizens and some (but not all) Chinese immigrants were considered "honorary" whites. But such a status, declared an official of the Department of Interior, did not extend to their "marrying or going to bed with a white woman." Moreover, he continued, it did not "mean that they are considered inferior—just different."[8] Such lunacies reflected the contortions of a state determined to regiment its majority population, and others on the margin who were not white.

Obviously, affected Africans, Coloureds, and Asians protested vehemently at these abominations. So did some white South Africans who believed in natural justice and human rights. But the Suppression of Communism Act of 1950 banned the South African Communist Party, one of the eldest across the globe, and permitted the minister of justice to declare any protestors communists. Anyone who was attempting to bring about political, industrial, social, or economic change within South Africa through "disorder or hostility" against whites was deemed a communist, and could be restrained. The law was also applied retroactively against anyone who had ever been a communist, whether or not they had renounced the party.[9] The Criminal Laws Amendment Act prohibited the incitement of violence. Furthermore, after 1962, the police could arrest suspects without charge and throw them into solitary confinement indefinitely and keep them incommunicado. The Sabotage Act of the same year construed sabotage to include carrying weapons or tampering with property. From 1967, terrorism became an all-inclusive offense that encompassed anything "harmful" to the white-controlled state.

Notoriously, the formidable South African security apparatus used banning orders to curtail fundamental freedoms. Banned individuals, confined to their homes, were forbidden to talk to or be seen with more than one other person at a time (while saving the state the costs of their incarceration and room and board). They had to report regularly to the police. Banned persons who died could not be quoted, for their banning orders remained. A prisoner might be released, and immediately be served with a banning order. Someone banned could not resume work in his or her profession; writers could not continue to be journalists or to write in any way. A black churchman preferred playing doubles tennis but was restricted by his banning order to singles since doubles would have constituted an "illegal gathering."

The National Party also tampered with educational opportunity, in 1953 taking control of schooling away from private and missionary organizations. The government further decided who could visit a library (or any place of entertainment). It censored publications and films, tapped telephone conversations, opened mail (like mine), bullied the valiant press, and used state-run radio to disseminate apartheid-favorable propaganda. In 1959, the government closed many hitherto unsegregated university doors to Africans; the country's major "open" universities had always welcomed Africans, Coloureds, and Asians, together with whites. Now Africans were largely restricted to brand-new ethnic higher-education facilities in thirteen freshly designated rural labor reservoirs called homelands, and demarcated as the (fictional) residences of the nation's sizable black population.

All of this harmful Orwellian legislation and active repression aroused the ANC to mount boycotts and protests, and to begin to organize itself underground. Nelson Mandela and Walter Sisulu were among the young lawyers, writers, and others who tried within the law to interpose their persons and their reason against the juggernaut of repression. Their efforts were aided and abetted by handfuls of compassionate and strong-minded white South Africans, some of whom were in fact real communists, but the bulk of the white electorate was less than alarmed; it welcomed the undemocratic nature of post-1948 South Africa.[10] Even the political parties who had lost to the National Party in 1948 largely stayed silent. In 1953, 1958, 1961, 1966, and 1970, the National Party increased its majority in Parliament. The only opposition in Parliament to National Party policies, and to the legal ratcheting up of apartheid in most of those years until 1974, was the doughty Helen Suzman. From 1961 she brightly held the torch of liberty and human rights high against the clamoring jeers and insults of 165 or so baying National Party legislative shock troops.[11]

Covering all shadow portfolios singlehandedly, with hardly any assistance, Suzman could barely even begin to stem the encroaching tide of offensive legislation, and its enforcement. She knew her facts, however, and used them in a rapier-like manner to skewer apartheid apologists. She peppered the Nats, as they were called, with questions—as many as 200 a year—that forced them to reveal (or almost to reveal) what they were doing. "How many Africans were arrested daily for pass law violations?" she asked. "What were the arrest breakdowns per city?" "How many Africans were beaten?" "How many were shot and wounded, or were killed?" She requested reports on the health of Mandela and other Robben Island inmates, and employed her parliamentary position to visit him and others and to view conditions for herself (and later to raise questions in Parliament so that the world would know what she had discovered). As Mandela later said after he emerged from the Island, "It was an odd and wonderful sight to see this courageous woman peering into our cells and strolling around our courtyard."[12]

Suzman used her status as an elected representative fully, and the Afrikaners' pride in the "legal" standing of their efforts at remaking society, to take as much advantage as conceivably possible of her legitimacy. She knew full well that the National Party government would only reveal to her and to the world what she as a consummate parliamentary tactician had a statutory right to know. "I did what I could, where I was, with what I had," she explained. Frightened often at what the apartheid machine and its security apparatus might do to her, she nevertheless was fearless and brave in many small as well as large ways throughout her years in opposition through 1989. Nothing stopped her, nothing daunted her. She was motivated, she said, by her hatred of bullies. She preferred "simple justice" and fairness. No one was happier to welcome Mandela from prison in 1990.

In and out of Parliament, in almost any and all situations and encounters, Suzman was a great wit and a compelling raconteur. She was also a consummate constituency politician, but the constituency that she served as a lone Progressive Party MP, and then after 1974 as one of a small group of newly elected Progressive Federal Party members of Parliament, was the entire nation of deprived Africans. Her telephone number was always listed; the calls would pour in, day and night, and she would attempt to assist Africans in retrieving their rights or to redress their apartheid-battered losses. Often, fortunately, her advocacy managed to achieve modest gains against the regime. Thousands, possibly hundreds of thousands, directly owed the recovery of their jobs, the realization of their pensions, their permits, and the enlargement of their hopes, to her untiring efforts. (I often overheard her side of the telephone conversations and was occasionally pressed into service as the answerer of incoming calls.) Some of those incoming messages, too, were obscene and threatening, especially the ones that disturbed her peace in the middle of the night. Her practiced response to those calls was to blow a police whistle down the offending telephone line, possibly deafening her caller.

Suzman never let the National Party and its adherents think that they were superior, or had gained even slight parliamentary ascendance. Apartheid was an abomination. Fortunately, and to the discomfort of the ruling party, she was the mistress of the deft riposte. When Prime Minister Hendrik Verwoerd, an architect of apartheid and the bullying leader of the National Party, noticed that Suzman had entered Parliament after her (original) United Party had lost all but her single seat in 1961, he turned to her and dismissively said: "I have written you off." But almost before he had finished such a derisive critique, she turned her acid tongue toward him and replied: "The whole world has written you off." She told Balthazar Johannes Vorster, then minister of justice and later prime minister, that he should try to visit his constituency "heavily disguised as a human being." To her, members of the ruling National Party were "that bloody mob." A government minister accused Suzman of embarrassing South Africa with her acerbic parliamentary questions. "It is not my questions," she staunchly replied. "It is your answers."[13] Throughout her long years jousting with the masters of apartheid, her voice called for dignity and tolerance at a time when the ruling party was running roughshod over human rights and civil liberties.

Sobukwe and Mandela

My first visit to South Africa took place just a few months before the Sharpeville Massacre made South African oppression of Africans and the cruelties of apartheid a widespread global concern. Whereas earlier outrages against Africans, Coloureds, and human rights had been noted by concerned Western governments and European and American concerned civil societies, hereafter apartheid—and what it was doing to South Africans—made the front pages of the world press, energized foreign boycotts of South African exports, and drove the National Party and its supporters into deeply defensive maneuvering positions and to a heightened surveillance of and antagonism toward the anti-apartheid movement internally and overseas.

Until 1948, the ANC and other African political bodies had demanded reform but eschewed militancy. Most leaders were established, bourgeois in outlook, and anxious not to storm the proverbial barricades. But, when Nelson Mandela came to Johannesburg from the Transkei in 1943, he quickly joined other young lawyers and professionals to establish an ANC Youth League. After the 1948 electoral disaster, the Youth League pushed the entire ANC to adopt a "Program of Action." In 1952, in concert with the South African Indian Congress, that led to a mobilized defiance of "unjust" extreme segregationist laws, including not carrying passes. Civil disobedience was the method, together with the courting of arrest and the crowding of jails. Unlike the British in India or in the Gold Coast, however, the apartheid government responded harshly. Thousands were imprisoned; Africans rioted in Johannesburg, Port Elizabeth, and in other cities. Later there were national strikes, passive resistance efforts, a boycott of schools, the defiance of pass laws by 20,000 women in Pretoria, and mass boycotts of buses and purchases of potatoes. Only those last two efforts of consumerism were successful, the others being largely overcome by intensive police roundups.

Africans were far worse off politically and socially in 1960 than they had been in 1948. Parliament had legislated even tougher restrictions than before, thousands of Africans sat in jail, 156 of their leaders were being tried under provisions of the Treason Act of 1956, Mandela and others were banned, and reversing apartheid in all of its cruel repugnance seemed difficult, if not impossible.

These trying times motivated Mandela to assume a greater leadership role within the ANC and for Robert Mangaliso Sobukwe, a slim, smiling-eyed, language teacher at the University of the Witwatersrand, to question the ANC's tactics. Sobukwe and close associates feared that the ANC's effectiveness was being compromised by its collaboration with the Indian Congress and the South

Figure 6.2. Nelson Mandela

African Communist Party. In 1959, Sobukwe and 25,000 followers broke with the ANC (and its own 100,000 adherents) and created the Pan-Africanist Congress (PAC). Both entities vied to demonstrate their superior appeal in March 1960, by organizing large-scale protests against the carrying of the hated passes. The PAC cannily scheduled its demonstration ten days ahead of the ANC's initiative.

Near Vereeniging, on the Vaal River in the southern Transvaal (now Gauteng), on March 21, 1960, thousands (from 3,000 to 20,000, accounts differ) presented themselves at the local police station without passes, inviting arrest. The police panicked, shooting and killing 68 and wounding 186. This was the Sharpeville Massacre, reports and photographs of which were flashed around the world. Within South Africa, African mobs rampaged in and around Soweto (Johannesburg) and Langa, near Cape Town. In Johannesburg, Cape Town, and Port Elizabeth, a week of mourning was accompanied by work stoppages sponsored by both the PAC and the ANC. Philip Kgosana of the PAC led 15,000 Africans on a march on Cape Town from Langa. The government declared a state of emergency, banned the PAC and the ANC, arrested Sobukwe and ANC leaders, and forcibly broke the strike.[14]

After Sharpeville, opposition to apartheid turned violent. Urban sabotage became common. Mandela's new Umkonto we Sizwe (Spear of the Nation, the armed wing of the ANC) attacked electricity substations and post offices. Poqo (Only Ourselves), the clandestine armed PAC subsidiary, bombed police stations, railway lines, and power plants. In 1962, Mandela, his co-conspirators, and Poqo's operatives were all arrested. By 1964, the state security forces had achieved effective control of the nation. After the infamous Rivonia trial, Mandela and a cohort of ANC leaders were imprisoned on Robben Island or in Johannesburg. Sobukwe was held also, and the PAC largely withered away while the ANC, backed by the Soviet Union, gathered itself abroad.

By 1970 or so, white South Africa had succeeded forcefully in discouraging the active expression of concerted dissent by conventional political means such as boycotts and mass protests. I arrived back in South Africa in the midst of what was to be a transitional period between important episodes of militant unrest. This transitional era was marked by the systematic harassment of white and any remaining black opponents, by enlarged and emboldened security forces, a deceptive surface calm, the gradual emergence of a new generation of urban and rural antagonists, and the establishment under Prime Minister Vorster, a onetime Nazi sympathizer, of a novel attempt to hoodwink the world by giving Africans rights in "homelands" and calling the cynical program "separate development."[15] Vorster also reached out to compliant leaders of independent Africa such as President Kamuzu Banda of Malawi. (See chapter 4.)

The dream of a successfully integrated society had faded. Yet the white-run National Union of South African Students (NUSAS) continued—often underground—to oppose government policies. In 1970, too, Stephen Biko and other black students broke away from NUSAS to create the South African Students' Organization (SASO) to emphasize black consciousness and black self-reliance.[16] Biko was then a student at the nonwhite medical school of Natal University. In 1972, SASO and the allied Black People's Convention and South African Students' Movement (SASM) gained adherents across the country, in secondary schools and universities. By the time of my return to South Africa, a younger generation of antagonists of apartheid had demonstrated a sense of self-esteem and rejected subjugation. Even so, the battle for the final disposition of South Africa was not yet fully joined, and would not be for another decade and a half; one side appeared implacably strong, even if opposed from within and derided from without.

My self-appointed task was to acquaint myself with as many of the actors as possible, and to learn about and assess the critical variables and battle lines.

A Recipe for Banning

Mandela and many of the key leaders of the ANC were breaking rocks and sewing mailbags on Robben Island in the early months of 1972, so it would be many years before I could interact with and interview them. But I had spent time with

Oliver Tambo, the exiled president of the ANC, in Cambridge, Massachusetts, and through Todd Matshikiza and T. George Silundika (of ZAPU) had met many ANC exiles in Lusaka.

Robert Sobukwe was out of jail, however, and rusticated to a "location" or township within Kimberley, the location of South Africa's great diamond hole and the origin of Cecil Rhodes' immense fortune. I had to go there from Johannesburg to research my later biography of that contested English imperialist, premier of the Cape Colony, conqueror of Zimbabwe and Zambia, and unwitting progenitor of segregation and apartheid. When I arrived, and checked into the staid Kimberley Hotel, I immediately sent a message to Sobukwe, and invited him to lunch at the hotel.

Rustication meant that Sobukwe could only leave the "location" during daylight hours, and had literally to be back inside the barbed wire fence of the compound by 6 p.m. After the Sharpeville Massacre, the government had immediately arrested Sobukwe and jailed him for three years for inciting protests. At the end of his sentence, the apartheid apparatus rushed through a special law to keep Sobukwe—a supposed threat to the apartheid state and someone whom Vorster labeled a dangerous "magnetic personality"—confined. He spent six more years on Robben Island before being banished to Kimberley in 1970.[17]

Thanks to an introduction from crusading investigative journalist and *Rand Daily Mail* deputy editor Benjamin Pogrund, later Sobukwe's biographer, Sobukwe, tall, imposing, immensely articulate, and charismatic, was willing to come to the hotel not once but twice to discuss how unpleasant and exacting his life had been since Sharpeville and prison and, paradoxically, how hopeful he still was that apartheid could be defeated by resilient and resourceful Africans. He and I ignored the stares from other hotel guests and the proprietors; Africans had never before routinely been served in the hotel. And certainly no one so notorious (and imposing) as Sobukwe had ever entered its doors. When I walked Sobukwe back to the edge of the barbed wire fence after each of our encounters, I wondered what would become of someone so bright, so reasonable, so gentle, so forgiving, so measured, and so likable. Sobukwe's humanity was obvious and appealing. By pillorying and humiliating Sobukwe, white South Africa was clearly (to me) missing a great opportunity to meet majority demands for self-rule intelligently.

Since outsiders like myself suspected that apartheid could never permanently block change and progress—that majority rule would eventually prevail—it made no strategic sense to treat persons like Sobukwe (or Biko or Mandela) as pariahs when they were indubitably the future leaders of an integrated nation. (Instead, Sobukwe languished under house and township arrest in the Kimberley location until his death in 1978 of lung cancer.)

In Johannesburg, Pogrund also introduced me to Raymond Louw, the courageous editor of the *Rand Daily Mail*, a beacon of light in the South African darkness, to Rex Gibson, one of his successors, and to Allister Sparks, another acerbic journalist and trenchant commentator on South Africa. I was to spend many convivial hours in future years with the Louw and Pogrund families, and with the wide circle of hard-hitting critics of apartheid that had managed to survive during South Africa's difficult years of narrowing freedom.[18] (The Suzmans and I watched the *Sandra Laing* film in Benjie and Anne Sassoon Pogrunds' living room, with windows covered.)

In order to appreciate the full measure of South Africa's so far successful security operations, Pogrund suggested that I try to see General Hendrik van den Bergh, the head of the fearsome and secretive Bureau of State Security (BOSS). (Van den Bergh imprisoned Pogrund briefly before they became nodding antagonists, with Pogrund the astute crusading journalist that he was and van den Bergh attempting to propagandize through Pogrund, too smart and too skeptical to fall for van den Bergh's glosses and embellishments.)[19]

Towering and confident, van den Bergh ushered me into a stark conference room at his headquarters in Pretoria. He sat at one end of a long table, me at the other end. Given his forbidding reputation and his position of enormous power within the apartheid regime, I expected him to be little forthcoming. Instead, he was voluble about preventing South Africa from being overrun by communists, about the virtues of separate development, and about how increasingly strong and comprehensive South African intelligence gathering was becoming under his watch. He clearly wanted me to carry a misleading message back to the United States that BOSS was formidable, prepared, less racist than anti-outlaw, and guided by a determination to preserve white dominance while gradually uplifting Africans. Since I knew that van den Bergh was very close to Prime Minister Vorster, who had only recently succeeded Hendrik Verwoerd as South Africa's head of government, I knew that my disinformation was coming from near to the apex of Afrikanerdom. Van den Bergh was also a confident and ruthless key figure in the Broederbond—the Band of Brothers—that had helped to chart political direction for the National Party. From him, Africans could expect no quarter. He was intent on winning, no matter how many innocent African lives were mangled or how many suspects were tortured until they "tumbled" out of high windows in BOSS' interrogation centers. Suzman called van den Bergh "South Africa's own Heinrich Himmler."[20]

Van den Bergh had been Vorster's closest confidant since they had both been interned for Nazi sympathies. When Vorster was Verwoerd's minister of justice in the early 1960s, van den Bergh created a secret service called Republican Intelligence to "protect" the National Party and Afrikaners from hostile outsiders and from the likes of the ANC and the PAC. In 1968, Republican Intelligence became the nucleus of BOSS, with van den Bergh thereafter successfully usurping prime functions hitherto held by military intelligence and the elite security police. But he won hardly any friends in the competing services as BOSS soon doubled in size. Although few South Africans were fully aware of his influence on Vorster and on policy developments generally, van den Bergh was the architect (along with Mulder, successively minister of information, interior, and plural relations) of South Africa's outreach to the rest of Africa, of its determination to consort effectively with Israel, and of its attempt to improve South Africa's image abroad. (That is presumably why he consented to see me.) Van den Bergh effectively was Vorster's crisis manager, but in the future his autocratic methods were to falter.[21]

In Cape Town, on this same visit, I spent nights with the leaders of NUSAS, and later quietly carried missives from them to contacts in New York; met Colin Eglin, leader of the Progressive Party (a friend whom I was to see often in later years); was introduced into the lively and exuberant free-thinking circle of Bennie Rabinowitz, another person who was to become a long-time friend; discussed anti-apartheid politics with Franklin Sonn and Alan Boesak, two teachers and—in time—Coloured political leaders (Sonn much later became President Mandela's ambassador to Washington); and started decade-long stimulating conversations with fellow academics at the Universities of Cape Town, the Western Cape, and Stellenbosch. Another fearless editor, Tony Heard of the *Cape Times*, was then exposing apartheid's cruelties as best he could; we were to see much of each other over succeeding years. Each of these and many other acquaintances in Cape Town, Kimberley, Johannesburg, and Pretoria enlightened me about aspects of apartheid that should have been obvious in their invidious impact on both blacks and whites, but that often were hidden in plain sight. Outside observers like myself needed all of the insights gleaned from interviews, casual encounters, social gatherings, and daily participatory observations to begin to draw conclusions about the desperate quality of life under apartheid, and about the hypocrisies that were integral to its existence and its propaganda. White rule was predicated on double-talk and doublethink, perpetual prevarication, and continuous cruelty.[22]

After returning from South Africa to MIT, where I had begun teaching political science and history in 1968, I reported on the opinion pages of both *Newsday* and the Sunday *Washington Post* that although there had been a few hopeful breaks in the rigid apartheid armor—judges had acquitted a few prominent Africans supposedly seeking the government's overthrow, the state-owned railways had begun tentatively to open up employment opportunities for skilled Africans, and South Africa had reached out to the rest of Africa and welcomed Banda with electrifying attention and honors—these were but glacial shifts that hardly portended the lessening of the impress of minority rule. Welcoming

Banda was a sales job meant to deceive the skeptical world; the acquittals were a fortunate aberration.

Both of my articles denounced "separate development" as a sham. This was a policy devised by Prime Minister Vorster, van den Bergh, and cabinet ministers such as Koornhof and Mulder, with the approval of the Broederbond, to give the semblance of autonomy to puppet homeland regimes (Bantustans) in order to pretend that South Africa was only for whites and that the satellite labor reservoirs were the real and the true homes of blacks. Hence the wild nomenclature of "plural development" as well as "separate development."

"Separate development" was outdated by 1980, and even Prime Minister Pieter W. Botha recognized that it was more useless fiction than helpful policy. "Even if the impoverished overcrowded pseudostates," I wrote, "had a future as quasi- or semiautonomous bodies . . . they ha[d] failed to attract Africans away from the urban areas." Indeed, Pretoria paid 80 percent of the costs of running even the so-called independent homelands.[23]

Most of the designated heads of the thirteen Bantustans were thoroughly vetted and mostly compliant satraps eager to cash in personally (and for their relatives) on the largesse of the state. But one homeland, that of KwaZulu (then the Zululand Territorial Authority, with a Zulu population of 4.5 million), was led by the magnetic, ambitious, and domineering Chief Mangosuthu Gatsha Buthelezi. I knew him from meetings in the United States, and met him once more near the Johannesburg (now the Oliver Tambo) international airport. At that session in a nearby Holiday Inn I urged him to make the Zulu Territorial Authority as democratic in reality and appearance as possible, in order to show the architects of apartheid how African leaders could govern well. But Buthelezi was quick to assure me that he would not let rivals win even one seat in the Zulu assembly. He had his dignity and authority to uphold.

Buthelezi even then abhorred separate development but told me that he had accepted the challenge nevertheless to work within the only framework "open to black political leaders." "I made it clear," he told me, "that the role I am now playing is that of bringing change within the framework of present government policy." Or so he hoped, vainly. He planned to take Zululand to "independence" in order to improve black lives and to give him leverage to change all of South Africa for the better. "They promised us human dignity," Buthelezi told me, but if they want to give it to us separately, then at least "it must be full human dignity as understood anywhere else."[24] Within what became the Zulu homeland, Buthelezi certainly attempted in succeeding years to give his people a fuller dignity than they could achieve elsewhere in South Africa. But doing so was again a mirage; homelands were a dead end, and separate development was a public relations exercise that served mostly and unsuccessfully to divert attention from the evils of apartheid.[25]

I said as much in the long Sunday *Washington Post* article, and also compared South African repression to what I had experienced in Haiti. In no other states where I had spent time researching politics was fear "so pervasive." In Port au Prince, its capital, and elsewhere in the republic ruled by dictator François (Papa Doc) Duvalier (whom I had interviewed at length in 1968), "Conversations could only be held in fast-moving motor vehicles. People lowered their voices in restaurants, talked out of the corners of their mouths, and listened for tell-tale clicks on their telephones."[26] My *Washington Post* article went on to urge the Nixon administration to refrain from aligning itself with those on Capitol Hill who ignorantly backed South Africa as a bastion of anticommunism important in helping to win the Cold War. The existential battle in South Africa was for its soul, and for the health, wealth, and sanctity of its many inhabitants who were not white, not Afrikaners, and thoroughly oppressed. The U.S. government needed to join the ultimately winning side, I said, for deeply moral as well as starkly strategic reasons. Sobukwe and even Buthelezi were important harbingers of what could be, together with Mandela and others once they were conceivably released from prison. Van den Bergh, however, represented to me (although I never said so in print) evil personified.

Because of the *Post* article, probably because I had consorted openly with Sobukwe, possibly because I had met the NUSAS leaders, and who knows what else, I was asked to visit the South African ambassador to Washington. He rebuked me personally, calling the *Post* contribution offensive and denigrating. I also received an official letter from Pretoria designating me as a "prohibited immigrant." I was henceforth banned from entering South Africa, from renewing my research on Rhodes, and from continuing to visit my new friends and acquaintances in South Africa. But being a prohibited immigrant did not mean that I could not follow events in South Africa, and comment on them in the press frequently and critically, until returning to that corner of the globe was again possible.

Challenges to Apartheid

When Arthur Ashe, an African American tennis star, played against South African whites in a tournament in Johannesburg (a van den Bergh ploy), I had to remind the U.S. public that apartheid regulations still prevented local blacks from using "white" facilities or moving about freely within their own nation. Julian Bond, chair of the National Association for the Advancement of Colored People, and John Lewis, celebrated survivor of beatings at Selma, Alabama, and a Democratic Congressman from Georgia, had also visited South Africa. And Buthelezi had been permitted for the first time to travel to other parts of Africa and to Europe and again to the United States. But apartheid was as vicious as ever, despite these cosmetic moves. "The color of a person's skin still governs," I wrote. "Even as he was welcoming Ashe, the minister of sport was forbidding local soccer matches . . . between African and white teams." The minister of interior was deporting pesky white missionaries and placing black clergy under house arrest. The visits of Ashe, Bond, Lewis, and others from outside hardly altered South Africa's "dreary official antagonism to African betterment and the sameness of continued racial intolerance."[27]

Those who wanted to do away with apartheid, I wrote, must hope for an unlikely internal revolution. The forces of repression remained strong, the ANC guerrilla operation gathering momentum in Zambia and Tanzania too weak, underground opposition within the country still protean (despite Biko's appeal), and a mass revolution inconceivable immediately. European boycotts of South African citrus exports ("out with Outspan") were symbolically important, but would not bring down the regime. Nor would oil embargoes, because only about 30 percent of the country's energy needs came from outside. Anyway, Iran and Indonesia were sanctions-busters, and were secretly supplying petroleum to South Africa. Moreover, South Africa was successfully using an old German process to refine crude oil from abundant low-quality coal. South Africans would, in any event, tighten their consumer belts long before they backed away from white supremacy. I was pessimistic, bitterly, but the American public and decision-makers should refuse, I said, to be gulled by obfuscation and diversion arranged by van den Bergh and his ilk.

Separate development was becoming more and more central, as well, to South Africa's attempt to sell itself, again cynically, to an unsuspecting world as a benevolent ruler of disparate peoples. It was proceeding to make its first Bantustan "independent." In late 1976, the Transkei, the major homeland of about 2.3 million Xhosa-speaking South Africans (many of whom really resided in urban areas; Mandela was of Xhosa lineage) became "independent," meaning that nominally it could set its own rules and could ignore security and similar restrictions set by its South African sovereign. Indeed, to celebrate its new autonomy, the Transkei decided to hold a conference on what it could and should do in the future. I was invited to participate. This was doubly useful because the Bureau of Intelligence and Research in the U.S. State Department had asked me to organize a major report on South Africa's homeland system, and I also needed to follow political developments in Namibia.

Since traveling to Umtata (now Mthatha), the capital of the Transkei, would mean a transit through Johannesburg, and a potential breach of my immigration ban, I took advice from John Barratt, my colleague and close collaborator who headed the South African Institute of International Relations, and from another friend, John Dugard, professor of law at the University of the Witwatersrand and a champion of African rights. They agreed that because the Transkei's independence was at stake, I'd probably be able to slip in transit from the Johannesburg airport to Umtata. And so I did.

But then there was the return transit, en route to Namibia (which South Africa still controlled, tightly). (See chapter 10.) Because there was no immediate flight to Windhoek, the capital of what was still South-West Africa, I was hustled by the immigration authorities into the hands of the police and ushered behind bars into a section of the airport transit hotel where South African security held culprits. I managed to pass a telephoned message to my wife, at home, and she contacted the U.S. Department of State. The next morning U.S. Ambassador William Bowdler arrived, to my happy surprise. We talked about what to do. I still hoped to travel to Namibia rather than directly home to Boston. A message eventually arrived. Mulder, then the minister of interior, summoned me to Pretoria for an interrogation. Where was I going? What did I want to do in Namibia? And so on.

Tapping a large pile of files on his desk, the bluff-faced Mulder told me that they were all about my "doings." I asked to see them to refute the information that they contained. He laughed and said that since the files were not his that he would have to consult "others" before making a decision on what to do with me. So I stepped out of the room, under guard, and waited. Finally, Mulder summoned me back into his presence and announced that, as a special favor, I could spend the night at a designated hotel near the airport (and off its grounds and out of police control) and then go on to Windhoek the next day. My prohibited immigrant status was revoked and I was now officially on parole within South Africa for the night (which I spent at a memorable dinner party at the Suzman house rather than at the designated hotel).

Thereafter, I could enter South Africa, but always with trepidation and fearful apprehension when I stood in the long immigration queues at the airport near Johannesburg. I could resume my research on Rhodes, complete what became a book on the homelands, and finish *Suffer the Future: Policy Choices in Southern Africa* (Harvard University Press) a book that appeared in 1980. I was also busy in those years writing in the press for American and European (and even South African) audiences on the struggle within South Africa.

The revolution that had seemed so remote a few years before had, as well, come a little closer. A few months before my visit to the Transkei, African schoolboys in Soweto had taken to the streets to protest their lack of educational opportunity, their compulsory instruction in Afrikaans—the language of the oppressor—and the social and economic constraints under which all blacks lived. This was the Soweto Uprising that engulfed twenty-eight townships and thirty-three square miles of the sprawling satellite city of Johannesburg and then spread across the country to enflame the ghettoes of Pretoria, Port Elizabeth, East London, Cape

Town, Ladysmith, Klerksdorp, and 150 other communities, plus all of the segregated university campuses that the government had created since 1959.

In June 1976, police fired into a large crowd of 20,000 schoolchildren who were marching through Orlando (within Soweto) in order to protest against their political and educational deprivations. A few days before, they had begun boycotting classes because of the government's insistence that elementary schools should begin teaching classes in Afrikaans, not English. With their consciousness having been raised by SASO and SASM, they had innumerable other grievances as well.[28] The recent removal of Portuguese colonial control of Mozambique and Angola also influenced militant black South African attitudes and hopes.

As violence proliferated from Orlando, with Africans marching in Cape Town, Johannesburg, and beyond, angry black youths destroyed *shebeens* (illegal bars), kept schools from receiving pupils well into 1977, and helped to diminish economic vitality across the land. Nearly 700 Africans and others, mostly under twenty-five years old and some as young as thirteen, lost their lives. Two-thirds were shot by the police. Another 4,000 or so were wounded. More than 1,000 were arrested and more than 200 young people under eighteen years old were detained. SASO and SASM were banned. So were the Union of Black Journalists, the Christian Institute, and *The World*, the country's leading black-run daily newspaper (with a circulation of about 178,000). Percy Qoboza, its thoughtful editor and a friend from his days as a Nieman Fellow at Harvard, was imprisoned first in a multistory security prison in Johannesburg, where I visited him as soon as possible, and later outside the city in Modder B, a notorious prison, where we talked several times through a wire grille for the allotted ten minutes.

Nthato Motlana, a trim and fit Fort Hare graduate with a ready smile who later became Mandela's personal physician, was also incarcerated after the Uprising. I had known Motlana well before Soweto rose up and celebrated with him by mail when he was finally permitted a passport to travel to the United States and to see the world earlier in 1976. Indeed, he was sitting at my breakfast table at a remote hilltop location in New Hampshire's White Mountains eating raisin bran and bananas when a BBC news broadcast alerted us both to the Soweto Uprising. Motlana made some quick telephone calls home to South Africa, cut short his visit to the United States, and hastily flew back to become one of the leaders of the Soweto Committee of Ten.[29] It attempted forlornly to end mayhem and achieve greater rights for striking Africans of all ages. On each of my subsequent visits to South Africa, I always spent time with Motlana in and out of Soweto.

Biko's ideological purity and his concerted call for self-reliance had helped to embolden students and even their elders during the Uprising and after. He explained that for Africans to be involved with and somewhat dependent upon whites, especially liberals, was a trap that prevented Africans from exerting

Figure 6.3. Nthato Motlana

their power and breaking the yoke of oppression. He opposed the rise of homeland leaders. He fought against the "realism" that seemed to motivate older black politicians. He did everything he could to uplift the self-esteem of a younger generation of South Africans who had come—he argued—to accept subjugation. But, after being banned for years, Biko was infamously killed by the police in 1977. His captors battered him (pathologists reported five brain lesions) and inflicted more injuries during a 750-mile desperate drive (with Biko shackled, naked, in the back of a Land Rover) en route to a prison hospital in Pretoria. "We end," said his family's counsel at the inquest, "with Steve Biko dying a miserable and lonely death on a mat on a stone floor."[30] That was a metaphor for the end of any semblance of decency in a South Africa run by apartheid apparatchiks.

The Southern Lusophone Factor

White-run, apartheid consumed, South Africa could no longer escape heavy global criticism. South Africa could no longer assume (although many of its political leaders probably did) that a minority of whites could forever control an increasingly enlarged and increasingly aggrieved and aggravated majority.

Equally, Africans could not expect that the Soviet-backed legions of the ANC in exile, even comforted by the Frente de Libertação de Moçambique's victory in Mozambique and Movimento Popular de Libertação de Angola's triumph in Angola, could overturn apartheid by invading from without, or dislodge the regime even by intermittent sabotage and targeted killings within the country. No colonial powers in Africa had ever been ousted by force alone, even in the Lusophone territories.

A military coup in Portugal itself, rather than guerrilla victories in the overseas territories, had helped Mozambique and Angola, and Cape Verde, São Tomé and Principe, and Guinea-Bissau to overcome their colonial overlords. But that coup at home in 1974 was a product of dissatisfaction with the overseas wars, with how thoroughly those interminable hostilities had harmed the economic growth and social betterment of mainland Portuguese, and with a desire on the part of younger officers to end the Antonio Salazar dictatorship that was limiting progress for Portuguese within Europe and the world.

In southern Africa, Lusophone revolutionary movements were poised to assume control: Soviet-supported Frelimo in Mozambique, led by Samora Machel and Joaquim Chissano, and the MPLA in Angola under the control of Agostinho Neto and Eduardo dos Santos, were already active against their overlords from bases in adjacent countries, with Cuban and Soviet backing. The coup in Lisbon enabled both movements to surge forward and take control of their respective territories despite the opposition of South Africa to both assumptions of power and despite South Africa's interventions in both former colonies on behalf of internal opposition movements.

In Angola, the MPLA for several years fought a rival non-Marxist contesting force, UNITA (União Nacional para a Independência Total de Angola). It was led by Jonas Savimbi, a southern Angolan who was supported and funded by South Africa and, for a time, by the United States. Diamonds in southern Angola were a rich resource that both contenders wished to exploit. Only well after independence in 1975 was the MPLA able with Cuban cooperation to overcome the Savimbi salient and to fold him and his movement into the new political structure of the country. By then it was pumping petroleum in large quantities, too, so the combat over diamond riches became less determinative. Savimbi also gradually forfeited his South African backing. With neighboring Namibia's independence in 1990, and the encompassing victory there of Swapo (see chapter 10), South Africa no longer needed a dissident and disruptive ally in Angola, so Savimbi lost his strongest backer.[31]

At the onset of its independence, Frelimo in Mozambique also was compelled to battle for hegemony within the country with a South African– and Rhodesian-funded proxy called Renamo (Resistência Nacional Moçambicana), led by Afonso Dhlakama. Kamuzu Banda's Malawi also helped Renamo. Even well after

Frelimo was unquestionably in control of the state, by 1990 anyway, Renamo still continued in political opposition, a complexity that effectively remained until Dhlakama's death in 2018.[32]

From Armageddon to Apotheosis

South Africa was vulnerable economically over the long term, but probably not in the short term even though new foreign investment was becoming limited. I counseled a number of American and Canadian firms during this period; new investments could not be considered secure. Existing investments might continue to make sense so long as their South African subsidiaries focused more and more on employee welfare and training, and became or remained providers of hospitable workplaces. If American-owned corporations wished to prosper, and ready themselves for the return (someday) of civility and majority rule in South Africa, they should better the lives of their workers and do everything possible to distance themselves from apartheid. That was a message delivered directly by me to U.S., British, Canadian, and occasionally even South African executives over much of the 1970s and 1980s.[33]

South Africa could still profitably sell its supplies of gold and diamonds on the world market. Platinum, ferrochrome, iron ore, and many more metals remained in demand and South Africa's mining industry was productive thanks to a plethora of underpaid and strictly regimented black workers. (Helen Suzman and I took an investigative tour one day—she in her official parliamentary role—of the crowded and insalubrious hostels in which single mine laborers were confined.) The country had dealt effectively with its petroleum needs, its electric generating system then worked, and labor supplies were abundant because of the hated pass laws and separate development. Potable water was not yet in short supply. Black labor on white-run farms also produced an abundance of maize, wheat, sugar, vegetables, and more. For whites, with the Vietnam War's demand for metals still robust, economic prospects were promising. For most Africans, especially those forced to reside in or go back to the homelands, living conditions were marginal, and unlikely to improve so long as their freedom of movement were curtailed along with restrictions on their freedom of occupation and denials of educational advancement.

Given white South Africa's determination to survive, and to maintain the onerous exactions of apartheid as long as possible, I counseled readers, opinion makers, congressional committees, the State Department, and corporate executives to expect a prolonged confrontation between good and evil for the soul of South Africa. The accession of Prime Minister Pieter W. Botha in 1978, succeeding Vorster, indicated no shift in Afrikaner thinking. He had served as defense minister for many years and was just as *verkrampte* ("narrow, cramped, closed minded") as his predecessor.

In the aftermath of the Soweto Uprising and Biko's tragic demise, Botha's South Africa confronted a tsunami of discontent. Black unemployment was rising; the young were restless and spoiling for positive change; even some of the homeland leaders were becoming feisty. Botha, I wrote, would likely try to tough it out, but he was both imperious and volatile as a leader, with a fierce temper. Even so, he seemed more aware than Vorster of apartheid's practical (not moral) weaknesses.[34]

Botha's mantra for his nation was "adapt or die." He condemned the Immorality and Mixed Marriages acts as unnecessary. He approved mixed sporting events and began removing such staples of the color bar as separate queuing lines at post offices. He permitted Africans to establish trade unions. (I spent hours discussing various improvements contemplated for African workers with Nic Wiehahn, Botha's principal, comparatively enlightened, advisor on industrial matters.) Bishop Desmond Tutu, later Archbishop and Nobel Laureate, and then Secretary of the South African Council of Churches, asked Botha to do more—to create a common citizenship within an undivided nation, to upgrade educational opportunities for blacks, and to abolish pass laws.[35]

In 1979 and 1980, African and Coloured schoolchildren protested almost daily against their denial of educational rights and for educational improvements. They clashed frequently with the police, fatalities followed, and an almost perpetual state of high tension pervaded the townships that surrounded South Africa's major cities. Older Africans and Coloureds stoned police vehicles, and even the sleepy mining center of Kimberley erupted in violence.

The children and their elders campaigned for better schools, better teachers, and more funding to supply educational facilities and learning materials equal to those of whites. (South Africa in 1980 was spending $1,000 per white child, $300 per Coloured student, and only $100 on each African pupil.) And despite sympathetic rhetoric from Botha, absolutely no improvements were implemented.

Botha was much more interested in keeping his white political supporters loyal. Moreover, he was intensely focused on preemptive strikes against ANC operatives in neighboring states, hence the increasingly bold attacks from the air on bases in Zambia and Angola, on assassinations and attempted kidnappings in Botswana, on attempts to cut off ANC infiltration routes through Eswatini (then Swaziland), and more. Indeed, his government concocted a "total strategy" against what he and military commanders called the red threat—the "total onslaught"—that supposedly was pointed dagger-like toward the heart of South Africa. This was the new securocratic state that Botha, with his lengthy ties to the defense establishment, believed would be his country's most formidable bulwark against assaults from without. At home, he and his associates also wanted to remove all protest leaders from society at all costs. (Hence the brutal murders of the Cradock Four, and many other atrocities later investigated by South Africa's Truth and Reconciliation Commission.)[36]

An admiral in charge of military intelligence introduced me to the "red threat" in 1982. In a large conference room in Pretoria, amid a gathering of more than fifty of his colleagues, the admiral attempted—in all seriousness—to persuade me (another act of disinformation) that Soviet communism was bent on destroying South Africa by thrusting from Tanzania southwestward to what became Gauteng. Indeed, the admiral had large charts showing the red threat with bright crimson arrows descending across the continent in South Africa's direction. I wanted to laugh, but of course could not. The idea that the reds were hounding South Africa was ludicrous on many levels; that menace was amplified, naturally, to provide a rationale for the "total strategy." When I talked (fairly often) to Foreign Minister Roelof (Pik) Botha (no relation to his boss), I sensed an awareness of how silly the securocratic ideology truly was, but the propaganda war may also have blinded some of the intelligence analysts to the true nature of the legitimate and inescapable threat to white South Africa.[37]

By the early 1980s, South Africa had largely lost the global public relations struggle. Internally, too, the coming of age of new post-Soweto university graduates had spawned the United Democratic Front (UDF), led by the likes of Archie Gumede, Oscar Mpetha, trade unionists such as Mohammed Valli and (later president) Cyril Ramaphosa, and several others. Inside the nation, it was able to do more to rattle the apartheid state through sabotage, fire bombings, and consciousness-raising than anything perpetrated by the ANC from outside. (The UDF was loyal to the ANC, however.)[38] The UDF also sponsored effective township rent and consumer boycotts, slowed liquor store sales, used funeral marches to campaign against the government, tried to hinder criminal gang activity in order win the trust and support of most urban Africans, and harassed the repressive forces of apartheid however and wherever it could. As a movement sprung from the innards of apartheid policy precipitated turmoil, the UDF "demonstrated that black groups, when capable of overcoming their differences, had the potential to immobilize white power in the townships."[39]

Pragmatic though Prime Minister Botha seemed, he remained committed to separate development, even pushing two small, impoverished homelands—Venda and Ciskei—to opt for "independence." I called the entire policy of homelandization, especially fake satrapy independence, a dark dead end. Ninety percent of Venda's income depended on remittances from South African urban workers; as a homeland it was run by a cabal of corrupt thugs reporting to a white "ambassador."[40]

An international commission on which I served recommended definitively against Ciskei's independence; instead, we advocated an ingenious arrangement linking African areas labeled "Ciskei" to surrounding white urban and farming areas, the innovative result being labeled a condominium and freed from all South African racial laws.[41] Both Prime Minister Botha and Lennox Sebe, the Ciskei's ruler, dismissed our report out of hand and quickly embraced independence for the tiny domain (pop. 700,000) along the country's southeastern coast.

The prime minister and several of his cabinet ministers (especially Koornhof, then Minister of Cooperation and Development) paid lip service to ameliorating the disparities in service, residence, social relations, schooling, and essential freedoms under which Africans lived their lives. But whatever alterations in black life ensued were minor, on the surface, and far less than Africans wanted and thought that they deserved.

The most dramatic of these reforms during the Botha effort was his introduction of a spankingly new constitutional dispensation for the nation. His contorted trilateral Parliament was inaugurated in 1983, after several years of discussion within the National Party and the Broederbond, white support in a referendum, and some bitter internal divisions. Dangerous and pernicious, this attempt to provide a modicum of autonomous self-government for the hitherto disenfranchised 2.9 million Coloureds and 860,000 Asian South Africans did nothing for 18 million black South Africans. It persisted in denying political participation to the majority. Even the other "nonwhites," with their separate parliamentary chambers, would only be able to debate matters pertaining to themselves—to their own communities. The parliamentary chamber for 4.7 million whites (the continuation of the existing national Parliament) would be able to outvote the other two chambers combined. Whites, in other words, would give up nothing. Once again apartheid South Africa was attempting to toy with the world, pretending that reform was in the air, when nothing of the sort was even remotely contemplated.

The Reagan administration and some foreign businessmen were indeed taken in, however, calling the parliamentary changes "better than nothing." The U.S. State Department saw these changes as a welcome first step. Some even believed that an African chamber could be added later. But that was never the design. Botha said repeatedly that Africans could expect neither political representation nor common treatment as citizens of South Africa (rather than in the homelands). Indeed, his administration continued to remove Africans from "white" areas. Africans obviously sought instead a nonfragmented South Africa in which they had equal rights and the opportunity to exercise a full and free franchise.

The bastions of apartheid were being buttressed, not removed. The new constitution also transformed Prime Minister Botha into an executive president with enhanced authority. Whites gained power. Coloureds and Asians gained a modest voice. Africans lost—once again. All that had happened was a repackaging. "No one in power," I wrote, "is concerning himself with or articulating a vision for South Africa that addresses the common concerns of all."[42]

Indeed, South Africa's absolute denial of the rights of the swelling majority had gone beyond enforced segregation toward perpetual exclusion. By attempting artificially to reconfigure apartheid without altering its core, the white government invited wholly unprecedented levels of indigenous asperity and retaliation. When desultory elections to the subsidiary parliamentary chambers were held in 1984, Africans watched angrily from the sidelines. In print, after several visits during those years to South Africa, and long conversations with Suzman and Frederik van zyl Slabbert and Alex Boraine, leaders in Parliament of the newly energized Progressive Federal Party, I argued that the nation was becoming more divided and tense, not less, and that Botha's government was digging its own political grave by refusing to begin accommodating Africans in a meaningful and honest manner.[43]

At home in the United States, I also battled intellectually against the Reagan administration's misguided policy of "constructive engagement." My colleague Chester Crocker was Assistant Secretary of State for Africa; it was his well-intended but misconceived policy that myself and many others sought to combat in the halls of Washington and elsewhere. Constructive engagement meant "sweet-talking" South Africa, the lifting of embargoes on a range of strategic exports, including nuclear fuel, and relaxing visa and other restrictions. I said that such a policy was and would increasingly be damaging to American goals in Africa and South Africa, and was also fundamentally harmful to South African black interests. And it would ultimately, I prophesied, be self-defeating. U.S. support for South Africa was doing almost nothing for Africans stuck in the maw of apartheid. Furthermore, U.S. policy predilections were driving Angola and Mozambique more fully into the Soviet orbit.[44]

South Africa's townships erupted at this time (1984) into rapid bursts of protest. That led inevitably to brutal and fatal battles between repressive police forces (reinforced by military contingents) and the youthful protestors. More than 600 Africans lost their lives in such clashes by early 1985; thousands were wounded. The government naturally responded by jailing the leaders of the UDF—"the very moderate black leaders with whom a government bent on reform would want to negotiate." But Botha called them communists (in line with the "total onslaught" mode of thinking). I concluded, again based on a recent visit and detailed conversations with Motlana, UDF leaders, and the white Progressives, that "until white South Africa agrees to negotiate with blacks for the lasting future of the country, cycles of violence and repression are certain to continue." Indeed, "Only a major effort to give blacks a stake in gradually evolving South Africa would do."[45]

Mandela as South Africa's Jailer

Reagan began to criticize South Africa for the first time, recognizing that "constructive engagement" was accomplishing too little. Botha also decided to cross the proverbial Rubicon, recognizing that the tide of failure was lapping at the once tidy shores of apartheid. In 1985, Botha gave a much-advertised, heavily hyped, and greatly anticipated speech about reforming South Africa, headlined "Crossing the Rubicon." Despite it being heralded beforehand as a major shift in official thinking, all it did (I was in South Africa at the time, listening with my Progressive parliamentary friends, mouths agape) was to dismay white liberals and black progressives. Botha startled his listeners by promising more repression, not less, and by offering only some very limited legislative modifications of apartheid's systematic denigration of black aspirations. The speech was underwhelming, a vivid testimony to the poverty of Afrikaner responses to a nation increasingly consumed by violent protest. It satisfied almost no one, at home or abroad. Because international investors and business conglomerate leaders were as appalled as Africans, I proposed that Botha's Rubicon speech had driven South Africa inexorably and probably terminally into tragedy.[46]

Botha and his close colleagues still believed that they could orchestrate and control change, and could do so without disrupting the even tenor of a white-dominated economy (an economy that depended on black labor, at every level, in every pursuit) and society. The difference between such tactical maneuvering and some fundamental strategic repositioning was profound. The creation of a tricameral Parliament and the Rubicon's limited social concessions produced results that were directly contrary to those intended and desired. The South African government simply could not hear the message of a South African drama that was racing pell-mell toward its denouement.

Constructive engagement was finished; the United States even imposed sanctions, albeit mild ones. Reagan's *volte-face* was important, but much more telling were the stern conditions increasingly being imposed by international businessmen with regard to investments in South Africa. The financiers of the West turned against South Africa, forcing its rulers to concentrate their minds and consider options that were starkly novel. Most efficacious, as it developed, were not the efforts of colleges and universities to demand disinvestment—to sell shares in companies that continued to do business in and with South Africa—but the decision of key banks in the United States to cease rolling over ninety-day loans to a government that hitherto—for decades—had routinely anticipated renewals without question. This last intervention hindered South Africa's fiscal liquidity and drove a key stake into the very belly of apartheid. Additional impalements followed official American bans on investment in South Africa (from 1986), bans against bank lending, and prohibitions of anything American that could contribute to South African military might. Congress placed embargoes on the import of raw materials such as ferrochrome and manganese from South Africa. It banned South African Airways from landing in the United States.[47]

Coetsee and a few others around Botha finally understood about 1985 that the absolute key to South Africa's future was locked away on Robben Island, where Mandela had cemented his legitimacy with older militants and also with the new younger post-Soweto generation. Botha even offered to free Mandela if he would renounce violence and take up residence in the Transkei, a plea of desperation that Mandela easily recognized and movingly rebuffed.

Africans, and Mandela and the ANC, would be satisfied by nothing less than fresh keys to the political kingdom. Whereas some black opponents might have been fobbed off in the 1970s by the dismantling of apartheid and some serious grants of political participation to true indigenous leaders, by 1985 there were no holding Africans back. Mandela, as I wrote on several occasions then and in succeeding years, was effectively South Africa's jailer. Only with his cooperation and agreement could South Africa move forward to the promised land of peace and cooperation. And only with Mandela's acquiescence could whites find a satisfactory place within what would certainly become an embattled and confused black-run, potentially multiracial, society.

Those were among my observations in 1985 and 1986, as I spent as much time as I could closely eyeing the South African dilemma and its end game. Whites could gain more for themselves the sooner that they embraced honest change, and negotiated its contours with Africans. The more that they procrastinated, the fewer options they would have. "Every week that the white government forfeits, the black opposition gains additional credibility."[48]

By the middle of 1986, nearly two years and 1,500 deaths into the tribulations of the townships, the apartheid government demonstrably had lost the initiative.[49] Yet Botha's only response was to keep detaining dissidents, a grand total of 3,000 being under lock and key by mid-1986. Townships were subject to curfews and police sweeps, to no avail.

Such actions led nowhere. Even a politically influential organization of Afrikaners and important business groups were advocating the introduction of a universal franchise, forgetting or not realizing that African leaders (in the UDF and the ANC both) would accept nothing less than a meaningful share of power. Mandela's release was every important African spokesperson's demand. Even Buthelezi refused to talk any more to the white government until it released Mandela.[50] The latter's blessing was imperative if South Africa were ever to move toward peace, and to prosper.

White South African opposition leaders such as Slabbert and a few Afrikaners who were fronting for the government began to meet clandestinely with the ANC in Africa, in Europe, and in the United States. It was evident, finally, that the ANC and Mandela were both integral to any resolution of the apartheid-induced crisis. Many of the critical leaders of the ANC were Marxists, but—after having visited with Thabo Mbeki and other ANC leaders in Lusaka—its top leaders were, wrote I, "thoroughly bourgeois." It was important, I said, to parley earlier rather than later with Mandela, his aging prison mates, and the ANC in exile.[51] But, as much as Botha and a few of his trusted ministers and officials were anxious to talk seriously with Mandela, the other prisoners, and Mbeki and others in the guerrilla camps, some Afrikaners revolted rightward, and Botha was compelled to confront a breakaway farther right-wing party, the Conservatives. A 1987 election and subsequent by-elections showed their strength as the Conservatives doubled their percentage of the white vote and replaced the Progressives as the official parliamentary opposition. Clearly, positive change in South Africa would not come through the (white) ballot box.

The economy at the same time was suffering from inflation and a depreciated currency, new shortages of foreign exchange, and the country's increasingly obvious isolation from the rest of the world, especially from the West and Japan. The government, reacting badly, cracked down on press freedom and detained African editors and acclaimed African moderates. In early 1988, Botha's regime was in full retreat from any previously contemplated accommodation of African political participatory aspirations. These *verkrampte* actions were, admittedly, taking place while closed-door discussions with Mandela were underway. (He had meanwhile been moved from Robben Island to a more comfortable prison on the mainland near Cape Town.)

Apartheid had failed and several of the sensible and pragmatic members of Botha's cabinet were fully aware that the game was up. By the end of 1988, harsh demographic and economic realities had overtaken dreams of white supremacy. Whites were fewer than 5 million. Africans were 21 million in number and doubling demographically every twenty years. Despite influx control and the other madcap strictures of apartheid, the cities were 75 percent black, and swelling in size daily. The country's GDP had stopped rising. Job growth had fallen behind population increases. Capital flight was steady. Formal unemployment for Africans was at least 50 percent. I calculated at one point that South Africa had not created a net new job in twenty years.

The fate of white South Africa, and the future of whatever the country was to become, were fully in Mandela's hands. "His legitimacy, reinforced and sanctified by white venom and long years of incarceration," was unique. South Africa was stalemated so long as Mandela was not free. Only Mandela could give South Africa a chance to emerge whole. He was "Botha's jailer."[52]

Botha's government was caught in a comprehensive prisoner's dilemma. Doing nothing would only postpone the days of reckoning, and diminish its bargaining position. But Botha feared the creeping white Right. It was clear to me and many others in and out of South Africa that Botha's only possible good choice was to release Mandela unconditionally (he would leave prison no other way), and to start bargaining with him about the future of the nation. Botha could then, I argued in print, transform himself from a rearguard survivalist into a statesman. But all of this line of argument was subsumed when Botha, seventy-three, suffered a (mild) stroke in early 1989 and was quickly replaced as the head of the National Party (and later president) by Frederik W. de Klerk, fifty-three, minister of national education and someone not previously active in the deliberations about Mandela and the nation's future. He possessed impeccable right-wing credentials, having spoken out frequently against scrapping social apartheid and having harassed multiracial universities. Therefore, I argued in the *New York Times*, South Africa had found its Nixon. "Just as President Nixon was able to go to China," so de Klerk could travel metaphorically to Soweto and Lusaka.

De Klerk was much less bedeviled than Botha by the hobgoblin of Afrikaner solidarity. I believed that he could and would make the necessary compromises with dogma and ideology that were required in a tense and economically weakened South Africa. What I did not know at the time, but learned afterward in discussions with him and his close associates, was that de Klerk—previously leader of the National Party in the Transvaal—had been strongly influenced by the Broederbond's thinking about South Africa's future. I predicted in 1989 that de Klerk would take "the great leap forward" and negotiate with Mandela. It was past time, and there were effectively no good alternatives.[53]

De Klerk, as he told me several years later, knew that he needed to act early, decisively, and boldly if he (and white South Africa) were to have any hope of guiding the nation toward a better future. (De Klerk was acting, he later told me, in order to create a livable and sustainable South Africa for his grandchildren.) Within four months, this process was well underway. Mandela took tea with Botha and visited de Klerk. Emissaries of the government were meeting with Mbeki in Lusaka and assuring him, so Mbeki told me, that Mandela's release would occur in 1990. Walter Sisulu was released from Robben Island in October 1989.

"The well-being of all in this country," de Klerk told Parliament in February 1990, was "linked inextricably to the ability of the leaders to come to terms with one another on a new dispensation. No one can escape this simple truth." He promised a "totally new and just constitutional dispensation in which every inhabitant will enjoy equal rights, treatment and opportunity in every sphere of endeavor."[54]

De Klerk released Mandela and unbanned the ANC and its other leaders. Yet bold strokes alone do not successful transitions make. De Klerk had to face down and contain the resurgent white Far Right (which remained a problem until after independence in 1994). He and Mandela, with subsequent deft assistance from Ramaphosa and Roelf Meyer, had to chart a course that led from release to a new constitution, elections, independence, reconciliation, justice, truth seeking, and the like.

De Klerk and his closest associates believed that even after Mandela's release and the welcoming home of ANC exiles and internal prisoners, whites could cleverly prevent full African dominance. De Klerk made none of his reforms "with the intention of putting himself out of power," Mandela subsequently wrote. "He made them for precisely the opposite reason: to ensure power for the Afrikaner in the new dispensation."[55] But Mandela, absolutely clear and steadfast, would not give way. Mandela had the top cards and, after immensely hard bargaining, Mandela always maintained a steady momentum that led to real change. No one could tamper with Mandela's legitimacy, his charisma, his genuine inclusionism—"We are all victors"—and his belief in black entitlement. Twenty-seven years in prison had prepared Mandela to lead even whites (as well as Africans) toward the rainbow nation's New Jerusalem.

A few crucial details still had to be finalized. De Klerk's government had to dismantle apartheid completely, which took until 1992. It was then possible for de Klerk to visit Nigeria, and for South African Airways to fly to numerous African capitals. Ambassadorial exchanges occurred. Europe started shipping petroleum products to South Africa after a seven-year boycott. World Cup competition welcomed South African cricketers back into its ranks. In 1993, Mandela allowed the globe's sanctions on South Africa to be lifted. South Africa had come in from the cold.

But all of these initiatives (and more) were theater compared to what was needed at home. Mandela and de Klerk and their representatives had serious conceptual differences. Negotiations broke down on numerous occasions in 1991 and 1992 over representation in the post-independence Parliament, over the rights that would be written into the new constitution, and—most of all— over the place of whites in the new South Africa. In 1992, the future joint Nobel Peace Prize winners called each other liars and deceivers. Mandela understood that de Klerk was worried about a right-wing military coup and was alarmed to learn that the National Party had earlier backed a "third force" that had murdered leaders of the UDF, bombed presumed opponents in neighboring nations, and even attempted to poison ANC leaders when they visited the United States. But some confidence was restored in late 1992 when de Klerk broke with Buthelezi's Zulu chauvinist Inkatha Freedom Party (which was causing mayhem in violent struggles against the ANC in townships near Johannesburg and in KwaZulu), and dismissed military hard-liners.[56] The masterstroke that gave de Klerk the confidence and assurances that he needed to deal fully with Mandela, however, was the preemptive calling of a referendum of mostly white voters in late 1992 that resulted in a massive victory for overwhelming positive change. Afterward, de Klerk and his team could negotiate with Mandela freely.

This victory constituted serious progress. But de Klerk and the ANC still disagreed over the extent to which the new South Africa would be a direct, one man, one vote, representative democracy. De Klerk and his team wanted safeguards for whites. Finally, Mandela persuaded de Klerk to give up a white veto over future parliamentary decisions. When it all came together thanks to the canny negotiations of Ramaphosa and Meyer, they left conclusive arrangements to be debated in a constituent assembly in 1993 and early 1994 that the ANC was sure to dominate.

After months of discussion, both sides accepted an entrenched justiciable bill of rights (vaguely on the American constitutional model, but with stronger and less ambiguous provisions). Specific clauses protected private property and established freedoms of religion, speech, and assembly. But Mandela refused to embrace the blanket amnesty for crimes perpetrated by whites during apartheid that some of de Klerk's people desired, and that later were incompletely addressed by the Truth and Reconciliation Commission that Tutu chaired and Boraine helped to run. The independence of the judges and courts were specified, and a constitutional court—embodying many of the features of American judicial review—was agreed upon (and has been much relied upon ever since). Whites and Buthelezi also obtained the partially decentralized system for which they advocated; former provinces were renamed and new ones created. Mandela and de Klerk also promised to forge a government of national unity after independence.

The new South Africa arrived in 1994, completing its remarkable transformation from unfree to free with great panache and enormous ease in April. In the nation's first expression of a complete franchise with 75 percent of eligible voters casting ballots, the ANC's proportional representation list (the ANC decided to adopt an extreme version of the Israeli method) won almost two-thirds of the total.[57] The feared white backlash receded, the security forces and the police stayed loyal (thanks to Mandela's inclusive leadership and his embrace of former white jailers and oppressors), and—in one joyous swoop of participatory democracy—the new South Africa arose from the ashes of apartheid. Mandela became president, with Mbeki anointed as his deputy (fatefully instead of Ramaphosa). Mandela and Mbeki now had to govern, addressing the myriad tough societal and economic problems that are discussed in the next chapter.[58]

Surviving State Capture

The Path Forward

Overturning apartheid for long-subjugated South Africans and transferring real power from whites to blacks followed a jarring, incessantly bumpy, route to the oft-promised land—the new Zion with its overflowing abundance of milk and honey. As the African National Congress (ANC), its fervent supporters, and President Nelson Mandela and Deputy President Thabo Mbeki soon learned, ousting the Afrikaner-led National Party from power and recovering from decades of ever more oppressive hegemony revealed a landscape littered with deeply rooted social and economic obstacles that resisted easy eradication.

South Africa in 1994 was a multiracial montage that for more than a century had been misgoverned; parts of the whole were advanced industrially, medically, and educationally. But most of the new nation was underdeveloped: all kinds of services to the majority were in many instances rudimentary or nonexistent. Only the white and some Asian and Coloured communities enjoyed advanced medical treatments and public health interventions. Educational opportunity disparities were huge and human accomplishments accordingly highly contorted. Even in the cities, wealthier sections enjoyed easily available potable water; poorer areas relied on widely spaced standpipes or privately and expensively delivered supplies. Wealthier areas were safer. Wealthier areas had improved paved streets. Even in rural South Africa, infrastructural provisions long reflected income and color distinctions, which naturally ran together.

A leader as sagacious as Mandela was bound to find governing the South Africa that he and Mbeki inherited from the fading de Klerk administration far more daunting, and far more challenging across so many more dimensions, than he or anyone else could have anticipated. Together, they discovered the many calamitous insufficiencies—deficits that would take decades to overcome—produced by apartheid and the segregationist decades that had preceded it. South Africa's population was growing far more rapidly than its economy; formal sector jobs were scarce and would remain so until ANC rule could encourage massive new investment. Poverty and crime were at very high levels,

Overcoming the Oppressors. Robert I. Rotberg, Oxford University Press. © Oxford University Press 2023.
DOI: 10.1093/oso/9780197674208.003.0007

and escalating. Decent housing was largely unavailable for Africans, most of whom subsisted at or below the national poverty line. Squalid, underresourced settlements surrounded each of the country's major cities and had become breeding grounds for disease and crime. Forty years of official neglect, sheer mismanagement, the legacy of youthful protests and boycotts of schools, and unrest in townships during the anti-apartheid era and because of skirmishes between ANC supporters and militants loyal to the Inkatha Freedom Party, all contributed to a massive educational deficit that desperately mortgaged South Africa's future. And then the HIV/AIDS pandemic arrived.

Mandela understood how important to the nation and his people was remedying each of these deficiencies. But at the head, initially, of a government of "national unity," sharing some authority with de Klerk and fearful that the defeated white minority could conceivably attempt to destabilize the new South Africa, Mandela opted instead to expend energy, political capital, and his full legitimacy on spiritual leadership and reconciliation.

As I commented at the time, "From his . . . agreement to head a government of national unity with the very whites who had oppressed him and his people to [his] insistence on the rights of minorities [Mandela] practiced the politics of inclusion with a passion that border[ed] on the evangelical," and made many converts. He refused to be politically correct or to genuflect before the altars of an exclusively African-controlled South Africa. He was determined to build a "united" nation, with all of its discordant parts knitted together as seamlessly as his crafty loom could manage. He demonstrated an unexpected and magnanimous sensitivity for the very persons and groups who had never respected Africans. This was "leadership of a high and visionary order."[1]

When white right-wingers in 1993 assassinated Chris Hani, a magnetic and much-admired key ANC military figure, Mandela knew that he had to prevent that killing from destroying the slowly emerging entente between blacks and whites that he and many others were forging on both sides of the main South African transitional fault lines. On radio, then still a medium of mass communication, he appealed for calm. "Now is the time for all South Africans to stand together against those who . . . wish to destroy what Chris gave his life for—the freedom of all of us."[2] He counseled his militant followers to join hands rather than pick up arms. He dealt in the same manner with those of his followers who preferred to keep fighting violently against the Zulu separatist Inkatha movement led by Chief Buthelezi. Emphasizing his own determination to lead and do right, Mandela addressed his followers in Katlehong, east of Johannesburg: "It is difficult for us to say when people are angry that they must be nonviolent. But the solution is peace, it is reconciliation, it is political tolerance." Furthermore, "If you are going to kill innocent people you don't belong in the ANC. Your test is reconciliation. Listen to me . . . I am your leader. I am going to give leadership. . . . As long as I am your leader, I will tell you, always, when you are wrong."[3]

To Reach Out and Reassure

Mandela's gift for acute emotional intelligence became even more telling in his dealings with his very tormentors and their allies during and after the arrival of democracy. Indeed, it was as a dedicated inclusionist, as a fervent conciliator, as a conscious bridger of color divides, and as an optimistic believer in the goodness of humans that Mandela excelled. He captured the imagination and affection of all of his countrymen and women. By his gestures, his symbolism, and his actions he persuaded South Africans of all colors that their novel national enterprise was worthwhile—that nation building was beneficial for all. He gave South Africans a strong sense of belonging to a worthwhile project that promised to uplift each person spiritually.

His human touch was remarkable, and genuine (as my wife and I had ample reason to know). His pleasure in reaching out and embracing disparate peoples, including very recent enemies, was dramatic and infectious. Early on, he called on former President Pieter W. Botha, a memorable conversation captured fully on television. He hosted a dinner for his former Robben Island jailor and the outgoing head of the country's apartheid intelligence service. He appointed a prison chief as ambassador. He lunched with the man who had prosecuted him for sabotage. He attended Dutch Reformed Church services in Afrikaans. He flew to a distant settlement to take tea with the widow of President Hendrik Verwoerd, one of the key architects of apartheid. But, most of all, Mandela's unexpected appearance at a decisive rugby match between the famed Springboks of South Africa, competing against New Zealand, startled and won the hearts of his new sports-mad rainbow nation, especially when he donned the Springboks' green and gold jersey and strolled dramatically to the center of the pitch to present the World Cup trophy to the astounded South African captain, an Afrikaner, with the crowd going wild and chanting "Nel-son" over and over.[4]

Mandela brought South Africa together. Although it was already a "nation" in a way that few other sub-Saharan polities were, even thirty years after the severing of their colonial ties, Mandela's inclusionary impress truly constructed his nation anew; he did everything in his charismatic power to give Africans, Coloureds, Asians, and whites a proud sense of belonging to a gifted enterprise and a larger whole. Those were among Mandela's lasting contributions to a reborn country to which he gave so much, and in which he believed so strongly.

That rich spiritual gift could never be matched by equal material contributions to the welfare and development of the state. The post-apartheid baleful legacy was too large and formidable, even for someone of Mandela's breadth and dedication. It proved overwhelming to Mbeki, as well, and to Mandela's later presidential successors.

Nevertheless, as president from 1994 to 1999, Mandela sought to remediate many of the daunting deficits that his administration had inherited. For a year or two he convened cabinet meetings and gave detailed instructions to his ministers. But Mbeki more and more exercised the operational reins of government. Mandela, surprisingly detail-oriented at first, gradually concerned himself less and less with the micro-accomplishments of his government. Instead, he worried appropriately about larger issues of economic modernization, peacemaking at home and abroad (Burundi, the Democratic Republic of Congo/Zaire, Lesotho, Libya, Nigeria), and societal reconciliation—always his policy priority.[5] "In effect, his was an imperial presidency that for the most part attempted to frame and to motivate the new South Africa rather than to set and to accomplish specific legislative objectives."[6]

The Democratic Opposition

With the transformation of South Africa from a minority-ruled, heavily discriminatory, and thoroughly regimented state to one with a liberal constitution, a charismatic and magnanimous head of state, and democratic instincts and intentions, initially it seemed that the persevering antagonists of apartheid—the Progressive Alliance particularly—had lost their political and moral relevance. Helen Suzman had retired from Parliament and smartly welcomed Mandela's freedom and his accession to the presidency. The many others in the Progressives cohort with whom I had long had close contact and innumerable political conversations—Alex Boraine, Colin Eglin, and Frederik van Zyl Slabbert—were all excited by the nation's positive new prospect for which they had each labored ingeniously and courageously. Each had helped in his or her several ways to usher in the striking collapse of apartheid and was anxious and active to help to assist the ANC in its massive social and physical reconstruction of a damaged nation. However, in the 1994 parliamentary poll the Democratic Party (as the Progressives had become), and now led by Zach de Beer in succession to Slabbert, won only 2 percent of the total vote, down dramatically from the 20 percent that it had received in the 1989 election (held under different electoral rules at the end of the apartheid era). The ANC took 63 percent of vote total in 1994, the white National Party 20 percent, the Inkatha Freedom Party 11 percent, the far right-wing white Freedom Front 2 percent, the Democratic Party 2 percent, and the Pan-Africanist Congress 1 percent.[7]

But not all facets of the ANC were as smooth and as sparkling as Mandela. Suzman and the other concerned observers knew that they had to remain vigilant. Indeed, as the corrupt urges in the ANC swelled to a crescendo (see below), as the ANC's determination to sweep holdover whites, especially Afrikaners, out of bureaucratic positions in various government departments and to replace them with less experienced affirmative action appointments became pronounced, and as Deputy President Mbeki and a number of his associates demonstrated autocratic tendencies (see pp. 164–65), the old Progressives, now the new Democrats, realized that the struggle for human rights, for freedom of expression and other fundamental freedoms, and for honest dealings, remained imperative and challenged. Suzman outside Parliament and Eglin and others, including new leaders like Tony Leon and Zach de Beer within the legislature, resumed their attempts to hold the new authorities to account.

As we shall see, the initial suspicions of these anti-apartheid campaigners, now morphed into traditional liberal democrats, had much to worry about on behalf of an increasingly concerned public. Many of Mandela's associates deviated far from the straight line of reconciliation and societal reformation that he espoused. They rightly employed several methods to grow the now broadened economy, to manage the state and state apparatuses to benefit all South Africans, and to return South Africa meaningfully to the global as well as the all-African stage. (I was delighted to welcome Franklin Sonn, for example, to Washington as South Africa's first post-independence ambassador.) But they behaved more imperiously than Suzman, Eglin, de Beer, and others thought wise. And they wheeled and dealt in a manner that the many of the anti-apartheid campaigners believed boded ill in terms of respect for human rights and civil liberties, the restored court system, and fiscal common sense. ANC adherents, many old Marxists returning home after long periods in enforced exile, also wondered then and later whether the ANC in power would reflect the idealism of their collective past dreams and hopes.[8]

Truth versus Justice

Boraine, a Methodist minister before becoming a politician, was instrumental in helping to enlarge Mandela's comprehensive vision of a reconciled and humane new South Africa to include a special and in many ways unique Truth and Reconciliation Commission (TRC) to uncover and expose the dark facts of apartheid, to report them to South Africans and to the world, and, critically, to make amnesty conditional on the full and truthful confession of abuses of human rights. It also investigated vicious acts within the ANC, and by ANC adherents, but neither well nor thoroughly.[9]

The concept of a TRC emerged out of an elaborate political compromise that rejected the outgoing regime's demand for blanket forgiveness and no retribution (no matter the heinous acts committed) in exchange for a mechanism (the TRC) that could grant conditional absolution for dastardly deeds only if the perpetrators provided a full accounting of long ago or relatively recent violations of human rights, incidents of torture, merciless killings, and more.

If a community wanted to prevent the recurrence of atrocity and if it further sought to cleanse itself of the corrosive effects of massive injuries to individuals and groups, then the investigations, hearings, and adjudications of a commission charged with obtaining the truth about past harms would be helpful, even necessary. Only through such an elaborate and iterative process could a community hope at the deepest possible level to understand what occurred and why, and under whose orders, thus forestalling anything similar happening ever again. Essential, however, was a conscientious and elaborate effort to recover the full truth of past events, no matter how compromising to the perpetrators and horrible in the retelling for those violated or for their next of kin. Truth commissions as a genre were intended to function preventively and restoratively.

Before South Africa's truth-seeking endeavor, there had been other jurisdictions across the globe where democracies had overturned brutal totalitarian/authoritarian regimes and the successor governments had sought healing more than retribution. The earlier efforts to unearth truth after wars in Argentina and Chile were especially instructive for the South African undertaking. Indeed, the Chilean endeavor greatly influenced the South African effort because it was premised on reconciling a national military-led period with the democratic era that followed. Archbishop Desmond Tutu, Mandela's chosen chair for the TRC, went even beyond the Chilean precepts to seek atonement as well as knowledge. Tutu asked whites to apologize and take responsibility for their evil actions during apartheid.[10]

The theoretical underpinning of the truth commission concept and questions about whether "truth" is discoverable retrospectively and whether justice can possibly be served by a truth commission exercise are best discussed elsewhere.[11] What was very different in South Africa, however, from previous truth commission exercises in Latin America and Asia was the TRC's insistence on letting all of apartheid's dirty laundry hang out in public view. The TRC's hearings were broadcast on television; the press was given full access; and the TRC's report (published in several volumes in 1998) was comprehensive. Some earlier commissions had held their inquiries and invigilated witnesses in camera, with no public record. Others shielded parts of the testimonies or provided only heavily redacted transcripts. "There can be no question that, at the most basic

Figure 7.1. Desmond Tutu

level, [the TRC] provided a shock education into the abuses of the state under apartheid," concluded the sometime editor of Johannesburg's *Sunday Times*.[12]

The TRC, as critics suggest, may have sacrificed "the pursuit of justice . . . for the sake of promoting some other social purpose such as reconciliation" and traded "criminal justice for a general social benefit" in a manner that was morally suspect.[13] But there were political needs and an overriding attempt to foster social harmony. That is, the South African commission operated in order to establish restorative justice, with no necessary intent to seek courtroom forms of retributive justice.

Tutu, Boraine, and their talented investigative and interrogative teams held more than 2,500 hearings, brought more than 2,000 perpetrators before the 21,000 victims whom they had wronged, and exposed innumerable sordid apartheid-inflicted brutalities. Those who testified fully often gained effective protection from prosecution. But whether society as a whole was cleansed and restored by the proceedings, and whether the TRC's actions enabled South Africans to come back together with a fuller appreciation of the sins of apartheid and learned how to move on as a reunited society, is much less clear. For Boraine, forgiveness was preferable to trials that would not only have been costly but could have caused further division in society. "Is it not . . . better," he asked, to "move forward into the future?"[14] Indeed, in the business of retrospective transparency and truth telling, the TRC is the leading model of its kind. It became one of the glittering jewels of Mandela's attempt to give his new rainbow nation a sense of united purpose and enhanced oneness.[15]

Transferring the Crown

Of all of the many consequential decisions of his presidential term, none was as significant as the choice of Mandela's successor. Mandela decided rather early in his incumbency that he preferred being a world statesman to orchestrating a (messy) and problematical reconstruction of South Africa. He was eighty-one, too, in 1999, and well deserved an opportunity to lead the world from the South African sidelines. At least, that is one way of configuring his retirement in favor of Mbeki, a decision made official at the ANC national congress in late 1997 and confirmed when the ANC won the 1999 parliamentary election.

Mandela had originally wanted to appoint Cyril Ramaphosa as deputy president and putative heir apparent in 1994, and still preferred Ramaphosa over Mbeki as late as the party congress. Yet Mandela was also loyal to the party, and the ANC's central committee strongly urged Mandela to choose Mbeki, son of an early ANC stalwart and, during his post–Sussex University years, the political commissar of the guerrilla training camps near Lusaka (where he and I first talked at length and warmly in 1989).[16]

Ramaphosa was younger, had never been a guerrilla, and was ethnically Venda, one of South Africa's least prominent groups. Mbeki was a Xhosa, South Africa's second largest ethnic grouping after the Zulu, as was Mandela. The fact that Ramaphosa had masterfully helped to lead the United Democratic Front in its "successful" internal struggle against the apartheid regime impressed ANC kingmakers (who had themselves mostly spent the apartheid years on Robben Island or in the external training camps) less than did Mbeki's time in the field and his camaraderie with those who had battled apartheid from outside. It mattered less to the elders that Ramaphosa had subsequently founded and led the National Union of Mine Workers and, since independence, had served effectively as the General Secretary of the ANC.

Even before the choice of Mbeki over Ramaphosa had been formalized, and after Mbeki, fifty-four, and a poised, well-tailored, meerschaum pipe smoker, had visited Harvard and spoken several times with me and addressed students, I praised his likely anointment: "Mbeki is not a Mandela clone," I wrote. "He is his own person, with a distinctive intellect and style which complements Mandela's. . . ." At Harvard, he assured audiences that he knew exactly how to achieve growth with equity, to manage the expectations of trade unionists and jobless Africans, and to reduce criminal violence. He said that he could build a "participatory consensus for good government on the foundation of [the] bitter anti-apartheid struggle." With each answer, I continued, "Mbeki displayed a thoughtfulness and a respect for complexity that [was] rare among national leaders in and out of Africa." However, I wondered whether Mbeki's analytical skills could compensate for his "lack of a common touch."[17]

As it later transpired, I was too confident that Mbeki could fill Mandela's immense footsteps. Mandela himself perceived potential flaws in his sometime protégé and warned against them. At the ANC's late 1997 congress that confirmed Mbeki's ascendance and his accession to the presidency of the ANC, Mandela waved a proverbial finger at Mbeki. "One of the temptations of a leader who has been elected unopposed is that he may use his powerful position to settle scores with his detractors, marginalize them, and in certain cases, get rid of them and surround himself with yes-men and -women." Implicitly rebuking the "high-handed" manner in which Mbeki had dealt with economic matters, Mandela said that voters should be able to criticize leaders without "fear or favour."[18]

After independence, when Black Economic Empowerment (BEE) was at its formative stage, Ramaphosa, forty-three, accepted that Mandela was unable to make him the official political heir. After skillfully negotiating the modalities of the white Nationalists' transfer of power to Mandela and the ANC, and overseeing the writing of the country's liberal new constitution, Ramaphosa might have asserted a claim on the deputy presidency and succession. Rejected by the party elders, he instead established a business with Nthato Motlana, my medical friend and Mandela's physician. They called it New African Investments Ltd (NAIL), and opened an unpretentious office in a northern suburb of Johannesburg. From that base Ramaphosa rose by 1999 to chair two corporate behemoths: the Anglo-American Corporation and South African Breweries, and to accumulate a spreading array of profitable investments.

We met one day at NAIL in early 1996 when it was evident (but not certain) that Mbeki would succeed Mandela and that Ramaphosa would be relegated to the political wilderness. I commiserated with him. "No matter," he replied with a long face and a rueful smile. "I will go into business, make money, and return to lead the country." How confidently prophetic! Later, freed as he was from politics, I bumped into him by chance on several occasions late at night in one of Johannesburg's better bookstores. We were both browsing the shelves for the latest analyses of South Africa or, in his case, for recent books on development economics and corporate strategy. Other African leaders might have profited by reading widely; to my knowledge, only Ramaphosa did so.

With the crown set securely on Mbeki's sturdy head after 1999, he felt himself free, and sufficiently master of South Africa's future, to impose his own considerable opinions on the nation. Mbeki was another wannabe closet autocrat with "no feel for democratic politics."[19] Never having competed for office before being tapped to be deputy president, he had much more faith in his own understanding of the world and the new nation's organizational necessities than he did in popular mandates or the popular will. He thought that he was bringing a centralizing efficiency to the affairs and workings of the ANC when, for the most part, his appointments to high political positions mostly favored those who would support his leadership, and not enhance integrity or intellectual honesty—as in combating HIV/AIDS, battling corruption, or curbing despotism in neighboring Zimbabwe.[20]

Doing Nothing for Zimbabwe

From the moment in 1999 when it was apparent that Zimbabwe's President Robert Mugabe had shifted from being a mere authoritarian to being a very high-handed despot (see chapter 9), through 2000 and 2001, when it became clear that he preferred to rig elections rather than to win them fairly, I pleaded with Mbeki and Frank Chikane, his chief aide and a former Kennedy School student, to intervene. Mbeki, and Chikane on his behalf, always assured me that he understood exactly what Mugabe was doing and appreciated the absolute need to return Zimbabwe to democracy. On the eve of a major meeting between Mbeki and South African business executives in 2001, Mbeki again promised me that he had the matter in hand—that he was about to tell the assembly of corporate leaders that Mugabe's dictatorial instincts and actions would be curbed; South Africa could hardly afford to have such an outrageous rogue state on its border. After all, as Prime Minister B. Johannes Vorster told Prime Minister Ian Smith in 1976 (see chapter 9), South Africa provided Zimbabwe's economic and logistical lifeline. South Africa's needs and preferences should take precedence.

More significantly, Mbeki flat out personally promised U.S. President George W. Bush that he would curb Mugabe—that he was fully in agreement with the U.S. official considered opinion that Mugabe was a menace to his own people and to the peace and stability of southern Africa. (See the discussion, quotations, and citations in chapter 9.)

Mbeki, like Zuma afterward, nonetheless did nothing with regard to moderating Zimbabwean political excesses. Mbeki paid Mugabe several visits, and talked big to outsiders, just as President Jacob Zuma later promised real action to U.S. Secretary of State Hillary Clinton. South Africa, as personified by its elected leaders (but not by some of its lower-level interlocutors) contentedly tut-tutted as Mugabe falsified electoral outcomes in 2002 and 2008, and then again in 2013. However, Mbeki did impose a unity government on Mugabe and Morgan Tsvangirai of the Movement for Democratic Change in 2009, after violence throughout Zimbabwe's major metropolises threatened to spread to and inflame cities in South Africa. But then Mbeki point blank refused to monitor Mugabe's failure to observe the letter and spirit of the compromise accord and his marginalization of Tsvangirai and the non-Mugabe half of the government of national unity.[21]

In a series of articles, I emphasized that Mbeki (and later Zuma) had immense leverage. South Africa under their command could cease deliveries of gasoline and diesel supplies, and could easily pull the electrical power plug. Then Mugabe would surely do South Africa's bidding. Or, at the very least, Mbeki or Zuma could use their bully pulpits to condemn Mugabe to the world, and bring his regime down that way.[22] But nary a serious complaint issued from high-level and very complacent Pretoria.

Johnston reckons that Mbeki chose to do so little in Zimbabwe because of his fears that the success of a post-liberation political party like the Movement for Democratic Change (MDC) would threaten the ANC by encouraging a similar, trade union-backed, competitor at home in South Africa. If an upstart political movement could displace Mugabe's ZANU-PF, the Democratic Alliance, the Economic Freedom Fighters, or something similar could do the same closer to home. This "was the stuff of exile generation nightmares."[23]

Whether or not that was the overriding reason for Mbeki's (and Zuma's) failure to make Zimbabwe behave and to ensure democratic outcomes in its near abroad (unlike South Africa's military interventions suppressing coups in Lesotho and the Comoros), South Africa's hands-off policy toward Zimbabwe meant the perpetuation of autocracy and kleptocracy there, plus untold hunger, joblessness, and human suffering. For Mbeki, too, his do-nothing policy contributed significantly to his precipitous loss of legitimacy and his ouster from the South African presidency in 2007.

Party Equals State

Mbeki internally led a typical sub-Saharan African insistence on equating party with state, a tendency toward imposing ANC "deployment" strictures and loyalty requirements to which even Mandela acquiesced.[24] Doing so for a time, at least, assisted Mbeki's desire to enunciate unchallengeable policy edicts and to stifle democratic stirrings within the dominant party. Much of the disarray in the ANC in 2022 can be traced back to Mbeki's leadership as deputy president and president, and to the momentum that pushed him out of power and Zuma into it. Even as Mbeki "centralized" decisions about who would be permitted to govern this or that province, he permitted each such satrapy to become a micro-autocracy, with the concomitant rise of tender fraud, outright embezzlement,

Figure 7.2. Thabo Mbeki

and other kinds of peculation. Likewise, with proportional representation giving the party and its head and its central committee total control over the choice of candidates for parliamentary election on the ANC list and ordinary members and citizens never being able fully and democratically to participate in the political process, constituencies had little real consequence. That reality meant that parliamentarians had little reason to listen to their supposed "constituents," only to the party bosses. (Proportional representation had originally been introduced as a modality to ensure that the voices of minorities would be heard, but all it did was to hand overweening power to the ruling party's bosses.)

Mbeki had moments as late as 2001 when, by using his centralized power within the party and the national megaphone of his forceful presidency, he might have halted the drift to wholesale corruption. But he never did, and the impulse to grab whatever officeholders could grab persists today.

Mandela had specifically warned about corruption in 1997, speaking to the party congress. Echoing Fanon, he criticized predatory elites "that have thrived on the basis of the looting of national wealth." He said that "careerism" might lead politicians (indeed!) to use their positions to make money illicitly.[25]

An Economic Dividend

Pathbreaking economic growth eluded the Mandela administration as it bedeviled the Mbeki, Zuma, and—so far—the Ramaphosa administrations that followed. Mandela early accepted that the old socialist nostrums would not propel South Africa upward. South Africa, he appreciated well before others in the ANC, could only deliver a satisfactory post-apartheid dividend to its struggling millions if it opened up its economy to trade and capital movements; more jobs—elusive as they were—could best alleviate poverty. Mandela shifted the ANC from a centralized market approach to a model closer to that of a free market. Fiscal responsibility, moreover, and macroeconomic steadiness would, he hoped, limit the flight of skilled whites and encourage new foreign investment.

Despite such mainstream intentions, and elaborate planning, per capita growth lagged population increases, sometimes by large margins, causing formal unemployment numbers to rise substantially. The gradually swelling labor force has long remained predominantly jobless, officially in the 27 percent range, from the 1990s to today, but more likely north of 40 percent. In any event, because of a whole range of problems with infrastructural requirements, rampant corruption, inconsistent investment policies, and demographic realities, no net new jobs have been created since about 1970.

The Reconstruction and Development Program (RDP) of the Mandela presidency accomplished sustainably little, in terms of new growth and new employment. The more conservative Growth, Employment and Redistribution Program (GEAR), its refined successor, was purposely more austere and more careful, establishing a pattern of benefit. The economy grew at 2.8 percent annually between 1994 and 2003, a respectable but insufficient rise. Inflation moderated. Debt service and debt levels overall improved. But, after the adoption of GEAR, inequality and poverty levels increased significantly. Gini-coefficient measurements rose from 1994 to 1999 by 2 percent, a substantially worse outcome than at independence.[26] These combined results could not provide formal sector wage employment sufficient for swelling numbers of high school leavers. Yet, on the plus side of the ledger, tax collection became more effective. Nearly 3 million new houses were built. New moneys were devoted to social services, and to sanitation and electrical power availability in the crowded peri-urban townships that accommodated most Africans. But it was also a period when the criminal justice system collapsed.[27]

Both the RDP and GEAR initiatives were intended to uplift the 25 percent of South Africans who somehow survived below the national poverty line and to improve the social welfare of all South Africans. But these programs and their successors could not completely overcome the country's revived command economy, the stranglehold of its inflexible trade union movement (allied as it always was with the ANC), the ruling party's lingering distrust of macroeconomic openness, and its hostility to the workings of a market economy (pace Mandela). Yet GEAR, and the Black Economic Empowerment and Equity Employment policies that accompanied it, did give entrepreneurial opportunities and wealth accumulation possibilities to a numerically sparse coterie of canny, aspiring, mostly young, middle-class black persons with ties to the ruling party—persons in Mbeki's own confident mode—while simultaneously curbing expanded employment opportunities in the public sector.

Largely at Mbeki's behest, the BEE scheme compelled white-owned enterprises, from those dominating the mining sector to smaller manufacturing concerns, to transfer substantial ownership shares to a cohort of well-connected black entrepreneurs. Without investing their own capital, a host of men and a few women became wealthy almost overnight. An elite class of black empowered entrepreneurs thus gained substantial roles in South Africa's most prosperous enterprises, with the state, and workers, gaining proportionally little.

The ANC insisted that "political liberation" should be followed by "economic liberation," that is, that blacks should benefit from "affirmative action" in employment, government contracts, and privatizations. Black boardroom involvement became a necessity for bidding on big government contracts, with quota-based affirmative action legislation being required for all tenders, licenses, and the unbundling of state-owned enterprises. Indeed, firms complying with substantial black ownership requirements obtained a 15 percent advantage when they bid for government contracts.

South Africa's chief diamond and gold magnate welcomed the BEE program: "It was vital to make it possible for black people to control some of the big companies in South Africa. It was the right thing to do—part of a necessary response to the efforts for peace made by Mandela and his colleagues. You felt business had to match their efforts. . . ."[28] What he and other corporate leaders accordingly did was to invite Africans of talent to join their boards, gifting them shares in the companies whose operations they oversaw.

Just as Ramaphosa, Tokyo Sexwale, and other bright, well-educated Africans swelled their bank accounts (and their herds of cattle or their numbers of expensive motor cars), so poverty grew throughout the republic. Neither GEAR nor BEE redistributed riches or trickled-up growth prospects. By making entrance into the fat cat ranks relatively easy, both initiatives may even have retarded entrepreneurial strivings that might have led to even more broadly distributed economic advances.

Export earnings from gold, diamonds, platinum, vanadium, manganese, and a host of other metals, dug and otherwise worked by millions of poorly paid African miners, continued under Mandela and his successors to drive the nation's economy. The burning of locally sourced coal together with hydropower imported from Mozambique and the Congo and the output of a small nuclear plant provided electrical generating capacity.

Although the ANC in exile had espoused transferring control of the mining and other productive sectors to the state, Mandela came to realize that a nationalization on the Zambian model might curtail prosperity and inhibit incoming foreign investment, as well as likely proving sclerotic for the overall national economy. Even so, as a percentage of South Africa's annual GDP, manufacturing has contributed less and less since 1990. Its contribution fell steadily from 21 percent to 12 percent between that year and 2019.[29] Mbeki and others would have preferred an upward movement on that chart.

Agriculture, deregulated in ways that industry never was, contributed importantly to South Africa's export earnings, to employment, and to the country's total GDP during these same early years. The RDP originally envisaged shifting 30 percent of the country's farm holdings from white to black hands, largely by encouraging willing seller–willing buyer arrangements, and by providing financing for black empowerment in this sector. Whites had obviously taken black lands in the nineteenth century and, by means of the punitive 1913 Native Lands Act, had forcibly pushed Africans off good soils while also prohibiting freehold tenure in the Transkei and the eastern Cape Province, where Africans had once tended profitable holdings. The ANC had indeed originated in opposition to the act and its adverse implications for African prosperity.

Mandela, and Mbeki later, advocated redressing past grievances and restoring Africans to the land. But Mandela was loath to undermine South Africa's agricultural productivity and the jobs and export earnings that were contributing so much to the country's prosperity. He was hardly anxious, as well, to push white (mostly Afrikaner) farmers off their lands, especially at a time when race relations were tense and harmony a problem. Nor could Mandela's successors easily solve the landlessness problem, leaving it as an open sore in 2022, with no easy resolution in sight.

One of the important factors that inhibited South African growth in the Mandelan and post-Mandelan years was the vast shortage of skilled indigenous persons.

At independence and for at least another decade the new South African nation sorely lacked the human resource abundance that it required to blossom and prosper. Economic growth in South Africa, as in Botswana after 1966 and Namibia after 1990, required vast numbers of skilled and well-educated personnel to staff and run an advanced economy, a large-scale bureaucracy, complicated parastatal institutions, a renewed diplomatic corps, and much more. But among the nation's 28 million Africans in 1990 there were fewer than 1,000 lawyers and 1,000 physicians, and only a handful of engineers and chartered accountants.[30] In the annual high school graduation examinations, 97 percent of whites received passing grades while only 42 percent (in 1990) and 38 percent (in 1993) of Africans received completion (matriculation) certificates. That apartheid-influenced performance meant that 118,000 Africans in 1994 and larger numbers in subsequent years through 2000 failed to matriculate or graduate from secondary school, and found themselves thrust on the tough employment market without official qualifications. They thus became destined for informal jobs of varying kinds—or criminal pursuits. Moreover, of the Africans who did pass their secondary school final examination, only 15 percent received marks high enough to qualify for university entrance, a result that persisted well into the first decade of the twenty-first century. By the next decade, however, with revisions to the matriculation examination and better teachers and teaching, 70 and 80 percent of South African taking that exam were passing, as in 2019.[31]

The Scourge of HIV/AIDS

The HIV/AIDS epidemic overwhelmed Mbeki, defined his presidency, weakened South Africa, and crippled millions of its afflicted citizens. When his presidency commenced in 1999, 25 percent of South African women already tested HIV-positive. Five years later, 5 percent more women were positive and death rates had soared by a factor of four. More than 10 percent of all South Africans had been infected with HIV, with 320,000 citizens dying in 2005 of HIV/AIDS.[32]

The epidemic was a calamity the likes of which southern Africa had never experienced, dwarfing in its lethality and death rates even the pneumonias, multidrug-resistant tuberculosis, malaria, and helminth diseases from which South Africans (and other Africans) already suffered supremely. The HIV-1 version that swept across eastern and southern Africa, somewhat sparing West Africa, was unusually virulent, sexually transmitted, and for long periods without effective remedies. Indeed, Mbeki initially derided the connection between HIV and AIDS, denying the efficacy of antiretroviral medicines as a "toxic" hoax benefiting only global pharmaceutical manufacturers. Mbeki imagined the AIDS hoopla as "an assault on Africa, and in particular on black male sexuality." Tuning himself nightly into the conspiracy theories of dissident "authorities" debunking what the world's infectious disease specialists were saying about HIV/AIDS, Mbeki for several years into his presidency pursued an obstinate course that kept needy South Africans from obtaining retroviral relief and made mockery of his own vaunted intelligence and, more importantly, pretensions to truthful leadership. Thousands of lives were accordingly lost, one careful study putting the unnecessarily forfeited number at 330,000, and another at 343,000.[33]

Poverty caused AIDS. Or so Mbeki declaimed. Others, including Mbeki's minister of health, promoted garlic as a miracle cure. Or she touted combinations of olive oil and lemon juice, beets, and herbal concoctions. Zuma later dealt with promiscuity and AIDS by "taking showers." The science behind HIV/AIDS was seriously flawed, said Mbeki, contradicting other South African politicians and most of the nation's known specialists. He insisted on doing research himself, succumbing as he did so to far-out and unsupported conspiracy theories propagated by pseudoscientific charlatans intoning on the World

Wide Web. Big Pharma was the culprit, and the agent of falsehood. Mbeki minimized the importance of "safer-sex" campaigns. Using his high office to resist the use of expensive azidothymidine (AZT) and nevirapine, helpful elsewhere, he believed that he knew better than experts, including local African scientists and physicians. They urged him without success to cease spreading falsehoods. But Mbeki believed in his own investigations. He resisted the calls of scholars and opposition politicians to relent. Johnston's perceptive analysis calls Mbeki an "intellectual cowboy."[34] Only when a Constitutional Court decision compelled him, grudgingly, to start treatment programs using antiretroviral medicines, and his cabinet piled on, did he relent. Mandela, a wiser and less opinionated out-of-office leader, helped to turn public opinion against Mbeki, eventually acting responsibly to save lives. Mandela believed that Mbeki was incorrect, morally and politically, "to question conventional science" and to prevaricate over therapeutic innovations rather than to follow "international best practice."[35]

The Constitutional Court decided against Mbeki in 2002. Throughout the remaining years of Mbeki's presidency, and well into Zuma's, the greater awareness of the etiology of HIV/AIDS and the greater availability of several antiretroviral medicines transformed HIV/AIDS from an invariably fatal into a chronic disease, capable of being held in check by the conscientious administration of newer forms of therapy. By 2008, and the end of Mbeki's term in office, AIDS fatalities in South Africa had plateaued at about 345,000. Eleven years later, deaths numbered 72,000; 7.5 million adults lived with HIV/AIDS.[36] Its prevalence within the population was 19 percent. In 2022, South Africans still contract AIDS at rates that remain among the highest in the world. But the disease can now be controlled. The lost years, even lost generations, are the result of Mbeki's temperamental misconceptions and his retreat into solipsism.

Feeding at the Trough, and Perdition

Corruption, using one's elected or appointed public prominence to acquire illicit personal benefits, had never been absent from South Africa when it was controlled by a series of white governments before and after 1910. Likewise, after acquiring power in 1994, ANC operatives at several levels sought to turn their new national, provincial, or municipal positions into rewarding opportunities.[37] Although Mandela may just possibly have been oblivious, all manner of ANC principals and managers began to peddle influence for profit. "More disturbing," Hartley tartly reports, "was Mandela's failure to turn the tide against post-apartheid corruption while it was still in its infancy. He was presented with several opportunities to do so, and, on each occasion, he allowed the ANC's worst instincts to rule over the intention of the new dispensation . . . to usher in a free and open society."[38]

Many hands pilfered from the national cash box. A police commissioner took kickbacks, for example, to protect criminals who constituted South Africa's version of the Mafia. Scarcity conditions avarice, at one fiscal end of the continuum, and procurements drive round the economy's new wheels, at another. Both imperatives stimulate corrupt conniving from near the political apex down to the lower bureaucratic ranks.

The biggest temptation of all for the new wielders of power, as it always has been elsewhere in the world, was security spending. Mbeki, possibly with Mandela's blessing, believed that South Africa's defense force was antiquated, little suited to one of Africa's more advanced and ambitious states. South Africa after apartheid was unable to project kinetic power even within its home country. As a result, Mbeki, consulting with Minister of Defense Joe Modise and with party chairman Zuma, another military man and the ANC's former chief of intelligence, authorized the purchase of submarines and frigates from France and Germany, rejecting a less expensive Spanish bid. South Africa also ordered new fighter aircraft from a Swedish/British consortium. About R30 billion ($7 billion) was involved in both arrangements, a proportion of which was destined by the manufacturers to go to Zuma and others for facilitating the arms purchases. (We shall eventually learn the details in Zuma's trial, still underway in 2022.) It seems that kickbacks, purloining of proceeds, special payments to the ANC, over-invoicing methods, and similar illicit mechanisms were involved, and that the amounts paid were higher than they might have been because of the need to reward the South Africans who had enabled the deal. In the context of grand corruption, ships and planes for cash was a common exchange. Equally damning was Mbeki's refusal to agree to an ANC parliamentary-inspired judicial inquiry as early as 2001. So there were cover-ups on top of cover-ups, the usual fate of whistle-blower-like attempts in the developing world to report and contain the graft of higher-ranking superiors.[39]

The Armsgate Scandal, as it was called, demonstrated that serious money could be acquired personally from political positions and political influence. Under Mbeki's purview, there were innumerable successive scandals at the national and provincial levels, and—as recently demonstrated—even at the municipal level. No one wanted to be left behind when the gravy train ran. Mbeki is unlikely to have benefited personally (I never managed to discuss this question with him), but he tolerated sleaze throughout the upper levels of the party and the provinces, presumably for political reasons—so as not to alienate too many would-be supporters. He may have sympathized, too, with the newcomers' greed—their desire to accumulate while the going was good. And such carefully calibrated patronage would support his ascendancy.

The arms deal came out from under the cover-up a year later, when investigators discovered that Zuma's longtime financial advisor had earlier solicited bribes worth R500,000 a year on behalf of Zuma from a French company. What followed was a dance of devils between Mbeki, the national president, and Zuma, his deputy president and erstwhile struggle comrade. Mbeki at first refused to permit prosecutors to charge Zuma—despite the testimony of the financial advisor. He wanted Zuma to resign. But Zuma dared Mbeki to fire him, which Mbeki finally did in 2005, after winning the 2004 parliamentary election on a joint ticket featuring both of them. The financial advisor was found guilty in that year of corrupt relations with Zuma. The sacking followed almost immediately, South Africa's prosecuting authority charging Zuma with corruptly profiting from the arms purchases.

In most situations, the now defrocked deputy president—a polygamist, a hearty, glad-handing man of all seasons—would have shortly thereafter have had his day in court and revealed all, or would have chosen to remain silent to protect the ANC and other potential miscreants. But none of that ensued. (A few years

Figure 7.3. Jacob Zuma

earlier, before the state indicted Zuma, I spent several days with Zuma at a conference in Britain; he was a man of big smiles, lots of gregarious swapping of tales with former President F. W. de Klerk, another attendee, but with very little in the way of salient contributions to the subject of the conclave. Zuma was easy to like for bonhomie, if not for his discourse.)

A different trial, in late 2005, acquitted Zuma of raping the HIV-positive daughter of a close acquaintance. He said that she had dressed provocatively. Zuma, then sixty-three, was compelled to concede, however, that he had engaged in unprotected sex, and that he had guarded himself against contracting HIV/AIDS by taking a post-coital shower.[40]

The taint of corruption hung over Zuma, and the ANC, until late 2007, when his campaign to oust Mbeki as president of the ANC bore fruition at an infamous congress of the party in Polokwane (Pietersburg). Zuma had started campaigning against Mbeki immediately after being called a corrupt conspirator. Mbeki's imperious manner had made enemies. So had his centralizing tendencies, keeping some aspirant ANC entrepreneurs from constructing their own edifices of financial well-being through provincial-level political officeholding.

Zuma was popular with less formally educated members of the ANC. (Originally chosen by Mbeki as deputy president because "this man of limited education and lack of open political ambition" was malleable and unlikely to pose a political threat, Zuma schemed all the while.)[41] His accession could also take the party back to its Zulu roots, and end the Xhosa (and professional) stranglehold on high office and the perquisites of such prominence.

Zuma may have been less able to converse smartly with European heads of government or American vice presidents than Mbeki, but he was a consummate old-school politician of the baby-kissing variety who could raise emotional temperatures among urban and rural South Africans alike.

Unceremoniously, Zuma's coalition ousted Mbeki from the ANC presidency in 2007, making Zuma the presumptive winning candidate for president after the scheduled 2009 national parliamentary election (South African presidents are chosen by the parliamentary majority). These politically intense machinations heralded an ignominious ending of Mbeki's career as a legitimate and legitimated national leader (he was subsequently to pursue a career as an African statesman), but they were even more destructive to good governance within the nation. The insidious forces of wholesale corruption, personified by Zuma's escape from perdition, could easily be celebrated and (despite pending court cases) thereafter enjoy the keys to the kingdom (both figuratively and literally).

As a political lame duck, Mbeki was still to suffer further indignity. In late 2008, a High Court judge dismissed Zuma's bribe-receiving indictment on technical grounds, moreover finding that Zuma could have reason to believe that he had been charged as a result of a political conspiracy. Mbeki had meddled in his case, the judge averred. The earlier discharge of Zuma from high office was termed "unfair and unjust."[42]

Immediately, the ANC's executive committee "recalled" Mbeki, a decision that Mbeki accepted with a prompt resignation even though only Parliament could really terminate his presidential term. Ironically, in 2009 the South African Supreme Court of Appeals overturned the High Court findings regarding Zuma, calling them unfounded and gratuitous. It reinstated the charges against Zuma, even as he was preparing for a national election and a putative accession to real power. (South Africa's National Director of Public Prosecutions decided to halt the case against Zuma in 2009, a few days before the national election. But on appeal, the High Court once more reinstated the charges in 2016, and Zuma's case was again before the country's judges.)

Capturing the State

Zuma and his supporters ran roughshod over the state that they captured on behalf of the "popular" forces of the ANC. These popular forces were unquestionably avaricious, especially when the head of state implicitly gave himself and them license to loot the state for personal gain. After Zuma led the ANC to victory in the 2009 elections (ANC, 66 percent of the popular vote, down from 70 percent in 2004; the Democratic Alliance, 17 percent, up from 12 percent; the Congress of the People—an Mbeki ally—7 percent; and three minor parties 6 percent), the floodgates of corruption opened wide. President Zuma, trusting to political impunity, placed allies in key posts. Meanwhile the ANC's tradition of (nearly always) protecting its own, and Zuma's wily maneuvers, kept the long arm of the law from disturbing his presidential authority.

Within months of the ANC's victory at the polls and his own accession to the state presidency, Zuma was building a $27 million private retreat in KwaZulu-Natal with state funds. He also purchased a $251 million jet to whiz around the country and the continent. At almost the same time, numerous parliamentarians were caught padding their expense claims, several going so far as to take expensive air trips on the taxpayer dime. South Africa's top cop and the head of the police crime intelligence unit gathered bribes from ordinary thieves and gang leaders; in 2010–2011, a reputed 50 percent of all motorists in Gauteng, the country's wealthiest province, were shaken down at least once by uniformed police. The head of South Africa's special crime-busting force, the Scorpions, supposedly pocketed a massive bribe from a white Zimbabwean fixer and money launderer close to Emmerson Mnangagwa (later Zimbabwe's president) to waive a host of indictments.[43] Transparency International reported that 68 percent of South Africans said that the police were "extremely corrupt."[44] Archbishop

Desmond Tutu, disgusted, told a university audience in 2011 "that our country with such tremendous potential is [being] dragged backwards and downwards by corruption, which in some instances is quite blatant."[45]

Provincial administrations, not to be outdone, were rife with fake jobs and fake purchases. Special payments, as in Limpopo Province, were doled out to no-show cronies. Ten percent of teachers drawing monthly salaries simply did not exist. "We thought that South Africa could be different," rued the head of the South African Communist Party in Limpopo. According to the younger brother of former President Mbeki, Limpopo was hardly unique: "It is all over the country." Further, "It [was] a general form of self-enrichment by the politically connected."[46]

The construction at Nkandla proceeded not so much in secret—locals and journalists suspected that official appropriations were being misused—but for several years as an integral contribution to security for the state president. It was only when Thuli Madonsela, South Africa's official Public Protector (ombudsperson) in 2014 labeled Zuma a fraudster, with instructions from her office that he must repay the nation most of the costs of the massive mansion, that South Africans began to realize that Zuma had engaged not in ordinary thefts from the state, but in serious kleptocratic grand corruption. Her pronouncement led neither to apology nor remorse on the part of Zuma; indeed, she was excoriated by the president and the ANC and, a year later, the minister of police absolved Zuma of any obligation to repay millions of rand. The minister claimed that the retreat's cattle kraal, chicken run, and sizable amphitheater were all needed for "security," along with a swimming pool. Two years later, however, Madonsela's criticisms made their way to the nation's Constitutional Court; it chastised Zuma severely, ordering him to reimburse the state for some of the (minor) expenditures on his palace.[47]

These rebukes to Zuma did little to check his appetite. Indeed, already South Africans learned that he had permitted a triumvirate of brothers from India to "capture" the state, that is, to gain special access for themselves to state contracts and corporate privileges in exchange for jobs and lucrative opportunities for Zuma, and for Zuma's sons. State capture is more than paying off greedy officials; it distorts government policy for personal gain—it becomes the perfection of grand corruption.[48]

Some of the Gupta-arranged clandestine endeavors had occurred, under cover, for several years as the brothers (Ajay, Atul, and Rajesh), and Zuma gained control of state-owned enterprises: a large dairy, a uranium mine, and a newspaper established for propaganda purposes. They set up advertising and television companies, contemplated an air service to India, and created business fronts to siphon even more state funds into their own and Zuma family pockets, as well as into ANC coffers. "The Gupta caprice demonstrates how an entire country can fall to foreign influences without a single shot being fired—especially when that country is ruled by a divisive president who is skilled at fueling racial resentments, willing to fire his own intelligence chiefs to protect his business interests, and eager to use his elected position to enrich himself with unsavory investors," commented one investigative report.[49]

In 2013, the Guptas flaunted their influence by flying over 200 guests from India to Johannesburg for a family wedding, and, especially, by gaining unusual and unprecedented permission to land their flights at a military airport outside the city. Not only were those arrangements irregular; later it transpired that the wedding proceedings had been funded by laundered monies from the Free State. The Guptas also attempted in 2017 to bribe a deputy minister of finance, claiming that they "owned" Zuma.

The Zondo Commission of Inquiry began hearing evidence in 2018 of the depredations of the Zuma-Gupta fraud alliance, and of all that the South African state had squandered while being "captured." The commission, chaired by Deputy Chief Justice Raymond Zondo, heard damning testimony throughout 2021 of how fully the Gupta machine had penetrated the offices and systems of the state under Zuma, and exactly how and how much money (possibly $7 billion) they had laundered through questionable entities connected with or beholden to the administration of the Free State. They also stashed some of their proceeds in Texas. (It is not yet evident how many millions or billions of purloined dollars found their way to President Zuma, but hefty proceeds were shunted into the open hands of his son Duduzane—one of twenty-three known offspring with five wives.)[50] In 2019, the U.S. Treasury's office of terrorism and financial intelligence imposed sanctions on the Gupta trio: "The Gupta family leveraged its political connections to engage in widespread corruption and bribery, capture government contracts, and misappropriate state assets."[51] (Meanwhile, the Guptas fled to Dubai, and were arrested there in early June 2022, pending extradition to South Africa.)

When the first three volumes of the Zondo Commission's findings were published early in 2022, more than 1,400 persons and institutions were cited for defrauding the state, and it offered numerous telling recommendations regarding procurement and other state practices. As a prominent South African commentator explained after reading the report's 874-page first volume: "The democratic state *was* captured; key institutions *were* looted as vast sums of public money were stolen. Former president Jacob Zuma and his motley network of exploited and exploitative allies *were* responsible."[52] The second volume called the Gupta efforts "a racketeering enterprise" and the illicit proceedings between 2009 and 2018 "a "systematic scheme of securing illicit and corrupt influence or control over the decision-making."[53] The final volume set out full details of exactly how Zuma and the Guptas captured and criminalized the state, and what the Ramaphosa government should do to make such corrupt dealings impossible in the future.

About the same time that these Gupta and capture revelations had added to the array of Zuma's alleged peculations—his conditioning of ministerial and other appointments on appropriate kickbacks and, in the case of the state security services, on protection for himself and his family—a South African corporate executive unrelated to the Guptas admitted proffering cash bribes (termed "monopoly money") to high-ranking members of the ANC executive and to stuffing $22,000 into a fancy handbag delivered to Zuma. An ANC cabinet minister separately appreciated receiving an annual Christmas basket that contained four cases of fancy whiskey, forty cases of beer, and eight slaughtered lambs, cut up. Not surprisingly, a researcher concluded that corruption was "deeply embedded" in the ANC at all levels. "In parts of the country it more closely resembles a criminal enterprise than a political parry. Tender corruption, the rampant plundering of state assets, and kickbacks have become the new normal."[54] These conclusions constituted a massive understatement of the real state of graft, fraud, and influence peddling in South Africa in the years after Mandela. During Zuma's presidency, at least $32 billion were stolen.[55]

In late 2020, Ace Magashule, secretary general of the ANC and a close comrade of Zuma, appeared in court charged with twenty-one counts of corruption, fraud, and money laundering. The various counts specified that he had received sums as large as $14 million and as small as $3,431 in exchange for various favors and contracts. He also regaled in taking taxpayer-funded trips to places as distant as Cuba. As party secretary general, Magashule oversaw the day-to-day running of the ANC's political and corporate machine, all the while proving himself a model wheeling-and-dealing kleptocrat. Magashule, a popular figure, headed the Free State government for more than a decade during Zuma's ascendancy. He also favored Zuma, rather than Ramaphosa, in the 2018 contested race for the ANC's top leader.[56] (See below, p. 186.)

South Africa's National Prosecuting Authority, unleashed by Ramaphosa's accession to the presidency, is still chasing other ANC operatives implicated in the Gupta-Zuma orchestrated theft of state resources. But whether the prosecutions, perhaps convictions, and a newly articulated animosity toward peculation by officials of the nation will moderate elected politicians' employing their offices primarily as tribute-collecting operations is yet to be seen. It all depends on the signals that Ramaphosa and his administration emit in 2022, and the extent to which the government is able to implement the Zondo reform recommendations.

Given a decade of strenuous state capture, it is no wonder that the latest Corruption Perceptions Index ranks South Africa even lower than its hitherto abysmal place on the annual scale. In 2021, it fell to seventieth place (of 180), with a score of 44 (of 100). That put it on par with Jamaica and Tunisia, and above Ghana and Hungary, but below China, Romania, and Montenegro. Among African countries, South Africa is the seventh least corrupt, well after the Seychelles, Cape Verde, Botswana, Rwanda, São Tomé and Principe, and Namibia—a dismal but realistic showing for a country so advanced and wealthy.[57]

Assessing Zuma's Presidency

Halfway through Zuma's two terms as president of South Africa, I brought a number of prominent and dispassionate South Africans together to analyze the state of the nation. Their considered assessments of how lamentably the country had failed to meet the heady promises of independence and how South Africa's governing elites still fell far short of satisfying the reasonable expectations of their constituents, echoed Archbishop's Tutu's earlier lament.[58] In 2022, the conclusions of those experts still suitably frame the national discontent, even under a very different successor. Many of the problems of the Mbeki and Zuma eras fester still, catalysts for reform.

Under Zuma, the economy grew far too slowly to generate the kinds of returns that could reduce unemployment, raise living standards, provide new housing starts, extend medical support, and create more and better educational opportunities. In 2013, South Africa's GDP only rose 1.9 percent compared to an average of 5.5 percent for the rest of sub-Saharan Africa. It did little better the next years and then fell sharply into recession for two years before increasing to 0.9 percent in 2018 and 1.1 percent in 2020. In 2021, its GDP swelled by 4.9 percent. With a labor force increasing each year under Zuma and afterward by 6 percent or more, these earlier measly growth numbers denominated great suffering, hunger, and societal distress, especially since only 43 percent of working-age adults held formal sector jobs in 2013, and an estimated 47 percent were formally employed in 2019. Through another optic, the official South African formal unemployment rate in 2021 was 34 percent, a number that many expert observers in South Africa believed was lower by perhaps 10 percent than it should have been.[59] In any event, however, shortages of jobs remain an unfortunate feature of South African reality well into 2022.

South Africa under Zuma and Ramaphosa remained dependent on exports for foreign exchange earnings, for large proportions of its GDP, for formal employment opportunities, and for the cash with which to exploit its primary resources. From underground, it still digs out large quantities of gold and fewer carats of diamonds. It mines iron ore, platinum, palladium, manganese, vanadium, ferrochrome, and much low-quality coal. It also sells motor vehicles, steel, electrical and mechanical machinery, citrus fruits, a little aluminum, and beer and spirits. Of about \$90 billion worth of exports, about 32 percent goes to Asia, 25 percent to Europe, 8 percent to the United States, and the remainder to its near abroad—to members of the African Union.

If South Africa could become a manufacturing powerhouse or an offshore service center it could offer jobs to the unemployed and alleviate poverty. But, surprisingly, South Africa's real costs of labor are higher than expected, making job creation in South Africa more difficult than in several Asian states as well as a number in Africa.[60] Despite massive unemployment, restrictive labor laws closely regulate how workers work. High minimum wage restrictions further curtail South Africa's ability to compete on cost grounds with Asian manufacturers—a legacy of the national trade union's close affiliation with the ANC. South Africa also loses to Asia because of educational deficits and skilling shortages. Then there are infrastructural impediments such as contorted and high-cost transportation bottlenecks and still unstable supplies of electricity. Corruption also hurts, sapping the sanctity of contracts and undermining the rule of law. High crime rates inhibit investment.

South Africa during the Zuma years was and is still one of the globe's least equal nations, a thin layer of whites and empowered black fat cats grabbed (and still hold) most of the country's old and new wealth. In terms of Gini-coefficient numbers, the country in 2013 and after fell into the 60 percent range, where 100 percent marks complete inequality. In 2018, the rate was 63 percent. The comparable figure for Brazil, a country where wealth is notoriously mal-distributed, is 53 percent. South Korea's number, at the other end of the continuum, is 31 percent. In 2013 and now, South Africa astonishingly (measured by the Gini coefficient) is a more unequal society than it was during the apartheid era.

Poverty is widespread despite the fact that more households than ever before have access to electric power (whenever Eskom, the beleaguered state monopoly producer, can supply it), potable water, improved sanitation, health clinics, and welfare grants. Old-age pensions support possibly as many as 20 million of the country's 57 million people. At the end of Zuma's first term, a full 44 percent of all households relied on social grants for everyday subsistence.

Despite such progress, and the persistent growth of consumer-driven middle-class accomplishments, respondents to periodic General Household Surveys wanted much more than they were receiving. "The standard [that people] expect seems to be rising faster than the pace at which the state can improve things."[61] People living in congested locations around most of South Africa's major cities expressed themselves loudly throughout the Zuma years demanding more water, improved sanitation, and steady power supplies.

They also asked for better schooling chances for their children. South African youngsters' standardized test results placed them near the bottom on all international measurement scales. According to the World Economic Forum, they ranked 146 of 148 in educational outcomes in 2014, lagging even several low-income African neighbors.[62] Only 40 percent of persons starting secondary school graduate; about 12 percent of those eventually taking the matriculation examination that caps secondary school now pass it with marks high enough to qualify for a university place. As in other sub-Saharan African countries, massive skills shortages were not addressed during the Zuma years, and remain unaddressed today. South Africa will continue to find it onerous to attract foreign or domestic investment without improving teaching, student persistence, and learning outputs at all levels, especially secondary and tertiary.

Blackouts, service interruptions, load shedding—whatever Eskom called its inability from Zuma's time onward—created inconvenience issues for consumers, but the more telling effects occurred in industry. Productive businesses had to shut occasionally, and so did mining operations. But the biggest, and the continuing problem, was unreliability. It was difficult in the teens for a mismanaged and thoroughly corrupted electricity generator to maintain the supply of steady power when plants burning coal had been under-maintained for years, imports from the distant Cahora Bassa hydropower plant on the Zambezi River in Mozambique were sporadic because of low water, and the entire enterprise had been turned over to political rather than technically qualified appointees. Wind and solar still contribute too little to the country's energy supply because of transmission line deficits and a failure, until very recently, to invest in alternative energy.

Massive un- and underemployment contributes in obvious way to poverty, health deficits, and crime. So does lax policing, poorly trained cops, underfunding of law enforcement, and the ease with which hardened criminals can traduce ordinary police persons and their superiors. Some time ago, when I took a celebrated police commissioner who had commanded cops in New York and Los Angeles to examine policing in South Africa, he was startled by failures to patrol, fear of combating crooks in the dark, and technological backwardness.[63]

South Africa's cities and townships had always been appallingly unsafe and insecure, even during the days of heightened surveillance under apartheid. Violent property crimes—aggravated robberies, business thefts, and car and truck hijackings at a rate of 225 per 100,000 people—placed South Africa in 2016 among the least secure jurisdictions in the world. Moreover, the statistics cannot fully characterize the extent to which South Africa is an unusually angry society, with strikingly high levels of violence accompanying crime. Rape is common, and vastly underreported. Recently, homicides numbered 16,200, placing South Africa among countries with highest domestic levels of murder. Most were of African males killing African males.

Elevated South African rates of homicide (as a proxy for overall crime levels) continued well into the Ramaphosa presidency. In 2020, even after the new president had begun to re-professionalize the policing and prosecution services, and had attempted to reduce graft, South African homicides on a per capita basis ranked tenth highest in the world, with 34 persons killed per 100,000 people. (El Salvador topped the deadliest list with 83 killings per 100,000, followed by Honduras [57], Venezuela [56], the US Virgin Islands [49], Jamaica [47], Lesotho [41], Belize [38], St Vincent [36], and St. Kitts [34].)[64]

Even as Mbeki had mistakenly let HIV/AIDS run amok among the South African population, so Zuma's own cavalier macho approach did little to reduce HIV/AIDS' lethality in the country. However, his administration eventually embraced the anti-retroviral medicines that converted South Africa's very high incidence of the disease to chronic rather than inevitably fatal status. Zuma's health authorities followed Botswana, supplying the necessary medicines generously, and at cost. But they had less success, relatively, with multiple drug-resistant tuberculosis—rife in high-density "locations" surrounding major cities and in some rural areas. Childhood perils such as diarrhea and pneumonia remain rampant, as does malaria. Paradoxically, too, South Africa now endures childhood obesity and diabetes at first-world levels.

Another casualty of the Mbeki/Zuma presidencies was the ANC's creeping loss of legitimacy as a founding liberation political movement. In 2014, the ANC still won parliamentary seats comfortably, but with a slightly reduced majority over the prior election in 2009. However, in 2018 the opposition Democratic Alliance (DA, previously the DP) gained seats and, more threateningly to the ANC, significantly strengthened its hold on the voters of the Western Cape Province and of Cape Town. It also made striking gains in Gauteng and Johannesburg, votes for the ANC in the cities of the industrial heartland (and Cape Town) slipping by 10 percent. Provincial and municipal vote totals also showed that the black middle class had begun to abandon the ANC.

The DA had long run Cape Town well. I tried to confirm what I had heard favorably from (mostly cynical) residents by interviewing ebullient Mayor Patricia de Lille and some of her key staff persons at length, and by confirming that many city services were better performed in Cape Town than inside other South African cities, even with the onset of a massive drought, and the rationing of water. But de Lille and her staff were up to those tasks, and many more, showing that South Africa could be run well, albeit so far more from outside the ANC orbit than within.[65]

On several occasions I also tried to understand why Parliament was so weak, why it failed over and over to curb the myriad mistakes of the ANC executive and why individual legislators refused or failed to provide the oversight of executives that is the main function of such a parliamentary body. The answer was two-fold: because of the manner in which it was constituted, and because of the nature of the ANC itself. Proportional list voting systems—and South Africa's is an extreme version—give unassailable power to party bosses, in South Africa's case to the president and the executive committee. They choose the persons on the upper (potentially winning) section of the party's candidate list. Names below the line (below the fifty-eighth percentage in the case of the 2019 poll) simply cannot achieve election. And party bosses determine who is placed where on the (winning) list. According to ANC practice, the central executive "deploys" its followers when and how it chooses. Obedience is assumed.

Correspondingly, there are effectively no constituencies (although the ANC has now created them arbitrarily), so "voice" is muted and parliamentarians naturally obey the party rather than their own instincts, their principles, or what they might think that their people want. Additionally, within Parliament, the ANC controls the order of business, and the daily proceedings, all to its own advantage. Even a Harvard Kennedy School student from a leading ANC family who had become Speaker of Parliament confessed to me that he was not completely in charge of the House of Assembly, as his counterparts across the English-speaking globe certainly can be. He had to take orders from the central executive of the party, no matter how ill-considered they were. Moreover, as in intolerant "guided" democracies or autocracies elsewhere, the ANC president and key ministers ignore or evade answering questions in plenary and even in committee meetings of Parliament. This deviation from the Westminster model of customary parliamentary behavior is not a recipe for democracy; more is it a recipe for authoritarianism.[66]

Parliaments, moreover, have the history and enunciated duty of providing oversight, curbing the excesses of the executive, and making extensive inquiries on the part of the general public. They have functioned that way for centuries, on the hoary English model. However, when the Special Committee on Public Accounts—among the two or three most important parliamentary institutions—appropriately tried in South Africa to investigate the unfolding Armsgate scandal in 2001, the party shut it down, threatening its ANC members with punishment.[67] That was almost the end of South African parliamentarians' ability to do their job.

This parliamentary weakness joined the steady slippage of the ANC as a ruling party. Its clear loss of popularity at the 2019 polls corresponded to what others and I had been hearing and reading in South Africa. Older ANC stalwarts, especially those who had joined the ANC from the South African Communist Party and remained staunch trade unionists, became dismayed at the corrupt maneuvering of the post-Mandelan ANC. Having hoped for societal transformation, many of these original supporters of Mandela and the ANC, some of whom had linked up with the ANC in exile, felt decidedly let down by the self-referential and incompetent governmental apparatus called the ANC.[68] Likewise, campaigners against apartheid who had joined the ANC in exile or had worked clandestinely for the ANC from safe niches within South Africa believed by the teens that moral decay had engulfed the ANC. Archbishop Tutu urged South Africa to try hard to "recover the spirit that made us great." (Tutu's death at ninety at the very end of 2021 brought thoughtful eulogies from within South Africa and throughout the world that emphasized his moral presence, his lament for the transforming ANC that was meant to be, and his oft-expressed dismay at the rise of a new ruling elite that was as self-serving as the oppressors of old.)

Mamphele Ramphele declared that South Africa under Zuma had lost its "moral authority and international respect." Indeed, she regretted that "the country of our dreams has unfortunately faded. . . . My generation has to confess to the young people of our country [that] we have failed you."[69] Many more disillusioned dissidents, including several ANC parliamentarians, complained in public and in person to me that the ANC had abandoned non-racialism for ethnically denominated patronage. Many were tired of waiting for the ANC to cleanse itself. It had lost its way.

Ramphosa's Resurgence

Righting the ANC and helping its ship to sail into more esteemed harbors were among the overridingly tough tasks that Ramaphosa inherited from Zuma. Especially facing Ramaphosa now is an urgent need to help the ANC to abandon "careerism," stop looting the state, cease behaving as if politics existed primarily to serve a predatory elite, and to begin fully to promote the national rather than the party interest—all admonitions to the ANC made by none other than Mandela, at the 1997 party congress.[70]

Ramaphosa returned to the ANC as an ordinary member of its National Executive Council in 2007, became deputy party president behind Zuma in 2012, four years into Zuma's incumbency, and deputy state president in 2014. He had spent ten very lucrative years in the political wilderness (1997–2007) while amassing board directorships, a sizable fortune, and herds of pedigree long-horned cattle from Uganda. Only when becoming deputy state president did he shelve his corporate career and divest himself of many of his investment holdings—but not his prized cattle.

When the Guptagate scandal emerged in its fullest form in 2017 and it became evident that corruption charges would inevitably overshadow Zuma's last months in the presidency, Ramaphosa was well placed within the ANC hierarchy to presume promotion to the party as well as the national presidencies. At the late 2017 ANC national congress, Zuma was as much a target of displeasure as Mbeki had been ten years earlier. But Zuma was unwilling simply to let Ramaphosa succeed him as easily as he had displaced Mbeki. Indeed, in order to have some hope of continuing to evade prosecution and censure, he proceeded to back a former wife and serving cabinet minister as the party's president, trusting that she would protect him from further investigation. Nkosasana Dlamini-Zuma had been Jacob Zuma's first wife and the mother of his four daughters. A physician, she later served in Mandela's cabinet as minister of health, as chair of the executive commission of the African Union, and as Mbeki's minister of foreign affairs and Zuma's minister of home affairs. She was a plausible counter candidate to Ramaphosa, and the ANC otherwise had too few senior leaders who were women. But she was also a candidate promoted by Zuma so that he could (presumably) be relieved of harsh court proceedings. Zuma well knew how to hamstring the police and prosecutors; there was every reason to believe that his ex-wife would willingly cooperate. Nevertheless, Zuma's terminal loss of legitimacy, and Dlamini-Zuma's own political weaknesses, doomed her candidacy. Ramaphosa, much more personally engaging, much better connected and backed by the labor movement, the media, industry, and opinion shapers who had known his talents and accomplishments over almost three decades, could count on significant support outside of the party. The ANC itself had to consider, too, that he alone could appeal to the legions of potential voters who presumably reviled Zuma's corruption, and might otherwise cease supporting the ANC electorally.

In late 2017, at another ANC national congress, Ramaphosa narrowly triumphed to become party president and the presumptive leading candidate for the national presidency in 2019. However, in a drama that was still occupying stage center in 2022, the six senior elected party positions beyond president were split evenly between backers of Ramaphosa and supporters of Zuma. Magashule was in Zuma's corner. So were Gwede Mantashe and Paul Mashatile. David Mabuza and Jesse Duarte voted for Ramaphosa. The eighty other members of the National Executive Committee fitted into one or the other of the disputatious camps.

To rid themselves of the Zuma albatross, too, the ANC executive committee had to "recall" Zuma, a demand that Zuma resisted until finally giving way with much backbiting and drama in early 2018. Ramaphosa accordingly took office and prepared for the 2019 national poll; his "toughest and most important task," I wrote at the time, was "to restore South Africa's belief in itself"—a process still ongoing in 2022. I also opined that he "must try to repair South Africa's social fabric first, and then ... rebuild accountability and transparency leading to trust." Moreover, " . . . without turning skeptical youths (half of the country, demographically) into believers willing to reject criminal pursuits for the possibility of jobs, South Africa will find it difficult," I wrote, "to rejuvenate itself after the last years of ... Zuma."[71] In 2022, that tension remains stark.

At the 2019 national polls the ANC triumphed with a reduced margin of 58 percent (down from 62 percent in 2014), the DA won 21 percent, and the Economic Freedom Fighters took 11 percent of the vote. Ramaphosa's character and his candidacy had saved the ANC from national ignominy while it lost control of several provinces and municipalities. In both Port Elizabeth (part of the Nelson Mandela Bay Municipality) and Johannesburg, the DA assumed control, together with their long domination of Cape Town and the Western Cape Province.

Ramaphosa in 2020 and 2021 started to reinvigorate South Africa's sense of national purpose and to promise, if not as yet necessarily to deliver, the kinds of public services that South Africans seek and that other nearby nationals, such as those living in Botswana and Namibia, enjoy. It was Ramaphosa's unfortunate leadership lot to "distribute the pain of extended austerity" and to cope with frightening vaccine insufficiencies as his country battled the Covid-19 pandemic—not necessarily to a standstill. Moreover, as a perceptive columnist wrote, "the alliance Ramaphosa leads [was] at war with itself" and South Africa's bureaucratic establishment was, alas, newly "hobbled and weak."[72]

These problems and problematics obviously made Ramaphosa's task of cleaning up after Zuma while holding off ANC opponents that much more difficult, controversial, and—to an inpatient public—easily misunderstood and easily criticized. Yet, what still stood out in 2021 and 2022 was Ramaphosa's undeniable personal integrity, his appointment of more qualified cabinet ministers than those chosen by Zuma, his willingness to recognize and accept the organizational and governance deficits that his administration had inherited, and his clear determination to make South Africa a better place. Testifying in 2021 about Zuma's failure to steer the ANC honestly and his defiance of an officially constituted inquiry, Ramaphosa carefully told the Zondo Commission on State Capture that "the position of the ANC on leaders and members who have been complicit in acts of corruption or other crimes [was compromised]. Their actions [were] a direct violation not only of the laws of the Republic, but also of the ANC constitution, its values and principles. Such members must face the full legal consequences of their actions."[73] South Africa's head of state made it clear that the rule of law must, and should, be maintained.

Ramaphosa's courage in the face of the pro-Zuma hostility of a proportion of the ANC executive, his determination to do right, and his evident emotional intelligence gave renewed hope to everyone who wanted South Africa finally to realize the advances and stability that Mandela promised his anxious countrymen in 1994. Ramaphosa, trying to overcome immense entropy within the ANC, showed time and again that he was his country's last best chance for progress. Only his leadership, it seemed, could assist South Africa in realizing the still unachieved peace dividend of the 1990s.

These sentiments, and his leadership of the nation, were sorely tested in July 2021. The Constitutional Court, in a triumphant exercise of judicial supremacy, ordered Zuma to spend fifteen months in jail for contempt of court—for repeatedly defying orders mandating testimony by him before the Zondo Commission (and for thus challenging the "normative" foundations of South Africa's rule of law.)[74] After Zuma turned himself in to serve his sentence, his supporters precipitated a week-long burst of rioting and looting throughout the cities of South Africa; Ramaphosa had to mobilize the army to restore order and calm, especially in Johannesburg and Durban. (Rioting led to at least 212 deaths and 118 violent confrontations between the police and protestors.) It was clear that Zuma's associates hoped that the disturbances (the worst in South Africa since rolling urban battles against apartheid) would bring down Ramaphosa's government and somehow make Zuma (and his coterie) powerful again.

Ramaphosa addressed the South African nation in mid-July: "It is clear now," he said trenchantly, "that the events of the past week were nothing less than a deliberate, coordinated and well-planned attack on our democracy. The constitutional order of our country is under threat." Furthermore, "These actions are intended to cripple the economy, cause social instability and severely weaken— or even dislodge—the democratic state. Using the pretext of a political grievance, those behind these acts have sought to provoke a popular insurrection."[75]

Months later, Ramaphosa and the ANC learned that the continuing battles between Zuma's followers and those who believed more in Ramaphosa's leadership intentions and accomplishments (amid the coronavirus pandemic) cost the party significant political support across wide swaths of the nation. Facing widespread despair over enduring corruption and decreasing service delivery (governance), for the first time in South Africa's post-apartheid history the ANC won less than 50 percent of the seats contested in municipal (or any other) electoral exercise. Only 47 percent, a historically low turnout, of the eligible electors cast ballots in the November 2021 poll.

More than 95,000 candidates ran for 10,468 mayoral positions and council seats in cities and towns in every province. New coalitions between the ANC and smaller parties had to be constructed to rule municipalities. Yet, many of the ANC's traditional rivals and allies also lost traction. The DA forfeited seats while the Inkatha Freedom Party gained support in KwaZulu-Natal and the Afrikaner Freedom Front Plus also added positions. On the eve of the poll, Ramaphosa told a campaign rally, "I see development everywhere."[76] But voters thought otherwise, buffeted as they were even before the arrival of the Omicron corona variant by pandemic restrictions, limited vaccination possibilities, shortages of staples, a weak economy, and renewed problems with water and electrical power availabilities.

Commentators wondered if South Africa, long regarded as sub-Saharan Africa's most advanced state, was in fact failing—failing its millions of constituents, failing the supporters of the ANC and other political parties, and failing those who had believed in the creation in the 1990s of a new and potentially flourishing rainbow nation. Neethling asked whether July's mayhem in KwaZulu/Natal and Gauteng, battles in the eastern Cape Province, and hostage taking of cabinet ministers in Pretoria indicated (along with high unemployment and electricity supply failures) that "the administrative, political, and economic systems have become so weak that key governmental functions [have] become inoperable or even [have] disintegrate[d]." Had there been sufficient betterments for the majority of South Africans since 1994?

The country was more racially just than in 1994 but much more violent, with those hostilities costing 19 percent of GDP. (The Global Peace Index placed South Africa as the 128th least peaceful country out of 161 nations rated.) Law enforcement agencies were simply not "up to the task" of providing security and safety to South Africans. So, in terms of at least this analysis, South Africa was far less "strong" than it once was and its "weakness" was beginning to trend toward a profound failure to perform fully for its peoples.[77]

At the end of the fifth month of 2022, South Africa's "official" death toll attributed to the coronavirus pandemic constituted 101,000 of Africa's total (and probably underreported) 254,000 deaths. Of Africa's 12.4 million cases, South Africa acknowledged 3.96 million at the same time.[78] Ramphosa's lockdowns probably kept those totals from becoming greater, but in mid-2022 he and his administration were still struggling to vaccinate citizens (only 25 percent having both jabs) in order more fully to lessen the impact of the disease in South Africa. (At that point, only 12 percent of the rest of Africa were vaccinated.) Ramaphosa was dealing far less than elsewhere in the world with a reluctance on the part of citizens to accept inoculation than he was with a sheer shortage of vaccines. He was also attempting (successfully only in 2022) to manufacture vaccines in South Africa for distribution to South Africans, and to break the lock on patents (and thus manufacturing) of the major Messenger RNA vaccine producers.

The polarized nature of the ANC executive committee means that someone as gifted as Ramaphosa cannot, even in 2022, lead South Africa as independently and forthrightly as he should and could. Having mixed support from the party's executive committee limits how bold Ramaphosa has been and can be. Nevertheless, Ramaphosa is of a generation that is more progressive, and more transformational than transactional in his approach than his erstwhile opponents within the party. Ramaphosa presumably knows that integrity matters more than ever, and that his success as a leader depends very considerably on breaking with the arbitrary and rather callous Mbeki and Zuma approaches to policy-making.

Rebuilding trust in the state and the party, especially after the devastation of the coronavirus and his own mixed success at weighing protection against the pandemic and maintaining the livelihoods of his constituents, is obviously essential.

Throughout 2021, and thanks to the coronavirus, the nation's economy teetered again on the brink of recession. In terms of per capita GDP since 1994, South Africa compared to the rest of the world had slipped by 20 percent. Even compared just to Africa, South Africa's lead over other countries had fallen considerably. In 1994, South Africa's per capita GDP was more than four times greater than China's, but in 2021 South Africa's was half of that of China. In 1994, South Africa generated more electricity per head than the rest of the world on average; in 2021 power production had receded to 60 percent of the global average. As compared to China, also, South Africa in 2021 generated only half of what China supplied per person, whereas in 1994 it produced six times more power than China. Life expectancy rates had also suffered as compared to world statistics.[79]

A trenchant analysis of South Africa's great economic slide (and very slow growth) from the relatively more prosperous years before the global crisis of 2008 blames most of South Africa's woes on its declining total factor productivity, especially in the electricity sector, other state-owned enterprises, and the export industrial sector. Even the mines, once South Africa's bulwark economically, produced less well in the recent decade than before 2011. "Economic policy," the report says, "needs without delay to tackle the microeconomic drivers of the country's productivity decline."[80] Too many production bottlenecks remain; foreign and even domestic investment will not revive unless South Africa is better managed and better governed.

Unfortunately, the trials of leadership in South Africa persist: jobs are hard to find; schooling still suffers from teacher quality, teacher absences, and teacher union obduracy. Pneumonia, HIV/AIDS, multidrug-resistant tuberculosis, malaria, and the coronavirus—and finally the Omicron mutation and whatever comes next—are morbid and fatal.

Patriarchy remains a prevalent obstacle to a broad-based uplift. Electrical power continues to arrive much too episodically, with load-shedding blackouts still frequent. Municipalities fail to provide basic services, mostly because of corruption and incompetence.[81] The paucity of affordable housing and reliable urban transport affects life chances and productivity. Ramaphosa also will need in 2022 and 2023 to battle the teaching trade unions to restore vigorous learning opportunities at the primary and secondary schooling levels, and to encourage foreign and domestic investment in order greatly to multiply available formal sector jobs. Stronger management needs to replace cronyism and patronage. Most of all, the state really was captured, distorted, and eviscerated under Zuma. Retrieving promise and rebuilding confidence are among Ramaphosa's most compelling objectives. Those of us who knew him in the 1990s say that he definitely is the man for this, and other, seasons unless the tentacles of sleaze and easy money have too enduringly rotted the innards of the new state.

Ramaphosa's South Africa also has a major problem of indebtedness. Its yearly growth prospects lag interest repayment requirements. Debt service furthermore crowds out spending on schools, health, roads, and the like. Moreover, comments a leading South African economist: "A state that cannot maintain a monopoly on the use of violence, that has an entrenched culture of corruption, and that also wants to open the spending taps, will not enjoy the confidence of investors. It will therefore see borrowing costs rise if it seeks to issue more debt, and the gap between growth rates and interest rates will widen further."[82]

Since he no longer need be diffident, having caught up with the Mbekis and Zumas of contemporary South Africa, and since of all of South Africa's leaders he is the only one with the acumen and legitimacy to reinforce Mandela's legacy, Ramaphosa should be poised (when the Covid pandemic becomes better controlled) to pull South Africa up by its proverbial bootstraps. Ramaphosa should be ready and willing (post-Covid) to focus fully on the needs of all of his peoples, not just ANC honchos and others in the party who are out mostly for themselves. (His battle to oust corrupt ANC grandees like Magashule continues.) South Africa really now has its last best chance to serve its citizens, and not just the whims of the political elite.[83] The Ramaphosa whom I knew in the 1990s could recreate a post-Mandelan South Africa; few others possess similar enduring leadership qualities. If he cannot, and if Ramaphosa's initiatives are thwarted or impeded by an ANC that continues to lust for outsized and effortless rewards and refuses to join him in embracing increased political participation, greater tolerance, and a concerted behavioral renaissance, South Africa could quickly regress to the sub-Saharan African mean in terms of governance quality and economic decay.

A strong sign of whether Mandela's South Africa will survive the tumult and distractions of 2021 and 2022 will come in December 2022, when the ANC decides whether to confirm Ramaphosa as its continuing leader.

8

Botswana

Africa's Democratic Exception

The southern African winter sun was giving out little warmth in the mid-1970s as President Sir Seretse Khama and I walked across a field toward the stadium in which he was about to educate an assembly of followers and listeners about good governance. The rise of petty and grand corruption, until then minor problems in Botswana in contrast to almost every other African country, still worried Khama. As we strolled to the stadium, accompanied at a distance by security personnel (in other African countries a president would have been driven, and would have been protected by a phalanx of guards) he told me that he had received reports that some of his own cabinet ministers and some possibly greedy senior civil servants were being tempted by the possibility of easy money. His talk, as I would soon hear, was to be a reiterated admonition to the people of Botswana against succumbing to or contributing to any forms of influence buying.

By the mid-1970s, Khama had been president and the much-respected leader of Botswana for nearly a decade. Unlike nearly all other great men leading their nations in sub-Saharan Africa in that era (and they were all men), Khama had dedicated his time in office to implanting an ethic of good governance. To do good, Khama asserted following Thomas Paine, was his religion.[1] At its critical core, good governance meant to Khama and his close associates an eschewing of corrupt dealings and the conscientious delivery of a range of expected services from emergency famine relief to new roads. Whereas neighboring apartheid-motivated South Africa, white-settler-ruled Zimbabwe, and African-run Zambia were all corrupt in their several ways, Botswana after nearly a decade was almost a sole outlier within the Organization of African Unity. On the mainland of Africa, it already stood out for its probity, its abstemious shunning of the fancy trappings of new ruling class pretensions, and its laser-like focus on expanding public services for all of Botswana's people, not just an ethnic minority or a ruling clique. All of that were Khama's doing, and a testament to his principled leadership and the example that he set personally.

As earlier chapters in this book have detailed, others of Khama's contemporaries presided over their states rather more grandly, with expressions of absolutism, and with appetites for personal enrichment. That was the prevalent

Overcoming the Oppressors. Robert I. Rotberg, Oxford University Press. © Oxford University Press 2023.
DOI: 10.1093/oso/9780197674208.003.0008

pattern throughout the continent during the 1960s, and more so during the 1970s and 1980s, before some attempted pushbacks and rearrangements (with little success) in the 1990s and thereafter.

Khama could easily have pursued similar goals. After all, he was a hereditary paramount chief and therefore had abundant traditional legitimacy. As paramount chief of the Bamangwato, the most populous of the Setswana-speaking ethnic groups that made up the majority of his constituents, and as the founder (along with a few others) of the ruling Botswana Democratic Party (BDP), Khama effortlessly could have followed the lead of Presidents Kwame Nkrumah in Ghana, Julius Nyerere in Tanzania, Jomo Kenyatta in Kenya, and Kenneth Kaunda closer to home in Zambia and fashioned a one-party system with himself as a president for life (as Kamuzu Banda was doing in Malawi). That is what liberationist leaders did, telling their citizens that they and their ruling parties knew best, and definitely knew what was developmentally most appropriate for a brand-new country-coming-into-being.

Even though I arrived well into the formative years of Khama's presidency to investigate what was becoming known as Africa's democratic and developmental miracle, the country as an embryonic state was still raw, and just beginning to establish itself internally and within Africa. Yet, by the mid-1970s, Khama's calm, steady, prudent methods had gained him growing circles of acclaim. (President Kennedy's first assistant secretary for state for Africa noted as early as 1961, after a visit, that Khama was "progressive or modern-minded," intelligent, and able.)[2] No political purges, common elsewhere in Africa, had occurred. No scandals had marred the BDP or besmirched Khama's retinue. Moreover, Khama and the BDP were holding and winning regular elections, thanks for the most part to their gradual delivery of improved educational, medical, and other essential services to the peoples of Botswana. In terms of the popular vote, the BDP won 68 percent in 1969, 77 percent in 1974, and 75 percent in 1979.[3] After Khama's death, despite internal feuds, the party consistently produced sizable majorities: 68 percent in 1984, 65 percent in 1989, 55 percent in 1994, 57 percent in 1999, 52 percent in 2004, 53 percent in 2009, 46 percent in 2014, and 53 percent in 2019 (when—see below, pp. 228–29—an outgoing president established a new party to contest the poll.)[4]

Even so, in the 1970s, Gaborone, the dusty new capital city along the old rail line between South Africa and Zimbabwe, was still small and unprepossessing, with government buildings, two hotels, a central commercial square, and empty fields that quickly intruded on both the administrative and the business areas. In the late 1970s and throughout the 1980s, Botswana hosted exiles and ANC guerrillas from South Africa. There were notorious South African military raids on guerrilla "safe" houses in Gaborone and elsewhere in the 1980s, and numerous air attacks on South Africans sheltering in Botswana, but, during my earliest visits, life in the country was seemingly tranquil, the way Khama wanted it. (For the attacks, and more, see chapter 9.)

Unlike so many other African heads of state, he had from the start hewn a non-ideological, understated, and very temperate path for his inexperienced people, and even for those of his followers and supporters who were worldly, conventionally well-educated, and anxious to emulate their African brethren farther north. He was of the country's cattle-owning aristocracy, which gave him credibility among that class and in the larger community of Tswana as well. Because of South Africa's antagonism toward him and his marriage, his anti-apartheid credentials were also easily established.

No one could gainsay Khama's patriotism, but there were critics to his left and voters to satisfy. Yet Khama enunciated principles, kept to them, demonstrated unquestioned personal integrity, and insisted that Botswana could become a model African nation despite (or because) of its unfortunate proximity to South Africa, South African–ruled Namibia, and Rhodesia (by which three hegemons it was almost entirely surrounded). Consequently, Khama and Quett (later Sir Ketumile) Masire, his very close associate and presidential successor, insisted from the beginning on doing everything within their and the fledgling nation's power to provide new educational opportunities for their constituents, relentlessly to upgrade their territory's rudimentary infrastructure, and to be active but prudent in modernizing what, before diamonds could be exploited, was still a thoroughly fragile and impoverished land.

As genial Archie Mogwe, Botswana's foreign minister and someone with whom I was in frequent contact during his many years in office (and later) as cabinet minister and ambassador, always reminded me: Khama and Masire were determined to establish a model country that could—in innumerable ways—put apartheid-run South Africa to shame. Botswana had to be holier and better run than its dominating neighbor.

A Unique Leader

Even more than George Washington, and much more in the mold of Lee Kuan Yew and Kemal Ataturk, the key markers of Khama's and their leadership were a vision of enhanced governmental quality and an inherent inclusivity that preceded that of Nelson Mandela's governance. Khama embodied integrity, transparency, accountability, self-mastery, and intellectual honesty, and displayed a committed and well-communicated sense of shared regard for the public interest. Unlike others, Khama communicated to his citizens that he was far less desirous of promoting his family benefits than he was of elevating the welfare of the country and its peoples. His restraint and his humility were genuine, and unusual in Africa. Even great humanists and personable leaders like Kaunda and Nyerere proved unable or unwilling fully to put their people's needs before their political parties' ambitions for power and hegemony.

Khama's leadership competencies always seemed instinctive and natural, but they may have been nurtured and reinforced by his heritage and training. After all, the disparate Tswana peoples had for centuries cherished consultative rather than arbitrary rule. Their traditional form of government was consensual. Like the *pitso* in Lesotho, the Tswanan *kgotla* embodied a gathering of all of a group's people (a kind of New England town meeting) around a chief for periodic discussions and the pursuit of tribal business. Admittedly, in practice the voices of "the people" were dominated by persons of influence within particular communities, with chiefs taking heed of the concerns of their near-peers, less often the thoughts of commoners. But the several layers of kgotla conclaves resolved disputes, advised village heads or superior chiefs on how plaintiffs and defendants should be treated and their cases resolved, and recommended how chiefs should impose responsibility for injuries or breaches of decorum. The kgotla further existed as a participatory escape valve for the airing of grievances, the articulation of requests for betterment, the raising of concerns that threatened communities and cried out for resolution, and circumspectly the prevention of chiefs and their associates from running amok with power. The kgotla functioned as a community parliament, a court of law, and in some respects as an administrative body.[5]

More than a century of Christian missionary preaching among the peoples of Botswana reinforced this ethos of listening, collaborating, and carefully bringing the opinions of a broader community into the decision-making arena. Many other African nations were also marinated in the missionary message, but the instructions of and life examples of the London Missionary Society (Congregational) pioneers impressed and acculturated five of the eight western Tswana peoples more formidably and in a more profoundly lasting manner than elsewhere on the continent. Certainly Khama, even though less a fervent disciple than a secular Christian, nevertheless grew up, was educated, and was thoroughly steeped in and conversant with the non-evangelical, comparatively non-judgmental, Congregational framework that conditioned the life and lives of most Tswana and their Kalanga, Sarwa, and other fellow citizens.

Khama's forefathers settled in what is now Botswana in the eighteenth century, and consolidated their control over comparatively hospitable territory along the eastern edge of the Kalahari Desert after beating back invaders of Zulu and Afrikaner descent, especially in the 1850s. Kwena Chief Sechele was among those who helped to lead the Tswana peoples during this crucial period, and is credited with assisting and collaborating with Ngwato Chief Khama III's efforts of resistance.

Beleaguered and fearing further attack from across what much later became a national boundary, they naturally welcomed the LMS missionaries from Scotland and England who came to save souls in the buffer borderlands; to translate the scriptures into Setswana; and to instruct their Setswana-speaking presumed parishioners in the meaning of biblical prescriptions, to read in their own tongue and in English, and to do sums. The missionaries also transferred vocational skills such as carpentry.

John Moffat was the leader of the doughty band of LMS adherents who settled among the transplanted Tswana near Kuruman and Mafeking, much later to become the chief towns of South Africa's Northern Cape Province. Within a few years, he and his family were joined by others from England and Scotland, including David Livingstone, a newly trained physician who yearned to explore and who married Moffat's eldest daughter.

Their collective influence and example, the morality and higher meaning of their message, and a sense that the missionaries could help to protect the Tswana in their new settlements soon led to conversions. Khama III, paramount chief of the Ngwato and Sir Seretse's grandfather, converted to Christianity in 1860, leading many of his people to follow. Chiefs of other Setswana-speaking ethnic groups soon joined Khama III in embracing the foreign creed. Together their disparate peoples formed Setswana-speaking Congregational churches.[6]

Whereas missionaries of various persuasions often found it excruciatingly difficult, if not impossible, elsewhere in Africa to make Christians of the disparate peoples among whom they settled, Moffat and his brethren tapped a comparatively receptive vein of openness to the new religious gospel and its meaning. Or perhaps the Tswana, given their need to keep Zulu and Ndebele warriors and Afrikaner attackers at bay, were anxious to gain allies and to embrace a new ideology, but one that in no way impinged punitively on their accustomed way of life. Indeed, the LMS preachers were more understanding of the folkways and mores of their new parishioners than the usual run of churchly interveners elsewhere on the continent. They respected those among whom they were sent to serve; missionaries elsewhere were often surprisingly impatient or intolerant of the peoples in whose midst they settled.[7]

The presence of missionaries and Khama III's consequent acquaintance with Western ways helped to lead him and other chiefs to accept the British establishment of the Bechuanaland Protectorate (not a colony) in 1885. The creation of a Protectorate was stimulated by Germany's acquisition of South-West Africa along Bechuanaland's western flank, but exactly what "protectorate" meant was not decided until 1891.[8] The imperial purpose of the Protectorate was to separate the rights and lands of the Tswana from the Germans and from the expansionist aims of the adjoining, Afrikaner-ruled, Transvaal Republic. Although the Tswana may also have welcomed the proclamation of the Protectorate as a means of forestalling the acquisitive land grabbing of Cecil J. Rhodes, the Kimberley diamond and Johannesburg gold-mining magnate, Rhodes nevertheless snaked a rail line from the diamond mines in South Africa northward along the edge of the Transvaal through the new Bechuanaland to the supposedly mineral-rich and newly conquered lands of the Ndebele (a Zulu offshoot) in modern Zimbabwe (and then on to and across Livingstone's Victoria Falls).[9]

The existence of a protectorate subsequently helped the Tswana peoples to avoid being absorbed into the Union of South Africa before and, after 1910, to resist the implanting of South African forms of racial segregation (well before the introduction of apartheid), and to maintain a cherished indigenous autonomy. But doing so could not prevent Bechuanaland from becoming dependent upon South Africa and its logistical infrastructure for nearly all of its consumer and other imports, such as fuel, and for much of the education of its young people beyond primary school. South Africa's mines provided almost the only source of formal sector employment for the bulk of Bechuanaland's young men, and hence for national earnings and potential improvements in standards of living.

Within the crucible of a nominal protectorate, the Ngwato and other Tswana learned to coexist alongside white-ruled South Africa. At home, within their own territorial domain, the Tswana became accustomed to the benign neglect of Britain, their colonial overlord. It administered the Protectorate, with its limited revenues, lightly, and individual governors and district commissioners (and their staffs) were respectful of Tswanan pursuits and preferences. A number even sought to elevate the lives and standards of their church-going subjects.

By 1930, when Sekgoma II, Seretse's father, died and passed the Ngwato throne to his nine-year-old son, the Ngwato and other Setswana speakers within the Protectorate were thoroughgoing parishioners, wedded to Christian morality, to the participatory practices of the kgotla, and to a largely rural, mostly pastoral existence on what could be considered the very periphery of the British Empire. It was during this period, suggests Botswana's second president, that the Tswana became very "process oriented."[10] That tendency reinforced the kgotla as a firm brake on arbitrary rule, and jibed well with the democratic values of the Congregational Church (echoed in Zambia by the advanced attitudes of the United Free Church of Scotland [Presbyterian], that nurtured Kaunda). (See chapters 1 and 2.)

The virtues of the kgotla and the imbued awareness and appreciation of ethical bright lines that accompanied the implantation of Congregationalism among the Tswana shaped the young Khama, heir to the Ngatwo chieftaincy but subject until attaining his majority to the stern regency and tutelage of his politically astute and ambitious uncle, Tshekedi Khama. But those two factors, plus the unquestioned conservative inclinations of his uncle, cannot alone account for the singularity of Seretse Khama and what he accomplished for the infant Botswana.

Nor can we ascribe Botswana's preference for democratic governance, antagonism to corruption, and trajectory of prosperity to its relatively small population (2.4 million in 2022) and to its alleged homogeneity as a nation. The different Tswana peoples could have demanded separate autonomies or caviled at the dominance of the Ngwato through Khama. After all, Somalia is no less homogenous than Botswana, with clan substituting for tribe. But Khama, unlike Somali President Siad Barre, never privileged one tribe over another, and no Tswana over Kalanga. He focused on building a nation, not on uplifting only the Ngwato. Unlike Jomo Kenyatta in Kenya, he never gave plum jobs and plum commercial opportunities to Ngwato (read Kikuyu) in preference to, say, Kgatla, Kwena, or Khururtse (read Kamba or Luo in Kenya).

The Maturing of Seretse

Tshekedi Khama groomed his orphaned ward for leadership from an early age. Young Seretse was trundled off to Lovedale School, the most distinguished mission-run educational enterprise in the eastern Cape Province of South Africa, through Standard V. There (and later at nearby Fort Hare University College) he was mentored by the learned Zachariah Keodirelang (Z. K.) Mathews, another Ngwato (but born in the Cape Province of South Africa). At that point, in 1935 (when he was fourteen), the slight, shy, somewhat mischievous teenager contracted tuberculosis, then and now a common South African affliction. After recuperating back among the Ngwato, Seretse went off to Adams College, a distinguished American Congregationalist secondary establishment near Durban. The next year he enrolled at the LMS' Tiger Kloof secondary school near Vryburg in the Northern Cape Province, much closer to home. Three years later, at eighteen, Seretse passed the Cape Junior Certificate examination, became a school prefect, actively boxed, played soccer, and showed versatility running track. Subsequently, after another year at Lovedale, Seretse attended Fort Hare, South Africa's premier tertiary institution for Africans. There, along with such classmates as Charles Njonjo of Kenya, Robert Sobukwe of South Africa (see chapter 6), and Ntsu Mokhehle of Lesotho (see chapter 1), he obtained his first BA degree, and also excelled at the high jump, rugby, and soccer.

African nationalist political feelings frequently found expression among Fort Hare students. Unlike so many others, however, in these student years of the early 1940s, Khama was drawn less to the message of the ANC, and more to nonracial or multiracial outlets of expression. However, there is evidence, too, that sometime during his three years at Fort Hare Khama became a proponent of African home rule and opposed continued control of Bechuanaland by whites.

In mid-1945, with World War II ended in Europe and transport overseas finally becoming possible, Khama sailed to Britain to enroll at Balliol College, Oxford, to study law. But that saga ended after a year when Khama's knowledge of Latin proved insufficient for a bachelor of civil laws degree. Instead, he began tutorials in politics, philosophy, and economics (then a relatively new Oxford undergraduate degree subject). But that also proved a dead end.

Exiled from the Kingdom

London in the immediate aftermath of war was still shell-shocked. Food of all varieties was short, and strictly rationed. Social services revived only slowly. The economy very gradually began improving. But amid this continued privation in the empire's hub, students from the colonies such as Khama, future Prime Minister Forbes Burnham from Guyana, Harry Nkumbula from Zambia (see chapters 1 and 2), and Njonjo lived in Nutford House, a hostel for overseas students. It was from Nutford House near Russell Square that Khama traveled every weekday to the Inner Temple, one of London's Inns of Court, where in 1947 he began eating obligatory ritual dinners and training in the law. This was a common and respectable route to becoming an accredited lawyer in Britain; annoyed at how he had been treated at Oxford, Khama soon settled into this orthodox manner of becoming an advocate.

Even before Khama had finished his studies, however, and qualified as a lawyer, he met Ruth Williams, a Briton, at a social event at Nutford House, wooed her, and married, assuming that they would both return together to Botswana so that he could assume his chiefly responsibilities. India and Pakistan had by that time become independent nations, there were modest nationalist stirring elsewhere, and the grip of the empire might—for the students at Nutford House at least—be imagined to be loosening. Plausibly, those who were from the colonies could contemplate a future with more numerous political possibilities than ever before.

Whether or not Khama realized that his marriage had profoundly altered the nature of his paramountcy and his role in Africa, it quickly transitioned him from obscurity to notoriety. His uncle and many senior Ngwato were furious, being strongly opposed to a white woman becoming their queen. British administrators in Bechuanaland were appalled at Khama's temerity. It took all of Khama's gentle persuasive powers and politicking skills, and months of on-the-ground efforts, to persuade the Ngwato kgotla in 1949 to bless his marriage.[11] That satisfied Britain's district commissioner in Serowe, the Ngwato capital, and his superiors (then based in Mafeking, now Mahiking).

Consternation ensued in Pretoria and London, however. Given the National Party's victory in the South African elections of 1948, and the onrush of apartheid with an about-to-be enacted strict ban on mixed marriages across any color lines (they had been illegal in the Union of South Africa between whites and blacks since 1923), British officials believed and were advised to think that Khama's nuptials would only inflame the Nats and worsen Anglo-South African relations. Prime Minister (later Sir) Godfrey Huggins in white-ruled Southern Rhodesia also opposed introducing a royal cross-racial marriage into a neighboring state. Indeed, Khama's betrothal unwittingly (or perhaps naively) undercut the prevailing political message that whites and blacks could not possibly live peaceably together in Africa.

Khama and Ruth's example of harmonious multiracialism as a path forward, at least for Botswana, today may seem prosaic and a matter of individual preference and choice. But it stirred southern Africa and caused even a Labour government in Britain to withdraw its approval of Khama's accession to the Ngwato throne and to compel his return to Britain, and exile. "Tribe and myself tricked by British Government," Khama telegraphed home to Ruth in 1950. "I am banned from whole Protectorate." Winston Churchill, then the leader of Britain's opposition Conservative Party, termed the whole business "a very disreputable transaction"—a sordid maneuver to appease South Africa.[12]

Khama and Ruth lived modestly in Britain until 1956, refusing to abdicate the chieftainship or to cooperate in any material way with various British attempts to displace him permanently, or to transport him to a position in Jamaica. Only if Britain gave him full liberty to return home to participate in the Protectorate's political emergence would Khama agree to renounce his claim to the Ngwato headship.

Such an amicable resolution of the Khama imbroglio only occurred as the passage of time made it apparent that the Nats could not be brought back from the brink of extreme racism, that their legislative implanting of apartheid would be relentless, and that the new prime minister of South Africa was even more Hitler-adoring than his predecessor. Moreover, South Africa was rolling out a pernicious separate development plan to create ethnic homelands or Bantustans (see chapter 6), and the possibility of the Protectorates of Bechuanaland, Basutoland, and Swaziland ever being transferred into South African custody had become moot. Moreover, and equally decisive, the discovery of promising mineral deposits on the edges of Ngwatoland could hardly be exploited with the chiefly succession unresolved.

As Britain's and France's West African colonial possessions were moving toward self-government, it further seemed retrogressively out of time and place to retard Bechuanaland's political emergence under the possible influence of someone whom officials from the British Colonial and Commonwealth

Relations offices had come to respect for his lack of bitterness, his honesty, and his "right judgement."[13]

Khama thus returned home in 1956 to help his people "to develop a democratic system, raise the standard of living, and establish a happy healthy nationhood."[14] That was Khama's creed, and one he elaborated upon and made the lodestar of the remainder of his life—to the lasting benefit of all of the peoples of Botswana.

We should note, however, that unlike so many of the liberationist leaders of early African nationalism, Khama may not have harbored a precisely articulated vision of how he would help the Tswana (and Kalanga) peoples to establish a meaningful democracy and a healthy nationhood. He had not devoted his years of exile to manifesto writing and political agitation (unlike the fulminations of Nkumbula and Kamuzu Banda against the Federal experiment in next door Southern and Northern Rhodesia, and Nyasaland). Nor had he made his home in Britain the center of exiled anti-colonial political ferment (as Banda had used his medical offices in London). But Khama's mind had nevertheless concentrated itself, and as he and Ruth returned to Serowe they were aware of Britain's and France's humbling at the Suez Canal by President Gamal Abdel Nasser, of Britain's increasingly open willingness to contemplate the loss of its overseas possessions, and of the rise in Britain of more modern trending politicians. Most all, conceivably, Khama's many years in exile had broadened his own personal horizons, and had contributed to a sense of destiny that was to propel his leadership in directions then and later uncommon among Africans. Whatever democratic instincts had been nurtured at Lovedale and Fort Hare multiplied in Britain, enlarged his vision and his sense of self, and prepared him to think less as a mere Ngwato chief and more as a potential African statesman. Via an unexpected route, Botswana and Africa had found a leader of unquestioned rectitude, resilience, and promise.

Becoming Free

From the late 1950s, first as the Ngwato delegate to the all-Botswana Joint Advisory Council and then as an elected member of the Protectorate's first African Advisory Council, Khama advocated rapid movement toward home rule, leadership for Tswana that was based on talent more than tribal affiliation, and the abolition of all of the forms of discrimination that had leaked into Bechuanaland from South Africa and Southern Rhodesia. That meant curtailing segregationist behavior along the Rhodesia Railways that cut from south to north and in the white border redoubts such as Lobatse and Francistown. It further meant integrating the schools of the Protectorate, obtaining equal pay for equal work in the civil service, and ending the demeaning practice of shops selling goods to Africans only through outside hatches, not over the counter. Interestingly, Khama preferred making such changes without confrontation so as not to drive whites from his nascent country. Khama then and later particularly wanted Botswana to offer political lessons to others, not to copy (draconian) solutions or methods developed farther north.

"I think it is time that we ourselves," he told the Council in 1958, "formulate a policy of our own which is . . . unique to us. . . . And that is a policy, perhaps, of even teaching those countries who profess to be more advanced than ourselves, that in as far as administration and race relationships they have more to learn from us than we from them. . . . We have ample opportunity in this country to teach people how human beings can live together."[15]

Khama's vanguard role in the emergence of modern Botswana was preempted in 1960, however, when a cadre of radically minded Tswana from non-Ngwato sections of the wider Tswana community created the Bechuanaland People's Party (BPP), the Protectorate's first modern political movement. Nkrumah and Ghana quickly acknowledged the BPP and regarded it and its founders as akin in southern Africa to the South African ANC and Joshua Nkomo's Southern Rhodesian African National Congress. Nkrumah even supplied vehicles and made it widely known after the 1960 All-African People's Congress in Accra that the BPP was its country's "authentic" freedom movement.

Khama derided the founders of the BPP as preachers of empty rhetoric, "promising everything and yielding nothing." In order to expose the falsehoods of those so-labeled hotheads, Khama, Masire, who was from the Ngwaketse ethnic branch of the Tswana people, and others in 1961 established the Bechuanaland Democratic Party (BDP) to advise the British rulers of the Protectorate on how best to achieve political progress in the territory.

In 1962, the BDP held its inaugural national congress. Khama naturally became its leader, ably supported and backed by Masire. He urged British administrators to establish a Legislative Council so that indigenous inhabitants of the Protectorate could begin helping to rule Bechuanaland. He also demanded "one man, one vote," but made it clear that the BDP favored cooperation over contestation as he and his party took their peoples forward to independence. Masire, later Botswana's second president and critical lieutenant to Khama during the founding years of the Republic, was a farmer, entrepreneur, school headmaster, and journalist who bonded with Khama after meeting him during the opening sessions of the Legislative Council.

Khama was prepared to achieve independence for his proto-state somewhat more deliberately than the experience in Malawi and Zambia, a posture that Nkrumah and others called "selling out." But Khama was never troubled by such accusations, nor moved by anything other than his own sense of what

Figure 8.1. Seretse Khama

the Tswana wanted, and at what pace. Then and later Khama was content to do what he thought was right, and not what clamoring core groups of constituents preferred. This posture foreshadowed Mandela's "I am your leader. I am going to give leadership. . . . As long as I am your leader, I will tell you, always, when you are wrong."[16]

Khama could envisage proceeding to independence even though his disparate peoples numbered only 600,000 within a domain the size of Texas or France that was two-thirds desert and for which few could envisage an obvious economic path to prosperity, much less self-sufficiency. But first he reckoned that he had to transform the BDP into a popular party with a national reach. He and Masire took to the hustings in 1963 and 1964, giving speeches and meeting villagers across the great breadth of the Protectorate. At a constitutional conference with the British administration in 1963 they insisted on the introduction of a parliamentary system, with no temporizing intermediate stages, full adult suffrage, and the termination of white and chiefly privileges. Unlike in other African states, the democratizing forces of Botswana were never resisted by the traditional chiefs, largely because they saw so many of their class concerns furthered by Khama. As well, his consultative methods, and Masire's, kept the kgotlas on the side of the new representative dispensation.

Whatever Nkrumah might have believed, Khama's careful, disciplined, and painstaking leadership brought the future Botswana to the brink of self-government. Thereafter, it was more a matter of enhancing his already broad popularity and unquestioned traditional and rational legitimacy in the minds of future voters. He insisted that the territory's capital move from distant Mafeking, in what had become South Africa, to Gaborone. Khama also demanded that the country that he was soon to govern should not prematurely Africanize its civil service, and that Botswana should pride itself on a non-politicized civil service, however staffed, but with an emphasis on competence, not skin color. He also welcomed foreign administrative personnel, many with legal or financial competencies and supplied by foreign foundations and other donors. As Khama told a distinguished American academic visitor in 1964, "Our [unique] role is not one of violence. We will achieve our independence without it. Our mission for Africa will be to demonstrate for our neighbor South Africa that we have a stable African government in which no man is discriminated against on racial grounds and in which the living standards of all are being raised."[17]

In 1965, in its inaugural parliamentary election, the BDP (twenty-eight of thirty-one seats) trounced the BPP (three seats) and a new Bechuanaland Independence Party (zero seats). The BDP won 80 percent of the popular vote, the BPP just 14 percent. Khama became prime minister under a British governor and, later in the year, led the legislature in voting for independence. A year later, with little fuss, Khama was president and Masire vice president and finance minister of the new Republic of Botswana. Khama appointed a cabinet of former headmasters and others whom Khama called persons of "good character." After a rather peaceful transition, formidable collective governing tasks were now the responsibility of Khama, Masire, and their associates.

To Build a Viable Nation

Because Britain had never lavished much administrative attention on the three small southernmost African protectorates, and because of their common paucity of natural resources (and wealth), Britain had long neglected the educational and medical needs of their inhabitants. Botswana, the physically largest and most sparsely populated of the three principalities, hence advanced toward independence with little in the way of basic infrastructure. Arteries were few in Bechuanaland, largely rudimentary earth tracks rather than gravel roads, with little by the way of macadam roadways except for seven miles' worth in the tiny urban settlements of Francistown and Lobatse, along the line of rail.

"Independent Botswana inherited," says one acerbic critic, "a colonial state not worth the name. It did not have an apparatus capable of promoting economic development; nor did it have an agricultural and industrial resource base to marshal for future development."[18]

Given its vast geographical spread, the overpowering Kalahari Desert, the concentration of most economic activity before about 1970 along the borders with South Africa and Southern Rhodesia (where the rails ran), and the territory's limited population size, it is no particular wonder that Her Majesty's Government saw only middling prospects for its former Protectorate when it handed the keys to the new kingdom to Khama in 1966. Britain felt that its parting gift of a fully outfitted abattoir (slaughterhouse) was appropriate and sufficient.

Exporting beef seemed the new Botswana's best hope of providing employment to its people and supporting the nation. There were about 1 million cattle, mostly munching alfalfa on Tswana-owned farms, but converting the beasts into bundles of exportable meat depended on the new regime's ability to combat common afflictions such as hoof-and-mouth disease (a big outbreak occurred in 1977), rinderpest, anthrax, cattle lung disease, and East Coast fever. Migrating wildebeest and buffalo sometimes infected cattle with these and other epizootic diseases. Additionally, in 1966 a prolonged drought held the new nation tightly in its grip; cattle were thirsty, deep wells few, and beasts were thin. Hence, one of the Khama administration's first post-independence tasks was to improve the health of the myriad herds, construct additional abattoirs, seek new markets, and hope and pray for steady and timely rains.[19]

At the time of independence, the American-based Roan Selection Trust was about to begin exploiting copper, nickel, and cobalt deposits near Francistown, but there was as yet no public hint of the gem diamonds plentitude that was to give Botswana such unexpected wealth toward the end of Khama's life and ever since.[20] The straitened circumstances of the new state encompassed hardly any manufacturing capacity or industry, little revenue from tourism, and but limited and episodic returns from the remittances that migrant contract laborers sent home from toiling deep underground in South Africa's gold mines. The average per capita annual GDP for Botswana in the 1960s was about $50.[21] Botswana was then one of the globe's poorest jurisdictions, a "basket case" in the terminology of the day.[22]

Botswana's economic takeoff was hindered in its incipient years by South Africa's control of its import and export routes and channels, by South Africa's domination of the regional customs and currency unions of which Botswana was an integral part, and by the common use of the South African rand as legal tender throughout the protectorates as well as in South Africa. Botswana could hardly run an independent economy under those circumstances; the imperfections and currency fluctuations of the much larger enterprise next door reduced Botswana's fiscal maneuverability, and hindered prospects for sustainable development. South African control of Botswana's currency was "too much for us," Masire remembered.[23]

That is why Quill Hermans, Governor of the Bank of Botswana, persuaded both Khama and Masire to break with the rand and establish the soon-to-be pula, Botswana's own fully convertible currency, in 1976. As Hermans subsequently explained the decision-making process to me, there was initial skepticism in Gaborone and London that Botswana could support its own currency, and that it would be taken seriously. But Khama and Masire both quickly grasped how getting out from under the hold of South Africa's Reserve Bank would let Botswana end the automatic importing of apartheid during South Africa's bouts of inflation and deflation; Botswana, in time wealthier per capita than South Africa, could gain fiscal strength by cutting cross-border ties. As Derek Hudson, Deputy Governor of the Bank of Botswana, later reported, Khama was content to rely on his experts; he did not need to micromanage decisions relating to the introduction of the pula: one day Hudson launched into a detailed microeconomic explanation of what having the pula would mean. "I was stopped short by the president. He said that because the board knew so much more about economic issues than he did, he would accept the board's recommendation on trust. My interview had lasted about 12 minutes. I was much impressed with President Seretse Khama's modesty."[24]

Botswanan society in those years (and since) was profoundly unequal. Twelve percent of Tswana owned 60 percent of all cattle, the movable bank accounts of rich Tswana. (Among the prosperous owners were Khama and his uncle, both men of enormous wealth by local standards.) Thirty percent of its people owned no cattle and were employed to care for the herds of others, in serf-like conditions. This was the peasantariat, a vast number of whom were compelled during the colonial period to toil in South Africa; until independence, Botswana functioned in many ways as a labor reservoir for its larger neighbor and, at home, as a supplier of inexpensive labor to the cattle-owning class.

Khama fully understood and embodied the powerful position in Botswanan life played by owners of cattle, the extent to which social status and social stability had long accompanied inequality, and the entitlements that flowed from skewed ownership of Botswana's most observable instruments of wealth.[25] But, big cattle owner though he was, Khama from the onset of national politics committed himself to championing the economic advance of all Tswanan citizens. Few ever accused cattle barons Khama or Masire of discriminating against up-and-coming entrepreneurs, or of providing hospitable conditions for rent-seekers—charges easily leveled against their peers in South Africa, Zimbabwe, Zambia, and Malawi.

Skilled Tswana were few: only a handful served in the upper ranks of the civil service. Twenty-two university graduates (including Khama), and about one hundred holders of secondary school graduation certificates, resided in the state. Fewer than 1,000 Tswana (mostly boys) attended secondary school, and in 1964 only twenty-seven had passed the formidable Cambridge Overseas secondary schooling examination. Of the twenty-seven, just thirteen passed with marks qualifying them for university. Furthermore, only one child in ten who completed primary school found a secondary school place, and there were further dropouts throughout the secondary school years. Trained local teachers were scarce at all levels, especially in secondary school classes.

These uncomfortable realities conditioned what Botswana could hope to achieve as a new state. They moderated the pace by which modernity and advanced political and other practices could be adopted. However, they also spurred Khama to expand educational facilities and educational opportunities as fast as budgetary limitations would permit. He and Masire understood that delivering betterment was a prime goal; without producing more and more secondary school and university graduates, Botswana could never develop economically. Nor could the BDP government hope to satisfy the material wants of its long-deprived constituents without a ramped-up focus on modern instruction. Khama's administration therefore doubled primary school enrollment between 1966, when there were only 170 primary schools throughout the territory, and 1998 when there were 300 schools, with 85 percent of eligible children in attendance. Botswana could count only three junior secondary and two senior secondary schools in 1966, but their numbers mushroomed under the new regime, secondary school enrollments rising exponentially from 1,500 in 1966 to 9,500 in 1976, 36,000 in 1986, and 140,000 in 1998.[26]

In 1982, Khama established a university in Gaborone (later with additional campuses in Francistown and Maun) to succeed the tripartite British-initiated higher educational institution for Lesotho, Swaziland, and Botswana that had been based in Roma, Lesotho, from 1964 until 1975. From 1975 to 1982, after Lesotho had taken over the Roma campus for its own national university, tertiary education in the other two former high-commission territories was organized as the University of Botswana and Swaziland, with separate campuses in each country until they went their separate national ways in 1982. In 2021, the University of Botswana taught 15,000 students at its three locations.

One of my successful Tswana PhD students from Boston University soon joined the new University of Botswana's history faculty, and was teaching there well into 2021. Another Boston University doctoral graduate founded and ran a private secondary school after serving for many years as the chief of Botswana's press office and presidential spokesperson. A Harvard undergraduate working with me on Africa was so entranced by Botswana's early promise that, after graduation, he traveled there first to teach in an experimental private secondary school of some acclaim, then to marry locally, and subsequently to establish and run Botswana's state-owned official development corporation.

Until the new university could produce trained personnel in sufficient numbers to meet public service employment needs, and to staff a variety of government-linked enterprises, plus positions in the private sector, Khama largely relied on the few men (and women, later) who had already gained higher degrees in South Africa or overseas, had matured in the Bechuanaland service, or were supplied by American, British, and Nordic institutions. The U.S. Peace Corps provided secondary-school teachers when Botswana had too few of its own; some Peace Corps persons even helped in the ministries and in negotiating contracts. Khama preferred no headlong imposition of affirmative action for Botswanans, no matter how popular giving jobs to locals would have been. To the consternation of leaders to the African north, for example, he decided after independence to retain a talented Afrikaner and naturalized citizen of Botswana who had been a district commissioner in service of the Bechuanaland Protectorate and who opted to stay after independence as his chief aide. Likewise, Khama appointed an Oxford-trained South African who had taken Botswanan citizenship at independence to be the top civil servant in the finance ministry. For a time, too, he kept Britons in charge of Botswana's police and fledgling army. Merit mattered to Khama more than skin color or the political appeal of fervent nationalism. Indeed, Khama (and Masire later) affronted some of his party colleagues in 1974 by elevating two technocrats—Mogwe and Gaositwe Chiepe, a woman who was to become Botswana's foreign minister as well as holding other cabinet positions—to ministerial posts ahead of ambitious BDP political operatives. As Masire recalled, ". . . we wanted the country to develop rapidly, so we needed to be sure we maintained the capacity to execute policies and projects well, even if the staffing was not entirely by citizens."[27]

In charge of creating the administrative core of the new nation—building capacity and competence for the gradually maturing national enterprise—Khama placed Philip Steenkamp, a (Kenyan-born) Afrikaner and recent district commissioner. After independence, Steenkamp became the administrative chief of the new nation and one of the two principal permanent secretaries in the presidential office, along with Mogwe. He was widely regarded as a tough taskmaster and as a no-nonsense, demanding, meticulous, and immensely hardworking loyal aide-de-camp to both Khama and Masire. Steenkamp praised both bosses: "We were friends and I really admired [Khama's] courage and ability. He was very competent and well-rounded. We are still to see a leader like him."

Steenkamp recalled that "localizing" (a euphemism for what, had it not been undertaken in Botswana, would have been termed "affirmative" action) the public service was a taxing assignment. "There was a lack of training facilities at the time and qualified people were very few and far between." Moreover, "The localisation of the police force and the setting up of the Botswana Defense Force

(BDF) presented their own challenges. We also had to walk a tight rope with South Africa. We never knew when the railway would stop running. That worried us because we had no decent north-south road." Of his own "main contribution" to Botswana, Steenkamp said that he was particularly proud of "establishing a public service that is honest."[28] Indeed, Khama, Masire, and Steenkamp together introduced a "coherent and professional code of conduct" that has withstood the passage of time and the original principals.[29] The standards of honesty that Steenkamp, especially, set were among the very highest in Africa—a benchmark that has served Botswana well and contributed to the country's high rating by governance indexes, anti-corruption indicators, and a host of other global measurement tools (see below, pp. 230–31).

Diamonds Become Forever

The character of the nation's public service contributed considerably to its beneficial economic performance. Equally important was Khama's careful leadership. In this sphere, Khama's most formative and telling decision naturally concerned diamonds. (Earlier, too, he and Masire had persuaded the country's key ethnic groups that revenues from minerals, originally just copper and nickel, should be attributed to the state, for the benefit of all of its peoples, not allotted just to the tribal areas where the discoveries had been made.)

Whereas the heads of petrostates such as Nigeria, Angola, and Equatorial Guinea saw the finding and exploitation of primary resources as welcome opportunities for political and military accumulation, whatever the desperate developmental needs of their impoverished citizens, Khama's leadership instincts focused squarely on how such a bonanza could be maximized to benefit the entire nation, not just the comprador class. In Ghana, Nkrumah and his associates had attempted to channel riches from gold and cocoa into personal pockets. So did Mobutu Sese Seko in Zaire/Congo try to accumulate returns from copper, cadmium, cobalt, diamonds, gold, and the like. Much later Robert Mugabe and his cronies in Zimbabwe grabbed a sudden find of diamonds for themselves, letting little of its benefits to trickle down to their constituents.

Khama behaved differently than his peers over potential rents and rewards from underground resources, as he did consistently in nearly all of the policy arenas where the future of the Tswanan people and of the nation were at stake. "We learned from the experience of other countries," Masire reported, "that possessing minerals did not automatically lead to economic development."[30] Moreover, as an authoritative analysis declared, "What is astonishing is that [Khama and Masire and their dominant class] managed to [accumulate benefits from minerals] without pervasive rent seeking or corruption."[31]

Prospectors for De Beers Ltd., the monopolistic diamond-prospecting and sales juggernaut that Cecil Rhodes and Alfred Beit had created in 1886, discovered diamonds at Orapa (west of Francistown and north of Serowe) in the lands of the Ngwato people in 1967 after twelve years following the trail of a small collection of rough diamond stones that had been located in a nearby dry riverbed in 1955. By 1969, the size and quality of the Orapa pipe had been proven, and a joint company called Debswana had been established that was 85 percent owned by De Beers and 15 percent by the very young, then weak and inexperienced, government of Botswana. Subsequently, two smaller diamond properties were located under the sandveld near Orapa and, in 1973, what became the globe's greatest source of gem diamonds and the country's eventual fount of prosperity was located at Jwaneng, west of Gaborone.

Rulers throughout Africa typically grabbed such sure and unanticipated signs of wealth for themselves, declaring that such treasures rightly belonged to their nations, not to the commercial concerns that had made the discoveries. Khama articulated the same message as early as 1973 but, deviating from other African heads of state and heads of government, he understood (unlike Kaunda regarding copper in Zambia) that Botswana could benefit substantially from De Beers' expertise, managerial skills, industrial savvy, and marketing genius. Instead of nationalizing the diamond mines, he carefully struck an elaborately negotiated partnership that significantly improved on the weak agreement of 1969. After very tough bargaining over four years, in 1975 Botswana and De Beers agreed, De Beers very reluctantly, to share Debswana, but with revenues from diamonds distributed 70 percent to the nation and 30 percent to the firm. Three years later, and well before Jwaneng became the most profitable gem diamond producer in the world, Khama's team and De Beers split the new mine's proceeds in the same manner.[32] Ever since, diamonds have contributed as much as 50 percent and for long periods 30 percent to the annual GDP of Botswana, with De Beers and Botswana operating their welcome revenue stream harmoniously. In the 1990s, when a quarter of the world's supply of gem diamonds derived from Botswana, it supplied two-thirds of the nation's export earnings and half of its revenues. In 2019, Debswana produced 23.3 million carats of diamonds. In 2021, in the midst of a $2 billion expansion of Jwaneng, miners unearthed a massive 1,098 carat stone, one of the largest ever found in Botswana. However, throughout the twentieth century, the copper-nickel complex at Selebi-Phikwe was by far the largest employer in the country (outside of government) even though its revenue benefits to the nation have always proven underwhelming.

Khama and De Beers decided in the twenty-first century to move the joint company's diamond-sorting and diamond-cutting operation from London to Gaborone, thus retaining more of the profits from diamonds within the originating nation, and adding to local employment attributable to diamonds. When

I toured the heavily guarded facility in 2012, shortly after it opened, Tswana men (and women!) were busily shifting what looked to a novice like rough, dull, stones with no glitter and little outward signs of brilliance into various piles of immense potential—approximately $6 billion worth annually.[33]

Botswana's high place on the good governance ladder, and its pursuit of democracy, certainly benefited from diamond proceeds. (Beef exports also contributed to Botswana's national income and the prosperity of its citizens. So, but to a much less impressive and important degree than had been expected, did copper and nickel add to wealth of the country.) But the obverse is equally correct: without having established prudent management as a national goal immediately after independence, without Khama's willingness to eschew the developmental mantras and socialistic shibboleths that were then driving other African countries into excess and error, and without his and Masire's confidence in their own leadership visions for the nation, the negotiations with De Beers might have gone awry, and its technical and marketing experience been lost. Botswana, additionally, could have squandered its unexpected prospects of major economic growth (off a very low base) by being greedy, or by unleashing the Dutch disease that so bedeviled Africa's petroleum producers. The Tswanan political elite could also have gorged themselves on easy rents as a consequence of diamonds. Instead, despite the difficulty of collecting income taxes in most of Africa, Khama and Masire early inculcated the very un-African pattern of making fat and fatter cats pay for privilege. Together, the president and his finance minister ran a tight, transparent, enterprise, with abundant accountability.[34]

The glimmer of real prosperity for all Tswana (not just for the elites, as elsewhere) strengthened Khama's ability to uplift his people and give them the kinds of advanced services and opportunities that were otherwise unavailable in similar severely challenged former British and French overseas possessions. Khama and Masire could thereafter attempt to narrow their embryonic nation's urban-rural divide, to improve its infrastructure, to generate employment within the territory rather than across the South African border, to contemplate a major expansion of educational and medical facilities, and to cease relying on British assistance. In fact, Khama was particularly proud to have avoided depending on handouts from London as early as 1972, when he and Masire emphasized the fiscal discipline that would serve them and the nation so well once revenues from diamonds began to flow. This ability to balance Botswana's budget without foreign aid was the result, too, of a careful analysis of the way in which Botswana was being shortchanged by the skewed allocation of revenues from the Southern African Customs Union. Once Masire and Hermans, then Permanent Secretary of the Ministry of Finance and Economic Development, convinced their counterparts in the other regional countries to reformulate revenue flows from customs and excise receipts, Botswana greatly increased its cash flow and the annual payments to its treasury.[35]

Unlike some other African countries, Khama and Masire believed strongly in old-fashioned parsimony, in avoiding extravagance, and in shying away from ostentation or the flaunting of privilege or position. Khama's motorcade consisted of his own car accompanied by the police, not the lengthy, traffic-stopping, road-hogging, never-ending parades of contemporaries such as Kamuzu Banda. Air travel, to the shock of other Africans, was accomplished for everyone but the president in coach class. Masire as vice president even arrived in Addis Ababa for a major conference, traveling coach and in the back; by the time that he had emerged from the aircraft in which he had traveled the red carpet had been rolled up and put away—to the embarrassment of his Ethiopian hosts. Ethiopians were accustomed to vice presidents and cabinet ministers traveling in style. Further, when Khama visited Pyongyang in the 1970s, he startled his North Korean hosts by playing billiards with his accompanying entourage and, once at least, stretching full length across the table to deal with an awkward shot, his Tswana retinue watching with admiration.[36]

Curing Corruption

The genuine modesty of leading Tswana (as in Khama allowing me to walk with him across the fields to his talk) reinforced another of his immense contributions to his country, the welfare of its citizens, and their ability to be industrious and entrepreneurially effective at the personal level. Khama, exactly like Lee Kuan Yew, determined from the beginning of his presidential reign to prevent Botswana from becoming corrupted and corrupt—to do everything within his power to avoid the curse of corruption that had so dramatically poisoned South Africa, Zimbabwe, Zambia, and almost every other member of the Organization of African Unity (later the African Union), especially ravaging the mineral and petroleum producers of the continent.

When it was a Protectorate, Botswana experienced little corruption. Some of the tendencies toward petty corruption in neighboring South Africa, and on the Rhodesia Railways that transited Botswana, may have crossed the border with its white staff or with the white-officered police forces that operated on both sides of the frontier. But grand corruption was doubtless inhibited by the Protectorate's poverty, and by the esprit de corps of the handful of British and Afrikaner officials who administered Bechuanaland before it became independent.

When he assumed presidential office, Khama was fully aware of the extent to which other African rulers, and their high officials, had compromised new governments by trading influence for cash, granting mining and other money-making concessions for hefty rewards, winking at embezzlements, and encouraging procurement kickbacks. Consequently, Khama (like Lee in Singapore) knew from the very beginning of his presidency that neither he nor his ruling party could afford to sully their prospects for economic growth, and their chances of achieving prosperity for the nation and its citizens, by condoning such corrupt practices as influence-peddling, theft of public resources, over-invoicing, contract padding, or nepotism. As he urged civil servants and others in my hearing in Gaborone to resist temptation, he knew that government employees in Botswana were intrinsically no less greedy than their counterparts elsewhere on the continent. Thus he readily concluded at the inception of the BDP's rule that it would be dangerous and foolish to condone even the most minor breaches of anti-corruption regulations.

Khama insisted from the beginning that his cabinet ministers pay their debts promptly and cover their overdrafts immediately. He was even tough on Masire when his close colleague was slow to repay a large bank borrowing. Likewise, he explained to his cabinet ministers that they must be vigilant in rebuffing any improper maneuvers, any questionable wealth-chasing ideas, and any compromised business dealings. When the nation's minister of natural resources committed suicide in 1976, Khama doubled down on sponsorship of anti-corruption activities. Sleazy dealings of any kind, Khama explained to parliament, his ministers, and their civil servants, undermined the nation-building exercise in which they were all engaged, and on which Botswana's future depended. In even plainer words, he urged everyone connected with the new national government to avoid imagining independence and a position of official importance as a route to personal enrichment. Corruption had no place in the infant former Protectorate, Khama articulated at meeting after meeting in the 1960s and 1970s.

Masire later recalled that their administration had worked very hard to avoid corruption, and then punished it severely when discovered. "Corruption is an evil," Masire explained later. "It is something that has really ruined the economy, the morals and everything of value in a society."[37] Masire also explained that the Tswana had inherited a need properly to account for all dealings, which helped. So did the existence of the kgotla, where citizens could complain, circulate rumors, point fingers, and excoriate presumed offenders.[38]

Of substantial importance in reducing corrupt dealings in Botswana was Khama's canny insistence on curbing the decision-making independence of his ministers. Lee warned his important associates against succumbing to blandishments, and demonstratively sacked any subordinates, even his deputy prime ministers, when they strayed—or even if their wives appeared to be wearing expensive jewelry.[39] Khama respected due process more than Lee, so rarely acted in a peremptory manner, but he did make it clear that ministers and highly placed officials had to consult other members of the cabinet and the president before making major moves that might privilege contractors or other contenders, especially in the mining arena, where diamond or coal concessions were being sought. "No, this is not something for one man on his own," Khama instructed one minister of mines. "It is too important. Even if you think it is right, if anything goes wrong, you must share the responsibility with your colleagues. . . ."[40] Full transparency at all times and at all levels was imperative.

In order to keep corrupt tendencies at bay, Khama and Masire also urged the prosecution of ministers and officials who—despite abundant cautions from on high—misappropriated funds or took advantage of their public positions for illicit private gain. One of those who was indicted and successfully prosecuted was Khama's cousin, a senior civil servant. According to Steenkamp, head of the civil service and permanent secretary to the president, when he apprised Khama that his cousin had been fiddling mileage reimbursement claims in a major way, Khama said: "He's not my cousin; he's your civil servant."[41] Another in the early years was a key personage in the BDP. A third was Masire's younger brother. In a fourth case, Masire terminated an assistant minister and the permanent secretary in the ministry of local government and lands even though the minister's criminal conviction was overturned on appeal.

Using these several methods, but more because of the impeccable example that Khama set, Botswana exited its first and succeeding decades of independence with comparatively little grand corruption and, as a result, no prevalence of petty corruption. Traffic police in Botswana did not bilk motorists as they did in Rhodesia and then Zimbabwe. The persons at the apex of institutional trees never expected or demanded the kinds of largesse that their contemporaries elsewhere extorted as their due. Botswana, certainly in my acquaintance, was always orderly, without roadblocks to shakedown harassed drivers or entire busloads of passengers. Obviously, the country and its people were not without fault, but Khama forced common avarice deeply underground. One of Khama's great contributions to the well-being of his country and, by example, to all of Africa, was his successful determination to expunge bribery, peculation, embezzlement, and all manner of self- and family dealing (not avarice) from the new nation that he led so sagely. Doing so contributed directly to good governance and to the lofty annual rates of growth that Botswanans enjoyed during much of the 1980s and 1990s, and well into the twenty-first century. Without Khama's insistence on ethical universalism as a mode of governmental being, and his rebuffing of the scourge of corruption, Botswana would not have become one of Africa's model states. Nor would the government of Botswana have been able to deliver such advanced political goods to its citizens.

The Democratic Determination

Equally critical, Khama—assisted in every detail by Masire—established a political culture that transformed Botswana from a post-colonial administrative state into one of Africa's rare specimens—a thoroughgoing democracy. When they together took Botswana to independence and then began to fashion a new state, they both understood that the preferred governmental model in West and East Africa was either militaristic or, at best, quasi-democratic, with nominal political participation by a territory's inhabitants but, actually, little choice or voice. States were centralized and economies planned. Countries from Côte d'Ivoire and Liberia in the northwest, Kenya and Tanzania in the east, and even Zambia, immediately to the north, all embraced varieties of guided democracy, sometimes with only show elections. This was a pattern that seemed to be working, seemed somehow to be satisfying popular aspirations, and mostly kept the first cohort of leaders firmly in power. But it was not an approach that appealed to Khama. He understood the available choices, and opted for transparency, accountability, genuine and full participation, and real representation. The "histrionics and fulminations of extremists outside this country will not help Botswana achieve its destiny."[42]

As Masire reported, "Seretse was a democrat through and through."[43] He was instinctively consultative, collaborative, and inclusive. Tolerance of others and tolerance in general were watchwords. He believed in an open society. "The essence of a democracy is an informed public," and Khama never deviated from that very fundamental democratic precept.[44]

Toward the end of his life, Khama admitted that "democracy, like a little plant, does not grow or develop on its own. It must be nursed and nurtured if it is to grow and flourish. It must be believed in and practiced if it is to survive." Democratic institutions, he continued, will not perpetuate themselves on their own.[45]

In a pronounced manner that demonstrated his singularity, Khama often declared that he and his new nation would never "tolerate autocracy of any kind." And, after visiting North Korea and China, he rebuked those who welcomed authoritarianism. "Dictatorships and tyrannical systems of government," Khama excoriated, "are hatched in the minds of men who appoint themselves philosophers, kings, and possessors of absolute truth."[46] That was not Khama's preference, and a singularly courageous choice for Africa at the time. Moreover, although many contemporary African leaders could have enunciated similar propositions, Khama was believable. He walked the walk, along with good talk.

Khama was equally scathing about the "mess" Africans elsewhere on the continent were making of their opportunities to rule. A state visit to Malawi, where Kamuzu Banda acted every inch the potentate and had crowned himself "for life," proved profoundly disturbing. So was the coming to power of a thug such as Idi Amin in Uganda. What Nyerere and Kaunda were attempting to do in and for their one-man-ruled countries seemed inappropriate and false. "The time has come," Khama said, "when we should [accept that] . . . [our failure] . . . is really due to our own mishandling of our own affairs"—a conclusion that Khama wanted Botswana to avoid.[47]

Khama was obliged, he always said, to build a nation, not just to inherit responsibility for an arbitrary geographical expression filled with people. He also knew that nations only came fully into being when their disparate peoples felt that they belonged to a worthy larger whole—to an entity that was more comprehensive than their birth ethnicity and that was composed of peoples from disparate regions (sometimes) speaking disparate languages. When peoples can be proud of belonging to their nation, and proud of its accomplishments, then it can be called one. Thus Khama was intent on unifying, not dividing, and on giving equal opportunities to all.

Meticulously, Khama sought from the first to eliminate tribalism, or any similar form of chauvinism. His vision included giving a collection of tribal kingdoms and a wealthy cattle-herding aristocracy a larger purpose—a sense of being integral to a greater whole. That meant knitting the speakers of Setswana and TjiKalanga together by giving them a mutual central purpose, a task that a number of African countries in 2022 still have not accomplished.

Whether or not he did so consciously, Khama understood that constructing a successful new nation depended on instilling a new political culture into and across the Tswana kingdoms and the Kalanga and Sarwa peoples. In a talk to Botswana's very first legislative assembly, Khama urged the members of parliament to help him foster a national spirit so that the peoples of the territory would think of themselves as one, not as a member of this or that ethnic group. Political institutions capable of holding the country together and advancing its democratic purpose could only come into being when he and Masire, and their associates, perfected new structures capable of delivering good governance and economic growth. Furthermore, this positive ethos could only be ensured by exemplary leadership of the kind that Khama pledged himself to provide, with Masire as a full and—for Africa—unusually successful partner.

According to Masire, "Seretse and I worked together very closely . . . Seretse and I were extremely candid and honest with each other. If I differed from him, he would reconsider his position. From the beginning, there was simply a fund of trust between us. . . ."[48] Khama slowed Masire down when necessary and led, with Masire supporting, in ways that could only be advanced by Khama alone. In the same manner, Khama mobilized his supporters, and even some opponents, behind a vision that was demonstrated and articulated in a consistent manner from before independence to the end of his presidency. He guided his ministers, rather than dictating to them, and always favored deliberative discussion.

Moreover, his principled maneuvers gained him legitimacy and a growing popularity the longer he served as president and the more his unique approach to governing produced the kinds of positive, incremental results that benefited most of the peoples of the country.

In terms of the critical competencies of transformational leadership, Khama advanced a vision, mobilized followers behind it, demonstrated unquestioned integrity, expressed an intellectual honesty equaled in Africa only by Mandela, behaved as a pragmatic traditionalist with fastidious prudence and self-mastery, and accomplished the supreme leadership task of infusing the peoples of Botswana with a sense of national purpose—a sense of belonging to something larger than themselves.[49] Few other African leaders have so far done so much. That is why only a handful of other African polities have as yet crossed the threshold of nationhood. Most are states, still becoming nations, with little ultimate sense of unity. Khama's greatest gift to his successors, and to his peoples, was the forging of a nation and the instilling of a political culture of democracy (to which being non-corrupt is intrinsic). Without Khama's leadership, seconded and continued by Masire, by Festus Mogae, by Ian Khama, and now by Mokgweetsi Masisi, Botswana would have struggled to surpass the African pre-institutional governance mean.

Matching the gifts to his people of nationhood, a sense of self, and important deliverables of good government such as security and safety, respect for human rights, educational opportunity, medical care, and clean water, Khama also catered to their material wants and aspirations. Thanks both to diamonds and to sensible management, but especially to good governance and a variety of fiscal and macroeconomic advances, Botswana prospered under Khama and his successors in ways equaled in Africa only by the island states of Mauritius, the Seychelles, and Cape Verde. Nothing on the mainland begins to compare to Botswana in the achieving of consistently high growth combined with the full pursuit of equality.

A searching inquiry by Acemoglu, Johnson, and Robinson credits Botswana's "spectacular" economic success to its good institutions and its enshrining of private property as much as to its natural resource abundance. Leith echoes their conclusions in his own inside examination of Botswana's prosperity. There were clear structural advantages that assisted Botswana's ability to prosper, but human agency—the decisive and honest manner in which Khama and Masire ran the nation—proved absolutely critical.[50] Khama and Masire produced a political culture that enabled positive political institutions of exemplary governance. In simpler terms, diamond wealth could easily have been squandered, pocketed, maldistributed, and deposited in vaults in Switzerland, not put to work in Botswana. Making it benefit the citizens of Botswana was Khama's goal, as was so much of instilled value in the infant Botswana.

The Masire Generation, and After

Khama suffered from diabetes and stomach cancer and died tragically young at fifty-nine, in mid-1980. But, by the time of his death, Botswana was well launched as a nation (no longer a state). It existed as a thriving political culture that espoused democracy and that already could count a legion of believers throughout the territory—all of them having been socialized gradually by Khama's message and by the benefits that democratic rule and good governance had bestowed on the fortunate country.

For the next eighteen years, Masire continued to construct a successful edifice on the firm foundations poured by Khama. Few other African states, especially in southern Africa, emerged in the 1980s and 1990s on such secure footings. Few were as blessed, as Botswana was, by such an ethos of exceptionality. Botswana under Khama's successors did not have to struggle to find its place in the world, to do the right and decent thing, to smart under the IMF's "structural adjustment" demands and the World Bank's restrictions, or to reconcile ethnic groups competing for primacy and perquisites. Khama established a framework within which nearly all of the peoples of Botswana could participate fully in the affairs of the country and pursue their personal dreams without the kinds of barriers and biases that barred even middle-class Africans elsewhere on the continent.

Masire's approach to leadership mirrored that of his senior partner. Hermans, who worked under him or with him for many years, said that he was a "keen" listener and a vice president and president who somehow mastered the briefs of nearly all of his subordinate ministries.[51] Stephen Lewis, one of Masire's key economic advisors, termed both Khama and Masire pragmatic, solution-oriented, and very consensus-directed. "The traditions of consultation in the kgotla were practiced at virtually every meeting, as these two leaders encouraged questions and dissenting views," Lewis asserted.[52]

Masire proved reluctant (unlike his peers farther north) to interfere personally in matters rightly subject to other political institutions, or to breach any separation of powers. In the celebrated case of a well-connected Tswanan entrepreneur who believed that the municipality of Gaborone owed him compensation because of a taking of eminent domain and asked Masire to issue a presidential directive in his favor, the president replied that it was up to the courts, not the executive, to decide.

When Masire was still vice president, he personally sought to subdivide a large plot near Gaborone to construct houses that he would try to rent in order to obtain income until he was ready to retire. But this project fell afoul at first of official municipal planning delays and bureaucratic obstacles to which his reaction (uncharacteristic for a politician in Africa) was: "I had to follow the rules just as any other Motswana would have to do."[53]

In terms of development, Khama and Masire turned their country into a splendid advertisement for beneficent state-arranged delivery of essential services. During their presidencies, initially with massive assistance from donors who sometimes had to be cajoled or instructed, Botswana constructed major modern roads where none existed previously. One traversed the nation from the South African border in the south to the Rhodesian frontier, south to north, and then continued farther north to Kasane and Kazungula on the Chobe and Zambezi Rivers. Other key arteries traversed the desert to Maun and Ghanzi (Gantsi) and then joined a Namibian route crossing that country to Walvis Bay. Masire wanted to put tolls on the Ghanzi road so that South African truckers would defray the costs of the road that Botswana had built, but Masire's minister of transport feared a rash reaction from ordinary motorists, and prevailed.

Khama and Masire constructed a number of abattoirs. They built schools and medical facilities. In the absence of private concerns rushing to invest in Botswana, they created state-owned commercial entities like the Botswana Housing Corporation (BHC) and the Botswana Development Corporation (BDC) to invest in the nation and jump-start a variety of important sectors that private investors were avoiding. Since there was little available accommodation for public servants in the protean capital of Gaborone, and in other towns that grew to become urban centers, the BHC paternalistically constructed flats and houses, and rented them out. At one point in the late 1990s, it owned 70 percent of all urban housing in the entire country. The BDC initiated a number of enterprises, most of which were necessary and did well, but Air Botswana was always heavily subsidized. Botswana's attempt to start its own brewery and motor vehicle assembly plant never succeeded, as well, largely because of South African private and state interference and undercutting. There were major labor productivity issues as well.

In a desiccated land, water is always short. One of the country's major early efforts was to build dams for power as well as for water distribution, in one significant and capital-intensive case to supply water to help operate the large (and never truly profitable) copper-nickel mine at Selebi-Phikwe.[54] Subsequently, there was a flurry of bore hole (artesian well) digging across large swaths of cattle country in order to make cattle herding more productive and less dependent on erratic rainfalls. (A large aquifer fortunately exists beneath the sands of central Botswana.) This was a controversial project, because of its alienation in many cases of communal land and the deprivation in too many cases of the privileges of poor Tswana who had been accustomed to using or dwelling on those same lands. It also deprived Sarwa and others of their rights. (See below, p. 221.)

The economy continued strong throughout Masire's long years in office, and afterward throughout the Mogae and Ian Khama presidencies, to deliver positive results, more and more building on high-end tourism, an embryonic assembling industry, expanded chilled beef exports, nickel, and the sparkle of gem diamonds. No non-petroleum-producing economy on mainland Africa did so well consistently from 1966 to 2008; Botswana increased its total GDP annually by about 4.5 percent over more than thirty years and an amazing 10.7 percent each year from 1974 to 1992. Even later, when diamonds were less profitable and the global economy slowed, Botswana still grew faster than its competitors at about 2.1 percent yearly.[55]

As president, Masire ensured that the wheels of prosperity kept turning. Thanks to the pact forged with De Beers, the shift from the rand to the pula, frugal management by his former ministry and the Bank of Botswana, local antipathy to corrupt behavior, and a firm rule of law that made contracts secure and minimized governmental interference, this was a compatible endeavor. In many ways the engine of this successful effort was the sensible and careful manner in which Masire and Festus Mogae's ministries of finance and planning development orchestrated Botswana's ambitions, and later, its wealth management. There were global and local economic setbacks in 1982 and 1991, and recurrent rainfall failures, but Botswana was able overcome those interruptions in ways that were unusual for fragile economies in Africa. Diamond profits were only a good cushion if they were well deployed and the cloth of the larger macroeconomy fashioned to Botswana's particular requirements.

Drought plagued the young Botswana acutely in the 1960s, in the late 1970s, and again in the 1980s, compelling the Khama and Masire administrations to turn to the World Food Program (WFP) for substantive relief; in the 1960s the WFP fed as much as half of the country's population. As Seekings shows, dealing with persistent drought in an already desiccated environment and rescuing small-scale farmers from famine led to a conservative national welfare policy of "workfare" that assisted poor citizens and ultimately led to a broad-based national old-age pension scheme.[56] In the 2000s, for electoral backing as well as humanitarian reasons, Mogae's government provided modest support, in cash and kind, to a surprisingly large proportion of the nation's people. Doing so bettered their life chances and somewhat mitigated inequalities between cattle owners and the new public servant elite at the upper end and the herdsmen, migrant laborers, and smallholders who had benefited much less fully from Botswana's great prosperity.

South Africa's inauguration of an African-led government in 1994 removed a previous impediment to growth, giving Botswana much more agency and a new freedom to pursue its own national interests without reproaches (or raids) from its neighbor. Botswana's average GDP per capita rose strikingly from $153 in 1970 to $3,000 in 1990, to $6,000 in 2005, and to $18,562 in 2020, ranking Botswana, per capita, as one of Africa's five wealthiest countries behind the

Seychelles and Mauritius.[57] In terms of inequality as measured by the Gini co-efficient, however, Botswana became only marginally less unequal (in terms of income distribution), improving from 54 in 1985 to 53 in 2019, according to the World Bank. Botswana was considered "one of the most socially unjust countries in the world."[58]

Of the peoples of Botswana largely excluded from the nation's rapidly growing, diamond-propelled, economic prosperity, the Sarwa, or San, were the most numerous and the most deprived. Harassed and scorned by Tswana and Kalanga, with many suffering for more than a century as involuntary serfs tied to cattle-proprietors and sometimes being "owned" by wealthy cattle merchants, other Sarwa had been accustomed to living in small groups and hunting and gathering at will across the sandveld of the western Kalahari and parts of the Okavango Delta. A very few owned cattle and goats. The Tswana discriminated against them during the Protectorate period, and their social disparity accelerated after independence when Tswana gained total control.[59]

Concerted contempt for Sarwa, and their forced relocation out of the Central Kalahari Game Reserve and other traditional settlement areas, accelerated in the 1970s and 1980s, when diamond prospecting occurred in the Game Reserve and when the country's Tribal Land Grazing Policy put pastoral land into private hands and fenced former communal holdings. Compelled removals of Sarwa began under Masire but the majority of the contested population shifts occurred during Mogae's presidency and continued throughout the second Khama's reign.

Mogae sought to confine some of the nomadic Sarwa peoples to "favorable" sites allocated to them by (an unsympathetic) government. The Sarwa (earlier called Bushmen and finally "San"), refused to do what they were asked to do, took the government to court, and battled forlornly for the freedom to subsist on their own, as they had in decades past. Yet, no administration conceded land rights to the Sarwa. Nor did any ever wish to acknowledge that the Sarwa, the Nama, the Tawana, the Lala, and other small groups (all lumped together as Remote Area Dwellers) could justifiably claim an indigenous status greater than that of the comparatively late-arriving Tswana.

The Sarwa tried to contest their systematic marginalization politically and legally; they gained support from international NGOs who hammered the Mogae and Ian Khama governments, mostly to little avail. Under President Masisi, however, the Sarwa were finally permitted to hunt game freely, and under Ian Khama they were provided with additional water resources. In 2021, the 66,000 Sarwa, the Khoe, and other associated peoples (numbering perhaps another 10,000 or so) remained the last to benefit from the Botswanan miracle and were deeply dissatisfied with the manner in which the government treated them and disposed of their interests.[60] The harassment of the Sarwa is a major blot on the otherwise positive accomplishments of Botswana's democracy.

Aside from such a stain, Masire, Mogae, and Ian Khama each gained credit by presiding during their periods in office over a relatively (for Africa) corruption-free environment. However, just as Seretse Khama understood that neither he nor the political cultural ethos with which he had imbued Botswana could banish greed entirely, during the 1990s Masire confronted several severe challenges to the nation's antagonism to corruption, and to Khama's and his own conscious efforts to keep their colleagues and associates from temptation. In his own case, a prominent motor dealer in Gaborone offered Masire shares in a new (and potentially very profitable franchise). On the surface, it seemed like a straightforward investment option for the president. "I declined," Masire wrote. " . . . the situation was exploitable. . . . Justice must not only be done but must be seen to be done." Masire also refused "no end of . . . offering[s] . . . to open secret bank accounts in Switzerland."[61]

In the early part of that decade, the general manager of a state corporation took massive bribes from construction companies for mostly unneeded or wasteful projects. Numbers of ranches were allocated to prominent persons under the newly introduced Tribal Grazing Program. A little later, a contract to supply textbooks for primary schools included major kickbacks to the officials involved (as a similar scam did in Malawi at about the same time). The heads of a rash of new parastatal bodies like the Botswana National Development Bank and the BHC were caught rent-seeking. Then—in a most serious threat to unity within the BDP because the corrupt endeavor involved a sitting vice president and his potential replacement—valuable land on the outskirts of Gaborone was transferred between ministerial co-conspirators through shadowy means. Finally, the president himself and several cabinet ministers were slow to repay loans to the National Development bank, violating one of Seretse Khama's sacred cautions.

After decades of esteemed public probity, Botswana had slipped into patterns familiar elsewhere on the continent. All of the usual crimes had been committed: abuse of office, preferential treatment for influential relatives and firms, tender fraud, the giving and taking of bribes, and graft. As yet, there was no "culture of corruption," but Masire and others worried. Indeed, all Botswana was unaccustomed to the scandals embroiling the ruling BDP.

What to do? Masire decided to accept advice from Hong Kong, hiring the deputy head of Hong Kong's notable Independent Commission Against Corruption (ICAC) to establish the Botswana Directorate on Corruption and Economic Crime (DCEC) and to work with parliament to pass a new legal framework, especially the Corruption and Economic Crime Act. It outlawed obtaining or receiving "valuable consideration" or special favors in exchange for permits and preferences to others. Searches and seizures of suspects were explicitly permitted. Moreover, as in Singapore, Botswana's DCEC was allowed to question public officials who were living above their means. "Unexplained" resources invited investigation. Legislation also permitted Masire to appoint an ombudsperson to answer complaints from the public.[62]

The existence of the Botswanan investigative commission, with its members appointed by the president and 300 staff employed as members of the civil service, not as independent contractors, was less powerful and less independent than its counterparts in Hong Kong and Singapore. Nevertheless, it played a useful role under Masire, Mogae, and their successors checking corrupt tendencies within the ruling party and the elected and appointed officials of the government.

The DCEC also strengthened ministerial service delivery capacities, tried to eliminate bureaucratic bottlenecks, and reduced the scope of official discretion, all in order to lessen opportunities at all levels to act corruptly. Furthermore, it helped each cabinet ministry and state-owned enterprise to establish its own mini-anticorruption or integrity units, learning from the ICAC's emphasis on preventing corruption as well as discovering it. The DCEC tried to produce a major critique of each of those bodies, helping in this manner to reform the country's motor insurance fund and a small business grant operation. But its most salient intervention altered the process of preparing construction contracts to be let to tender.[63]

In terms of individuals, the DCEC completed investigations of a very senior official who was suspected of illegal transfers of public land, of Debswana's managing director, of the head of the state public procurement agency who had allegedly awarded contracts to his relatives, and of three cabinet ministers who had given state-owned equipment and contracts to themselves. The DCEC claimed a 75 percent conviction rate from about 2000 to 2013; however, many of those found guilty were small-time operators, bigger fish often being acquitted on appeal to the state's High Court. Furthermore, during the presidency of Ian Khama, nearly all of the national contracts to supply bread to schools across the land and to prisons came suspiciously from a bakery owned by a prominent member of the ruling party based in Lobatse. The head of a state procurement board awarded a sizable contract to his nephew. Other high officials also succumbed to nepotism. (See below.)

In modern times, clearly, Botswana had slipped somewhat toward the African mean in terms of fraud. Yet its institutions were functioning, and the levels of impunity for politicians and higher public servants seen elsewhere were almost entirely lacking in Gaborone and beyond. In society at large, too, Seretse Khama's message still resonated: pilfering from the state was abhorrent; taking unfair advantage of public positions to gain private wealth or position was harmful to the state and its supporters, and shameful in the eyes of the public. Corruption in the 2010s and in 2020 had not yet, and may never, become a default way of life, as in Nigeria or Equatorial Guinea. Botswana and its people had crossed the normative boundary by at least 2000 into a thoroughgoing appreciation of ethical universalism.[64]

When Transparency International began producing its Corruption Perceptions Index in the mid-1990s, Botswana always ranked as the least corrupt country on the continent and, for many years, the thirty-fourth least corrupt nation on the world ranking table. Khama clearly had dampened the baleful expression of greed and Masire and Mogae had continued to deny politically connected Tswana impunity. By the end of Masire's presidency in 1998, there was little doubt that indulging in corruption—the abuse of an elected or appointed public position for private benefit—affronted values that Tswana had come to hold dear.

Indeed, when leading politicians in Botswana were accused of improper actions in the 1990s, Masire's answer was to marginalize them, take at least two presumed heirs apparent out of the line of presidential succession, send some cases to the attorney general for prosecution, and reconfigure the upper echelons of the ruling BDP. Indeed, charges of corrupt behavior led surprisingly to Masire's fateful decision to transform Mogae, an Oxford-trained public servant, into a politician, a vice president, and then to back him for the presidency of the republic in 1998. (Masire also had to propose amendments to the country's constitution to mandate presidential term limits and the automatic succession of vice presidents to the top post.)[65]

Mogae had been director of economic affairs in the 1970s, permanent secretary in the ministry of finance and development planning, executive director for Anglophone Africa at the International Monetary Fund, governor of the Bank of Botswana, and permanent secretary to the president before being picked by Masire as his likely successor—in part because he belonged to none of the BDP's contending factions. Masire "respected Mogae's intelligence, humility, unassuming manner and also because Festus didn't come across as a person with any particular wish to be president."[66]

HIV/AIDS

The Masire and Mogae presidencies had to contend with the apex of the HIV/AIDS pandemic. For much of the era from 1995 to 2015, and possibly longer, Botswana produced one of the largest case loads (per capita) in the world, with deaths for a decade or more sapping the abilities of the sparsely populated state to stanch the spread of HIV/AIDS. It proved difficult to end, or even to reduce, the proliferation of the affliction throughout the country. As much as 37 percent of Botswana's population was infected at one point in the early twenty-first century, with 26,000 dying in 2001 alone. Masire regretted not having acted earlier and more effectively to stem the scourge's spread after the first case appeared in 1985.[67] Ultimately, after a method of slowing the spread of the disease was produced in Europe and the United States, Mogae made a progressive decision to offer free antiretroviral treatments to all of those affected, and disease numbers slowly fell. The HIV prevalence rate at its peak in 2000 was 26 percent of all adults, falling in 2019 to 21 percent of adults, still the fourth highest in the world.

Mogae's response to HIV/AIDS contrasted tellingly with that of President Thabo Mbeki in South Africa; the latter refused for several years to acknowledge that HIV/AIDS was sexually transmitted. Mbeki also harkened to HIV/AIDS deniers and their antiscientific messages on social media. Like Jacob Zuma, his presidential successor, Mbeki recommended quack cures like massive ingestions of garlic, refusing for too long to make antiretroviral medicines easily and freely available to his suffering constituents. (See chapter 7.) Thousands of lives were lost unnecessarily in South Africa, and saved in Botswana—a testament not only to Mogae's good sense but to the leadership example that Seretse Khama and Masire had introduced and instilled.

Despite such alarming HIV rates, the Masire, Mogae, and Ian Khama governments remarkably presided over steady improvements in the nation's public health services and, accordingly, in its steady increases in population numbers, in the diminution of other deadly diseases, and in the opening of clinics and hospitals across the land. In the first Khama's day, Botswana's accredited hospitals numbered eight and its health clinics about fifty. By the end of Masire's presidency, there were thirty well-maintained hospitals, 300 clinics, and roving mobile medical centers that made public health services available at 650 stopping places. Eighty percent of Botswana's people were within a fifteen-kilometer walk of at least a mobile clinic.

A proxy for a population's health outcomes is life expectancy. Another is infant mortality, and a third is the rate of maternal deaths in childbirth. Average life expectancy in Botswana rose from 54 in 1970 to 69 in 2018, compared to the all-Africa average in 2018 of 61; and 60 in the Democratic Republic of Congo (DRC); 61 in Zimbabwe; 63 in Namibia; 64 in Ghana, Zambia, and South Africa; 66 in Ethiopia; and 74 in Mauritius. Infant mortality numbers fell strikingly from 87 per 1,000 live births in 1970 to 23 per 1,000 in 2009 and back higher to a surprising 32 per 1,000 in 2019. By 2021, that figure was receding, to 28.1.[68] Numbers elsewhere per 1,000 were Nigeria, 74; Chad, 69; DRC, 66; Zambia 42; Zimbabwe 38; Ethiopia 37; Ghana 34; Kenya 32; Namibia 31; South Africa, 28; and Mauritius 14. The average infant mortality rate in sub-Saharan Africa in 2021 was 49.3 per 1,000 births.[69]

The sub-Saharan average maternal mortality rate fell as well from 289 in 1998 to 144 deaths per 100,000 live births in 2019. In 2015, Sierra Leone reported among the highest maternal deaths in the world at 1,360 per 100,000; Nigeria,

814; Kenya, 510; Zimbabwe 443; Ethiopia 353; Namibia 265; Zambia, 224; South Africa, 138; Botswana 129; and Mauritius 52.

As Botswana grew richer, it also spent more and more funds on medical remediation, especially during the HIV/AIDS epidemic, and obtained improved results across all metrics as compared to earlier years and as compared to the other countries of Africa, even a well-developed place like South Africa. According to the numbers, Botswana from Seretse Khama's time forward brought about systematic improvements in health outcomes, a welcome and telling political good.

Challenges to the BDP

Except for 1994, when corruption cases and turmoil within the BDP resulted in opposition victories in thirteen of the thirty-one parliamentary contests, the ruling party has usually overcome challenges to its political dominance with some ease. Within the party, however, "northerners" at times felt outmaneuvered for preeminence by "southerners" in a manner that Khama would not have welcomed. The elevation of Mogae to the vice presidency also disturbed the even tenor of political dispensation within the ruling party.

Even so, Mogae presided judiciously, dispassionately, during his allotted eight years. HIV/AIDS became his major concern, and land issues concerning the Sarwa proved a significant perturbation that he (and his successors) never solved to the satisfaction of international critics and the grieving Sarwa themselves. He was low-keyed, modest in the tradition of prior presidents, rarely ruffled. I sat in his presidential office with him on several occasions marveling at his seeming insistence on consultative democratic procedures, accentuated pragmatism, and an understated but real criticism of excesses among neighboring potentates like Mugabe, Sam Nujoma in Namibia, and Frederick Chiluba and his successors in Zambia. One afternoon, during a crisis at the University of Botswana, with an American vice chancellor departing, I asked him whom he favored as the next vice chancellor of the institution. He was its chancellor (in nearly all African universities, national presidents make major decisions as chancellors) and therefore in charge of choosing its leader, something other African heads of state took as their right. Mogae's answer to me was simple: "I have not been told so far whom the university council and faculties prefer." It was not his decision to make. That kind of steadfast attention to the roles of a president as a democratic norm giver and norm perpetrator were recognized when he won the infrequently awarded Ibrahim African Leadership Prize in 2009.

Yet the prize givers somehow overlooked Mogae's egregious assaults on academic freedom and freedom of expression; in 2005, he deported an elderly Australian University of Botswana full professor who had taught politics there for fifteen years, had roundly criticized the government's handling of the Khoe and Sarwa removals, and advocated boycotting Botswana over its treatment of those marginalized members of Botswana's peoples. Even so, the dissident was hardly a threat to peace and security, nor to anything else. Since Mogae refused to provide a reason for the expulsion of Kenneth Good, even during lengthy proceedings, it is still hard to know why intelligence officials and the national security council urged Mogae to deport Good, and plead presidential prerogatives in court. But the rough treatment of an expatriate academic hardly accorded either with Seretse Khama's methods or with Mogae's frequently expressed sentiments about respect in Botswana for the four essential freedoms.[70]

Another Succession

Mogae had chosen Ian Khama as his vice president and successor in order to unify the BDP and to prevent assertive longtime party grandees from reaching high office. But Mogae could not have known that Ian Khama would hew to a different leadership model than those who preceded him.

A closet autocrat (as I had noted in 1977, when we sat together to celebrate his father's honorary degree at Harvard University's commencement)—others would call him merely "rigid" and "introverted"—was constrained in office somewhat by his father's legacy and the democratic political culture that his father had introduced and Masire had reinforced. Ian Khama's two terms in office were notable for an appropriate and loudly voiced opposition to the Mugabe regime's excesses in Zimbabwe, for his insistence on forgoing traditions of consultation within the ruling party and the nation in favor of tighter presidential control, for a personalizing of the presidential position, for favoring cronies, and for the consequential growth of unexpected corrupt dealings among close associates. Members of his coterie were called tenderpreneurs for their ability to gain lucrative state contracts, like the bread supply arrangement in Lobatse.[71]

To the dismay of Masire and Mogae, Ian Khama, a young general in Botswana's Defense Force before becoming Mogae's vice president, altered a pattern of cherished policymaking that had devolved to the officials and ministers responsible for particular areas of administration the prerogative of initiating proposed legislative innovations. Deviating from this accustomed pattern, Ian Khama established parallel military-like structures within the executive that gave him novel authority to plan and authorize social and economic departures from existing practice. The result was a "near paralysis of institutions." They could no longer operate without their directions being orchestrated from State House. This change was apparent in many contested areas, including the provision of housing, restrictions on the consumption of alcohol, methods of poverty eradication, and innumerable others. Indeed, Ian Khama, considered a "polarizing populist" by some associates, gave priority to his own "pet projects," a few of which were populist in intent. He resisted grand demands by the country's labor unions and was slow to compromise with political opponents. But, that said, Ian Khama was much more appreciated in rural than in urban Botswana. The intelligentsia was particularly concerned when he gave wide rein to his military intelligence and security services, a worrying first for Botswana.[72]

Under Ian Khama's predecessors, parliament had rarely exerted a strong check on the executive, but the first Khama, Masire, and Mogae had always paid its members heed, and consulted with them.[73] Ian Khama chose to tread a different path. He also deployed his position as the nominal Ngwato chief (his father had renounced the throne before entering politics) to overcome opposition expressed during kgotla sessions.

Two critics suggest that "since Ian Khama assumed office, his administration . . . managed in a manner that enfeeble[d] state institutions and propped up his personal image. This . . . promoted a personality-oriented development policy-making where policies are styled in his name and not in that of the state. Institutions of the state or the state itself are relegated to an inferior position in the governance framework." Moreover, "He became a law unto himself."[74]

The central government began to solve problems that had previously been handled at the local level. His father's mode of leadership was decisively different, especially regarding district and village concerns. Afrobarometer surveys showed increasing public distaste for what respondents perceived as one-man rule.[75] Even former President Mogae was outspoken: He told the local news media that Ian Khama was a "disappointment," prone to "tantrums" if he did not get his way.[76]

Ian Khama allegedly chose Masisi to succeed him thinking that since the inexperienced Masisi had come late to politics and had no large BDP following, that he would let his predecessor be the dominant power behind the throne. (Masisi, the son of a BDP parliamentarian, took a master's degree in education from Florida State University. When back in Botswana he ran a small business and reformed school social studies curricula for UNICEF, and then entered politics in 2009, wining a primary contest.) But Ian Khama's calculation of subservience foundered on the rocks of ambition and party loyalty, just as it did with the selection of John Magufuli to head the ruling party slate in Tanzania and of Abiy Ahmed in Ethiopia to run its leading party.

Masisi, becoming president in 2018, muscled Ian Khama's henchmen out of power, and encouraged prosecutors and the DCEC to investigate and try some of Ian Khama's associates. Not only did the supposed "puppet" reject Ian Khama's continued influence, but Masisi, ignoring Khama's advice, lifted a ban on elephant trophy hunting and approved the rescinding of laws against homosexuality. The BDP took thirty-eight of fifty-seven directly elected seats in the parliamentary elections of late 2019, cementing Masisi's and the BDP's continued power in Botswana and overcoming Ian Khama's unprecedented attempt to lead a coalition of opposition parties against his father's BDP. Masisi claimed a return to the methods and governing approaches of the first Khama, Masire, and Mogae. Masisi, fifty-eight, thus became a new champion of political continuity.[77]

The Masisi Presidency

His immediate tasks after the election and throughout 2021 and into 2022 were somehow to maintain Botswana's relative victory over the coronavirus pandemic (308,000 cases and only 2,700 recorded deaths by the end of May 2022) and the ominous Omicron variant that was discovered in late 2021 in both Botswana and South Africa. Only when Africa is more fully vaccinated (Botswana by mid-2022 had inoculated 57 percent of its population, a southern African best) will tourists return and employment presumably return to its pre-Covid-19 levels.[78] The sale of diamonds has also been slowed globally by coronavirus worries.

Short and long term, Masisi in 2021 strove to find employment for the country's many jobless young people—the country's biggest challenge after coping with the fallout from the pandemic. (Botswana's formal unemployment rate in 2020 was 18 percent, high historically but low compared to South Africa, Zimbabwe, Zambia, and many other African states.) Only the end of the pandemic and the return of tourism will alleviate joblessness, but Masisi may also be able to invent other methods of promoting economic uplift. One, announced in mid-2022, was to ban the import of most agricultural products from neighboring Namibia, to "protect" Botswana's own growers of vegetables and other foodstuffs from competition despite the all-Africa free trade agreement that Botswana had signed in 2021.

Masisi's Botswana, well regarded in Africa for its educational accomplishments, also presents a number of unexpected and hitherto overlooked schooling challenges. According to the World Bank in 2019, "In Botswana only about half of ten-year olds can read and understand a simple story—in America the rate is 92 percent." The results in the rest of Africa were even more grim. Teachers lacked training, curricula were out-of-date and "over-stuffed." The result was that about 90 percent of Ethiopians, 82 percent of Ugandans, 79 percent of South Africans, and 75 percent of Senegalese suffered from an inability to "understand a simple age-appropriate test." Covid-19 in 2020 and 2021, with schools closed for substantial periods of time and social distancing mandated, hardly made schooling issues more tractable, but Botswana (and Zambia) experimented with novel catch-up programs that may have helped. Botswana (as well as South

Africa) obviously cannot expect striking improvements in employment numbers if potential workers suffer from literacy and educational weaknesses.[79]

Although Botswana should be considered a dominant-party democracy, there have been sufficient battles within the BDP, as typified by primary contests, to strengthen the notion that Botswana is incontestably a democracy both in form (which many African polities can claim) and in spirit and practice (which many cannot). Moreover, when the party split and Ian Khama led a frontal assault on the BDP's hegemony after being its de jure and de facto hard-driving leader for eight years, voters backed a return to an older style, or at least to a somewhat restored sense of the BDP despite Ian Khama's evident ability to please villagers. Unlike Prime Minister Lee Hsien Loong in Singapore, son of founding prime minister Lee Kuan Yew, the young Khama pushed his personal program, and those of his air force buddies, in an assertive manner that constituents and party members ultimately rejected.[80]

Despite this turmoil, or maybe because Botswana ultimately remained wedded mostly to the chaste, anti-corrupt, democratic direction of their early rulers, Freedom House rates and has always rated Botswana among the "free," not the unfree or partly free polities of Africa. Yet, on a 100-point scale, in 2020 Botswana scored only 72 on the Freedom in the World index. In the same list, Cape Verde rated more highly at 92; Mauritius, 89; Ghana, 82; South Africa, 79; and Namibia, 77. The lower African scores include the Central African Republic, not free, 10; Eswatini, 19, not free; Rwanda, 22, not free; Ethiopia, 24, not free; Kenya, 48, partly free; Côte d'Ivoire, 51, partly free; Zambia, 54, partly free; and Malawi, 62, partly free.[81]

According to my Index of African Governance and its successor Ibrahim Index, Botswana has virtually always ranked among the highest, best-governed, countries in Africa. In 2005, it ranked third, after Mauritius and the Seychelles, with a score of 73 of 100. Two years later, it fell to fourth, after Cape Verde, with a score of 72.7. From 2010 to 2019, the Ibrahim continuation of my index scored Botswana at 66 of 100, reflecting the onset of Ian Khama's changes. It slipped to fifth in the rankings and maintained essentially the same total score through 2019. Mauritius' scores over the same period were 77; Cape Verde 72–73; the Seychelles 64–72; Tunisia 62–70; Ghana 64; Namibia 62–65; Senegal 59–63; and South Africa 67–66.[82]

Botswana remains an African exception. In 2022, having weathered the aberrant Ian Khama presidency and his subsequent attempts to organize politically against the ruling BDP, it settled back into the largely consensually driven mode that the first Khama and Masire together initiated. The tendencies toward authoritarianism, corruption, and neglect of citizens' needs that are still common in neighboring states such as Zimbabwe, and were prevalent in South Africa under Jacob Zuma and Malawi under the presidencies of the brothers

Mutharika, Bingu wa and Peter, remain muted—but not absent—in Botswana. The value system that the first Khama developed and conveyed to his followers still prevails, despite troubling rumors that Masisi and several cohorts are feathering their own nests financially.

Whatever the truth of those rumors, in 2022 Masisi presided over a country that, with all of its legacy successes and unparalleled stability, was more politically divided than ever in its history. In the 2019 election, the ruling BDP lost heavily for the first time in northern areas of the nation while winning handily in southern constituencies. That meant that its erstwhile rivals—the Botswana Patriotic Front, the Botswana National Front, the Botswana People's Party, the Alliance for Progressives, and the Botswana Congress Party, all gathered loosely under the Umbrella for Democratic Change (UDC)—theoretically had much more viability as an opposition electoral force than ever before. At the end of 2021 the combined opposition parties demonstrated their intrinsic strength, at least in rural Botswana, by winning eight of eleven contested constituencies in elections for local council seats. The BDP struggled to hold on to just three (two in the south and one in the north), showing how the country's democracy was working and how the ruling party was falling out of favor in villages.[83]

As I wrote elsewhere—during Mogae's era—"Thanks to the vision of Sir Seretse Khama," Botswana's political culture continues "firmly participatory . . . ethically-oriented, and committed to service delivery . . . in stark contrast to many of its neighbors, where education and health for the people are sacrificed on the altar of defense spending, jobs for the big guys, lavish palaces . . . corrupt payoffs, and a macroeconomic framework designed to benefit elites." I concluded, "It is not so much that Botswana is remarkably well run, it is that is run for its people, not for a ruling clique or a band of well-connected crooks. Other Africans deserve so much."[84] Whereas many of the countries of Africa rank low on the governance and corruption perception scales, Botswana performs well on behalf of and for its citizens. It is still a leading model for Africa.

9
The Promise of Democracy Lost
Zimbabwe

South Africa's canny long-serving foreign minister, Roelof (Pik) Botha, and Neil van Heerden, his astute chief strategist, assured me—with no hesitation and great confidence—that apartheid intelligence was absolutely sure that Methodist Bishop Abel Muzorewa (backed by South Africa and in league with Prime Minister Ian Smith's breakaway Rhodesian government), would defeat Robert Mugabe's Zimbabwe African National Union (ZANU) in the upcoming elections to end white rule in Zimbabwe. We were talking in Botha's office in Cape Town in February 1980; the poll was scheduled for later in the month, after British-brokered peace talks the previous year in London had produced a plan to end a bitter civil war and craft a lasting peace.

My understanding, as I conveyed it forcefully to Botha and van Heerden, was starkly different. Because Mugabe had the backing of nearly 80 percent of Zimbabwe's electorate—the Shona people—and because Muzorewa (albeit also CiShona-speaking) was contemptuously viewed everywhere throughout the dying Rhodesia as a sellout—he stood no chance. Mugabe would triumph easily and overwhelmingly, I explained patiently to Botha and van Heerden.

I had taken no opinion surveys, but I had just returned from a lengthy visit to Rhodesia—my first in eight years. With independence looming and the British government overseeing the election, Lord Soames (the interim British governor) and his chief aides (one of whom was a former Northern Rhodesian district commissioner and a close friend) had managed to secure my entry into the former colony despite an enduring prohibition by the outgoing Rhodesian authorities.

Stirring Nationalist Fervor

As early as 1960, the segregated but mostly complacent Rhodesia that had existed so perfectly for whites throughout the first half of the twentieth century was beginning to reverberate with potential threats from the north. White politicians felt in the 1960s that they had their backs to the wall, especially as the other two sections of the lamentable Federation of Rhodesia and Nyasaland had moved toward independence and Southern Rhodesia was obviously next

Overcoming the Oppressors. Robert I. Rotberg, Oxford University Press. © Oxford University Press 2023.
DOI: 10.1093/oso/9780197674208.003.0009

Map 9.1. Zimbabwe and Botswana

in the decolonization queue. Congo's independence from Belgium and British Prime Minister Harold Macmillan's stark warning that the "Wind of Change" was coming to southern Africa and that it was a "political fact" hardly gave white Rhodesians any comfort.[1]

After Cecil J. Rhodes' British South Africa Company had defeated the Ndebele under Paramount Chief Lobengula and subdued both Ndebele and Shona militant oppositions, whites occupied what became Southern Rhodesia in the 1890s. Whites from Britain and Britons from South Africa, plus a number of Afrikaners, Irish, Scots, Jews, and other Europeans, put down roots there in the decades before company control was transformed into settler home rule in 1923. Tens of thousands joined them in succeeding decades, especially in the 1950s. Collectively, they had pushed Africans off the best soils, introduced a strict color bar, and then carved out prosperous Virginia tobacco, maize, cotton, sugar, and wheat farms throughout the more salubrious and well-watered parts of the lands that they had taken tragically from Africans. In the cities, whites created infant industries and followed mercantile pursuits; they constructed sprawling farm homes and mansions in the cities on the sprawling sub-tropical plateau that they now called home. Many knew no other lives. Whereas Africans to the north— from Ghana and Senegal to Kenya and Zambia—were gaining power and creating independent countries, the Southern Rhodesian (white) government was "committed to repress any African attempts to subvert white authority."[2]

Africans in Southern Rhodesia had come rather late to embrace nationalist politics. Although an African National Congress had existed within the colony as a welfare society from 1921, and a successor movement had been established in 1934, it was not until 1948 that African political aspirations gained noticeable voice. The Rev. Thompson Douglas Samkange and Benjamin B. Burombo resuscitated the African National Congress, led a failed general strike of workers and tenant farmers against segregation, and protested the idea of a federation when it was first mooted in the same year.

Meanwhile, Joshua Mquabuko Nkomo, who had attended government schools near Bulawayo (Southern Rhodesia's second city) before entering high school at Adams College, the famed Congregationalist secondary school in Natal, had emerged as a potential nationalist leader. After Adams, he trained as a social worker at the Jan Hofmeyr School of Social Science in Johannesburg and participated in South African African National Congress (ANC) meetings. Returning home, he became Rhodesia Railways' first welfare worker, later the head of its union.

In 1952, Nkomo attacked the Federal concept and became secretary of an All-African Convention that had been created in Southern Rhodesia to oppose federating Central Africa. Soon George Nyandoro, Dunduzu Chisiza, and James Chikerema, the founders of the City Youth League (subsequently the Southern Rhodesia African National Youth League)—an urban movement of younger militants—realized that they needed to broaden their political reach beyond Salisbury (Harare) to politicize the rest of the country. They sought the support of what was left of the old Congress, based mostly in Bulawayo. Just as Chipembere believed that Malawi needed a Banda-like figure, so the Youth Leaguers asked Nkomo, forty-four, to be their leader. He assumed the presidency of the rejuvenated Southern Rhodesian African National Congress in 1957 and, assisted by the younger men, demanded full participation by Africans in the government of the territory and loudly attacked segregation and racial discrimination.

The new Congress campaigned against the loss of African rights in the rural areas, and spoke out against the Federation. Nkomo met with President Nkrumah's representatives in Ghana, and his younger associates voiced criticism of the government of Southern Rhodesia wherever and whenever they could. But there is little evidence that the Congress constituted much of a threat to white domination in early 1959, when disturbances in Nyasaland provoked a Federal military response, the declaration of an emergency there and in Zambia, the arrest of more than 300 Southern Rhodesian Congress members, and the banning of the local Congress. (See chapters 1 and 4.) Prime Minister (Sir) Edgar Whitehead said that the Southern Rhodesian Congress had plotted with Kamuzu Banda of Nyasaland.[3]

Nkomo only escaped capture because he was on his way back from Accra, diverting after the arrests to London, where he lived for more than a year. In his absence, however, Michael Mawema, Stanlake Samkange (son of the minister), and Tarcisus George Silundika, a budding anthropologist, created the National Democratic Party (NDP) in 1960 to replace the Congress. They were soon joined by Herbert Chitepo, Southern Rhodesia's first black barrister by the Rev. Ndabaningi Sithole, by editor Leopold Takawira, and by Enoch Dumbutshena, then a journalist and later chief justice. Nkomo returned home in late 1960 to assume the presidency of the new nationalist organization. But Whitehead's government soon arrested the NDP's key members, and riots broke out in Bulawayo, Gweru, and Harare that led to the loss of African lives. The Southern Rhodesian parliament then passed draconian legislation meant to keep "law and order" in revolutionary times.

A year later, at a constitutional conference in London, Nkomo agreed—he thought reasonably—to a new political arrangement for Southern Rhodesia that was devised by Whitehead to end Britain's veto of discriminatory Rhodesian legislation in exchange for African seats in a reconstituted local parliament and a smooth glide path toward white-dominated self-government. Of the new legislature's sixty-five seats, Africans would hold fifteen. Nkomo, believing that some advance was preferable to none, accepted the proposal and prepared for an upcoming election.

But Nkomo misjudged his supporters. I was standing on the tarmac at Salisbury airport along with hundreds of others to welcome him back from London when the crowd voiced its extreme displeasure at Nkomo's weak responses. He had "caved in," they said, to British and Rhodesian expediency. Nyandoro, Chikerema, and many of the other leaders of Congress wanted nothing less than the full franchise that Malawians were about to exercise and that Zambians were strongly demanding. Nkomo immediately renounced the agreement, his party conference did the same, and together they pronounced an all-out political attack on the Whitehead government, forfeiting an admittedly incremental but very limited political opening for Africans. Southern Rhodesia, Nkomo and his followers proclaimed, was to become an African, not a multira-cial, nor a nonracial country.[4]

Later in 1961, the Congress decreed a progressive rejection of all things associated with whites and white rule. Africans were to go without shoes on Sunday, to attend political rallies without shoes or socks, and to participate in strikes against British-owned businesses. In retaliation, Whitehead's government banned the NDP. Nkomo, who was in Tanzania, quickly returned home and established the Zimbabwean African People's Union (ZAPU) as its successor.[5]

It was after witnessing these political maneuverings (and hardly knowing or even sensing that Nkomo's reneging on the 1961 constitution would lead in four years to a unilateral declaration of independence [UDI] by white politicians much more anti-African than Whitehead), that I appraised Nkomo's ineffectual leadership skills for an American audience. His detractors, I said, decried his "love of comfort and good living," his affable way with whites, his moderation, his tendency to vacillate, and an absence of any burning intensity such as that expressed by Zambia's future President Kenneth Kaunda. Moreover, Nkomo's "joyful girth [gives] no answer to those in Central Africa who . . . preach austerity. Most of all, Nkomo was a SiNdebele speaker, with strong support in Bulawayo and throughout Matabeleland. But that represented only about 20 percent of the territory's people, and many of the younger, up-and-coming, nationalists were CiShona speakers and unlikely to follow Nkomo's so far much too gentle leadership of the freedom movement."

Many of those CiShona speakers, quietly at first and then argumentatively later, voiced dissatisfaction with Nkomo's ability to lead them to the promised land of independence. Nyandoro, Chikerema, and Chitepo were critics. So was Sithole. And then there was an ascetic, tough-talking, forty-one-year old Jesuit-schooled CiShona-speaking teacher who had recently returned from training in Ghana, with a Ghanaian wife. This was Robert Gabriel Mugabe, a critic of Nkomo's selling-out and a passionate critic of soft living, alcohol consumption, and smoking. In late 1961, he had become publicity secretary of the NDF. After conversations with him and many meetings in Harare, I touted him as someone with the requisite skills and the personal drive to replace Nkomo and—in time—to take a faltering Rhodesia "down more desperate paths" to independence.[6] Law Professor Claire Palley was also impressed with Mugabe's mind and his intellectual rigor: "He had this ability to listen to argument, then dissect it, take it to bits."[7] What neither she nor I discerned was exactly how ambitious and ruthless he was, how immoral he was, and how those character defects would ultimately drive almost all Zimbabweans into poverty and compel many to flee to more hospitable lands.

Mugabe and a number of CiShona-speaking militant members of the Southern Rhodesia Congress soon decided that Nkomo was indeed moving too slowly and hesitantly. There was an undercurrent of distrust of a SiNdebele speaker, too. His detractors expressed themselves within Congress and publicly in Harare and beyond. I often met with many of those militants, including Mugabe, who sought a rupture with Nkomo. In 1963, these sentiments led to the creation of ZANU, led initially by Sithole, with Mugabe as its general secretary. The rift between SiNdebele and CiShona nationalists was wide; it was to grow even wider despite later efforts by Presidents Kaunda and Nyerere to bring the vitriolic contending forces together to combat a common enemy. (See below, pp. 243–44)

In 1964, the Southern Rhodesian government, by now under the right-wing leadership of Winston Field, jailed most of ZANU's top echelon. The ZAPU leadership was also detained, with Nkomo rusticated to remote Gonakudzingwa, in southeastern Zimbabwe. Those actions, and a raft of new restrictive legislation, made it much easier for whites in Rhodesia to believe that they could hold back from their own beaches the tides of indigenous home rule that had crested earlier that year in Malawi and Zambia. But even incarcerating their principal opponents was not enough. The colonial overlord was still able to promote pro-African endeavors.[8]

UDI and Civil War

An audacious UDI in late 1965 followed, an alarming turn in the wheel of postcolonial misfortune. Critics of that white Rhodesian gambit led by Prime Minister Ian Smith wanted Prime Minister Harold Wilson's British government to put down the rebellion forcibly. After all, technically, Southern Rhodesia (not Rhodesia) was still a British colony even though it had been self-ruling since 1923. But Wilson's advisors believed myopically that sanctions and blockades of fuel deliveries from Indian Ocean ports in Mozambique could quickly bring Smith and his rebels to their senses. Moreover, Britain and the United States would refuse to purchase Rhodesian minerals (ferrochrome, platinum, and more) and Virginia tobacco and sugar. In Washington, President Johnson was focused on Vietnam and only a few senior diplomats wanted to act militarily. They opted to do no more than to follow the British faltering lead.[9] Rhodesia would soon sue for peace. Or so Whitehall averred.

Britain failed to appreciate that both Portugal and South Africa would support Smith's breakaway regime and supply it with petroleum and other goods by rail and road. The Japanese and others would purchase minerals. In a seminar at Harvard's then Center for International Affairs, I also had to provide a geographical lesson to a baffled Sir Hugh Foot (Baron Caradon), Britain's Permanent Representative to the United Nations and an accomplished diplomat. Barricading oil at Beira, where most of Rhodesia's oil transited inland, would hardly stop petroleum shipments via Lourenço Marques (Maputo); a rail line entered Rhodesia from that port and could easily replace Beira as an entrance and exit point for white Rhodesia. Foot had not realized that there was such a third rail line in addition to the one from Beira and the one that ran north from South Africa through Botswana to Plumtree and on to both Victoria Falls and Harare.

The embargoes and sanctions never worked. All they did was to encourage autarkic self-reliance (at which the 230,000 white Rhodesians became very expert and resilient). Beleaguered Africans, especially nationalists and others who crossed borders to join the militant exiles, abandoned peaceful protest inside the country and mounted a vigorous insurgency: ZANU was backed by China and ZAPU was financed by the Soviet Union.[10]

As the guerrilla movements gained strength inside and outside Rhodesia, Britain tried several multi-pronged unsuccessful diplomatic initiatives to negotiate an end to Smith's separation. But when Wilson's Labour government was defeated by the Conservative Party, led by Edward Heath, in 1970, Smith turned Rhodesia into a republic. The stage was then set for strenuous negotiations led by Foreign Secretary Sir Alec Douglas-Home. In late 1971, he and Smith drafted a new constitution that legitimized the usurpation of power of 1965, gave Rhodesia independence under whites, and provided some limited participation for the 5.5 million African majority, but only over an interminably long estimated fifty- to sixty-year period of transition.

In exchange for a blessing by Britain, the Heath government insisted (to appease opponents in Britain and the United States, and to mollify horrified Africans) on an elaborate survey of indigenous opinion. If that canvas favored the proposed massive constitutional gift to whites, Douglas-Home's arrangements would be ratified. If not, Rhodesia could not so easily come in from the cold. The ascertaining of opinion was to be accomplished by a special commission headed by Baron Pearce, former British Lord of Appeal in Ordinary and head of Britain's Press Council; and including the Fifth Baron Harlech (Sir David Ormsby-Gore), a British Conservative politician; and Sir Glyn Jones (late governor of Malawi and one-time colonial secretary in Northern Rhodesia). Fifteen other British commissioners took testimony throughout the country.

The sittings of the Pearce Commission fortunately coincided with my return to Rhodesia in early 1972 after a formative visit to South Africa (discussed in chapter 6). Even an outsider like me realized that black Zimbabweans would not willingly accede to a white-crafted proposal that would defer *parity* in decision-making (not majority rule) in their own country for as long as sixty years. (Smith insouciantly proclaimed that Africans would never achieve majority rule in his son's lifetime.) So exactly what subterfuge were the British Tories and their Rhodesian counterparts promoting?

Nevertheless, ZANU could leave nothing to chance. Since Mugabe and his collaborators were still incarcerated, a then well-respected moderate, Bishop Abel Muzorewa, was recruited to be the (temporary) spokesman for African discontent. Among those who mobilized Africans and African opinion to support Muzorewa's dissent, and to prepare all manner of Zimbabweans to testify appropriately to the Pearce Commission, was my PhD student Eddison Zvobgo, and Edson Sithole, a young lawyer. Zvobgo had just been released from seven years in jail for opposing UDI, and Sithole was the country's second African to have been admitted to the local bar. He had emerged from detention, along with Zvobgo, and was in 1975 to be abducted mysteriously by the Rhodesian police, never to be seen again. Zvobgo, however, survived to become Mugabe's minister of justice (along with occupying other ministerial positions).

In preparation for the hearings before the Pearce Commission, Zvobgo and Sithole, with me in tow, spent days and nights in Highfield, Salisbury's second-oldest high-density (ghetto) section of the Rhodesian capital city. They knocked on doors, encountered passersby in the streets, and vigorously (with me observing) explained the need to provide a resounding "no" to the question of constitutional change.

When the hearings themselves began, I managed to obtain a seat to observe submissions to the Commission as it sat in a courtroom in downtown Salisbury. Jones smiled knowingly when he saw me among the avidly attentive spectators. (See also chapter 2.)

The African National Council, created and led by Muzorewa, testified that its rejection of the proposed constitution was "unanimous." Africans could not under any circumstances "accept a settlement whose result, directly or indirectly [would legalize the] . . . unilateral declaration of independence." Zvobgo asked the impassive commissioners whether Rhodesian blacks "could be expected to be the only human beings requesting rule by a minority?" Later, in Rhodesia's remote eastern highlands, Chief Rekayi Tangwena waggled his finger at a startled commissioner and reminded him, "The children of the Queen are doing much wrong here. Let them be put in jail."[11]

When I was not observing the Commission, or moving about the city with Zvobgo, I researched my biography of Cecil Rhodes. Doing so meant examining voluminous evidence—letters to Rhodes from his contemporaries—in the Rhodesian archives. (For want of time, I could not complete my work on that visit, but expected shortly to return and to continue perusing the archival material in both Rhodesia and South Africa.)

At night, I retreated to the famed, historic, Meikle's Hotel in downtown Salisbury, just off what was then called Cecil Square. A big sign at the front door instructed patrons to check their long guns at the door. The atmosphere throughout Harare and other cities was obviously tense, strained, and radically polarized. After all, Rhodesia/Zimbabwe was at war, with both ZANU and ZAPU warriors having begun to harass outlying white-run farms and to threaten Smith's followers with all-out mayhem.

Soon, especially after the Pearce Commission returned a resounding negative finding and the proposed constitution became null and void, the war warmed considerably. By the beginning of 1973, South Africa's influential *Cape Times* wrote that it was no longer unlikely that a Vietnam-type situation would grow in Zimbabwe.[12] ZANU, the primarily Shona guerrilla movement, menaced white farmers in the northern and eastern sections of the country, primarily from training camps in Zambia and distant Tanzania. ZAPU, the mostly Ndebele nationalist organization led by Nkomo, was active in western Zimbabwe, from bases in Zambia. Together, from about 1973, both movements (demanded by Kaunda) established a Joint Military Command to coordinate ambushes and other attacks, and to learn from and work with Frelimo, Mozambique's experienced liberation movement and its operatives.

The war was no plaything between 1973 and 1979. Whites armed themselves to the hilt, and even innocent Africans were endangered. Many young Zimbabwean Africans, even those still in secondary school, fled the cities to join ZANU and ZAPU in the bush.[13] There were no shortages of eager recruits, especially after both nationalist movements were strengthened by the release from prison after eleven years of Mugabe and Edgar Tekere. Together they escaped overland to Mozambique in 1975. Both ZANU and ZAPU grew stronger in subsequent years, especially with Soviet and Chinese financial backing and training and the moral and material support of Zambia, Tanzania, and Mozambique—finally independent of Portuguese colonial rule (see chapter 6).[14]

A Prohibited Immigrant

Unfortunately, I was compelled to observe much of the course of the war and its innumerable brutalities, as well as the assiduous and vicious efforts of outnumbered whites to forestall a successful African invasion, either from Zambia, Mozambique, or Tanzania.

After I returned home from my African investigations in 1972, I naturally wrote critically in the American and South African press about what I had seen, and how odious and Canute-like the Rhodesian white machinations would prove to be.

I had settled back into teaching responsibilities and graduate student supervision at MIT when Rhodesian Attorney General Piet K. van der Byl sent me a very polite, formal letter announcing that I was henceforth a "prohibited immigrant." I could no longer come to Rhodesia. There ensued a six- or seven-letter exchange, with me innocently asking, "Why?" and van der Byl explaining that he could provide no reasons. Naturally I responded, and reminded him of his father's long and warm relationship with Sir Stewart Gore-Browne, my own illustrious late friend. Van der Byl wrote back, essentially saying, "Nice try, but no dice." We went back and forth some more, but fruitlessly (and mostly for my own amusement). Clearly my activities with Zvobgo and Sithole had triggered a Rhodesian intelligence response. So had various press articles of mine critical of Rhodesia.[15]

For the next eight years I was compelled to follow the unraveling of Rhodesia from outside, to defer archival research on Rhodes, and to keep closely in touch with the fortunes of ZANU and ZAPU, and the guerrilla war generally, from Lusaka—where I met often with Silundika of ZAPU—or from Dar es Salaam, where Zvobgo and his comrades had relocated.

At various intervals Smith agreed to talk about regularizing his regime. In 1973 and 1974, he and Muzorewa had talks about holding talks. But there was no urgency until the demise of Portugal as a colonial power and the shift in control of Mozambique to Frelimo, headed by Samora Machel. After all, an African-ruled Mozambique could clearly deny the use of its harbors to anything destined for Rhodesia, which it soon did.

To Smith's surprise, too, South Africa was content to tolerate a revolutionary government in Mozambique while simultaneously funding and organizing Renamo, an anti-Frelimo resistance movement advised by its own special forces and Rhodesian military operatives; that awareness gave little permanent comfort to Smith and his collaborators. Moreover, Smith suspected that he could no longer count on the unquestioned support of his patron to the south. As a client state, his satrapy could easily be jettisoned, or bartered away for a larger objective. Indeed, by about the mid-1970s, South African Prime Minister Vorster and General Hendrik van den Bergh, his chief security advisor, decided that waging war in Rhodesia for Rhodesians was far more dangerous than defending their own heartland. If South Africa could help to arrange a peaceful transfer of power in Rhodesia/Zimbabwe, doing so could buy South Africa time and, conceivably, stability.

President Kaunda in Zambia also needed stability—desperately. His country's role as a key front-line state was causing great economic pain. Playing host to a collection of private (ANC, ZANU, ZAPU, and SWAPO) armies posed dangers as well as severe costs.

Kaunda (and Nyerere, who also hosted Zimbabwean guerrillas in Tanzania) was particularly anxious in the mid-1970s to unify and toughen the ZANU and ZAPU political operatives whom he sheltered in Zambia. At his behest, the two movements nominally came together under an African National Council umbrella, but neither of the opposing movements had much enthusiasm for this enforced solidarity.

Nor was ZANU itself consolidated in Lusaka or in the combatant camps. Indeed, in early 1975 the rivalries between the eastern (Manyika) and southern (Karanga) Shona factions within ZANU erupted, leading to the assassination of Chitepo—ZANU's putative leader in Lusaka—and the arrest by Zambian police of a clutch of ZANU activists. Chitepo may have been working more closely with ZAPU leaders in Lusaka, as Kaunda preferred but more radical ZANU operatives disdained. Whatever its origins and motivations, the killing of Chitepo was an inside job, and Josiah Tongorara, leader of the military wing of ZANU, was suspected of engineering it—possibly on behalf of or in concert with others in the militant wing. But no definitive suspect has ever been charged despite local arrests, an official commission of inquiry, and careful investigations by Dumbutshena. British officials in Lusaka viewed Chitepo as "a victim of circumstances . . . who fell victim to his more radical comrades, who saw him as a liability."[16] His demise, moreover, made Mugabe's rise to prominence that much more plausible. A key rival had been eliminated, conveniently but possibly fortuitously.

Kaunda was meanwhile exploring a diplomatic initiative. Vorster and Kaunda together tried to bring peace to Rhodesia at a conference at Victoria Falls in 1975. South Africa brought Smith to the table and the Zambians delivered ZANU and ZAPU. But the South Africans could not reduce Smith's intransigence. ZANU believed that it had the means and the motives to follow Frelimo's success in Mozambique with powerful war strikes of its own into northern and northeastern Rhodesia, ultimately to break the back of white resistance. ZANU also suspected that Kaunda and Vorster favored Nkomo over ZANU. So that largely wild attempt to broker peace never really had much of a chance.[17]

Ruthlessness and Victory

After Mozambique won its independence from Portugal in 1975, and ZANU moved many of its forward bases into that country's Tete corridor, I was also able to converse directly with Mugabe by telephone. I was in Maputo and he was up the coast in Quelimane, trying to gain control over ZANU and to marginalize Tongogara and other military leaders of the guerrilla movement.

In a long telephone conversation over a scratchy line, Mugabe assured me in 1976 that he was a socialist but that he had seen what Frelimo's socialism had done to retard Mozambique's post-independence development. He would not repeat the Frelimo mistakes, he assured me. Mugabe had lived in Ghana and he knew better than to follow the flawed Nkrumah model of corrupt state dominance. He would rule Zimbabwe, an advanced economy, after its coming independence as a committed democrat and as someone who respected essential freedoms. He also promised to organize a fully participatory representative democracy that would permit capitalism to lift Zimbabweans up by their bootstraps. So far, I thought, so good. Mugabe, the consummate dissembler and diplomat, always sounded reasonable and intelligent, confirming what Palley and others had earlier noted. American Congressman Stephen Solarz, who served on the Foreign Affairs Committee, visited Mugabe in Quelimane about this time, and came away with a distinctly favorable impression. A British diplomat in Maputo also found him very reasonable: "I found him quite impressive and likeable . . . but rather mild and modest with nothing of the swagger or the ruthlessness of Machel."[18] Little did we all know or anticipate the autocratic actions that were to come.

Later that year, appalled that the Soviet-backed and Cuban-reinforced MPLA had triumphed in Angola despite South African and American support for UNITA, U.S. Secretary of State Henry Kissinger (with British encouragement) persuaded Vorster to help bring Smith and Rhodesia to heel in order to forestall a similar debacle in Rhodesia The United States, said Kissinger, "will not tolerate another massive Cuban move."[19] Thus, pushed, possibly even threatened, by Vorster (with Kissinger very active in the background) on behalf of South African realpolitik, Smith intimated on television that trying to transform Rhodesia into a multiracial, ultimately black-run, state might be useful, given Kissinger's assurances that he and Vorster would protect white interests. Smith's white followers were appalled, Africans surprised and puzzled.[20] And a few weeks later, Smith was rapidly backtracking, complaining that the possibility of anointing Mugabe as his successor would be a disaster for the country.

Thanks to Kissinger's energetic and rather Machiavellian initiative, Britain convened a meeting in Geneva in late 1976 with Smith, Nkomo, Mugabe, Muzorewa, Ndabaningi Sithole (as the head of a breakaway rump ZANU), and

Figure 9.1. Robert Mugabe

Chikerema on behalf of the Front for the Liberation of Zimbabwe. But incentives for a deal were insufficiently robust; Smith was not yet ready to negotiate his own political demise and the capitulation of white Rhodesia. Likewise, ZANU, with about 5,000 combatants in training, was unwilling to see its battlefield advantages dissipated at the negotiating table. Indeed, ZANU and ZAPU both broke with Muzorewa, Sithole, and the others even before the Geneva meeting. Thereafter, because Muzorewa (who now considered himself a powerful political actor) insisted on working with Smith (and partnered with him in 1979), the main political movements of the future Zimbabwe regarded Muzorewa as a turncoat.

By the end of the Geneva meeting, Mugabe and Nkomo were the acknowledged leaders of a future Zimbabwe. Nkomo, with his first-mover advantage and a politically moderate posture that appealed to Kaunda, was a presumptive heir to Smith—not Muzorewa or Sithole. Nyerere's view was different from Kaunda's: "Nkomo won't fight, the Bishop wants to preach, and Sithole is a write-off."[21] Nyerere and Machel preferred Mugabe because they knew that the guerrillas in the field favored him. Indeed, in Geneva Mugabe had greatly enhanced his stature with the ZANU military figures. He was more obdurate than Solarz or others expected, and that strong approach appealed at least to the ZANU cadres. Mugabe refused, for example, to countenance a Kissingerian arrangement that would have given Rhodesian whites a governance role during the transitional period before independence. Mugabe emerged from Geneva much stronger than he had entered even though Nkomo, according to British diplomats, still believed that he could "control" Mugabe.[22]

Nkomo and Mugabe and their movements were forcibly yoked together by the Organization of African Unity (OAU), which supplied some funds, and because of the strenuous demands of both Kaunda and Nyerere that the leaders and their activists should cooperate. But there was never any love lost between the principals, and little amity among the personnel in the field. Nkomo treated Mugabe in public as someone definitively junior; Mugabe, the younger man, disdained Nkomo's pretensions. Mugabe devoted himself in these last years of the 1970s to strengthening his own precarious power within a ZANU that was divided between so-called progressives (largely unpersuaded as they were of Mugabe's legitimacy) and "conservatives" who reckoned that Mugabe was their rightful leader.

Mugabe and his backers suspected that Nkomo would cut a deal behind their backs with Smith and Muzorewa—a goal that the British government and its negotiators seemed to prefer. Nkomo regarded Muzorewa, Sithole, and Chikerema, and their ilk, as "liars" and "black weaklings," but because of his national political insecurities, might have been susceptible to a partnership that gave him unquestioned primacy.[23] (Smith, meanwhile, was attempting to bring friendly Africans into his government to provide fake multiracial cover.) Nkomo also realized after Geneva that he needed some kind of British-sponsored arrangement if he were to emerge as the first leader of a free Zimbabwe. He appreciated, much more than all of the outsiders, that he and his adherents could never emerge victorious if the transitional process culminated in a free election. Mugabe's supporters were too numerous, too antagonistic to an endeavor led by men from Matabeleland.

Although ethnic differences had meant little in Southern Rhodesian and Rhodesian black politics in the early 1960s, by 1978—with real power and spoils coming closer—the identity differences between the followers of Nkomo and Mugabe, and between the two leaders themselves, became sharply pronounced. After all, the character differences between the two, and their policy disagreements, were of long standing.

By 1978, thanks to Chinese and some intermittent Soviet and East European backing, ZANU's military might encompassed about 8,000 soldiers with abundant small arms and rocket launchers; its operations had elevated the ongoing costs of the Rhodesian defenses and severely damaged white morale. Casualties were numerous on both sides. Preemptive Rhodesian strikes into Mozambique hardly held ZANU back. Whites, many of whom had left their rural farms on the hard-to-protect frontier, were crowding into the safer cities. Others were emigrating en masse.

In the field, ZANU was far stronger than ZAPU despite stout Soviet and Cuban support for ZAPU, fresh backing from Kaunda, and renewed energy on Nkomo's part. Small squads penetrated into northwestern Rhodesia from Zambia and were able to shoot their way south toward Bulawayo. But, in contrast to ZANU's 8,000 combatants, ZAPU's guerrillas in the field probably numbered no more than 6,000. The Patriotic Front that Kaunda had imposed on ZANU and ZAPU existed more on paper than in combat.[24]

Although it was clear to many perceptive outsiders, and even to Smith's intelligence operatives, that the African nationalists were going to win the battle for Rhodesia, and soon, Smith and his close associates still imagined that they could create a multiracial facade that would postpone the evil day, hold South Africa on their side, and keep Rhodesia white-ruled for a decade or so. Legerdemain constituted a way to forestall black domination—or so they imagined.

Thus, in early 1978, Muzorewa, Ndabaningi Sithole, and Chief Jeremiah Chirau joined Smith's executive council as co-leaders of Rhodesia. Their close followers became co-cabinet ministers with the existing white cabinet ministers. Although a continuing parliament, filled with whites, retained its legislative functions, the executive council began exercising authority in the war-torn country. It dismantled the legal underpinnings of segregation, voiding the Land Apportionment Act that had forced Africans off desirable farming terrain, ended separate schooling for blacks and whites, established a minimum wage, and approved a new (but white devised) constitution giving Africans seventy-two of one hundred seats in the lower house of a new parliament and twenty of thirty seats in the upper house. The constitution gave whites a veto over legislation, however. Overall, the new arrangement was designed cleverly to convey only circumscribed power to Africans, with key cabinet portfolios remaining in white hands.

Muzorewa professed being open to having Nkomo and Mugabe join him in the new Rhodesian charade. The British government particularly wanted Nkomo to consider such an amalgamation of his ZAPU interests with those of Muzorewa and Smith. Indeed, in mid-1978, Nkomo met secretly with Smith, but refused to abandon Mugabe. Nigeria preferred Nkomo's ascension, too, and for months tried to broker an agreement for Nkomo to enter a new Rhodesian government and become its first black premier. But these intricate maneuverings, which for a time separated Kaunda and Nyerere, came to naught. The OAU (and especially Nyerere and Machel) would not approve sidelining Mugabe, perhaps for fear of Nkomo's fronting for the Soviets and Cubans. Or, more likely, the OAU preferred Mugabe because they believed Nkomo too weak (see above, p. 244) to win an effective peace and rule Zimbabwe energetically.

Elections under the interim internally constructed constitution took place in early 1979. Muzorewa's United African National Congress won 67 percent of the black vote, worth fifty-one lower-house seats. Sithole's rump ZANU took twelve seats, a stand-in ZAPU party won ten seats, and Chirau none. Muzorewa ended up as prime minister of Rhodesia, with ten of the cabinet positions, Smith five, and Sithole and a ZAPU stand-in party two each.

This multiracial government, with whites still pulling many of the crucial levers of power, might have suited an earlier decade. But by the end of the 1970s, nothing Muzorewa—who looked like Smith's puppet—could do could end the war, appease the guerrillas, or satisfy the political aspirations of the bulk of Zimbabwe's population. Nor could massive Rhodesian attacks on ZANU and ZAPU camps in Angola, Mozambique, and Zambia alter the legitimacy and firepower of the guerrillas. Ninety percent of Rhodesia remained under martial law. Even cities were unsafe, and whites and Africans traveled throughout the country only during daylight and only in escorted convoy. Ambushes were frequent. Whites drove with machine guns or pistols close at hand. Nkomo's men even employed heat-seeking Soviet SAM-7 ground-to-air missiles to shoot down two internal civilian flights of Air Rhodesia, killing 107 passengers. Such mayhem, and massive military patrols by the defenders, consumed the Muzorewa/Smith regime's limited capital; at about $1.5 million a day in 1978 and 1979, a small country such as Rhodesia could hardly sustain such a disproportionate fiscal drain. The price was much too steep; a fragile economy with half of its labor force on patrol and away from gainful pursuits could hardly endure war without end.

The formidable Margaret Thatcher became prime minister of Britain in 1979. A few months after gaining office, she insisted on a new attempt to negotiate peace in Her Majesty's pariah dominion. Especially, she sought a sure method of testing the rival claims of Mugabe and Nkomo, and of Muzorewa, in the voting booth rather than on the battlefield. She, like Botha, may have been told that Muzorewa could or would win a fair contest. She brought all competing sides to London in September 1979. Lord Carrington, Britain's foreign secretary (assisted by some clever tapping of the telephones of all of the African parties) presided resolutely for three months over what became a decisive knocking of collective heads. Throughout these long months Zvobgo operated as Mugabe's spokesman. He had Mugabe's ear and was under instruction to speak a consistently tough line to the media. "His flair for producing the quick and easy quote for pressmen, and performing for the television cameras was very conscious." At one point he urged Prime Minister Thatcher "to jump into the Thames."[25] (In London at the time, I conferred almost daily with Zvobgo, and learned at second hand how much pressure Carrington was putting on Mugabe to parley openly, and to compromise.)

To the surprise of those who had experienced Rhodesian and Zimbabwean intransigence since 1965, Carrington managed by gifted gamesmanship (and that inside intelligence) to persuade Muzorewa to break with Smith, and to let Carrington transfer power to a British governor (Lord Soames) who would organize new elections in 1980. Carrington insisted that Mugabe and Nkomo cooperate—and accept a diminished and temporary, but real role for whites. With Kaunda's assistance, Carrington also overrode Mugabe-Nkomo worries that South Africa would intervene against the Patriotic Front and neutralize its military advantages. Carrington promised that Soames and Commonwealth troops would leash the Rhodesian air force and keep South Africans troops (five battalions were in Rhodesia, wearing Rhodesian uniforms) from interfering.[26] ZANU and ZAPU would join a ceasefire. Upon their agreement, he would lift sanctions by Britain, and the United States would follow suit, enabling the Zimbabwean economy to recover.

Tongogara, the accomplished Marxist-trained general who commanded ZANU's military force with a firm hand, participated in the London conference. He was Mugabe's only real rival for political supremacy in the soon-to-be-realized independent Zimbabwe. But he never made it back to Harare. Just after Christmas, 1979, a suspicious automobile accident took his life while he was returning to Zimbabwe from his stronghold in rural Mozambique. Tongogara's demise, combined with the brutal earlier assassination of Cbitepo, left Zimbabwe and ZANU devoid of potential contenders for primary leadership. Mugabe had outlasted—or removed—his rivals.[27]

Later, Mugabe saw that hostile critics within the party, and within the independent country, suffered mysterious road crashes. Sometimes the tires on automobiles would suddenly fly off; sometimes there were foreign elements placed in petrol tanks. As a US ranking official later recalled, judges "would all of a sudden find themselves in automobile wrecks and things like that. It was pretty nasty."[28] Zvobgo believed in the early 2000s that he was targeted, but survived. (Subsequently, too, there was the horrific shooting and burning by Mugabe and Mnangagwa loyalists of General Solomon Mujuru, who stood in the way of Grace Mugabe's political ascendance.)[29]

The election outcome in late February 1980 startled the South Africans, Smith's people, and Muzorewa's followers, exactly as I had intimated to Botha.[30] There was evident intimidation by ZANU forces in the eastern and central parts of the country, but nevertheless, given Shona predominance on the voting rolls, Mugabe and ZANU emerged with 63 percent of the vote and fifty-seven of the one hundred parliamentary common-roll seats. (Mugabe had insisted on running as ZANU, not as part of the Patriotic Front, leaving ZAPU isolated and adrift. Mugabe wanted to show electoral strength in order to sideline contenders for national primacy.) Nkomo and ZAPU obtained 24 percent and twenty seats. Muzorewa's party only received 8 percent of the votes and three seats. Smith's Rhodesian Front won the twenty seats that were reserved on the white roll, and were to be extinguished in ten years. The stage was set perfectly for Zimbabwe's independence in mid-April 1980, ninety years after Rhodes set his imperial sights on the territory to which he gave his name. There was much to be accomplished by a new administration of Africans. With Mugabe's promises to me much in mind, I was as hopeful as Lord Soames (who was prepared to overlook electoral breaches by ZANU), Lord Carrington, and Her Majesty's now relieved government.

Promises Not Kept: The Early Years of Independence

At independence in 1980, Zimbabwe possessed the human and physical resources to produce an outstanding African success story. Its economy was the most balanced on the continent, with vast agricultural promise and great potential wealth underground: its mining sector already unearthed ferrochrome, gold, nickel, copper, asbestos, and coal. Its 5,000 white-owned farms employed 400,000 African laborers. Together they grew great surpluses of food crops as well as export-quality Virginia tobacco, beef, cotton, and sugar. Mugabe and his followers had also inherited an impressive physical infrastructure: roads, rails, and telecommunications in the pre-internet age were of high standard compared to the rest of sub-Saharan Africa (north of South Africa). It possessed thermal and hydroelectric generating capacity, well-managed game reserves welcoming to tourists (now that the war was over), capable administrators, and more indigenous university graduates per capita than any other place on the continent.

Given such a fortunate legacy, the Mugabe regime's prime task was to uplift the ordinary Africans who had suffered so much and for so long under white settler domination. At first it chose a model of multiracial growth that eschewed the Marxist rhetoric of the liberation struggle, and which conformed pretty much to the assurances that Mugabe had conveyed to me in 1976. It also emphasized a major expansion of educational opportunity, opening new schools at all levels, training new cadres of teachers, and spending large developmental sums in this sector. "By 1990 Zimbabwe had the highest rate of literacy in Africa. In the first five years after Independence, we built a new school every day. We built a modern hospital in every District with a national network of referral hospitals and 1600 basic health centers. In this frantic effort we had the support of the world."[31] Zimbabwe rapidly turned guns into butter.

As Mugabe himself declared on the literal eve of independence, "Our majority rule could easily turn into inhuman rule if we oppressed, persecuted or harassed those who do not look or think like the majority of us. Democracy is never mob-rule. It is and should remain disciplined rule requiring compliance with the law and social rules. Our independence must thus not be construed as an instrument vesting individuals or groups with the right to harass and intimidate others into acting against their will."[32]
Certainly not!

At first, Mugabe ostensibly ran the young Zimbabwe in an even-handed manner, constrained as he was by the provisions of the 1979 constitution that gave whites a parliamentary say and prevented him from becoming an executive president until 1987. I saw him often in those early years when I was in Harare meeting with Zvobgo and Nathan Shamuyarira—minister of information and my old friend from my first days in Africa. Shamuyarira had visited me and my family in Cambridge, too, while he was completing a doctoral dissertation at Princeton University.

Yet there were troubling signs, discernible early in the reign of the new Zimbabwean administration. The government purchased a South African–owned press operation that controlled Zimbabwe's only daily newspapers, exerted official authority over all radio and television broadcasts, and threatened to nationalize the marketing of minerals. Mugabe also began talking about turning Zimbabwe, as soon as he could, into a one-party state on the Tanzanian and Zambian models. Mugabe's instincts, and the ruthlessness that I had not anticipated, tended more and more toward authoritarianism. Shamuyarira, who knew better, began rationalizing these excesses in conversations with me (a pattern that continued over the next twenty years as Mugabe's assaults on civil liberties and human rights became more frequent). But Zvobgo shrugged, appreciating that he could do nothing to hold Mugabe back. A few years later, when Zvobgo was Minister of Mines, I asked him how he prevented Mugabe from interfering in the decisions made within Zvobgo's portfolio. He explained with a smile that he always told Mugabe what he was doing, rather than asking for permission to take a particular course of action. Most of the time Mugabe, busy with other matters, failed to reply.

This method might have worked for other subordinates, but few tried it. Additionally, Mugabe was rightly focused on moving the major levers of transformational influence, and in consolidating his personal ascendancy in the same way that he had moved against Tongogara and others. He was determined to create a single-party state, eliminating potential opposition. For that reason, as well as his all-consuming enmity toward Nkomo, he moved swiftly to crush any potential dissidence in Matabeleland.

The most egregious of Mugabe's many harmful actions filled the early months of 1983 with mayhem, and continued well into 1984. Mugabe sent the North Korean–trained Zimbabwe army's Fifth Brigade into Matabeleland in southwestern Zimbabwe to suppress alleged opposition among SiNdebele-speaking citizens who—presumably—backed Nkomo. This was ethnic cleansing at its most extreme. Under Mugabe's direct order, and with future president Emmerson Mnangagwa and frequent cabinet minister Sydney Sekeramayi orchestrating the attack, at least 20,000 non-combatant Ndebele were slaughtered. Many Ndebele were bayoneted. Entire villages were set alight. The Fifth Brigade visited unspeakable atrocities, including gang rapes, on many thousands more, choosing villages to destroy and villagers to torture and extirpate presumably because of their inferred ZAPU affiliations. In CiShona the operation was termed *Gukurahundi*, or cleansing ("the spring rains that wash away the chaff").[33]

The country's Conference of Roman Catholic Bishops, several of whom were black, formally condemned these wanton brutalities. So did the Catholic Commission for Justice and Peace. The Anglican Bishop of Matabeleland termed the attacks genocide: "It seems to be the deliberate and indiscriminate revenge on the Matabele people . . . a policy of genocide."[34] Mugabe called members of the local archdiocese traitors and meddlers, and silenced any criticisms within his own party. He also extolled the killings. Shamuyarira said that the statement by the Catholic bishops was "irresponsible, contrived and propagandistic." The Fifth Brigade, he declared, was bringing "peace and relief" to the region. Because of Britain's support for the Mugabe regime that it had spawned, the U.S. critique of these genocidal acts was mostly muted and private; other embassies were also quiet, taking their lead from the official British response to ignore the massacre that Mugabe had initiated. As Meredith wrote, this was not the only but the most dangerous early example of Mugabe's determined ruthlessness, matched by the ruthlessness of Mnangagwa (whom I came to know later) and of Colonel (later General) Perence Shiri, who commanded the battalion.[35]

My own published commentary was naturally critical of the immense harm that Mugabe was wreaking on innocent citizens in his alas successful attempt to depress Ndebele support for Nkomo and ZAPU. Yet I was starkly wrong in my hopeful and temporizing concluding sentence: "It is too soon to lump Zimbabwe with the Zambias and the Zaires of today's debt-ridden and democratically-stunted Africa, but the signs of early trouble are present."[36]

In fact, it was not soon enough. In 1984, Zimbabwe took further backward steps when Mugabe and his followers began to exchange Western-style, market-oriented, multiparty rule for a single-party socialist state tightly controlled by ZANU's "politburo" and central committee—the former's members (the new "comrades") being appointed by Mugabe.[37] They did not rush to oust the South African, European, and American investors who drove the nation's economy, especially its mining sector. Nor did they then use available British funding to replace white farm ownership with African freeholders. All of these developments would come after 1990, when twenty white followers of Smith would lose their guaranteed seats in parliament and untrammeled political hegemony would be ZANU's to dispose.

But first Mugabe needed to co-opt Nkomo and to eliminate what was left of ZAPU as a rival political party after the wanton massacres of 1983–1984. He did so at the end of 1987 by persuading Nkomo, a spent political force by this point, to merge ZANU and ZAPU into what became known as the ZANU-PF (Patriotic Front), with Mugabe firmly in control as an executive president (no longer as prime minister). The merged party also gave Mugabe the right to run both the party and the nation in an autocratic manner, to disburse all patronage, make all appointments, and start consolidating what became a dictatorship. Zimbabwe, I wrote at the time, "had fallen into the same trap" as so many of its lamented and failed predecessors in Africa. Mugabe was knowingly forfeiting the advantages of a country with wealth and educated citizens, and great promise. Even though the Afro-socialist model had failed dramatically in Tanzania, Zambia, and Ghana, and even though those and many other African states were dismantling their socialist approaches, regretting overvalued currencies and stultifying import restrictions, Mugabe was insistent on pressing ahead with a failed model, presumably to give him and his associates greater opportunities for rent-seeking and infernal arbitrage.[38]

Elsewhere in Africa, plausible semblances of democracy were returning, albeit in fits and starts. But not in Zimbabwe, which was forging its own dark path. It became harder than ever before to disagree with Mugabe. As the state's

Central Intelligence Organization (CIO) grew in size and power, Mugabe more and more employed instruments of intimidation and patronage to keep senior (and junior) politicians in line. With the media and television/radio tightly run, lucrative commercial opportunities in the president's gift, and internal opposition quelled, Mugabe emerged in the 1990s as an unquestioned despot concerned less for the welfare of his constituents than for feeding his own personal and the ruling party's appetite for unquestioned control and broad fiscal reward.

In the early years of Mugabe's reign, his wife Sally Hayfron (they met at the Takoradi Teacher Training College in Ghana) is credited with restraining some of the president's pretensions of grandeur, as well as his personal avarice. But Sally suffered with kidney disease from the late 1980s and died in early 1992. By the tine of Sally's death, a typing pool secretary—Grace Marufu—had borne Mugabe a son. Many local observers associate Grace's acquisitive influence on Mugabe with his decisive turn to predation and wholesale corruption throughout the 1990s and after.

Edgar Tekere, a onetime major figure in the liberation struggle and in ZANU, bravely threatened Mugabe's omnipotence in the 1990 presidential contest, being opposed to a one-party state. He lost in a possibly rigged result, and was soon sidelined.[39] Later in the decade, Margaret Dongo, a sometime youthful freedom fighter and onetime CIO operative who knew Mugabe's abuses of power at close hand, served for five years as a lone voice of criticism within parliament. (She then became a student of mine at the Harvard Kennedy School and was full of lurid tales of how Mugabe and his cronies had benefited from an upsurge of corruption.)[40]

ZANU kept winning parliamentary and presidential elections (each held separately) throughout this period, but the ZANU victories at the polls were hollow, Mugabe usually succeeding against token or jailed opponents. It was obvious long before, but by 1996 Mugabe was unquestionably running an autocracy masquerading as a democracy.[41]

Throughout the 1990s, Mugabe steadfastly refused the entreaties of some of his cabinet ministers and kept the national economy firmly closed. Many colleagues saw the error of their previous ways and urged Mugabe to privatize state-owned enterprises and to launch a period of growth. But time and again Mugabe rebuked them, just when neighbors were opening their economies, and prospering. From 1995 to 2000, Zimbabwe's annual GDP per capita fell from $620 to $510. Government deficits ballooned. Medical and educational services collapsed, not for the last time. The percentage of the labor force without formal employment rose to 60 percent and inflation soared from 26 percent per annum in 1995 to 55 percent in 2000. Zimbabwe's dollar slumped against the U.S. dollar. Foreign exchange weaknesses caused persistent shortages of petroleum, cooking oil, kerosene, and some staple food commodities. Electricity blackouts became common.

Much of this economic and fiscal deterioration resulted from corruption that grew rampant from about 1992. State procurements almost always included shares for Mugabe, Mnangagwa, and many others in the ZANU leadership. Everyone in power was taking a cut of everything and anything on which they could lay their grasping tentacles.

Mugabe and all of his acolytes became more and more acquisitive in the last half of the 1990s. He and his new wife commandeered Air Zimbabwe commercial aircraft and flew frequently to Europe, South America, and Asia, purchasing fancy goods as they traveled, and buying houses and flats in Britain, Hong Kong, and Singapore. At home, the government gave more and more construction contracts to consortia controlled by the president's nephew. For years, little had been procured without government officials at the top and lower down receiving their cuts. Nothing could be signed or arranged without State House, usually assisted by Mnangagwa as a go-between, profiting and profiteering.

Mugabe even arranged a lucrative retirement package for himself; the Presidential Benefits and Retirement Amendment Bill of 1998 enabled him to continue to enjoy his then current luxurious lifestyle indefinitely—at taxpayer expense. His spouse and children (legitimate and illegitimate) earned handsome rewards as well. That was in addition to free housing, transport, clothing, medical, and security allowances—all tax free.

"Long-lived leaders and governments," I wrote sanctimoniously, "sometimes do themselves in. When they demonstrate contempt for their constituents, and the people more generally, the ends of their hegemonies may be predicted."[42] Or so I may have wished.

Sure enough, but not conclusively, riots broke out in early 1998, especially in Harare. The rioters protested the impoverishment of the country, thanks to mismanagement and corruption. Costs of living had spiraled out of control. The local currency had collapsed again, and more dramatically. Food prices, especially that for staple maize meal, had reached unprecedented high levels. These developments largely followed Mugabe's personal assault on his nation's most productive export sectors for ostensible political gain.

Even though 40 percent of all agricultural earnings came from the farms owned and managed by whites (all acting on earlier government assurances and permits), Mugabe began to confiscate 1,500 of those holdings, promising to settle landless blacks on those maize and tobacco lands. But he did so without funds with which to place Africans on the many profitable estates that he and his sponsored thugs were seizing violently from hapless white farmers. Trying to play the racist card, a tactic that had worked for him in earlier, less sophisticated, times, Mugabe forced black laborers off the commandeered farms and greatly curtailed the agricultural sector's ability to keep growing and harvesting crops. He also managed to repress the riots, but only for a time.

Invading the Congo

This rush to accumulate large rewards accelerated, too, when Zimbabwe's army and air force moved under Mugabe's orders to assist Democratic Republic of Congo President Laurent Kabila's resistance of Rwandan invaders in late 1998.

First 6,000 and then another 7,000 crack Zimbabwean troops moved into the Congo provinces of Shaba and Kasai without even a nod to the Zimbabwean cabinet or approval by parliament. Zimbabwean political and military leaders rushed to defend Congo's rich cobalt, copper, diamond, and gold mines; Mugabe and his associates personally benefited while the costs of the mercenary force were borne by the Zimbabwean taxpayer. Looting was the goal, whether or not Kabila survived.

Shortly after the arrival of Zimbabwean military detachments in the Congo, I was in Zimbabwe attempting to arrange a Harvard economic advising mission to support the efforts of Herbert Murerwa, its Harvard-trained finance minister, and occasionally seeing Mugabe. One afternoon in Murerwa's opulent office I asked the minister how he planned to pay for the soldiers and the equipment who had been sent northward to preserve Kabila's shaky presidency. I knew that Zimbabwe at this point was effectively bankrupt because of Mugabe's misman-agement of the national economy and his hostile attitude to foreign investors. (Mugabe had also promised vast pensions to so-called war veterans in order to pay off potential protesters.) I knew, too, that ZANU-PF was stealing everything that was not tied down. "How are you going to cover the vast expenses of the incursion?" I asked innocently. Murewa's reply was enormously instructive: "I have no idea," he confessed. "I have not been told." In other words, the economic czar in State House (Charles Utete) who answered to Mugabe and made many fateful fiscal decisions, had not yet bothered to consult Murerwa. All of these developments, as I quickly learned, were sure signs of an autocracy decaying, and of a corrupt edifice that knew few limits. Greed had become a dominating driver of personal and national interest. And so it was to remain.

Invading the Congo was hardly popular on the streets of Harare and Bulawayo. Indeed, this arbitrary exercise of presidential discretion soon added to the misery of ordinary Zimbabweans. The price of imported petrol (gasoline) rose by 67 percent; cooking oil and bread costs also escalated. Bus fares increased by 100 percent, helping further to impoverish commuters. Since all of these penal-ties paid by laboring Zimbabweans could easily be traced to the Congo exercise, constituents grumbled, and did so loudly.

When they learned that drinking water was scarce in Harare because the government had run out of funds to purchase a key water pump, they grew angrier. Then they realized that Mugabe, after a sixteen-day trip with his second wife to Libya and Europe, was constructing several expensive mansions for Grace, the consort. She was increasingly referred to as "Grasping Grace"—even by Shamuyarira to me in private. To top it all, ZANU's mayor of Harare was building a $1.5 million personal edifice. The displeasure of everyday Zimbabweans became palpable. Few on the streets in the capital could understand why Mugabe had sent troops to fight an expensive campaign (costing $5 million a week) in the Congo aimed at propping up unpopular President Kabila at a time when Zimbabwe at home was desperately short of cash. "Greed on the part of politicians is taken for granted," I wrote, but hardly welcomed.[43]

Morgan Tsvangerai, the head of the Zimbabwe Confederation of Trade Unions, watched the protests that roiled the streets of Harare in late 1998 and early 1999. I stood with him outside Meikle's hotel observing marching workers and suggested that it might be time for him to lead an all-out assault on the dictatorship that was immiserating Zimbabweans. The labor movement was the only institution that Mugabe did not in some material way control. Tsvangerai commanded the only mass of people who conceivably could oust Mugabe and—plausibly—could prevent police and military detachments from securing his throne. But Tsvangerai assured me then, as he did many times later, that the time was not ripe—that he and his followers were not yet strong enough to mount an all-out battle for Zimbabwe's future.

The moment for action might have come a little later when Zimbabwean troops in the Congo mutinied, and, at home, when sixty-three officers plotted a military coup against the Mugabe regime. The *Standard*, an innovative newspaper that the government did not own, revealed both occurrences. That immediately led army generals to grab Mark Chavanduka, editor of the paper, and Ray Choto, a journalist who had uncovered the coup, and to take them (without warrants) to a military interrogation center outside of Harare. Brutally tortured by military intelligence personnel assisted by CIO operatives, they were finally dumped back into Harare after several days of enduring electric shocks. They were then in very poor shape, as attested by two African medical specialists. The minister of defense said that they could not have been tortured; they must have "scratched" themselves.

Zimbabwe's High Court had ordered the writers to be released from military detention, but to no avail. After Chavanduka and Choto had finally been let go, and students and professionals had marched on parliament to protest the detaining and torturing of journalists, three judges of the Supreme Court (one white and two black) urged Mugabe to punish the soldiers and the CIO and to affirm the rule of law and condemn torture. (Chavanduka subsequently came to Harvard as a Nieman Fellow, where I saw him often. Choto gained a senior position at Voice of America in Washington; we talked about the descent of his country.)[44]

Mugabe's tirade against the judges, journalists who "think they can tell lies," and foreign "spies"—"British agents"—was to be expected. In a radio broadcast to the nation he also declared that if the journalists had not acted "dishonestly" they would not have been tortured. They had "forfeited the right to legal protection." And the judges had behaved impertinently—"an outrageous and deliberate act of impudence"; he invited them to resign. "The law is what I say it is," Mugabe declared.[45]

The First MDC Crusade

In the wake of these tragic events, and with his trade union movement officially prohibited from mounting demonstrations, Tsvangerai initiated a broad campaign to counter Mugabe's attempt to revise the national constitution. New provisions permitted Mugabe to take land from whites without compensation, and to amend the constitution in other ways that were intended to give Mugabe greater legal freedom to act arbitrarily. Zvobgo, as minister of justice, had prepared many of the amendments, including one that would have held future presidents to two, rather than unlimited terms in office. Zvobgo assured me that his intention was to curb presidential power, but reining in Mugabe was hardly possible in the best of circumstances.

Tsvangerai, by now the head of a new Movement for Democratic Change, and many others campaigned against the referendum in early 2000 that was expected to ratify the constitutional changes that Zvobgo had initiated and Mugabe wanted. But, to the consternation of the regime, voters turned them down. ZANU and Mugabe had never before lost any kind of electoral contest.

The Wages of Despotism

This rebuff to Mugabe and his men signaled the start of a concerted final battle that has still not ended between darkness and light in Zimbabwe, between adequate and bad governance, between integrity and deceit, and between those who were wholly and irredeemably corrupt and those who preferred to steal from the people only now and then.

For the next seventeen years, until ousted by generals and Mnangagwa, Mugabe and Grace steadily looted state coffers, gave license to subordinates to take what they could when they could, tossed the weak and struggling state onto the economic ash heap, ignored inflation levels that soared as high as 1 billion percent, and cared little that millions of their people starved.

Instead, Mugabe tried like despots always do to threaten his opponents and blame outsiders and troublemakers for ills that he himself had created. In 2000, he refused to "brook any court impediments to our land acquisition program. . . ." Courts "belong to the people . . . [and are] not allowed to go against our quest for full sovereignty." Despite what "racists" say, "We are right and we are just." The British government was an enemy, so ZANU-PF was obliged to "safeguard the nation and prevent its subjection once again to racist rule. . . ." He continued: "I am not preaching violence . . . but the fight that they want, we will give them twice as much."[46]

Zimbabwe has never recovered from its foreign exchange shortages and near bankruptcy during the Congo debacle. It also wasted massive amounts placating (mostly fake) veterans of the *chimurenga* or bush battle against Rhodesia with large pensions. But an even bigger and lasting drag on economic growth was Mugabe's angry riposte to the loss of the 2000 referendum. He proceeded over the next seven years mercilessly to uproot the remaining white farm owners who were growing food for the country's citizens and contributing mightily to export earnings. Steadily, several thousand farmers who had employed Africans and grown maize and tobacco were forced to flee without compensation when African rent-a-thugs invaded and harassed their homesteads, collapsing the employment of hundreds of thousands of innocent workers and tenant farmers.[47] Few of those who were invited onto the confiscated lands knew how to till the soil and nurture crops; many if not the majority of farms were given to (or taken by) politicians loyal to Mugabe, and permitted to decay. It was and is a tragedy of lasting consequence.[48]

Mugabe and ZANU-PF stole every election from 2000 to 2015, and won again in 2019 by questionable means.[49] As Zvobgo informed me confidently in 2000, ZANU-PF would never let itself lose an election. By arranging constituencies to benefit the ruling party, by massaging the voter's roll, by using the military to intimidate opposition voters, by controlling all media outlets, by stuffing ballot boxes, by orchestrating the counting of results, and by employing violence to deprive the MDC of clear victories, ZANU-PF blatantly captured the presidential and parliamentary elections of 2000, 2002, and 2005. Tsvangerai and the MDC hardly stood a fair chance.

Throughout these long years of deprivation, the citizens of Zimbabwe had less and less voice; political participation was effectively nil, coinciding with a cascading collapse of the country's economy that, through 2008 and into 2009, turned a thriving middle-income country into one that was desperately poor—a "basket case," to quote a pejorative appellation applied first to Bangladesh during the Cold War. Mugabe couldn't have cared less. I wrote that after knowing

Mugabe much earlier and seeing him off and on during the twentieth century, I finally realized by the early 2000s that absolute power indeed corrupted absolutely. "Tirelessly ruthless, unscrupulous, and canny, Mugabe remain[ed] of sound and scheming mind, full of seductive charm, and widely feared." I continued: "Like former Haitian dictator François (Papa Doc) Duvalier [whom I had interviewed at length and about whom I had written much of a book], he intimidates his close associates. . . ." He was indeed "venal," I said, his perpetrated destruction of Zimbabwe since 1998 testifying, I wrote, "to the lasting power of [his] curse."[50]

Despite all the adverse manipulations, ZANU-PF was so sufficiently discredited that Tsvangerai and the MDC actually won the 2008 parliamentary election outright. But the country's electoral commission, loyal to Mugabe, refused to honor the result. In consequence, after ensuing turmoil and concerted regime-fomented violence, the regional Southern African Development Community (SADC) intervened in 2009 to impose a unity government on the bitterly contested nation. The MDC and ZANU-PF were meant thereafter to share power meaningfully, but Mugabe—as usual—was devious and clever. Accepting Tsvangerai under the unity agreement as prime minister, he made sure during the four years that the unity arrangement persisted that there would be little unity (despite promises), even less partnership, and a continued denial of political and human rights. SADC protocols to the contrary, Mugabe continued throughout this period to hold tightly to the levers of power, running roughshod over the unity compact. As MDC Minister of Finance Tendai Biti said so colorfully in early 2010, "ZANU-PF . . . continue[s] to urinate on us."[51]

Mugabe put control of security in the hands of the powerful military Joint Operations Command and excluded the MDC. The top brass of the army and the air force remained loyal to Mugabe, having been permitted to continue to enjoy profits from procurement fraud and mining deals. From at least 1998, Mugabe had enmeshed securocrats (military and police elites) in a dense web of state-sponsored corruption. They had looted cobalt, cadmium, gold, and diamonds in the Congo and then helped Mugabe and Mnangagwa profit egregiously from the Marange alluvial diamond deposits of eastern Zimbabwe.[52]

For the parlous people of Zimbabwe, the only saving grace of the unity government was not—as might have been anticipated—a respite from the ruinous attacks on civilians by the police and military. Nor did farm invasions cease and commercial agricultural production resume. Further, the skimming of resources from profitable gold and platinum mining enterprises persisted.

But the decisions of Minister of Finance Biti, following up the abolition of Zimbabwe's own (worthless) dollar currency with the imposition of tight budgetary controls (except over the expenditures of Mugabe's own office!), proved immensely effective. With the U.S. dollar, the South African rand, and other national stable currencies circulating freely, previously empty shop shelves filled up with food and scarce imported gasoline and diesel fuel became available—at least to elites with hard foreign currency. The once-frozen economy warmed. It was only during the 2009 to 2013 era that most of Zimbabwe was governed for its inhabitants, and not exclusively for the ZANU-PF ruling class.

Biti paid long-suffering civil servants, teachers, and medical personnel much more than they had previously realized. With new money in their pockets to spend, the resulting multiplier effect boosted incomes generally. Zimbabwe revived significantly during the years of supposed unity, possibly by as much as 5 percent a year.

These positive developments were all to the good, and beneficial to the nation so long as Tsvangerai and Biti could keep Mugabe, the key cabinet ministers that he still controlled, and the reigning securocrats from perpetuating the massive fiscal profligacy and higher degrees of grand corruption that they had perfected in earlier decades. This turned out to be a Sisyphean battle. Additionally, because of the way in which some of the MDC appointees succumbed to Mugabe's seductive offers of patronage, and big ministerial automobiles, it was never clear that the MDC turned the potential of participating in the joint government to its own longer-term political advantage. Biti told me that he was able to exercise only limited oversight of State House, the military, and ZANU-PF financial maneuverings.

Many of Tsvangerai's supporters pleaded with him to be more assertive (as did I on five or six occasions) in opposing Mugabe within the joint government and in positioning the MDC part of the union as a full alternative administration. As for the possibility of going from unity to regime change through a purple or rose revolution, Tsvangerai firmly believed that Mugabe's security apparatus was too strong. Active mass protests fostered by the MDC, Tsvangerai asserted, would be met with overwhelming force, thousands of deaths, and seas of blood. He wanted none of it.

For those and similar cogent reasons, Tsvangerai and the MDC never created a dramatic alternative to ZANU-PF hegemony. They became comfortable in office and, when it came time to contest the 2013 elections, they still had little control over police and military detachments. Intimidation prevailed, as in previous electoral contests. I called the election "cleverly rigged." Burgis suggests that massive financial support from Central Asian criminal oligarchies, illicit mining operations in the Democratic Republic of Congo, and Chinese intelligence operatives eased Mugabe's buying of voters and ensuring military loyalty.[53] But Tsvangerai foolishly also agreed to take his people to the polls before the voting roll had been purged of the dead and the duplicates, and before constituency delimitations had been reformed. Outwitted by ZANU-PF machinations, he led the MDC to a striking loss.[54]

Beyond Unity

In this period, and earlier and later, South Africa under President Zuma aborted several golden chances to intervene and save Zimbabwe from itself. "Instead, they let him [Mugabe] run roughshod over his captive nation."[55] Because South Africa during President Mbeki's time in office until late 2007, afterward under Zuma, and again immediately after the 2017 coup in Harare, had imponderable leverage over Zimbabwe because of its economic might and its influence through SADC, it could have limited Mugabe and later Mnangagwa's political options, and corralled their despotic instincts. But Mbeki, particularly, was not anxious to curb a dictatorship. I pleaded with him and key members of his presidential entourage—to no effect. Mbeki told businessmen in Johannesburg in 2002, and me in the same and later years, that he had everything under control and would soon bring Mugabe's leadership to its senses. Mbeki said the same to President George W. Bush. "Thabo completely understood," reported the U.S. Assistant Secretary of State for Africa, "that Mugabe had to go, and his response and guarantee was 'leave it in my good hands and I will take care of this issue, and within six months we'll have a completely different political dynamic in Zimbabwe.'"[56] But nothing along those lines ever occurred. (See also chapter 7.) Nor did Zuma exhibit any desire to meddle with a regime as corrupt as his own. Furthermore, when I asked President Paul Kagame of Rwanda, no shrinking violet, to take on Mugabe through the African Union, he also demurred. It was not his concern. Nor did the leaders of the African Union ever do more than mutter darkly about Mugabe's "eccentricities," and ignore the oppression of his own people.

Twenty-first-century Zimbabwe was hardly the country that Mugabe inherited in 1980. An analysis by the well-respected Center for Global Development estimated in about 2005 that the purchasing power of the average Zimbabwean had receded to 1953 levels.[57] In 2015, the World Bank calculated the once-wealthy nation's per capita GDP at no more than $250, calling it the third poorest country across the planet. Life expectancy levels had also fallen from about sixty years in the twentieth century to a low of thirty-six years.[58]

Mugabe's policies and his neglect of the national interest had destroyed what had been a prosperous, if unequally distributed, national enterprise. Corruption had sapped the very innards of productivity, reduced incentives for investors, and fattened the lives mostly of the politically connected elite. Mugabe had presided over the full-scale decay of his country's once highly regarded educational and medical infrastructure. At several points during the 2000s and even into the 2010s, hospitals in the big cities lacked sutures, basic medicines, and—for months when they were on strike for decent pay—junior physicians. To obtain service in the supposedly free government hospitals, anyone seeking medical attention had to dig into her or his wallets—in advance. After all, the state paid nurses and physicians only pittances.

At several critical junctures in the twenty-first century, Zimbabwe's poverty was accentuated by periodic droughts that hardly made agricultural life easier, and twice or thrice for years at a time the World Food Program (WFP) indicated that it was feeding one-third or more of the nation's entire population. Again in the 2018–2021 period, only WFP supplies prevented millions of Zimbabweans from starving.

Another one-quarter or so of the population emigrated to South Africa, Botswana, Zambia, and Mozambique—to any place that would take fleeing émigrés. A common practice for visitors from Zimbabwe to Cape Town or Johannesburg was brightly to ask the most accomplished waiter in a local restaurant where in Zimbabwe he or she was from. Nearly always, the waiters had been teachers in Central Mashonaland, the heart of Zimbabwe, and had emigrated when the government no longer paid their salaries. Well-trained nurses and midwives flocked to London for the same reason.

Given Zimbabwe's economic meltdown, massive capital flight, the loss of liquidity in the nation's commercial and banking sectors, and pronounced deflation, Mugabe and his ministers flew to Beijing in 2014, hoping for a massive bailout—probably in the $4 billion range. No other donor or international institution would entertain such an entreaty. President Xi Jinping and his officials agreed to help restore Zimbabwe's crumbling infrastructure, especially its shambolic power and water systems. They also continued to invest in farming, having leased land and sent Chinese smallholders to till plots near Chinoye in Central Mashonaland. China purchased more of Zimbabwe's minerals as well, trade totals doubling to more than $1.1 billion yearly.[59] But even the injection of Chinese cash from purchases and investments could not prevent the country's continued deterioration. Mismanagement and corruption were too ingrained and decay too pervasive.

Grasping Grace

In the years after 2013, Mugabe, ninety, was suffering from prostate cancer and flying often to Singapore for treatment. Meanwhile, his nation's economic performance again suffered from neglect and perverse incentives. Grace Mugabe also became more and more influential within the party, taking advantage of her position close to the throne.

By 2017, she was publicly grooming herself as her aging husband's successor, gaining a self-vaulted prominence in public affairs, fulfilling the long-ago claim by ZANU-PF bigwigs that she truly was "Grasping Grace." Factions formed within ZANU-PF—those allied with Grace, assuming that she would be a winner—and those putting their money on Mnangagwa and his own ties to security chief General Constantino Chiwenga.

Mnangagwa, with whom I had conversed across the years at ZANU-PF events and embassy receptions, had in the years after 2013 mounted a systematic charm offensive directed at the diplomatic community, at businessmen, and foreign journalists. He attempted assiduously to improve his unsavory reputation with non-Zimbabweans, and with anyone who was willing to dismiss his reputation as a determined thug. (In his home Masvingo constituency, he kept losing elections for parliamentary seats.) After all, Mugabe was aging and more and more capricious in his actions. Indeed, Mnangagwa carefully begin to plot his own survival and succession, whenever "the old man" would falter and, as it developed, when Mugabe's younger wife showed politically acquisitive tendencies.

It was evident to close observers of Zimbabwe by late 2014 that Grace Mugabe, forty-nine, was angling for preeminence. She pushed aside the chairwoman of the ZANU-PF Women's League, publicly attacked the woman who was Zimbabwe's vice president and nominal heir apparent, and persuaded the University of Zimbabwe (over which her husband presided) to grant her a doctoral degree for a thesis that others wrote. She also started holding her own political rallies across the country, using the presidential helicopter. Buses were suddenly adorned with big posters of her, looking formidable.[60] Meanwhile, too, she ousted villagers from prime land near Mazowe in order to develop a vast dairy enterprise.

Fearful of what Grace Mugabe was doing, and conscious that Mugabe was becoming more frail and unsteady and repetitive in public, Mnangagwa and Chiwenga, probably with some Chinese backing, arranged a palace coup in late 2017 that removed the Mugabes from office and, effectively confining them to quarters, ended a thirty-seven-year reign of unrelieved malignity. But as lawyer and former Minister of Education David Coltart remarked, "We have removed a tyrant, but not yet a tyranny."[61] Ex-President Mugabe died at ninety-five in Singapore in 2019.

Mnangagwa promised to revive industry, to bring farming back to its old glory (and to compensate the whites who had been pushed off their lands), to promote industry, and to create an honest administration—but not a return to the rule of law—that would benefit all Zimbabweans. He made those same promises in 2018, when campaigning against a weakened MDC (Tsvangerai having died earlier in 2018) in the national elections that his reimagined ZANU-PF won easily, 145 to 65 parliamentary places. But, with the new ZANU-PF government trying some of the same discredited currency games that Mugabe's men had played so disastrously in the 2000s, inflation ratcheted up to 800 percent per annum in 2019 and 2020, imports became short, hunger again stalked the rural areas, and journalists, celebrated novelists, and politicians were jailed for speaking badly of ZANU-PF and of drawing attention to widespread corruption in the struggle to reduce deaths from the coronavirus.[62] In 2021, after the government began auctioning access to foreign exchange and letting the local currency depreciate, inflation levels fell to single numbers, and imported goods became more widely available.

The Crocodile's Jaws

Mnangagwa, known for decades as "the crocodile" because of his merciless depredations and his long years as Mugabe's enforcer and "bagman," was hardly an improvement on Mugabe as far as the life chances of ordinary Zimbabweans were concerned.[63] When the coronavirus came to Africa, his corrupt leadership hardly made anyone's life better. Indeed, the suffering of the long-pummeled Zimbabwean people exceeded those of most other Africans in so many ways that the afflictions of the coronavirus were just more fatal straws on the battered backs of the populace.

At the beginning of June 2022, with the Omicron variant having invaded Zimbabwe, the country's total number of cases since the beginning of the pandemic totaled 253,000, with an acknowledged 5,507 deaths.[64] Those were relatively modest numbers, even for an Africa that may not be able to report all cases and mortalities and for a country with faltering health services. More than 31 percent of the population was fully vaccinated, which was a much better total than for numerous other African countries.

Whereas Zimbabwe would have been considered relatively well governed in the early to mid-1980s, it rapidly lost such esteem as the failures of Mugabe and his government grew palpable in the 1990s. By the time of the first compilation of the Index of African Governance in 2000, Zimbabwe's ratings had already begun to slip. In that year, Zimbabwe ranked 21st of 48 states in sub-Saharan Africa, with the Seychelles, Mauritius, and Botswana in the top three spots, and the Democratic Republic of Congo, Angola, and Somalia in the bottom three. Zimbabwe's overall score in that year was 52.7 of 100, falling slightly in 2002, when it ranked 26th (again of 48). Three years later, Zimbabwe had receded to 31st place, just above equally despotic Equatorial Guinea, Guinea, Swaziland, and Togo. Its score was a solid 52.0, whereas top-ranked Mauritius scored 86.2 and bottom-ranked Chad, the Democratic Republic of Congo, and Somalia ranged in their scores from 38.0 to 28.0. By 2009, Zimbabwe had fallen backward to 45th place (of 53), with a diminished score of 47.3. The listings for that year placed it just above Angola, Eritrea, and the Central African Republic. Throughout the 2010s, Zimbabwe demonstrated little improvement and, in 2018, it ranked

39th of 54, with a raw score of 44.7. Two years later, the index mysteriously rated Zimbabwe as improved, in 33rd place with a score of 47.[65]

On the complementary and well-respected Corruption Perceptions Index (CPI) of Transparency International, in 2006 Zimbabwe ranked 130th of 160. In 2020, it had fallen to 157th place of 180, with a low score of 24 of 100. That score had not changed materially for a decade and it placed the country even with Honduras, just better than Nicaragua, and slightly above Madagascar. It was categorized throughout as "highly corrupt," somewhat countering Zimbabwe's relatively elevated result on the governance index.[66] Another 100 or so other relevant indexes of governance and corruption all place Zimbabwe toward the bottom of their scales, confirming what the CPI and the governance index show.

The CPI develops its scores and rankings from carefully curated perceptions of experts, many of them local. But it cannot indicate how regimes facilitate and pursue corrupt opportunities and exactly how political elites (kleptocrats for the most part) acquire their spoils and through what devious means. In the case of Zimbabwe, a locus of egregious and odious practices of grand corruption since at least 1985, such precise information has been almost impossible to obtain, except anecdotally. However, in very late 2020 an assiduous (and secretive) group of knowledgeable local researchers produced—first for private distribution and second for publication in South Africa—a remarkable document that lays out in excruciating detail how most (but not all) of the thieving from the public occurred, and who connived with whom. Its main and very telling contribution is to detail the various "cartels" (aka criminal gangs of politicians and entrepreneurs) who arranged and organized most of Zimbabwe's grand corruption under the knowing gaze of President Mnangagwa and Vice President Chiwenga, plus other securocrats and high-level politicians who are part and parcel of the criminalized political/security cartels that still steal from Zimbabwe in 2022.[67]

The sixty-four-page "Cartel Power Dynamics in Zimbabwe" report declares that Mnangagwa was at the center of an intricate web of syndicates that specialized in large-scale, venal theft from the public. It traced the mechanization of greed from at least the invasion of the Democratic Republic of Congo in 1998 onward, showing many of the persons and schemes that successfully purloined from the coffers of the state (and thus from citizens). According to the study, as much as $3 billion yearly was siphoned across Zimbabwe's borders illicitly. Another $1 billion was lost annually by intra-Zimbabwean fraud schemes. More than $1.5 billion worth of gold and diamonds was smuggled out of the country each year. Hoards of improperly acquired wealth consequently were banked overseas, in one or more supposedly secure locations.

That investigation offered many direct examples of grand corruption. One prosaic but illustrative one was the purchase by the Zimbabwe National Road

Authority of more than forty motorized graders from the most expensive rather than the least expensive bidder, costing the country millions of dollars that presumably found their way as kickbacks into well-connected hands. An intermediary purchased 162 buses for $59,000 each and sold them to a government-controlled entity for $212,000 each. In 2018, to cite one year, even Zimbabwe's auditor-general said that 82 percent of government expenditures were "irregular."[68]

Mnangagwa's presidency has hardly improved the country's probity, a result that reflects the malign confluence of Zimbabwe's contemporary despotism and the ultimate failure of the Mugabe dictatorship to achieve anything constructive and lasting for its sorely tried people. The Mugabe-Mnangagwa cabal may be credited over at least four decades with the massive worsening of life chances and life opportunities for nearly all of its people.

Inflation returned with a vengeance in 2022, as well, hitting 61 percent in early 2022 and escalating later to more than 131 percent in May after the government touted the returned Zimbabwe dollar as the authorized currency. "The Zimbabwe dollar is the worst-performing currency in the world."[69] (One US dollar purchased 400 Zim dollars in May.) The roads in Harare were massively potholed, with maintenance having been forsaken. Municipal water supplies were scarce. Wealthy Zimbabweans could play currency games in order to shop; poorer Zimbabweans reduced their food purchases. The nation's treasury printed $3.4 million worth of bills in May and gave them to a well-connected local oligarch so that he could acquire state-owned mines, presumably at the behest of ruling political elites.[70]

Only the politically well connected, and their crooked associates, have prospered in a land potentially of plenty. For young Zimbabweans, half of the population, jobs were still scarce; indeed, many job seekers found that they had to pay bribes to secure positions, and then to keep them.[71] Formal employment levels were as low as 10 percent; job seekers were forced to bribe, or offer sex, or to work informally at the sides of streets and beyond. "A fixer known as Banga works with a top manager at the fertiliser company. He has agents who look for clients in different places and collect bribes from the job seekers to pass on to the manager," reported *Aljazeera*. Its investigation also uncovered numerous women from whom sex was demanded before they could obtain jobs; some ended up HIV-positive.[72]

The end of this oppression and economic decline is not at hand, especially given the scourge of the continuing coronavirus and the weaknesses and lack of unity within the opposition MDC. Indeed, the MDC splintered in 2021 and, under Nelson Chamisa, the Citizens' Coalition for Change bloc took nineteen of twenty-eight seats contested in special by-elections early in 2022. Nine were won by ZANU-PF candidates. Whether the rise of a new popular party in the shadow of the old promises political change through the ballot box is uncertain. ZANU-PF remains in control of the national levers of power, and of the forces of repression, intimidation, and economic patronage.

By mid-2022, the parlous state of Zimbabwe was reminiscent of the impossible days of 2008; Zimbabweans had hoped never to revisit the rampant mismanagement, widespread fraud, economic collapse, spreading hunger, and forlorn hopelessness that had typified the bottomless slough of the Mugabe epoch. Zimbabwe also owed China $1.1 billion, with no way to pay. In the words of a trenchant analyst and former U.S. ambassador: "Conditions for the people of Zimbabwe continue to go from bad to worse. Triple digit inflation shows no signs of slowing. Over half of the country lives in poverty. Its corrupt government lurches from disinterest in the population's pain to rosy projections for growth based on pure fantasy to clumsy interventions like the recent short-lived edict banning banks from lending."[73]

President Mnangagwa's avaricious administration had merged the state with the security forces; was attempting to marginalize and dismantle civil society, Russian style, in order more fully to control dissension and criticism; and was extending its use of violence to reinforce its control of the desperate and volatile country. "There will be nothing remotely resembling a level playing field as the 2023 elections draw near."[74]

Zimbabwe's profoundly poor governance still needs to be overcome so that democracy will prevail and provide better returns for all of its abused peoples. But exactly how improved opportunities for growth and freedom would be realized remains the toughest of questions.

10

Namibia

Throwing Off the Long Yoke

Just as official white South Africans believed during the apartheid era that they could postpone or somehow manage the inevitability of majority rule in their own country, and in Rhodesia/Zimbabwe, so they defied the United Nations and held tightly after World War II to the nominal UN Trust Territory of South-West Africa despite its overwhelmingly indigenous population and the rise in and after the 1960s of a vigorous nationalist movement—the South-West African People's Organization (SWAPO).

For many decades, the apartheid regime treated that distant desert territory, the size of two Californias but with a total population just over 1 million in 1970 (and only 60,000 whites), as a spurious fifth province of South Africa, with representation in the South African parliament and juridical coverage to match.

South Africa tried to ignore the reality that its rule in South-West Africa was fundamentally transient, and a profoundly illicit occupation after the demise of the League of Nations. South Africa regularly brushed aside such legal niceties and UN resolutions and preferred even well after the Soweto Uprising at home to tighten its grip on the former German colony. Naturally, apartheid-consumed South Africa supported the white farmers and merchants who lived in South-West Africa, some descended from the Germans who had conquered and settled the colony, but most of Afrikaner heritage.

Strategically, South Africa in the 1960s, 1970s, and 1980s regarded South-West Africa as a buffer against African and supposedly communist invaders (especially after Cubans helped the Movimento Popular de Libertação de Angola (MPLA) sustain power in Angola after 1975 and battle Jonas Savimbi's União Nacional para a Independência Total de Angola (UNITA), covertly funded by South Africa. South-West Africa contained mineral riches (copper, zinc, lead, diamonds, and uranium). It bolstered and buttressed Afrikaner domination in the region. Furthermore, allowing a liberation movement aligned with its own African National Congress (ANC) to gain power in South Africa's backyard, and in a territory long ruled by South Africa, would obviously embolden the ANC and harm morale among whites in South Africa itself. Lastly, but increasingly relevant later in the pre-independence era, South-West Africa was a massive

Overcoming the Oppressors. Robert I. Rotberg, Oxford University Press. © Oxford University Press 2023.
DOI: 10.1093/oso/9780197674208.003.0010

Map 10.1. Botswana and Namibia

bargaining chip to be deployed to protect apartheid and its perpetrators from the putative "total onslaught." (See chapter 7.)

South Africa's military planners naturally believed that their best defensive redoubts should be situated as far to the north as possible of their own physical borders. That would keep distant the "total onslaught" organized by the Soviet Union and Red China and advanced by their insurgent proxies such as SWAPO, the ANC, and ZANU and ZAPU, and also by the MPLA and Mozambique's Frelimo. (See chapter 7.) Additionally, South Africa's air force, and secret operatives, preemptively attacked insurgent SWAPO and ANC training camps in Zambia, and later in Angola and Mozambique. They further raided Botswana to intimidate its people and their rulers, and to make the costs of harboring anti-apartheid "rebels" punitive. The apartheid regime pursued individual dissidents in Europe and the Americas. After Portugal receded from its African colonies, South Africa sponsored indigenous movements (UNITA and Renamo) hostile to the Soviet-supported parties who came to power in 1975 in Angola and Mozambique.

Keeping full control of South-West Africa to safeguard white rule in South Africa was fundamental to South African official thinking, especially during the premierships of Balthazar Johannes Vorster and Pieter W. Botha (1966–1978 and 1978–1989). They and their principal security operatives hence motivated a concerted, brutal and brutalizing, rearguard, anti-insurgency battle against SWAPO in what was to become Namibia, and farther north, and a clandestine and often deadly combat against supposed SWAPO sympathizers inside South-West Africa itself. Telephones were tapped, letters opened, listening bugs were placed in private spaces, and those who were thought to oppose South Africa's plans for South-West Africa were watched closely, often intimidated, and sometimes eliminated.

Just as Ian Smith in Rhodesia (backed for a time by South Africa) had enlisted Bishop Muzorewa as a friendly African front man to forestall a real transfer of power (see chapter 9), so in South-West Africa the sovereign overlord attempted for much of what became a pre-independence struggle period of twenty-five years to foist a locally white-run (but South African backed) faux multiracial alternative on the inhabitants of South-West Africa, the powers of the world, and the UN.

For decades, sometimes despite promises and carefully drafted agreements, South Africa refused to give up—to acknowledge that it had even less standing in South-West Africa than the usual colonial overlords who had conquered and administered much of Africa since the late nineteenth century, and no conceivable right to rule its residents. Even less did South Africa have any right in international law to have effectively annexed the sometime mandatory territory to South Africa or to have governed it as if it were integral to the dominion of South Africa.

South Africa Seizes Control

During much of the nineteenth century, what was to become central Namibia was fought over by Nama (a mixed pastoral group of different backgrounds and strong connections to Namaqualand in the northwestern reaches of the Cape Province of South Africa) and by Herero, competing for control over good grazing lands in a region that was ecologically fragile, agriculturally compromised, and 90 percent desert or near-desert. The cattle-herding Herero had earlier taken land from the Damara, largely subjugating them. Farther north, the Ovambo peoples (with seven sub-groups) crossed the border with modern Angola and occupied the arable and comparatively well-watered grasslands of a triangle-shaped salient in northern Namibia's only zone remotely suitable for crop growing.

The interest of whites in Namibia—long after visits by Portuguese explorers—was first focused on deep beds of guano along its coastal islands and the slaughter of whales and seals along the shores of the Atlantic Ocean. Then, by mid-century, missionaries from Britain, Finland, and Germany arrived. The Finnish Mission Society proselytized among the dominant Ndonga branch of the Ovambo, followed by German Roman Catholic orders and English Anglicans, working among other Ovambo clusters. The German-speaking Rhenish Missionary Society began to preach the Gospel to the Herero and the Nama.

German merchants followed their fellow missionaries. By late 1885, the German government (with British acquiescence) had extended its "protection" to all of what is now Namibia, minus the pedicle that extends to the Zambezi River. That geographical anomaly was recognized as an integral part of South-West Africa by the terms of the omnibus Anglo-German agreement of 1990.[1]

German soldiers constructed a fort in what became Windhoek, long the Namibian capital, only in that year, and did little to disturb the pursuits of local inhabitants until 1893, when the Germans felt themselves strong enough to massacre Nama residents of Kaptein Hendrik Witbooi's Hornkranz settlement near Rehoboth and to begin to compete with the Herero, one branch of which was conquered in 1896. Throughout this decade, the German colonizers dispossessed Nama, Herero, and other local competitors of their agricultural and pastoral lands, and attempted to open the conquered territory to German immigrants. The German administration of its newest colony constructed railways inland from Atlantic coastal ports in the southern and central highlands; a trickle of immigrants followed.

Starting in 1903, but bitterly and viciously between 1904 and 1906, German troops put down a concerted Herero rebellion fueled by harsh labor demands and extensive confiscations of valuable pastoral lands. This forcible repression led to the annihilation of the Herero and Nama peoples. After issuing an "extermination order," Germans killed about 65,000 of 80,000 Herero and 10,000 of 20,000 Nama herders and agriculturalists, pursuing fleeing Africans into the Kalahari Desert. Germans raped women, poisoned wells, burned crops, and established concentration camps. These outrages constituted one of the modern world's earliest genocides, with many deaths occurring in the camps or from starvation and disease. (In 2021, Germany admitted responsibility for the genocide, apologized, and agreed to pay Namibia $1.4 billion in compensation over ten years.)[2]

The extirpation of so many Herero and Nama dramatically altered the population balance between southern and northern Namibia, leaving the Ovambo largely outside of heavy German control until after 1911. The Herero and

Nama, however, were regimented and segregated, compelled to carry identity documents or passes, and forced to labor under harsh conditions for their new overlords.

The predatory and the fledgling developmental aspects of German colonial rule ended abruptly with the onset of war in Europe and the Allied decision to oust Germans from all of their African colonies. After the massacres, sparsely populated Namibia then included about 80,000 indigenous inhabitants and 15,000 Germans, many of whom were repatriated and others interned when, at the behest of Britain, South African forces invaded in 1915 and imposed their own government and rules of law.

Although the new occupiers wished simply to incorporate the ex-German colony into the Union of South Africa, U.S. President Woodrow Wilson and British Prime Minister David Lloyd-George absolutely refused to approve such an annexation because of the Union's harshly offensive policies of segregation and its color bar. Instead, after hard bargaining at the Versailles Peace Conference, the newly established League of Nations granted South Africa the right to administer Namibia as a Class-C mandate. What that meant on paper was that South Africa was responsible to the League for running Namibia as "a sacred trust of civilization" so as to uplift those who were "not yet able to stand by themselves...."[3]

In practice, however, South Africa relentlessly ignored its mandatory responsibilities and promises and ran South-West Africa as if it had been annexed. (Walvis Bay and twelve small offshore islands had already become an official part of the Union in 1910.) The new colonial officials placed the interests of whites, and incoming white settlers, above those of the indigenous inhabitants, promoted white integration, promulgated or carried over from the Union segregationist legislation such as the Native Administration proclamation and Master's and Servants laws, and compelled Africans to continue to carry passes. The South Africans deputed to organize their new "province" refused to return to the Herero and Nama the lands taken from them by the Germans, and consigned both peoples to arid reserves. The Nama and Herero soon rebelled once more, and were again defeated, this time with the aid of punitive aerial bombardments. One of the Herero indigenous stalwarts was tried for treason, which meant that South Africa had successfully to persuade its own Supreme Court that South African sovereignty extended into South-West Africa.[4]

That it did, and that the power of the Permanent Mandates Commission of the League of Nations was limited, meant that South Africa henceforth ruled its new "province" almost without hindrance as a segregated addition to the Union itself. The Commission and a special 1936 investigation by a South African body declared, however, that South Africa was hardly fulfilling its "sacred trust" obligations and signally failing to advance the welfare of the majority of Namibians.[5]

South Africa too easily managed to confiscate the limited good grazing lands that remained in African hands and transfer them to whites. It effectively erected social and economic barriers to blacks, marginalized almost all indigenous women's pursuits and traditional livelihoods, and compelled Africans to work for whites and to migrate to South Africa itself to labor on its gold mines—massively disrupting customary pursuits and economic endeavors.[6] Educational opportunity and medical care for Africans were neglected, just as they were within the Union proper.

From 1925, when whites (then numbering about 27,000) gained autonomy for their own affairs, the "province" was run by a legislative assembly of eighteen white members, with a South African administrator able to veto actions of the local parliament.

This anomalous mandate-ignoring posture, with the outright subjugation of the very peoples whom the mandate was intended to uplift, prevailed until the end of World War II. During those decades of world depression and coming hostilities, Namibia largely persisted outside of the global trading system and world order. Cattle and sheep raising was a primary industry, as was fishing in the Atlantic Ocean, diamond mining in the south of the country, and some copper extraction in the north.[7] Only the relatively numerous Ovambo were for the most part spared by their remoteness from Windhoek and the comparative fecundity of their agricultural activity from the exactions of South African oversight and insistent settler demands for farm labor.

The United Nations and a New World Order

South Africa refused to recognize the authority of the United Nations. Under Chapter XII of the charter of the United Nations, mandates under the League of Nations became Trust Territories to be run under authority delegated by the Trusteeship Council of the new global body. South Africa said it would not abide by that shift in oversight, claiming that its mandate disappeared when the League was dissolved in 1946. South Africa wanted to fold Namibia bodily into its own corpus but (and fortunately), given the implacable opposition of the United Nations and its major founding fathers, South Africa essentially decided to delay annexing Namibia or making any overtly formal changes (or reversions).

Nevertheless, when the National Party achieved victory in the 1948 parliamentary polls in South Africa, the new apartheid-driven conservatives buttressed their majority by allocating six seats in the Union's House of Assembly to representatives from South- West Africa. In the same year, the Assembly transferred many of the rights vested in the governor-general of South Africa to itself; South Africa's parliament hence controlled what happened "legally" and otherwise in South-West Africa. In 1949, the South West Africa Affairs Amendment Act gave the new "province" two seats in South Africa's Senate, thus buttressing the National Party's Senate majority. In 1954—despite United Nations' objections—South Africa took any authority over "native affairs" in South-West Africa away from the "province" and transferred it to South Africa's new ministry of Bantu Administration and Development. Then, in 1969, parliament's South-West Africa Affairs Act abolished South-West Africa's legislative assembly and gave all power over the future Namibia to South Africa's own elected officials in Pretoria.

This was the high-water mark of South African domestic imperialism. Its near abroad was entirely within the National Party's apartheid-motivated jurisdiction—whatever the bureaucrats and busybodies of the UN wanted to say. For the next ten years, the fundamental nature of South African control over Namibia remained largely on its apartheid-extended course. All major decisions affecting the territory were made in Pretoria, not in Windhoek, and none of the important decision-makers was South-West African. Even the important posts in the South-West African civil service were filled from South Africa, not locally, with Africans naturally consigned to the lowest levels of this bureaucratic apparatus.

Rural Namibia was officially divided, as it was in South Africa, into so-called homelands or Bantustans. Ovamboland began officially in 1968, with its seven ethnic divisions, becoming "self-governing" in 1973, with SWAPO and others boycotting the first local elections. Next-door Kavangoland became "self-governing" in 1973, and East Caprivi in 1975. The Damara had a Representative Authority, ignored by most Damara, from 1977. So did the Nama, the Basters, and the Coloureds enjoy some forms of "home rule." The Herero, however, adamantly refused to accept a homeland; its leaders were among the petitioners at the United Nations who repeatedly beseeched the UN to exercise its authority within Namibia.[8]

Until 1977, even the black-filled towns of the "province" were run by municipal councils or village management boards controlled by whites—all reporting to the South African minister of local government. Two copper- and diamond-mining towns were administered by their commercial corporations. In terms of the prevailing law, serious crimes were tried by magistrates appointed by South Africa, with Roman-Dutch law prevailing. But the country's African chiefs and African councils also ran a parallel legal system along customary lines, with appeals heard in a special court of appeal "advised by" a South African "Bantu commissioner."

Schooling was limited. In the 1970s, there were ten secondary schools and nearly 300 full primary schools. In 1977, however, only ninety-seven indigenous Namibians successfully passed the examinations that concluded their high school educations. In the next year, the future Namibia could count only twenty-eight black university graduates, one with a DPhil degree from the University of Oxford. In 1978, 107 of the "province's" 112 physicians were white, four were of mixed race (Baster), and one was an African. Three lawyers were African.

Throughout the years when this administrative integration of South-West Africa and South Africa was being pursued persistently by the apartheid state, the UN was hardly passive in its response, despite having nothing more formidable than moral authority to enforce its preferences. In the 1950s, an ad hoc committee of the General Assembly failed to broker a settlement with South Africa as the latter refused repeatedly to recognize two special committees charged with trusteeship oversight of the former South-West Africa mandate. South Africa asked for a partition of the country, but the UN refused.

The General Assembly referred the stalemate to the International Court of Justice. It ruled in 1950 that since the mandate had lapsed, so had South Africa's rule in South-West Africa. In two later cases the Court also ruled against South Africa. But in 1966, the Court produced a muddy decision that, in effect, enabled South Africa to continue prevaricating in its attitudes toward the UN and world order.[9]

This failure to alter South Africa's trajectory within Namibia led inexorably to SWAPO's turn to guerrilla warfare and, within the UN system, to a series of initiatives to regain control of the ex-mandate's destiny. In 1968, the Security Council told South Africa to withdraw from Namibia (which the UN had renamed) immediately. In 1969, it recognized the legitimacy of the struggle of Namibians against South Africa, and did so again in 1971.

South Africa reacted to the increasingly assertive role of the UN General Assembly, and to the office of the UN Secretary-General, at first by denying the UN any role in its domestic imperial affairs and then by trying to create a mini-assembly of homeland leaders to which South Africa pretended to transfer some internal authority. But these defensive maneuverings were soon overtaken by the final crumbling of Portugal's colonial empire. It collapsed in 1975, Angola was soon an independent, and a Soviet-friendly nation soon threatened Namibia's long northern flank. Tempting fate, South African forces even invaded Angola in 1975, presumably with the objective of crippling the MPLA, installing UNITA in its stead, and blocking any movement of Cuban mercenary soldiers toward Namibia. But the South Africans, fearful of losing whatever support from the Western powers that they thought they had, turned back at the gates of Luanda, having ultimately accomplished little of consequence for themselves or their proxies. Nor had they forestalled SWAPO, which was soon to set up elaborate training camps in a now newly secured Angola.

After the incursion into Angola, South-West Africa became even more exposed than ever before. South Africa had demonstrated its might, but to no lasting result. It had also lost credibility in world affairs. Thereafter, South Africa was compelled to abandon its redoubt approach in favor of what its strategists imagined could be a clever method of diverting and subverting the attention of the hostile world. After all, South-West Africa in the 1970s, more than ever, constituted an essential and possibly not so formidable buffer between the imperiled homeland and its global foes. Moreover, the Security Council demanded repeatedly that South Africa exit South-West Africa. In late 1978, it adopted declarative Resolution 435, which was to govern UN-Namibian relations thereafter. Resolution 435, with the Soviet Union abstaining and China absent in the UN Security Council, said that all parties should stand down, agree to a ceasefire, and permit the UN to organize free and fair elections to establish which group or groups were to rule Namibia.

The Turnhalle Initiative

South Africa's first response to the Security Council was to send more of its military into Namibia. By 1977, as many as 47,000 South African soldiers were based there. Large sections of the "province's" north were placed under emergency regulations; soon about half of Namibia's entire African population was subjected to oppressive restrictions enforced by the South African military from camps throughout Ovamboland. Nearly 20,000 Africans were forced to remove themselves from homes along the Angolan border. Soon South African security forces made wholesale arrests of presumed SWAPO collaborators across Ovamboland.

Its second answer to the Security Council, and to critics of South Africa everywhere, was an attempt to establish an internal settlement that could be foisted on world opinion as a multiracial solution to the Namibian issue. South Africa summoned a constitutional conclave in 1975 and 1976 that met in Windhoek and was called the Turnhalle Conference after the converted German assembly hall in which it met periodically, for weeks at a time. Whites from the Legislative Assembly and blacks from the various puppet homeland authorities came together, but without representatives from SWAPO or several other indigenous political parties.

The overall leader of this South African sponsored artificial effort was Dirk Mudge, a consummate white politician, farmer, and businessman of local repute. Clements Kapuuo, paramount chief of the Herero; pastor Cornelius Ndjoba, an Ovambo; and Ben Africa, a pro–South African Baster physician, joined him. Mudge was more supple and inventive than his fellow whites, and often had to drag them, and South African political and security overseers, to agree to give the black and brown delegates to the Turnhalle Conference meaningful social and representational concessions. Most of the whites, drawn from the ranks of the Assembly, preferred a government that would appear to represent the ethnic groups of Namibia but which would be run (as Smith was arranging in Rhodesia) only by whites, with strong, unbreakable, long-term ties to South Africa. Everyone else at the conference sought a broadly representative multiracial dispensation. Mudge kept urging the delegates to merge white and black interests for the good of Namibia. Even so, despite his modernizing views, Mudge throughout acted as an agent for South Africa, and aimed to perpetuate its ultimate control.

The Turnhalle Initiative produced a draft constitution for the territory that called for three tiers of government. Each ethnic group would create and run their local authorities. Combinations of ethnic groups would also govern new regions. The national governing body would be selected from and by the regions. It would exercise responsibility for foreign affairs, defense, and finance. Education, health matters, and other functions closer to individual communities would be organized at the regional level.

These arrangements may have seemed tidy to those who approved them and to those outsiders who were intended to be impressed. But there were obvious fundamental flaws. The regions were based on the ten former homelands, many of which were sparsely populated. Most of all, much of the country would remain in white hands; the eleventh region was deemed to be the white "homeland," and it comprised all of the cities and farming areas occupied by whites. Eighty-two thousand whites would dominate the Turnhalle version of Namibia. Additionally, the seven Ovambo-speaking groups in the north would be vastly under-represented in the proposed new Turnhalle legislature and in the executive council, with its representatives equal in number to those from the smaller and larger ethnic groups (with a mere extra seat for the Ovambo). Mudge would become executive president of the whole, with extensive powers. But South Africa would retain final control over foreign policy, defense, transport, finance, and internal security. Furthermore, Namibia would effectively remain segregated. The color bar remained, de facto.[10]

These plans, designed to extend white control over the kinds of functions that most affected whites and buttress the continued policies of segregation, fooled few outside observers and pleased hardly any Namibians. It was evident that since voting for the central government would be based on ethnic group parity, whites (about 11.6 percent of the total population in 1977) would have much more say than they could be expected to have under anything that approximated a "one man, one vote" result. South Africa and Mudge in fact had devised a scheme to limit the role of the numerically dominant Ovambo and other northern peoples and to supplement white hegemonic influence by essentially incorporating the numerically challenged southern groups into their bloc.

The delegates, perhaps believing or led to believe that the contemplated new arrangements would actually satisfy their constituents and succeed in forestalling SWAPO, further planned to declare Namibia independent at the end of 1978. (UN Security Council Resolution 435 was the world body's response.)

How they, Mudge, or South Africa (which carefully orchestrated the Turnhalle Initiative) imagined that this complicated ploy would sustain white rule in Namibia is not evident. Since President Carter had replaced President Ford, there was a new American focus on human rights, globally. The Turnhalle outcome was therefore defective; it would not automatically attract international approval. Quite the reverse, in fact. Not by any stretch of the imagination, I thought and wrote at the time, could the Turnhalle outcome do anything but provoke SWAPO guerrillas from bases in Angola and Zambia to redouble their cross-border incursions. Backed by Cuban military contingents and Soviet training and funding, SWAPO would likely ramp up its attempt to attack South African and white installations within Namibia. This was exactly what SWAPO intended, said Sam Nujoma, SWAPO'S leader, when I interviewed him at some length in Lusaka, and began a conversational relationship of many decades. (From that first meeting and throughout all of our subsequent interactions, it was clear to me—and many others—that Nujoma would brook little internal opposition and would deal intolerantly and roughly with those who questioned his tough-minded dominance of the liberation effort.) SWAPO's intentions and credibility could not be ignored even if South Africa were militarily far superior and ferociously determined.

Nor, after I visited Namibia itself during the Turnhalle deliberations, could Mudge or others persuade me differently. Mudge projected confidence in his vision for a white-run but friendly black-engaged Namibia, all under a sheltering South African umbrella. My evident skepticism only redoubled his efforts to persuade me of the wisdom of his artfully constructed and cannily developed method of keeping Namibia out of Nujoma's and SWAPO'S nationalist hands.

When conversing in Windhoek, Swakopmund, and Tsumeb in those protean days, and especially when I met at lunch in Die Südwester Stube (down a side alley in central Windhoek) with men who were German, English, Irish, Afrikaner, Herero, Damara, and sometimes Ovambo by birth and dedicated Namibians by conviction, they all felt that the Turnhalle Initiative was a mere diversion, hardly worth the time and immense labor that had been devoted to its creation and articulation. Lawyers, advocates, judges, future ministers of finance and attorneys general, German-speaking farmers, Herero and Afrikaner businessmen, and leaders of the several African and mixed-race communities came to these informal friendly lunch discussions, all talking together in their own mutually understood languages (and largely mostly foreign to me). But that was at least one snapshot of Namibia at which I always marveled: mutual intelligibility and conviviality despite their disparate home languages and their varied ethnic heritages. Namibia, as I discovered often, was an unusual African country, much more cosmopolitan (and much more truly religious) than most. It was indeed a "rainbow" nation in embryo.

Traveling by car across the vast, open country on multiple occasions, initially together with my wife, reinforced the observation that a productive future was likely once Namibia could rid itself of South African interference. My visits to Ovambo villages; the old-fashioned copper mines of Tsumeb and Rossing's giant open-pit uranium oxide excavation operation near Swakopmund; days spent at the De Beers diamond-pumping installations along the southern coast; marvelous sunrises observed while climbing the towering, sun-dappled sand dunes at Sossusvlei and their counterparts outside of Walvis Bay; the long drive across the Namib desert to see the so-called White Lady (actually of a San man) rock paintings at Daures/Brandberg (and others); inspection of the Portuguese-erected pillars along the long Atlantic Ocean coast; speech-making in Swakopmund and Windhoek; and days spent in Katutura and the other the high-density suburbs ringing Windhoek; forays onto sheep and cattle (and ostrich) farms; a detailed examination of Windhoek's unique industrial water-recycling plant (which turned out potable supplies); and touristic expeditions to the country's vast fauna-filled Etosha and Waterberg National Parks made it evident to me that Namibians left to their own devices could overcome what had been an oppressive colonial past, and prosper. Years later, I also managed to introduce family members to the myriad fauna and avifauna wonders of Zambezi (once the eastern Caprivi), especially along the once-contested riparian zone of the Chobe River.

The Rise of SWAPO

After the early twentieth-century massacres of Herero and Nama, the Ovambo always dominated what was to become Namibia because of their vast numerical superiority (nearly 50 percent of twentieth-century totals), and possibly because of the intensive manner in which various mission groups taught and preached among them. Indeed, by the late 1950s there were a number of Ovambo living and working the Cape Town area. Foremost among them was Herman Toivo ya Toivo, an Ndonga born about 1924 and educated by Finnish Lutherans. He had served in South Africa's Native Military Corps during World War II, becoming a teacher after the war and subsequently finding work as a railway policeman, a clerk on a manganese mine, and a gold miner. In Woodstock, inside Cape Town, he found employment in a furniture factory.

Another was Andreas Shipanga, also from the Ndonga grouping of Ovambo and another migrant trained by the Finnish Lutherans. He taught primary school in Ondongwa in Ovamboland, traveled north to Lobito in Angola in 1954, found employment on the Copperbelts of the Congo and Zambia, and clerked in Zimbabwe. Continuing his peregrinations, he worked on an underground gold mine near Johannesburg and found his way to Cape Town, where he was employed as a clerk for an insurance company.

In 1958, together with Toivo and Solomon Mifima, of the Kwanyama branch of Ovambo, Shipanga founded the Ovambo People's Organization (OPO) to battle against South African–sponsored contract labor practices that were sapping Ovambo family life and drawing legions of men (without their families) to harsh workplaces in Namibia and to the mines of South Africa. Toivo additionally recorded a petition decrying South African sovereignty in Namibia and forwarded it to the UN. That resulted in his peremptory deportation back to Windhoek, where he mobilized support for the new political organization. The South African administration in the territory promptly transported him again, this time back home to his Ndonga village and confined him there, under house arrest, until 1961. Five years later, tried for subversion under South African security law, he was sentenced to twenty years to be served (along with Mandela and Sisulu, among many others) on Robben Island. Additional Namibians joined Toivo on Robben Island, and innumerable others were to follow.

Toivo thus became the most notorious, and acclaimed, of Namibia's first political prisoners. (Much later, after his release from Robben Island in 1984, we spent time together in New York and in Windhoek; open and cheerful, always with a gracious sparkle in his eyes, he told me that warders on Robben Island smuggled newspapers and writings into the prison; he therefore knew appreciatively of many of us who were writing during those dark years about Namibia and its repression.)

The Ovambo-initiated opposition to South African rule, and Toivo's recorded petition, had been preceded by other petitions for redress to the League of Nations and then to the Trusteeship Council of the UN by Herero Paramount Chief Hosea Kutako, Nama chief S. Hendrik Witbooi, and crusading Anglican missionary Michael Scott. In 1955, Jariretundu Kozonguizi, a Herero student at Fort Hare University College in South Africa, where the ANC was active, established the South-West African Progressive Association.

When Kozonguizi returned home to Namibia and Toivo had been detained, he and other Herero, including Chief Clemens Kapuuo, formed the South-West African National Union (SWANU), the protean nation's first truly national political body. Soon, it grew out of its Herero base to include key figures of

Damara and Nama heritage and, notably, Ovambo such as Sam Nujoma, of the Ongandjera Ovambo subgroup. Also trained by Finnish missionaries, Nujoma was then working in and near Windhoek on the South African Railways as a clerk. Afterward, he clerked for the Windhoek municipality and in a wholesale store.

SWANU organized mass protests in 1959 against the removal of residents (paralleling what South Africa had done in such a draconian manner in Sophiatown and District Six) from the Old Windhoek Location and their relocation into the new town of Katutura on the outskirts of the capital. Nujoma, who was also a member of OPO, came to prominence during the ensuing demonstrations, which led to a boycott of public buses, movie theaters, and beer halls. Buildings were burned and at least eleven Namibians were killed by police reprisals. A year later, Nujoma was in New York at the UN, presenting a petition against South African oppression in Namibia. When he realized that SWANU and Kozonguizi, who had fled Namibia after the Katurura riots and had been campaigning across Europe against South African control, were becoming effective Herero rivals of anti–South African activity by Ovambo, Nujoma became determined to transform OPO into SWAPO. Nujoma and others worried, too, that by attracting support from China, Kozonguizi and SWANU were undermining efforts to encourage UN intervention against South Africa.

Nujoma became SWAPO's unquestioned leader in 1962. The Soviet Union backed SWAPO and Nujoma from about this time—to rival China's fostering of SWANU—and that sponsorship remained essential to SWAPO until Namibia was liberated.

Namibian recruits made their way to the Soviet Union for training. The initial SWAPO attacks on South-West Africa began in 1966. From 1966 to 1979, first with Algerian and Soviet, and later with Cuban, assistance, SWAPO tried to infiltrate small detachments of guerrillas into the Caprivi Strip (Zambezi Province) from adjacent Zambia and across the border with Angola. But real success was fleeting, especially because of the strength of South African defenses but also because SWAPO's numbers were always more limited than its ambitions. In 1978, SWAPO could mobilize no more than 5,000 trained personnel; South Africa in those days had up to 50,000 troops in the "province." South Africa also possessed formidable surveillance capabilities.

By 1978, too, Nujoma had gained unquestioned control of SWAPO and its central committee. The fact that Soviet financial and military backing was funneled through him naturally strengthened his hand. Periodic grumbling by new, youthful recruits in Zambian or (later) Angolan training camps, and complaints about corruption and resource pilfering, were brutally repressed. SWAPO's detainee camps became notorious. When Shipanga, then third in command within SWAPO, led one of these protests against Nujoma's leadership in 1976, he was arrested along with nine other SWAPO dissidents and nearly 1,000 putative soldiers, extradited illegally to Tanzania, and held in close confinement in Dodoma Central Prison for a year.

By 1978, when the Turnhalle Initiative had threatened to declare Namibia independent under its contrived auspices, the UN and the Organization of African Unity, predecessor to the African Union, recognized only SWAPO as Namibia's authentic movement of liberation. Inside the country, too, Daniel Tjongarero, a Herero, Peter Katjavivi, an Oxford-trained Herero, and Misheck Muyongo, a Caprivian, pursued SWAPO'S goals, acknowledging Nujoma's command of their independence movement.

Meanwhile, in Windhoek especially, the Turnhalle delegates led by Mudge had become the Democratic Turnhalle Alliance (DTA). Moderate, and opposed to both the DTA and SWAPO but willing to work with SWAPO, was the Namibia National Front (NNF), an amalgam of what remained of SWANU (which had renounced Marxism); the white-led, liberal, and anti-DTA Federal Party; and the Damara Council. (Kapuuo was assassinated mysteriously in Katutura in 1978.)[11] Shipanga had made his way back to Namibia and formed the SWAPO-Democrats (SWAPO-D), a new political grouping that was allied loosely to the NNF, antagonistic to both South Africa and SWAPO, and mostly opposed to Nujoma's tight-fisted (and allegedly corrupt) rule. Despite his Ovambo (and Ndonga) ethnic credentials and his role in creating OPO, Shipanga was hardly popular either in Namibia or within SWAPO during the late 1970s.

On the eve of elections called to ratify the Turnhalle procedures in 1978 and solidify continued South African hegemony within the "province," Shipanga became the object of well-meaning international attention because of his Ovambo credentials, his opposition to Nujoma, and as a result of his position as someone who had broken with Soviet support. Although I was assured by my contacts in Windhoek, and by militants such as Tjongarero and Katjavivi, that Shipanga had no substantial local following, there were many prominent outsiders who considered lending financial and other backing to Shipanga's cause. South Africa's foreign ministry and its security forces thus sought to promote and use Shipanga. I told Foreign Minister Botha and several of his key associates that they were wasting their time—to no avail. But in more benign quarters influential persons were equally beguiled. I had to explain to the heads of De Beers and the Anglo-American Corporation, with their significant diamond properties in Namibia, that backing Shipanga would accomplish nothing. Likewise, when a wealthy American magnate with mining interests across Africa asked me to join him, his corporate associates, and Shipanga on a gentle cruise around Manhattan Island, I had to explain privately to the mogul that Shipanga—a plausible and upstanding nationalist—simply had no way of marshaling forces in Namibia capable of competing with the appeal of a formidable and popular liberationist movement such as SWAPO. Shipanga was far more suave and easy to relate to than Nujoma, but he was but a convenient straw dropped into the Namibian political whirlpool to divert its waters away from Soviet-supported nationalists. Financing his cause would be wasteful.

The Contact Group

South Africa had long attempted to keep Namibia to itself, and out of the global public eye. But the victory of President Carter in 1976, and his appointment of Ambassadors Andrew Young and Donald McHenry to key American representational positions at the UN, quickly elevated the Namibian issue to a higher diplomatic level than ever before. Together, they demanded an absolute end to South Africa's attempt to pass power to Mudge and the Turnhalle delegates. Prime Minister Vorster in 1977 met with McHenry and diplomats from Germany, Canada, Britain, and France—henceforth known collectively as the Contact Group—and, advised by General Hendrik van den Bergh (see chapter 6), Neil Barnard of South Africa's National Intelligence Service, and Foreign Minister Botha, decided that crafting a solution that both protected South Africa and appeased the Contact Group made better sense than proceeding pell-mell with the Turnhalle project. Vorster halted the drive toward home rule and finally acknowledged the obvious standing of the UN with regard to Namibia and its future. He also appointed a judge from the Orange Free State as administrator-general to assume total control of Namibia, responsible solely to South Africa.

For the remainder of 1977 and throughout 1978 (and afterward), when I was in close contact with McHenry and frequently in Namibia, Vorster and Pik Botha apparently hoped that they could somehow persuade the Contact Group and the UN to validate a version of the Turnhalle-crafted internal solution. Meanwhile, of course, South Africa backed UNITA in Angola, pounded SWAPO camps whenever it could, and fiercely sought to rout SWAPO supporters inside the country—all efforts of South Africa's military to undermine Vorster's concessions.

Whether motivated by a newly conceived self-interest, a sense of realism, fear, or duplicity, in early 1978, South Africa finally agreed to a devolution plan put forward by McHenry and the Contact Group. SWAPO was not enthusiastic, and kept hedging, but McHenry obtained assent to the plan from Nujoma. By mid-1978, all sides had agreed to elections to a new constituent assembly supervised by the UN, a major reduction of South African military numbers, and the arrival of a large force of UN troops to keep the peace and ensure a free and fair poll. Success for the Contact Group! I celebrated it (prematurely) along with so many other hopeful well-wishers.

Two months later, however, Vorster resigned (as a result of a domestic political scandal), bringing forward as his successor Pieter W. Botha, until then minister of defense and a *verkrampte*-minded opponent of concessions to the Contact Group, the UN, and SWAPO.[12] Botha (no relation to his foreign minister) effectively ditched the Namibian agreement with the Contact Group and, defying the UN, scheduled local legislative assembly elections for the end of 1978. The contemplated poll, by proportional representation, was a blatant (and falsely premised) attempt to demonstrate that DTA-promoted goals and policies represented mainstream Namibian opinion. The balloting was a ploy intended by its prospective results to keep SWAPO indefinitely outside the national gates.

SWAPO, the NNF, and SWAPO-D all boycotted the faux voting exercise. That enabled the DTA to win approximately 82 percent of the 268,000 votes cast, or forty-one of the fifty seats available. Newly formed minor parties of the right and the center filled the other places. But, as I wrote, "The election itself led nowhere."[13] By the time that the votes had been counted, the revolutionary Islamist regime of Ayatollah Ruhollah Khomeini had deposed the Shah of Iran; that shift meant the loss—South Africa assumed—of the covert petroleum lifeline that had helped to sustain South Africa's industrial economy and its war effort for more than a decade. Despite the DTA's electoral triumph, Botha's government suddenly agreed to accede to the provisions of UN Resolution 435 and to transfer power to the UN and, after an internationally supervised real election, to SWAPO. The Contact Group and most observers viewed such an electoral exercise as a fitting way of giving the indigenous peoples of the lapsed mandate a direct path to self-government.

South Africa, however, changed its mind as rapidly as its sudden accession had startled McHenry and others. Four months after accepting the meaning of Resolution 435, and weeks after the Smith-Muzorewa pact in Rhodesia had given whites in that colony a seeming lifeline, Prime Minister Botha and his advisors believed that they could successfully shift their own hold on Namibia to a new, relatively open-minded and well-connected, administrator-general and to Mudge (heading the DTA) in a manner that could satisfy domestic opinion and prove sufficiently plausible to stiff-arm the Contact Group and the UN. What were they smoking?

By mid-1979, the new DTA-dominated Namibian National Assembly began to make laws for the supposed state and even to amend or overturn South African racially discriminatory legislation that had earlier applied to Namibia. The color bar was lifted, despite right-wing white opposition. Urban housing segregation and separation in hotels, bars, holiday resorts, and so on, were abolished. Apartheid's demise in Namibia came effectively and quickly on paper, and much more gradually in practice. These were welcome advances, nevertheless, but they came far too late to serve South Africa or white Namibia's political purposes.

There was to be no concocting an effective method of sneaking out from under obligations to the UN and, more significantly, from the geopolitical realities of decolonization.

Mudge and Gerrit Viljoen, the Broederbond leader and recent Rector of Rand Afrikaans University (now the University of Johannesburg) who had become Prime Minister Botha's agent in Namibia as the new administrator-general, possibly failed to appreciate that their new arrangements appealed more to the fragmented and little-populated ethnic interests that had joined whites in the DTA than they did, or possibly could, to the Ovambo, massively underrepresented as they were in the DTA's National Assembly.[14] In my friendly talks with Mudge and Viljoen, I urged them unsuccessfully to come to terms with the reality of SWAPO's hold on the hearts and minds of the overwhelming majority of Namibians. I also tried, again forlornly, to suggest that they were both misjudging the movement's core. Most of the SWAPO leadership cadre that I had known in New York, in Lusaka, or even within the country itself, were more bourgeois in their aspirations and inclinations than they were (fierce) Marxists. Instead, they embodied the aspirations of a long-subdued people who wanted nothing more unusual than a chance (like Africans farther north on the continent) to rule themselves. Since South Africa would itself have to follow the same path, why not be magnanimous and sensible in Namibia—and soon?

SWAPO was indeed an Ovambo-centered nationalist movement, but it also had significant, if not majority backing, from Damara, Herero, Nama, Lozi speakers in the Caprivi, and nearly every non-white ethnic constituency in the country. Despite being a military movement based externally, SWAPO still had a tight network of supporters within the putative nation. I met with many of the internal leaders quietly whenever I was in Windhoek, or in Ovamboland. Likewise, SWAPO had a host of white sympathizers, certainly in Windhoek, and I talked with them as well. The South Africans who were clinging to Namibia through their proxies could hardly escape the prevailing demographical realities, and the translation of those realities into political legitimacy. But such were American ideas. Mudge and Viljoen were still trying to craft an escape route that would perpetuate white survival and hegemony on South Africa's northwestern flank.

The Tortuous Final Road to Success

As I was to discover, a successful transfer of power to true Namibians would take place only once the appropriate international stars were aligned propitiously, once major domestic shifts in South Africa itself occurred, and once South Africa had exhausted all manner of possible alternatives, no matter how contorted. Indeed, once Ronald Reagan, with sympathetic views regarding white rule in

South Africa, became president of the United States in 1981 and "constructive engagement" became a toothsome policy intended to nudge South Africa toward improvements at home and devolution in Namibia, the previous momentum toward agreement faltered. The Reagan administration obliterated the Contact Group's forward motion and darkened the formerly starry skies. By pandering to the South Africans, I wrote, Washington was giving South Africa an unquestioned negotiating advantage and prolonging "the many agonies and losses of life in southern Africa." I also asked, skeptically, if "an upright, determined American administration [could] persuade a coy, worried, and wily South Africa to come to terms over the fate of Namibia" when its energetic predecessor could not.[15]

SWAPO as an aggressive guerrilla movement could not on its own compel South Africa to negotiate with the United States, the Contact Group, or the UN. Even though the military costs to South Africa of maintaining Namibia as a well-protected redoubt were ruinously expensive, at about $500,000 a day, South Africa for much of the 1970s and 1980s was prepared to maintain a formidable security apparatus and to supplement it in Namibia with a brutal clandestine internal offensive, including assassinations of prominent whites as well as blacks, regimentation, strict curfews in Ovamboland, and the callous deprivation of fundamental human rights. The Ovambo-Kavango-Caprivi area remained under effective martial law from 1977 to 1989, with indefinite detentions without trial and very limited access to family or lawyers.

As Namibian Supreme Court Judge David Smuts, with whom I became acquainted in the 1980s when he was a courageous advocate for the dispossessed and the founding director of Namibia's Legal Assistance Centre, has demonstrated and chillingly documented so thoroughly, South Africa's clandestine offensive encompassed top-secret executions of unarmed civilians (for no reason except blundering into a South African patrol), the murder of a former prisoner returned from Robben Island during a political rally in Katutura by security forces acting under cover, the detention without charge of refugees from SWAPO bases in secret South African camps, torture (in one of many cases that Smuts investigated, a man in the Ovambo district was accused by the South African military of feeding insurgents, and was waterboarded and more), other torture cases in which electric shocks were the main form of abuse, secret South African laws designed to eliminate elementary judicial oversight of questionable defense force brutalities, attacks on attorneys who assisted accused prisoners or were thought to oppose the security forces, obstruction of legal remonstrations and court proceedings, denial of access to defense attorneys, the killing of SWAPO soldiers inside Namibia even after the Contact Group and the UN had brokered a peace settlement with South Africa, and—finally—the assassination outside his home in Windhoek in 1989 of a well-respected lawyer and SWAPO member by a South African Defense Force covert unit called in oxymoronic language the

Civil Cooperation Bureau (CCB). The magnetic man gunned down by a state death squad was Anton Lubowski, whom I had visited in his home a few weeks before. The CCB's remit was "maximal disruption of the enemy," as Smuts demonstrated so effectively in pursuing this and so many other vicious attempts by South African covert and intelligence operations to hinder SWAPO's ultimate victory in Namibia.[16]

These destructive, ceaseless attacks on defenseless Namibians, massive and interminable violations of fundamental human rights, raids on the ground and from the air on SWAPO bases and SWAPO detachments, hostility to Angola, military support for UNITA against the Angolan government, and a boisterous propaganda barrage served to intimidate civilians but could not deter backing for SWAPO, keep SWAPO from gaining followers, or limit SWAPO incursions across the Angolan border. South African security operations made life difficult for even the hardiest village Ovambo, converting much of the area just south of the Angolan border into a heavily conflicted and dangerous war zone. But it only gained South Africa a brief mirage of time.

Knowledgeable and loyal South African officers and officials may have believed during the 1980s that by holding off SWAPO legions and harassing Angola that they were creating a lasting internal solution to the Namibian puzzle. But, in effect, as I realized during visits to Namibia in the middle 1980s, South Africa and its DTA proxy were merely going round and round in inconsequential circles. Seeking to avoid the inevitable (as in South Africa itself) by fair and mostly foul means was an unlikely and forlorn attempt to stem the tides of decolonization and to delay seeking outcomes beneficial to all. Moreover, nothing that happened inside the country could bring about a result favorable to all of those who had interests in Namibia unless bargaining became transparent and all contending parties could be held genuinely accountable.

Because the constructive engagers in the early 1980s were giving more aid and comfort to the South Africans than the latter had any right to expect, this going round and round became the frustrating game for much of the remainder of the decade. Vice President George H. W. Bush befriended South Africa officially; South African military and intelligence personnel were permitted to go back and forth between Pretoria and Washington, strategizing; the Reagan administration's Department of Commerce authorized the sale of once-embargoed military materiel to South Africa (for use in Namibia). At the UN, the United States vetoed resolutions intended to curb South Africa's actions in Namibia. But still there was no forward movement by Botha's government, under siege internally in South Africa from the United Democratic Front, but more confident than before thanks to American support. South Africa somehow believed that it could endure UN sanctions and the tightening international anti-apartheid noose.

In return for constructively engaging with South Africa, Washington intended to forge a workable agreement over Namibia's future. But South Africa—for at least a few years—had different ideas and refused to agree even to the generous terms that the Reagan team proffered. Cruelly, too, the policy of constructive engagement in effect legitimized the presence of Soviet, Cuban, and East German military and intelligence involvement in the southern African region. The Cold War continued, but the Marxist operations also intended their MPLA proxy in Angola to strengthen its hold on that oil-rich country and for its SWAPO affiliate to prevail in Namibia. "The peace of southern Africa is . . . threatened more by the unchecked exercise of South African military might," I argued, "than by Soviet machinations or the presence . . . of Cuban troops." South Africa's anxieties about a Red-directed "total onslaught" were less formative than "its own attempts to unsettle the region. . . ." In the same article in the *New York Times*, I indicated that South Africa had destroyed SWAPO bases in southern Angola and materially limited SWAPO'S ability to strike into Namibia. South Africa, I revealed, had gained control of a 160-mile-deep salient of southern Angola and, as result of its patronage and support of UNITA, even larger swaths of central and southeastern Angola—a very effective buffer zone.[17] (The White House also backed UNITA as a non-communist ally in the Cold War; President Reagan and Republican lawmakers even attempted to sell Stingers—portable, heat-seeking antiaircraft missiles—to UNITA to assist its struggle against the MPLA and stimulate a local arms race, an idea I and others testified against before Congress. Doing so for me led to a major confrontation with Richard Cheney, then a verbally abusive congressman from Wyoming.)[18]

South Africa was also attacking its opponents in Botswana and Zambia, sponsoring resistance to Mugabe's reign in Zimbabwe, and funding the Renamo insurgency in Mozambique against its Soviet-backed, post-Portuguese rulers. Southern Africa, including Namibia and Angola, remained in an alarming twilight zone, thanks to the Reagan administration's policy of constructive engagement and its cosseting of South Africa's retributive struggle for survival. That approach even encouraged a foolhardy South African military strike on an American-owned oil-pumping facility in northern Angola in 1985 and a South African commando raid on ANC safe houses in sleepy Gaborone, Botswana's tiny capital. These external assaults matched the Botha government's refusal to cope with its own internal spasm of violence. Constructive engagement was hardly accomplishing much by way of positive change; by stiffening South Africa's resolve it had worsened conditions for millions throughout the region and retarded a diplomatic settlement of the Namibian problem.[19]

Admittedly, unlike in pre-independence Zimbabwe, where both ZANU and ZAPU became sufficiently dangerous on the *chimurenga* battlefield to compromise the lives and livelihoods of the Rhodesian settler minority, SWAPO could never create a comparable atmosphere of menace for white Namibians. Its incursions hardly threatened the distant diamond-vacuuming operations in the far south, the large white-owned pastoral establishments in central Namibia, or the fisheries offshore. Residents of the major cities of Windhoek and Swakopmund remained largely sheltered by their distance from the war front. Even tourism, not yet as international as it was to become, was little affected by guerrilla incursions. Only SWAPO forays into the Ovambo and Caprivi regions, the mining of roads and bombing of northern administrative buildings, and the assassination of collaborators kept the South African security forces busy and the border areas on edge. This weakness on the part of the exiled militants put a greater burden on international actors and international pressure to bring the Namibian stalemate to an end.

The truly decisive series of events that turned Namibia toward independence were the internal crumbling of the Soviet Union, the growing expense of feeding and sheltering 55,000 Cuban soldiers in Angola, and South Africa's realization of its own ultimate political weaknesses, plus an acute balance-of-payments problem thanks to banking decisions in New York. Perestroika decapitated the Soviet Union and led to its abandonment of the MPLA in Angola and of SWAPO. Soviet retrenchment also meant that South Africa could help to send the Cubans home from Angola if it ceased supporting UNITA. The stars finally aligned themselves in favor of a lasting brokered settlement of the Namibian conflict.

Forging Independence

Toward the end of 1988, I predicted that Namibia could be free in the next year.[20] In a parley with the UN, the United States, Angola, and Cuba, South Africa agreed before the close of the year to withdraw its remaining contingents from Angola and scale back its occupying legions in Namibia itself. A smallish UN Transitional Assistance Group (UNTAG) led by Finland's gifted Martti Ahtisaari (later Nobel Peace laureate and President of Finland) replaced the South African administration of Namibia and began an energetic and tactically adroit transfer of power from white to black. Smuts calls Ahtisaari "immensely professional and diplomatic," in the face of immense South African (mostly) military perfidy.[21]

This transition was no easy task, however. I was in Windhoek and Klein Windhoek (where UNTAG was based) fairly frequently, consulting with Ahtisaari and his team of seconded officials from thirty nations and learning about the many obstacles to independence that could still be erected to slow, or even to attempt to derail, the agreed-upon movement from the older to a newer political dispensation.

The South Africans were still playing a series of retrogressive games. They subsidized almost any kind of local group that claimed to be opposed to SWAPO, and many did, and indulged in combative skirmishes long after hostilities were supposed to be over. SWAPO's leadership, allowed back into Namibia to organize and campaign prior to a defining election, wisely distrusted South African intentions and actions. All sides refused to play fair, especially the South-West African Police Force. There were innumerable intrigues, with UNTAG, Ahtisaari, and his key British and Irish adjutants trying to confound those (even SWAPO) who would seek unfair advantage. UNTAG, particularly its military detachment, hence had to keep a close eye on both South African and SWAPO forces to make sure that each obeyed UN rules, intimidated no one, and campaigned in an honest manner for the decisive late 1989 constituent assembly elections.[22]

Even South Africans in Namibia and Mudge and his DTA followers knew that SWAPO would likely sweep the poll in Ovamboland, where 700,000 of Namibia's 1.4 million people resided. But those who joined South Africa in opposing SWAPO sought to keep the liberation movement from winning two-thirds of the seats in a Constituent Assembly, and thus the ability to write Namibia's new constitution in what non-SWAPO contenders assumed would be a Soviet-inspired, Marxist-inclined manner. The Kavango (90,000) and the Caprivi (50,000) were presumed to be pro-SWAPO, as well, so the DTA and its allied smaller parties sought electoral support from among 65,000 white farmers and businessmen, 45,000 Baster farmers, 40,000 mixed background Coloureds, 35,000 San, and 9,000 Tswana. The DTA grouping also hoped to obtain voting support from among the 90,000 Damara, 85,000 Herero, and 50,000 Nama living mostly in central Namibia, but many of SWAPO's long-esteemed leaders, including several who had lobbied furiously at the UN on behalf of Namibian independence, were of Damara and Herero descent.

After a vigorous campaign closely observed by UNTAG and, episodically, by me accompanying UNTAG managers, SWAPO won more than 57 percent of the poll, giving it forty-one places in the seventy-two-seat Constituent Assembly. The DTA, with twenty-one seats, became the official opposition, together with five smaller parties (of the forty-five contesting). South Africa was relieved that SWAPO had proved less popular than feared, taking less than two-thirds of the assembly positions. (The Constituent Assembly became the National Assembly after independence.)

What would SWAPO do now that it was finally in power and could write a constitution for the country that it had long planned to govern? I was not in Namibia during this period but had been assured throughout the run-up to the poll, and after its victory, that SWAPO intended to show skeptics inside and outside the country that their fears were unfounded, that its leaders indeed possessed the bourgeois, normalizing, imperative about which I had written and had earlier attempted to reassure Mudge, Viljoen, Pik Botha, American Congressmen, and the Reagan and Bush U.S. State Departments.

The true test of victorious nationalism came in the writing of the new constitution in such a manner that it would ensure conditions conducive to good governance. Just as Cyril Ramaphosa had a major role in drafting South Africa's liberal blueprint, so Hage Geingob, SWAPO's formidable chief representative in New York, a former student at Temple University in Philadelphia and Fordham University and the New School in New York, and the head of the UN Institute for Namibia—which had trained Namibians for the era when they would be in charge—oversaw the drafting of the Namibian charter.

Nujoma, soon to become president, extended the hand of recognition to the DTA and its smaller allies. He and his winning team accepted in the Assembly the need for a justiciable bill of rights that would safeguard against the fears of Namibia's many minorities. Horse-trading during the drafting process there was. But, ultimately, Namibia's constitutional writing convention produced one of the most liberal national constitutions ever written, foreshadowing what South Africa would do a few years later. The new platform for Namibian rule sanctified private property, produced conditions favorable to foreign investment, enshrined protections for human rights and civil liberties, mandated an independent judiciary, and provided for both an auditor-general and an ombudsperson to try to guarantee accountability and transparency.

Namibia became Africa's fifty-second independent nation in early 1990, shortly after Mandela was finally released from his long detention and about the same time that the Soviet Union became defunct. President Nujoma, as he now was, and Prime Minister Geingob, a Damara who was much later to become president, convened a multiracial, pan-ethnic cabinet, and proceeded to inaugurate a governing process that was more practical than ideological, and surprisingly willing to cater to the needs of domestic and foreign investors. The SWAPO government accepted the importance of the country's white-dominated commercial sector, Nujoma going out of his way to avoid alarming major, mostly foreign-owned, export producers.[23]

Consolidated Diamond Mines, a subsidiary of South Africa's De Beers Ltd., then contributed 30 percent of the new nation's GDP and 13 percent of all tax revenues, and was its largest private employer. A subsidiary of Britain's Rio Tinto Zinc Ltd. produced uranium oxide at Rossing; its share of export earnings, employment, and taxes was just below that of the diamond operations. Pilchards and sardines, caught offshore, were other major earners, together with pelts of karakul lambs. But Nujoma and his team also had to maintain good relations with South Africa: nearly all of Namibia's food imports and its transportation networks (air, rail, road, and harbors) flowed across the southern border with South Africa; most of its tourists were South African. And South Africa during the long war had been subsidizing the Namibian budget. Possibly Nujoma's strongest confidence-building measures were to put straight-laced Otto Herigel, a German-descended entrepreneur and SWAPO supporter (and part of our innumerable luncheon discussions in Die Südwester Stube), in charge of the finance ministry and economic development and to install Hartmut Ruppel, another person of German background and a longtime human rights campaigner, as Namibia's first attorney general.

The New Namibia

Namibia worked. That was my verdict as early as 1992. There were more pluses than minuses, considering how Nujoma, Geingob, and their associates were delivering governance to their followers and the many others who lived in Namibia. In comparison to other African countries, especially nearby Zimbabwe, Nujoma and his cabinet ministers initially conveyed a responsible leadership message. After a flurry of pretension, Nujoma limited the length and duration of presidential motorcades and downplayed at least some of the usual pomp, more similar to the Botswanan model than that of Malawi or Zambia. Nujoma lived with less ostentation than many of his presidential peers (excepting Botswana and Mandela's South Africa). He received a delegation of protesting white farmers without decrying them or criticizing their motives. On several occasions, too, he saw me in State House and smiled broadly when I conveyed a message from former President Oscar Arias of Costa Rica asking him if he would stand down the nation's armed forces in order to devote more funds to education and health and spend less on the military, following the enduringly successful Costa Rican experiment. He told me that he indeed would be happy to follow that lead, because Namibia had no more enemies and no more wars to fight but, he added, "How then would the nation feed the ex-soldiers?" Having an army helped sop up unemployment, Nujoma sagely reminded me. Moreover, and much more the reason, Nujoma relied on his military establishment to keep order in the event of internal discord, in case of some unlikely South African attack, or to use it later to harass Botswana and intervene in the Congo.

During the 1990s, Namibia sought to be a progressive developing democracy, with increasing attention devoted to upgrading health and other human services, to multiplying schools and educational opportunities as rapidly as possible, and in transforming an old teacher-training institution into a new university. Katjavivi, whom I had known for more than a decade, became its first head and, together with some local and some seconded staff from overseas, tried with only a minimum of state funding to fashion an early version of a serious tertiary endeavor. The Ford Foundation asked me to advise Katjavivi as much as I could, so many of my visits to Namibia during the 1990s were devoted to the protean university, and to helping Katjavivi focus the institution's educational mission on achievable targets, and on subjects and skills that Namibia desperately needed.

South Africa, as a mandatory power and after, had paid very little attention to educational advancement in its fifth "province." As a result, trained indigenous teachers, lawyers, physicians, engineers, surveyors, locomotive drivers, water specialists, agricultural extension personnel, ichthyologically oriented scientists or technicians, and hospitality and tourism experts were all in very short supply. The new university could not make up in its instruction for South Africa's deficient colonial rule, but under Katjavivi's leadership it certainly began earnestly and energetically in the 1990s to close the gap. In other social areas, however, there was far more pious talk than genuine action.

Diversification of employment was another issue with which the young Namibia had to contend. It inherited a country where 55 percent of all formal jobs were in national and local government. Under SWAPO's rule, pre-independence patronage issues in the civil service became even more acute than before. Moreover, whatever level of bureaucratic competency had existed under South African rule was soon compromised by the flight of many long-time technocrats back to South Africa, and by the understandable lack of experience of their local successors.

In the political realm, many Namibians hoped that Nujoma, despite his rough background and ruthless reputation, would emerge as one of the more publicly interested of African leaders, and would preside over the new republic in ways similar to Presidents Sir Seretse Khama and Sir Ketumile Masire in neighboring and equally sparsely populated Botswana—where corruption was frowned upon, and had become rarer than in any other state of mainland Africa. But Nujoma had his own style, and quietly from the first ran a tight-fisted state. During his fifteen-year reign, most contrary voices were stilled. He attempted to stifle media criticism, as well as being hostile to any divergent voices within SWAPO. He tried, particularly, to cow *The Namibian*, a feisty Windhoek newspaper that investigated suspected wrongdoings in the new administration, battled Nujoma's tight control when necessary, and ultimately emerged as a doughty advocate for the rights of all Namibians.

In 2000, Nujoma said that *The Namibian*, and Gwen Lister, its pioneering editor, had criticized him and SWAPO too much. They had opposed his standing for a third presidential term in contravention of constitutional limits. So his government stopped official advertisements in the newspaper, and ordered officials not to buy or read it. A year later, he appointed himself information minister (in addition to being president) and proceeded to turn the Namibian Broadcasting Corporation into a propaganda machine. Throughout the remainder of his presidency, Nujoma tended to copy Mugabe's predilections in Zimbabwe, both rulers being enemies of press freedom. (He also often defended Mugabe's despotism within the Organization of African Unity, the African Union, and the Southern African Development Community.) In 2002, Nujoma even declared that "the public would be better served . . . if the press merely served as a 'tool' to transmit government information."[24] Fortunately, *The Namibian*'s coverage of the country was not obstructed by the government boycott, its editors were fearless, and Nujoma's successors were more temperate and/or less easily offended.

Nujoma certainly favored the dominant party state, with a "big man" at its apex. From late 1994, after SWAPO gained two-thirds control of the Assembly in elections, he and it reigned supreme for the next eleven years, and for a further two years as he retained his headship of the party. Accountability to the citizenry correspondingly diminished and, according to authoritative analyses, loyalty to party, and patronage for "comrades," took precedence over any feelings for the broader public interest.[25] A privileged elite rapidly gained prominence, and accumulated perquisites and wealth. SWAPO as an institution and Nujoma as a leader showed little tolerance for opposition. Accordingly, in the 1999 and 2004 Assembly and presidential polls, SWAPO increased its parliamentary hold, gaining and then holding three-quarters of the seats.

Opposition to Nujoma's tight grip over SWAPO and Namibia was building, however. In 2004, when he anointed as his successor Hifikepunye Pohamba, a rather colorless cabinet minister unswervingly loyal to the outgoing president, without much internal party discussion, SWAPO's politburo exploded. Toivo and several other highly placed SWAPO operatives seeking more modern and more democratically inclined leadership tried instead to nominate Hidipo Hamutenya, long-serving Minister of Trade and Industry and subsequently Minister of Foreign Affairs, as president instead of Pohamba. Hamutenya, a determined graduate of American and Canadian universities and a cocky cabinet minister with whom I kept in close contact whenever I was in Windhoek, was too ambitious and too "new school" for Nujoma and his coterie despite (or because of) his potent Ovambo credentials.

Hamutenya's candidacy was initially thwarted within the cabinet, from which body he was summarily dismissed. Later, when he rebelliously formed a rival Rally for Democracy and Progress (RDP) party in 2007, prior to the 2009 elections, he and his associates were denounced by Nujoma and SWAPO as traitors, agents of imperialism, and "pawns acting in the interest of regime change."[26] Physical clashes between rival factions followed, public rallies by the new party being prohibited on spurious grounds. In the 2009 national balloting, SWAPO won 74.3 percent of the vote, or fifty-four of seventy-two seats, and the RDP a surprising 11.1 percent, or eight seats, polling very well in Windhoek and Rehoboth. In the separate presidential contest, Pohamba received more than

75 percent of the votes, Hamutenya only 10 percent. However, Hamutenya had won an Assembly seat, and served in parliament until the 2014 balloting, when he and his party were roundly defeated by SWAPO, and by Geingob, the presidential candidate. (Hamutenya died in 2016, a year after rejoining SWAPO.)

As confirmed by these several elections, and by later ones, Namibia, like so many of its neighbors, was a state with a dominant single party, a true representative democracy having yet to be achieved. Some call it a minimalist democracy, and refer to the continuation of structural violence as a means of denying full political participation by its citizens.[27] For a long time, too, Namibia held political prisoners as a result of a failed 1998–1999 Caprivi (now Zambezi) secessionist movement and SWAPO's preference for repression over reconciliation. Minority concerns and interests had a hard time being heard before the 2020 municipal and regional elections (see below, p. 302).

The party remained supreme, as before, but in 2014, non-Oshiwambo-speaking adherents of SWAPO gained a new, and surprising, prominence within the institution. Until then, the party was ethnically monolithic at its apex, certainly so long as Nujoma was in office. Under Pohamba, persons of other ethnic backgrounds became more prominent, as they had been during the long run-up to independence. Yet few outsiders anticipated the revolution within the revolutionary movement that occurred in 2014. Unlike other African liberation movements such as those in Zambia, Malawi, Kenya, and Zimbabwe, where the dominant ethnic groups retained permanent control of high offices within their ruling party and their governments, at that year's party congress, SWAPO became one of the few African founding parties to transfer power within the party to a representative of another ethnic group. In this case, after an internal struggle, the party chose Geingob, a Damara, to succeed Pohamba. Geingob, its first prime minister but sidelined and exiled by Nujoma early in the twenty-first century, had been rehabilitated as cabinet minister under Pohamba, rising finally to the premiership. In 2015, after a smashing victory at the polls, Geingob inaugurated a government that still included many Ovambo ministers but also, for the first time, gave political prominence to Damara and Herero colleagues. The party remained mostly supreme, and Geingob, as a long-time powerful member of the ruling elite, resumed the leading role that he had played in the 1990s. The old SWAPO guard continued in charge. Nonetheless, Geingob's elevation broke the Oshiwambo-speaking hold on the party's topmost hierarchy.

Nujoma's reign was not particularly progressive, and Pohamba's ten years (2005–2015) as chief executive proved a largely steady continuation of the Nujoma paradigm, The distinction between the state and the party continued to be blurred and Pohamba, like his predecessor, had no compunction about conflating the two, and emphasizing how pernicious and unpatriotic was criticism from the press or from civil society. Still, his regime otherwise adhered more than many contemporary African hegemonic parties to the rule of law, and protected an independent, if somewhat untrained, judiciary. During his incumbency, Pohamba's regime became more tolerant and permissive of dissent. He "truly made Namibia a much better . . . [and] more humane and inclusive society."[28]

Geingob's first term in office did little to strike out in new directions. Nor did he manage to reduce unemployment or to make Namibia a more equal, socially responsible, state. With a new generation of young people voting in 2019, Geingob's failure noticeably to uplift his people may have led to a slide in SWAPO's appeal; in the balloting contest of that year SWAPO only won 56 percent of the vote, its lowest total since 1989.

Possibly, too, after three decades of SWAPO hegemony, numbers of Namibians had become disaffected by SWAPO's antipathy to criticism and its restrained approach to social advances. The party's appeal was marred, as well, by a tendency (albeit much less pronounced than in Zimbabwe) for its rulers to take advantage of their elected positions for private gain, and to distribute opportunities for personal enrichment to clients in the small country's sovereign political and corporate networks.

Graft and Scams

The specter of corruption reared its compromising face early in Nujoma's tenure, and poisoned the Namibian body politic ever after. Soon after independence, a number of prominent members of the new ruling class became implicated in public scandals. By the standards of Nigeria or the Congo, graft and bribery in Namibia may have been of comparatively limited scale, but it immediately disturbed public opinion, especially in a relatively impoverished, rather religiously influenced, and chaste territory accustomed more to austerity and modesty than to sleaze. In 1994, for example, the auditor-general, reporting to parliament, accused the government of "sweeping corruption under the carpet."[29] He and other investigators pointed to profitable eco-tourism franchises having been transferred to patrons of the president. Concessions in the reviving offshore fisheries industry had been allocated suspiciously to cabinet ministers. The nation's ombudsman revealed that the foreign ministry harbored serious scams, including the purchase of expensive motor vehicles in a dubiously circuitous and unfairly expensive manner. Over-invoicing in the ministry was widespread. Additionally, some of the new ministers had fenced off farms and drilled deep wells for themselves at government expense. Most of all, the president and parliament refused to take much note of these official indications that the nascent republic's ministers and officials were thieving from taxpayers.

Nujoma ignored the findings of the auditor-general and the ombudsman. He also decided that he required (and deserved) an expensive $25 million French jet aircraft to be used for travel within the country but more so that he could arrive in style at all-African meetings. Subsequently, the press was filled with accusations that Nujoma had acquired a diamond mine for himself in the Congo after Namibian troops went there to assist President Laurent Kabila's defense of his regime against a Rwandan invasion. (See also chapters 7 and 9.)

Whether or not Nujoma and his successors have more or less been on the take, or at least permitted their subordinates to feast lavishly from the fatted calf, Transparency International's Corruption Perceptions Index (CPI) has always placed Namibia among the better (but not the best) African anti-corruption performers on the continent. Behind the Seychelles, Botswana, Cape Verde, and Rwanda, and regularly well ahead of South Africa, Namibia ranked from the earlier years more highly than all but those few other African examples. In 2011 (in earlier years the CPI employed a divergent methodology), Namibia ranked 57th of 180 global states, well after Botswana (32nd), Cape Verde (41st), Rwanda (49th), and the Seychelles (50th), but just ahead of the Czech Republic and Malaysia. In that year South Africa was placed 64th on the list. For the remainder of the decade, Namibia's raw scores and rankings against its African peer group stayed almost level. In 2020, the CPI list of African nations began with the Seychelles (27th), followed by Botswana (35th), Cape Verde (41st), Rwanda (49th), and Mauritius (52nd). Namibia dropped to 57th place (with a score of 51 of 100). It lost rankings in one year, from 2019. That put Namibia a few places above Armenia and Cuba. South Africa was 69th on the same list for 2020.[30]

The CPI ratings for Namibia were always much more favorable in this century than those given subjectively by locally based "experts," commentators, and diplomats. In 2017, too, when I was in Windhoek to renew acquaintances with President Geingob (meeting with him in the pretentiously over-built new State House), Speaker of the House of Assembly (as he had become) Katjavivi, Judge Smuts, and long-time academic colleagues, the local newspaper was filled with tales of corruption at the city's international airport. Indeed, Geingob had recently sacked several of the high-ranking accused. Lunch table discussion even linked some of the then current sleaze conditions to the president himself. According to the Heritage Foundation's 2020 Index of Economic Freedom, there were "significant weaknesses in [Namibia's] transparency and government accountability, and a majority of Namibians regard[ed] the level of corruption as very high."[31] The new Index of Public Integrity (IPI) rated only a handful of sub-Saharan African countries in 2019 (of the 117 nations listed); South Africa took the 38th place and Namibia fell well behind in the 49th slot, but still ahead of other polities on the sub-continent, including Botswana, surprisingly low down on this list in 83rd place.[32] In 2021, the same index placed South Africa 33rd, Namibia 79th, and Botswana 85th.[33] Belying what locals saw and knew, and gossiped about, in comparison to its peers in the African Union, conditions in Namibia otherwise generally elicited a perception of limited graft among those who supplied ratings to the CPI and the IPI.

Even comparatively minimal corrupt dealings inhibit rapid development, however, and, after independence Namibia's economic growth trajectory was curbed by procurement fraud, special licensing deals, bribes for special permits, and the usual kinds of influence peddling that attracted special rewards. Additionally, Namibian advances during and after the first decades of independence slowed because of poor demand for uranium oxide, by the continuing hostilities in Angola between the MPLA and UNITA that reduced tourism revenues before the end of the twentieth century, and by falling prices for copper, lead, and zinc. Diamonds continued to be a mainstay of Namibia, as they are today, and a major contributor to the nation's GDP.

In 1994, the Anglo-American Corporation ceded control of Consolidated Diamond Mines, assembled in 1920, to the new republic; together they established a partnership styled as the Namdeb Mining Corporation, with revenue allocations among the partners being revised in 2011. In 2020, Namdeb remained the republic's largest non-public service employer, with 1,800 personnel on its payroll. Its gem exports contributed about 50 percent of the nation's foreign exchange earnings and as much as 12.5 percent of annual GDP. Rio Tinto's vast (and then mothballed) uranium oxide complex was sold to China's National Uranium Corporation in 2018, resuming its role as a key contributor to the nation's tax income, earnings, and jobs. Additionally, Namibia still mines gold, zinc, and a little copper. The opening of an expanded container terminal at Walvis Bay (which Namibia acquired from South Africa in 1994) facilitates transport overseas and helps boost incomes. The overall economy remained hindered, however, by its ties to the South African rand currency, which was weak in modern times, and by Namibia's dependence for a sizable percentage of its revenue base on revenues (weak in 2019–2021) derived from its participation in the Southern African Customs Union. Moreover, since for so many decades Namibia has obtained nearly all of its consumer goods from South Africa, the nation has been slow to develop local manufacturing capacity, or even to beneficiate many of its valuable minerals.

Namibia, a country with little rainfall except in the north, also suffered in the 1990s and ever since from unexpected periods of global warming droughts that largely destroyed subsistence farming prospects and made the raising of the cattle, sheep, and goats on which the majority of Namibians depend that much less sustainable. The fishing industry was slow to revive, too, after overfishing and poaching by Chinese and European trawlers. (Despite Chinese depredation, the

SWAPO government increased its commercial ties to China during the Geingob administrative years after 2015, especially in 2020 and 2021.)

Even so, the harvesting of monkfish, horse-mackerel, hake, pilchards, sardines and other fish offshore attracted increasing foreign and local commercial attention, starting about the time that Geingob became prime minister for the second time and just before the start of his two presidencies. A large Icelandic fisheries conglomerate discovered from about 2012 that by bribing the Namibian minister of fisheries and marine resources and the minister of justice, the chair of Namibia's state-owned Fishcor, and contributing to SWAPO party coffers, that it could gain favored access to the quota allocations that were granted by the fisheries minister. *Aljazeera*, which used the testimony of a Icelandic whistleblower to spur an investigation of corruption in Namibia's modern-day fisheries enterprise, believes that the Icelandic conglomerate spent about $10 to $12 million to secure its privileges. Other estimates suggest that as much as $600 million shifted into official Namibian hands, and SWAPO's exchequer, from foreign companies seeking legal access to Namibia's offshore waters during the 2010s.[34]

At about the time of the 2019 national elections in Namibia, *Aljazeera* tested its findings about corruption in the Namibian fishing industry by posing as a Chinese corporation seeking to obtain lucrative fishing rights in Namibian waters. For $500,000 paid to the head of Fishcor and $200,000 to the minister of fisheries, allegedly for SWAPO election expenses, the fake Chinese concern received what it sought. *Aljazeera* filmed much of the bargaining for bribes.[35]

Namibia's police arrested the minister of fisheries, the minister of justice (who owned corrupt fishing companies), the chair of Fishcor, two Namibian businessmen, and several other highly placed miscreants. Protesters on the streets of Windhoek also urged the head of Namibia's Anti-Corruption Commission, who had done nothing to uncover or investigate the "fishrot" arrangements, to resign. The extent to which any of these illegal emoluments made their way to, or were intended to enrich, higher-ups in the party and the state is not known. President Geingob was implicated as a recipient of funds by one of the lawyers who testified, however.[36] Certainly, the extent and duration of the Icelandic scheme testified to a depth of graft that has never been fully captured by CPI figures. The ministers and other schemers were still awaiting trial in mid-2022.

As the Fishrot cases were being investigated, in April 2021, the minister of defense, a former naval officer, admitted to owning a significant, hitherto secret, undeclared foreign bank account in Hong Kong. Moreover, the account, containing "illicit proceeds," was first registered about 2009, at the time of a major arms purchase from China. Kickbacks from Chinese sellers were presumably a feature of the N$1.8 million ($124,000) deal. The minister resigned.[37]

Despite economic setbacks and these recent waves of corruption, in the twenty-first century Namibia's rulers produced surprisingly robust macroeconomic returns for the country, thanks to diamonds, and thanks to relatively careful management of the overall economy. By 2020, economic growth, which had peaked at 6.5 percent per annum in 2015, and then fallen (along with South Africa) to below 1 percent, was cresting 2 percent and growing strongly before the coronavirus epidemic hit southern Africa and stifled global trade. The Index of Economic Freedom had downgraded the country in the mid-2010s, but by 2020 it rated Namibia as the seventh most free nation in sub-Saharan Africa (and ninety-sixth globally), after the usual subjects—Mauritius, Rwanda, Botswana, the Seychelles, Cape Verde, and (a surprise) Tanzania. Namibia rated highly for labor freedom and business freedom, with very low scores for fiscal health and government integrity.[38]

Per capita GDP, for all of its flaws as a measure, grew from $2,136 (unadjusted for inflation) in 2000 to $5,318 in 2010, to $10,064 in 2019, falling in 2020 and 2021, when Namibia slid into recession. According to Bloomberg News, Namibia's official unemployment rate of 33.5 percent—probably an underestimate—was the highest in Africa in 2021, with Nigeria second and South Africa third.[39] Moody's, the credit rating agency, in late 2020 downgraded Namibia's fiscal apparatus to "below junk" status. Furthermore, even in recession, the country's still comparatively elevated GDP per capita figure masked severe income inequality, measured by Gini-coefficient results (from World Bank Development Group household surveys) that showed how well the country's new elites had prospered since independence relative to their less favored brethren. Fat cats had gained wealth and, despite abundant talk, oft-promised land redistribution had never occurred on a serious scale. Namibia's Gini score of 59 of 100 (in 2015) was much less favorable than other sub-Saharan states such as Malawi, Mauritius, and Rwanda, and somewhat worse than Botswana, but better (in terms of inequality) than South Africa.[40] According to the latest United Nations Human Development Report, "Over half of employed Namibians earn less than US$ 95 (N$ 1,400) a month. Even among those in paid employment this amounts to less than the average per capita income for sub-Saharan Africa."[41] Melber decries the "crypto-capitalist, petty-minded, self-enriching black elite," that exploits "the public purse" and is responsible for turning Namibia into one of the world's most unequal societies, with 40 percent of the population living below or close to the national poverty line.[42]

Transparency is a major component of and marker for governance. When my graduate students and I at Harvard University's Kennedy School of Government began systematically to measure governance—the delivery of essential government services—across the globe, Namibia rated well in ways that obscured or took too little account of the defects in SWAPO's muddled administration of the country. According to the mostly objective series of measures that we developed, however, Namibia from 2000 always scored near the top of the countries of the continent. It was "safe and secure," the government had not directly undermined the rule of law, and voters had "voice," albeit within a controlled environment. In that first year's compilation of the Index of African Governance, Namibia rated fifth highest, after the Seychelles, Mauritius, Botswana, and South Africa, with a total score across the five rating categories of 70.7 (out of 100). In 2005, it fell to seventh place, being overtaken by Gabon and Cape Verde, and its score slipped to 67.0, putting it just above Ghana and Senegal. By 2007, Namibia's rating had receded to eighth place, but with a score of 69.2, slightly ahead of South Africa, São Tomé and Principe, and Gabon. In that last year it was marked down because of a very low score (43.1) in the "sustainable economic opportunity" category, and a low rating (60.6) for "human development." The Seychelles and Mauritius, for example, had very much higher scores for both categories, and the totals for Botswana and South Africa were both better than Namibia's in those areas. Its highest score (88.8) was for "safety and security." By 2017, using a somewhat altered methodology, Namibia ranked fourth on the index's list of all fifty-four African nations, with a total score of 68.6, meaning that there had been a rating improvement over the decade relative to its peers. Mauritius was the top-ranking African polity in that year, as it had been consistently, in 2017 with a total score of 79.8.[43]

As a tribute to Namibia's development under SWAPO and its first three presidents, average life expectancy as a proxy for improving health standards reached 63.7 years in 2020, substantially higher than Nigeria, Angola, Mozambique, and Zimbabwe, and many poorer African countries, but lower than Botswana (69.6 years) and South Africa (64.1 years). Maternal mortality rates per 100,000 live births, another robust proxy measure of national well-being, improved from 1998 to 2017 from 329 to 195, demonstrating the effective delivery of health services to Namibia's people. Over roughly the same period, Botswana's average rate of maternal mortality fell from 260 to 144, with both nations coping with the ravages of HIV/AIDS, tuberculosis, and malaria. The percentage of Namibia's population with ready access to supplies of potable water—a further measure of effective service delivery—was estimated to be 91 percent in 2020, but only 34 percent of the population had ready access to improved sanitation. Botswana's comparable figures were 97 percent and 64 percent, whereas beleaguered Zimbabwe's totals were 64 percent and 36 percent.

Under Geingob, Namibia at first survived the 2020/2021 coronavirus pandemic with fewer cases and deaths than its neighbors. In March 2021, Namibia's 40,000 cases and 430 deaths placed the country at the lower end of Africa's otherwise tragic results; its deaths per 100,000 population were 17.3, compared to more than 100 in Peru and other parts of South America and 60 to 80 in Europe and the United States. Neighboring Botswana, with a similarly sized population of 2.5 million, reported only 31,000 cases and 332 deaths, whereas South Africa (another neighbor) suffered 1,500,000 cases and 51,000 deaths over the same period, or 86 per 100,000.

But these relatively un-malign outcomes shifted at the end of 2021 with the arrival of the Omicron variant and the ramping up of Delta-delivered morbidity. Namibia listed about 134,000 confirmed cases of Covid-19 at the end of the year, and 3,600 acknowledged deaths.[44] In a country of 2.3 million people, these numbers reflected badly on the country's administrative efforts to curb the coronavirus. They compromised Geingob's leadership, and led to popular grumbling about SWAPO's failures to keep its people safe.

These feelings were compounded by the coronavirus pandemic's devastating curtailing of tourism, an economic mainstay, the slowing sales of diamonds, and a reduction of uranium exports. Youth unemployment, a problem before the pandemic, became much worse, with likely future political and national morale problems. Feeling distinctly prosperous in 2019, at the end of 2021 Namibia's people felt themselves much less well off.

Nation-Building and Fragmentation

The first three presidents of Namibia created a political culture, with strengthened political institutions, that by 2021 had transformed a post-colonial state, with all kinds of emerging issues, into a mostly modern nation. That is an accomplishment that very few other sub-Saharan African polities have managed. Nigeria, Kenya, Uganda, Ghana, Senegal, and the rest are still states (not nations), and overwhelmingly pre-institutional. In such states, the executive has overweening power, parties dominate, and legislatures are weak. Botswana transitioned from pre-institutional to institutional status relatively rapidly because of the consummate founding leadership of Sir Seretse Khama. Nujoma chose not to follow that route, but his successors helped to make Namibia the accomplished, if still internally unequal state that it is, with functioning political institutions and expectations among its citizens to match. Protests in Windhoek against the "Fishrot" revelations demonstrated the extent to which Namibians now hold their leaders and government to account.

Geingob and SWAPO's diminished electoral majority in 2019 in fact testified to Namibia's growing maturity as a politically more open, more pluralistic, and more integrated state than it was during its first twenty-nine years. It also indicated how relatively jaundiced the electors had become because of SWAPO's perceived marginalization of its main urban constituency, in Windhoek. Influence peddling also diminished SWAPO's legacy appeal. "The results were driven by corruption, governance failures and abuse of office," according to a careful observer of Namibia.[45]

All of these factors, plus the unfolding Fishrot scandal, contributed mate-rially to further SWAPO losses when regional and local government balloting occurred in late 2020. SWAPO suffered major defeats for the first time. Voters chose a young activist as mayor of Windhoek. In the fourteen regional authority contests, SWAPO's poll numbers dropped precipitously from 83 percent in 2015 to 57 percent in 2020. Two southern councils preferred a new party called the Landless People's Movement. A central council opted for the Independent Patriots for Change (organized by a charismatic SWAPO defector). A bellwether northwestern region voted for the People's Democratic Movement. In three other regions SWAPO forfeited its absolute majority. None of these alternative parties had much of a following before 2019, with SWAPO hitherto being, and behaving as, a hegemonic single party. It can no longer make such claims, especially with Geingob's diminished popularity.

Among other responsibilities, regional councils appoint three members each to parliament's upper house. Those appointments accordingly diminished SWAPO's control of the National Council (the upper house) and its parliamen-tary hegemony.

At the municipal level, of Namibia's fifty-seven jurisdictions, SWAPO maintained full control of only twenty (as against fifty-two previously), with its overall vote totals falling to 40 percent from 73 percent in 2015. After the crushing poll, SWAPO no longer runs Swakopmund and Walvis Bay, and its seats on the Windhoek council fell from twelve to five of fifteen.[46]

Namibia in 2022 is much more politically fragmented, and possibly more po-litically free, than ever before. (Additionally, Namibia has that African rarity, a free press.) SWAPO is no longer as thoroughly dominant as it was in the first two postliberation decades. Afrobarometer survey results show a precipitous de-cline in SWAPO's legitimacy. Several of the new political parties that are poised to continue gaining support in 2022 and beyond appeal to ethnic constituen-cies. The National Unity Democratic Organization is a Herero electoral vehicle. The United Democratic Front caters to Damara interests. The Landless People's Movement expresses the concerns of the Nama. The Congress of Independent Patriots draws its support from Windhoek and Walvis Bay, although the young activist mayor of Windhoek is allied with the Affirmative Repositioning Movement. The national project that Nujoma began to perfect, and Pohamba and Geingob sustained, seemed unfinished in 2021, and in danger in 2022 of becoming less Ovambo-led, and possibly more internally contentious, than ever before.[47]

After such two telling electoral failures, Geingob's stature as a leader obvi-ously suffered, especially as compared to the relatively unchallenged reigns of his (Oshiwambo-speaking) predecessors. Whether he can as a president steeped in and beholden to SWAPO's liberationist legitimacy move the party in a direction that is more open-minded, consultative, inclusionist, intolerant of corruption, and indeed transformational, is the key question for the remainder of Geingob's final time in office. Answers will determine whether Namibia delivers as much good governance to its people as Botswana, and effectively more positive outcomes than Zambia, Malawi, and South Africa. Amid the unfolding Fishrot corruption scandal, the afflictions of the Covid-19 pandemic, and diminished economic success, Geingob's ability to lead responsibly and successfully is bound sorely to be tested.

Fortunately for him and for Namibia, the French petroleum multinational firm Total and the Dutch/British firm Shell discovered sizable gas and oil deposits off the nation's shores in early 2022. Returns of more than $3.5 billion from an estimated 3 billion barrels of undersea petroleum could be realized in this decade. That bonanza immediately led the Geingob government to create a sovereign wealth fund, Norwegian style, into which all of the presumed bountiful proceeds will be deposited. Oil prices on world markets may fall, of course, and the kinds of rent-seeking that have bedeviled other petroleum-pumping endeavors in Africa may limit how much of the country's new wealth actually benefits Namibia's poor. Geingob has an opportunity to follow Botswana's favorable example, not Angola's, and to retrieve much of his lost popularity. Overall, the oil and gas discoveries may permit Namibia and Namibians to become much more prosperous than ever anticipated.

11
Leaders of Integrity Conquer Africa's Consummate Challenges

The destinies of the peoples of southern Africa have largely been, and are still, determined by the predilections and political strategies of those men and women who emerged after 1964 as its leaders. Structure and contingency are always important, but in the southern African and African contexts, national outcomes, the delivery of governmental services (governance) to citizens, and even personal welfare satisfaction levels have each been (and continue to be) supremely influenced by the designs and self-interests of the black rulers who replaced the white oppressors, and by the numerous heirs of those early liberation-era pioneers.

Nothing has influenced the life chances and resulting social and economic outcomes in southern Africa since independence more than the personal preferences of political elites and, invariably, those of the men (with one exception) who ruled the states of southern Africa in the post-colonial era. We can search for structural factors that drove one regime after another into governmental error. We can suggest complicated political reasons why policies went awry, why successive governments failed to deliver quantities and qualities of essential services to their constituents. We can blame the brutalities of apartheid, neglect and oppression at the hands of varied colonial overlords, the IMF's imposition of structural adjustment conditionalities, mining companies' corporate preferences, white farmer prejudices, shifting climatic disasters, and resistant ethnic competition for many of the flawed or self-serving responses of the past half century in southern Africa. But an exacting examination of the post-independent decades in southern Africa instead concludes that presidents and prime ministers were far more influential, even massively hegemonic, than they were and are in more settled countries such as those in Scandinavia, in the United Kingdom, or in the United States. In those latter places, usually it matters only marginally who—especially in parliamentary systems—is prime minister or president. Good and bad candidates often change places. From World War II to 2021, Italy experienced sixty-five prime ministers and governments, with good and bad decisions being made and unmade and with institutions beyond the executive sharing the wielding of power.

Overcoming the Oppressors. Robert I. Rotberg, Oxford University Press. © Oxford University Press 2023.
DOI: 10.1093/oso/9780197674208.003.0011

In Africa, however, as the preceding chapters in this book have demonstrated over and over, the character of the executives—their ambitions, senses of self, received information, understanding of world forces, and ideological biases— exerted a preponderant influence on the ways in which states organized them- selves, appealed for support, acculturated citizens, and attempted mightily (or by mischance) to alter human outcomes.

From the very first, executives in southern Africa's states (with two exemplary exceptions) privileged the exercise of arbitrary power over consensus building, acquiescence and conformity over open debate and dissent, and self-interest over the national interest. Becoming president by election in each of the English- speaking jurisdictions of southern Africa (as in much of the rest of sub-Saharan Africa) conferred an instantaneous ability to give orders, decide fairly arbitrarily to make nation-shattering decisions, and determine the ideological overarching superstructure for millions of constituents. (Kaunda even had his "Little Red Book.") Admittedly, presidents had to win the acquiescence of party central committees and politburos, but imprisoning dissenters and providing wells of patronage often made second-guessing a president treasonable, and physically and politically unwise.

Winning the presidency often equaled opportunity—in one case to build a democracy and produce positive economic and social results for voters and followers, in another to knit the brutalized fabric of a country together so that people could once again live productively side by side. Elsewhere, for most of the modern heads of state in southern Africa, gaining presidential office equaled a main chance to prosper at the expense of fellow citizens. A presidential acces- sion betokened a major opportunity to self-aggrandize by abusing the power of public office for private and family gain. Furthermore, in an atmosphere where sharing or alternating power was a distinctly foreign concept, zero-sum tenden- cies prevailed. One's time in office was a time "to eat"—to slay the fatted calf and live off of its accumulated meat and bones.

Fanon's coruscating critique of colonial rule and of black peoples' subju- gation formatively influenced many liberation struggles in Africa, as well as the Black Power movement of the United States; Stokely Carmichael was among those whose own endeavors gained strength from Fanon's analysis. Fanon was clear-eyed about how those being liberated might themselves turn on their own, and profit in terms of wealth and power from their own ascendance: "Before independence, the [new] leader generally embodies the aspirations of the people for independence, political liberty, and national dig- nity. But, as soon as independence is declared, far from embodying in concrete form the needs of the people in what touches bread, land and the restoration of the country . . . the leader will reveal his inner purpose: to become the general president of that country of profiteers impatient for their returns . . . the national bourgeoisie." Moreover, whether prescient in 1961 or simply cynical, Fanon goes on to suggest that the new leader's "honesty . . . crumbles away little by little." The leader, suggests Fanon, ranges himself more and more "on the side of the exploiters." The state therefore sank back "inevitably into neo-colonialist lines." Fanon's experience was in the French West Indies and metropolitan France, and in the 1950s in Algeria, Tunisia, Ethiopia, Ghana, Guinea, and Mali. The old colonial state would somehow manage, he saw, to regain effective economic and political influence through the bourgeois indigenous leaders who had obtained freedom for their subjects. He had little first-hand experience of southern Africa, where anti-colonial battles were only just commencing, and could not exactly predict how the old oppressors would be replaced by oppressors of the same ilk. Yet Fanon prophesied that the new leaders would enrich themselves at the expense of the poor, becoming immoral dictators.[1]

Only a few politicians (before several current ones) sought high office in southern Africa in order to make the lives of others better. Most sought to gain and then to hold onto power, and to accumulate cash and other advantages for families and relatives. Abrogating constitutional prohibitions and running for re-election after two terms sheltered wealth and protected presidents from being held liable by successors (as several of our cases were, any way).

The spoils of a presidency are rich, and tempting. The benefits of political primacy obviously are legion, as earlier chapters of this book have adumbrated. And, naturally, they are hard to forsake. Frederick Chiluba, Edgar Lungu, Bakili Muluzi, Peter Mutharika, and Jacob Zuma left office only reluctantly and are now judged less on how much they accomplished for their nations and more on what they stole and permitted others to pilfer.

This concluding chapter discusses the meaning and importance of leadership in southern Africa and Africa, and how to nurture leaders on the Khama model. It examines the kleptocratic scourge of corruption, which permeates all of the states of southern Africa, except Botswana. It discusses the nature of good governance and how the refusal to govern on behalf of all peoples leads to poorer material and spiritual outcomes, and even to state failure. This chapter tries to explain, once more, the essence of Botswana's exceptionality in Africa as well as in southern Africa.

The last part of this chapter looks ahead: What are the choices that leaders and their constituents have as two of the region's countries soon celebrate sixty years of independence and the others enter their fifth and fourth decades of freedom from colonial oppression? Where will responsible leadership take these collections of still disparate peoples? What roles will they, can they, play in the modern world?

The Trials of Leadership

Effective leadership separates endeavors that succeed from those that fail. Imaginative political leadership is especially salient, and too often lacking in the polities of the developing world. Effective and imaginative political leadership delivers stability and a dampening of intercommunal violence; inhibits conflicts between competing ethnic, religious, or other interest groups; encourages macroeconomic advances; attracts foreign investment; presides over job growth in the formal sector and poverty reduction more broadly; and enables entire peoples to advance socially.

Because the nations of the developing world often lack fully rooted systems of democracy, who leads makes more of a difference than it does in the developed parts of the planet. In the developed world, political institutions are a deeply implanted and frequently counterweights to even the most authoritarian-minded executives. In such places the necessity of good governance is taken for granted, the independence of judges is assumed, open economic practices are common, and democratic political cultures are of long standing. Not so in most lower-income and protean states, where survival is frequently at risk, poverty is endemic, and there is little or no experience with power sharing or power alternation. Thus, the value added of responsible, enlightened, leadership is much greater (and much more critical) in those regions of the globe where democratic political cultures and respect for political institutions are still rare and embryonic, where human capacity is more prospective than robust, and where educational opportunities continue constrained.

Indeed, it is precisely in less privileged polities that exemplary political leadership is more rather than less essential. Who leads makes a bigger difference in fractured, fragile, lower-income, scrabbling, nation-states than it does in stable, settled ones. Comparing outcomes between states, and even within many states, emphasizes that proposition. Matching leaders in the states of southern Africa over time shows the major difference that leaders made: Ramaphosa versus Zuma in South Africa; Kaunda versus Chiluba in Zambia, Chakwera versus Kamuzu Banda in Malawi, and Seretse Khama versus Ian Khama in Botswana, are illustrative pairings.

Effective leadership in any context is the employment largely of informal means to gather followers or potential followers to embrace, authorize, and promote initiatives that improve the likely success of an endeavor in which they are all mutually engaged. Better leaders show constituents the way forward and persuade them to follow. They cajole them. They mobilize collective efforts on behalf of mutually desirable objectives.

Gifted political leaders offer a vision of societal betterment, mobilize their adherents behind that vision, and themselves act with integrity and transparency so as to forward the initiatives that stem from an articulated program of social uplift. In order to accomplish such progressive goals, realize her vision in full, and advance the welfare of citizens, a committed leader listens assiduously to the voices of followers and opponents alike, courageously counters propositions that are self-serving, transparently puts the public interest before private interests, and carefully uses the legitimacy of her elected or inherited office to satisfy broad rather than self-contained accomplishments of value to an entire community. Great leaders, moreover, are emotionally intelligent, possessing empathy, "reflexive self awareness," and a "self-adeptedness" that connects them meaningfully and genuinely to their followers and enables them to gather support for their visions of change.[2]

Fundamental core competencies strengthen a political leader's ability to accomplish her goals and to produce uplifting social and economic outcomes for all. Foremost among the core competencies is the formulating of a comprehensive vision that enables positive collective national and personal growth and the accomplishment of material advances of benefit to current and future generations of citizens. Articulating a comprehensive and innovative vision, selling it well, and mobilizing citizens behind it are true tests of committed leaders. "Without projecting . . . a compelling and transforming vision, political leaders cannot guide their peoples and nations persuasively." In that case, they are "reduced to presiding or governing without really leading."[3]

Accomplished and courageous leaders enlarge their blueprint for the future into a vision that responds to the needs of constituents. But courageous leaders also need to explain how that vision will benefit citizens and constituents—to sell its virtues—and then to energize citizen backing for the objectives of the vision. Otherwise, little momentum ensues, and what might have been intended to be a transformational endeavor becomes a humdrum political exercise that falls flat. Skeptical Singaporeans supported Prime Minister Lee Kuan Yew's expansive vision only when they realized that his initiatives actually delivered real economic and social improvements, and that his recipe for major shifts in behavior and operating principles could indeed revolutionize the accomplishments of the city-state and their own personal life chances.

What Lee outlined, and the results that followed, were thoroughly transformational. Such leaders innovate, challenge settled expectations, motivate, and induce higher levels of performance than ever before. They raise community consciousness, engage citizens in endeavors that demand new emphases on national goals that are greater than individual interests, and enlarge the focus of their followers in ways hitherto unimagined.

Few leaders rise to the transformational level. The majority are instead transactional in their leadership operations and actions. They are incrementalists—traditional managers and "business as usual" politicians. In elected office, they most often focus on perpetuating themselves and their political parties, winning elections, and out-maneuvering rivals. Whereas transformational leaders alter the frameworks of existence, transactional leaders act within existing frameworks. Lee describes transactional leaders: "If you just do your sums—pluses, minuses, credit, debit—you are a washout."[4]

Embracing a comprehensive vision that energizes whole citizenries converts what otherwise might be a transactional national experience into something decidedly transformational. But stimulating followers also depends on several kinds of competencies that reinforce a political leader's message, and strengthen her legitimacy in the eyes of voters and a broad citizenry. Being genuinely inclusive is essential, as President Nelson Mandela demonstrated, to show that a leader cares about the nation, not just her own interest or ethnic group. The best leaders know how to listen, for the most committed followership comes as a result of a leader's empathy and her ability to be consultative and interactive.

Leaders who demonstrate integrity in every sphere, as well as intellectual honesty, and prudence in their utterings and manner, gain the trust of their citizens and enable a ruler and the inhabitants of a country to forge a modern social contract that benefits all. Moreover, consummate political leaders give their citizens a transcendent feeling of belonging to an enlarged enterprise; they provide a sense of purpose and purposefulness that enables persons to enjoy enhanced self-worth.[5]

These criteria help us to evaluate more than a half century's worth of political development in Botswana, Zambia, and Malawi, forty years of Zimbabwean rule, and thirty-plus years of political change in Namibia and South Africa. Today's living standards in each of the countries and objective measures such as life expectancies, infant mortality rates, GDP numbers, school persistence and graduation rates, Corruption Perceptions Index (CPI) ratings, and governance index rankings all reflect the impact of leadership successes and failures over several decades—both relatively against their own internal benchmarks and against the scores of their African peer group.

Except for Botswana, where far-seeing visionary leadership vaulted a desperately poor and underprivileged outlier into the top levels of African attainment, the others largely suffered from inadequate kinds of transactional leadership. South Africa after Mandela, for example, vastly underperformed its potential. So did the others, especially Zambia until late 2021. Malawi can accurately plead intense poverty and limited resources, but Kamuzu Banda and his corrupt successors depreciated what limited opportunities for social and economic improvement might have been successful. In each country the quality of leadership was telling. In Botswana's case (as the discussion in that chapter demonstrates) the sense of good governance that Khama instilled has lasted, to the enduring benefit of his people. In Zambia's case, those benighted presidents who followed Kaunda simply doubled down on his errors of commission and omission, leading inexorably to the autocracy of President Lungu. The successors to Kamuzu Banda in Malawi pledged to make a positive difference. But, as in the Zambian case, they misgoverned and proceeded to steal almost without impunity. Possibly President Chakwera will steer Malawi back along a more promising course and President Hichilema will do equally well in Zambia.

Such assertions emphasize why leaders are so important in those parts of the world where political institutions are imperfectly established and where democratic political cultures have as yet to be implanted. When Kaunda and UNIP abolished political parties other than their own and Kamuzu Banda declared himself president for life in a single-party state, there were no robust political institutions to cry foul. Civil society was embryonic in both cases. Moreover, the security forces and party-sponsored thugs in both countries were heavy handed. In Malawi, even mild religiously inspired dissidents were imprisoned, thrashed, and killed.

Likewise, Zimbabwe—a well-educated and prosperous place at the time of independence—first grew economically and educationally because of Mugabe's initial inclinations. Then his regime's ruthlessness and ethnic cleansing proclivity, as demonstrated in Matabeleland and afterward, became the national norm. Corruption levels escalated, white farmers became scapegoats and political fodder, and presidential obstinacy and perversity drove a country to its knees, with bouts of million, billion, and trillion percent inflation. His successors are little better. Impoverished Zimbabwe today is what self-indulgent and narcissistic leaders have made it.

South Africa and Namibia are also products of leaders who refused to follow Mandela's example, discarded consensus politics, and allowed corrupt dealings to replace the inclusive model that Mandela had espoused (and that Khama and Botswana had proved effective). In both cases, the political institutional check that parliaments should have played were neutered by party structures and the hegemonic power that party heads exercised in their own, rather than the public's, interest.

Ultimately, as we review the political and economic vicissitudes of southern Africa since independence—since the overthrow of white oppressors—we can pinpoint particular errors of leadership that were costly: nationalizing the copper mines at the wrong time in the wrong way without any appreciation of better options for Zambia; and refusing capriciously to permit Malawian farmers to grow cash crops such as peanuts, once a rewarding pursuit in the Central Province, are but two examples. Even more calamitous was Mugabe's mindless decapitation of white-run agriculture, a profitable and productive sector of an otherwise flailing national economy that employed 400,000 indigenous Zimbabweans and provided fiscal multipliers and societal ballast that ferrochrome and gold and diamond exploitation did not.

Embryonic political cultures that might have been massaged and adapted to local needs so as to uplift Zambia, Malawi, Namibia, and Zimbabwe were rejected by key politicians, to be replaced by several varieties of autocracy and self-serving decision-making. This was even true for South Africa, a long-established nation (whereas the others were newly imagined and newly created) where citizens awaited post-independence social and economic dividends that never arrived. The political elites and the empowered new black entrepreneurial class pocketed most of the rewards (as in Namibia) and redistributed too little to the majority of their fellow citizens. These unfortunate results followed from the leadership initiatives of politicians who were more interested in themselves and their backers and associates than in the welfare of citizens. Each of these leaders might have looked over their shoulders at Botswana, but each "knew better" and calculated his/her responsibilities to citizens very differently.

We can say that these were human failings and that Khama's and Masire's methods represented human successes. But Khama and Masire were also intellectually honest as well as being materially honest and straightforward. The others, even gentle and well-intentioned Kaunda, proved incapable of learning from the experiences of others on the continent and farther afield, something of which Khama became acutely conscious. Muluzi had the benefit of talented and non-partisan advisors, as did Chiluba, but both ignored tutelage and recommendations that interfered with their own instincts to accumulate. In twenty-first-century Zambia, Sata and both Mutharikas behaved in much the same way despite Peter Mutharika's academic background and long professional experience in the United States.

Khama, perhaps because of his chiefly heritage, was acutely self-aware of an existential responsibility to better the lives and prospects of his people. Heads of other countries uttered the same verities, but only occasionally embodied similar senses of purpose and sovereign obligation. Mbeki sometimes spoke as if he felt a burden of paramountcy, but with less conviction.

Transformational and Transactional Leadership

Hence this book's exploration of what leaders have and have not done to advance the welfare of their citizens. Earlier chapters revealed that many leaders lacked Khama's and Masire's clear-eyed vision of how to make progress and improve the lives of their constituents. Most were concerned primarily with ensuring that they or their parties would win the next election; Khama and Masire were intent on transforming all aspects of their admittedly small-scale national enterprise.

By focusing on staying in power rather than on delivering political goods, others were concerned to limit rather than to enhance political participation (as in early Malawi and Zambia, and throughout all of Zimbabwe's independent decades). Aside from Botswana, and even in South Africa until recently, ruling parties claimed monopolies on wisdom; they knew what was right for their peoples.

Each, except for Khama, was a consummate transactionalist. True, Kamuzu Banda was as well a reactionary when it suited him and his acute sense of self-importance; Chipembere only too tardily realized what an arrogant traditionalist and anti-transformationalist he had recruited for Malawi. Kaunda had some transformational aspirations but could never chart an unimpeded path toward their realization.

The rest were incrementalists through and through. They cut deals, took advantage of their high positions whenever and wherever they could, and focused their political talents on winning elections and moving their cronies into positions of significance. Many were unscrupulous as well as being greedy. Whatever did an American law professor think he was doing when he tried to keep his dead brother "alive" in order to cheat a vice president (and Malawi's peoples) of her constitutional rights? Why did Mbeki fly in the face of scientific consensus to adopt and promote errant conspiracy theories about HIV/AIDS?

Mandela was no saint, but he could separate wrong from right, which hardly any of his non-Botswanan compatriots apparently could. And only Khama and Mandela gave their peoples (and all Africans) a sense of being a part of a noble enterprise of exceptionality. South Africans stood tall thanks to Mandela's example and his leadership. So did and do the peoples of Botswana (despite the slippages of Khama's son and heir). Zambia and Malawi may be entering those hallowed precincts now. But in South Africa's case, Mandela was saddened by Mbeki's failure to leave his ego and his sense of self-importance behind, and then was revolted by Zuma's acquiescence in state capture and surreal sleaze. Southern Africans have been poorly served by most of their leaders, even by the non-flamboyant presidents of Namibia.

In most analytical settings, emphasis would be placed as much on those interests and interest groups who competed for national prominence as on the mindsets and self-empowering political objectives of the individuals who gained and then exercised authority within southern African state boundaries. But, because of the inordinate impress of leadership visions and leadership endeavors on daily life within the countries of southern Africa, and because the political, economic, and social trajectories of each of the countries that we have discussed at length depend for future direction on executive actions and initiatives, we cannot pretend that leadership agency has not thus far been a dominating force within southern Africa. Entire sets of results—whether constituents go hungry, succumb to pestilence and disease, attend school, hold jobs (and which jobs?), are able to purchase sufficient food staples, and participate effectively in politics, are heavily influenced by the policy choices made every day by the persons who preside over the countries of southern Africa.

Much of Africa, and southern Africa except for Botswana and South Africa, is still largely pre-institutional, with political cultures that disperse little power away from the executive. Being pre-institutional means that political institutions such as legislatures and judiciaries, civil society, and the fourth journalistic estate, are still embryonic. Such states are not yet fully nations; they are still building their nations (as Seretse Khama in Botswana consciously strove to do) out of the multiple ethnic components situated within their colonially derived borders. The concept of being a part of a nation, and of professing more than loyalty to a language group, is still abuilding. Consequently, executive authority carries more weight and the self-interests of heads of state overwhelm any understanding of a commonweal.

Self-interest, and kleptocratic behavior, can easily dominate when a sense of mutual purpose is absent. What Khama accomplished over fewer than two decades of masterful leadership was to give his people a stake in their government as their government, not as the exclusive pursuit of political elites lording over them from on high. By advancing the public interest as the highest and best goal of government, and by making corrupt dealings the exception rather than the societal expectation or norm, he was able to introduce an ethos of good governance that concomitantly gave political institutions other than the executive importance and heft. Only a few other post-colonial African countries have achieved this same level of neo-Nordic political development, and, aside from the historically separate case of South Africa, no other southern African state has yet established a national purpose, a national identity, and a political culture with institutional safeguards on the model pioneered by Botswana.

Good Governance

Good leadership creates good governance, positive service delivery outcomes for a territory's inhabitants. As Khama's decisive role in Botswana's evolution from poor protectorate to wealthy nation suggests, transformational leaders establish beneficent political cultures that are conducive to the growth of positive practices of governance. Lee did the same in Singapore and, had he stayed in the presidency in South Africa for a second term, Mandela might have made an equal contribution. Kaunda (like Nyerere in Tanzania, Jomo Kenyatta in Kenya, Nkrumah in Ghana, and Félix Houphoüet-Boigny in Côte d'Ivoire) might easily have done the same, but each flubbed his great opportunity to implant the kinds of governance regimes that, arguably, would have profited his citizens and provided the kinds of strong political, economic, and social platforms upon which great institutions could have been built. Instead, almost alone among his contemporaries (except for those in Mauritius and Cape Verde) Khama guided his peoples down paths of probity and public service that led to estimable political goods provisioning and among the highest per capita incomes on mainland Africa.

Governance is performance, the delivery of quantities and qualities of essential services (political goods) by a constituted authority at national, provincial, and municipal levels. Citizens rightly expect that governmental bodies exist principally to ensure ever better and broader kinds of services. A sense of social contract now prevails in nearly all modern political jurisdictions that implies, for example, that the modern state may govern the governed and its rulers rule only if they secure the consent of the governed—a consent that is contingent on the state meeting the essential needs and desires of its inhabitants.[6]

Those essential needs are the political goods of security and safety, a justiciable rule of law, accountability and transparency, open political participation, respect for and the observance of fundamental human rights and civil liberties, sustainable economic development (including a stable money and banking system, effective and accessible arteries of commerce, and access to modern methods of communication such as broadband and mobile telephones), and a panoply of human development attributes such as educational opportunity, medical care, potable water supplies, modern sanitation, and more. Modern states are constituted to provide such political goods, and to the extent or not they do, we say that a polity is well or less well governed. Indeed, rather than estimate subjectively whether a political entity is thus supplying the political goods that its inhabitants demand and require, I established a published formal measurement scheme (originally the Index of African Governance and now the Ibrahim Index of African Governance) in 2007 that scores the extent to which the governments of Africa actually work for their peoples, and supply political goods.[7]

I argue, too, that governance is a much better and fuller optic than "democracy" with which to gauge a political jurisdiction's ability and willingness to serve its citizens and produce better lives and livelihood outcomes with and for them. "Democracy" is hard to measure objectively, and subjective methods of approximating the quality and quantity of a nation's democratic practice are supremely prone to selection and observer bias.

The perceived difficulty of deciding conclusively whether, say, Malawi or Zambia were more democratic, and to what extent and in what areas, led me with successive cohorts of my Harvard Kennedy School graduate classes to devise a more comprehensive, more objective, assessing mechanism that could tell us both the relative rankings of countries anywhere on a citizen satisfaction scale and, more important, could diagnose in what granular respects a country was falling short. Subjective inspections of democratic procedures and efforts could not. For example, a proxy for more or less election fairness is difficult to construct. So is more or less respect for fundamental human freedoms, tolerance of dissent, and the like. Governance, with its original fifty-seven major categories of analysis and many more sub-categories, and with a focus on outputs, not inputs such as budgetary allocations, gives us a comprehensive ability to examine what governments do and fail to do.

According to the 2019 iteration by the Ibrahim Index of African Governance of my approach, Botswana's scores from 2010 through the Index's latest year show a consistent 66–67 score out of 100 across the decade. (It ranked 5th of 54 in 2019, overall.) South Africa's rating fell slightly from 66.7 to 65.8 and it placed 6th. Namibia (7th) was greatly improved in 2019, from 61.7 to 65.1. Zambia (21st) started at 52 in 2010, rose to 55 in 2015, and fell back to 52 in 2019. Malawi (23rd) over the same period has retreated from 52.8 to 51.5. Zimbabwe (33rd) began the decade at 38.7 and ended it at 46.1. (Mauritius scores at the top with 77, Cape Verde rates 75, and the Seychelles follows with 72 in 2019.)[8]

As we have seen in earlier chapters, Botswana scores highly; Khama and his successors have delivered estimable quantities and qualities of political goods. Relatively to other African entities, so have Namibia and South Africa over at least two decades, despite all of the issues that previous chapters have examined. Zambia's ranking plummeted during Lungu's lamentable presidency (for reasons explained in chapter 3), Malawi has consistently rated mediocre (although Chakwera's incumbency may elevate its scores), and dictatorial Zimbabwe has always placed near the bottom of the Indexes because of Mugabe's despotism and the corrupt authoritarian tendencies of his tough successor.

These measurement methodologies, and a number of complementary attempts to assess the provision of particular political goods to citizens, reveal the extent to which the ruling classes of southern Africa (Botswana excepted) have largely and consistently denied their assorted citizenries opportunities to prosper, to be schooled, to enjoy good health, and to progress as fully and as rapidly as their counterparts elsewhere in the world. Freedom House's Freedom in the World index, a subjective instrument that measures a complementary proxy for democracy, shows Zimbabwe as not free, Malawi and Zambia as partly free, and Botswana, Namibia, and South Africa as free.[9]

The UN Development Program's Human Development Index (HDI), which combines life expectancy, expected and mean years of schooling, and gross national incomes per capita into a composite evaluation of well-being (and an approximation of governance) starkly shows both the accomplishment differences within southern Africa and the relatively poor scorings of Africa compared to the rest of the world's countries. Norway leads this latest iteration of the HDI, followed by Ireland, Switzerland, and Hong Kong. In Africa, the best performers are the island states of Mauritius and the Seychelles in 66th and 67th place, respectively. Botswana is next in Africa, ranking 100th of 189 countries, followed in southern Africa by South Africa 114th, Namibia 130th, Zambia 146th, Zimbabwe 150th, and Malawi 174th.[10] The contribution of leadership in those countries to economic returns for at least the elites was a big part of these rankings.[11]

The 2020 Legatum Prosperity Index, which is similar to the African Index of Governance in its categories of analysis, rated Botswana 82nd of 167 countries, South Africa 87th, Namibia 88th, Zambia 123rd, Malawi 132nd, Zimbabwe 143rd. (The United States was ranked 18th on this list and Mauritius 44th and the Seychelles 51st.)[12] Again, GDP results influence the ratings.

As these indexes, and the findings of a plethora of similar rating and scoring methods show, Botswana has performed acceptably for its citizens. So has South Africa and Namibia, but given South Africa's head start nationally, its access to wealth and experience, and its infrastructurally advanced capacity, South Africa's relative performance underwhelms according to these several assessment methods, probably because of the governance weaknesses perpetrated by Mbeki and Zuma as well as its negative economic GDP growth in recent years. Additionally, these different evaluation instruments all underscore the proposition that good governance produces beneficial outcomes—across several dimensions—for citizens. Furthermore, analyzing the detailed nature of "governance" allows governments, civil societies, donors, and researchers to ascertain exactly in what areas a government is performing well and in which areas it merits improvement.

State Failure and Leadership Responsibility

Poor scores of governance also indicate polities that are likely to fail. There is a compelling operative syllogism that opens with a state providing fewer and fewer essential services to its citizens. The state then loses legitimacy in the eyes of a minority or of a section of the population that feels deprived of good governance and, often, believes itself discriminated against. That leads to insurgency, separatism, and—in time—the outbreak of civil conflict. In 2022, the Central African Republic, the Democratic Republic of Congo, Ethiopia, Nigeria, and South Sudan were failed states by the criteria elaborated in my previous detailed exploration these phenomena.[13] Countries such as Chad, Guinea-Bissau, and Zimbabwe exist on the cusp of failure, but are not yet quite "failed" despite—as my theory explains—delivering only paltry quantities and qualities of political goods to their constituents. But they do not harbor full-blown civil wars, a decisive indicator of insecurity and thus failure. Nigeria was a special case of failure in 2021 and 2022 because of the several violent civil conflicts (including the Boko Haram emergency) within its midst and, especially, because of the increasing insecurity of citizens across all regions of the populous polity.[14]

According to my definition of how failure may be determined, there are only a few "strong" states in Africa—the Botswanas, South Africas, Ghanas, and Senegals of the continent. Aside from the failures and near failures, most of the entities of sub-Saharan Africa are classified as "weak," with the scale of weakness shading naturally from "almost strong" to "almost failed." New leadership efforts may make Malawi less "weak" than under its several corrupt heads of state. The same should happen as Zambia under Hichilema overcomes its despotic interlude under Lungu. To reiterate, these categories of analysis are helpful more if they are used to diagnose problematic areas and to seek ways to fix shortfalls than when they are used to label adversely and to denigrate national strivings.

Governments exist in theory and in practice to serve their citizens. Otherwise, they act illegitimately. In Africa, of course, the actual nation-state experiment (as this book shows) has produced mixed results, with some governments (including several discussed in this book) prioritizing outcomes for leaders over results for citizens. In Africa as a whole, as in southern Africa, most nation-states have over six decades served their constituents inadequately while simultaneously benefiting and enriching governing elites. Their Gini-coefficient showings are all at the very high, high, or medium (Malawi and Zimbabwe) parts of the Gini continuum, meaning that economic returns skew against the majority of residents.[15]

That last proposition follows from the observation that many of the leaders of Africa and southern Africa favor their own interests and the interests of their dominant political parties and the preferences of their families, their lineages, or their ethnic groups over the general public interest. If they come from a majority or dominant ethnic or language group, they often single out the members of such a special constituency for favorable consideration, as Kamuzu Banda did in Malawi, Chiluba and his successors, especially Lungu, did in Zambia, as Mugabe always did in Zimbabwe, and as Nujoma and Pohamba did in Namibia. The social contract between the ruled and rulers breaks down (as it has in southern Africa) when the governors are seen as unfairly favoring a particular ethnic congeries for jobs and opportunities and denying equal chances to others, a discriminatory inclination that often leads to state breakdown and violent conflict. It can even lead to the possibility of state failure.

Just as some Russians remember harsh Soviet rule fondly, and some Brazilians still recall twenty years of dictatorship with nostalgia, so this generation's citizens in countries such as Zambia and Zimbabwe, and possibly earlier under the Mutharikas and Kamuzu Banda in Malawi, may feel and have felt ill-served by their new ruling classes. Yet incomes generally are higher, except in Zimbabwe;

schooling opportunities, and medical responses and social services are largely greater than they were, especially in Botswana and South Africa. Most of all, where perceived oppression continues, the oppressors are locally bred, and (usually) more easily replaced. These are all continuing questions, however, and ones that southern Africa's growing middle class, southern Africa's ever more vibrant civil societies, and its better governments are well placed to address.

In summary, high governance scores are correlated with higher per capita incomes, better educational and public health outcomes, lower rates of crime, and the absence of internal conflict. Likewise, the prevalence of civil conflict(s) reflect declining or persistently low levels of governance, low scores on the subcategories of political participation, respect for human rights, rule of law, and human development, and little sustainable economic progress. The objectively least well governed countries in Africa—the countries with the lowest governance scores—are also the least free, the least democratic, the most internally conflicted, the most prone to insurgencies (Islamist or other), and the ones with the most annual deaths in civil wars. Furthermore, all of these last countries are wildly corrupt, according to the CPI. Indeed, as the prior chapters have shown, corrupt southern African countries by definition lack transparency and accountability. The more corrupt they are the more they deprive their constituents of the opportunity to prosper, to be safe and secure, to go to school and be educated through at least secondary school, to receive reasonably advanced medical care, to have access to potable water and waterborne sanitation, and to be able to convey agricultural products to markets using good, safe roads.

The Corruption Curse

Corruption is much more than a moral failing. As the abuse of public positions or public trust for private gain, corruption greatly distorts priorities, privileges rents over the commonweal and, by shoveling public funds into personal pockets, deprives schools, hospitals, agricultural extension services, road making, bridge repairing, and myriad other essential services of substantial revenues. Loss to annual national GDP of 2 or 3 percent is the common estimate of corruption's toll on economic growth achievements; the World Bank estimates that more than $1 trillion is paid out each year in bribes. The World Economic Forum says that the global annual cost of corruption is about 5 percent of total planetary GDP, possibly as much as $2.6 trillion. Global Financial Integrity suggests that $7.8 trillion was diverted illegally from emerging economies between 2004 and 2013 as a result of tax evasion, graft, and other criminal activity.[16] Southern Africa's comparable total is only a fraction of that amount, but certainly billions of dollars are lost each year in the sub-region to varieties of peculation, influence peddling, and rent-seeking. Mugabe's impoverishment of his state and its people is merely the most obvious example of meretricious kleptocratic behavior. So is Zuma's grifting and graft, dating from the 1990s and continuing throughout his presidency. Cashgate showed what forensic accountants could discover of plunder by parliamentarians and cabinet ministers in Malawi. Massive bribing of responsible ministers in Namibia to secure fishing quotas reveals the kinds of illicit behavior that had long been buried in public.

Previous chapters have detailed much of this incessant corruption, and its economic harm. But we may never know exactly how much has been stolen, how many worthy projects were stalled or sidelined because of corrupt alternatives and opportunities. All we know for certain is that nearly all earlier presidents and prime ministers in the region beyond Botswana since 1964 have stuck their hands in the till for personal or party gain, and that they would now do so again. Zuma's retirement estate in KwaZulu-Natal is a good example of how to parlay a lofty elected position into (immense) illicit and intense personal reward. Another is Chiluba's use of state funds to purchase suits and shoes, and his wife's attempt to walk off with state silver, carpets, and the like.

Corrupt polities can only persist if heads of state reward associates and followers with opportunities to steal as forms of patronage, as over and over again in Zimbabwe, and as in Muluzi and the Mutharikas' Malawi. But because such patronage binds even officers and perhaps soldiers to back a corrupt president or prime minister, whole critical areas of governmental activity may be neglected—to the detriment of economic growth, the equitable distribution of resources to villagers or urban dwellers, steady supplies of medicines in hospitals, and so on. In some of our countries, effective responses to the coronavirus pandemic were also reduced thanks to pilfering by officers of the state.

Many pages of this book allude to or explicitly mention instances of grand corruption—the (usually) kleptocratic maneuvers that slipped official funds into private pockets. The theft of Marange diamonds by Mugabe and his cronies, including the current president and vice president, is but one egregious example of padding one's own income at the expense of a nation. But, less obvious and equally damaging, is what Muluzi did to take control of lucrative sugar and trucking monopolies without proper tenders or competition. Then there were all of the innumerable construction contracts that were allocated systematically and spuriously to friends of heads of state in several countries. Malawi's political elite profited from hoarding pilfered maize from the national marketing board and then selling tons of it for inflated prices during a massive famine. South African political leaders took kickbacks on sizable defense contracts and, almost everywhere, clever tenderpreneurship has contributed to higher prices for consumers, to projects unfinished or shoddily completed, to waste, and to immense private gain. Chinese-sponsored efforts proved no exception.

Nothing contributed more to the decay of southern African politics than the focus of ruling elites on what could be gained personally—rather than for how an entire nation might be elevated—by governmental actions that the state (and its leaders) controlled. This meant elaborate projects primarily to collect kickbacks, ventures that benefited politicians without helping the country, the granting of mineral concessions in exchange for large sums that could be deposited in personal accounts, and even contracting for such supplies as unneeded school exercise books in order collect profits from over-invoicing. A telling example is the massive spiral staircase in the thirteenth palace that Kamuzu Banda was constructing when he was voted out of office. Italian workmen in the palace in Lilongwe told me that Cecilia Kadzamira, Banda's consort, insisted on redoing the perfectly well crafted banisters of the staircase eighteen times in order to collect kickbacks over and over.

Corruption corrodes a state, shredding its moral fabric, and undermining its fundamental legitimacy. When everything is on sale to high bidders, and honest dealings are rare or nonexistent, citizens lose faith (as they should) in the fundamental purpose of the state. The social contract fades, nation-building deteriorates, and citizens strive for themselves alone, not for some collective interest. Trust vanishes, as does the sense of belonging to a common enterprise that defines stronger forms of leadership.

Botswana's limited corruption has strengthened the state's ties to its citizens, contributed significantly to its remarkable growth trajectory over fifty years, and managed steady and remarkable returns to citizens from gem diamond mining that would under a more corrupt regime have been stolen or dissipated. Seretse Khama, unwittingly copying Lee in Singapore, realized that the practice of corruption would weaken his young and fragile state, preventing it from maturing in a healthy manner. He learned from the mistakes of others in Africa, and also realized that conveying a sense of and belief in integrity would solidly pave the only possible road to prosperity and the achievement of a solid stature in the world of less-responsible nations. Personal integrity was essential, to send a strong message, to strengthen legitimacy, and to remove the kinds of temptation that would, if his ministers succumbed, have led to the destruction of the regime's compact with the people.

Other rulers and other political systems were more intent, as we have seen, on plunder and arranging situations conducive to plunder. Kaunda may not have pilfered himself, but his associates did (probably much more extensively than he ever appreciated). Once sleaze was tolerated implicitly, or at least not punished brutally (as in Singapore) there were few limits (despite a well-managed Anti-Corruption Commission). That was the case in Malawi, and in South Africa from the Mbeki era onward. Fortunately, in contemporary South Africa Ramaphosa has been struggling to curb the avariciousness of his African National Congress colleagues after their many years of successful thieving.

In the 2019 CPI rankings, Zimbabwe took up the rear with a score of 24 (out of 100) in 158th place (of 180 nations); Malawi, 31 and 123rd; Zambia, 34 and 113th; South Africa, 44 and 70th; and Namibia, 52 and 56th filled out the southern African list. That Zimbabwe ranks twenty-two places above the absolute bottom of the list means that places like Somalia, South Sudan, Sudan, Equatorial Guinea, Guinea-Bissau, both Congos, and Burundi are just that much more corrupt even than Zimbabwe, with scores from 20 down to 9. Malawi's ranking just below Zambia shows the extent to which the presidencies of the Mutharika brothers (in Malawi) and Sata and Lungu (in Zambia) emphasized purloining from the public. Ratings for South Africa and Namibia may not fully capture recent revelations, but scores for both fell considerably from previous annual compilations. Botswana retained its second-from-the-top place on the list (61 and 34th) among all of the African performers, after the Seychelles, 66 and 27th.[17] This is a continuing tribute to the ethos that Seretse Khama created and passed on to his successors; it has endured despite periodic attempts by potentially greedy politicians to seek greater flexibility in their dealings and aspirations.

A Crisis of Contemporary Political Leadership

Across southern Africa, as throughout the rest of the continent, there have been too few leaders of the stature, vision, and transformational accomplishments of Khama, Masire, and Mandela. Possibly Hichilema, Chakwera, and Ramaphosa will emerge as successful transformationalists, but just as the brightness of potential leadership stars like Prime Minister Abiy Ahmed in Ethiopia and Tanzania's President John Magufuli soon dimmed as they turned authoritarian, and lost their stature and legitimacy, so we must pause to see whether Hichilema, Chakwera, and Ramaphosa can consolidate their power and succeed in governing their respective countries in pathbreaking and leadership-ennobling manners.

Ramaphosa is more of a known quantity, and his auguries are positive (as chapter 7 has indicated), but he may not be able to overcome sclerotic forces within the ANC that seek daily to constrain his forward-looking initiatives. Hichilema and Chakwera are far less politically tested. Moreover, all three heads of state, and the others, still have to contend with the pernicious lasting consequences of the coronavirus pandemic.

Their predecessors everywhere but in Botswana lacked integrity (Mandela excluded), and lacked the navigating skills, self-mastery, and robust levels of analytical and emotional intelligence that characterized the approaches of Khama, Masire, Mogae, and Mandela and enabled each of those presidents to tap into and then enlarge the authentic needs of their citizens. None was ostentatious. None abused authority for personal gain or to distribute patronage prerequisites and other emoluments. All were—as Masire wrote about Khama—thoroughgoing democrats, observing both the spirit and the letter of rules of law and consultative practices.[18] Each, Mandela possibly excepted, brought substantial material gain to their country's citizens by emphasizing good governance procedures, by emphasizing the sanctity of the rule of law, and by eschewing corruption.

Botswana is the southern African and African country where leadership behavior and leadership guidance made an extraordinarily positive difference in term of outcomes—in terms of creating raised living standards and of giving citizens a sense of belonging to a larger and uplifting enterprise. (Mugabe is the poster boy for the negative impact of leadership.) Both Khama and Masire, carried forward by Mogae, further emphasized the importance of "tolerance" as a mode of governance, of accepting differences among Botswana's peoples, and of coping with dissimilar patterns in the rest of Africa.

The peoples of each of the other country experiences examined in this book suffered under leaders less accomplished and less public-spirited than those in Botswana. Following Mandela but deviating from his model, Mbeki and Zuma ignored the key lessons of his leadership from 1990 to 1999 and proceeded to govern transactionally and narrowly. They displayed little self-mastery during and about the HIV/AIDS epidemic or with regard to the acquisitive instincts of their associates and cronies. Indeed, in South Africa, Malawi, and Zambia, escalating levels of corruption sapped the moral energies of national populations, inhibited new investment and marginalized existing entrepreneurialism, and forfeited the progressive advances that might have brought real rewards in the decades before the coronavirus pandemic arrived so devastatingly.

Mbeki chose at first to downplay the importance of HIV/AIDS, denied that it was transmitted sexually, and explored preposterous alternative causes and remedies, hence delaying treatment possibilities for myriad sufferers. He ignored the seriousness of Mugabe's crimes against humanity in Zimbabwe and the social and economic deterioration occurring there and, indeed, even that occurring within his own country. He overlooked mounting corruption scandals in South Africa, paving the way for Zuma to incapacitate the nation and devalue its citizens. Zuma permitted the whole to be "captured" by a cabal of sharp-eyed mercenaries intent on merciless plunder. Under Zuma, now hopefully to be righted by Ramaphosa, poverty spread, the wage gap between rich and poor blacks widened, educational and medical outcomes deteriorated, crime rates grew, electrical power availability fell strikingly, housing starts were few, and xenophobia and interethnic conflicts became more common. Tragically, the sense of belonging and nation-hood that Mandela injected into South Africa's body politic was eroded, if not erased, by the Mbeki and Zuma failures of leadership. Ramaphosa has much to retrieve and regain, but with limited time and the Omicron and subsequent co-ronavirus variants to battle.

Much the same can certainly be said about the other troubled countries of southern Africa, certainly about Malawi, where Chakwera has much quickly to accomplish if he is set his nation securely on a sure path to harmony and growth. Zambia's future is now much more propitious, thanks to the ouster of Lungu and the positive rhetoric of Hichilema. President Hage Geingob in Namibia took office with much promise, and was re-elected on the basis of the progres-sive improvements that he had begun. But the spread of corruption, as in all of the other countries, bar Botswana, has compromised even his governance achievements in Namibia. Nor can the Mnangagwa government claim more than a modest transactional shift from the lamentable long rule of Mugabe, his mentor and predecessor. When a country is steeped in graft and its population badly beaten down (when not all of its members have fled elsewhere), the wages of sinful leadership become apparent—again with no end in sight.

A central issue for leaders everywhere in the developing world, and in southern Africa, is how they most effectively and most sensibly can lift their peoples up. Sometimes that is neither their interest nor their concern; venal leaders instead consciously seek and then use political office mendaciously to criminalize the state in order to securitize the hold of a cadre or cabal. More often, leaders in Africa want good outcomes for their peoples, but together with especially good outcomes for themselves and their cohort. With equal frequency, African heads of state may be well meaning, but practice so few of the arts of modern leadership and governance that they fall prey to persuasive panaceas or formulistic recipes that little advance their citizens socially, and politically.[19]

According to World Bank, the effects of the coronavirus pushed the eco-nomic performance of the countries of southern Africa deeply into the negative column in 2020 and 2021: Botswana by 9 percent and South Africa by 8 percent. Namibia's growth, the Bank says, receded by 8 percent in 2020. Malawi edged up by 1 percent in 2020. Zambia went backward in 2020 by 5 percent. Zimbabwe slumped by 20 percent in 2020.[20] Each of these economies was expected origi-nally to grow in 2022, but the spread of the pandemic has made the parlous per-formance of these countries more lasting. Moreover, populations are all growing by greater percentages, making job finding immensely difficult.

The emerging urban middle classes of southern Africa seek better leader-ship and stronger governance than their fathers and mothers experienced. They seek robust rules of law, much more transparency and accountability and much less corruption, more educational resources, and fuller attention to redressing the social and economic deficits within their countries. They want positive improvements and recognize that a revamped and more responsive leadership is required in order to upgrade the lax performances of nearly all of their national governments. According to surveys by the Pew Research Center, the members of Africa's increasingly powerful and numerous middle classes consciously seek the material and spiritual benefits that their counterparts in Asia, Europe, and the Americas enjoy.[21] Middle-class southern Africans have attended universities and been employed outside of Africa; social media gives them intimate connections to the rest of the world. Thanks to mobile telephones, Africa is no longer apart, or cut off. African aspirations, accordingly, are those of their peers elsewhere. How to compel political decision-makers to serve the middle class as well as satisfying the popular demands of less sophisticated, less worldly segments of a nation's total population is one of the vexing problems of today's Africa.

Building Leadership Capacity

More gifted leaders could remedy the ills of the continent and its peoples, especially in the diverse polities and societies of southern Africa. Thus far, recruitment methods have been haphazard. Even in Botswana, presidents more than parties or the electorate as a whole have chosen heirs apparent, and made them vice presidents before in time they automatically became presidents. That mechanism worked effectively when Masire groomed Mogae as his successor, to the annoyance of other politically ambitious members of the ruling BDP, but not when Mogae passed the baton to Ian Khama and Khama to Masisi.

Elsewhere, Mnangagwa removed his longtime mentor in a coup to prevent Mugabe from trying to convey position and power to "Grasping Grace," his much-disliked First Lady. And little fundamental change has since ensued. Zambians and Malawians largely followed a modified Botswanan method in selecting successors to Chiluba and Muluzi (who had both come to prominence after voters in both countries had rejected the founding fathers and their liberationist political movements). Namibia kept its succession within the dominant political party, but significantly passed the reins to a longtime insider who stemmed from outside the nation's most populous ethnic group.

By the 1990s, if not well before, politicians, critics, and researchers all acknowledged the decisively important contribution of the leadership factor to African national success, or something less. Indeed, as earlier paragraphs in this chapter have emphasized, the more leadership was acknowledged as a significant political variable, the more reforming the selection and training of political leaders appeared essential.

Consequently, almost twenty years ago I gathered together a group of experienced and highly placed African political leaders to attempt to think through how best to build capacity for African leadership development. In the aftermath of Mugabe's cataclysmic abuse of authority in Zimbabwe; the atrocities of Idi Amin in Uganda and Emperor Jean-Bédel Bokassa in Central Africa; and the smothering of people's voices in Kenya, Uganda, Guinea, Equatorial Guinea, and Chad; mayhem in Somalia; Marxist brutality in Ethiopia; and the enormous excesses of military rule in Nigeria, the need for a more responsible and public obliging class of leader became urgent. At least so it seemed to me.

In order to check and critique my own analysis of Africa's perceived leadership failings at a time when I was both espousing the need for better leadership in and for sub-Saharan Africa and also beginning to articulate a theory of governance (rather than democracy) as a way to calibrate Africa's successes and failures, I turned for advice and recommendations to well-respected, thoughtful, former President Julius Nyerere of Tanzania, and then to President Mogae of Botswana, with whom I was then in close contact. Nyerere and I met in Arusha and spent many hours agreeing that the leadership problem was grave and that establishing some kind of academy to train future political leaders made estimable sense. (He and I also mused, inter alia, about his own errors as a powerful president of Tanzania; he rued collectivizing the Gogo, nationalizing sisal plantations, and failing to curb the more avaricious of his political allies and subordinates.)[22] Mogae had far less to be apologetic about since he had only recently become president of Botswana. Later, however, he roundly criticized his own successor (see chapter 8) and deplored all that Africa's earlier leaders had wrought. They started off well, he said, but then "something happened."[23]

Lee Kuan Yew brightly opined that "this attribute called leadership is either in you or it is not." He continued: "I do not think you learn leadership."[24] Nevertheless, Nyerere, Mogae, and I firmly believed that quality leadership could be nurtured. We hypothesized that aspirant politicians—junior members of parliaments and parties—would naturally try to emulate those who had preceded them in gaining political prominence unless newly formulated interventions could show them a better and more public interested road to elected office and political power than the often compromised path pursued by their elders (such as Mugabe). Mogae had grown into leadership as a disciple of Khama and Masire; Nyerere had learned to lead on the job, after only a handful of years preparing. Moreover, eminent researchers of leadership offered abundant theoretical support for our nurture rather than nature proposition.[25]

Nyerere agreed in early 1999 to command our attempt to strengthen African leadership. But when he sadly died later that year, I turned to Mogae. He said, however, that a sitting national president should not shoulder such a critical, but apt to be contested, effort. So I turned to Masire, out of office and retired, who readily assented to chair the task force of distinguished Africans that he and I agreed should decide exactly how the dearth of good leaders in Africa might be remedied, and fashion an effective response. Together we recruited former Nigerian head of state General Yakubu Gowon; Vice President Moody Awori of Kenya (elder brother of one of my long before Harvard students); former prime minister (and future president) Hage Geingob of Namibia (whom I had known in New York and Namibia); former Sierra Leonean minister of finance and UN Undersecretary General James Jonah, a longtime acquaintance; thoughtful Peter Anyang' Nyong'o, Minister for Planning and National Development, Kenya; Najib Balala, Minister for Gender, Sports, Culture, and Social Services, and former mayor of Mombasa, Kenya; Matthews Chikaonda, former minister of finance and governor of the Reserve Bank, Malawi; Ali Khalif Galaydh, former prime minister, Somalia; and General Abdulrahman Kinana of Tanzania, Speaker of the East African Legislative Assembly, and a former Kennedy School student.

We met first in Gaborone, then at Harvard's Kennedy School, and a third time in Mombasa, Kenya. In the last city we established the African Leadership Council, crafted a mission statement and a Code of African Leadership, and devised a curriculum for a proposed training course or courses on "Capacity Building for Elected African Leaders."

"Good leadership is a precious commodity," read the opening sentence of the Council's Mission Statement. In order "to further high quality elected leadership in Africa," it continued, "the African Leadership Council shall

- Assist the African Union, NEPAD [the New Partnership for Africa's Development, a project of South Africa's Mbeki], the United Nations, and individual leaders, as requested, [to improve] leadership best practices;
- Organize capacity building for elected African leaders;
- Maintain and update the Code of African Leadership;
- Organize forums on and research about African leadership;
- Meet regularly as a Council to review the state of African leadership and make recommendations, as required."

The Code asked that good leaders obey twenty-three commandments:

- Offer a coherent vision of individual growth and national advancement with justice and dignity for all;
- Seek to be transformational more than transactional;
- Encourage broad participation of all levels of society, including all minorities and majorities, and emphasize the deliberative nature of the best democratic practices;

- Demonstrate in their professional and personal lives deep respect for the letter and the spirit of all provision of a nation's constitution, including abiding strictly by term limits;
- Lead by example and teach to acquaint her/his peoples with respect for dissent, the ideas of others, and the importance of disagreement between political parties and individuals;
- Enforce rulings of all courts and independent tribunals and emphasize the independence of the judiciary so as to bolster the rule of law;
- Respect international conventions and international laws;
- Promote transparency and encourage and adhere to internationally common forms of accountability;
- Recognize that leaders are accountable for their actions and that no one is above the law nationally and internationally;
- Accept peer review [as contemplated by NEPAD];
- Promote policies aimed at eradicating poverty and enhancing the welfare and livelihoods of citizens within an appropriate macroeconomic framework;
- Strengthen and improve access to education and health care;
- Respect all human rights and civil liberties;
- Demand and work for peaceful and lawful transfers of power;
- Promote and respect the separation of powers by ensuring financial autonomy of the judiciary and parliament, and to ensure that the judiciary and parliament are free from unlawful interference by the executive;
- Adhere to a strong code of ethics and demand the same from all subordinate officials and cabinet ministers;
- Refrain from using their office for personal gain and avoid (and declare) all conflicts of interest and personal assets;
- Specifically abandon corruption and expose those acting in their personal capacity who violate national laws and practices against corruption;
- Ensure human security;
- Respect freedom of religion, freedom of the press, freedom of assembly, and of expression.

The preamble to the Code asserted that "too many African leaders [had] forgotten these [the Code's] underlying principles. Too many [had] moved from elections to preemptory methods of rule, forgetting their roots, forgetting the critical principles of democracy, and forgetting how the erosion of democratic methods ultimately leads to corruption, poverty, and antagonism between different ethnic groups or peoples." It went on to assert that conflict stemmed from "bad governance," and bad governance was a direct product of faulty individual leadership. When African countries prosper, it said, "intelligent, forward looking, selfless, democratic leadership" had been the decisive contributing factor. Furthermore, the Council "believe[d] that absolute standards of leadership [were] both appropriate and attainable." Conscious, it affirmed, "that Africa's poor are getting poorer and that good governance is essential for successful economic development," the Council put itself in the vanguard of fundamental reform. "Improved leadership is important and just."[26]

The Code, press attention to the Mombasa Declaration, and the intrinsic legitimacy and esteem of the persons who came together as a Council (and opened the door to others) spoke to the need for fundamental reforms in the way that African countries were managed and their leaders carried out their elected responsibilities. But, recognizing that fine words and hortatory expressions could hardly break existing patterns of behavior or, overnight, revolutionize the nature of political leadership on the African continent, we chose to try to sunder existing paradigms of leadership development by building capacity among Africans who aspired to higher positions in their governments but who were still at a presumably still malleable and teachable junior levels in their parliamentary or other political systems.

We wanted to introduce likely future cabinet ministers and heads of government to the values of good governance, personal probity, consensus building, strong listening, and the many other core competencies (see above, pp.304–309) that would strengthen their own abilities to lead, and lead responsibly and well. We envisaged an African-wide competitive selection process and a series of training programs over at least a few years that would create a cadre of acculturated young future leaders who would look to each other for reinforcement and socialization rather than to the autocrats or corrupted politicians who were otherwise likely going to be their role models. We saw our program as nurturing, and creating an esprit de corps for young African political leaders that would in many respects be modeled on the long-established collectivity (and methods of selection) of Rhodes Scholars.

We even went so far as to prepare an ambitious curriculum for our training modules: we wanted the best and brightest of future African leaders to study leadership itself, best practices, the meaning of governance, the basics of public management, democratic procedures, methods of coalition building, rule-of-law fundamentals, the content and importance of ethics, basic macroeconomics, and so on.

After we finished our deliberations in Mombasa and dispersed to our various countries, Masire and I continued to promote the causes of the Council. Masire talked to a number of audiences about the results of the Council meeting and about how, together, we hoped to develop new kinds of African leaders. So did I. Several of the others returned home to assume even more important political positions than they had held when we met. Balala and Nyong'o both moved up the ministerial pecking order in Kenya, Chakaonda became head of the powerful state-run Press Corporation, an industrial and service conglomerate, in Malawi. Geingob, out of favor when we met, again became Namibia's prime minister and, in 2015, its president. (See chapter 10.)

Transforming the way in which leaders were recruited and nurtured in Africa depended more on eleemosynary assistance, however, than on our uplifting bromides in Mombasa. The Council deputed me to fund it and its activities, and to raise the large sums that would be required to undertake the capacity-building exercises envisaged, even in a preliminary way. The usual sources of foundation funding were all receptive. But several years of effort on behalf of the Council yielded varieties of deep interest, albeit no firm offers of support. The Council and its capacity-building scheme still awaits backing; certainly the need is as great as it ever was, as this dissection of the political, economic, and social evolution of southern Africa has made evident.

As the contents of this book, and especially the analyses of this chapter, have demonstrated, good leadership too often has been a hit-or-miss proposition. To prosper, to enjoy successful lives for all citizens throughout the region, to improve schooling opportunities, and to secure upgraded public health outcomes, Botswanan-type leaders in the mold of Seretse Khama and Masire are desperately needed. The African Leadership Council advanced a plan to supply such women and men, and to socialize them in the arts of leadership. For the health, welfare, and important uplift of southern Africa (and sub-Saharan Africa as a whole) we must still find a way to do so. The vicissitudes of the coronavirus pandemic, and Africa's consequential economic collapse, makes the need for gifted leadership that much more compelling.

Confronting Southern Africa's Future

The peoples of southern Africa survived the HIV/AIDS epidemic thanks to medical and treatment advances and, in Botswana, because of the forthright actions of its leaders. In 2020 and 2021, the Covid-19 pandemic affected South Africans far more than the inhabitants of many neighboring countries. Ramaphosa led well, locking down his country for long stretches throughout 2020 and 2021, and combating the Omicron mutations well into 2022. Elsewhere, mask wearing, social distancing, and the youthfulness of whole national populations kept case and death numbers relatively low. For many months Namibia and Botswana registered hardly any fatalities from the disease. Even Zimbabwe, with eviscerated hospital care and shortages of potable water and many basic medical supplies, initially avoided unexpected levels of mortality from the pandemic. But, in late 2021, a new variant of the disease, holiday partying, and public laxness caused new waves of excess deaths (e.g., more deaths from all ailments than in pre-Covid-19 months). With vaccine availability severely limited throughout 2021, a sudden increase in deaths from the coronavirus occurred in each of the southern African territories. Malawi and Zimbabwe lost prominent cabinet ministers. So did South Africa.[27]

In 2022 and beyond, exceptional leadership of the quality that only Botswana (and maybe today's South Africa, Zambia, and Malawi) has enjoyed or enjoys will be more essential than ever before. Coping with the coronavirus pandemic is obviously a first charge on leadership. Second, and just as important, the economic downturn that accompanied the pandemic has severe short-term consequences that may linger for years and impair a return to pre-pandemic levels of progress. Existing and new leaders will be judged on how well they can guide their countries back to prosperity and to greater levels of economic equality. Minimizing the impact of climatic change—the droughts and floods, the erratic and ill-timed falls of rain—will be within the ambit of leadership actions despite the inability of human agency to make it rain less or more, or at the most propitious moments.

Ahead there are innumerable critical challenges to leadership in southern Africa. But in addition to keeping citizens healthy and alive, well fed, and productive (with a sense that they are significant parts of a greater national and global whole), the one inescapable phenomenon on which too few political leaders in southern Africa (or Africa) are focusing is the dramatic demographic shift that is underway everywhere on the continent. Because the peoples of southern Africa are wealthier and better educated (on average) than their counterparts farther north, the southern African nations are growing much less rapidly than are such places as Nigeria, Tanzania, the Democratic Republic of Congo, or even outliers like Burkina Faso. But southern Africa's population is exploding nevertheless, and few leaders are aware of the major potential difficulties ahead.

Malawi, Zambia, and Zimbabwe are all doubling in people numbers over the next thirty years. Botswana, Namibia, and South Africa will grow less dramatically, according to the estimates of the UN Division of Population, but they, too, are swelling in size. In each of the southern African cases, a demographic explosion means that national populations will remain youthful. The median age in nearly all cases will for the next thirty years (and beyond to the end of the century) hover from the early twenties to the late twenties until about 2060.

That youth bulge poses particular problems in each country. Young people require jobs if there is to be some kind of demographic dividend for southern Africa during the next half century. From whence are those jobs to come? Will foreign, or even domestic, investors create those new jobs? What should southern African nations be doing to help create new employment opportunities?

Schooling, the more thorough the better, is one remedy. More vocational-type education is another. Helping girls persist into and through secondary school is an essential third. Today, whereas most young southern Africans attend primary school, fewer girls than boys persist into secondary education, and very few go on to some level of tertiary training. More and better education (a major need throughout the region, and beyond) will help to provide the skills necessary for productive levels of employment and for the expansion and diversification of employment opportunities. Enlarging today's limited capacity for manufacturing throughout the region depends on skills acquisition at an accelerated speed. Reduced fertility rates and slower population growth depends upon the schooling of girls, and especially on educating girls with renewed intensity.

Truly transformational leadership can focus entire peoples on managing and taking advantage of the realities of population growth. Even transactional leaders will need to pay attention. Otherwise, massive numbers of thwarted job seekers will turn to uncomfortable aspects of the informal employment sectors in each southern African country; crime rates will soar; southern African countries and their leaders will face a host of new, or newly exacerbated, social concerns. The Islamist-inspired insurgency in northern Mozambique could even spread to other parts of southern Africa.

Along with increased numbers overall, more and more persons will flee from farms to cities and towns. Southern African cities will enlarge—some to bursting point—and become less and less manageable. Already, Harare cannot always provide clean water to its inhabitants. Some southern African cities suffer electrical shortages, blackouts, and load shedding. Providing adequate supplies of waterborne sanitation is a continuing problem. Only forward planning, which depends on local and national leadership, can prevent these kinds of problems from overwhelming much of southern Africa in the future. Cape Town ran out of water in 2019, before leaders could react effectively. Lusaka, Kitwe, Lilongwe, Harare, and Windhoek will experience the congestion and service delivery issues that South African cities have long known. Forward-thinking political leaders are required to prepare the peoples of southern Africa to manage and surmount such problems.

As this chapter and this book have indicated, if the peoples of southern Africa are to join the peoples of the rest of the continent and the rest of the globe in realizing their full human potential, if they hope to contribute meaningfully to the progress of our planet, then their own leaders must show the way. Collections of people cannot find the best solutions on their own, or with the welcome and often well-intended assistance of donors. They require political leaders to offer visions and mobilize citizens to pursue the best possible, the most exciting, paths to progress. Absent qualities akin to truly transformational leadership, the countries of southern Africa (even South Africa) will forfeit this generation's key challenges. There is almost no time to lose, and almost no greater responsibility for estimable political leadership.

Acknowledgments

Joanna Hermione Henshaw Oakeshott, my beloved late wife, shared much of this story. Our extended honeymoon took us through Dakar, Ougadougou, Accra, Lagos, Enugu, and Kano, and then on to the central focus of this book—Lusaka, Blantyre, Zomba, Harare, and more of Central Africa. We were together with Kamuzu Banda, Aleke Banda, and Dunduzu Chisiza during the last Nyasaland elections. On many occasions we drove Zambia's dusty Great North Road before it was paved en route to Mpika, Shiwa Ngandu, Kasama, Chinsali, and Abercorn (now Mbala), and talked often with President Kenneth Kaunda and First Lady Betty Kaunda in State House. We traveled to Johannesburg and Cape Town, before I was banned in apartheid South Africa, and even ventured overland to Dar es Salaam, and via muddy back roads to Mbeya, Rungwa, Dodoma, and eventually to Kampala. We lived together in Karen, outside Nairobi, as well. We experienced much of this book's African odyssey together. In Cambridge, Massachusetts, too, Joanna and I entertained Kamuzu Banda, Kenneth Kaunda, Sir Stewart Gore-Browne, Helen Suzman, Alex and Jenny Boraine, Benjie Pogrund and Anne Sassoon, Nthato Motlana, Masauko Chipembere, and many other distinguished Africans, dignitaries, politicians, and students. Those were the best of times, together.

Joanna would have been one of this book's most helpful critics. Nonetheless, the book's verisimilitude has been greatly enhanced by a number of close and exacting readers, each of whom is a well-published regional and a country or multicountry expert.

My writing and rewriting of *Overcoming the Oppressors* has thus greatly benefited from Roger Southall's thorough critiques of and comments upon the South African, Zimbabwean, Botswanan, Namibian, and concluding chapters. Justice Richard Goldstone likewise kindly reviewed the South African chapters. Bruce Bolnick, who spent years attempting to strengthen the economies of independent Zambia, Malawi, Mozambique, and Zimbabwe, generously read the Malawian, Zambian, Zimbabwean, and concluding chapters. His many suggestions, and those of Richard Goldstone and Roger Southall, have helped measurably to make large sections of this book more authoritative, more nuanced, and more complete. Jeff Ramsay lent his expertise on and long experience examining and participating in Botswana's political and social emergence to the further crafting and focusing of that chapter. André du Pisani, another colleague greatly involved in and knowledgeable of the maturation of modern Namibia, provided extremely valuable critiques to improve that chapter. So did David R. Smuts, a Supreme Court judge in Namibia and someone deeply involved in much of that country's liberation struggle. The responsibility for the book's contents obviously remains mine, but among the perfected parts are those that Bolnick, du Pisani, Goldstone, Ramsay, Smuts, and Southall generously helped to fashion. As each knows, I am enormously grateful for the many small and large ways in which their suggestions have made this book more precise and balanced in its portrait of oppressors and oppression. Additionally, two anonymous and significantly helpful reviewers read initial drafts of the first five chapters, plus the one on Zimbabwe, and helped me to improve those sections and, indeed, the whole book.

During the long coronavirus pandemic libraries, even the greatest ones, were closed to browsers and many critical materials were hard to retrieve. Fortunately for me, at important moments of bibliographical scarcity, Mary Brinton and Ellen McDonald rose to the challenge. Brinton helped with some difficult downloads from privileged sources; McDonald used her librarian's knowledge to acquire key items and to download others. Alice Story retrieved important articles, too. This book is the richer for their efforts, and I remain very grateful. Some essential chapters could not have been completed without their timely assistance.

My daughters Rebecca, Nicola, and Fiona added their own important insights to the book after perusing different drafts; so did Dylan, my eldest grandson, and Cornelia Cook Johnson. I am appreciative of their careful readings and criticisms, and of questions from Quinton, another grandson, who originally urged me to think about what was to become this volume as we followed trails and avifauna through the wilds of Argentina and Brazil.

Throughout decades of research, travel, and participatory observation in southern Africa I was blessed with good friendships and generous hospitality. Libby and Tony Ardington, Jenny and Alex Boraine, Selma and Jules Browde, Firle Davies, Sue Drummond Haley, Jean and Raymond Louw, Bennie Rabinowitz, Anne Sassoon and Benjie Pogrund, June and Peter Stutley, and Helen Suzman each graciously welcomed me into their homes on innumerable memorable occasions. Without their multiple kindnesses, my life on the road would have been less interesting and enjoyable, and this book less well informed. I thank them all.

Joanna G. Cloutier, my eldest granddaughter, skillfully prepared the artistic sketches of African personalities that grace this book's pages. Dylan A. Gattey deftly used "Mapbox"—www.mapbox.com—to create the five maps that illustrate the book's contents. He and I thank the inventors of Mapbox for simplifying and strengthening the making of maps for public display and use.

I hope new readers, and many political leaders and concerned citizens of southern Africa, will learn from and enjoy this book's message as much as my daughters and grandchildren, and the other experts and friends to whom I am enormously indebted, claim that they have.

R. I. R.
June 17, 2022

Notes

Chapter 1

1. For details and a much fuller discussion, see Rotberg, "The 'Partnership' Hoax: How the British Government Deprived Central Africans of Their Rights," *Journal of Southern African Studies* XLV (2019): 89–110.
2. On Africans and the colonial administration and administrators, see Samuel N. Chipungu, "African Leadership under Indirect Rule in Colonial Zambia," in Chipungu (ed.), *Guardians in Their Time: Experiences of Zambians under Colonial Rule, 1890–1964* (London: Macmillan, 1992), 50–73.
3. Welensky, quoted in *Bulawayo Chronicle*, April 13, 1950. See also Roy Welensky, "Toward Federation in Central Africa," *Foreign Affairs* XXXI (1952): 142–149. A very perceptive appreciation of Welensky's motives and upbringing is presented in Frank Barton, "Portrait of a Failure: Sir Roy Welensky," *Africa South* III, no. 4 (1959): 64–69.
4. Godfrey Huggins, quoted in *Northern News*, December 4, 1951. The "rider and his horse" motif is cited often. Enoch Dumbutshena, *Zimbabwe Tragedy* (Nairobi: East African Publishing, 1975), 51, wrote that Huggins uttered that revealing phrase in Gatooma (Kadoma) in 1952. Clyde Sanger, *Central African Emergency* (London: Heinemann, 1960), 47, mentions it, too. For the governor of South Rhodesia's friendly gloss on this speech, see Sir John Noble Kennedy to Sir Percivale Liesching, January 11, 1950, document 46 in Philip Murphy (ed.), *Central Africa*, vol. I: *Closer Association, 1945–1958* (London: Stationery Office, 2005), 130. Huggins' views on partnership are mentioned in Lewis H. Gann and Michael Gelfand, *Huggins of Rhodesia: The Man and His Country* (London: Allen & Unwin, 1964), only in a footnote, 229. But his offensive speech is never discussed therein.
5. Huggins, quoted in *Northern News*, March 26, 1959.
6. Cyril Dunn, *Central African Witness* (London: Gollancz, 1959), 119. See also Colin Leys, *European Politics in Southern Rhodesia* (Oxford: Clarendon, 1959), 272.
7. Kenneth Kaunda, "Rider and Horse in Northern Rhodesia," *Africa South* III (July–September 1959): 52.
8. Jaspar Savanhu to Roy Welensky, 1962, quoted in Rotberg, "Welensky's Last Stand: The Multi-racial Experiment in Central Africa Is Finished," *New Republic*, September 24, 1962. See also Prosser Gifford, "Misconceived Dominion: The Creation and Disintegration of Federation in British Central Africa," in Gifford and William Roger Louis (eds.), *The Transfer of Power in Africa: Decolonization, 1940–1960* (New Haven: Yale University Press, 1982), 403; T. R. M. Creighton, *The Anatomy of Partnership: Southern Rhodesia and the Central African Federation* (London: Faber, 1960), 127–202.

9. Hastings Banda to Roy Welensky, May 29, 1949, in J. R. T. Wood, *The Welensky Papers: A History of the Federation of Rhodesia and Nyasaland* (Durban: Graham, 1983), 119.

10. Donald R. Siwale, in Northern Rhodesia, African Representative Council, *Proceedings*, April 15, 1950; Siwale, African Representative Council, *Proceedings* 6 (1951): 13; Lipalile, *Proceedings* 8 (1952): 7. Siwale and I were later frequently in correspondence, especially in 1962–1964.

11. Petition of January 22, 1951, N/0002/2, Lusaka archives.

12. Minutes of the Executive Committee of the Nyasa African Congress, April 8–9, 1950, Zomba archives.

13. The proceedings of these bodies were all reviewed by the author in the relevant provinces and districts during the early 1960s, when my notes were compiled. But not all of the minutes and proceedings have made it into the official archives in Lusaka.

14. Siwale, African Representative Council, *Proceedings*, 6 (1951): 13; Lipalile, *Proceedings*, 8 (1952): 7.

15. Hastings Kamuzu Banda, speaking at a public meeting at Church House, Westminster, January 23, 1953.

16. See Philip Murphy, "Introduction," in Murphy, *Closer Association*, lii.

17. Paul Sikazwe, Northern Provincial Council, *Proceedings*, 1950. Also Donald R. Siwale, letter to the author, October 6, 1963; interview with Chief Mwase at his boma, September 14, 1962.

18. N/2193/2: Minutes of the Chinsali Association, December 29, 1951, and February 16, 1952, Lusaka archives; Orton Chirwa, paraphrased in Wood, *Welensky Papers*, 209.

19. For details see Rotberg, *Black Heart: Gore-Browne and the Politics of Multiracial Zambia* (Berkeley: University of California Press, 1977).

20. Quoted in Rotberg, *Black Heart*, 113.

21. Nadine Gordimer, "Zambia," *Holiday*, June 1966, 86.

22. Stewart Gore-Browne, in Legislative Council, *Debates* 45 (May 27, 1943): 71–74; 46 (November 23, 1943): 27.

23. Stewart Gore-Browne, in *Debates* 48 (August 9, 1944): 92, 96–97.

24. Stewart Gore-Browne to C. W. W. Greenidge, Secretary, Anti-Slavery Society, April 21, June 17, 1949, Gore-Browne Papers, Bodleian Library, Oxford. For the Capricorn Africa Society, see Rotberg, "Partnership Hoax," 101–102. For a more favorable view of the Capricorn Society, see Bizeck Jube Phiri, "The Capricorn Africa Society Revisited: The Impact of Liberalism in Zambia's Colonial History, 1949–1963," *International Journal of African Historical Studies* XXIV (1991): 65–83.

25. Stewart Gore-Browne, writing in the *Northern News*, December 21, 1954; Gore-Browne, letter to the editor, *Manchester Guardian*, December 20, 1954; Gore-Browne to Dame Ethel Locke-King, July 1, 1955, Gore-Browne Papers.

26. Quotations all from Rotberg, *The Rise of Nationalism in Central Africa: The Making of Malawi and Zambia, 1873–1964* (Cambridge, MA: Harvard University Press, 1965), 293–294.

27. See David C. Mulford, *Zambia: The Politics of Independence, 1957–1964* (Nairobi: Oxford University Press, 1967), 69–76.

28. "Application for Registration . . ." in B. S. Krishnamurthy (comp.), *Cha Cha Cha: Zambia's Struggle for Independence* (Lusaka: Oxford University Press, 1972).

29. Rotberg, "Gandhi's Tactics Pushed in Africa," *New York Times*, February 24, 1959.

30. Quoted in Rotberg, "Central Africa: Test of Multiracial Rule," *New Republic*, April 9, 1962.

31. "Zambia Congress Banned: All Leaders Arrested," *Northern News*, March 13, 1959; Andrew Sardanis, *Africa: Another Side of the Coin* (London: Tauris, 2011), 60–61.

32. There is a riveting handwritten account by Kaunda narrating "How I was Arrested," on March 12, 1959, and dated April 25, 1959 (from Kabompo) in Krishnamurthy, *Cha Cha Cha*. The same collection also includes Kaunda's attempt by means of a writ of habeas corpus to resist his arrest in Kabompo and transport to Lusaka on May 23, 1959, and Governor Benson's "Restriction Order" on Kaunda, dated March 11, 1959 and stamped "secret."

33. Richard Hall, *Zambia* (London: Pall Mall, 1965), 187.

34. Transcript of a taped interview with Sikota Wina, December 14, 1967, Luwingu, RIR files, 24–28. This may be the only inside account of the Farmhouse meeting cabal. But also see Hall, *Zambia*, 186–189. My examination of the supposed Farmhouse plot is Rotberg, "'Murder Incorporated': The Plot to Kill Whites in Northern Rhodesia (Zambia)," *Journal of Imperial and Commonwealth History* (2022)forthcoming.

35. Sanger wrote about this period in his *Our Golden Years in Africa: From the Congo to Zimbabwe* (Ottawa: Sanger, 2021), 30–32.

36. Kaunda to "Dear Comrades," April 28, 1959, RIR files.

37. See Rotberg, "Basutoland 1962," *Africa Report*, February 1962.

38. For these men and this period, see George Roberts, *Revolutionary State-Making in Dar es Salaam: African Liberation and the Global Cold War, 1961–1974* (Cambridge: Cambridge University Press, 2021). See also Rotberg, "Africa's Liberation Generation," *Journal of Modern African Studies* (2022)forthcoming.

39. For the full story, see Michael F. Lofchie, "The Zanzibari Revolution: African Protest in a Racially Plural Society," in Rotberg and Ali A. Mazrui (eds.), *Protest and Power in Black Africa* (New York: Oxford University Press, 1970), 924–967.

40. See John H. Spencer, *Ethiopia at Bay: A Personal Account of the Haile Selassie Years* (New York: Reference Publications, 1984).

Chapter 2

1. Gore-Browne to Sir Donald MacGillivray, March 15, 1960, Gore-Browne Papers, Bodleian Library, Oxford.

2. Rotberg, *Black Heart: Gore-Browne and the Politics of Multiracial Zambia* (Berkeley: University of California Press, 1977), 312–313.

3. Kaunda to RIR, June 1, 1961, RIR files.

4. Richard Hall, *Zambia, 1890–1964: The Colonial Period* (London: Longman, 1976), 193. For the Liberal Party and like organizations, see Bizeck Jube Phiri, "The

Capricorn Africa Society Revisited: The Impact of Liberalism in Zambia's Colonial History, 1949–1963," *International Journal of African Historical Studies* XXIV (1991): 65–83.

5. Kaunda to Gore-Browne, April 28, 1961, Gore-Browne Papers. See also the good discussion of the Monckton Commission and Federal concerns in Hall, *Zambia*, 138–143.

6. Rotberg, *Black Heart*, 316.

7. Andrew Sardanis, *Africa: Another Side of the Coin: Northern Rhodesia's Final Years and Zambia's Nationhood* (London: Tauris, 2011), 107.

8. According to Hall, *Zambia*, 154, the UFP and Nkumbula had cut such a deal in 1961.

9. The definitive study of the 1962 elections is David C. Mulford, *The Northern Rhodesian General Election 1962* (Nairobi: Oxford University Press, 1964).

10. Sardanis, *Africa*, 164.

11. Adam Smith (D. D. Raphael and A. L. Macfie, eds.), *The Theory of Moral Sentiments* (Oxford: Oxford University Press, 1976), 237. See also the discussion in Rotberg, *Transformative Political Leadership: Making a Difference in the Developing World* (Chicago: University of Chicago Press, 2012), 31–34.

12. For a contemporary commentary on the effects of sanctions, see Richard Hall, *The High Price of Principles: Kaunda and the White South* (London: Hodder & Stoughton, 1969), 161–165. See also Andrew Roberts, *A History of Zambia* (London: Heinemann, 1976), 227–233; Douglas G. Anglin, *Zambian Crisis Behaviour: Confronting Rhodesia's Unilateral Declaration of Independence, 1965–1966* (Montreal: McGill-Queen's University Press, 1994).

13. Rotberg, "Tribalism and Politics in Zambia," *Africa Report*, December 1967.

14. For the Arusha Declaration, see George Roberts, *Revolutionary State-Making in Dar es Salaam: African Liberation and the Global Cold War, 1961–1974* (Cambridge: Cambridge University Press, 2021), 66–99. See also https://disa.ukzn. ac.za/sites/default/files/pdf_files/Acn2967.0001.9976.000.029.1967.4.pdf.

15. Quoted in Hall, *High Price of Principles*, 47–48.

16. Cherry Gertzel, Carolyn Balies, and Morris Szeftel, "The Making of the One-Party State," in (Gertzel, ed.), *The Dynamics of the One-Party State in Zambia* (Manchester: Manchester University Press, 1984), 10.

17. Quoted in Rotberg, "Tribalism." See also Roberts, *A History of Zambia*, 246. For the doctrine, see Kenneth David Kaunda, *A Humanist in Africa* (Nashville: Abingdon Press, 1966), 19–47.

18. Sardanis, *Africa*, 200.

19. Alex Callinicos and John Rogers, *Southern Africa after Soweto* (London: Pluto, 1977), 112.

20. See Mark Bostock and Charles Harvey, "The Takeover," in (Bostock and Harvey, eds.), *Economic Independence and Zambian Copper: A Case Study of Foreign Investment* (New York: Praeger, 1972), 145–188.

21. Frantz Fanon (Constance Farrington, trans.), *The Wretched of the Earth* (1961; New York: Grove Press, 1963), 133.

22. See Cranford Pratt, *The Critical Phase in Tanzania, 1945–1968: Nyerere and the Emergence of a Socialist Strategy* (Cambridge: Cambridge University Press, 1976), 227–264.

23. Interview with Kaunda, October 28, 1997, in Lusaka, RIR files.

24. Sikota Wina told me in late 1967 that UNIP was very democratic, and Kaunda very consultative, until the Mulungushi Conference of 1967. Thereafter, he more and more gave orders and expected to be obeyed. Transcript of taped interview with Wina, December 14, 1967, RIR files.

25. Details and quotation in Callinicos and Rogers, *Southern Africa after Soweto*, 271, 274–276.

26. See Gertzel, "Dissent and Authority in the Zambian One-Party State 1973–1980," in Cherry Gertzel, *Dynamics*, 81–82.

27. For an additional insight, see Miles Larmer, *Living for the City: Social Change and Knowledge Production in the Central African Copperbelt* (Cambridge: Cambridge University Press, 2021), 274–275.

28. Carolyn Baylies and Morris Szeftel, "Elections in the One-Party State," in Gertzel, *Dynamics*, 49–51.

29. Rotberg, "Zambia Struggles with the Plight of Have-Not Nations," *Christian Science Monitor*, October 1, 1982.

30. Russell to RIR, private emails, April 20, September 9, October 25, 2015. See also Rotberg, *The Corruption Cure: How Citizens and Leaders Can Combat Graft* (Princeton: Princeton University Press, 2017), 158–160.

31. "Tiny Rowland," *Economist*, July 30, 1998, https://www.economist.com/obituary/1998/07/30/tiny-rowland. See also Tom Bower, *Tiny Rowland: A Rebel Tycoon* (London: Heinemann, 1993).

32. Sardanis, *Africa*, 30.

33. Callinicos and Rogers, *Southern Africa after Soweto*, 123–131.

Chapter 3

1. See Ndangwa Noyoo, *Social Welfare in Zambia: The Search for a Transformative Agenda* (London: Adonis & Abbey, 2013), 268–283.

2. Andrew Sardanis, *A Venture in Africa: The Challenges of African Business* (London: Tauris, 2007), 99, 121.

3. Inter-Parliamentary Union, "Zambia," accessed July 18, 2022, http://archive.ipu.org/parline-e/reports/arc/2359_91.htm.

4. See Bruce R. Bolnick, "Early Sequencing of Financial-Market Liberalization Interest Rate Policy, 1992–1994," in Catharine B. Hill and Malcolm F. McPherson (eds.), *Promoting and Sustaining Economic Reform in Zambia* (Cambridge, MA: Harvard Kennedy School, 2004), 215–236.

5. For the gory details, and more, see Rights and Accountability in Development, "Zambia: Deregulation and the Denial of Human Rights," March 2000, https://www.raid-uk.org/sites/default/files/zambia-dereg-summary.pdf;   Rights   and

Accountability in Development, "Anglo American plc: Adherence to the OECD Guidelines for Multinational Enterprises in Respect of Its Operations in Zambia," January 2002, https://www.raid-uk.org/sites/default/files/oecd-request-anglo.pdf; Rights and Accountability in Development, "Privatisation in Zambia: What It Means for the Majority," 1996, accessed July 18, 2022, https://www.raid-uk.org/sites/default/files/zambia-factsheets.pdf; Zambia Consolidated Copper Mines, "Privatisation—Progress Report as at 30 June 1997," RIR files.

6. See Amnesty International, "Zambia: Forcible Exile to Suppress Dissent," April 1997, https://www.amnesty.org/download/Documents/156000/afr630041997en.pdf.

7. "Court Restores Kaunda's Zambian Citizenship," *Independent* online, October 20, 2000, https://www.iol.co.za/news/africa/court-restores-kaundas-zambian-citizenship-51273. See also Erica Frantz, *Authoritarianism: What Everyone Needs to Know* (New York: Oxford University Press, 2018), 96.

8. Transcript and notes of interview with Kenneth Kaunda, October 27–28, 1998, in Lusaka, RIR files.

9. Amnesty International, "Zambia: Misrule of Law. Human Rights in an Emergency," March 2, 1998, https://www.amnesty.org/download/Documents/152000/afr630041998en.pdf.

10. "Death of Kaunda's Son 'An Assassination,'" *Irish Times*, November 5, 1999, https://www.irishtimes.com/news/death-of-kaunda-s-son-an-assassination-1.246692.

11. Andrew Sardanis, *Zambia: The First Fifty Years* (London: Tauris, 2014), 153. World Bank officials in the late 1990s believed that Princess Nakatindi was complicit in running narcotics into Zambia while she was minister of tourism. But these allegations may have been promoted by Michael Sata, another cabinet minister under Chiluba and later president of Zambia.

12. Donald G. McNeil Jr., "Zambia Gazes at the Power Elite's Dirty Laundry," *New York Times*, January 30, 1998, https://www.nytimes.com/1998/01/30/world/zambia-gazes-at-the-power-elite-s-dirty-laundry.html.

13. See Human Rights Watch, "Zambia: Elections and Human Rights in the Third Republic," December 1996, https://www.hrw.org/reports/1996/Zambia.htm; Roy Clarke, quoted in Stephen Chan, *Grasping Africa: A Tale of Tragedy and Achievement* (London: Tauris, 2007), 57.

14. Sata, quoted in Patson Chilemba, *The Post*, March 6, 2010.

15. Notes of interview with Chiluba, July 14, 1997, in State House, Lusaka, in RIR files.

16. See Rotberg, *The Corruption Cure: How Citizens and Leaders Can Combat Graft* (Princeton: Princeton University Press, 2017), 160. Much of this section draws on material in *Corruption Cure*, 161–165.

17. All of these details, and more, emerged during Chiluba's trials. See "Judgement in the Case of *Attorney General of Zambia v. Meer Care & Desai*," quoted in John Hatchard, *Controlling Corruption: Legal Approaches to Supporting Good Governance and Integrity* (Cheltenham: Edward Elgar, 2014), 72.

See also Jotham C. Momba, "Economic Reforms, Corruption and the Crisis of Governance in Zambia: The Dilemma for the Donor Community," in Kwame Frimpong and Gloria Jacques (eds.), *Corruption, Democracy, and Good Governance in Africa* (Gaborone: Lightbooks, 1999), 195–196.

18. John Hanks, *Operation Lock and the War on Rhino Poaching* (Johannesburg: Penguin, 2015), 33–35, 83–84.

19. Russell to RIR, personal email, October 25, 2015.

20. Testimony of Paul Russell, Cape Town, January 18, 2015, RIR files.

21. "Chiluba to Pay $57m—Smith," *Lusaka Times*, June 29, 2007, https://www.lusa katimes.com/2007/06/29/chiluba-to-pay-57m-smith. For good commentary, see Sardanis, *Zambia*, 166–174.

22. *Southern African Report*, March 6, 2009, 5; "Regina Chiluba Found Guilty and Sentenced," *Lusaka Times*, March 3, 2009, https://www.lusakatimes.com/2009/03/03/8974/.

23. Jotham Momba, quoted in "Court Clears Ex-President Chiluba of Graft Charges," Reuters, August 18, 2009, https://www.france24.com/en/20090818-court-clears-ex-president-chiluba-graft-charges-.

24. Sardanis, *Zambia*, 121, 154.

25. See the authoritative account, Sishuwa Sishuwa, "Surviving on Borrowed Power: Rethinking the Role of Civil Society in Zambia's Third-Term Debate," *Journal of Southern African Studies* XLVI (2020): 471–490.

26. Electoral Institute for Sustainable Democracy in Africa, African Democracy Encyclopaedia Project, "Zambia: 2001 Presidential Elections Results," April 2021, https://www.eisa.org/wep/zam2001resultsp.htm.

27. Electoral Institute for Sustainable Democracy in Africa, African Democracy Encyclopaedia Project, "Zambia: 2006 Presidential Elections Results," April 2021, https://www.eisa.org/wep/zam2006resultsp.htm.

28. Electoral Institute for Sustainable Democracy in Africa, African Democracy Encyclopaedia Project, "Zambia: 2008 Presidential Elections Results," April 2021, https://www.eisa.org/wep/zam2008results.htm.

29. https://www.google.com/search?q = Zambia + GDP+per + capita+ 2011&oq = Zambia + GDP+per + caoita+2011&aqs = chrome..69i57j33i10i22.

30. Erin Conway-Smith, "Zambian Election Results Check Chinese Influence in Africa," *Global Post*, September 25, 2011, https://www.pri.org/stories/2011-09-25/zambian-election-results-check-chinese-influence-africa.

31. *The Economist*, "Not as Bad as They Say," October 1, 2011, https://www.economist.com/middle-east-and-africa/2011/10/01/not-as-bad-as-they-say; Rotberg, *Africa Emerges: Consummate Challenges, Abundant Opportunities* (Cambridge: Polity, 2013), 165. Sata spoke to students at Harvard about China in Africa alongside Mia Farrow and Samantha Power.

32. https://www.hrw.org/news/2011/11/03/zambia-workers-detail-abuse-chinese-owned-mines#.

33. These last two paragraphs adapted liberally from Rotberg, *Things Come Together: Africans Achieving Greatness in the Twenty-First Century* (New York: Oxford University Press, 2020), 156–157, which in turn draws upon Rotberg, *Africa Emerges*, 165–168. See also Rotberg, "China's Quest for Resources, Opportunities, and Influence in Africa," and a dozen other chapters in Rotberg (ed.), *China into Africa: Trade, Aid, and Influence* (Washington, DC: Brookings, 2009), 1–20.

34. Sata, quoted in Conway-Smith, "Zambian Election Results."

35. Chipembo, quoted in Sardanis, *Zambia*, 188–189.

36. For CPI ranks and scores for the various years, see, e.g., Transparency International, "Corruption Perceptions Index," https://www.transparency.org/en/cpi/2014.

37. Transparency International, "Corruption Perceptions Index," https://www.transparency.org/en/cpi/2020.

38. How Edgar Lungu Stole Client's Money Leading to His Suspension from LAZ," *Zambian Observer*, March 19, 2019, https://www.zambianobserver.com/ruling-of-the-legal-practitioners-committee-of-the-law-association-of-zambia-against-mr-edgar-chagwa-lungu/.

39. NDTV news, "Edgar Lungu Wins Zambian Presidential Election," January 25, 2015, https://www.ndtv.com/world-news/edgar-lungu-731879.

40. See Rotberg, "Africa Plagued by Third Term-itis," *Diplomat and International Canada* (October–November 2015), 50–53.

41. Sishuwa Sishuwa, lecturer in modern history, quoted in "Zambia Is Starting to Look Like Zimbabwe, the Failure Next Door," *Economist*, November 14, 2020.

42. Filip Warwick, "Zambia 2019 Copper Output Drop Due to New Mining Taxes," S & P Global Platts, December 27, 2019, https://www.spglobal.com/platts/en/market-insights/latest-news/metals/122719-zambia-2019-copper-output-drop-due-to-new-mining-taxes-com.

43. Grieve Chelwa, "China Blamed for Zambia's Debt, but the West's Banks and Agencies Enabled It," *Mail & Guardian* (Johannesburg), November 18, 2020, https://mg.coza/africa/2020-11-18.

44. *Africa Confidential* claimed in 2018 that Zambia was hiding its true debt total, which was closer to 100 percent than 51 percent of GDP. *Africa Confidential*, April 20, 2018.

45. Trevor Hambayi, "African Countries Are Having a Risky Affair with Eurobond Debt and It Could End Very Badly," Quartz Africa report, October 31, 2017, https://qz.com/africa/1115944/utm; *Economist*, "Lungu's Largess: Zambia Was Already a Case Study in How Not to Run an Economy," May 2, 2020.

46. Andrew M. Fischer, "Haemorrhaging Zambia: Prequel to the Current Debt Crisis," *Developing Economics* blog, November 24, 2020, https://developingeconomics.org/2020/11/24/haemorrhaging-zambia-prequel-to-the-current-debt-crisis/.

47. "Lessons from Lusaka," *Economist*, September 15, 2018.

48. Tom Burgis, *Kleptopia: How Dirty Money Is Conquering the World* (New York: HarperCollins, 2020), 278–280. Apparently, ERNC purchased the smelter mostly to launder illicit profits that then could be siphoned back to its owners, cheating shareholders.

49. "Lungu's Largesse," *Economist*, May 2, 2020.

50. Sylvia Masebo, quoted in Jon Sharman, "Zambian Foreign Minister Resigns over 'Swelling' Corruption within Country," *Independent* (London), January 3, 2018, www.independent.co.uk/news/world/africa/zambia . . . a8140151.html.

51. Reuters Staff, "Zambia Owes Nearly $27 Billion in Foreign and Local Public Debt," October 20, 2021, https://www.reuters.com/article/zambia-debt/zambia-owes-nearly-27-billion-in-foreign-and-local-public-debt-idUSKBN2HA2L5.

52. Muna Ndulo, a leading Zambian legal scholar, quoted in "Zambia," *Economist*, May 2, 2020.

53. Rotberg, "Zambia's Unexpected Election Result Marks a Welcome Change for Africa," *Globe & Mail*, August 23, 2021.

54. BBC News, "Zambian President Inherits Empty Treasury," September 1, 2021.

55. Dickens Olewe, "Hakainde Hichilema: Zambia's New President Inspires African Opposition Leaders," BBC News, August 24, 2021.

56. International Monetary Fund, "Updated: IMF Staff Reaches Staff-Level Agreement on an Extended Credit Facility Arrangement with Zambia," Press Release no. 21/359, https://www.imf.org/en/News/Articles/2021/12/06/pr21359-zambia-imf-staff-reac hes-staff-level-agreement-on-ecf.

57. Hichilema, quoted in News Now, December 11, 2021, https://www.newsnow.co.uk/ h/World + News/Africa/Zambia.

58. https://www.google.com/search?q = ZAmbia + coronavirus&oq = ZAmbia + coronavirus&aqs = chrome..69i57j0i13l3j0i13i457j0i13i30l4.51.

Chapter 4

1. Circular letter from Sangala of October 1, 1943, Zomba archives. For more on Sangala and early Malawi political movements, see Rotberg, *The Rise of Nationalism in Central Africa: The Making of Malawi and Zambia* (Cambridge, MA: Harvard University Press, 1965), 181–192.

2. Constitution of the Nyasaland African Congress, mimeo. copy, December 20, 1944, RIR files.

3. These details, and more, are set out in Rotberg, *Rise of Nationalism*, 186–189. Information about Banda's early years was confirmed by his universities and colleges, but transcripts proved unavailable. Discussions with the Rev. Hanock Phiri, Banda's uncle, were helpful. However, I never managed an in-depth discussion with Banda himself about his pre-independence past.

4. "Note of a Meeting . . . between the Secretary of State and a Delegation from the Nyasaland African Congress . . . ," June 3, 1948, mimeo., RIR files.

5. Banda and Harry Nkumbula, "Federation in Central Africa" (unpub. typescript), May 1, 1949, RIR files. For Banda's private life and romantic affairs in London and Edinburgh, see Edwin Munger, *Touched by Africa* (Pasadena, CA: Castle Press, 1983), 251–253.

6. Verbatim report of a public meeting at Church House, Westminster, London, January 23, 1953, Lusaka archives.

7. See Colin Baker, *Seeds of Trouble: Government Policy and Land Rights in Nyasaland, 1946–1964* (London: British Academic Press, 1993), 174–186.

8. Quoted in *Report of the Nyasaland Commission of Inquiry*, Cmnd. 814 (1959), 12–13.

9. Chipembere (Rotberg, ed.), *Hero of the Nation: Chipembere of Malawi, an Autobiography* (Blantyre: Kachere Press, 2001), 295.

10. See Fernand van Langenhove, *Consciences Tribales et Nationales en Afrique Noire* (The Hague: Institut Royal des Relations Internationales, 1960), 382–384.

11. Foe the name, see Philip Short, *Banda* (London: Routledge, 1974), 126.

12. For Aleke K. Banda, see Short, *Banda*, 126.

13. See Rotberg, "The Malawi News," *Africa Report*, December 1963.

14. Andrew Ross, "Some Reflections on the Malawi 'Cabinet Crisis' 1964–65," *Religion in Malawi* VII (1997): 5.

15. Lucy P. Mair, *The Nyasaland Elections of 1961* (London: Athlone, 1962).

16. For the atmosphere of the club, see Paul Theroux, *Dark Star Safari* (Boston: Houghton Mifflin, 2003), 305–307. In the archives we were researching John Chilembwe's 2015 rebellion and, in the process, discovered what became my edited version of George Simeon Mwase, *Strike a Blow and Die: Race Relations in Colonial Africa* (Cambridge, MA: Harvard University Press, 1965).

17. For Chisiza, see Colin Cameron, "Dunduzu Kaluli Chisiza (1930–1962): A Brief Personal Perspective," *Society of Malawi Journal* LXIX (2016): 1–7. Cameron hints that Kamuzu Banda had reason to, and may have had Chisiza killed, with the crash only looking like an accident. My last interview with Chisiza was on August 8, 1962, in Zomba; notes in RIR files.

18. Kamuzu Banda, in official Nyasaland *Hansard*, May 29, 1964, 93.

19. Dunduza Chisiza, *Realities of African Independence* (London: Africa Bureau, 1961), 11.

20. On Taiwan and China, see John K. Cooley, *East Wind over Africa: Red China's African Offensive* (New York: Walker, 1965), 97–98.

21. See also Short, *Banda*, 203–205.

22. Chipembere, interview, quoted at length in Short, *Banda*, 200.

23. Full text in Chipembere, *Hero of the Nation*, 39. Second quotation from Rotberg, "Masauko Chipembere," *Harvard Magazine* May–June 2010, 42.

24. See Short, *Banda*, 215–230.

25. Ross, email to Rotberg, August 5, 1999.

26. Rotberg, "Introduction: Nationalist by Design, Chipembere and the Making of Malawi," in Chipembere, *Hero of the Nation*, 43.

27. Quoted in Short, *Banda*, 262. The year was 1966.

28. Quoted in Short, *Banda*, 264.

29. See Paul Theroux, "The Killing of Hastings Banda," in Theroux, *Sunrise with Seamonsters* (Boston: Houghton Mifflin, 1985), 65–66, 73.

30. The Censorship Board still existed when Theroux visited in 2002. See his *Dark Star Safari*, 314.

31. Rhoda E. Howard Hassman, "Jehovah's Witnesses: Neglected Victims of Persecution," *The Conversation*, March 24, 2019; "Jehovah's Witnesses Complain They're Persecuted in Malawi," *New York Times*, March 5, 1975; Ken Jubber, "The Persecution of Jehovah's Witnesses in Southern Africa," *Social Compass* XXIV (1977): 121–134 https://journals.sagepub.com/doi/10.1177/003776867702400108; Grenna Kaiya, "The Role of the Churches in Human Rights Advocacy: The Case of Malawian Members of the Jehovah's Witnesses . . . ," unpub. master's thesis in Diakonia, Diakonhjemmet University College (Oslo, 2013).

32. Lupenga Mphande, "Dr Hastings Kamuzu Banda and the Malawi Writers Group: The [Un]Making of a Cultural Tradition," *Research in African Literatures* XXVII (1996): 8625.

33. Paul Chiudza Banda, "Regime Policing and the Stifling of the Human Rights Agenda: Late Colonial and Post-colonial Malawi, 1948–Present," in Nicholas K. Githuku (ed.), *A Tapestry of African Histories: With Longer Times and Wider Geopolitics* (Lanham, MD: Lexington Books, 2021), 252–256.

34. See Rotberg, "Paul Kagame: Rwanda's Despot?," *Diplomat and International Canada*, Summer 2021.

35. Alan Cowell, "Deaths Bring Air of Menace to Malawi," *New York Times*, July 7, 1983.

36. See, e.g., Amnesty International, *Report 1987*, 69–71.

37. Director of Public Prosecution v Banda . . . and Others, www.malawilii.org/mw/judgment/supreme-court-appeal/1997/2.

38. David Robinson, "Renamo, Malawi, and the Struggle to Succeed Banda: Assessing Theories of Malawian Intervention in the Mozambican Civil War," *Eras* XI (2009), accessed September 17, 2021, https://www.academia.edu/3098090; Karl Maier, "Mozambican Army Gains as Neighbors Lend Increasing aid: Government Now Has Malawi's Support in Drive against Rebels," *Christian Science Monitor*, March 25, 1987.

39. Harri Englund, *Visions for Racial Equality: David Clement Scott and the Struggle for Justice in Nineteenth-Century Malawi* (Cambridge: Cambridge University Press, 2022), 271.

40. Bruce and Doreen Bolnick were driving from Lusaka through western Malawi to the Nyika plateau during the balloting exercise. "It was exhilarating to see the energy of the common people in every village and their joy at having the right to vote." Bruce Bolnick to RIR, January 15, 2021.

Chapter 5

1. Inter-Parliamentary Union, "Malawi," accessed July 20, 2022, http://archive.ipu.org/parline-e/reports/arc/2195_94.htm.

2. A Harvard-supplied educationist was advising Muluzi and the ministry of education.

3. Bruce R. Bolnick, email to RIR, January 17, 2021.

4. World Bank, "Mortality Rate, Infant (per 1,000 Live Births)," accessed July 20, 2022, https://data.worldbank.org/indicator/SP.DYN.IMRT.IN?locations = MW.

5. Aleke Banda's fax to me was gratifying. "We are delighted to see . . . this . . . very good Report and I wish to congratulate your team for making such a thorough evaluation of the Malawi economy." Banda to RIR, January 11, 1995.

6. Rotberg, Shirley Burchfield, Richard Goldman, Lester Gordon, Theo Lippeveld, Michael Roemer, and Christopher Shaw, "Trickle-Up Growth," HIID, November 22, 1994. Bruce R. Bolnick kindly lent me his copy of this document, as well as many other relevant contemporary materials from his formative time in Malawi as director of the HIID Malawi Economic Management and Reform (MEMAR) program.

7. Rotberg et al., "Trickle-Up Growth," 3.

8. Rotberg et al., "Trickle-Up Growth," 7.

9. Rotberg, "Malawi Can Get By—with a Little Help from Its Friends," *Christian Science Monitor*, December 27, 1994; Rotberg, "Malawi Struggles to Undo Years of Corruption," *Boston Globe*, August 11, 1994.

10. Donald Snodgrass, "Economic Growth and Poverty Reduction in Malawi: Contrasting Approaches," June 13, 1995; Michael Roemer, "Deregulation, Diversification and the Private Sector," June 13, 1995, unpub. HIID papers, Bolnick files.

11. Charles Mann, "Higher Yields for All Smallholders through 'Best Bet' Technology: The Surest Way to Restart Economic Growth in Malawi," March 1998, Soil Fertility Network Results Working Paper, 6–8, Bolnick files.

12. Recounted in Paul Theroux, *Dark Star Safari* (Boston: Houghton Mifflin, 2003), 299.

13. Alexander Newa, "Stambuli Arrested," *The Nation* (Blantyre), June 23, 1997.

14. https://www.facebook.com/494524227355140/posts/how-bakili-muluzi-killed-kalonga-stambuliand-got-away-with-itformer-president-ba/1665253596948858, May 12, 2020.

15. "How Bakili Muluzi Killed Kalonga Stambuli . . . and Got Away with It," *Malawi News Network*, May 13, 2020, https://malawinewsnetworks.com/2020/05/13/how-bakili-muluzi-killed-kalonga-stambuli-and-got-away-with-it-part-2.

16. Mustafa Hussein, "Combating Corruption in Malawi: An Assessment of the Enforcing Mechanisms," *African Security Review* XIV (2005): 4.

17. H. Masauko Chipembere (Rotberg, ed.) *Hero of the Nation: Chipembere of Malawi, an Autobiography* (Blantyre: Kachere Press, 2001).

18. For the early reception of the ACB, see Isaac C. Lamba, "Controlling Corruption in Africa: The Case of Malawi," in Kwame Frimpong and Gloria Jacques (eds.), *Corruption, Democracy, and Good Governance in Africa* (Gaborone: Lightbooks, 1999), 261–264. For the Malawi ACB and what it did, see also Bruce R. Bolnick, "Fighting Corruption in Africa: Lessons from Malawi," *Harvard Journal of African American Public Policy* VIII (2002): 8–11.

19. ACB, "Investigations Report on Petroleum Control Commission," 42–45, RIR files.

20. ACB, "A Report on Allegations of Corruption in the Award of a Pre-shipment Inspections Contract," 18, RIR files.

21. Hannes Hechler and Bea Parkes, "Annual Review of DFID/RNE Malawi's Anti-Corruption Bureau Support Programme," 2010, 16, RIR files.

22. Rotberg, "The Starving of Africans," *Boston Globe*, June 26, 2002.

23. David Hall-Matthews, "Tickling Donors and Tackling Opponents: The Anti-corruption Campaign in Malawi," in Sarah Bracking (ed.), *Corruption and Development* (New York: Palgrave Macmillan, 2007), 86–87; Associated Press, September 8, 2002; "Malawi: Ex-Minister Arrested over Sale of State Grain," reliefweb, October 28, 2004, https://reliefweb,int/report/Malawi/Malawi-ex-minister.

24. Hussein, "Combating Corruption in Malawi," 3.

25. Nixon S. Khembo, "National Integrity Systems: Malawi 2004," Transparency International Country Report, 2004, 9.

26. Millennium Consulting Group, "Governance and Corruption Baseline Survey, Malawi, 2005" (Lilongwe, 2006), 7; UN Economic Commission for Africa, "African Governance Report" (2005), 150.

27. Transparency International, "Corruption Perceptions Index," accessed July 20, 2022, https://www.transparency.org/en/cpi/2003.

28. Muluzi, quoted in BBC News, "Malawi President 'a Bad Choice,'" April 5, 2005.

29. Quoted in Hall-Matthews, "Tickling Donors," 77.

30. https://www.google.com/search?q=Malawi+GDP+2009&oq=Malawi+GDP+2009&aqs=chrome..69i57j0i15i22i30j0i390l4.7185j0j7&sourceid=chrome&ie=UTF-8.

31. Hall-Matthews, "Tickling Donors," 83.

32. "President of Malawi Moves to $100m Palatial Residence," *Irish Times*, December 23, 2004, https://www.irishtimes.com/news/president-of-malawi-moves-to-100m-palatial-residence-1.1171076?mode = amp. See also chapter 4.

33. PricewaterhouseCoopers audit report, https://www.google.com/search?q=Malawi+Cashgate+Audiot+report&oq=Malawi+Cashgate+Audiot+report&aqs=chrome..69i57j33i10i160j33i10i299.7437j0j7&sourceid=chrome&ie=UTF-8. See also, https://www.unodc.org/documents/corruption/LimaEGM2018/Presentations/Case_Gate_Scandal_in_Malawi_-_Victor_Samuel_Chiwala.pdf.

34. Quoted in Rotberg, "Protests Erupt in Malawi," ThinkAfricaPress.com, August 4, 2011.

35. Rotberg, "Protests Erupt in Malawi." See also Stephen Chan, "Bingu wa Mutharika Obituary: President of Malawi Who Went from Reformer to Despot," *Guardian*, April 7, 2012, https://www.theguardian.com/world/2012/apr/07/bingu-wa-mutharika-obituary-malawi.

36. "Malawi: Red Carpet for Dead President," *Mail & Guardian*, March 15, 2013, https://mg.co.za/article/2013-03-15-00-malawi-red-carpet-for-dead-president/.

37. Rotberg, "A New Kind of Leader for Malawi," *Ottawa Citizen*, February 24, 2013.

38. Rex Chikoko, "Malawi 'Theft' Balloons to R540m," *Mail & Guardian*, February 13–19, 2015; Godfrey Mapondera and David Smith, "Malawi President Sacks Cabinet over Corruption Scandal," *Guardian*, October 13, 2013; https://www.globalsecurity.org/military/world/africa/mw-corruption.htm.

39. Jimmy Kainja, "What Drives Corruption and Why It Won't Disappear Soon," *The Conversation*, October 1, 2015.

40. BBC News, "Malawi Election: Peter Mutharika Wins Presidential Vote," May 30, 2014, https://www.bbc.com/news/world-africa-27646181.

41. Peter Mutharika, official transcript, speaking to the Council on Foreign Relations, New York, September 24, 2015.

42. Dan van Veen, "Former Malawi AG Superintendent Elected President," Assemblies of God, July 8, 2020, https://news.ag.org/News/Former-Malawi-AG-Superintendent-Elected-President.

43. Court judgment quoted in Andrew Harding, "Malawi Election: What the Annulment Means for Democracy Across Africa," BBC News, February 5, 2020, https://www.bbc.com/news/world-africa-51369191.

44. BBC News, "Malawi Opposition Leader Lazarus Chakwera Wins Historic Poll Rerun," June 27, 2020, https://www.bbc.com/news/world-africa-53207780.

45. Golden Matonga, "Meet Norman Chisale, Malawi's Richest Bodyguard," *Mail & Guardian*, March 7, 2021, https://mg.co.za/africa/2021-03-07-meet-norman-chis ale-malawis-richest-bodyguard.

46. Winston Mwale, "Inaugural Address by the State President of the Republic of Malawi, His Excellency Dr. Lazarus McCarthy Chakwera," Africa Brief, July 6, 2020, https:// africabrief.substack.com/p/inaugural-address-by-the-state-president.

47. Transparency International, "Corruption Perceptions Index," accessed July 20, 2022, https://www.transparency.org/en/cpi/2021.

48. https://www.google.com/search?q = coronavirus + in+malawi&oq = coronavirus + in+Malawi&aqs = chrome.0.0i512j0i22i30l7j0i39. See also Rotberg, "The Pandemic Won't End without Vaccinating Poorer Countries," *Globe & Mail*, March 22, 2021.

49. Lameck Masina, "Malawi President Reviews His 100 Days in Office," VOA, October 8, 2020, voanews.com/africa/malawi-president-reviews-his-100-days-office.

50. *Quartz Africa Weekly Brief*, December 5, 2021.

51. Grace Phiri, "Renewed Hope for Low Wage Earners," *Nation* (Blantyre), December 24, 2020, https://www.mwnation.com/renewed-hope-for-low-wage-earners/.

52. President Chakwera, quoted in Reuters, "Malawi Fires Labour Minister, Arrests Officials over Misuse of COVID Funds," April 19, 2021; Madalitso Wills Kateta, "How Corruption Derails Development in Malawi," *Foreign Policy*, May 21, 2021, https://foreignpolicy.com/2021/05/21/how-corruption-derails-development-in-mal awi/?utm_source = PostUp&utm_medium = email&.

53. AFP, "Malawi Arrests Former Minister, Bank Chief for Lying to IMF," *Guardian*, December 8, 2021, https://guardian.ng/news/malawi-arrests-former-minister-bank-chief-for-lying-to-imf/#:~:text = Malawi%20police%20have%2.

54. Lameck Masina, "Malawi Businessman Convicted for 2019 Attempt to Bribe Judges," VOA, September 10, 2021, https://www.voanews.com/a/6221526.html.

55. Dudu Douglas-Hamilton, head of counter-wildlife trafficking at the Elephant Crisis Fund, quoted in Rachel Nuwer, "Kingpin Heads to Prison as Malawi Brings Down a Wildlife Crime Cartel," *New York Times*, October 19, 2021.

56. AFP, "Malawi Leader Names New Cabinet, Retains Most Ministers He Fired," Seychelles News Agency, January 27, 2022, http://www.seychellesnewsagency.com/ articles/16199/Malawi%20leader%20names%20new%20cabinet%2C%20reta ins%20most%20ministers%20he%20fired?utm_source=dailybrief&utm_medium= email&utm_campaign = DailyBrief2022Jan27&utm_term = DailyNewsBrief.

57. Gift Trapence, deputy chairperson of the Human Rights Defenders Coalition of Malawi, quoted in Masina, "Malawi Businessman Convicted." VOA, September 10, 2021.

Chapter 6

1. See Roger Southall, *The New Black Middle Class in South Africa* (Auckland Park, South Africa: Jacana, 2016), 30–37. On the "legal" undergirding of apartheid, see Ian

Loveland, *By Due Process of Law: Racial Discrimination and the Right to Vote in South Africa, 1855–1960* (Oxford: Hart Publishing, 1999), 226–332.

2. See Saul Dubrow, *Racial Segregation and the Origins of Apartheid in South Africa, 1919–1936* (New York: St. Martins, 1989); John W. Cell, *The Highest Stage of White Supremacy: The Origins of Segregation in South Africa and the American South* (New York: Cambridge University Press, 1982).

3. See T. Dunbar Moodie, *The Rise of Afrikanerdom: Power, Apartheid, and the Afrikaner Civil Religion* (Berkeley: University of California Press, 1975), 234–258; Hermann Giliomee, *The Afrikaners: Biography of a People* (Charlottesville: University of Virginia Press, 2003), 447–496.

4. Hermann Giliomee, "The Growth of Afrikaner Identity," in Heribert Adam and Giliomee, *Ethnic Power Mobilized: Can South Africa Change?* (New Haven: Yale University Press, 1979), 114–122, esp. 116. Giliomee finds the first printed use of the term "apartheid" to date from 1929, in what was then the Orange Free State. Giliomee, *The Afrikaners*, 454. See also 464–479 in the same source.

5. For the entire chilling apparatus of apartheid, see the magisterial analysis, John Dugard, *Human Rights and the South African Legal Order* (Princeton: Princeton University Press, 1978). Also see Heribert Adam, *Modernizing Racial Domination: The Dynamics of South African Politics* (Berkeley: University of California Press, 1971), 37–52.

6. For what Sophiatown once was, see Don Mattera, *Sophiatown: Coming of Age in South Africa* (Boston: Beacon Press, 1987); Tom Lodge, *Black Politics in South Africa* (Johannesburg: Ravan, 1983), 91–114.

7. Quoted in Rotberg, "Apartheid: Changes Are on the Surface," *Washington Post*, May 14, 1972.

8. Rotberg, "Apartheid."

9. See Anthony S. Mathews, *Law, Order and Liberty in South Africa* (Berkeley: University of California Press, 1972), 53–115.

10. For the important role of civil society protest, and especially of the women who maintained vigils to protest against the outrages of apartheid, and created "advice centers" to help the most deprived and most afflicted cope with such injustices as the pass laws, see Noel Robb, *The Sash and I: A Personal Memoir and a Tribute to the Black Sash* (Claremont, South Africa: Robb, 2006).

11. In addition to Suzman's own memoir, the warm, informative, and compelling essays in Robin Lee (ed.), *Values Alive: A Tribute to Helen Suzman* (Johannesburg: Jonathan Ball, 1990), provide rich and rewarding material about her immense contribution to South Africa's political evolution during and after apartheid. Especially compelling are the chapters by Irene Mennell (on how thoroughly Suzman prepared to confront the apartheid juggernaut), Neville Alexander (on her important visits to Robben Island, where he was a prisoner), Colin Eglin (on their Progressive years together in combat), Harry Oppenheimer (on his crucial support for her brave efforts), and John Dugard (on her practical attacks on National Party legislative sophistry). The collection also contains E. J. Kahn's famous *New Yorker* article on his visit to Suzman and South Africa in the mid-1980s.

12. Mandela, *Long Walk to Freedom* (Boston: Little, Brown, 1994), 382; see also Sheila Cohen, "Suzman's Relationship with Mandela," *Helen Suzman*, accessed July 20, 2022, https://www.cortland.edu/cgis/suzman/mandela.html.

13. Quotations in the above paragraphs are from Rotberg, "Helen Suzman: Biographical Memoir," *Proceedings of the American Philosophical Society* CLV (March 2011): 116–117. See also Suzman's compelling autobiography, full of great stories: *In No Uncertain Terms: A South African Memoir* (New York: Knopf, 1993), especially 88–111. For Verwoerd, Alexander Hepple, *Verwoerd* (Harmondsworth, UK: Penguin, 1967).

14. For the Massacre and the events and thinking leading up to it, see Benjamin Pogrund, *Sobukwe and Apartheid* (Johannesburg: Ball, 1990), 110–147; Philip Frankel, *An Ordinary Atrocity: Sharpeville and Its Massacre* (New Haven: Yale University Press, 2001), 51–180; Gail M. Gerhart, *Black Power in South Africa: The Evolution of an Ideology* (Berkeley: University of California Press, 1978), 173–256.

15. For insights into Vorster's personality. See Anthony Hazlitt Heard, *The Cape of Storms: A Personal History of the Crisis in South Africa* (Fayetteville: University of Arkansas Press, 1990), 133–139.

16. For Biko's many intellectual and spiritual contributions to South Africa's liberation, see the essays in Andile Mngxitama, Amanda Alexander, and Nigel C. Gibson (eds.), *Biko Lives! Contesting the Legacies of Steve Biko* (New York: Palgrave, 2008); Millard Arnold (ed.), *Steve Biko: Black Consciousness in South Africa* (New York: Random House, 1978), xiii–xx.

17. For the Vorster quotation and Suzman's battle to free Sobukwe, see her *In No Uncertain Terms*, 214–215.

18. For an early study of the press and its critical role in apartheid South Africa, see Richard Pollak, *Up Against Apartheid: The Role and Plight of the Press in South Africa* (Carbondale: Southern Illinois University Press, 1981).

19. See Benjamin Pogrund, *War of Words: Memoir of a South African Journalist* (New York: Seven Stories Press, 2000), 146, 247–249.

20. Rotberg, "Helen Suzman," *116*. For van den Bergh's standing and role in the Broederbond, see Ivor Wilkins and Hans Strydom, *The Super-Afrikaners: Inside the Afrikaner Broederbond* (Johannesburg: Jonathan Ball, 1978), 10–11. See also Kenneth W. Grundy, *The Militarization of South African Politics* (Bloomington: Indiana University Press, 1986), 42–43; Giliomee, *The Afrikaners*, 582–583.

21. See Rotberg, "The Process of Decision-Making in Contemporary South Africa," *CSIS Africa Notes*, December 28, 1983.

22. For Eglin, see Colin Eglin, *Crossing the Borders of Power* (Johannesburg: Ball, 2007).

23. Rotberg, "South Africa under Botha: How Deep the Change?," *Foreign Policy* XXXVIII (Spring 1980): 130.

24. Buthelezi, quoted in Rotberg, "Apartheid." For Buthelezi's rise to power, and much else, see Ben Temkin, *Buthelezi: A Biography* (London: Cass, 2003). See also the speeches collected in M. Gatsha Buthelezi, *Power Is Ours* (New York: Books in Focus, 1979).

25. See also Jeffrey Butler, Rotberg, and John Adams, *The Black Homelands of South Africa: The Political and Economic Development of Bophuthatswana and KwaZulu* (Berkeley: University of California Press, 1977), 76–90.

26. Rotberg, "Apartheid." But see also Rotberg, *Haiti: The Politics of Squalor* (Boston: Houghton Mifflin, 1971), 227–228.

27. Rotberg, "Apartheid—Strong as Ever," *Newsday*, February 3, 1974.

28. See John Kane-Berman, *Soweto: Black Revolt, White Reaction* (Johannesburg: Ravan Press, 1978); Noor Nieftagodien, *The Soweto Uprising* (Athens: Ohio University Press, 2014).

29. For Motlana, see Jill Johnson and Peter Magubane, *Soweto Speaks* (Johannesburg: Donker, 1979), 87–89.

30. Sir Sydney Kentridge, QC, quoted in Donald Woods, *Biko* (London: Paddington Press, 1978), 255. Woods, disguised, went on the run within South Africa, and then escaped to London, after exposing Biko's murder. I caught up with Donald and Wendy Woods in London, where we lamented together about conditions in South Africa.

31. John Marcum, *The Angolan Revolution*, (Cambridge, MA: MIT Press, 1969 and 1978), 2v, is the complete story.

32. For Renamo, Alex Vines, *Renamo: Terrorism in Mozambique* (London: James Currey, 1991). For the struggle, see William Finnegan, *A Complicated War: The Harrowing of Mozambique* (Berkeley: University of California Press, 1991).

33. I organized a summer seminar on South Africa at MIT for a dozen years during the 1970s and 1980s. It was attended primarily by senior executives from American and British companies—BP, Heinz, Johnson & Johnson, Mobil, Texaco, and such—with business in South Africa. A few South Africans also participated in the week-long course. One of them was Basil Landau, head of the Union Corporation. Decades later, I learned that Landau had been spying for the apartheid government. Brooks Marmon discovered while perusing the files of Pieter W. Botha at the University of the Free State that Landau had reported back fully to Pretoria on the "leftist" discussions held in the seminar. Marmon to RIR, May 25, 2022, personal email.

34. Rotberg, "The South African Succession," *Christian Science Monitor*, September 26, 1978.

35. Rotberg, "To Lead South Africa Out of Despair," *Christian Science Monitor*, October 22, 1980. I met with the always bright-eyed and positive-thinking Tutu on a number of occasions in South Africa, in the United States—where he could be glimpsed strolling to a religious retreat center near my Harvard University office—and in the UK. For an assessment of Wiehahn's influence, see Danelle van Zyl-Hermann, *Privileged Precariat: White Workers and South Africa's Long Transition to Majority Rule* (Cambridge: Cambridge University Press, 2021), 116–151.

36. For a chilling elaboration of the Nationalist's security apparatus and its odious methods, see Jacob Dlamini, *The Terrorist Album: Apartheid's Insurgents, Collaborators, and the Security Police* (Cambridge, MA: Harvard University Press, 2020). On the Cradock murders, see Christopher Nicholson, *Permanent Removal: Who Killed the Cradock Four?* (Johannesburg: Wits University Press, 2004). "Total onslaught" was enunciated by P. W. Botha on January 5, 1983. The Soviet Union was behind total onslaught "in order to enslave us here in South Africa." See Nicci Young, "The Soviet Union, South Africa and the ANC: Why Worry?," *Hemispheres* XI (1987–88): 33.

37. For more on the "total onslaught," see Grundy, *Militarization*, 49–53.

38. For an excellent commentary on the UDF, see Allister Sparks, *The Mind of South Africa* (New York: Knopf, 1990), 337–347; Shaun Johnson, "'The Soldiers of Luthuli': Youth in the Politics of Resistance in South Africa," in Johnson (ed.), *South Africa: No Turning Back* (Bloomington: Indiana University Press, 1989), 94–150. The definitive study on the UDF is Jeremy Seekings, *UDF: A History of the United Democratic Front in South Africa, 1983–1991* (Athens: Ohio University Press, 2000).

39. Stephen M. Davis, *Apartheid's Rebels: Inside South Africa's Hidden War* (New Haven: Yale University Press, 1987), 95.

40. Rotberg, "South Africa's Homelands Policy—a Dead End," *Christian Science Monitor*, October 17, 1979.

41. See Rotberg, "South Africa's Latest Homeland—a New Approach," *Christian Science Monitor*, February 12, 1980.

42. Rotberg, "The Face of Change in South Africa," *Boston Globe*, August 15, 1983.

43. Rotberg, "South Africa's Winter of Reform," *Christian Science Monitor*, July 23, 1982. See also Frederik van zyl Slabbert, *The Last White Parliament* (Johannesburg: Jonathan Ball, 1985), 53–86.

44. For one view of constructive engagement, see Christopher Coker, *The United States and South Africa, 1968–1985: Constructive Engagement and Its Critics* (Durham: Duke University Press, 1986), 111–127.

45. Rotberg, "South Africa: Domestic Turmoil," *Christian Science Monitor*, March 28, 1985; Rotberg, "South Africa under Botha," 131.

46. Rotberg, "Satisfying South African Blacks," *Christian Science Monitor*, August 10, 1985.

47. I welcomed these impositions, but urged Reagan to demand the release of Mandela and to invite Oliver Tambo, acting ANC president, to the White House. Rotberg, "What to Do about South Africa," *New York Times*, July 15, 1986.

48. Rotberg, "What Botha Should Do Now to Save South Africa," *Christian Science Monitor*, December 5, 1985.

49. See the telling study of the Alexandra uprising, Belinda Bozzoli, *Theatres of Struggle and the End of Apartheid* (Athens: Ohio University Press, 2004). See also Mzwanele Mayekiso, *Township Politics: Civic Struggles for a New South Africa* (New York: Monthly Review Press, 1996), which is all about Alexandra.

50. A committed anti-apartheid activist, Buthelezi in the mid-1980s was also attempting to put his Zulu-based Inkatha Movement forward as a viable negotiating alternative to what he called "the ANC Mission in Exile." He called for the release of Mandela, but also claimed to favor nonviolent protest rather than ANC-promoted violence. He also claimed implausibly that Inkatha was "the largest political organization ever to have been formed in the history of South Africa." See Mangosuthu G. Buthelezi, "South Africa's Future—Violence or Negotiation?," *The World and I*, March 1987, 144. The article is the text of a speech that Buthelezi delivered to the Washington, DC-based Heritage Foundation on November 14, 1986.

51. Rotberg, "Pretoria Must Deal with Black Leaders," *New York Times*, October 27, 1986.

52. Rotberg, "Mandela's Prisoner," *Boston Globe*, August 29, 1988.

53. Rotberg, "Has South Africa Found Its Nixon?," *New York Times*, March 14, 1989.

54. De Klerk, quoted in John F. Burns, "South Africa's New Era; Mandela to Go Free Today; De Klerk Proclaims Ending of 'Chapter' after 27 Years," *New York Times*, February 11, 1990, https://www.nytimes.com/1990/02/11/world/south-africa-s-new-era-mandela-go-free-today-de-klerk-proclaims-ending-chapter.html. For Helen Suzman's take on this speech and the ending of apartheid, see her *In No Uncertain Terms*, 268–270. See also Alex Duval Smith, "Why FW de Klerk Let Nelson Mandela Out of Prison," *Guardian*, January 30, 2010, https://www.theguardian.com/world/2010/jan/31/nelson-mandela-de-klerk-apartheid.

55. Mandela, quoted in Marc Lacey, obituary of "F. W. de Klerk, Architect in Scrapping Apartheid," *Boston Globe*, November 12, 2021.

56. For the mayhem caused by Buthelezi and his legions, see Adrian Guelke, *South Africa in Transition: The Misunderstood Miracle* (London: Tauris, 1999), 89–111.

57. Full details in the next chapter.

58. There is much on Ramaphosa in the next chapter.

Chapter 7

1. Rotberg, "The Politics of Language, Identity, and Race," *Christian Science Monitor*, February 29, 1996; Rotberg, *Ending Autocracy, Enabling Democracy* (Washington, DC: Brookings Press, 2002), 481.

2. Nelson Mandela, *Long Walk to Freedom* (Boston: Little, Brown, 1994), 530.

3. Quoted in Tom Lodge, *Mandela: A Critical Life* (New York: Oxford University Press, 2006), 179–180.

4. See Ray Hartley, *Ragged Glory: The Rainbow Nation in Black and White* (Johannesburg: Jonathan Ball, 2014), 56. The 2009 movie *Invictus* captures this World Cup moment well. It was based on John Carlin, *Playing the Enemy: Nelson Mandela and the Game That Made a Nation* (New York: Penguin, 2008). Archbishop Desmond Tutu coined the name "rainbow nation" to describe the new South Africa.

5. In attempting to decide whether South Africa should help to resuscitate the Congo after Laurent Kabila's guerrilla movement and Rwandan legions had overthrown the despotic regime of Mobuto Sese Seko in 1997, Mandela's government (motivated by Mbeki) sent me, on behalf of a Harvard Institute of International Development mission, to determine whether the incoming junta could absorb aid from and was worthy of South African support. I met with the incoming minister of finance, a PhD agricultural economist from the University of Kentucky. He stuck out his hand and brightly asked: "What have you brought for me?" I made clear that we did not do business that way, reported to Mbeki accordingly, and returned to Harvard.

6. Rotberg, *Transformational Political Leadership* (Chicago: University of Chicago Press, 2012), 62; Mark Gevisser, *A Legacy of Liberation: Thabo Mbeki and the Future of the South African Dream* (New York: Palgrave, 2009), 247.

7. See Tom Lodge, "The South African General Election, April 1994: Results, Analysis and Implications," *African Affairs*, XCIV (1995): 471–500.

8. For a provocative assessment of the essence of the ANC, see Anthony Butler, *The Idea of the ANC* (Athens: Ohio University Press, 2012), 92–118.

9. See Roger Southall, "Securing the Transition? Whites and the TRC," in Southall, *Whites and Democracy in South Africa* (Woodbridge, UK: James Currey, 2022), 61–74; Terry Bell, with Dumisa Buhle Ntsebeza, *Unfinished Business: South Africa, Apartheid and Truth* (London: Verso, 2003), 285–295.

10. Tutu, quoted in *Boston Globe*, August 7, 1998.

11. These questions are discussed at length in Rotberg, "Truth Commissions and the Provision of Truth, Justice, and Reconciliation," in Rotberg and Dennis Thompson (eds.), *Truth v. Justice: The Morality of Truth Commissions* (Princeton: Princeton University Press, 2000), 1–21, and in the many other chapters in that book, including several by members of the TRC.

12. Hartley, *Ragged Glory*, 65.

13. Amy Gutmann and Dennis Thompson, "The Moral Foundations of Truth Commissions," in Rotberg and Thompson, *Truth v. Justice*, 24–26. See also Elizabeth Kiss, "Moral Ambition within and beyond Political Constraints: Reflections on Restorative Justice," in *Truth v. Justice*, 68–98.

14. Boraine, quoted in *Boston Globe*, September 9, 1998. But see also the thorough analysis of the TRC's impact, and what it failed to accomplish, in Fanie du Toit, *When Political Transitions Work: Reconciliation as Interdependence* (New York: Oxford University Press, 2018), 101–113.

15. On the origins and meaning of the rainbow nation, see Carolyn E. Holmes, *The Black and White Rainbow: Reconciliation, Opposition, and Nation-Building in Democratic South Africa* (Ann Arbor: University of Michigan Press, 2020), 45–55.

16. See Gevisser, *Legacy of Liberation*, 339.

17. Rotberg, "Mandela's Heir Apparent Is Different in Style but Similar in Skill," *Boston Globe*, September 30, 1996.

18. Mandela, quoted in Gevisser, *Legacy of Liberation*, 261. As Gevisser indicates, the relationship between Mbeki and Mandela greatly deteriorated when Mbeki became, in Mandela's eyes, an imperious leader, just as Mandela had warned against. There is a slightly differently worded version of Mandela's speech to the ANC congress in "Mandela Hands the Baton to Mbeki," BBC News, December 20, 1997, http://news.bbc.co.uk/1/hi/41252.stm.

19. Alexander Johnston, *In the Shadow of Mandela: Political Leadership in South Africa* (London: Tauris, 2020), 180.

20. See Andrew Feinstein, *After the Party: Corruption, the ANC and South Africa's Uncertain Future* (London: Verso, 2009), 119.

21. See Derek Matyszak, *Law, Politics and Zimbabwe's "Unity" Government* (Harare: Konrad-Adenauer Stiftung, 2010), 1–15.

22. Rotberg, "Only Mbeki Can Restore Sanity to Zimbabwe," *Financial Times*, December 7, 2004; Rotberg, "Mbeki Is Avoiding the Right Course on Zimbabwe," *Financial Times*, May 18, 2003; Rotberg, "Zimbabwe's Spreading Misery," *New York Times*, May 14, 2001. See also Feinstein, *After the Party*, 104–110.

23. Johnston, *Shadow of Mandela*, 188.

24. President Kaunda told me that his one "big mistake" was merging party and state. Interview with Kaunda, October 27, 1997, Lusaka, RIR files.

25. Mandela, paraphrased and quoted in Anthony Sampson, *Mandela* (New York: Knopf, 1999), 533.

26. Adam Habib, *South Africa's Suspended Revolution; Hopes and Prospects* (Athens: Ohio University Press, 2013), 80–82; Roger Southall, *The New Black Middle Class in South Africa* (Auckland Park, South Africa: Jacana, 2016), 96–98.

27. Gevisser, *Legacy of Liberation*, 342.

28. Harry Oppenheimer, quoted in Barbara Slaughter, "South Africa: The Fraud of 'Black Empowerment,'" World Socialist Web Site, May 25, 1999, https://www.wsws.org/en/articles/1999/05/anc-m25.html.

29. "South Africa Manufacturing Output 1960–2022," Macrotrends, accessed July 23, 2022, https://www.macrotrends.net/countries/ZAF/south-africa/manufacturing-output.

30. Rotberg, "South Africa's Bold Initiative for Nonracial Education," *Christian Science Monitor*, February 22, 1993; Rotberg, "After the Elections, South Africa Must Focus on Education," *Boston Globe*, February 25, 1994.

31. "South Africa's Matric Pass Rate: 2008 to 2019," BusinessTech, January 7, 2020, https://businesstech.co.za/news/government/364476/south-africas-matric-pass-rate-2008-to-2019/.

32. Statistics from "At a Glance: HIV in South Africa," Be in the Know, accessed July 21, 2022, www.avert.org/safricastats.htm. See also Nicoli Nattrass, "Aids and the Scientific Governance of Medicine in Post-apartheid South Africa," *African Affairs* CVII (2008): 157–176.

33. Pride Chegwedere et al., "Estimating the Lost Benefits of Antiretroviral Drug Use in South Africa," *Journal of Acquired Immune Deficiency Syndromes*, October 16, 2008; Nattrass, "Aids," 159–170.

34. Johnston, *Shadow of Mandela*, 188.

35. Gevisser, *Legacy of Liberation*, 289.

36. Jeanette Kurian Birnbaum, Christopher J. L. Murray, and Rafael Lozano, "Exposing Misclassified HIV/AIDS Deaths in South Africa," *Bulletin of the World Health Organization*, February 17, 2011; https://www.avert.org/professionals/hiv-around-world/sub-saharan-africa/south-africa.

37. For a careful exposé of ANC-directed corruption at the municipal level, see Mcebesi Ndletyana, *Anatomy of the ANC in Power: Insights from Port Elizabeth, 1990–2019* (Cape Town: HSRC Press, 2020).

38. Hartley, *Ragged Glory*, 68.

39. See Feinstein's trenchant *After the Party*, 139–184.

40. For lurid details, see Douglas Foster, *After Mandela: The Struggle for Freedom in Post-apartheid South Africa* (New York: Liveright, 2012), 238–239.

41. Adekeye Adebajo, *Thabo Mbeki* (Athens: Ohio University Press, 2016), 74.

42. Judgment of Justice Chris Nicholson, in Gevisser, *Legacy of Liberation*, 334–335. See also Johnston, *Shadow of Mandela*, 329 n. 14.

43. Tom Burgis, *Kleptopia: How Dirty Money Is Conquering the World* (New York: HarperCollins, 2020), 72–73, 355.

44. "Something Very Rotten," *Economist*, June 23, 2012.

45. Tutu, at the University of the Western Cape, quoted in *Southern African Report*, February 25, 2011.

46. Moeletsi Mbeki, quoted in Lydia Polgreen, "South Africa Suffers as Graft Saps Provinces," *New York Times*, February 18, 2012. For more on corruption's destructive legacy, see du Toit, *Political Transitions*, 113–114; Hennie Van Vuuren, *South Africa, Democracy, Corruption, and Conflict Management* (London: Legatum, 2014).

47. Chief Justice Mogoeng Mogoeng, quoted in Norimitsu Onishi, "Zuma's Spending on Home Is Ruled Unconstitutional," *New York Times*, April 1, 2016. See also Marianne Merten, "Flouting the Law Crux of Nkandla," *The Star* (Johannesburg), August 4, 2015; Johnston, *Shadow of Mandela*, 244. On the startling announcement that charges against Zuma were to be dropped, see Hartley, *Ragged Glory*, 206–207.

48. See Ivor Chipkin and Mark Swilling, *Shadow State: The Politics of State Capture* (New York: New York University Press, 2018).

49. Karan Mahajan, "'State Capture': How the Gupta Brothers Hijacked South Africa Using Bribes Instead of Bullets," *Vanity Fair*, March 2019. See also Micah Reddy and Sam Sole, "The Guptas and Coal: How State Capture Hobbled Alexkor, Part 2," amaBhungane, December 20, 2021, amabhungane.org/stories/211220-the-guptas-and-coal-how-state-capture-hobbled-alexkor-part-2/.

50. The first volume of the Zondo Commission's report was published early in 2022: Judicial Commission of Enquiry into State Capture, *Report*, I, https://www.gov.za/sites/default/files/gcis_speech/Judicial%20Commission%20of%20Inquiry%20into%20State%20Capt.

51. BBC News, "South Africa's Gupta Brothers Sanctioned by US over 'Corruption,'" October 10, 2019, https://www.bbc.com/news/world-africa-50003150.

52. Richard Calland, "State Report Chronicles Extent of Corruption in South Africa: But Will Action Follow?," *The Conversation*, January 6, 2022.

53. Greg Nicolson, "State Capture Central: How Transnet Became the Hub of the Gupta Looting Frenzy," *Daily Maverick*, February 2, 2022, https://www.dailymaverick.co.za/article/2022-02-02-state-capture-central-how-transnet-became-the-hub-of-the-gupta-looting-frenzy/.

54. Angelo Agrizzi, quoted in Norimitsu Onishi, "Monopoly Money: Detailing Cash and Car Bribes to South African Leaders," *New York Times*, January 30, 2019; James Hamell, "Why the ANC Itself Is the Chief Impediment to Ramaphosa's Agenda," *The Conversation*, December 14, 2019, www.theconversation.org.

55. Monica Mark, "A. N. C. Leader Faces Charges of Corruption in South Africa," *New York Times*, November 14, 2020.

56. For much of the Magashule story, see Pieter-Louis Myburgh, *Gangster State: Unraveling Ace Magashule's Web of Capture* (Cape Town: Penguin, 2019).

57. Transparency International, "Corruption Perceptions Index," accessed July 21, 2022, https://www.transparency.org/files/content/pages/2021_CPI_Report_EN.pdf.

58. The results of our consultations near Cape Town are in Rotberg (ed.), *Governance and Innovation in Africa: South Africa after Mandela* (Waterloo, ON: CIGI, 2014). The book contains fourteen chapters mostly by recognized South African academic authorities.

59. Risenga Maluleke, "Quarterly Labour Force Survey: Q2:2021," Statistics South Africa, accessed July 21, 2022, http://www.statssa.gov.za/publications/P0211/Presentation%20QLFS%20Q2_2021.pdf.

60. Rotberg, *Things Come Together: Africans Achieving Greatness in the Twenty-First Century* (New York: Oxford University Press, 2020), 97, from which most of the paragraph derives.

61. "The Dole Toll," *Economist*, August 31, 2013.

62. See the thorough analysis in Ann Bernstein, "South Africa's Key Challenges: Tough Choices and New Directions," in Rotberg, *Governance and Innovation*, 44–45.

63. Commissioner William J. Bratton, in Rotberg, "Preface," in Rotberg and Greg Mills (eds.), *War & Peace in Southern Africa: Crime, Drugs, Arms, and Trade* (Washington, DC.: Brookings, 1998), ix; Rotberg, "South Africa's Looming Crisis," *Diplomat and International Canada*, Spring 2016, 63.

64. "Murder Rate by Country 2022," World Population Review, accessed July 21, 2022, https://worldpopulationreview.com/country-rankings/murder-rate-by-country; Rotberg, "South Africa's Looming Crisis," 63. See also the compelling review of these problematics in Colin Bundy, *Short-Changed? South Africa since Apartheid* (Athens: Ohio University Press, 2014), 116–136.

65. De Lille later became Minister of Public Works in the Ramaphosa national government.

66. See Rotberg and Jennifer Erin Salahub, "African Legislative Effectiveness," *North-South Institute* (Ottawa), on-line report, 2013.

67. Feinstein, *After the Party*, 174–184.

68. See Roger Southall, "Democracy at Risk? Politics and Governance under the ANC," in Rotberg, *Governance and Innovation*, 57–80.

69. Tutu, quoted in Christopher Torchia, "South Africa Debates Persistent Troubles since End of Apartheid," *Boston Globe*, April 13, 2013; Lynsey Chutel, "Even in Retirement, Desmond Tutu Remained South Africa's Moral Compass," *New York Times*, December 26, 2021; Isabella Kwai and Lynsey Chutel, "'A True South African Giant': Tributes for Desmond Tutu, a Force for Harmony," *New York Times*, December 26, 2021; Ramphele, former vice chancellor of the University of Cape Town and World Bank executive, quoted in David Smith, "Ramphele Launches Challenge to South Africa's ANC," *Guardian*, February 18, 2013; Ramphele, quoted in Rotberg, "Can a Breakaway Movement Reclaim Mandela's Legacy?," *Globe & Mail*, March 25, 2013.

70. Mandela, quoted in Sampson, *Mandela*, 533.

71. Rotberg, "Zuma Goes, Ramaphosa Comes: A Move That Should Save South Africa," *Globe & Mail*, February 14, 2018.

72. Jonny Steinberg, "Rampaphosa's Sense of Reality Rules Out the Autocrat's Overreach," *Business Day*, February 25, 2021.

73. Ramaphosa, before the Zondo Commission, quoted in Christina Goldbaum, "South African President Testifies before Commission Investigating Corruption," *New York Times*, April 29, 2021.

74. Mcebisi Ndletyana, "Jacob Zuma Isn't a Man with a Cause. Just a Wily Politician Trying to Evade the Law," *The Conversation*, June 30, 2021. After serving only two

months of the sentence for contempt, a corrections commissioner friendly to Zuma gave him a medical parole –a "get out of jail" card. But in December 2021 a High Court judge decreed that the medical parole had been issued incorrectly and sent Zuma back to prison to resume serving his interrupted sentence. Zuma's trial for corruption resumed in 2022.

75. "If We Stand Together, No Insurrection or Violence in SA Will Succeed—Ramaphosa," News24, July 16, 2021, https://www.news24.com/news24/southafrica/news/in-full-if-we-stand-together-no-insurrection-or-violence-in-sa-will-succeed-ramaphosa-20210716.

76. Ramaphosa, speaking in Tembisa, in John Eligon and Lynsey Chutel, "South Africa's Leader Is on Mission to Restore Faith in Liberation Party," *New York Times*, November 1, 2021. For the election results, Lynsey Chutel, "A.N.C. Suffers Worst Election Setback since Apartheid Ended," *New York Times*, November 5, 2021.

77. Theo Neethling, "South Africa's Political Risk Profile Has Gone Up a Few Notches: But It's Not Yet a Failed State," *The Conversation*, December 14, 2021. The Global Peace Index is produced by the Institute for Economics and Peace of Sydney, Australia.

78. https://www.google.com/search?q = south + africa+coronavirus&oq = South + Africa+coronavirus&aqs = chrome.0.0i131i433i512j0i131i433i457i512j0i512l8.790.

79. Dawie Roodt's analysis and charts, in "South Africa's Decline in 13 Graphs," BusinessTech, accessed July 21, 2022, https://businesstech.co.za/news/business-opinion/533364/south-africas-decline-in-13-graphs/amp/.

80. Ricardo Hausmann, Federico Sturzenegger, Patricio Goldstein, Frank Muci, and Douglas Barrios, "Macroeconomic Risks after a Decade of Microeconomic Turbulence: South Africa 2007–2020," WIDER Working Paper 2022/3, January 2022.

81. See "The Stench of Corruption," *Economist*, June 2, 2021.

82. Ann Bernstein, "Wise Economic Management Rises above Pressure in Budget Policy Statement," South African Centre for Development Economics, December 1, 2021,https://www.cde.org.za/wise-macroeconomic-management-rises-above-pressure-in-budget-policy-statement/#msdynttrid=-gEAnTRD9BamPloal-ZIRe2RuyUburlZWSY-CMbcbuU.

83. Rotberg, "Can Ramaphosa Save South Africa?," *Diplomat and International Canada*, Summer 2018, 70–71.

   Ramaphosa still had satisfactorily to explain why a vast trove of dollars was discovered in and later stolen by thieves from a couch in his country retreat.

Chapter 8

1. See Thomas Tlou, Neil Parsons, and Willie Henderson, *Seretse Khama, 1921–1980* (Gaborone: Botswana Society, 1950), 61.

2. G. Mennen Williams, quoted in Tlou et al., *Seretse Khama*, 49, 53.

3. "The BDP's 1969 vote was significantly down from its 1965 landslide of 80%. Scholars have generally attributed this to the decision to confront directly royal power with reforms which effectively reduced the powers of the chiefs, notably their ability to

allocate land, while making them subordinated figureheads in local government structures. This resulted in Bathoen II leading other disgruntled royals into the BNF, which then ran against the BDP from what could be described as both revolutionary Marxist and rural reactionary positions." Jeff Ramsay to RIR, email, March 7, 2021.

4. See Chris Brown, "Botswana Votes 2019: Two-Party Competition and the Khama Factor," *Journal of Southern African Studies* XLVI (2020): 703–722.

5. For the kgotla and what it represents as an institution, see Diana Wylie, *A Little God: The Twilight of Patriarchy in a Southern African Kingdom* (Hanover, NH: Wesleyan University Press, 1990), 100–107. Jeff Ramsay adds, "At the core of kgotla discourse is the concept of 'Mmualebe oa bo a bua la gagwe,' which roughly translates as even bad words have to be heard, i.e. a genuine injunction of freedom of speech. The kgotla used to exclude women and malata 'serfs' but were otherwise fairly open. In many tribes there was a history of chiefs courting commoner support as a counterweight to the royal relatives or other ambitious headmen." Ramsay to RIR, March 7, 2021.

6. See also Paul Landau, *The Realm of the Word: Language, Gender and Christianity in a Southern African Kingdom* (Portsmouth, NH: Heinemann, 1995).

7. See Rotberg, *Christian Missionaries and the Creation of Northern Rhodesia* (Princeton: Princeton University Press, 1965); J. Mutero Chirenje, "Church, State, and Education in Bechuanaland in the Nineteenth Century," *International Journal of African Historical Studies* IX (1976): 401–418.

8. See Barry Morton and Jeff Ramsay, "The Invention and Perpetuation of Botswana's National Mythology, 1885–1966," accessed July 22, 2022, https://www.academia.edu/ 15645705/The_Invention_and_Perpetuation_of_Botswanas_National_Mytholog y_1885_1966; Jeff Ramsay, "The Establishment of the Bechuanaland Protectorate," in Wayne Edge and M. H. Lekorwe (eds.), *Botswana Politics and Society* (Cape Town: Schaik, 1998), 62–98.

9. Rhodes and the British South Africa Company's negotiations with, and bullying of, Khama III are described in A. J. Dachs, "Rhodes' Grasp for Bechuanaland, 1889–1896," *Rhodesian History* II (1971): 1–10; Paul Maylam, *Rhodes, the Tswana, and the British: Colonialism, Collaboration and Conflict in the Bechuanaland Protectorate, 1885–1899* (Westport: Greenwood Press, 1980). Prior to the Protectorate, in 1888 the British High Commissioner of the Cape Colony had proclaimed what is now northern Botswana to be a part of a new "sphere of influence" to keep the region north of the twenty-second parallel free of German, Afrikaner, or Portuguese claims. But that joined the Ngwato area together with that of the Ndebele domain in what was to become Zimbabwe.

10. Quett Ketumile Joni Masire (Stephen R. Lewis, ed.), *Very Brave or Very Foolish? Memoirs of an African Democrat* (Gaborone: Macmillan, 2006), 35.

11. Wylie, *Little God*, 184.

12. Tlou et al., *Seretse Khama*, 100, 101. See also the fuller story of the marriage in Susan Williams, *Colour Bar: The Triumph of Seretse Khama and His Nation* (London: Allen Lane, 2006).

13. Quoted in Tlou et al., *Seretse Khama*, 113.

14. Quoted in Tlou et al., *Seretse Khama*, 148.

15. Khama, speaking at the Central Advisory Council, https://www.aluka.org/stable/10.5555/al.sff.document.nujac195804?searchUri=.

16. Mandela, addressing his angry supporters in Katlehong, east of Johannesburg, in 1993, quoted in Tom Lodge, *Mandela: A Critical Life* (New York: Oxford University Press, 2006), 179–180. See also chapter 6.

17. Khama, quoted in Edwin S. Munger, *Bechuanaland: Pan-African Outpost or Bantu Homeland?* (London: Oxford University Press, 1965), 2.

18. Abdi Ismail Samatar, *An African Miracle: State and Class Leadership and Colonial Legacy in Botswana Development* (Portsmouth, NH: Heinemann, 1999), 95.

19. M. Hubbard, "The Beef Cattle Industry," in M. A. Oomen, F. K. Inganji, and L. D. Ngconco (eds.), *Botswana's Economy since Independence* (New Delhi: McGraw-Hill, 1983), 134–151.

20. For some of the early troubles and complications of the copper project, see M. Charles Tibone, "The Shashe Nickel-Copper Project," in Oomen et al., *Botswana's Economy since Independence*, 238–251.

21. But see Festus G. Mogae, "A Review of the Performance of Botswana's Economy," in Oomen et al., *Botswana's Economy since Independence*, 19–28.

22. See Samatar, *African Miracle*, 62.

23. Masire, *Very Brave*, 158.

24. Derek Hudson, "My Recollections of the Introduction of Botswana's Pula Currency on 23 August 1976," in *Botswana Notes and Records* L (2018): 310. For more on the pula and how Botswana carefully managed currency valuations, see Laura Alfaro, "Botswana: A Diamond in the Rough," in Alfaro, *Global Capital and National Institutions: Crisis and Choice in the International Financial Architecture* (Singapore: World Scientific, 2010), 50.

25. On the meaning of Botswana's cattle complex or cattle fixation, see the fascinating discussion in Ornulf Gulbrandsen, *The State and the Social: State Formation in Botswana and Its Precolonial and Colonial Genealogies* (New York: Berghahn, 2012), 112–117.

26. Masire, *Very Brave*, 220–221.

27. Masire, *Very Brave*, 154.

28. Steenkamp, quoted in Bashi Letsididi, "A Conversation with Philip Steenkamp," *Sunday Standard*, October 28, 2007, also in *Botswana Notes and Records* L (2018): 320.

29. Samatar, *African Miracle*, 190.

30. Masire, *Very Brave*, 146.

31. Samatar, *African Miracle*, 177.

32. See Alfaro, "Botswana," 48–49; Debswana Managing Director Lewis G. Nchindo, "Diamonds in Botswana," in Oomen et al., *Botswana's Economy since Independence*, 233–238; Joe Nocera, "Diamonds Are Forever in Botswana," *New York Times*, August 8, 2008.

33. BBC News, "Botswana: De Beers Moves Diamond Sorting to Gaborone," August 15, 2012, https://www.bbc.com/news/business-19268851.

34. See the important discussion in J. Clark Leith, *Why Botswana Prospered* (Montreal: McGill-Queen's University Press, 2005), throughout, especially 112–120.

35. Derek Hudson, "Quill Hermans' Role in the Development of Botswana alongside Seretse Khama and Quett Masire," *Mmegi*, March 20, 2015; also appeared in *Botswana Notes and Records* L (2018).

36. Tlou et al., *Seretse Khama*, 334.

37. Masire, quoted in Amisha Padnani, "Ketumile Masire, 91; Shaped and Led a Vibrant Botswana," *New York Times*, January 7, 2017.

38. Masire, "Economic Opportunities and Disparities," in Masire, *Very Brave*, 239. See also Rotberg, "Leadership Alters Corrupt Behavior," in Rotberg (ed.), *Corruption, Global Security, and World Order* (Washington, DC: Brookings Institution Press, 2009), 352–353.

39. Francis T. Seow, *To Catch a Tartar: A Dissident in Lee Kuan Yew's Prison* (New Haven: Yale University Press, 1994), 20.

40. Khama, quoted in Masire, *Very Brave*, 240; Rotberg, "Leadership Alters Corrupt Behavior," 351–354.

41. Steenkamp, quoted in Bashi Letsididi, "A Conversation with Philip Steenkamp," *Sunday Standard*, October 28, 2007, also in *Botswana Notes and Records* L (2018): 310.

42. Quoted in Tlou et al., *Seretse Khama*, 280, 282. On accountability, Richard L. Sklar, "On Democracy and Development in Botswana," in John Holm and Patrick Molutsi (eds.), *Democracy in Botswana* (Athens: Ohio University Press, 1989), 276.

43. Masire, *Very Brave*, 103.

44. Masire, *Very Brave*, 56.

45. Quoted in Tlou et al., *Seretse Khama*, 364.

46. Tlou et al., *Seretse Khama*, 252.

47. Khama, speaking in New York, quoted in Tlou et al., *Seretse Khama*, 360.

48. Masire, *Very Brave*, 48. See also Tlou et al., *Seretse Khama*, 103.

49. For the theory, and exposition, see Rotberg, *Transformative Political Leadership: Making a Difference in the Developing World* (Chicago: University of Chicago Press, 2012), 20–35.

50. Daron Acemoglu, Simon Johnson, and James A. Robinson, "An African Success Story: Botswana," in Dani Rodrik (ed.), *In Search of Prosperity: Analytic Narratives on Economic Growth* (Princeton: Princeton University Press, 2003), 85–88, 104–106; Leith, *Why Botswana Prospered*, 102–112.

51. Reported in Samatar, *African Miracle*, 102.

52. Stephen R. Lewis Jr., "Remarks at President Q. J. K. Masire's 90th Birthday," Carleton College, July 25, 2015, https://www.carleton.edu/president/lewis/speeches-writings/90th/.

53. Masire, *Very Brave*, 238.

54. Re the mine, see E. Philip Morgan, "Botswana: Democratic Politics and Development," in Gwendolyn M. Carter and Patrick O'Meara (eds.), *Southern Africa in Crisis* (Bloomington: Indiana University Press, 1977), 221.

55. See Alfaro, "Botswana," 41.

56. Jeremy Seekings, "The Effects of Colonialism on Social Protection in South Africa and Botswana," in Carina Schmitt (ed.), *From Colonialism to International Aid: External Actors and Social Protection in the Global South* (London: Palgrave, 2020), 109–135.

For a dissection of welfare polices in Botswana and, especially, of its "workfare" policies, see also Seekings, "Building a Conservative Welfare State in Botswana," WIDER Working Paper 83 (Helsinki, 2017).

57. "GDP Per Capita, PPP (current international $), World Bank, accessed February 24, 2021, https://data.worldbank.org/indicator/NY.GDP.PCAP.PP.CD.

58. Samatar, *African Miracle*, 189.

59. On discrimination (forced) assimilation, and Tswana domination—complex and touchy subjects—see Gulbrandsen, *State and Social*, 212–215.

60. "Indigenous World 2020: Botswana," IWGIA, May 7, 2020, https://www.iwgia.org/en/botswana/3575-indigenous-world-2020-botswana.html. See also the authoritative and critical chapter "Dispossession and Subordination of the San," in Kenneth Good, *Diamonds, Dispossession and Democracy in* Botswana (London: James Currey, 2008), 103–142. There is a useful map at 104. For background, see Mazonde Isaac Ncube, "The Basarwa of Botswana: Leadership, Legitimacy and Participation in Development Sites," *Cultural Survival*, September 1996, culturalsurvival.org/publications/cultural-survival-quarterly/basarwa-botswana-leadership-legitimacy-and-participation.

61. Masire, *Very Brave*, 242.

62. See Gabriel Kuris, "Managing Corruption Risk: Botswana Builds an Antigraft Agency, 1994–2012," Princeton University, Innovations for Successful Societies Program, 2013, 1–2; Charles Manga Fombad, "Curbing Corruption in Africa: Some Lessons from Botswana's Experience," *International Social Science Journal* LI (1999): 241–254.

63. See Andrew Briscoe and Quill Hermans, *Combating Corruption in Botswana* (Gaborone: Ebert Foundation, 2001), 91–105.

64. But see the sharp dissenting views of Good, *Diamonds, Dispossession and Democracy*, 3 ff.

65. See Ian Taylor and Kenneth Good, "Unpacking the 'Model': Presidential Succession in Botswana," in Roger Southall and Henning Melber (eds.), *Legacies of Power: Leadership Change and Former Presidents in African Politics* (Cape Town: HSRC, 2006), 51–72.

66. Botsalo Ntuane, "President Festus Mogae: The Regent Who Became King," *Sunday Standard*, November 4, 2007, and in *Botswana Notes and Records* L (2018): 334.

67. Masire, *Very Brave*, 238. For the numbers, Alfaro, "Botswana," 52.

68. "Botswana Infant Mortality Rate 1950–2022," Macrotrends, accessed July 22, 2022, https://www.macrotrends.net/countries/BWA/botswana/infant-mortality-rate#:~:text = The%20current%20infant%20mortality%20rate,a%202.37%25%2.

69. "Africa Infant Mortality Rate 1950–2022," Macrotrends, accessed July 22, 2022, macrotrends.net/countries/AFR/africa/infant-mortality-rate#:~:text = The%20infant%20mortality%20rate%20for,a%202.6%25%20decline%20from%202020.

70. See Ian Taylor, "The Limits of the 'African Miracle': Academic Freedom in Botswana and the Deportation of Kenneth Good," *Journal of Contemporary African Studies* XXIV (2006): 101–122.

71. See Monageng Mogalakwe, "Botswana at 50: Democratic Deficit, Elite Corruption and Poverty in the Midst of Plenty," *Journal of Contemporary African Studies* XXXV (2017): 1–14.

72. Kenneth Good, "The Presidency of General Ian Khama: The Militarization of the Botswana 'Miracle,'" *African Affairs* CIX (2009): 315–324.

73. On parliamentary weakness, see Patrick Molutsi, "Botswana's Democratic Institutions: Their Strength and Prospects," in Sue Brothers, Janet Hermans, and Doreen Nteta (eds.), *Botswana in the 21st Century* (Gaborone: Botswana Society, 1994), 29.

74. Robert M. Molebatsi and Nelson Sello, "Parallel Policy Structures in Botswana: From Devolution to Centralisation under Ian Khama's Administration, 2008–2018," *Botswana Notes and Records* L (2018): 261, 264 (earlier quotations from 260).

75. See Molebatsi and Sello, "Parallel Policy Structures," 264. See also Enole Ditsheko, *Wrestling Botswana Back from Khama* (Gaborone: np, 2019).

76. Mogae, quoted in Lynsey Chutel, "Botswana Election Won by President Despite Rift with Predecessor," *New York Times*, October 25, 2019.

77. Barry Morton, "How Masisi Outsmarted Khama to Take the Reins in Botswana," *The Conversation*, November 6, 2019; Chutel, "Botswana Election."

78. https://graphics.reuters.com/world-coronavirus-tracker-and-maps/countries-and-territories/botswana.

79. "Education in Africa: Covid-19 Spurs Catch-up Classes," *Economist*, April 10, 2021.

80. For the Lee method, see Rotberg, *Transformative Political Leadership*, 93–119. For the 2019 election, see Brown, "Botswana Votes," 703–722.

81. Freedom House, https://freedomhouse.org/countries/freedom-world/scores, 2020.

82. Rotberg and Rachel Gisselquist, *Strengthening African Governance: Index of African Governance, Results and Rankings* (Cambridge, MA: World Peace Foundation, 2007, 2009); http://iiag.online/app.html?loc=AO|BF|BI|BJ|BW|CD|CF|CG|CI|CM|CV|DJ|DZ|EG|ER|ET|GA|GH|GM|GN|GQ|GW|KE|KM|LR|LS|LY|MA|MG|ML|MR|MU|MW|MZ|NA|NE|NG|RW|SC|SD|SL|SN|SO|SS|ST|SZ|TD|TG|TN|TZ|UG|ZA|ZM|ZW&meas=GOVERNANCE&view=table, 2019.

83. Jeff Ramsay to RIR, email, December 19, 2021.

84. Rotberg, "Lessons from Botswana," *Christian Science Monitor*, March 3, 2003.

Chapter 9

1. See Harold Macmillan, *Pointing the Way: 1959–61* (London: Macmillan, 1971), 156.

2. Rotberg, "From Settler Rhodesia to African Zimbabwe," in Rotberg, *Ending Autocracy, Enabling Democracy: The Tribulations of Southern Africa* (Washington, DC: Brookings Press, 2002), 48. For white attitudes and approaches, see Colin Leys, *European Politics in Southern Rhodesia* (Oxford: Clarendon, 1959), 275–278. For a careful examination of the impact of settler policy on Africans, see Robin Palmer, *Land and Racial Domination in Rhodesia* (Berkeley: University of California Press, 1977); Leonard Leslie Bessant, "Coercive Development: Land Shortage, Forced Labor, and Colonial Development in the Chiweshe Reserve, Colonial Zimbabwe, 1938–1946," *International Journal of African Historical Studies* XXV (1992): 39–65.

3. For the fall of Prime Minister Garfield Todd and his replacement (with Welensky's help) by (Sir) Edgar Whitehead—and what those machinations meant for the future of Southern Rhodesia, see Roger Southall, "If Only: Missed Opportunity or Inevitable Fate in Rhodesia?," *Canadian Journal of African Studies* LIII (2019): 368–369; Susan Woodhouse, *Garfield Todd: The End of the Liberal Dream in Rhodesia* (Harare: Weaver Press, 2018).

4. For details, see John Day, "Southern Rhodesian African Nationalists and the 1961 Constitution," *Journal of Modern African Studies*, VII (1969): 221–247; Jan Olssen, "A Crucial Watershed in Southern Rhodesian Politics: The 1961 Constitutional Process and the 1962 General Election" (unpub. MA thesis, University of Gotland), 2011; James Barber, *Rhodesia: The Road to Rebellion* (London: Oxford University Press, 1967), 79–85.

5. Timothy Lewis Scarnecchia, *Race and Diplomacy in Zimbabwe: the Cold War and Decolonization, 1960–1984* (Cambridge: Cambridge University Press, 2021), 27, has a different time line for the creation of ZAPU.

6. Rotberg, "From Moderate to Militant," *Africa Report*, March 1962.

7. Palley, quoted in Martin Meredith, *Our Votes, Our Guns: Robert Mugabe and the Tragedy of Zimbabwe* (New York: Public Affairs, 2002), 29.

8. A good source for the various maneuvers for control of the rebel African political movements in the months before Mugabe and others returned to Harare from Dar es Salaam and were tried for sedition is David Smith and Colin Simpson, *Mugabe* (London: Sphere, 1981), 44–50.

9. For the American debate and position, see Mark Atwood Lawrence, *The End of Ambition: The United States and the Third World in the Vietnam Era* (Princeton: Princeton University Press, 2021), 267–270.

10. For UDI and the African response, see Alois S. Mlambo, *A History of Zimbabwe* (Cambridge: Cambridge University Press, 2014), 149–193.

11. Quoted in Rotberg, "Great Britain Hasn't Solved the Rhodesian Problem Just Yet," *Newsday*, March 19, 1972.

12. See Rotberg, "Southern Africa May Be the World's Next Guerrilla War Zone," *Newsday*, February 8, 1973.

13. See Ngwabi Bhebe and Terence Ranger (eds.), *Soldiers in Zimbabwe's Liberation War* (London: James Currey, 1995).

14. For bitter ethnic and personal rivalries within each of the Zimbabwean exile movements, see Scarnecchia, *Race and Diplomacy*, 39–41. The formation of the Front for the Liberation of Zimbabwe is also discussed there.

15. For a laudatory biography of van der Byl, see Hannes Wessels, *PK van der Byl: African Statesman* (Brixton, South Africa: 30 South, 2010). The book's subtitle must surely be oxymoronic.

16. Quoted in Scarnecchia, *Race and Diplomacy*, 51. On the assassination of Chitepo and Tongogara's involvement, see also Smith and Simpson, *Mugabe*, 75–79; Alex Callinicos and John Rogers, *Southern Africa after Soweto* (London: Pluto, 1977), 127–129. For Solomon Mujuru's possible role in the assassination, and abundant detail about Tongogara's contribution, see Blessing-Miles Tendi, *The Army and Politics in*

Zimbabwe: Mujuru, the Liberation Fighter and Kingmaker (Cambridge: Cambridge University Press, 2020), 56–67. Luise White, *The Assassination of Herbert Chitepo: Texts and Politics in Zimbabwe* (Bloomington: Indiana University Press, 2003), also contains important material.

17. For the then relevant machinations, see Douglas G. Anglin and Timothy M. Shaw, *Zambia's Foreign Policy: Studies in Diplomacy and Dependence* (Boulder: Westview, 1979), 276–302.

18. Charles de Chassiron to Laver, July 26, 1976, quoted in Scarnecchia, *Race and Diplomacy*, 71. Much of what Mugabe told me he also repeated to U.S. Assistant Secretary of State for Africa William E. Schaufele Jr. in November 1976, on the sidelines of the Geneva conference. See Scarnecchia, *Race and Diplomacy*, 109.

19. Kissinger to Lusaka embassy, February 7, 1976, quoted in Scarnecchia, *Race and Diplomacy*, 57. Mark Chona, on behalf of Kaunda, was instrumental in gaining Kissinger's attention and urging him to prevent Cuban interference in Rhodesia.

20. For an extensive review of U.S. policy attitudes to UDI and the Smith regime, and for Kissinger's role, see Gerald Horne, *From the Barrel of a Gun: The United States and the War against Zimbabwe, 1965–1980* (Chapel Hill: University of North Carolina Press, 2001), 156–166.

21. Foreign and Colonial Office correspondence, February 25, 1976, in Scarnecchia, *Race and Diplomacy*, 68.

22. On this last point, see the conversation reported in Scarnecchia, *Race and Diplomacy*, 127.

23. Nkomo, quoted in Scarnecchia, *Race and Diplomacy*, 145–146.

24. For penetrating details about the *chimurenga* or bush war, with an emphasis on operations results (from both sides), see Jakkie K. Cilliers, *Counter-insurgency in Rhodesia* (Dover, NH: Croom Helm, 1985). Among the most detailed discussion of the war is Eddison Zvobgo's unpublished dissertation for a Fletcher School (Tufts University) doctoral degree. The degree was never granted, but the lengthy dissertation is in RIR files: "Chimurenga: A Study of Patterns and Phases in the Use of Political Threats, Arson, Intimidation, Violence, Terror and Armed-Struggle by African Liberation Movements in Southern Rhodesia . . ." (1977).

25. Quoted in Smith and Simpson, *Mugabe*, 123.

26. See Emizet F. Kisangani and Jeffrey Pickering, *African Interventions: State Militaries, Foreign Powers, and Rebel Forces* (Cambridge: Cambridge University Press, 2022), 214.

27. On Tongogara, and Tongogara's demise, see for his death, https://allafrica.com/stories/202112280381.html; for theories about his demise; "Zimbabwe: Tongo Murdered for Saying Mugabe Would Be 'Total Disaster' for Zim—Dabengwa," New Zimbabwe.com, June 21, 2018, https://allafrica.com/stories/201806210771.html.

28. Walter Kansteiner, interview with Michelle Gavin, "Africa in Transition," Council on Foreign Relations, blog, January 5, 2022.

29. See Rotberg, "Who Killed Solomon Mujuru? The Mystery in Zimbabwe Deepens," ThinkAfricaPress.com, February13, 2012. The definitive account, for now, is Tendi, *Army and Politics*, 264–296, who reviews the probabilities, indicates chillingly how he was likely killed, but assigns no final responsibility.

A supposed defector from the ZANU ministry of transport once showed up in my Harvard Kennedy School office and told me in detail how he had been instructed to sabotage automobiles of persons whom the regime wanted to eliminate. I was never able, unfortunately, to ascertain the veracity of his account, nor much about him and his asylum travails in the United States.

30. Kamuzu Banda had made the same prediction, for the same reasons, in conversation with Prime Minister Thatcher, quoted in Scarnecchia, *Race and Diplomacy*, 211.

31. Eddie Cross, "Understanding the Zimbabwe Economy," March 21, 2021, email to various recipients.

32. Mugabe, address to the nation, April 17, 1980, quoted in Gugulethu Moyo and Mark Ashurst, *The Day after Mugabe: Prospects for Change in Zimbabwe* (London: Africa Research Institute, 2007), 18–19.

33. See Suzanne Verheul, *Performing Power in Zimbabwe: Politics, Law, and the Courts since 2000* (Cambridge: Cambridge University Press, 2021), 43. U.S. Ambassador to Zimbabwe Robert Keeley believed that 30,000, not 20,000, was the likely number of casualties. Cited in Scarnecchia, *Race and Diplomacy*, 306. For the Fifth Brigade and its functions, see Jocelyn Alexander, JoAnn McGregor, and Terence Ranger, *Violence and Memory: One Hundred Years in the "Dark Forests" of Matabeleland* (Oxford: James Currey, 2000), 217–224.

34. Bishop Henry Karlen to Mugabe, February 12, 1983, quoted in Scarnecchia, *Race and Diplomacy*, 275. See, for contemporary reports of the atrocities, Nick Davies, "The Massacre That Misfired," *Guardian*, February 23, 1983. See also Ian Phimister, "The Making and Meanings of the Massacres in Matabeleland," *Development Dialogues* L (2008): 199–218; Hazel Cameron, "The Matabeleland Massacres: Britain's Wilful Blindness," *International History Review* XL (2018): 1–19; the Catholic Commission on Justice and Peace, "Breaking the Silence, Building True Peace: A Report on the Disturbances in Matabeleland and the Midlands, 1980 to 1988," February 1997, http://davidcoltart.com/wp-content/uploads/2006/10/breakingthesilence.pdf.

35. Meredith, *Our Votes, Our Guns*, 59–73.

36. Rotberg, "Signs of Trouble Lurking in Zimbabwe," *Boston Globe*, April 18, 1983.

37. A thorough analysis of Mugabe's socialist economic maneuvers is found in Tony Hawkins' trenchant "Zimbabwe's Socialist Transformation," *Optima*, XXXV (1987): 184–195.

38. Rotberg, "A Gradual—but Decisive—Step Backward in Zimbabwe," *Christian Science Monitor*, August 17, 1984; "Zimbabwe's Rhetoric at Odds with Reality," *Boston Globe*, October 14, 1984; "Zimbabwe and the Socialist Embrace: Roaring Backward into One-Party Rule," *Christian Science Monitor*, January 14, 1988.

39. See Edgar Tekere, *A Lifetime of Struggle* (Harare: SAPES, 2007).

40. See "Margaret Dongo," in African Feminist Forum, accessed March 1, 2021, http://www.africanfeministforum.com/margaret-dongo/.

41. Rotberg, "Democracy in Africa: The Ballot Does Not Tell All," *Christian Science Monitor*, May 1, 1996.

42. Rotberg, "Zimbabwe's Leader Takes Care of His Own," *Christian Science Monitor*, February 17, 1998.

43. Rotberg, "Mugabe's Dictatorship Erodes," *Christian Science Monitor*, December 8, 1998. For an astute blow-by-blow of Rwanda's invasion of Laurent Kabila's Congo and the response by Mugabe that startled President Paul Kagame, see Philip Roessler and Harry Verhoeven, *Why Comrades Go to War: Liberation Politics and the Outbreak of Africa's Deadliest Conflict* (New York: Oxford University Press, 2016), 387–389. See also Tom Burgis, *Kleptopia: How Dirty Money Is Conquering the World* (New York: HarperCollins, 2020), 50–51, 280.

44. For detentions and police treatment of detainees abusively, see the chapter on that subject in Verheul, *Performing Power*, 107–121.

45. Rotberg, "Corruption and Torture in Mugabe's Zimbabwe," *Boston Globe*, February 14, 1999; Angus Shaw, "Zimbabwe Leader Accuses Judges," Associated Press, February 7, 1999, https://apnews.com/article/f04fdc9a722d9c801af244025de79 551. See also Meredith, *Our Votes, Our Guns*, 150–154; George Hamandishe Karekwaivanane, *The Struggle over State Power in Zimbabwe: Land and Politics since 1950* (New York: Cambridge University Press, 2017), 228–229.

46. Quoted in Rotberg, *Ending Autocracy*, 236–237. For a sensitive discussion of the role of courts and justice in the twenty-first century, see Verheul, *Performing Power*, 51–59 ff.

47. For a detailed analysis of the farm seizures and what motivated Mugabe in attacking such a productive portion of his national economy, see Charles Laurie, *The Land Reform Deception: Political Opportunism in Zimbabwe's Land Seizure Era* (New York: Oxford University Press, 2016). For a colorful account of the farm invasions, see Paul Theroux, *Dark Star Safari* (Boston: Houghton Mifflin, 2003), 354–360. Andrew Meldrum, an engaged American journalist living in Zimbabwe, also observed and interviewed many besieged white farmers and their antagonists. See his *Where We Have Hope: A Memoir of Zimbabwe* (London: John Murray, 2004), 129–140.

48. "A senior member of Zimbabwe's land reform agency told me that he had been well aware at the time that Mugabe's policy would be a disaster. He also knew that a very reasonable alternative was available: allowing white farmers to remain on the land while breaking up and redistributing their holdings. For example, retain 200 or 500 hectares of a 10,000 hectare farm and redistribute the rest. But he feared that speaking up would get him killed—very likely true." Bruce Bolnick, email to RIR, January 22, 2021.

49. U.S. Assistant Secretary of State for Africa Walter Kansteiner remembered in 2022 that Mugabe "stole" elections continuously. Interview with Michelle Gavin, "Africa in Transition," Council on Foreign Relations email blog, January 5, 2022.

50. Rotberg, "Mugabe uber Alles: The Tyranny of Unity in Zimbabwe," *Foreign Affairs* LXXXIX (2010): 11. See also Rotberg, *Haiti: The Politics of Squalor* (Boston: Houghton Mifflin, 1971). On how corruption became so pervasive, see Ruth Weiss, *Zimbabwe and the New Elite* (London: British Academic Press, 1994), 185–190.

51. Rotberg, "Mugabe uber Alles," 10. For the 2008 election, and violence writ large, see Lloyd Sachikonye, *When a State Turns on Its Citizens: Institutionalized Violence and Political Culture* (Auckland Park, South Africa: Jacana, 2011), 62–78; Derek Matyszak, *Law, Politics and Zimbabwe's "Unity" Government* (Harare: Konrad-Adenauer Stiftung, 2010), 46.

52. Partnership Africa Canada, "Reap What You Sow: Greed and Corruption in Zimbabwe's Marrange Diamond Fields," Partnership Report, November 12, 2012.

53. Burgis, *Kleptopia*, 277, 336. Gifts from kleptocrats also greased electoral wheels in 2008.

54. Rotberg, "Lessons from the Field: Plunder and the Perils of Mugabe's Zimbabwe," *Africa Up Close*, Woodrow Wilson International Center for Scholars, February 16, 2015. The full study of why and how Mugabe and ZANU-PF out-maneuvered Tsvangirai and the MDC is contained in Stephen Chan and Julia Gallagher, *Why Mugabe Won: The 2013 Elections in Zimbabwe and Their Aftermath* (Cambridge: Cambridge University Press, 2017), 37–47.

55. Rotberg, "Zimbabwe: A Captive Nation," *Cape Times*, February 24, 2014.

56. Walter Kansteiner, recalling the conversation, interview with Michelle Gavin, "Africa in Transition," January 5, 2022.

57. Michael Clemens and Todd Moss, "Costs and Causes of Zimbabwe's Crisis," *CGD Notes*, July 2005, https://www.cgdev.org/sites/default/files/2918_file_Zimbabwe_Crisis.pdf.

58. Rotberg, "Lessons from the Field."

59. Rotberg, "Mugabe Goes to China," *China-US Focus*, September 4, 2014; Rotberg, "Chinese Farmers on African Land," *China-US Focus*, October 20, 2016; www.chinausfocus.com/.

60. Rotberg, "First Lady's Ominous Rise in Zim," *Cape Times*, November 21, 2014; Rotberg, "Grace Mugabe's Recklessness May Spark a Deadly Presidential Succession," *Globe & Mail*, November 13, 2017.

61. David Coltart, quoted in Rotberg, "A Corrupt Pattern Keeps Repeating," *Boston Globe*, December 3, 2017.

62. On the currency games, see Roger Southall, "Bond Notes, Borrowing, and Heading for Bust: Zimbabwe's Persistent Crisis," *Canadian Journal of African Studies* LI (2017): 389–405.

63. For revelations about the role of the notorious Billy Rautenbach in providing illicit funds for Mnangagwa, see Burgis, *Kleptopia*, 49–53, 72–73, 276–278, 336.

64. https://www.google.com/search?q=ZIMBABWE+CORONAVIRUS&oq=ZIMBABWE+CORONAVIRUS&aqs=chrome..69i57.4671j0j7&sourceid=chrome&ie=UTF-8.

65. https://mo.ibrahim.foundation/prize/laureates/festus-gontebanye-mogae.

66. https://www.transparency.org/en/cpi/2020/index/zwe.

67. Mark Heywood, "Zimbabwe: Explosive Cartel Report Uncovers the Anatomy of a Captured State," *Maverick Citizen*, February 9 and 10, 2021 (two parts), https://www.dailymaverick.co.za/article/2021-02-09-zimbabwe-explosive-cartel-report-uncovers-the-anatomy-of-a-captured-state.

68. "Report of Cartel Dynamics in Zimbabwe," ScribD, January 2021, https://www.scribd.com/document/493789960/Power-Dynamics-02-FEB-2021-Optimized, 13–21.

69. "Zimbabwe Central Bank Revises Inflation Target as Prices Soar," Bloomberg, May 30, 2022, https://www.businesslive.co.za/bloomberg/news/2022-05-30-zimbabwe-central-bank-revises-inflation-target-as-prices-soar.

70. Felix Njini and Antony Sguazzin, "Tycoon Seen Scoring from Zimbabwe's $3.4 Billion Off-Budget Debt," March 23, 2022, Bloomberg, https://www.bloomberg.com/news/articles/2022-03-23/tycoon-seen-scoring-from-zimbabwe-s-3-4-billion-off-budget-debt#xj4y7vzkg.

71. Chris Muronzi, "Paying to Get Paid: Young Zimbabweans Trade Money, Sex for Jobs," *Aljazeera*, May 19, 2022, https://www.aljazeera.com/features/2022/5/19/paying-to-get-paid-young-zimbabweans-trade-money-sex-for-jobs.

72. Muronzi, "Paying to Get Paid."

73. Michelle Galvin, "Africa in Transition," *Foreign Affairs* blog, June 1, 2022.

74. Galvin, "Africa in Transition."

Chapter 10

1. See Rotberg, *A Political History of Tropical Africa* (Boston: Harcourt Brace, 1965), 276.

2. See Rotberg, "Namibia's Push for Reparations from Germany Could Have Lessons for Other Nations," *Globe & Mail*, August 28, 2020.

3. Article 22 of the Covenant of the League of Nations, in John Dugard (ed.), *The South West Africa / Namibia Dispute* (Berkeley: University of California Press, 1973), 67.

4. See Isaak I. Dore, *The International Mandate System and Namibia* (Boulder: Westview, 1985), 63–74.

5. See John H. Wellington, *South West Africa and Its Human Issues* (Oxford: Oxford University Press, 1967), 307–308; Nicholas H. Z. Watts, "The Roots of the Controversy," in Rotberg (ed.), *Namibia: Political and Economic Prospects* (Lexington: Lexington Books, 1983), 3–5.

6. See Patricia Hayes, Jeremy Silvester, Marion Wallace, and Wolfram Hartmann (eds.), *Namibia under South African Rule: Mobility & Containment* (London: James Currey, 1998).

7. For a trenchant examination of Namibian agricultural enterprise and South Africa's attempt to use the "reserves" that it had created as labor reservoirs, see Wolfe W. Schmokel, "The Myth of the White Farmer: Commercial Agriculture in Namibia, 1900–1983," *International Journal of African Historical Studies* XVIII (1985): 93–108.

8. On petitions, see Peter H. Katjavivi, *A History of Resistance in Namibia* (Trenton: Africa World Press, 1990), 34–40.

9. See Dugard, *South West Africa*, 128–215.

10. For the Turnhalle ploy, and much more, see André du Pisani, *SWA/Namibia: The Politics of Continuity and Change* (Johannesburg: Jonathan Ball, 1985), 283–332, 377–381.

11. Jan-Bart Gewald, "Who Killed Clemens Kapuuo?," *Journal of Southern African Studies* XXX (2004): 559–576.

12. For the enforced resignation of Vorster because of clandestine attempts to buy influence overseas and create surreptitious news outlets at home, see Rotberg, "South Africa under Botha: How Deep the Change?," *Foreign Policy* XXXVIII (Spring 1980): 130.

13. Rotberg, *Suffer the Future: Policy Choices in Southern Africa* (Cambridge, MA: Harvard University Press, 1980), 222.

14. For an extensive discussion of Viljoen's role as chair of the Broederbond, see Ivor Wilkins and Hans Strydom, *The Super-Afrikaners: Inside the Afrikaner Broederbond* (Johannesburg: Jonathan Ball, 1978), 8, 14, 23 ff.

15. Rotberg, *Ending Autocracy, Enabling Democracy: The Tribulations of Southern Africa* (Washington, DC: Brookings, 2002), 125; Rotberg, "Namibian Soap Opera: Is South Africa Ready to End It?," *Christian Science Monitor*, June 8, 1981.

16. David Smuts, *Death, Detention and Disappearance: A Lawyer's Battle to Hold Power to Account in 1980s Namibia* (Cape Town: Tafelberg, 2019); the final quotation is from 304.

17. Rotberg, "On Southern Africa," *New York Times*, December 10, 1982; Rotberg, "Why the Russians Can Fish in Southern Africa's Troubled Waters," *Christian Science Monitor*, March 8, 1983. For the South African military side of the war, see Richard Dale, *The Namibian War of Independence, 1966–1989: Diplomatic, Economic and Military Campaigns* (Jefferson, NC: McFarland, 2014), 93–104. For a defense of constructive engagement, see Chester Crocker, *High Noon in Southern Africa: Making Peace in a Rough Neighborhood* (New York: Norton, 1993).

18. See Rotberg, "Angolan Sting," *Christian Science Monitor*, April 10, 1986. The Stingers were sent instead to Afghanistan, to help Afghans fight against the Soviet occupation and then to be employed by the Taliban against Afghans.

19. Rotberg, "U.S. & South Africa," *Christian Science Monitor*, June 24, 1985.

20. Rotberg, "Is Namibia on the Peace Train?," *Christian Science Monitor*, September 15, 1988.

21. Smuts, *Death*, 283. For Ahtisaari's views on how to mediate conflicts, see Katri Merikallio, *Making Peace: Ahtisaari and Aceh* (Juva, Finland: WS Bookwell Oy, 2006), 137–144.

22. For South African skullduggery, see Terry Bell, *Unfinished Business: South Africa, Apartheid and Truth* (London: Verso, 2003), 268–270.

23. For an overview of the transition period, see David Lush, *Last Steps to Uhuru: An Eye-Witness Account of Namibia's Transition to Independence* (Windhoek: New Namibia Books, 1993).

24. Adam Posluns, "Namibia: Undoing Press Freedom," Committee to Protect Journalists, accessed October 29, 2020, https://cpj.org/reports/2002/10/namibia-oct02/.

25. Henning Melber, *Understanding Namibia: The Trials of Independence* (London: Hurst, 2014), 63.

26. Melber, *Understanding Namibia*, 70.

27. Melber, *Understanding Namibia*, 85, 92.

28. David Smuts to RIR, email, April 5, 2021.

29. Quoted in Rotberg, "Growing Clouds of Corruption Threaten Namibia's Progress," *Christian Science Monitor*, August 9, 1994.

30. https://www.transparency.org/en/cpi/2020/index/mys; https://www.transparency.org/files/content/pages/2019_CPI_Report_EN.pdf; https://www.transparency.org/en/cpi/2011.

31. Heritage Foundation, Index of Economic Freedom, 2020, accessed October 29, 2020, https://www.heritage.org/index/country/namibia.

32. Index of Public Integrity, accessed October 30, 2020, https://integrity-index.org/.

33. https://www.google.com/search?q=index+of+public+integrity+2021&oq=index+of+public+integrity+2021&aqs=chrome..69i57j33i160.7517j0j7&sourceid=chro.

34. Sonja Smith, "After 'Fishrot' Scandal, Namibia Earns Little from Auction," October 1, 2020, https://apnews.com/article/virus-outbreak-cabinets-southern-africa-atlantic-ocean-africa-a76187d1567cf9837ae1acf89c5db196.

35. James Kleinfeld, "Corruption Prevailing," *Aljazeera*, December 1, 2019 https://www.aljazeera.com/news/2019/12/1/exclusive-corruption-in-namibias-fishing-industry-unveiled.

36. https://www.occrp.org/en/daily/13669-leaked-affidavit-implicates-namibian-president-in-fishrot-scandal.

37. Shinovene Immanuel, "Defence Minister Resigns," *Namibian*, April 6, 2021, https://www.namibian.com.na/100525/read/Defence-minister-resigns.

38. https://www.heritage.org/index/country/namibia.

39. https://www.bloomberg.com/news/articles/2021-03-15/nigeria-unemployment-rate-rises-to-second-highest-on-global-list#:~:text = The%20oil%20producer%20surpassed%20South,leads%20the%20list%20with%2033.4%25.

40. World Bank, accessed October 30, 2020, https://data.worldbank.org/indicator/SI.POV.GINI?locations = NA; https://data.worldbank.org/indicator/NY.GDP.PCAP.PP.CD, accessed 3/3/21.

41. André du Pisani to RIR, March 18, 2021.

42. Melber, *Understanding Namibia*, 177.

43. Rotberg and Rachel Gisselquist, *Strengthening African Governance* (Cambridge, MA: World Peace Foundation, 2007, 2009).

44. https://www.google.com/search?q=namibia+coronavirus&oq=Namibia+coron&aqs=chrome.0.0i512j69i57j0i512j0i457i512j0i22i30l6.5290j0j7&sourceid=chrome&ie=UTF-8.

45. Henning Melber, "Namibia's Democracy Enters New Era as Ruling Swapo Continues to Lose Its Lustre," *The Conversation*, December 6, 2020.

46. Melber, "Namibia's Democracy."

47. Henning Melber, "Why, 31 Years after Independence, Namibians Aren't in a Festive Mood," *The Conversation*, March 17, 2021.

Chapter 11

1. Frantz Fanon (Constance Farrington, trans.), *The Wretched of the Earth* (1961; New York: Grove Press, 1963), 134–136. See also Irene L. Gendzier, *Frantz Fanon: A Critical Study* (New York: Pantheon, 1973), 219, 221, for an important gloss on Fanon's thinking and intellectual development.

2. Howard Gardner, *Changing Minds: The Art and Science of Changing Our Own and Other People's Minds* (Boston: Harvard Business Review Press, 2006), 39, 108; Gardner,

Frames of Mind: The Theory of Multiple Intelligences, 2nd ed. (New York: Basic Books, 2004), 239.

3. Rotberg, *Transformative Political Leadership: Making a Difference in the Developing World* (Chicago: University of Chicago Press, 2012), 21.

4. Lee, quoted in James Minchin, *No Man Is an Island: A Portrait of Singapore's Lee Kuan Yew* (1986; London: Allen & Unwin, 1990), 343.

5. For a detailed examination of these concepts, and a setting out of the full argument, see Rotberg, *Transformational Political Leadership*, 21–38.

6. See the extended argument in Rotberg, *Things Come Together: Africans Achieving Greatness in the Twenty-First Century* (New York: Oxford University Press, 2020), 61–63; Rotberg, "The Governance of Nations: Definitions and Measures," in Rotberg (ed.), *On Governance: What It Is, What It Measures, and Its Policy Uses* (Waterloo: CIGI Press, 2015), 7–22.

7. See Rotberg and Rachel M. Gisselquist, *Strengthening African Governance: The Index of African Governance, Results and Rankings* (Cambridge, MA: World Peace Foundation, 2007, 2008, 2009), 3v.

8. https://iiag.online/app.html?v = mG7Bg_Dv, 2019.

9. https://freedomhouse.org/countries/freedom-world/scores, 2020.

10. http://hdr.undp.org/en/content/latest-human-development-index-ranking, 2020.

11. https://www.google.com/search?q=human+development+index+2020&oq= HUman+Development+INdex+2020&aqs=chrome.0.0i457j0l9.

12. https://www.prosperity.com/globe#MUS, 2020.

13. The full argument is contained in Rotberg, "The Failure and Collapse of Nation-States: Breakdown, Prevention, and Repair," in Rotberg (ed.), *When States Fail: Causes and Consequences* (Princeton: Princeton University Press, 2004), 1–50.

14. See Rotberg and John Campbell, "The Giant of Africa Is Failing: Only Nigeria Can Save Itself—but the United States Can Help," *Foreign Affairs*, May 31, 2021; "Nigeria Is a Failed State," *Foreign Policy*, May 27, 2021.

15. https://data.worldbank.org/indicator/SI.POV.GINI?locations = ZG. Note that the World Bank's Gini figures are not current in each case. Some, because of the way in which Gini coefficients are created, date back to 2015 and 2017. Zimbabwe's relatively low number (44.3) may reflect outdated data.

16. Numbers are from the Organisation for Economic Co-operation and Development, CleanGovBiz, "The Rationale for Fighting Corruption," Background Brief, 2014, 2, https://maritimecyprus.com/wp-content/uploads/2017/09/oecd-1.pdf; Joseph Spanjers and Dev Kar, "Illicit Financial Flows from Developing Countries: 2004–2013," Global Financial Integrity, December 8, 2015, https://gfintegrity.org/report/illicit-financial-flows-from-developing-countries-2004-2013/; Richard Rose and Carolyn Peiffer, *Paying Bribes for Public Services: A Global Guide to Grass Roots Corruption* (Basingstoke: Palgrave Macmillan, 2015), xi, 1, 10.

17. Transparency International, Corruption Perceptions Index, 2019, https://www.transparency.org/en/cpi/2019/index/chl.

18. See chapter 8.

19. Rotberg, *Transformational Political Leadership*, 173.

20. World Bank, Global Economic Prospects, 2021, accessed July 24, 2026, http://pubd ocs.worldbank.org/en/389631599838727666/Global-Economic-Prospects-January- 2021-Analysis-SSA.pdf.

21. https://www.pewresearch.org/global/2015/07/08/despite-povertys-plunge-middle- class-status-remains-out-of-reach-for-many.

22. For Nyerere's last years, see Paul Bjerk, *Julius Nyerere* (Athens: Ohio University Press, 2017), 127–148.

23. Mogae, quoted in Geoffrey York, "Foundation Unable to Hand Out Ibrahim Prize for Third Time in Six Years," *Globe & Mail*, October 15, 2012.

24. Lee, quoted in Han Fook Kwang, Warren Fernandez, and Sumiko Tan, *Lee Kuan Yew: The Man and His Ideas* (Singapore: Marshall Cavendish, 1998), 101, 231; Michael D. Barr, *Lee Kuan Yew: The Beliefs behind the Man* (Richmond: Surrey, 2000), 124.

25. Warren G. Bennis and Burt Nanus, *Leaders: Strategies for Taking Charge* (New York: Collins, 1997), 207, summarizes the research. "Major capacities and com- petencies of leadership can be learned. . . ."

26. African Leadership Council press release, March 20, 2004, https://www.belfercen ter.org/publication/african-leadership-council; Masire, "Good Leadership," speech delivered at the Eskom Business Leaders Forum, Johannesburg, October 13, 2004, unpub., RIR files. See also Rotberg, "Strengthening African Leadership: There Is Another Way," *Foreign Affairs*, LXXXIII (July–August 2004): 14–17.

27. See Siddhartha Mukherjee, "The Covid Conundrum," *New Yorker*, March 1, 2021, 18– 24; Rotberg, "The Horsemen of the African Apocalypse," *Diplomat and International Canada*, Spring 2021.

For Further Reading

Acemoglu, Daron, Simon Johnson, and James A. Robinson, "An African Success Story: Botswana," in Dani Rodrik (ed.), *In Search of Prosperity: Analytic Narratives on Economic Growth* (Princeton: Princeton University Press, 2003), 80–102.

Adam, Heribert, *Modernizing Racial Domination: The Dynamics of South African Politics* (Berkeley: University of California Press, 1971).

Adam, Heribert, and Hermann Giliomee, *Ethnic Power Mobilized: Can South Africa Change?* (New Haven: Yale University Press, 1979).

Adam, Heribert, and Kogila Moodley, *South Africa without Apartheid: Dismantling Racial Domination* (Berkeley: University of California Press, 1986).

Adebajo, Adkeye, *Thabo Mbeki* (Athens: Ohio University Press, 2016).

Alexander, Jocelyn, JoAnn McGregor, and Terence Ranger, *Violence and Memory: One Hundred Years in the "Dark Forests" of Matabeleland* (Oxford: James Currey, 2000).

Alfaro, Laura, "Botswana: A Diamond in the Rough," in Alfaro, *Global Capital and National Institutions: Crisis and Choice in the International Financial Architecture* (Singapore: World Scientific, 2010), 46–70.

Anglin, Douglas G., and Timothy M. Shaw, *Zambia's Foreign Policy: Studies in Diplomacy and Dependence* (Boulder: Westview, 1979).

Arnold, Millard (ed.), *Steve Biko: Black Consciousness in South Africa* (New York: Random House, 1978).

Baker, Colin, *Revolt of the Ministers: The Malawi Cabinet Crisis, 1964–1965* (London: Tauris, 2001).

Baker, Colin, *Seeds of Trouble: Government Policy and Land Rights in Nyasaland, 1946–1964* (London: British Academic Press, 1993).

Barber, James, *Rhodesia: The Road to Rebellion* (London: Oxford University Press, 1967).

Barber, James, and John Barratt, *South Africa's Foreign Policy: The Search for Status and Security, 1945–1988* (Cambridge: Cambridge University Press, 1990).

Barton, Frank, "Portrait of a Failure: Sir Roy Welensky," *Africa South*, III (1959): 64–69.

Bell, Terry, *Unfinished Business: South Africa, Apartheid and Truth* (London: Verso, 2003).

Bender, Gerald J., James S. Coleman, and Richard L. Sklar (eds.), *African Crisis Areas and U. S. Foreign Policy* (Berkeley: University of California Press, 1985).

Benson, Mary, *Nelson Mandela: The Man and the Movement* (New York: Norton, 1986).

Bhebe, Ngwabi, and Terence Ranger (eds.), *Soldiers in Zimbabwe's Liberation War* (London: James Currey, 1995).

Bjerk, Paul, *Julius Nyerere* (Athens: Ohio University Press, 2017).

Bolnick, Bruce R., "Fighting Corruption in Africa: Lessons from Malawi," *Harvard Journal of African American Public Policy*, VIII (2002): 8–11.

Boraine, Alex, Janet Levy, and Ronel Scheffer (eds.), *Dealing with the Past: Truth and Reconciliation in South Africa* (Rondebosch: IDASA, 1994).

Bostock, Mark, and Charles Harvey (eds.), *Economic Independence and Zambian Copper: A Case Study of Foreign Investment* (New York: Praeger, 1972).

Bozzoli, Belinda, *Theatres of Struggle and the End of Apartheid* (Athens: Ohio University Press, 2004).

Briscoe, Andrew, and Quill Hermans, *Combating Corruption in Botswana* (Gaborone: Ebert Foundation, 2001).

Brothers, Sue, Janet Hermans, and Doreen Nteta (eds.), *Botswana in the 21st Century* (Gaborone: Botswana Society, 1994).

Brown, Chris, "Botswana Votes 2019: Two-Party Competition and the Khama Factor," *Journal of Southern African Studies*, XLVI (2020): 703–722.

Bundy, Colin, *Short-Changed? South Africa since Apartheid* (Athens: Ohio University Press, 2014).

Burgis, Tom, *Kleptopia: How Dirty Money Is Conquering the World* (New York: HarperCollins, 2020).

Buthelezi, Mangosuthu Gatsha, *Power Is Ours* (New York: Books in Focus, 1979).

Butler, Anthony, *The Idea of the ANC* (Athens: Ohio University Press, 2012).

Butler, Jeffrey, Richard Elphick, and David Welsh (eds.), *Democratic Liberalism in South Africa: Its History and Prospect* (Middletown: Wesleyan University Press, 1987).

Butler, Jeffrey, Robert I. Rotberg, and John Adams, *The Black Homelands of South Africa: The Political and Economic Development of Bophuthatswana and KwaZulu* (Berkeley: University of California Press, 1977).

Callinicos, Alex, and John Rogers, *Southern Africa after Soweto* (London: Pluto, 1977).

Cameron, Colin, "Dunduzu Kaluli Chisiza (1930–1962): A Brief Personal Perspective," *Society of Malawi Journal*, LXIX (2016): 1–7.

Carlin, John, *Playing the Enemy: Nelson Mandela and the Game That Made a Nation* (New York: Penguin, 2008).

Carter, Gwendolyn M., and Patrick O'Meara (eds.), *Southern Africa in Crisis* (Bloomington: Indiana University Press, 1977).

Chan, Stephen, *Robert Mugabe: A Life of Power and Violence* (Ann Arbor: University of Michigan Press, 2003).

Chan, Stephen, and Julia Gallagher, *Why Mugabe Won: The 2013 Elections in Zimbabwe and Their Aftermath* (Cambridge: Cambridge University Press, 2017).

Chipembere, Henry Masauko (ed. Robert I. Rotberg), *Hero of the Nation: Chipembere of Malawi, an Autobiography* (Blantyre: Kachere Press, 2001).

Chipkin, Ivor, and Mark Swilling, *Shadow State: The Politics of State Capture* (New York: New York University Press, 2018).

Chipungu, Samuel N., "African Leadership under Indirect Rule in Colonial Zambia," in Chipungu (ed.), *Guardians in Their Time: Experiences of Zambians under Colonial Rule, 1890–1964* (London: Macmillan, 1992), 50–73.

Chisiza, Dunduza, *Realities of African Independence* (London: Africa Bureau, 1961).

Chiume, Murray William Kanyama, *Autobiography of Kanyama Chiume* (London: Panaf, 1982).

Chiume, Murray William Kanyama, *Banda's Malawi: An African Tragedy* (Lusaka: Multimedia Publications, 1992).

Clegg, Edward, *Race and Politics: Partnership in the Federation of Rhodesia and Nyasaland* (London: Oxford University Press, 1960).

Coker, Christopher, *The United States and South Africa, 1968–1985: Constructive Engagement and Its Critics* (Durham: Duke University Press, 1986).

Coltart, David, *The Struggle Continues: 50 Years of Tyranny in Zimbabwe* (Johannesburg: Jacana, 2016).

Cooley, John K., *East Wind over Africa: Red China's African Offensive* (New York: Walker, 1965).

Creighton, T. R. M., *The Anatomy of Partnership: Southern Rhodesia and the Central African Federation* (London: Faber, 1960).

Crocker, Chester A., *High Noon in Southern Africa: Making Peace in a Rough Neighborhood* (New York: Norton, 1993).

Dale, Richard, *The Namibian War of Independence, 1966–1989: Diplomatic, Economic and Military Campaigns* (Jefferson, NC: McFarland, 2014).

Davis, R. Hunt (ed.), *Apartheid Unravels* (Gainesville: University of Florida Press, 1991).

Davis, Stephen M., *Apartheid's Rebels: Inside South Africa's Hidden War* (New Haven: Yale University Press, 1987).

Day, John, "Southern Rhodesian African Nationalists and the 1961 Constitution," *Journal of Modern African Studies*, VII (1969): 221–247.

de Klerk, Willem, *F W de Klerk: The Man in His Time* (Johannesburg: Jonathan Ball, 1991).

DeRoche, Andrew, *Black, White, and Chrome: The United States and Zimbabwe, 1953 to 1998* (Trenton: Africa World Press, 2001).

DeRoche, Andrew, *Kenneth Kaunda, the United States, and Southern Africa* (London: Bloomsbury, 2016).

Dlamini, Jacob, *The Terrorist Album: Apartheid's Insurgents, Collaborators, and the Security Police* (Cambridge, MA: Harvard University Press, 2020).

Doran, Stuart, *Kingdom, Power, Glory: Mugabe, ZANU and the Quest for Supremacy, 1960–1987* (Midrand: Sithatha Media, 2017).

Dore, Isaak I., *The International Mandate System and Namibia* (Boulder: Westview, 1985).

Dubrow, Saul, *Racial Segregation and the Origins of Apartheid in South Africa, 1919–1936* (New York: St. Martins, 1989).

Dugard, John, *Human Rights and the South African Legal Order* (Princeton: Princeton University Press, 1978).

Dugard, John (ed.), *The South West Africa / Namibia Dispute* (Berkeley: University of California Press, 1973).

Dumbutshena, Enoch, *Zimbabwe Tragedy* (Nairobi: East African Publishing, 1975).

Dunn, Cyril, *Central African Witness* (London: Gollancz, 1959).

Eglin, Colin, *Crossing the Borders of Power* (Johannesburg: Jonathan Ball, 2007).

Englund, Harri, *Visions for Racial Equality: David Clement Scott and the Struggle for Justice in Nineteenth-Century Malawi* (Cambridge: Cambridge University Press, 2022).

Fanon, Frantz (trans. Constance Farrington), *The Wretched of the Earth* (1961; New York: Grove Press, 1963).

Feinstein, Andrew, *After the Party: Corruption, the ANC and South Africa's Uncertain Future* (London: Verso, 2009).

Finnegan, William, *A Complicated War: The Harrowing of Mozambique* (Berkeley: University of California Press, 1991).

Fombad, Charles Manga, "Curbing Corruption in Africa: Some Lessons from Botswana's Experience," *International Social Science Journal*, LI (1999): 241–254.

Foster, Douglas, *After Mandela: The Struggle for Freedom in Post-apartheid South Africa* (New York: Liveright, 2012).

Frankel, Philip, *An Ordinary Atrocity: Sharpeville and its Massacre* (New Haven: Yale University Press, 2001).

Franklin, Harry, *Unholy Wedlock: The Failure of the Central African Federation* (London: Allen & Unwin, 1963).

Gann, Lewis H., and Michael Gelfand, *Huggins of Rhodesia: The Man and His Country* (London: Allen & Unwin, 1964).

Gann, Lewis H., and Thomas H. Henriksen, *The Struggle for Zimbabwe: Battle in the Bush* (New York: Praeger, 1981).

Gendzier, Irene L., *Frantz Fanon: A Critical Study* (New York: Pantheon, 1973).

Gerhart, Gail M., *Black Power in South Africa: The Evolution of an Ideology* (Berkeley: University of California Press, 1978).

Gevisser, Mark, *A Legacy of Liberation: Thabo Mbeki and the Future of the South African Dream* (New York: Palgrave, 2009).

Gewald, Jan-Bart, "Who Killed Clemens Kapuuo?" *Journal of Southern African Studies*, XXX (2004): 559–576.

Gifford, Prosser, "The Creation and Disintegration of Federation in British Central Africa," in Gifford and William Roger Louis (eds.), *The Transfer of Power in Africa: Decolonization, 1940–1960* (New Haven: Yale University Press, 1982), 387–416.

Giliomee, Hermann, *The Afrikaners: Biography of a People* (Charlottesville: University of Virginia Press, 2003).

Godwin, Peter, and Ian Hancock, *"Rhodesians Never Die": The Impact of War and Political Change on White Rhodesia, c. 1970—1980* (New York: Oxford University Press, 1993).

Good, Kenneth, *Diamonds, Dispossession and Democracy in Botswana* (London: James Currey, 2008).

Good, Kenneth, "The Presidency of General Ian Khama: The Militarization of the Botswana 'Miracle,'" *African Affairs*, CIX (2009): 315–324.

Grundy, Kenneth W., *Confrontation and Accommodation in Southern Africa: The Limits of Independence* (Berkeley: University of California Press, 1973).

Grundy, Kenneth W., *The Militarization of South African Politics* (Bloomington: Indiana University Press, 1986).

Guelke, Adrian, *South Africa in Transition: The Misunderstood Miracle* (London: Tauris, 1999).

Gulbrandsen, Ornulf, *The State and the Social: State Formation in Botswana and Its Precolonial and Colonial Genealogies* (New York: Berghahn, 2012).

Habib, Adam, *South Africa's Suspended Revolution; Hopes and Prospects* (Athens: Ohio University Press, 2013).

Hall, Richard S., *The High Price of Principles: Kaunda and the White South* (London: Hodder & Stoughton, 1969).

Hall, Richard S., *Zambia* (London: Pall Mall, 1965).

Hall, Richard S., *Zambia, 1890–1964: The Colonial Period* (London: Longman, 1976).

Hall-Matthews, David, "Tickling Donors and Tackling Opponents: The Anti-corruption Campaign in Malawi," in Sarah Bracking (ed.), *Corruption and Development* (New York: Palgrave, 2007), 77–102.

Hartley, Ray, *Ragged Glory: The Rainbow Nation in Black and White* (Johannesburg: Jonathan Ball, 2014).

Hawkins, Tony, "Zimbabwe's Socialist Transformation," *Optima*, XXXV (1987): 184–195.

Hayes, Patricia, Jeremy Silvester, Marion Wallace, and Wolfram Hartmann (eds.), *Namibia under South African Rule: Mobility & Containment* (London: James Currey, 1998).

Heard, Anthony Hazlitt, *The Cape of Storms: A Personal History of the Crisis in South Africa* (Fayetteville: University of Arkansas Press, 1990).

Holm, John, and Patrick Molutsi (eds.), *Democracy in Botswana* (Athens: Ohio University Press, 1989).

Holmes, Carolyn E., *The Black and White Rainbow: Reconciliation, Opposition, and Nation-Building in Democratic South Africa* (Ann Arbor: University of Michigan Press, 2020).

Horne, Gerald, *From the Barrel of a Gun: The United States and the War against Zimbabwe, 1965–1980* (Chapel Hill: University of North Carolina Press, 2001).

Hussein, Mustafa, "Combating Corruption in Malawi: An Assessment of the Enforcing Mechanisms," *African Security Review*, XIV (2005): 91–101.

Irwin, Ryan M., *Gordian Knot: Apartheid and the Unmaking of the Liberal World Order* (Oxford: Oxford University Press, 2012).

Johnson, Jill, and Peter Magubane, *Soweto Speaks* (Johannesburg: Donker, 1979).

Johnson, Shaun (ed.), *South Africa: No Turning Back* (Bloomington: Indiana University Press, 1989).

Johnston, Alexander, *In the Shadow of Mandela: Political Leadership in South Africa* (London: Tauris, 2020).

Jubber, Ken, "The Persecution of Jehovah's Witnesses in Southern Africa," *Social Compass*, XXIV (1977): 121–134.

Kane-Berman, John, *Soweto: Black Revolt, White Reaction* (Johannesburg: Ravan, 1978).

Karekwaivanane, George Hamandishe, *The Struggle over State Power in Zimbabwe: Land and Politics since 1950* (New York: Cambridge University Press, 2017).

Karis, Thomas, and Gwendolen M. Carter (eds.), *A Documentary History of African Politics in South Africa, 1882–1964*, 4 vols. (Stanford: Hoover, 1972–77).

Kathrada, Ahmed, *No Bread for Mandela: Memoirs of Ahmed Kathrada, Prisoner No. 468/64* (Lexington: University Press of Kentucky, 2011, orig. pub. 2004).

Katjavivi, Peter H., *A History of Resistance in Namibia* (Trenton: Africa World Press, 1990).

Kaunda, Kenneth David, "Rider and Horse in Northern Rhodesia," *Africa South*, III (July–September 1959): 52–56.

Kaunda, Kenneth David, *A Humanist in Africa* (Nashville: Abington Press, 1966).

Kaunda, Kenneth David, *Zambia Shall Be Free* (New York: Praeger, 1962).

Kisangani, Emizet F., and Jeffrey Pickering, *African Interventions: State Militaries, Foreign Powers, and Rebel Forces* (Cambridge: Cambridge University Press, 2022).

Kitchen, Helen (ed.), *South Africa: In Transition to What?* (New York: Praeger, 1988).

Kotzé, D. A., *African Politics in South Africa, 1964–1974* (Pretoria: Schaik, 1975).

Kriger, Norma J., *Guerrilla Veterans in Post-war Zimbabwe: Symbolic and Violent Politics, 1980–1987* (Cambridge: Cambridge University Press, 2006).

Krishnamurthy, B. S. (comp.), *Cha Cha Cha: Zambia's Struggle for Independence* (Lusaka: Oxford University Press, 1972).

Lake, Anthony, *The "Tar Baby" Option: American Policy toward Southern Rhodesia* (New York: Columbia University Press, 1976).

Lamba, Isaac C., "Controlling Corruption in Africa: The Case of Malawi," in Kwame Frimpong and Gloria Jacques (eds.), *Corruption, Democracy, and Good Governance in Africa* (Gaborone: Lightbooks, 1999), 258–267.

Langenhove, Fernand van, *Consciences Tribales et Nationales en Afrique Noire* (The Hague: Institut Royal des Relations Internationales, 1960).

Larmer, Miles, *Living for the City: Social Change and Knowledge Production in the Central African Copperbelt* (New York: Cambridge University Press, 2021).

Larmer, Miles, *Rethinking African Politics: A History of Opposition in Zambia* (Farnham: Ashgate, 2011).

Laurie, Charles, *The Land Reform Deception: Political Opportunism in Zimbabwe's Land Seizure Era* (New York: Oxford University Press, 2016).

Lee, Robin (ed.), *Values Alive: A Tribute to Helen Suzman* (Johannesburg: Jonathan Ball, 1990).

Leith, J. Clark, *Why Botswana Prospered* (Montreal: McGill-Queen's University Press, 2005).

Leys, Colin, *European Politics in Southern Rhodesia* (Oxford: Clarendon, 1959).

Leys, Colin, and Cranford Pratt, *A New Deal in Central Africa* (London: Heinemann, 1960).

Libby, Ronald T., *The Politics of Economic Power in Southern Africa* (Princeton: Princeton University Press, 1987).

Lijphart, Arend, *Power-Sharing in South Africa* (Berkeley: Institute of International Studies, University of California, 1985).

Lipton, Merle, *Capitalism and Apartheid: South Africa, 1910–84* (Aldershot: Gower, 1985).

Lodge, Tom, *Black Politics in South Africa since 1945* (Johannesburg: Ravan, 1983).

Lodge, Tom, *Mandela: A Critical Life* (New York: Oxford University Press, 2006).

Loveland, Ian, *By Due Process of Law: Racial Discrimination and the Right to Vote in South Africa, 1855–1960* (Oxford: Hart Publishing, 1999).

Lush, David, *Last Steps to Uhuru: An Eye-Witness Account of Namibia's Transition to Independence* (Windhoek: New Namibia Books, 1993).

Maharaj, Mac, and Ahmed Kathrada (eds.), *Mandela: The Authorized Portrait* (Kansas City, MO: Andrews McMeel, 2006).

Mair, Lucy P., *The Nyasaland Elections of 1961* (London: Athlone, 1962).

Mamdani, Mahmood, *Neither Settler nor Native: The Making and Unmaking of Permanent Minorities* (Cambridge, MA: Harvard University Press, 2020).

Mandela, Nelson, *Long Walk to Freedom* (Boston: Little, Brown, 1994).

Marcum, John, *The Angolan Revolution*, 2 vols. (Cambridge, MA: MIT Press, 1969 and 1978).

Marks, Shula, and Stanley Trapido (eds.), *The Politics of Race, Class, and Nationalism in Twentieth Century South Africa* (New York: Longman, 1987).

Martin, David, and Phyllis Johnson, *The Struggle for Zimbabwe: the Chimurenga War* (London: Faber, 1981).

Marx, Anthony W., *Lessons of Struggle: South African Internal Opposition, 1960–1990* (New York: Oxford University Press, 1992).

Masire, Quett Ketumile Joni (ed. Stephen R. Lewis), *Very Brave or Very Foolish? Memoirs of an African Democrat* (Gaborone: Macmillan, 2006).

Mathews, Anthony S., *Law, Order and Liberty in South Africa* (Berkeley: University of California Press, 1972).

Mattera, Don, *Sophiatown: Coming of Age in South Africa* (Boston: Beacon Press, 1987).

Matyszak, Derek, *Law, Politics and Zimbabwe's "Unity" Government* (Harare: Konrad-Adenauer Stiftung, 2010).

Mayekiso, Mzwanele, *Township Politics: Civic Struggles for a New South Africa* (New York: Monthly Review Press, 1996).

Melber, Henning, *Understanding Namibia: The Trials of Independence* (London: Hurst, 2014).

Meldrum, Andrew, *Where We Have Hope: A Memoir of Zimbabwe* (London: John Murray, 2004).

Meli, Francis, *A History of the ANC: South Africa Belongs to Us* (1988; London: James Currey, 1989).

Meng, Anne, *Constraining Dictatorship: From Personalized Rule to Institutionalized Regimes* (Cambridge: Cambridge University Press, 2020).

Meredith, Martin, *Our Votes, Our Guns: Robert Mugabe and the Tragedy of Zimbabwe* (New York: Public Affairs, 2002).

Mhanda, Wilfred, *Dzino: Memories of a Freedom Fighter* (Harare: Weaver, 2011).

Michel, Eddie, *The White House and White Africa: Presidential Policy toward Rhodesia during the UDI Era, 1965–1979* (New York: Routledge, 2019).

Michelman, Cherry, *The Black Sash in South Africa: A Case Study in Liberalism* (London: Institute of Race Relations, 1975).

Miller, Jamie, *An African Volk: The Apartheid Regime and Its Search for Survival* (Oxford: Oxford University Press, 2016).

Mitchell, Nancy, *Jimmy Carter in Africa: Race and the Cold War* (Stanford: Stanford University Press, 2016).

Mlambo, Alois S., *A History of Zimbabwe* (Cambridge: Cambridge University Press, 2014).

Mngxitama, Andile, Amanda Alexander, and Nigel C. Gibson (eds.), *Biko Lives! Contesting the Legacies of Steve Biko* (New York: Palgrave, 2008).

Mogalakwe, Monageng, "Botswana at 50: Democratic Deficit, Elite Corruption and Poverty in the Midst of Plenty," *Journal of Contemporary African Studies*, XXXV (2017): 1–14.

Moodie, T. Dunbar, *The Rise of Afrikanerdom: Power, Apartheid, and the Afrikaner Civil Religion* (Berkeley: University of California Press, 1975).

Moore, David, *Mugabe's Legacy: Coups, Conspiracies and the Conceits of Power in Zimbabwe* (London: Hurst, 2021).

Moyo, Gugulethu, and Mark Ashurst, *The Day after Mugabe: Prospects for Change in Zimbabwe* (London: Africa Research Institute, 2007).

Mueller, Lisa, *Political Protest in Contemporary Africa* (Cambridge: Cambridge University Press, 2018).

Mulford, David C., *The Northern Rhodesian General Election, 1962* (Nairobi: Oxford University Press, 1964).

Mulford, David C., *Zambia: The Politics of Independence, 1957–1964* (Nairobi: Oxford University Press, 1967).

Mungazi, Dickson, *Colonial Policy and Conflict in Zimbabwe: A Study of Cultures in Collision, 1879–1979* (New York: Crane Russak, 1992).

Munger, Edwin S., *Bechuanaland: Pan-African Outpost or Bantu Homeland?* (London: Oxford University Press, 1965).

Munger, Edwin S., *Touched by Africa* (Pasadena, CA: Castle Press, 1983).

Murphy, Philip (ed.), *Central Africa*, I: *Closer Association, 1945–1958* (London: Stationery Office, 2005).

Muzorewa, Abel, *Rise Up and Walk: The Autobiography of Bishop Abel Tendekai Muzorewa* (London: Evans, 1978).

Myburgh, Pieter-Louis, *Gangster State: Unraveling Ace Magashule's Web of Capture* (Cape Town: Penguin, 2019).

Nattrass, Nicoli, "Aids and the Scientific Governance of Medicine in Post-apartheid South Africa," *African Affairs*, CVII (2008): 157–176.

Ndletyana, Mcebesi, *Anatomy of the ANC in Power: Insights from Port Elizabeth, 1990–2019* (Cape Town: HSRC Press, 2020).

Ndlovo-Gatsheni, Sabelo (ed.), *Joshua Mqabuko Nkomo of Zimbabwe: Politics, Power, and Memory* (London: Palgrave, 2017).

Ndlovo-Gatsheni, Sabelo (ed.), *Mugabeism? History, Politics and Power in Zimbabwe* (New York: Palgrave, 2015).

Nicholson, Christopher, *Permanent Removal: Who Killed the Cradock Four?* (Johannesburg: Wits University Press, 2004).

Nieftagodien, Noor, *The Soweto Uprising* (Athens: Ohio University Press, 2014).

Nkomo, Joshua, *Nkomo: The Story of My Life* (London: Methuen, 1984).

Noer, Tom, *Cold War and Black Liberation: The United States and White Rule in Africa, 1948–1968* (Columbia: University of Missouri Press, 1985).

Ntsebeza, Lungisile, *Democracy Compromised: Chiefs and the Politics of Land in South Africa* (Leiden: Brill, 2005).

Onslow, Sue (ed.), *Cold War in Southern Africa: White Power, Black Liberation* (London: Routledge, 2009).

Oomen, M. A., F. K. Inganji, and L. D. Ngconco (eds.), *Botswana's Economy since Independence* (New Delhi: McGraw-Hill, 1983).

Pallotti, Arrigo, and Ulf Engel (eds.), *South Africa after Apartheid: Policies and Challenges of the Democratic Transition* (Leiden: Brill, 2016).

Palmer, Robin, *Land and Racial Domination in Rhodesia* (Berkeley: University of California Press, 1977).

Payne, Richard J., *The Nonsuper Powers and South Africa: Implications for U. S. Policy* (Bloomington: Indiana University Press, 1990).

Phillips, Howard, *UCT under Apartheid: From Onset to Sit-In, 1948–1968* (Johannesburg: Ravan, 2022).

Phimister, Ian, "The Making and Meanings of the Massacres in Matabeleland," *Development Dialogues*, L (2008): 199–218.

Phiri, Bizeck Jube, "The Capricorn Africa Society Revisited: The Impact of Liberalism in Zambia's Colonial History, 1949–1963," *International Journal of African Historical Studies*, XXIV (1991): 65–83.

Pisani, André du, *SWA/Namibia: The Politics of Continuity and Change* (Johannesburg: Jonathan Ball, 1985).

Pogrund, Benjamin, *Sobukwe and Apartheid* (Johannesburg: Ball, 1990).

Pogrund, Benjamin, *War of Words: Memoir of a South African Journalist* (New York: Seven Stories Press, 2000).

Pollak, Richard, *Up against Apartheid: The Role and Plight of the Press in South Africa* (Carbondale: Southern Illinois University Press, 1981).

Raftopoulos, Brian, and Tyrone Savage (eds.), *Zimbabwe: Injustice and Political Reconciliation* (Harare: Weaver Press, 2005).

Ranger, Terence O., *Bulawayo Burning: The Social History of a Southern African City, 1893–1960* (London: James Currey, 2010).

Robb, Noel, *The Sash and I: A Personal Memoir and a Tribute to the Black Sash* (Claremont, South Africa: Robb, 2006).

Robinson, David, "Renamo, Malawi, and the Struggle to Succeed Banda: Assessing Theories of Malawian Intervention in the Mozambican Civil War," *Eras*, 11 (2009): 1–22.

Roessler, Philip, and Harry Verhoeven, *Why Comrades Go to War: Liberation Politics and the Outbreak of Africa's Deadliest Conflict* (New York: Oxford University Press, 2016).

Ross, Andrew, "Some Reflections on the Malawi 'Cabinet Crisis' 1964–65," *Religion in Malawi*, VII (1997): 1–12.

Rotberg, "Africa's Liberation Generation," *Journal of Modern African Studies*, LX (2022): 1–23.

Rotberg, "Africa's Mess, Mugabe's Mayhem," *Foreign Affairs*, LXXIX (September–October 2000): 47–61.

Rotberg, *Black Heart: Gore-Browne and the Politics of Multiracial Zambia* (Berkeley: University of California Press, 1977).

Rotberg, *The Corruption Cure: How Leaders and Citizens Can Combat Graft* (Princeton: Princeton University Press, 2017).

Rotberg, *Ending Autocracy, Enabling Democracy: The Tribulations of Southern Africa* (Washington, DC: Brookings Press, 2002).

Rotberg, "Failed States in a World of Terror," *Foreign Affairs*, LXXXI (July–August 2002): 127–141.

Rotberg, "The Failure and Collapse of Nation-States: Breakdown, Prevention, and Repair," in Rotberg (ed.), *When States Fail: Causes and Consequences* (Princeton: Princeton University Press, 2004), 1–50.

Rotberg (ed.), *Governance and Innovation in Africa: South Africa after Mandela* (Waterloo, ON: CIGI, 2014).

Rotberg, "Helen Suzman: Biographical Memoir," *Proceedings of the American Philosophical Society*, CLV (March 2011): 116–117.

Rotberg, "Leadership Alters Corrupt Behavior," in Rotberg (ed.), *Corruption, Global Security, and World Order* (Washington, DC: Brookings Institution Press, 2009), 341–356.

Rotberg, "Mugabe uber Alles: The Tyranny of Unity in Zimbabwe," *Foreign Affairs*, LXXXIX (2010): 10–15.

Rotberg (ed.), *Namibia: Political and Economic Prospects* (Lexington, MA: Lexington Books, 1983).

Rotberg (ed.), *On Governance: What It Is, What It Measures, and Its Policy Uses* (Waterloo, ON: CIGI, 2015).

Rotberg, "The 'Partnership' Hoax: How the British Government Deprived Central Africans of Their Rights," *Journal of Southern African Studies*, XLV (2019): 89–110.

Rotberg, *The Rise of Nationalism in Central Africa: The Making of Malawi and Zambia, 1873–1964* (Cambridge, MA: Harvard University Press, 1965).

Rotberg, "Strengthening African Leadership: There Is Another Way," *Foreign Affairs* LXXXIII (July–August 2004): 14–17.

Rotberg, *Suffer the Future: Policy Choices in Southern Africa* (Cambridge, MA: Harvard University Press, 1980).

Rotberg, *Things Come Together: Africans Achieving Greatness in the Twenty-First Century* (New York: Oxford University Press, 2020).

Rotberg, *Transformative Political Leadership: Making a Difference in the Developing World* (Chicago: University of Chicago Press, 2012).

Rotberg and Greg Mills (eds.), *War & Peace in Southern Africa: Crime, Drugs, Arms, and Trade* (Washington, DC: Brookings, 1998).

Rotberg and Dennis Thompson (eds.), *Truth v. Justice: The Morality of Truth Commissions* (Princeton: Princeton University Press, 2000).

Sachikonye, Lloyd, *When a State Turns on Its Citizens: 60 Years of Institutionalised Violence in Zimbabwe* (Johannesburg: Jacana, 2011).

Samatar, Abdi Ismail, *An African Miracle: State and Class Leadership and Colonial Legacy in Botswana Development* (Portsmouth, NH: Heinemann, 1999).

Sampson, Anthony, *Mandela* (New York: Knopf, 1999).

Sanger, Clyde, *Central African Emergency* (London: Heinemann, 1960).

Sanger, Clyde, *Our Golden Years in Africa: From the Congo to Zimbabwe* (Ottawa: Sanger, 2021).

Sardanis, Andrew, *Africa: Another Side of the Coin* (London: Tauris, 2011).

Sardanis, Andrew, *Zambia, the First Fifty Years: Reflections of an Eye Witness* (Oxford: Blackwell, 2014).

Scarnecchia, Timothy Lewis, *Race and Diplomacy in Zimbabwe: The Cold War and Decolonization, 1960–1984* (Cambridge: Cambridge University Press, 2021).

Scarnecchia, Timothy Lewis, *The Urban Roots of Democracy and Political Violence in Zimbabwe: Harare and Highfield, 1940–1964* (Rochester: University of Rochester Press, 2008).

Schmokel, Wolfe W., "The Myth of the White Farmer: Commercial Agriculture in Namibia, 1900–1983," *International Journal of African Historical Studies*, XVIII (1985): 93–108.

Seekings, Jeremy, "The Effects of Colonialism on Social Protection in South Africa and Botswana," in Carina Schmitt (ed.), *From Colonialism to International Aid: External Actors and Social Protection in the Global South* (London: Palgrave, 2020), 109–135.

Seekings, Jeremy, *UDF: A History of the United Democratic Front in South Africa, 1983–1991* (Athens: Ohio University Press, 2000).

Serfontein, J. Hennie P., *Brotherhood of Power: An Exposé of the Secret Afrikaner Broederbond* (London: Rex Collings, 1979).

Shamuyarira, Nathan, *Crisis in Rhodesia* (London: Deutsch, 1965).

Short, Philip, *Banda* (London: Routledge, 1974).

Slabbert, Frederik van zyl, *The Last White Parliament* (Johannesburg: Jonathan Ball, 1985).

Slabbert, Frederik van zyl, and David Welsh, *South Africa's Options: Strategies for Sharing Power* (Cape Town: David Philip, 1979).

Smith, Charlene, *Robben Island* (Cape Town: Struik, 1997).

Smith, David, and Colin Simpson, *Mugabe* (London: Sphere, 1981).

Smuts, David, *Death, Detention and Disappearance: A Lawyer's Battle to Hold Power to Account in 1980s Namibia* (Cape Town: Tafelberg, 2019).

Southall, Roger, "Bond Notes, Borrowing, and Heading for Bust: Zimbabwe's Persistent Crisis," *Canadian Journal of African Studies*, LI (2017): 389–405.

Southall, Roger, "If Only: Missed Opportunity or Inevitable Fate in Rhodesia?," *Canadian Journal of African Studies*, LIII (2019): 368–369.

Southall, Roger, *The New Black Middle Class in South Africa* (Auckland Park, South Africa: Jacana, 2016).

Southall, Roger, *Whites and Democracy in South Africa* (Woodbridge, UK: James Currey, 2022).

Southall, Roger, and Henning Melber (eds.), *Legacies of Power: Leadership Change and Former Presidents in African Politics* (Cape Town: HSRC, 2006).

Sparks, Allister, *The Mind of South Africa* (New York: Knopf, 1990).

Sparks, Donald L., and December Green, *Namibia: The Nation after Independence* (Boulder: Westview, 1992).

St. Jorre, John de, *A House Divided: South Africa's Uncertain Future* (Washington, DC: Carnegie Endowment, 1977).

Stedman, Stephen John, *Peacemaking in Civil War: International Mediation in Zimbabwe, 1974–1980* (Boulder: Rienner, 1991).

Stultz, Newell M., *Afrikaner Politics in South Africa, 1934–1948* (Berkeley: University of California Press, 1974).

Summers, Carol, *From Civilization to Segregation: Social Ideals and Social Control in Southern Rhodesia, 1890–1934* (Athens: Ohio University Press, 1994).

Suzman, Helen, *In No Uncertain Terms: A South African Memoir* (New York: Knopf, 1993).

Tamarkin, Mordechai, *The Making of Zimbabwe: Decolonization in Regional and International Politics* (London: Cass, 1990).

Taylor, Ian, "The Limits of the 'African Miracle': Academic Freedom in Botswana and the Deportation of Kenneth Good," *Journal of Contemporary African Studies*, XXIV (2006): 101–122.

Tekere, Edgar, *A Lifetime of Struggle* (Harare: SAPES, 2007).

Temkin, Ben, *Buthelezi: A Biography* (London: Cass, 2003).

Tendi, Blessing-Miles, *Army and Politics in Zimbabwe: Mujuru, the Liberation Fighter and Kingmaker* (Cambridge: Cambridge University Press, 2020).

Theroux, Paul, *Dark Star Safari* (Boston: Houghton Mifflin, 2003).

Theroux, Paul, "The Killing of Hastings Banda," in Theroux, *Sunrise with Seamonsters* (Boston: Houghton Mifflin, 1985), 63–75.

Thompson, Carol B., *Challenge to Imperialism: The Frontline States in the Liberation of Zimbabwe* (Boulder: Westview, 1986).

Tlou, Thomas, Neil Parsons, and Willie Henderson, *Seretse Khama, 1921–1980* (Gaborone: Botswana Society, 1950).

Toit, Fanie du, *When Political Transitions Work: Reconciliation as Interdependence* (New York: Oxford University Press, 2018).

Trabold, Bryan, *Rhetorics of Resistance: Opposition Journalism in Apartheid South Africa* (Pittsburgh: University of Pittsburgh Press, 2018).

Vambe, Lawrence, *From Rhodesia to Zimbabwe* (Pittsburgh: University of Pittsburgh Press, 1976).

Van Rooyen, Johann, *Hard Right: The New White Power in South Africa* (London: Tauris, 1994).

Van Vuuren, Hennie, *South Africa, Democracy, Corruption, and Conflict Management* (London: Legatum, 2014).

Van Zyl-Hermann, Danelle, *Privileged Precariat: White Workers and South Africa's Long Transition to Majority Rule* (Cambridge: Cambridge University Press, 2021).

Verheul, Suzanne, *Performing Power in Zimbabwe: Politics, Law, and the Courts since 2000* (Cambridge: Cambridge University Press, 2021).

Vines, Alex, *Renamo: Terrorism in Mozambique* (London: James Currey, 1991).

Watts, Carl P., *Rhodesia's Unilateral Declaration of Independence: A Study in International Crisis* (Basingstoke: Palgrave, 2008).

Weiss, Ruth, *Zimbabwe and the New Elite* (London: British Academic Press, 1994).

Welensky, Roy, *4000 Days: The Life and Death of the Federation of Rhodesia and Nyasaland* (London: Collins, 1964).

Welensky, Roy, "Toward Federation in Central Africa," *Foreign Affairs*, XXXI (1952): 142–149.

Wellington, John H., *South West Africa and Its Human Issues* (Oxford: Oxford University Press, 1967).

White, Luise, *The Assassination of Herbert Chitepo: Texts and Politics in Zimbabwe* (Bloomington: Indiana University Press, 2003).

White, Luise, *Unpopular Sovereignty: Rhodesian Independence and African Decolonization* (Chicago: University of Chicago Press, 2015).

Wilkins, Ivor, and Hans Strydom, *The Super-Afrikaners: Inside the Afrikaner Broederbond* (Johannesburg: Jonathan Ball, 1978.

Williams, Susan, *Colour Bar: The Triumph of Seretse Khama and His Nation* (London: Allen Lane, 2006).

Williams, Susan, *White Malice: The CIA and the Covert Recolonization of Africa* (New York: Public Affairs, 2021).

Windrich, Elaine, *Britain and the Politics of Rhodesian Independence* (New York: Africana, 1978).

Wood, J. R. T., *The Welensky Papers: A History of the Federation of Rhodesia and Nyasaland* (Durban: Graham, 1983).

Woodhouse, Susan, *Garfield Todd: The End of the Liberal Dream in Rhodesia* (Harare: Weaver Press, 2018).

Woods, Donald, *Biko* (London: Paddington Press, 1978).

Wylie, Diana, *A Little God: The Twilight of Patriarchy in a Southern African Kingdom* (Hanover, NH: Wesleyan University Press, 1990).

Young, Kenneth, *Rhodesia and Independence: A Study in British Colonial Policy* (London: Eyre & Spottiswoode, 1967).

Index